PRINCIPLES OF COMMUNITY PSYCHOLOGY

Principles of Community Psychology

PERSPECTIVES AND APPLICATIONS

Third Edition

Murray Levine
Douglas D. Perkins
David V. Perkins

New York   Oxford
OXFORD UNIVERSITY PRESS
2005

Oxford University Press

Oxford   New York
Auckland   Bangkok   Buenos Aires   Cape Town   Chennai
Dar es Salaam   Delhi   Hong Kong   Istanbul   Karachi   Kolkata
Kuala Lumpur   Madrid   Melbourne   Mexico City   Mumbai   Nairobi
São Paulo   Shanghai   Taipei   Tokyo   Toronto

Copyright © 1987, 1997, 2005 by Oxford University Press, Inc.

Published by Oxford University Press, Inc.
198 Madison Avenue, New York, New York, 10016
www.oup.com

Oxford is a registered trademark of Oxford University Press

Library of Congress Cataloging-in-Publication Data

Levine, Murray, 1928–
    Principles of community psychology: perspectives and applications/Murray Levine,
David V. Perkins, Douglas D. Perkins.—3rd ed.
        p.   cm.
    Includes bibliographical references and index.
    ISBN 0-19-514417-1 (cloth: alk. paper)
        1. Community psychology. 2. Community mental health services. I. Perkins, David
V. II. Perkins, Douglas D. III. Title

    RA790.55.L48 2004
    362.2'2—dc22   2004049525

Printing number: 9 8 7 6 5 4 3 2 1

Printed in the United States of America
on acid-free paper

To Seymour B. Sarason and the spirit of the Psychoeducational Clinic. To my wonderful wife and partner Adeline, my eminently satisfactory sons and their families, and our grandchildren, Arie, Ellen, and Eli.

M.L.

To Jo and Jianmei, Cynthia, and the memory of Vic; their adaptability, curiosity, creativity, and appreciation for cultural diversity and moral justice inspired my contributions to this book.

D.D.P.

To Linda, my wife and partner, whose support and understanding made my contributions to this book possible.

D.V.P.

Contents

Foreword

Prior to this edition, this book was unrivaled for its scope and depth of the obvious and not-so-obvious psychological implications of what American communities are: what problems they face, how they do and do not change. What this new edition makes abundantly clear is that what we call a community is glaringly porous: in the modern, highly technical, mobile world, a community is affected by events near and far from its borders, events that are psychological, sociological, economic, political, and legal. Yes, this is a book written by and for psychologists, but it draws upon the social sciences as no other book in the field. I would go so far as to say that this edition makes clearer than previous editions that this is more than a book about the American community. It is about America. Although this is truly a scholarly book, it is the opposite of a dull one. That is no small achievement. Beginning with the first chapter ("Life *Is* a Soap Opera") the writing is clear and stimulating. The details are many, but they are never divorced from the contents from which they emerge and which they illuminate. This is not a dry text but a lively, stimulating one. It is more than an introduction to community psychology. Social, developmental, and clinical psychologists will be well rewarded by reading this book because (without saying so) it makes a mockery of conventional specialties whose labels mask a degree of overlap too long ignored.

Seymour B. Sarason
Stratford, CT

Preface

This new edition represents not only an update of the past eight years in the field of community psychology, but also a substantial expansion in focus from the first two editions. Each chapter reviews the recent literature; includes updated references; and presents the latest empirical work, current issues and events, and some of the relevant policy debates surrounding them.

The introduction has been substantially expanded by adding some definitional grounding in what community psychology is and is not and in some of the fundamental principles and values in the field, along with the overview of the organization of chapters. The population parameters in the first full chapter, "Life *Is* a Soap Opera," were updated based on the 2000 Census and other currently available social indicators and national surveys. Many new illustrative boxes replace more dated ones. An example in chapter 1 is a review of "Psychosocial Adaptation to Health Problems: The Case of Genital Herpes."

Chapter 2 on the history of community psychology has been expanded to include not only the field's origins in the Community Mental Health movement, but also the "Influence of Applied Social Psychology and the War on Poverty," and a new box on issues and research surrounding homelessness. Chapter 3 presents the guiding conceptual orientation of the book, based on Dohrenwend's contextualized model of stress, and includes updated references. Chapter 4 includes a new box on behavior-environment congruence in Geel, Belgium, which illustrates the ecological principles of adaptation and niche. This box is based on material that was not grouped together or highlighted in the last edition as well as some new material.

Chapter 5 has been substantially expanded and reorganized around three psychological conceptions of the environment— perceived social climates, behavior settings, and social roles—toward a delineation of both social *and* physical environmental influences on behavior and well-being, as well as behavior settings as a melding of social and physical contexts. The social environment includes not only social climates and roles, but also key community "social capital" concepts such as citizen participation and empowerment, sense of community, and neighboring, which have been studied extensively in community psychology but received less attention in previous editions. All of these concepts are illustrated in a revised box on the classic Fairweather Lodge social experiment.

Chapter 6 on labeling theory and the sociology of deviance has been updated and a new section on the use of law to reduce stigma added. In chapter 7, we have included new research findings on adaptation, crisis, coping, and social support, and added a box on "Pollyanna and the Glad Game" as an apt but largely forgotten historical antecedent to the literature on coping.

In chapter 8, we have updated the section on HIV/AIDS prevention and the boxes on Project Head Start (and now early Head Start) and on preventing child maltreatment as an illustration of the problem of false positives. We have also added a box on a successful school-change effort as well as new sections on schools as a locus of prevention and on community-based health promotion. Chapter 9 on self-help/mutual assistance groups has been revised and updated.

Chapter 10 includes two new sections. One is on organizational change, development, and learning; and the other is on problems in planned change on a statewide level. The latter focuses on the so-called "Texas miracle" of educational reform. Chapter 11 on school desegregation as a societal-level intervention has been updated and includes two new sections on political and legal events since desegregation and on future problems in this arena. In chapter 12, on community-level change, we have greatly revised and expanded the section on community development and created an up-to-date box discussing the Center for Health, Environment, and Justice and the Environmental Justice Movement.

Finally, chapter 13 still focuses on science, ethics, and the future of community psychology, but it has been greatly expanded. In addition to updating the sections on ecology and science and the ethics of community intervention, we have added two new sections on making community psychology more interdisciplinary and on recognizing developments in community psychology outside the United States and the need to increase international communication and collaboration in the field. We have also added a box that presents a new ecological-psychopolitical model as one direction for future work in the field.

In sum, while no single text can provide all things to all readers, we think that, compared to previous editions, this book is even more reflective of the entire breadth of community psychology, from its origins, to the latest trends, to a future that is bright with new ideas and an expanding vista of issues to address.

Acknowledgments

The following material was used with permission of the author and publisher.

Figure 3–1 from B. S. Dohrenwend (1978), Social stress and community psychology. *American Journal of Community Psychology, 6,* 1–14. Copyright 1978, Plenum Publishing Corporation. Reprinted with permission.

Figure 5–1 from C. Timko and R. H. Moos (1991), "A typology of social climates in group residential facilities for older people." *Journal of Gerontology, 46,* S160–169. Copyright 1991, The Gerontological Society of America. Reprinted with permission.

Table 5–1 from G. W. Fairweather, D.H. Sanders, H. Maynard, and D. Cressler (1969), *Community life for the mentally ill.* Chicago: Aldine. Reprinted with permission.

Figure 5–2 from Perkins, D. D. , & Long, D. A. (2002). Neighborhood sense of community and social capital: A multi-level analysis. In A. T. Fisher, C. C. Sonn, & B. J. Bishop (Eds.), *Psychological sense of community: Research, applications, and implications* (pp. 291–318). New York: Kluwer Academic/Plenum Publishers. Reprinted with permission.

Figure 6–1 from T. J. Scheff (1984), *Being Mentally Ill: A sociological theory* (2nd ed.). New York: Aldine de Gruyter. Copyright 1984 by Thomas J. Scheff. Reprinted with permission.

Figure 7–1 from S. Cohen and T. A. Wills (1985), "Stress, social support, and the buffering hypothesis." *Psychological Bulletin, 98,* 310–357. Copyright 1985, American Psychological Association. Reprinted with permission.

Figure 8–1 from P. J. Mrazek and R. J. Haggerty (Eds.), *Reducing Risks for Mental Disorders: Frontiers for Preventive Intervention Research.* Copyright 1994 by the National Academy of Sciences. Courtesy of the National Academy Press, Washington, D.C. Reprinted with permission.

Figure 12–1 from Perkins, D. D., Crim B., Silberman, P., & Brown, B. B. (2004). Community development as a response to community-level adversity: Ecological theory and research and strengths-based policy. In

K. I. Maton, C. J. Schellenbach, B. J. Leadbeater, & A. L. Solarz (Eds.), *Investing in children, youth, families, and communitues: Strengths-based research and policy* (pp. 321–340). Washington, DC: American Psychological Association. Reprinted with permission.

PRINCIPLES OF COMMUNITY PSYCHOLOGY

Introduction: An Overview of Community Psychology

What Is Community Psychology?

Community psychology represents a new way of thinking about people's behavior and well-being in the context of all the community environments and social systems in which they live their lives. Our intention in this book is to develop that way of thinking and to show how the perspective is applicable to a very wide range of contemporary problems.

One of the most exciting aspects of community psychology is that the field is still developing and defining itself. It is not easily reduced to the traditional subdisciplines in psychology for several reasons. First, community psychologists simultaneously emphasize both *applied service delivery* to the community and *theory-based research*. Second, they focus, not just on individual psychological makeup, but on *multiple levels of analysis*, from individuals and groups to specific programs to organizations and, finally, to whole communities. Third, community psychology covers a broad *range of settings and substantive areas*. A community psychologist might find herself or himself conducting research in a mental health center on Monday, appearing as an expert witness in a courtroom on Tuesday, evaluating a hospital program on Wednesday, implementing a school-based program on Thursday, and organizing a neighborhood association meeting on Friday. For all the above reasons, there is a sense of vibrant urgency and uniqueness among community psychologists—as if they are as much a part of a social movement as of a professional or scientific discipline.

The new and disparate areas of community psychology are thus bound together by a singular vision: that of helping the relatively powerless, in and out of institutions, take control over their environment and their lives. Community psychologists must, however, "wear many hats" in working toward the creation of social systems which: (1) promote individual growth and prevent social and mental health problems before they start; (2) provide immediate and appropriate forms of intervention when and where they are most needed; and (3) enable those who have been labeled as "deviant" to live as dignified, supported, and empowered lives as possible, preferably as contributing members of the community.

For example, a community psychologist might (1) create and evaluate an array of programs and policies which help people control the stressful aspects of community and organizational environments; (2) assess the needs of a community and teach its members how to recognize an incipient problem and deal with it before it becomes intractable; or (3) study and implement more humane and effective ways for formerly institutionalized populations to live productively in society's mainstream.

What Isn't Community Psychology?*

It may be useful to describe community psychology by distinguishing it from other disciplines with which it is closely allied. As we will explain more fully below, community psychology is like public health in promoting healthy environments and lifestyles, in considering problems at the population (not just individual) level, and, especially, in adopting a preventive orientation. That is, community psychologists try to prevent problems before they start, rather than waiting for them to become serious and debilitating. But community psychology differs from public health in its concern with social and mental, as well as physical health, and the quality of life in general.

In many ways, community psychology is like social work, except that it has a strong research orientation. Community psychologists are committed to the notion that nothing is more practical than rigorous, well-conceived research directed at social problems.

Community psychology is like social psychology and sociology in taking a group or systems approach to human behavior, but it is more unabashedly applied than those disciplines and more concerned with using psychological knowledge to resolve social problems.

It borrows techniques from industrial and organizational psychology, but tends to deal with community organizations, human service delivery systems, and support networks. Plus, it focuses simultaneously on the problems of clients and workers as opposed to solely the goals and values of management. It is concerned with issues of social regulation and control, and with enhancing the positive characteristics and coping abilities of relatively powerless social groups such as the poor, minorities, children, and the elderly.

*We thank Marybeth Shinn for many of the ideas in this section.

As discussed in chapter 2, although some community psychologists came from, or were trained in, social psychology, the most important field of comparison for understanding community psychology is *clinical psychology*. Community psychology shares clinical psychology's action orientation and its goal of helping people in distress. An important difference between the community and the clinical orientation is the helping person's point of intervention, in terms of both location and timing. Community psychology arose largely out of dissatisfaction with the clinician's tendency to locate mental health problems within the individual. Community psychologists are more likely to see threats to mental health in the social environment, or in lack of fit between individuals and their environment. They focus on health rather than on illness, and on enhancing the competencies of individuals, small groups, organizations, communities, or higher policy levels. This focus on the person-in-environment is also emphasized by community psychologists outside the United States (e.g., Orford, 1992; Thomas & Veno, 1992).

The timing of intervention also helps to distinguish community psychology, which is more proactive, from clinical psychology, which is more reactive. One of the cofounders of community psychology, Emory Cowen, liked to illustrate this with an anecdote that by the time a child sees a therapist, there has already been a long process of difficulty, informal help-seeking, and frustration on everyone's part—the child, the family, teachers, friends. In most cases, the clinical psychologist cannot deal directly with the early stages of this process, but enters the picture at the end, after the problem has worsened, become more complicated and difficult to solve. The community approach and this book deal with all that came before.

Clinical psychology did produce the community mental health movement, which served as a kind of launching pad for community psychology. The community mental health movement has been characterized by efforts to deliver services in the local community instead of in a hospital or clinic, to emphasize services other than long-term hospitalization, and to use outpatient services as much as possible. The community movement is also dedicated to the development of innovative services and working relationships with other agencies in the community, for the client's benefit. We no longer follow the policy of isolating the repulsive deviant in pursuit of some chimerical goal of cure. Those adopting the community mental health perspective work to support people in the local community. When hospitalization does occur, the goal of treatment is not to cure illness, but to restore the individual's equilibrium so that he or she may be returned to the community as rapidly as possible.

This preference for community-based, in contrast to institution-based, treatment constitutes not only a perspective but also an ideology or a set of beliefs that characterize community psychologists. In contrast to the clinical perspective, the community perspective directs more attention to the conditions of life for the person who is the client. The clinical perspective leads us to be primarily concerned with the person's inner life and perhaps his or her relationships to family or close friends. The community perspective may incorporate such concerns and interests, but it also leads the helping person to be concerned about living conditions—the availability of housing, employment, recreation, medical care, and transportation. Once the concerns extend far enough to examine the client's network of support, the community psychologist is focusing on the community, a larger unit than the individual or the family.

Examining successes and failures of mental health practices of the past and present, we become even more aware of the extent to which our service system is embedded in the political structure. An understanding of funding streams is critical in understanding what happens to clients. Especially for the heaviest users of services, those who are seriously and persistently mentally ill, we find that many problems of living are related to welfare policies and laws. In adopting a community psychology perspective, we must use theoretical conceptions that extend beyond those useful in understanding an individual (e.g., diagnostic categories, psychodynamics, traits, and so on) and incorporate larger units of analysis.

Principles of Community Psychology

Community psychology is not only a professional and scientific discipline. It is also a philosophical or value orientation that is applicable to virtually any field or profession. The community perspective challenges traditional modes of thought. It avoids "blaming the victim" for problems or labeling people as "deviant" (chapter 6) and looks at whole ecological systems, including political, cultural, and environmental influences, as well as focusing on institutional and organizational factors (see chapters 4, 5 and 10). Acknowledging that many groups and individuals are suspicious of, or intimidated by, professionals, the community approach encourages client/citizen participation and recognizes the demand for local empowerment, bureaucratic decentralization, and self-help/mutual aid (chapters 9 and 12). It simultaneously stresses the utility of research, not only for theory development, but for program evaluation and policy analysis—and the omnipresence of values (implicitly or explicitly) throughout society and even science (see chapters 11 and 13). An important aspect of the community orientation is its appreciation of the authority of historical and structural contexts (chapter 2). Community psychology values and celebrates cultural diversity (chapter 11). Throughout the book, we show how community psychology emphasizes community and personal strengths and competency, as opposed to weaknesses and pathology.

Some of the viewpoints or theories in the community perspective have been more thoroughly elaborated than others. One important area of theory and research is the human stress process, its environmental causes (and how they can be prevented), how individuals and groups vary in how they cope with it (including the use of family, friends, and others for social support), and what kinds of negative, and even positive, outcomes can occur (Dohrenwend, 1978; see chapters 3 and 7).

Community psychology also emphasizes ecological thinking, which leads us beyond trying to change individuals to consider ways to improve the fit, or interaction, between persons and environments, which can have as important an effect on behavior and well-being as each factor has separately (see chapter 4). The ecological viewpoint requires "a concern with the relationships of individuals to each other as a community; as a differentiated social grouping with elaborate systems of formal and informal relationships" (Mann, 1978, p. x). The community perspective includes a "focus on broader ecological levels than the level of the exclusive treatment of the individual" (Heller & Monahan, 1977, p. 16).

A paradigm shift has occurred in that both the questions we must ask and the methods used to obtain answers have changed (Rappaport, 1977). It is necessary to develop research bases for informed intervention, but it is not sufficient. If psychology and social science are to be relevant and useful for the solution of social problems, then conceptual and research approaches will have to broaden to take into account the historical, social, economic, and political contexts within which policies are developed and implemented (Sarason, 1974, 1981a, 1981b, 1982a).

Although community psychologists tend to advocate social more than individual change, one can have less than radical aims and remain within the community orientation. Most psychologists following the community perspective see it as their mission, not to just tear down outmoded ideas and practices, but to help create or improve service organizations and other institutions. They work to achieve the goals of providing humane, effective care and less stigmatizing services to those in need while enhancing human psychological growth and development.

To make human service organizations more effective and more humane, community-oriented psychologists are interested in creating new settings and services consistent with the ecological perspective. That perspective, and the actions that flow from it, differ from the medical model in which the person in need defines his or her own problem and then seeks out help from a professional helper, most often on a fee-for-service basis. The medical model is useful for many people and for many problems. However, the medical model with its emphasis on highly trained professionals is unable to provide for all in need. Moreover certain forms of care may contribute to the perpetuation of problems because of the way problems are defined in the medical model as residing exclusively within the boundaries of an individual.

In the ecological perspective, human behavior is viewed in terms of the person's adaptation to resources and circumstances (see chapter 4). From this perspective, one may correct unsuccessful adaptations by altering the availability of resources. Thus new services may be created, or existing strengths in social networks may be discovered and conditions changed to enhance the use of resources. A good example is the way legal and cultural barriers to resources were eliminated as a result of antidiscrimination and voting rights legislation starting in the 1950s. The increased number of African Americans in professional, managerial, and technical occupations, the increase in income among middle- and upper-class African Americans, and the increased number of African American students in colleges and professional schools can be attributed to the civil rights movement. The increasing number of young, unemployed African American males, the correlated increase in single-mother families, and the concentration of social problems such as crime in certain urban areas can be attributed at least in part to a changing job market and the loss of access to jobs, a critical resource for favorable adaptation (Wilson, 1987). From this perspective, solutions to problems in living do not require more professional therapists; instead community psychologists try to work through a variety of institutions and with people who may not have advanced training in the mental health professions to improve and develop resources. The ecological perspective encourages a search for resources instead of a search for psychopathology. It encourages us to view others as having strengths that may be put to good use in the service of their own development if resources are available. It may not be necessary to undo psychopathology first.

Community psychologists have also rallied around the theme of prevention (chapter 8). The concept of prevention comes from the field of public health. Public health professionals argue that the greatest advances result from preventing diseases instead of treating them after they occur. Deadly scourges have been all but wiped out by inoculations and modern sanitary methods. Our increased average length of life, and our better health throughout a longer fraction of that life span, are both more attributable to preventive than to therapeutic measures. The public health model leads us to seek out the causes of pathology and to act to prevent them by either modifying environmental conditions or strengthening the person. It is not clear that the public health model can be adopted wholly when we deal with social and mental health problems. However, it does provide a set of goals and a way of thinking that direct our attention to issues other than individual psychopathology and its treatment.

The concept of prevention offers different times and places for intervention. It asks us to think about whether it might be possible to take action before the undesirable behavior actually appears, or in the alternative, learn to position assistance—resources—so that problem resolution can occur very early in the history of a problem. As clinicians we are generally called in after an intolerable situation has developed for an individual or a family. In the preventive perspective, we are encouraged to think systematically about the beginnings of the process that results in a person defining him or herself, or being defined by others, as a "case."

Preventive approaches also require us to function in new organizational settings. Historically, the setting for mental health professionals was the clinic, the hospital, or the private practice office. In preventive work using the community perspective, it becomes necessary to leave familiar settings and learn to live, work, and adapt in environments that are at best unfamiliar or uncongenial, and at worst may be actively hostile to strangers and to change efforts, no matter how benignly intended. It is necessary to work with and through schools, welfare departments, recreation facilities, the mass media, the legislative and the political process, and people representing many varied interests and values.

Community psychology directs attention to the larger context within which plans are developed and implemented. The possibilities for gaining resources must be carefully evaluated. The political climate supporting one type of programming at one time and another at another time must be understood. What is feasible at one time and under one set of political and economic conditions may often be approached only with great difficulty at another time or under other circumstances (Levine & Levine, 1992). Competition among agencies and groups for the same pool of limited resources becomes a crucial factor influencing what kinds and amounts of resources will be available and to whom. When we adopt the community perspective, our professional concerns necessarily broaden.

In this book we will examine some of the theories and programs in community psychology, and some of the research related to them. We are interested in showing the interrelationships among problems and theories and in trying to develop as systematic a framework as we can for thinking about problems and their solutions. At this point in the development of the field, we can try to convey an orientation and a way of thinking. Hard knowledge is in short supply, and may never be sufficient to satisfy the most "hard-nosed" critics. The problems of interest to this field will persist, however, and we will continue to develop better—if imperfect—ways of addressing them. When those of us working in this field in the early 1960s began, we were innocent of the questions as well as of the answers. Now at least we are developing an intellectual framework within which diverse experiences make some sense. We can at least ask questions that are more meaningful than ones we were able to ask 40 years ago.

Organization of Chapters

The content of the book is organized as follows. The first two chapters establish a philosophical and temporal context for community psychology. Chapter 1 examines the nature and scope of issues and problems facing the field and discusses the implications of a view that asserts that the definition of a problem involves its situational context. Chapter 2 reviews the historical background of this perspective. Chapter 3 presents Barbara Dohrenwend's unified model of the community psychology field and the various activities it endorses, on which the rest of the book elaborates. Chapters 4 through 7 describe and assess the major conceptual foundations of community psychology, including principles of ecology, conceptions of behavior in a social and physical context, labeling theory, and the increasingly useful concepts of stress and support. These concepts are also used to design programs for those who need long-term assistance with chronic problems.

The remainder of the book gives more attention to applications of community psychology principles while maintaining the focus on concepts. Chapter 8 outlines and discusses community psychology's perspective on prevention. This chapter pays particular attention to interventions involving individual competence building and interventions to reduce risks in important settings such as schools. Some of the ideas derived from prevention are applied in chapter 9 to the condition of people who need help on a more chronic, long-term basis. Self-help groups offer an important alternative to traditional clinical services in the way they conceptualize problems and the nature of their approach to overcoming a problem.

The remaining chapters elaborate on these issues. Chapter 10 considers the problem of change at the level of individual settings and organizations. Creating new settings and changing existing settings are both discussed, along with two illustrative case studies. Perspectives in community psychology also offer insights into the process of change at larger levels. School desegregation, for example, the focus in chapter 11, was a change of nationwide proportions in which psychologists and other social scientists played a relatively important role. Chapter 12 examines the nature of problem definition in a community context and some of the alternative interventions (e.g., within community development there are both professional planning and grassroots organizing models) that follow from different definitions. Chapter 13 completes the book with a community perspective on scientific research and the ethics and politics of intervention. We hope that everyone who reads this book will learn from it, but if we only stimulate the reader to think about these issues our most essential objective will have been accomplished.

I

ORIGINS OF COMMUNITY PSYCHOLOGY

1

Life *Is* a Soap Opera

A number of years ago there was a popular television program called *Queen for a Day*. Contestants competed by listing a catalog of personal miseries, tragedies, and catastrophes that they and their families had endured. The show was considered a vulgar display pandering to the morbid curiosity of the general public; its popularity was embarrassing if not puzzling. *Queen for a Day* was but one manifestation of the same deep interest in the plight of individuals and families who struggle with personal, familial, medical, psychiatric, legal, and economic problems that lead millions to read Ann Landers, and watch Oprah, Geraldo, and many others every day.

We are all intrigued or titillated by the complexities of human relationships depicted on daytime TV programs watched by tens of millions of people. Programs such as *Oprah, Montel, Jenny Jones* and, at a more sensational level, *Jerry Springer*, show us tragedy, conflict, and dilemmas of living. Advice columnists daily offer suggestions to people who are involved in complex family, friendship, romantic and employment relationships and dilemmas, and such columns enjoy an immense readership. On the radio, Dr. Laura daily solves moral and interpersonal dilemmas experienced by her listeners. Judge Judy and several similar programs bring other conflicts to our attention in a context of legal disputes. These are buttressed by the daily soap operas that have faithful followings and depict similar complexities of living, but with fictional characters.

Such TV programs and newspaper features are like the ever-popular soap operas but with real people as the actors. They chronicle for the American public the impact of death, disease, accident, divorce, crime, complex family relationships, and sundry tragedies in the everyday lives of the fictional characters. The popularity of soap operas is not explained by the loneliness of homemakers who fill their drab existences by experiencing vicariously the exciting lives of the beautiful, glamorous figures who populate televisionland. Soap operas do more than dispel boredom. The stories or myths that are the staple fare of the soap operas and advice programs and columns touch on universal themes. They provide an opportunity for catharsis, and teach, as all good myths do. Their lesson is that the tragedies of life are inevitable and, if not surmountable, then at least are to be endured with dignity.

We think that soap operas and their real-life counterparts are popular not only because they are entertaining but precisely because they are a way of understanding life. Life itself is the soap opera. The popularity of the television version simply reflects that fact. By looking at life as a soap opera, we can develop a better understanding of our cultural concern with psychological well-being, the demand for psychological services, the emphasis on crisis and coping in the contemporary professional literature, and the recent proliferation of self-help and social support groups. We may well come to a different view of what is "normal," in the sense of typical or not unusual. Moreover, problems are not distributed randomly in time, space, and among populations. By adopting an ecological perspective, community psychologists can have roles in developing, implementing, and evaluating programs designed to help people coping with problems.

An important theme of this book is that problem definitions themselves offer insights into social phenomena. For example, does a mental or emotional problem reside entirely inside a person or does it also become tangled in the specific events and situations immediately surrounding him or her? The simple statistics to follow suggest that multitudes are struggling with critical problems in living; struggle with life's problems is the rule, not the exception and not a consequence of individual deficits or personality flaws. Some events (e.g., death) are inevitable, but many are consequences of other social changes. In the absence of normative means of dealing with those challenges, adapting to changes is a special problem.

If struggles with critical problems are normative then public services built on the assumption that serious problems in living are the exception have no chance of serving the full public need. Problems of living are not the exception at all; any such conception does a disservice to the people living through the events and is a definition of the problem that inevitably leads to ever-increasing frustration and victim-blaming. To understand why old ways of waiting for problems to arise and then expecting professionals to react and solve them are inadequate, and why alternate forms of service, alternate personnel, and prevention are all necessities, we have only to turn to statistics describing the frequency of problems in living.

It will help in making sense of these statistics to understand the concepts of prevalence and incidence. *Prevalence* refers to the number of new and old instances of some problem in the population at a given point in time (called "point prevalence"), or alternatively the number active at any time during a specified interval ("period prevalence"). *Incidence* refers to the number of new cases coming into the population over a period of time, usually one year.

The Incidence and Prevalence of Problems in Living

We will present data from several sources, including statistics about people receiving psychiatric treatment and other prevalence estimates for mental disorders, epidemiological and survey estimates of certain maladaptive behavior patterns (e.g., alcohol abuse), disadvantaged social conditions (e.g., widowhood, poverty), and the implications for mental health of several contemporary social and cultural trends. Many items in this catalog of problems resemble those listed on measures of "stressful life events." The prototype scale was developed by Holmes and Rahe (1967; see chapter 7). In the following presentation figures may not always add up exactly. Figures obtained from different sources vary from each other, and extrapolations from population figures may be taken from different bases in different years. However, that does not alter the picture of general trends that we want to present.

Average household size. To appreciate fully the impact of the figures, keep in mind that the average household in the United States in 2000 consisted of 2.59 individuals: 281,421,906 people, living in 105,480,101 households (U.S. Bureau of the Census, 2000, Table DP-1). (The average household size is not fully descriptive because many people live alone and many others live with more than two other people, but for our purposes the average will do.) Thus for each individual affected by a given condition, on average, nearly two other people were also affected to some degree. For example, research has documented the stresses and burdens of living with a depressed adult (Coyne et al. 1987; Coyne, Thompson & Palmer, 2002) or a disabled sibling (Breslau & Prabucki, 1987; Pit-Ten Cate & Loots, 2000). In one study, measured well-being in caregivers of those with schizophrenia varied with variations in patient symptom severity (Travers, White, Boscoe, & McDonnell, 2001), as did the caregivers' physical health as measured by visits to the emergency room, hospitalizations, and doctor appointments for themselves (White, Travers, Boscoe, & McDonnell, 2001).

Institutionalized Population

This population includes people in psychiatric hospitals, institutions for people with mental retardation, elderly people in nursing homes, hospitals for chronically ill people, schools and hospitals for people with mental and physical disabilities, hospitals and wards for drug/alcohol abuse, youth in residential facilities, and the prison population. All of the people in these institutions receive care from trained staff. The size of the institutionalized population changes from time to time. In the 2000 census, 4,059,039 people were in such institutions. More were living in group homes for people with mental or physical disabilities, in halfway houses for drug/alcohol abuse, or in shelters for the homeless. The census counts each of those persons as noninstitutionalized and living in the community. Each person however, is in need of care, and is a problem to themselves and to family members. We will describe these populations separately below.

Psychiatric hospitals. At one time, the large psychiatric hospital was the mainstay of the mental health system. With deinstitutionalization (see chapter 2), the population of state and county psychiatric hospitals dropped from about 550,000 in the 1950s to about 79,000 now, including patients in veterans hospitals, and in psychiatric wards in general hospitals. The large state institution is all but gone. Some have closed, but in other states large hospitals have been reorganized and downsized. There are fewer beds overall in psychiatric hospitals, but occupancy rate is increasing, suggesting more use (National Association of Psychiatric Health Care Systems [NAPHCS], 2001).

Because of admissions and discharges during the year, the average daily census doesn't accurately reflect how busy the hospitals are. There were about 2 million admissions to inpatient treatment services in 1997 (Milazzo-Sayre, Henderson, Manderscheid, Bokossa, Evans, & Male (2001). Current therapeutic practices and economic considerations reduce the length of stay and increase patient turnover. The average length of stay in hospitals was about ten days in 2000 (NAPHCS, 2001). The turnover results from short-term success in treatment, but is also due to economic considerations. Two-thirds of psychiatric hospitals transfer patients for economic reasons. Those without insurance are transferred to public hospitals and community mental health centers (Doctor's Guide, 1997).

Many admissions were for short-term stays in psychiatric units of general hospitals, which often transfer to state and county facilities those who don't respond quickly to treatment. Many more patients were admitted to outpatient treatment (5.5 million), showing that the locus of care is now in the community (Milazzo-Sayre, et al., 2001). Nonetheless, if we add the 2 million admissions to mental hospitals, the 5.5 million admissions to outpatient care, and the 171,000 admissions to residential care (facilities for youth), we obtain a figure of 7.67 million admitted to mental health care. If we consider that both patients and their families are affected, using our multiplier of 2.59, and assuming no duplicate admissions, we can say that 19.9 million people in any year, or about 7 percent of the population, are affected by being institutionalized or having a family member institutionalized.

Facilities for people with mental retardation. In 2000 there were 189,900 residents of facilities (institutions, group homes, etc.) that provided 24-hour care for those with mental retardation (AFSCME, 2002). There has been a decline in the number of people in state institutions due to the emphasis on community-based practice. Today, the number is about 54,000. However, many more are living in small group homes, in foster care, or in other residences. There also has been a shift from public to private care. There are 86,225 residential settings; only 2.1 percent are state operated. The rest are state funded but operated by private for-profit or nonprofit agencies. If we estimate an average of six persons per residence, about 517,350 persons are served in such facilities (AFSCME, 2002).

Facilities for the elderly. There were 16.6 million Americans over age 75 in the United States in 2000. Most live in the community, and most are self-sufficient. However, some responsibility for their care falls on adult children who provide a variety of services for their elderly parents. Many adult children find gratification in fulfilling a filial duty, but many put in very long hours and experience stress.

The institutionalized population includes 1,720,500 elderly persons living in nursing homes or similar residential facilities. The number in institutions has dropped in recent years due to enhanced community and in-home services. Some elderly living in the community need varying degrees of help which they receive from services such as Meals on Wheels or at-home nursing care.

Nursing homes now have a higher concentration of more disabled people because Americans are less likely to use nursing home care today (National Center for Health Statistics, 1997). People in nursing homes need varying amounts of supervision or personal help with bathing, eating, using toilet facilities, dressing, money management, shopping, or walking. Based on a prevalence of 19.8 percent for some mental disorder among elderly living in institutions (Surgeon General's Report, 2001a), about 340,000 residents of nursing homes should receive some psychiatric attention. We don't know how many actually receive care.

Out-of-home residential care. Many children and adolescents are also in residential care. In 2000 there were 128,279 youth in public and private juvenile justice facilities. In 1999 there were about 568,000 children in foster care (U.S. General Accounting Office, 1993; National Clearinghouse on Child Abuse and Neglect, 2001; see section on foster care below). Many children were placed in foster care as a result of abuse or neglect.

Jails and prisons. The number of people in federal and state prisons and in jails (pretrial or short-term holding centers) has been increasing rapidly. In the year ending June 30, 2002, for the first time, the number of persons in jails and prisons exceeded 2 million. There were 665,475 inmates in jail custody (short term facilities, generally less than one year), and there were 1,426,118 prisoners in state and federal prisons (long-term facilities generally more than one year.) Women were 6.7 percent of the prison population and 11.6 percent of the jail population (Harrison & Karberg, 2003). About two-thirds of the women and 56 percent of the men have children (Snell & Morton, 1994). Those children need care, but the extent to which their difficulties are directly related to having a parent in prison has not been documented.

Because of the "criminalization of the mentally ill" (Teplin, 1984; 2001; see chapter 4), a large number of people with mental illness are in prisons and jails. Hilts (1992) claimed that the Los Angeles city jail held more mentally ill inmates than the largest remaining mental hospital in California. Conditions in many prisons and jails are very poor.

In 1993, there were 647 deaths in jails, 36 percent of them suicides. Twenty-six percent of jurisdictions with jails holding more than 100 inmates were under court order to improve conditions because they were so poor (U. S. Bureau of Justice Statistics, 1990; Perkins, Stephan, & Beck, 1995). In 1999 there were 283,000 inmates with mental illness in prisons and jails, and one-fourth of female prisoners report having a mental illness (Minnesota Public Radio, 2000). Services in prisons and jails are of variable quality.

Overall estimate. The 2000 Census reported that 4,059,039 people were in institutions. Using our multiplier of 2.59 for household size, we estimate that an additional 6,453,872 people are living with the fact that some household member is institutionalized. Note that this number does not take into account patient care episodes and psychiatric care in general hospitals. If we reduce the number by 25 percent because of repeated admissions, we are still left with at least 5 million additional persons who are affected each year. The 2000 census counted people living in group homes and similar facilities as living in the community. Using a conservative estimate, there are about three-quarters of a million people who are not living fully independently and receive care from a paid caretaker in the community. That means that about 4.8 million people have severe enough problems that they are under care. If we use our household size multiplier of 2.59, we estimate that in the United States, 12,432,000 people are either in institutions, in group care in the community, or are affected family members.

Outpatient Mental Health Care

We now examine estimates of the number of persons identified as having psychiatric disorders exclusive of those who are in group homes or institutions. These persons can receive treatment on an outpatient (or "ambulatory") basis. We have estimates of the number of adults with mental health problems from several door-to-door epidemiological sampling surveys using standardized self-report questionnaires that identify people with psychiatric diagnoses. Table 1–1 presents an estimate averaged over two large-scale studies using that methodology.

According to the 2000 Census there were 149.8 million people between the ages of 18 and 54. If the one-year prevalence of any disorder is 21 percent, then 31.5 million experienced symptoms in the previous year severe enough to qualify for a diagnosis. There were also 59,266,437 people age 55 or older. If the one-year prevalence rate for any disorder is 19.8 percent, then 11.7 million persons more qualify for a diagnosis. If we multiply the total number (31.5 + 11.7 = 43.2) by our household size estimate (2.59), we arrive at a figure of 111.9 million people whose symptoms in the previous year warranted a diagnosis, or who lived with someone who qualified for a diagnosis. That means

Table 1–1
Best Estimate, One-Year Prevalence, for Ages 18–54 and 55 or Over

Disorder	Best Estimate (%)	
	18–54	55+
Any anxiety disorder*	16.4	11.4
Any mood disorder**	7.1	4.4
Schizophrenia (and nonaffective psychoses)	1.5	0.6
Somatization	0.2	0.3
Antisocial Personality Disorder	2.1	0.0
Anorexia Nervosa	0.1	0.0
Severe cognitive impairment	1.2	6.6
ANY DISORDER	**21.0**	**19.8**

*Phobias, general anxiety disorder, panic disorder, obsessive compulsive disorder, PTSD
**Manic-depressive episodes, unipolar, bipolar, and dysthymia
Source: U.S. Surgeon General's Report on Mental Health, 2001a, chapters 4 and 5

that about 40 percent of the population (112/281 million) is affected. We have not yet taken into account the prevalence of disorder among children or the numbers affected by alcohol and drug abuse counted separately from those with mental health problems.

The service system. The U.S. Surgeon General defines the mental health service system as consisting of four sectors, as shown in Table 1–2: the specialty mental health sector (psychologists, psychiatrists, social workers, nurses), the general medical/primary care sector (family physicians, nurse practitioners, medical specialists), the human services sector (social welfare, criminal justice, educational, religious, and charitable services) and the voluntary support system (self-help groups and organizations).

We estimated that 43.2 million people experienced symptoms warranting a diagnosis in the previous year. However, there were only a total of 9.67 million admissions to inpatient and outpatient services in 1997 (Milazzo-Sayre, et al., 2001). That means that only about a fifth of those with symptoms severe enough to warrant a diagnosis were seen in the specialty mental health system. Of course, some may have been seen in private offices by mental health practitioners, and they would not show up in a census of hospitals and clinics. Actually, a very large percentage of professional care is devoted to those with less serious problems. Narrow et al. (1993) report that 46 percent of those receiving ambulatory help did not have a current diagnosis, and about 9 percent also had no lifetime history of diagnosable mental disorder.

Millions of Americans see physicians, but, except for nurse practitioners, the vast majority of physicians (80% or more) do not inquire

Table 1–2
Percent Using Mental Health Services in One Year and
Sources of Service

	Adults *15.0**	*Child/Adol* *21.0**
Specialty Mental Health Sector	5.5	9.0
Medical/Primary Care Sector	5.5	<1.0
Human Services Sector	5.0	17.0
Voluntary Support Network	3.0	<1.0

*Figures add to more than 15% or 21% because some use more than one type of service.
Source: U.S. Surgeon General's Report (2001a), chapter 2

about emotional/behavioral or cognitive functioning in routine examinations (Healthy People 2010, Priority Area 6, 6.13). It is difficult to judge how well ordinary medical care meets patient mental health needs.

The mental health system imposes many barriers on those seeking care. Many Americans (16%) either have no insurance or their benefits for mental health care are highly limited. Many Americans, and especially members of some racial and ethnic groups, perceive care as stigmatizing and avoid contact with the mental health system. These are all limits of the provision of care in the medical model (see below).

Illnesses or problems in living? Looked at in this way, these data (enhanced by our multiplier for family involvement) indicate that over 40 percent of the noninstitutionalized population may be affected by mental health problems. Is that large a percentage of the population "sick" or struggling with emotional and mental disorders of themselves or others close to them? We don't think so. Some have questioned the validity of the diagnostic questionnaires used in surveys, suggesting they overestimate the prevalence of disorder. The epidemiological rate is considerably smaller if the count is limited to those with a more severe symptom picture. However, we believe that the definition of subjective distress as a mental health problem, or as a "diagnosable disorder," reflects the influence on the field of the medical model of care. This definition limits our vision because it directs us to think in terms of treating disorders instead of understanding what in fact are ubiquitous problems in living.

Alcohol and Substance Abuse

Alcohol. Although many individuals have dual diagnoses of both mental disorder and substance abuse, alcohol and substance abuse problems are counted separately by epidemiologists. About half the population (46.6%) uses alcohol. According to the Substance Abuse and Mental Health Services Administration (SAMHSA, 2001), 20.6 percent of the population age 12 and over (46 million people) participated in binge drinking (five or more drinks on the same occasion at least once in the previous 30 days), and 5.6 percent or 12.6 million people reported heavy drinking (five or more drinks on the same occasion at least five days in the previous 30). Young adults (ages 18–25) were most likely to binge or drink heavily. Almost 10 million drinkers were under the legal age of 21. Except among the youngest drinkers, males were more likely to binge or to drink heavily than females. The rates among males and females were comparable in the underage group. About 10 percent of teens admit to drinking heavily on a weekly basis. College students drink more than noncollege students of the same age. Driving under the influence of alcohol is most frequent among those 18 to 25, almost 20 percent of whom said they drove under the influence in the previous year. College administrators may worry about those numbers, but college students themselves don't seem to consider drinking a serious problem. Intervention and prevention programs may be running counter to the students' attitude that drinking is not a problem.

In 1996 there were 1,466,300 arrests on charges of Driving While Intoxicated (DWI); the number is substantially less than ten years ago, suggesting that preventive efforts can be effective. Driving under the influence of alcohol occurs most often among those 18 to 25. Almost 20 percent of people that age said they drove under the influence in the previous year. In addition to traffic accidents and fatalities associated with alcohol use, about 36 percent of convicted offenders had been drinking at the time of their offense. Alcohol was involved in about two-thirds of cases of intimate violence (i.e., between spouses, lovers, etc.; Bureau of Justice Statistics, 1998).

In 1991, the U.S. Department of Health and Human Services said that about 18 percent of adults (which, when extrapolated to 2000, is 38.7 million people) lived with an alcoholic when they were children and about 9 percent of adults have been married to or have lived with an alcoholic (American Public Health Association, 1991). If we take the figure of those who drink heavily as an estimate of those with an alcohol problem (12.6 million) and multiply that number by average household size (2.59), 32.6 million people or about 12 percent of the population have an alcohol problem or are living with someone who has an alcohol problem.

Substance abuse. Illicit drugs are nonprescription or prescription drugs taken for the psychological effect rather than for any medicinal purpose. In 2000, 6.3 percent of those over age 12, or about 14 million people, used an illicit drug in the month prior to the survey interview. About three-quarters use marijuana, but about 5.7 million Americans use other illicit drugs either alone or in combination with marijuana. About 18 percent of college students use illicit drugs. Of marijuana users in 2000, 34.7 percent used on 100 days or more, and 11.7 percent used on 300 days or more in the previous year.

A new drug problem seems to have emerged as a consequence of the widespread use of Ritalin and similar substances for medical treatment of children and adolescents. About 3 percent of high school seniors reported methylphenidate obtained from friends or on the street was used recreationally. On college campuses it is used as a party drug. There have been reports of adults who take their children to several physicians to obtain prescriptions, then sell or trade the pills for other drugs on the street (Woodworth, 2000).

The rate of use of illicit drugs among pregnant adolescents is 12.9 percent; there are potential consequences for their newborns. In 1999 there were 198,400 arrests of juveniles for drug abuse violations (SAMHSA, 2001). About a fifth of all state prison and local jail inmates (372,104 persons) were convicted or were charged with a drug offense. There were about 7.8 million admissions annually for treatment of drug problems in state and local facilities receiving federal funds. If we treat this number as reflecting a "revolving door" with many readmissions, and reduce it by a third, we would still have 5.3 million individuals hospitalized for treatment of a drug problem. Applying our multiplier for household size, we estimate that 13.7 million people received drug treatment or were living with someone receiving drug treatment.

Crime and Victims of Crime

Crime victims suffer distress that may last a long time (Ross, 1993). Our knowledge of the frequency of crimes also leads us to feel anxious lest we may become victims. The rates of fear of crime range from 20 percent in smaller cities to 48 percent in cities such as Washington, DC, and Chicago. In 2001, 3,027,000 males and 2,716,000 females age 12 or older reported they were a victim of some crime. With male victims the perpetrator was a stranger in 55 percent of cases, while for female victims the perpetrator was a stranger in 32 percent of cases (Rennison, 2002). Only about half of violent victimizations and 37 percent of property crimes were reported to the police. Regarding overall violence by intimate partners (rape, sexual assault, robbery, aggravated assault, simple assault), 588,940 females or 5.0 per thousand were victims while 103,220 males or 0.9 per thousand were victims in 2001. Most frequent were simple assaults (71.6% for females; 48.7% for males); no sexual assaults or rapes were recorded for males. Intimate violence has gone down considerably for both males and females (by about 49.3%) from 1993 to 2001. The rate for male victims declined by 41.8 percent (Rennison, 2002).

The experience of criminal victimization can have important psychological consequences ranging from discomfort for a short period to a long-term post-traumatic stress disorder that may be disabling (Ross, 1993). A telephone survey of women 18 years of age and older reported that 21 percent said they had been a victim of a completed or an attempted rape, of sexual molestation, robbery, or aggravated assault. Victims experienced nervous breakdowns, thought of suicide, and made suicide attempts at a far higher rate than nonvictims. Those who were victims of a crime reported most often that their symptoms appeared after the episode of victimization, not beforehand (Acierno, Brady, Gray, Kilpatrick, Resnick, & Best, 2002). About a third of all victims of violent crime sustained physical injury, and had some medical costs. Medical costs sometimes continue for a long period of time after the injury. About 8 percent of victims lost time from work, an average of 3.4 days per crime. The average economic loss of a crime in 1992 was well over $500 per victim (Klaus, 1994). The person's symptoms may show up on surveys as evidence of mental or emotional disorder, but the precipitating incident may be criminal victimization that would not be detected in the typical psychiatric epidemiological survey.

Arrests. In addition to victims, a large number of people are arrested for crimes and experience stress for that reason. (Serving a term in jail is the fourth most stressful event on the Holmes and Rahe scale.) In 1999 law enforcement officials arrested 2.5 million persons under age 18 (Snyder, 2000). About a quarter were female, and 32 percent were under age 15. About 17 percent were charged with an offense included in the Violent Crime Index, and about 29 percent were charged with a Property Crime Index offense. Almost 200,000 youth were arrested for a drug offense. Juvenile courts handled 1,757,404 delinquency cases in 1998 (Stahl, 2001). That number does not include tens of thousands of status offense cases (runaways, truants, incorrigible children) who may also be processed through juvenile or family courts and are often diverted to the service system. These are not counted among the cases of delinquency.

Problems of Children and Adolescents

Psychiatric diagnosis. The problems of children and adolescents are not included in most of the figures cited previously. The prevalence rate among children 9 to 17 of any disorder is 20.9 percent. Based on the 2000 census, that means that 7.5 million children ages 9 to 17 have symptoms warranting a diagnosis. The prevalence is probably higher among poorer and inner-city children than among those living in more well-to-do areas (Institute of Medicine, 1989). Those figures don't include younger children who may have diagnoses of ADHD, or mental retardation, who are not counted in this survey. No one knows how many children are diagnosed as ADHD and are receiving Ritalin, and Aderall or related medications. Recently 11 million prescriptions were written for methylphenidate, and 6 million more for amphetamines for children (Woodworth, 2000).

However, assuming a lower prevalence rate of 10 percent for children under school age, we should add another 3.4 million children to the total. Adding the two estimates (7.5 million + 3.4 million = 10.9 million) and using our multiplier of 2.59 we arrive at a total of 28.2 million children and people in their families affected by some mental or emotional disorder. The prevalence rate drops to 11 percent if we count only those with significant impairments at home, in school or with peers, and to 5 percent if we count only those with extreme functional impairment (U.S. Surgeon General, 2001a).

Education-related problems. Children's problems emerge in educational settings and involve intellectual competence as well as issues of and adjustment to classrooms. In 1999–2000, 6,195,000 children were enrolled in public special education facilities (National Center for Education Statistics, 2001). The total includes 568,000 preschool children served under new amendments to the Individuals with Disabilities Education Act and the Elementary and Secondary Education Act. The four categories of specific learning disability—speech or language impairment, mental retardation, and serious emotional disturbance—account for nearly 80 percent of the children with problems. Using our multiplier, we can say that 15.6 million children and family members are dealing with a handicapping condition.

However, school-based programs for serious emotional disturbances are identifying and serving only a very small proportion of those in need. The number of those served does not take into account children who are not sufficiently disturbed (or disturbing) to be classified as educationally handicapped or seriously emotionally disturbed, but whose teachers may consider them maladjusted. According to the Surgeon General (2001b) each year about 21 percent of the child and adolescent population use mental health services, mostly through school-based providers. As with adults, however, the formal mental health service system serves only a small percentage of children in need, and a large share of its resources serve those with a lesser degree of need.

Child abuse and neglect. The problem of child abuse and neglect first surfaced in the mid-1960s. States responded by passing legislation requiring professionals who work with children to report suspected child abuse and neglect to either child protection authorities or to the police. Following the Child Abuse Prevention and Treatment Act of 1974, all states created state central registries and hotlines that took calls from ordinary citizens as well as mandated professionals. In 1999 almost 2 million reports, involving about 3 million children, were investigated by Child Protective Services (CPS; U.S. Department of Health and Human Services [DHHS], 2001). Of the investigated cases, 29.2 percent were substantiated by the local CPS investigation. Because more than one child is frequently involved in a report, there were about 780,000 child victims. Reported and substantiated cases represent only a fraction of the cases of abuse, and among those investigated and judged to be unfounded, there were probably some false negatives. Nonetheless, on an annual basis 2.2 million children and their families are involved in a child maltreatment investigation, at best not a benign event in their lives.

Reports of sexual abuse have decreased in recent years. In 1999, however, they constituted about 11 percent of all reports, of which about 40 percent were substantiated upon investigation (DHHS, 2001). A very high proportion of sex abuse victims suffer short-term emotional upset, and a smaller number (perhaps 20%) suffer long-term damage (Rind, Tromovich, & Bauserman, 1998; Finkelhor, 1990; for the controversy surrounding the Rind et al. article, see Sorotzkin, 2003). A history of abuse is associated with many problems—educational deficits, acting out, sexual problems later in life, criminality, and abuse of one's own children. Fortunately, most victims are resilient and overcome their difficulties. The numbers above refer to events reported on an annual basis. The prevalence of people who have suffered abuse at some time in the past and who continue to have some aftereffects must be quite high.

Children are victimized in familiar ways (e.g., assault) even more than adults. Children also experience relatively unique forms of victimization ranging from corporal punishment to abduction (Finkelhor & Hashima, 2001). About 750,000 incidents of corporal punishment occur each year in U.S. schools, with serious consequences for at least some children (Hyman, 1995). Sibling assault is experienced by over 50 million children (Finkelhor & Dziuba-Leatherman, 1994; Finkelhor & Hashima, 2001). Reactions to these experiences, which do not count as child abuse, are not typically taken into account in psychiatric epidemiological surveys.

The U.S. Advisory Board on Child Abuse and Neglect (1993) said that the child protection system is in a state of crisis. The problem of abuse and neglect is a national emergency, and the foster care system is overwhelmed. The problem has been exacerbated by the number of "crack" and cocaine babies and babies who are infected with the human immunodeficiency virus (HIV). Only a small proportion of investigated cases receive any service. The board has also recommended a complete overhaul of the existing system of child protection.

Medical Problems and Chronic Illness

Personal injury or illness, the sixth most stressful life event on the Holmes and Rahe list, is fairly common. In 1999, there were 31.2 million hospital discharges, with an average stay of 5.0 days (National Center for Health Statistics, 2001). Obviously there were even more hospital admissions, since some patients died before leaving the hospital. Using our multiplier, over 80 million individuals and their families were affected by an illness requiring hospitalization. In 1999, there were 102.8 million emergency room visits, of which 37.6 percent were injury related. Using our multiplier, 97.4 million people were affected by an emergency room visit for an injury.

A large number of Americans suffer from chronic disorders that limit their functioning in one or more areas of life (U.S. Bureau of the Census, 1998). For example, 32.6 million suffer from arthritis, 22.5 million are hearing impaired, 8.7 million have diabetes, 11.9 million have migraine headaches, 14.9 million have asthma, 21.1 million have heart conditions, 30 million have high blood pressure, and 31.8 million deformities or orthopedic impairments. Many of these conditions are age-related and also have socioeconomic correlates.

In 1997, 5.5 million males and 5.8 million females ages 16–64 had a "severe" work disability (U.S. Bureau of the Census, 1997; Table 27). Another 3 million males and 3.2 million females had a nonsevere work disability; many of these individuals were working despite the disability. Using our multiplier of 2.59, we can say that 45.3 million persons are coping with their own chronic physical limitations or with a member of the household who is limited in some significant degree by a chronic problem. The number is increased substantially when we count in those with various chronic conditions not counted as work disabilities (Breslau & Pabrucki, 1987).

Sexually transmitted diseases (STDs). Sexually transmitted disease may no longer be the social disgrace it once was, but it remains embarrassing at least, seriously disabling or even lethal at worst. Contracting an STD is a stressful event that has enduring consequences for personal relationships and sexual behavior. In 2000, 702,093 cases of chlamydia were reported, about a fifth of them in males (Centers for Disease Control, 2001). Although treatable today, the disease is associated with pelvic inflammatory disorder in women and consequent infertility. In 2000 there were 238,196 cases of gonorrhea but, fortunately, only 5,979 cases of syphilis. There are estimates of between 500,000 and 1 million new cases of genital herpes annually, with several million recurrences each year (see Box 1–1). Knowledge that one has an STD causes distress and perhaps guilt among those who want to conceive, but cannot because of disease-related infertility. Psychiatric epidemiological surveys do not take into account the presence of sexually transmitted disease for the distress they measure.

In 2002 over 800,000 people were infected with HIV in the United States alone, and nearly half a million Americans had died of AIDS (Acquired Immune Deficiency Syndrome; Centers for Disease Control, 2001). Many more persons have been exposed to HIV, the virus that

Box 1–1. *Psychosocial Adaptation to Health Problems:*
        The Case of Genital Herpes

The general public may be well aware of the Human Immunodeficiency Virus (HIV) that causes Aquired Immune Deficiency Syndrome (AIDS). Yet there is another sexually transmitted disease that
has quietly reached pandemic proportions in the United States. Estimates are that 21.9 percent of the population over age 12 (approximately 50.5 million people) are infected with genital herpes simplex
virus (HSV-2). The rate is increasing and is highest among young
adults. In 2000, about 200,000 initial office visits to physicians were
for genital warts, and 175,000 initial visits were for herpes infections
(National Center for HIV, STD and TB Prevention, 2000, 2002).

Herpes is accompanied by lifelong, sometimes painful, eruptions
of genital lesions and increased likelihood of HIV transmission. If acquired in pregnancy the condition can lead to fatal neonatal infection. Although it is manageable, its discovery is undoubtedly a
stressful life event with enduring consequences. The symptoms and
prognosis for HSV-2 are not nearly as serious as for AIDS. Because
HSV-2 is as yet incurable, however, its prevention and people's
adaptation to it are more behavioral than medical problems. Studying those problems and their solution may lead to more effective
programs to prevent and live with HIV and other STDs.

Herpes is also an emotional problem. There is evidence that
those with HSV-2 experience more distress when first infected than
people with other STDs and those with recurrent HSV-2 experience
even higher levels of distress (Green & Kocsis, 1997). Young adults
with HSV-2 experience lower self-esteem, problems with everyday
life, and more psychopathology. Those with frequent recurrence of
symptoms may feel their life is out of control. Those afflicted long-
term often have serious problems in their relationships, not only
with sexual partners but also with family and friends (Green &
Kocsis, 1997). In addition to isolation, other effects include feelings of
helplessness, depression, and poor performance at school or work
(Swanson & Chenitz, 1990).

As suggested by the Dohrenwend stress model we present in
chapter 3, there are several ways in which psychological research can
address this problem. One way is to study mechanisms and programs for preventing infection. For example, adolescent women who
drink heavily have a substantially higher risk of HSV-2 infection
(Cook, Pollock, Rao, & Clark, 2002). Furthermore, as with HIV, condom use and counseling about avoiding sex when a partner has lesions can prevent women's HSV-2 infection (Wald et al., 2001). These

findings suggest that programs addressing sexually transmitted diseases and risk and protective behaviors should target young women, especially those with alcohol problems.

Another approach is to examine the role of stress in the recurrence and worsening of herpes outbreaks. Many studies have linked stress and the recurrence of HSV-2 symptoms, although it is often impossible to know whether stress is worsening the disease or the disease is causing more stress—most likely each exacerbates the other. Sources of stress for herpes patients include worry over the future course of the disease, fear of rejection, and fear of transmitting the disease (Swanson & Chenitz, 1990). There are also troubling ethical dilemmas—such as whether to have sex, when, with whom, and whether a partner should be informed—which are complicated by not knowing for certain when one is contagious. These may result in "psychosocial disability" because the patient withdraws from the possibility of intimacy (Swanson & Chenitz, 1990).

As discussed more generally in chapter 7, various coping strategies and social-support mechanisms studied by community psychologists suggest other approaches to dealing with stress associated with HSV-2. Social support is generally related to better psychological adjustment in terms of self-esteem, depression, sexual adjustment, and distress over the disease (Manne & Sandler, 1984). Certain cognitive coping mechanisms (negative thoughts, wishful thinking, and self-blame) and repeated use of disease-management strategies are related to worse adjustment (Green & Kocsis, 1997; Manne & Sandler, 1984; Swanson & Chenitz, 1990).

The types of cognitive coping and support used make a difference, however. Aral et al. (1988) found that avoidant coping strategies (e.g., denial) and social support from a counselor were related to worse adjustment to HSV-2, whereas other cognitive coping strategies and *partner* social support were positively related to adjustment. Cassidy, Meadows, Catalan, & Barton (1997) found that problem-focused coping (e.g., planning, active coping) and emotion-focused coping (e.g., positive reinterpretation, growth) were associated with fewer recurrences of symptoms. Participation in herpes support groups may have mixed effects. They appear to help those with HSV-2 maintain the use of coping strategies but do not necessarily help with depression or feelings of distress over time (Manne, Sandler & Zautra, 1986). This may happen because those who are more stressed by the disease join and stay in support groups longer, however. As the prevalence of genital herpes continues to grow, it is clear that more research into its prevention and psychosocial consequences and adaptation is needed.

causes AIDS. Eighteen states and two territories have confidential reporting laws, so we don't know the precise number of infected people who do not have the disease. There are ethnic, gender, and socioeconomic correlates of AIDS infections. The rates are much higher among African Americans (66/100,000) and Hispanics (25.6/100,000) than among whites (7.6/100,000), Native Americans (8.8/100,000) and Asian–Pacific Islanders (3.4/100,000).

This devastating disorder is now manageable using expensive medications, which are complicated to take (a problem in itself). AIDS is correlated with psychological distress and presents problems of adaptation to the hundreds of thousands who are afflicted and their families and friends. Moreover, in the absence of medical means of preventing the disorder, prevention depends on behavioral change and lifestyle change. Although the manifestations are primarily medical in nature, the problems of prevention and adaptation are social and psychological (Reppucci, Woolard, & Fried, 1999; interventions to prevent AIDS/HIV are discussed in chapter 8).

Disasters

The terrorist attacks on the World Trade Center in New York City and the Pentagon in Washington, DC, on September 11, 2001, cost three thousand lives, including those of several hundred firemen, police, emergency medical, and other rescue workers. The dollar losses in property and in lost business were in the billions, and the consequences will be felt for many years to come.

We can get a feeling for the disruption in the lives of affected people of any disaster by seeing the kind of assistance the Federal Emergency Management Agency (FEMA) provided in the aftermath of the 9/11 attack: temporary housing assistance, low interest loans to small businesses, replacement of lost personal possessions, reimbursement of medical bills, mental health and crisis counseling, disaster unemployment assistance, food stamps, recovery activities (search and rescue teams), state and local government costs for debris removal, and emergency protective measures (FEMA, 2002).

Hundreds of thousands of people each year are affected by human-made and natural disasters, resulting at least in inconvenience and some degree of fear, but potentially resulting in death, severe injury, the necessity to change living arrangements or to start one's life anew, and in some cases enduring psychological distress (Luce, Firth Cozens, Midgley, & Burges, 2002; Zusman & Simon, 1983). Fire killed 3,250 persons and injured 17,175 in 1998. Property losses amounted to 4.4 billion dollars. Young children and the elderly are most vulnerable to death by fire. Nineteen percent of mass deaths took place in hotels, boarding houses, rooming houses, and in facilities for the aged. Burn injuries have a high rate of fatality, and the consequences of severe burns endure (American Academy of Pediatrics, 2000).

While natural disasters do not take many lives, comparatively speaking, many individuals and communities are affected. Floods cause about 100 deaths a year but result in $2 billion in damages, to say nothing about the psychological and economic cost to people who evacuated their homes. Earthquakes can also result in devastating property damage, although in the United States not many lives are lost. Hurricane Hugo in the southeastern United States caused 60 deaths and $7 billion in damages. The hurricane caused inland flooding and many were dislocated temporarily. Landslides, volcano eruptions, and wildfires take few lives fortunately, but property damage is high and people's lives can be affected for a long time because of volcanic ash, debris, mud, rocks, and threat of flooding due to loss of vegetation.

Rescue workers risk death and injury and are affected as they work under grueling conditions, coping with people who are injured, in pain, with bloody, mangled, or burned bodies. Think of the firemen and rescue workers sifting through the wreckage at the World Trade Center looking for remains of victims and of brother firemen who lost their lives in the rescue attempt. Mental health workers who volunteer in disasters can find themselves providing more support for the rescue workers than for the victims of disasters.

Technological advances have created the possibility of new kinds of disasters. Nuclear plant accidents at Three Mile Island, near Middletown, Pennsylvania (Perrow, 1984), and Chernobyl, outside Kiev, Ukraine, made real the danger of an accidental nuclear disaster. There are a large number of nuclear plants in the United States, and fear of the possibility of a nuclear accident, or a terrorist attack against nuclear facilities, crosses the minds of many children and adults (Rabow, Hernandez, & Newcomb, 1990; Schwebel & Schwebel, 1981; Vriens, 1999). The Love Canal episode (A. Levine, 1982; see also chapter 12), in which a leaking, abandoned toxic waste dump site threatened the safety of a residential area, brought that hazard to public attention. More than 80,000 hazardous waste sites have been identified in the United States. Ninety percent pose a threat of contamination to the water supply of nearby communities. The Center for Health Environment and Justice (2002; see chapter 12) issued a report based on computer mapping techniques showing that hundreds of schools, serving thousands of children all over the country, are located within half a mile of a superfund site (one designated as particularly hazardous by the EPA or by the state). For example, in Massachusetts 818 schools, serving 407,000 children, are located within half a mile of a contaminated site. In New York, 235 schools serving 142,738 children are located within half a mile of a contaminated site (Center for Health, Environment and Justice, 2002).

Although a clear relationship to adverse health effects remains to be fully documented, untold thousands live with a background threat to their health, safety, and economic well-being. The impact of technological disasters is as much psychological as it is physical (Wandersman & Hallman, 1993), but a community's problems are every bit as real in the technological as in the natural disaster (Edelstein, 1988; see chapter 12). The silver lining around the dark cloud of natural disasters, accidents, and terrorist acts may be that they provide a kind of "natural experiment" that helps us understand and appreciate both individual and community responses to environmental threats and the healing role of family, friends and neighbors in the form of social support (Kaniasty, Norris & Murrell, 1990; Norris & Murrell, 1988; Norris, Phifer & Kaniasty, 1994; see chapter 7). They also point to the strong emotional bonds we feel toward particular places as symbols of our country, our communities, and even our self-identities (Brown & Perkins, 1992). We generally take these place attachments for granted until they are threatened or disrupted by not only disasters but also crime, residential mobility, and many of the other life events catalogued in this chapter. Because disasters affect whole communities at once, however, they highlight humans' inherent and simultaneous identities as individuals and members of a community and our need for stability in the face of inevitable change (Brown & Perkins, 1992).

Marriage and Parenting

Marriage and parenting are major life goals achieved by most people, although in recent years some have been rethinking the place of children in their life plans (Hacker, 2000). However, marriage is the seventh most stressful of Holmes and Rahe's 43 events, and parenthood is the fourteenth. Both events are major life transitions posing myriad problems of adjustment. In the United States, most people marry at least once; by age 40, 87 percent of women and 82 percent of men have married. In 2001, there were 2,363,000 marriages involving 4,726,000 individuals.

Many people who marry (and many who don't) have children, another important life transition. In 2001 there were 4,045,000 live births (Centers for Disease Control, 2001b). Today, families make up 69 percent of households, in contrast to 1970 where they made up 81 percent (Fields & Casper, 2001). Thirty-nine percent of nonfamily households have one or more children. There were 12 million one-parent families in 2000, 2 million single-father families and 10 million single-mother families. Many single-parent families experience economic distress. Thirty percent of single-mother households have incomes under the poverty line, as do 16 percent of single-father households. In contrast, the median annual income of married householders is well over

$50,000. President Bush's advisers have offered policies to promote marriage, but not proposed policies to deal with the lack of desirable mates (employed, not in prison or jail—see our discussion of the Male Marriageable Pool Index in chapter 3) by increasing employment and education opportunities.

About 33 percent of all live births were to unmarried mothers, and about 75 percent of all births to teens were out of wedlock (U.S. Bureau of the Census, 1998, Tables 92–106). Although it is possible for many single parents to be competent and raise healthy children, a young single mother who has a child out of wedlock will be coping with considerable stress. Her chances of completing high school are considerably less than those of someone who postpones the birth of her first child until later. Young unmarried mothers are more likely to smoke and use drugs or alcohol during pregnancy, are less likely to have good prenatal care, and are more likely to have a low birth weight baby. All of these factors presage a difficult future for many of the young mothers and their children.

An increasing number of children are living with grandparents. Four and a half million children are living in 2.4 million grandparent-headed households. Many of these grandparents are divorced, widowed, or living on fixed incomes. Many have serious health problems, or their energy is insufficient to keep up with young children. Some communities are developing services geared to the needs of the grandparent parent. (Hudnall, 2001).

Abortions. Not all pregnancies are desired. In 1997 there were 1,186,039 legal abortions. Although abortion rates have declined in recent years, 81 percent of abortions are received by unmarried women and 20 percent by women under 19. Sexually active teens not using contraception have a 90 percent chance of becoming pregnant within a year; about 19 percent of sexually active teens (about 1 million) become pregnant each year. About 30 percent of their pregnancies are terminated by abortions, but about 500,000 teens give birth each year. Recent declines in births and abortions reflect changes in sexual behavior among teens. It is difficult to say whether the changes involve better contraceptive use, delay in initiating intercourse, reduced sexual frequency in fear of sexually transmitted diseases, changes in norms toward abstinence, changes in welfare laws limiting the attractiveness of having a child and going on welfare, or laws requiring parental participation in the abortion decision (Alan Guttmacher Institute, 1999).

Pregnancy, abortion, and having a child at a young age are stressful events and challenge adaptive coping in young women and their families. We have less information about the putative fathers. This set of stressful life events is not tracked in psychiatric epidemiological surveys.

Fetal and infant mortality. There are many more pregnancies than live births. In addition to those terminated by abortion, about 16 percent of pregnancies end in miscarriages or stillbirths. Those who wanted to be pregnant undoubtedly suffered emotional distress upon the loss, but bearing a child is no guarantee that the child will live and grow up. The infant mortality rate has been declining, but in 1995 nearly 30,000 infants died before their first birthdays (U.S. Bureau of the Census, 1998).

Infant morbidity and birth defects. For some sizable number of families, the birth of a child may signal the beginning of an enduring struggle with a chronic disorder, requiring an emotional adaptation on the part of the family and long-term planning for coping with the special problems that will inevitably arise. Each year over 100,000 infants are born with some birth defect (Physicians Committee for Responsible Medicine, undated). Many others have congenital diseases (e.g., cerebral palsy, muscular dystrophy, cystic fibrosis) that involve continuous coping with medical, financial, and emotional problems over a lifetime.

Adoptions. Recently there have been approximately 120,000 adoptions each year, about 46 percent of them by kinfolk or a stepparent (National Adoption Information Clearinghouse, 2000). About 38 percent of adoptions are made through private for-profit or nonprofit adoption agencies. Public adoptions from foster care to permanent homes account for about 16 percent of adoptions. An increasing percentage (estimated at 8–34 percent) of adoptions are by single women, and about 10,000 adoptions a year are children from foreign countries. The foster care system is unable to place many abused, neglected, or "special needs" children with physical or emotional handicaps, even though parental rights have been terminated and the children are available for adoption. Many social service agencies and family courts have made special efforts to increase the rate of adoptions of children in foster care who are eligible for adoption. Most adoptions work out well. However, about 5 percent of children referred for psychiatric treatment are adopted (Kadushin, 1980). Moreover, there are about 6 million adoptees in the population. About 100,000 a year reach age 18, and many of those start to search for their birth parents, creating a new problem of adaptation for the adoptees and for the birth parent when found.

Foster care. There were about 568,000 children in foster care in 1999 (National Clearinghouse on Child Abuse and Neglect Information, 2001). The courts removed most of them from their homes because their parents abused or neglected them or were unable to care for them. Including adopted children, about 600,000 children a year enter new families, many after having endured stress or trauma in their natural families. Of those in foster care, 36 percent were white, 42 percent were African American, 15 percent were Hispanic, and 7 percent were of other racial or ethnic groups. In 1999 about 286,000 children entered foster care while only 244,000 left. The demand for foster care homes is high, even though about a quarter of foster care placements are with relatives. Of those who left foster care, about 60 percent returned home and another 12 percent went to a relative or legal guardian. Only 16 percent were adopted and 8 percent were emancipated ("aged out"). States no longer had responsibility for those 20,000 youth, who were then on their own. A high proportion of these children in foster care have emotional problems, and few services are available for them (Horan, et al., 1993).

Divorce

In 1998 there were 1,136,000 divorces, with an average of one child per divorce (U.S. Bureau of the Census, *Statistical Abstract of the U.S.*, 2002). Divorce and separation are the second and third most stressful events, respectively, on the Holmes and Rahe scale, and are correlated with many physical and psychological difficulties (Bloom, Asher, & White, 1978; Lee & Hunsley, 2001). Changing divorce laws have had strong, adverse economic consequences for many divorced women (Smock, Manning, & Gupta, 1999). Women who are younger at the time of divorce and do not have children may be less adversely affected (Jacob, 1989). In addition to having reduced incomes, child support payments can be a continuing source of conflict after a divorce; a great many women receive no child support or receive it irregularly. In 2000, women on average received about 60 percent of the child support payments due under divorce settlements. The picture has been improving because of tougher enforcement efforts, which adds to the stress of divorce or remarriage for those who owe the support payments (Garfinkel, McLanahan, Meyer, & Seltzer, 1998).

Although the majority prove resilient and cope successfully, for about 20 percent of children of divorce there are long-term consequences for psychological development. Divorce is at least a short-term stressful life event, and for some the conflict generated by divorce persists. About 10 percent of divorces involve custody fights, and 6–25 percent of divorces are "high conflict" cases with repeated recourse to litigation about custody, visitation, and support payments. These fights take up a disproportionate amount of court time that may continue for years, involving repeated legal encounters (Clingempeel & Reppucci, 1982; Elrod, 2001), and children's adjustment is poorer when former spouses are in conflict (Emery, 1982; Elrod, 2001). At present, perhaps 25 percent of the young adult population are children of a divorce. The problems with divorce can continue through a lifetime. Divorced parents encounter each other at religious confirmations, graduations, marriages, and the births of grandchildren. The confrontation may be compounded in emotional difficulty if the first marriage broke up because of an extramarital affair with the second spouse. Divorce may also affect the formerly married couple's parents if the divorced person with or without children asks to return to the parental home. Moreover, divorce may affect grandparents who wish to maintain a relationship with grandchildren, even though the parents are divorced and in conflict. It's no wonder that divorce ranks so high on stressful life events scales.

Each year the number affected by divorce is large—2.2 million adults, and about 1 million children. If only 10 percent of divorces are high conflict, and the period of conflict lasts three years, at any given point the prevalence of people affected by high conflict divorces must be on the order of a million or more adults and children. Members of this group are high consumers of professional services for therapy, and for child custody evaluations. While under stress, their psychological states do not necessarily warrant psychiatric diagnoses. Again, our psychiatric epidemiological methods don't track the source of dysphoric feelings that the diagnostic scales measure.

About 75 percent of divorced people remarry. In a third or more of all marriages at least one of the spouses was previously married. However, remarriage is also problematic. About 60 percent of remarriages end in divorce. About 65 percent of remarriages include children from the previous marriages. About 22 percent of children under 18 live in two-parent households in which one of the parents is a stepparent. Thus many people face the often difficult problem of becoming a parent of someone else's partially grown child and blending the new spouse into other family affairs (e.g., a daughter's marriage). By one estimate, one out of three Americans is now a stepparent, a stepchild, a stepsibling,or some other member of a stepfamily (Stepfamily Association of America, 2000). At least one company has created greeting cards especially for blended families. The high rate of divorce and remarriage has also created conflict within various religious denominations over whether divorce is disapproved or approved in the Bible ("until death do us part", but see Deuteronomy 2:1–5) and whether ministers should be permitted to perform marriage ceremonies for those previously married whose ex-spouses are still alive.

Economics and Employment

Inadequate income. It is truly said that it is better to be rich and healthy than sick and poor. Poor people have more problems than those with more money. Socioeconomic status is consistently related to health outcomes (Adler, et al., 1994; Chen, Matthews, & Boyce, 2002), and several events involving financial problems are in the top half of Holmes and Rahe's list. A great many people regularly struggle with inadequate incomes. The Social Security Administration developed a poverty index for individuals and families. It is based on what the Department of Agriculture says is a minimally adequate nutritional diet multiplied by three on the assumption that poor people spend one third of their incomes on food. The index assumes that the homemaker will be an expert shopper, cook, and manager who never eats out (Fisher, 1992). The index is adjusted annually based on changes in the cost of living. In 1999 the poverty line for a family of four was $18,022. In 1999, 32.3 million people lived in families with incomes below the poverty line. Poverty is not distributed randomly in the population. In 2000 the median income of white families was about $48,950 while that of Hispanics was about $33,000 and that of African Americans about $30,000. Even though the economic situation of African Americans and Hispanics has been improving, the probability of an African American or a Hispanic family falling below the poverty line is about three times that of a white family.

The situation is especially difficult for single-parent families. In 2000 there were 3.6 million female-headed households with incomes below the poverty line (U.S. Bureau of the Census, 2000, Table QT-03). In addition to other stresses of living without a partner, these families struggled with inadequate financial resources.

Welfare and income dependency. In 1996, responding to widespread dissatisfaction with the existing welfare program, Congress passed the Personal Responsibility and Work Opportunity Reconciliation Act. The Act contained strong incentives to move from welfare to work, offered support for families moving from welfare to work, gave the states financial incentives to reduce unmarried pregnancies, and introduced lifetime time limits for people to remain on welfare. The program changed its name from Aid to Families with Dependent Children (AFDC) to Temporary Assistance for Needy Families (TANF; Haskins, Sawhill, & Weaver, 2001).

The change in law had a profound effect on the number of people receiving welfare payments. In 1995, 4.8 million families and 13.4 million individuals received welfare payments. In 2000, the number of families had dropped by 53 percent to 2.27 million, and the number of individuals receiving payments had dropped by 57 percent to 5.8 million people. The number of never-married mothers in the workforce increased and poverty among households headed by single women and their children declined (Haskins et al. 2001). About 60 percent of those who left the welfare rolls obtained work and were earning an average of $8 an hour, but only half had employee benefits and about 20 percent had no health insurance. About one quarter return to the welfare rolls and continue to use up their allotment of federal assistance. A year after leaving the welfare rolls, 40 percent are jobless. (Haskins et al., 2001; Acs & Loprest, 2001).

Welfare reform is associated in time with a drop in the rate of teen births and unmarried births, but many factors in addition to welfare reform contribute to that decline. Even though former welfare recipients now in the workforce are somewhat better off economically and psychologically in terms of self-esteem, we don't know the effect on children. (Haskins et al., 2001). Welfare reform has had some success, but it remains to be seen what happens in an economic downturn, or what happens to families who run through their federal or state time limits for remaining on welfare.

In 2000 about 6.6 million persons received Supplemental Security Income (SSI) payments because they were aged, indigent, blind, or otherwise disabled and did not qualify for Social Security payments. Of this number more than 60 percent were disabled. Many were former mental patients or individuals with mental retardation or developmental disabilities. Disabled persons received a monthly payment of $545 in 2002. Couples received $810 (Social Security Online, 2003). Some states supplement these amounts and recipients are eligible for Medicaid and food stamps. Efforts to make the disability eligibility rules more stringent may result in removing some from the SSI rolls, but then many of those people are not truly competitive in the workforce, and may have a hard time making ends meet.

Homelessness. Homelessness is one result of poverty and is increasing among women and children (Shinn, 1992). The homeless population changes from time to time. Many find homes and new people enter homelessness. At any point in time, between 500,000 and 600,000 are homeless (Urban Institute, 2000). The odds of a poor person being homeless at some time in his or her life may be as high as one in six. About 15 percent of the homeless population consists of female-headed households with children under 18. From 20 to 50 percent of these families entered homelessness because they were fleeing from domestic violence or abuse. A third of the children suffer from depression, and about a quarter have at least a borderline conduct disorder. It is difficult to provide for children's education while they are homeless. Of the adults, two thirds have either a mental illness or an alcohol or other substance abuse problem. Homelessness is not only due to people's deficits. There is insufficient low-income housing, and homeless people don't have the resources to pay rent in advance or to pay security deposits. Many are unemployed and don't have references to show prospective landlords.

Even when they have homes, poor people live in less desirable residences than do wealthier people. Zahner, Kasl, White, and Will (1985) report a correlation between the presence of vermin in the home, particularly rats, and measures of psychological well-being in minority women. Conditions associated with poverty were associated with psychological symptoms of a kind that are measured in epidemiological surveys. Had the research team just measured anxiety, they would have reported high levels of disorder instead of responses to unhealthy living conditions.

Unemployment. In recent years the unemployment rate has ranged from a low of 4.9 percent to 7.2 percent (U.S. Bureau of the Census, 1998, Table 646). In 2002, when the unemployment rate was 5.8 percent, there were 8,378,000 people unemployed (Bureau of Labor Statistics, 2003). Unemployment insurance cushions the economic shock for many, but for others unemployment triggers depressive reactions or feelings of worthlessness and requires some adaptation to unaccustomed free time. With a prolonged recession, many begin to exhaust their unemployment benefits, meaning they have to fall back on savings or take much less desirable jobs. Plant closings affecting entire communities present new problems of adaptation not only to those who lose jobs, but also to those whose communities are affected because of new social problems or because people move away.

Beyond unemployment, 38,540 businesses filed for bankruptcy in 2002 (American Bankruptcy Institute, 2003). Most were small businesses, but each one represented the dashed hopes of entrepreneurs, their employees, individuals and their families, affected their livelihoods, and forced some rethinking of a major life activity. The collapse of a giant corporation such as Enron where thousands of employees lost their pension savings is tragic because of failed expectations, anger, depression, and loss of trust.

Debt. Almost all families have some form of debt (e.g., mortgage, credit cards, car loan). As might be expected from the numbers of people with low incomes and our credit economy, many have debts they cannot easily repay. In 2000, 1.2 million bankruptcy petitions were filed in the federal courts. That same year, consumer debt of all kinds totaled $1.456 trillion, with another $5.2 trillion in mortgage debt (Lawless, 2001). In 1997, $1.236 trillion in installment debt was more than 30 days in arrears (U.S. Bureau of the Census, 1998, Tables 820, 821). Using our multiplier for household size, it is safe to conclude that millions of debtors and family members are affected by a delinquent debt. Given the ever rising level of consumer debt, collection industry employment is expected to grow at a faster than average rate for all industries (Bureau of Labor Statistics, 2000–2001). Credit counseling and debt consolidation services are also growing, although some may involve predatory practices.

Student indebtedness rose sharply after 1992 when the rules changed to open the federal student loan program to more students (Scherschel, 1997). Debt varied depending on the type and amount of schooling, as Table 1–3 shows.

The face amount of the debt does not show how much the former

Table 1–3
Average Student Debt of Those Finishing Their Degrees in 1995–1996*

Type of School	Mean Debt ($) (Not counting interest)
BA	
Public 4 year	11,950
Private 4 year	14,290
Masters	
Public 4 year	15,110
Private 4 year	21,410
Doctorate	
All Institutions	20,490
Professional (Law, medicine, business school, etc.)	
Public 4 year	46,830
Private 4 year	49,540

*Adapted from Table 1, King, 1998

student will repay over time, and loans begin accruing interest charges six months after students finish their degrees. The world is not fair: students coming from families with incomes over $70,000 attending four-year public colleges ($9,290) borrowed 26 percent less than those coming from families with incomes of less than $30,000 ($12,250). The differential (19%) was somewhat less for those attending four-year private colleges ($15,240 borrowed when the family earned under $30,000, $12,360 when family income was over $70,000; King, 1998). About half of student loan debtors said they were extremely or very burdened by loan payments ("like having a mortgage without a house"). On the positive side, however, over two-thirds agreed the investment was worth it for personal growth and for career development (Baum & Saunders, 1998).

How much worse would it be to owe large sums of money with nothing but a bad credit report to show for it? Identity theft, where the perpetrator fraudulently obtains and uses credit in another person's name, is one of the fastest-growing crimes reported to the Federal Trade Commission. On occasion the perpetrators are known to the victims, being members of the same family, including even parents who run up bills on their children's credit cards (Irvine, 2002). In 2002 alone the FTC recorded 161,819 victims of identity theft (most often credit card fraud) (http://www.consumer.gov/sentinel/sentinel-trends/), and as with other financial crimes many cases go unreported or even undetected.

Work, money, and family. We have been experiencing great changes in the nature of work, and in the composition of the labor force, and in child care arrangements. Women will continue to make up about 47 percent of the labor force in coming years (U.S. Bureau of the Census, 1998, Table 645). The increase of women in the workforce raises concerns about sexual harassment and discrimination. A great many continue working during pregnancy. This trend to work during pregnancy and when the child is very young has had no adverse effect on the sharp decline in infant and maternal mortality in the last century (Centers for Disease Control, 1999). A majority (65%) of women with young children under six now work, as do 79 percent of those with school-age children (Mothers in the Labor Force, 1955–2001). About 60 percent of women who worked while pregnant returned to work within six months of the child's birth, and those who continued to work ended up with higher pay at age 30 than those who left the workforce when their child was born (Smith & Bachu, 1999). The averages conceal great variability in these patterns by race, class, education, marital status and availability of benefits on the job.

About half of families with children under 13 had child care expenses. In 1997, they paid an average of $286 a month, or 9 percent of the earnings of a two-parent family. Single parent households paid 16 percent of their earnings in child care (Giannarelli & Barsimantov, 2000). In addition to paying for child care, many worry about the adequacy of the care provided for their children. The lack of affordable day care means that many "latch key" children are unsupervised after school. Most school-age children are cared for in after school programs or by relatives. However, 5 percent of children between ages six and nine care for themselves while their mothers are working, and 10 percent of children that age spend some time caring for themselves. Of those a little older (10–12 year olds), nearly one in four takes care of him- or herself while their mothers are working. The amount of time in self-care increases as the children's age increases. (Capizzano, Tout, & Adams, 2000). The implications of these patterns of child care for children's adaptation and coping remain to be studied carefully. Does a lack of adequate supervision after school among older teens contribute to delinquency or, among older adolescents, create opportunities for sexual contact?

There also may be changing patterns of family relationships based on earnings. Married women contribute about 45 percent of family earnings income and so do women living with a man in a couple relationship. The averages conceal the fact that 14.9 percent of married women earned $5,000 or more than the male in the relationship, as did 21.5 percent of women in unmarried couples. We don't know how many "househusbands" there are, but 4.7 million men between the ages of 25 and 50 (about 16% of 30 million marriages in that age range) had no personal earnings from wages and salaries. Some of these men may be disabled, self-employed or have other sources of income (Fields & Casper, 2001). Nonetheless, there are numerous examples to show that there are many exceptions to the conventional pattern of a man earning substantially more than a female partner earns.

The distribution of earnings and the amount of time spent at work undoubtedly has consequences for family relationships. Most women with young children are now working. What constitutes appropriate sex role behavior? How should authority and responsibility for the household and for children be shared? How does the share of household income each party brings in affect these relationships? (Crouter & McHale, 1993; A. G. Levine, 1977). These issues can be of critical concern for community psychologists considering interventions, for family therapists, and for clinical psychologists.

The changing nature of work and of work-related values. Since the end of World War II, the United States has been changing from an industrial to a service economy, from producing goods to providing services (Fuchs, 1968). Where once we were a nation of farmers, now about 3 percent of the workforce is engaged in farming. The changes have been so marked, especially in recent years, that the Bureau of Labor Statistics has had to change its occupational classification system to take into account new jobs and new industries (Bureau of Labor Statistics, 2001). Changes in the distribution of employment can have profound cultural and social effects. As Fuchs (1968) put it:

> Changes in the industrial distribution of employment have implications for where and how men live, the education they need, and even the health hazards they face. Indeed it has been written that when man changes his tools and his techniques, his ways of producing and distributing the goods of life, he also changes his gods. (p. 184)

As one example, agricultural employment now constitutes about 1 percent of all jobs. But only 31 percent of farmer income derives from farmwork. Even farms are changing: "niche farms, hobby farms, hunting preserves, dude ranches, you-pick operations and bread-and-breakfast operations" all require different skills than farming in the old-fashioned sense of the term (Veneman, 2001). Of new jobs coming into the market, professional and related occupations are expected to grow the fastest between 2000 and 2010. Construction, maintenance and repair, and production occupations are expected to have only modest growth. Low-paid service occupations will have one of the highest growth rates in the economy. Computer-related jobs will increase by over a million in the next decade, but the positions will be found in all industries.

The new jobs coming into the economy will require more education. In 2000, 21 percent of the jobs required a bachelor's level of education. By 2010, 29 percent of the new jobs will require that level of education. In 2000, about 8 percent of jobs required a post-secondary degree (vocational or associate), but by 2010, 13 percent of the new jobs will require that level of education. At the same time, in 2000, 71 percent of occupations required only on-the-job training, but by 2010, only 58 percent of the new jobs can be filled by people with little special training. In other words, completing post-secondary educational courses will become ever more important for competing in the job market (Hecker, 2001). If having a good job is essential to making a healthy adaptation as an adult, we really need to examine educational opportunities for members of different segments of our population, including opportunities for retraining as the work environment changes. There may be a role for community psychologists interested in prevention.

The work world is changing in other critical ways. Once, workers' wages were directly tied to output, as in piecework. The worker only received wages or a fixed salary. Today, 27 percent of total compensation is in benefits: paid vacation; sick and personal leave; unpaid family leave; health and life insurance; dental, vision and prescription drug plans; retirement and savings benefits, including 401k plans; child care provisions; bonuses and stock options (Bureau of Labor Statistics, 2001). The change in compensation means the employed person is tied to the employer in many different ways. The significance of having a job for one's lifestyle is heightened by all of the other issues related to working. It also means that losing a job has an intensified significance for the employee and his or her family. It is critical for community psychologists to appreciate the full significance of the tie to the world provided by the job. Those interested in social change, personality, and values can ponder the significance of the compensation package to work relationships and to other social values.

Leisure Time and Value Changes

In the United States, leisure time and industries catering to those with leisure are important. From 1990 to 1998, the population increased by 8.6 percent from 249.9 million to 271.3 million; recreational expenditures increased by 74 percent in the same period. These figures do not reflect the cost of travel for leisure activities. Sixty percent of air travel is for leisure, not business. People are spending much more of their personal resources on recreational and leisure time activities and they have the time to do it. About a third of our time and about a third of our expenditures are for leisure activities (Academy of Leisure Sciences, undated). This change in the value we place on leisure and the resources we devote to it may have an effect on the work ethic. Shortening the workweek is a possible solution to chronic unemployment. The long-range trend may well move us toward greater leisure time availability in the future. With shorter hours, increased vacation time, and a shorter lifetime work span with earlier retirement, the average person today has an estimated 45,000 more free hours available during a lifetime than a counterpart 100 years ago (DeGrazia, 1962), although for those working two jobs to make ends meet, leisure may be a promise unfulfilled.

These figures reflect a normative change that must be accompanied by a change in the value system. The current political debate emphasizing that we are having a "cultural war" is a manifestation of this problem of responding to changing values. Change affecting basic institutions is invariably stressful as we seek to reach a new social equilibrium. The problem is to develop a version of the good life that is well articulated, well internalized, and supported by other social and financial resources, a set of problems which community psychologists may help solve.

Summary. Having to cope and struggle with problems in living is more the rule than the exception. The problems documented in regularly kept statistics are similar to those that appear in stressful life events scales (see chapter 7). At any given moment, a large number of people are affected by acute and chronic illness and accidents; by disasters of one sort or another; or by problems related to crime, delinquency, drug addiction, and alcoholism. Marriage, divorce, and parenthood have their own special problems, and large numbers of Americans have serious financial problems as well. The work setting has introduced new problems and new opportunities, and increasing leisure also poses problems for adaptation.

We conclude that a large number of people regularly experience stressful events. That conclusion is an alternative to the view that there is a high prevalence of *DSM* disorders. The ecological perspective leads us to examine the frequency and distribution of the stressful life events in the population instead of just examining the rate and distribution of individual psychopathology. Later in this book we will argue that the ecological perspective may provide us with a better basis to develop and implement prevention programs.

Aloneness in American Society

Many Americans face their problems in relative isolation (Putnam, 2000). Putnam documented the decline in civic and social life in America, especially since the 1970s. He claims the decline represents a decline in "social capital"—"connections among individuals' social networks and the norms of reciprocity and trustworthiness that arise from them" (p.19). Here we will focus on statistics dealing with lifestyle and living arrangements that supplement Putnam's position and suggest that when "the soap opera" events arise, many Americans cope alone.

Death. The loss of a loved one because of death also stands high on the scale of stressful events and is followed by consequences similar to those involved in the loss of a relationship in divorce or separation. On the Holmes and Rahe (1967) list of stressful events, death of one's spouse was the single most stressful event one could experience. Death of a family member was among the top five most stressful events, and death of a close friend was in the top half. These events are relatively common.

For most people bereavement is a fact of life. Only those who themselves die young escape the pain of losing someone they love through death. About 2.41 million died in the 12 months ending in June 2001. Women live longer than men; there are 11,056,000 women who are widowed, 8.65 million of them over 65, but only 2.1 million men over 65 who are widowers (U.S. Bureau of the Census, 1998, Table 62). Because eligible women far outnumber eligible males in that age range, a widow in particular is unlikely to find a new partner.

There were at least 29,199 suicides in 1999, and probably many more, since suicide is underreported. Thirteen percent of completed suicides are among those 15–24 years old (McIntosh, 1999). Just as each type of relationship has special meaning, so too does each type of death carry with it a special kind of pain for those who are left behind (National Academy of Sciences, 1984, p. 4). There are many adverse health effects of bereavement, including increased mortality, depression, drug and alcohol abuse, cardiovascular disease, and accidents (Sakaguchi, 2001).

Residential mobility. Americans move frequently. Between 1999 and 2000, 43.4 million people moved (16% of the population). Renters move more than homeowners, and college age and younger middle-age people move more than other groups. Poorer people move more often than higher income persons. Long distance moves especially disrupt existing networks of relationships and require the development of new networks. Social relationships may be disrupted for adolescents; children who move even short distances (20–25% of school age Black, Hispanic, and Asian and Pacific Islanders) face the problem of adapting to a new school (Schacter, 2001).

Living alone. In 2000 some 26,724,000 people lived alone. More women than men lived alone (14,361,000 versus 9,613,000, respectively). At younger ages, more men than women lived alone, but among those 65 years and older, 2.4 million men, but 7.4 million women lived alone. Not all were necessarily isolated, but no one from whom they could receive support in time of need was sharing the household.

Because women live longer than men, women cannot count on developing another monogamous heterosexual relationship once having experienced a loss of relationship because of a death or a divorce that might have occurred when the woman was as young as 40. Divorced and widowed women may have friends, parents, relatives, and children to rely on for emotional support, companionship, and other aid. These figures confirm, however, that the ideal image of a married couple coping with the problems of life together does not fit the picture for substantial numbers of Americans, and particularly for substantial numbers of women.

Gender and psychological distress. Epidemiological research has established that women are diagnosed twice as often as men as having one or another anxiety disorder. With the exception of bipolar disorder, which may have a strong genetic component, women are diagnosed as having mood disorders twice as often as men (U.S. Surgeon General, 2001a).

We believe the gender difference is better described by using ecological rather than diagnostic conceptions. Emphasizing diagnosis and illness obscures the conditions of living for women and men. Women are more likely to be struggling with "soap opera" problems in living (Mirowsky & Ross, 1995), and to be struggling with those problems alone (a conclusion whose implications will be explored further in chapter 7). One consequence of aloneness may be a heightened tendency to reach for professional care when experiencing distress related to frequently occurring life events. However, a solution focusing on diagnosis and the need for mental health services obscures the financial stresses, the aloneness, and lack of support that many women experience.

The Availability of Professional Care

"Normal" life is indeed a soap opera for most people who muddle through without formal help. But how much formal help is available to those who need it? Albee's (1959) pioneering work for the Joint Commission on Mental Illness and Health alerted us to the problems of providing sufficient personnel if treatment is delivered by professionally trained staff through designated mental health organizations.

Our best estimate is that in 2000 there were approximately 72,000 doctoral-level clinical psychologists providing services in health service facilities and in private practice settings. In 2000 there were 468,000 social work jobs. It is difficult to say how many social workers have BA-level degrees and how many have MSW degrees. We will guess that about half have MSW degrees. There were about 29,300 psychiatrists. Most of these (70%) are in office-based practice, and only 20 percent (5,860) work in hospitals. In 2000, 21,000 MA-level personnel were employed as marriage and family counselors, and 441,000 held other counseling jobs. Of those classified as counselors, 46 percent were educational, vocational or school counselors. About 25 percent were rehabilitation counselors, 15 percent mental health counselors, and about 14 percent substance abuse counselors. Only a few of these work in private practice. There were about 4,000 members of the American Psychiatric Nurses Association. About 4 percent characterize themselves as therapists, about 4 percent as case managers, and 11 percent said they were in private practice. In addition, there are a large number of clergy who provide services either as pastoral counselors or as part of their ministry. The mental health fields are also growing. The Occupational Outlook Handbook lists these as occupations expected to grow at an above average rate in the next ten years.

In the previous editions of this book we engaged in an exercise to show that the number of professional mental health worker hours per person in need is very small. It is more difficult to undertake the exercise today because of the sharp increase in the number of psychologists, social workers, and counselors and the difficulty in defining the services the workers provide. A substantial number provide only diagnostic, referral, and supervision services, but little direct treatment. Others are basically administrators rather than treating personnel.

Moreover with the advent of managed care, it is more difficult to estimate the true availability of services because of insurance limits and controls on the use of services. One study of managed behavioral health care companies reported a wide range of results:

> outpatient followup within thirty days after hospital discharge for depression ranged from 39 percent to 92 percent; hospital readmission rates for all mental health diagnoses ranged from 2 percent to 41 percent; the proportion of patients with schizophrenia who received a minimum of four medication visits ranged from 15 percent to 97 percent; and the proportion of children less than 12 years of age who received at least one family visit ranged from 13.3 to 99 percent. Managed behavioral health companies were more consistent in their capacity to *limit* treatment, ranging from 65 to 100 percent in limiting visits for adjustment disorders to fewer than 10. (Varmus, 1998, p. 2)

The apparent arbitrariness and uncertainty about treatment decisions must make treatment less accessible, and must add to the anxiety and uncertainty experienced by patients, their families, and by providers.

Nonetheless, it is clear that some shortages of treatment services are indeed acute. New Mexico, for example, passed legislation over the objection of psychiatrists to permit psychologists to write prescriptions with specialized training and with medical supervision. The law was justified in New Mexico partly on the grounds that it took as long as six weeks for a patient in that state to see a doctor (Ault, 2002).

Whatever the treatment hours, they are not readily available to all. There are important regional differences in the distribution of mental health services. Professional mental health workers are concentrated in urban and suburban areas where people have higher incomes, more education, and better insurance coverage. In addition, many psychiatrists in public mental health facilities are foreign-trained, speak English poorly, and are employed in state facilities because licensing requirements are modified for employees of public facilities. Many areas of the country are almost totally without specialized mental health services. The shortage of personnel trained to work with children and the elderly is also very great. In some places, minority and bilingual patients may go without treatment because insufficient numbers of trained personnel speak the language (Snowden, 1982), a problem that is relieved when such personnel are available (O'Sullivan, Peterson, Cox, & Kirkeby, 1989).

Mental health services are in short supply for the 1.57 million residents of nursing homes (where up to 75 percent are estimated to have some degree of mental illness), partly because the institutions are not very gratifying places for professionals to exercise their skills. Neither are the institutions where more than 2 million others reside (e.g., prisons, jails, juvenile justice facilities, institutions for people with mental retardation). Recall, there are only 5,860 psychiatrists working full-time in hospitals. Most others are in office practice and are available only a few hours a week for other consulting.

Depending on the assumptions, we can arrive at figures of minutes or even seconds per week available to those who might be dealing with crises of living consequent to chronic and acute illness, employment and financial problems, or problems of death, divorce, and other separations. We have said nothing about the nearly 8 million children estimated to be in need, nor have we considered at all the problems in living consequent to transitions in adult life.

On numbers alone it is apparent that professionally trained personnel will never be available in sufficient numbers in the present mode of service delivery to meet even a fraction of the potential demand for mental health services.

Problems of the Medical Model

Availability aside, the medical model of service delivery is also a problem. The fee-for-service medical model is built on the assumption that most problems can be handled by acute, episodic interventions limited in time and with an enduring effect. Help provided with those assumptions will not serve the needs of the many millions who suffer from chronic physical problems. Even when treatment for a physical disorder is stabilized, the patient and the family have to work out their adaptations to the limitations imposed by the condition. If we add those involved with the mental health, criminal justice, or welfare systems, we must concede that many problems are chronic and will not readily give way to acute, episodic interventions. In the words of Stanton Coit, one of the founders of the American settlement house movement,

> If we consider the vast amount of personal attention and time needed to understand and deal effectively with the case of any one man or family that has fallen into vice, crime or pauperism, we shall see the impossibility of coping with even these evils alone, unless the helpers be both many and constantly at hand. (Coit, 1891, quoted in Levine & Levine, 1992, p. 61)

The medical model also implies a passive help giver who waits for the client to define his or her own need and then to request help. It assumes that people seeking help know the kind of help available, find the help culturally acceptable, and that they are "acceptable clients" (can pay the fee, have insurance, have the proper condition, etc.) to the help givers. We know that most persons with disorders are not treated. Every practitioner is aware that a relatively large proportion of people referred for mental health treatment fail to follow through. For those people treatment is not psychologically available.

The medical model assumes that professionals are competent and that personal or social characteristics of the professional do not matter (Dawes, 1994). However, cultural, racial, ethnic and language characteristics of either the provider or the recipient can be barriers to help (Giordano & Giordano, 1976; Snowden, 1982). The service system also sorts clients in complex ways by age, race, gender, and ethnicity. The dynamics of such sorting are unclear, but it is clear that the use of various components of the service system varies by factors that probably have only a tangential bearing on clinical condition (Milazzo-Sayre, et al., 2001).

A psychotherapist's productivity is improved by clients who are ready and willing to use psychotherapy. In the free market system provided by the fee-for-service model, the YAVIS (young, attractive, verbal, intelligent, successful) client is preferred. Ryan's (1969) demonstration that a substantial proportion of the case load of private psychiatrists in Boston consisted of college-educated women between the ages of 25 and 35 who lived in a few census tracts in Boston is a case in point. Contemporary services are not equally available to all who might need them, and some clients are better prepared than are others to use the services that are offered. Although we know something about the use of hospitals and clinics, we know very little about who uses the services of private practitioners in their private offices. Torrey, Wolfe, and Flynn (1988) believe that mental health professionals have opted to deal with less serious problems in private settings. In their view, private sector mental health services have skimmed off the easiest and most profitable patients and have left the more difficult problems to the public sector, which may have fewer and less well-trained staff to treat them.

Health insurance and psychotherapy. With greater availability of health insurance coverage for mental health services, less well-off people sought mental health care (Becker, Stiles, & Schonfeld, 2002). Consumers are organizing to see that managed care doesn't result in the rationing of care, and inadequate care (Malloy, 1995). Even with these changes, reliance on a public policy of trying to provide many more professional mental health workers will not come close to meeting public need. Alternatives are clearly necessary, and these shall be considered throughout this book. Over and beyond the limitations of the medical model and its treatment technologies, the medical model approach doesn't help us to think about changing existing institutions, creating new ones, or taking social or political action to modify oppressive social conditions that contribute to peoples' problems in living.

Disorders or problems in living? In the medical model, affective and behavioral responses to problems in living are called *disorders*, and professional services are *treatment* for those disorders. A subtle implication may be that because help is provided through professional services, the events that led the individual to seek help are unusual and should not have occurred. Higher recent estimates for the prevalence of mental disorders reflect a higher than expected incidence of relatively brief symptom episodes, especially anxiety and substance abuse (Regier et al., 1993), and we noted earlier that an estimated 46 percent of people who seek ambulatory help for mental health problems are not sufficiently impaired to warrant any current diagnosis (Narrow et al., 1993). For many of these people the implication may be that feelings of anxiety, tenseness, or depression in relation to problems in living should not occur.

In 1999 the pharmaceutical industry shipped over $15 billion worth of drugs affecting the central nervous system, about 22 percent of the value of all pharmaceuticals shipped. A survey of physicians and psychiatrists showed that prescriptions for psychotropic medications rose sharply between 1985 and 1994. A high number of prescriptions (20.4 million) were for antidepressants (Pincus et al., 1998). For many, the widespread use of Prozac is a chemical solution for feelings related to problems in living.

An emphasis on professional assistance may undermine confidence in one's ability to cope, whether alone or with the assistance of a friend, neighbor, or relative. Furthermore, the conception that professional help should be available for problems in living may undermine the sense of responsibility one person feels for another or that a network or a face-to-face community might feel for one of its members; if a professional is available to take care of the problem, then send the problem to the professional who is paid to do the job.

Having said this, we want to back away from that position slightly, for we do not mean to give credence to some romantic notion that any nonprofessional is for that reason alone a more effective person than any professional, or that professionals do not have valuable knowledge, experience, and special services to offer. Moreover, the essential aloneness of many in American society (Putnam, 2000) limits the utility of the idea that one can always rely on friends, neighbors, or relatives, or even on the local bartender or hairdresser for help (cf. Cowen, 1982). As Jane Addams (1910) put it, too many seem to have "lost that simple and almost automatic reponse to the human appeal, that old healthful reaction resulting in activity from the mere presence of suffering or helplessness" (p. 71).

The self-help movement, so prominent in the present day (see chapter 9), is an example of a person-to-person, nonprofessional, nonstate-supplied service. The U.S. Advisory Board on Child Abuse and Neglect (1993) has recommended a thorough review of the child protection system to make help more readily available in neighborhoods, and to encourage neighbors to help neighbors. Their recommendation recognized the inadequacy of the present system and the necessity to involve more of the community in solving individual problems of caring for children.

Even if most life crises and associated emotions are transient (Dohrenwend & Dohrenwend, 1969), the resources available to help mediate life crises can make the difference between an unfavorable outcome, an outcome that merely restores the individual's preexisting functioning, and an outcome that leaves the individual a better, stronger person for having coped successfully with distress.

Severe, chronic disorders exist in all countries and cultures. The causes of some disorders are consistent with a medical disease model (Dohrenwend et al., 1992). Many problems require highly specialized resources, trained personnel, and special facilities. Although it is certainly true that a great many people have problems, it is not true that all of their problems are the same or that all problems will yield to or be ameliorated by the same solutions. An emphasis on the problem person distracts from considering the resources to mediate stressful life events, and the social and community action that may be necessary to bring about change.

We need an epidemiology of life events in addition to an epidemiology of disorders. An epidemiology of life events calls attention to conditions in the social order that might be remediable by social and community action, or suggest how we might position resources to be available in time and space when people are coping with problems. A focus on disorder is less useful in that respect, and may limit the universe of alternatives in which we search for solutions.

Attitudes and ideologies. We are not sure that we know in a cultural sense how to face the soap opera of life. We probably do not prepare ourselves and our children well enough to cope with life's difficulties. Rossman (1976) points out that the best-selling self-help books are in those areas in which our socializing institutions have grossly failed us—marriage, giving birth, parenting, divorce, living with illness, and sexuality. There is a clue to prevention in this fact. Those who look to education and preparation for coping to provide individuals with the additional personal resources to reduce the worst consequences of life's stresses may have much to tell us.

These particular directions—providing public resources in a way that empowers and does not undermine person-to-person responsibility and caring, encouraging face-to-face mutual assistance, teaching people to cope, helping to develop meaningful and satisfying life views that can be lived out in a supportive social organization, and taking action to change oppressive social conditions and institutions—offer important possibilities for dealing with the soap opera of life beyond relying exclusively on specialized professional services.

Summary

To recapitulate, professional mental health personnel are not now, and never will be, available in sufficient numbers to provide assistance for the tens of millions who are daily coping with stressful problems in living. Moreover, our medical model delivery system will be available in a psychological and social sense to relatively few people. Psychoactive medications may relieve symptoms of anxiety and depression, but do little to help individuals cope with ongoing problems in life. For some, relief from affective distress, or a reduction in pathological thinking consequent to the relief of distress, may be sufficient to enable them to adapt. For others, chemical relief of distress may be only a small step in helping them deal with day-to-day problems.

In any event, large numbers of people cope with significant problems in living on a daily basis. Many cope alone, living in relative isolation from others who might provide emotional support, an opportunity to see problems differently, or more concrete assistance. Furthermore, broad social and cultural changes continuously add to the difficulties confronting many segments of the population. As we have noted, the problems in living discussed here appear on stressful-life-events scales and are correlated with psychiatric symptoms and physical illness (Rabkin & Streuning, 1976). We can arrive at similar estimates of the potential psychological need whether we use epidemiological studies of *DSM* diagnoses or a problems-in-living and stressful-life-events perspective. We have a different focus when we look at an epidemiology of "cases" as against an epidemiology of events. Cases lead us to treatment of individuals. An epidemiology of situations and events offers broader possibilities for thinking about helpful or preventive interventions. We obviously need to think our way through alternate analyses of the problems before us. In our opinion, an individual psychological orientation and the medical model seriously limit our thinking, while the view that life is a soap opera opens new vistas for the development of therapeutic and preventive services. In the following chapters we will be examining some alternatives and the concepts and the research related to them. As a group, these topics comprise our view of what is called community psychology.

2

The Origins of
Community Psychology

This chapter examines the seminal social and historical context for community psychology that was provided primarily by the community mental health movement, and the important place of community concepts in contemporary mental health practice. We review the history of mental health care to show how much our methods of providing care are closely embedded in our culture, in our political system, and in how we pay for the care. We briefly touch on trends in social psychology and other areas that also led to community psychology.

Both community psychology and community mental health emerged in the mid-1960s during a period of great ferment not only in the mental health fields but also in society at large (see Wilson, Hayes, Greene, Kelly, & Iscoe (2003) for an extensive review of these issues). The successful civil rights movement of the 1950s and 1960s began with the Supreme Court's desegregation decision in *Brown* v. *Board of Education* (1954), and became a model for feminists and other groups to use in attacking social inequities in many areas of society. The 1960s Kennedy-Johnson War on Poverty stimulated assaults on a wide variety of social problems, including poverty, crime, delinquency, unemployment, poor education, mental retardation, welfare inequities, and troubles in prisons. In this period new questions were raised regarding both social problems and their solutions.

President John F. Kennedy's address to Congress in 1963 was an important starting point for he announced a bold, new approach to the care of people with mental illness and mental retardation. Kennedy, whose sister suffered a botched brain operation and was left institutionalized for life, advocated reducing the censuses of mental hospitals and reintegrating people with mental illness into the community. He also called for the prevention of personal waste and misery and the promotion of positive mental health. Kennedy's new approach to mental health policy, quickly labeled community mental health, emerged as a direct consequence of post–World War II developments. However, there is always a "before-the-beginning" (Sarason, 1972), a distant and a more recent history that needs to be examined to appreciate watershed policies like the Kennedy program.

The community mental health movement was a reform of the state hospital which had been the mainstay of the mental health system until the end of World War II. Having evolved from seventeenth-century poorhouses and workhouses designed to care for chronically dependent people, state hospitals continued to provide refuge to various dependent populations well into the 1950s (Vogel, 1991). The following history shows how political, economic, social, welfare, professional and legal issues affect mental health care. History helps us see matters which cannot be understood when we focus only on the psychopathology of those we label mentally ill.

Origins of Mental Health Care in the Welfare System[1]

The welfare and mental health systems are inextricably connected. Many people served by the mental health system have a limited ability to care for themselves. The community mental health program was designed to support such people in the community rather than treat them in hospitals. A person discharged to the community may require housing, food, clothing, medical care, vocational training, recreation, transportation, and some degree of supervision, all requiring money. If a person considered disabled because of mental illness is unable to work, under our current system, the local, state, or federal government provides the needed funds. Although we may not want to characterize income provided to people with mental illness as welfare, such support does amount to providing for those who cannot entirely provide for themselves.

The break up of feudalism and the Elizabethan Poor Laws. The mental health system in its modern form can be traced to the breakup of feudalism, and passage of the Elizabethan Poor Laws in 1601, the grandmother of all welfare programs (Slack, 1995).

The feudal system broke up beginning about the fourteenth century, changing the system from one of mutual obligation between noblemen and all those who lived under their control to a "market economy" relying on wages. The employer now owed his employee wages for time worked, but not much else. Those who couldn't earn wages, or didn't earn enough to save for bad times fell through the cracks. Over the next 200 years, economic downturns and seasonal changes in the need for labor provoked restless movements of people from the country to the cities, and from place to place.

The Elizabethan Poor Laws, passed between 1597 and 1601, were the Queen's and Parliament's answer to the question of who was responsible for the care of dependent persons. These laws placed first responsibility on the family for the care of its own, but also established the principle of community responsibility for the poor. If parents couldn't support their children, or children couldn't support their elderly parents, then local government had a responsibility to care for them. Each parish was directed to appoint an overseer of the poor. The overseer was charged to build and maintain almshouses ("indoor" relief), provide for relief in the home ("outdoor" relief), and establish public works programs. Each parish was required to raise taxes for these purposes. Widows, orphans, the elderly, people with mental retardation, physical disabilities, or mental illness were all eligible for help. Once citizens were taxed for these programs, however, the treatment of all poor people became harsher. The reciprocity of mutual obligation was lost.

By the nineteenth century about 10 percent of the English population was housed in these institutions, despite the fact they were terrible places, designed to prevent the "welfare bums" of the day from taking advantage of the community's largesse. These institutions intermingled the poor with the mad and the bad.

Mental hospitals and the first mental health revolution. The eighteenth century is called the Age of Enlightenment because of its triumphs in science. Although poor and mentally ill people continued to live in almshouses and similar facilities, the middle class began providing for their own in private institutions. "Lunatic hospitals," such as London's St. Mary of Bethlehem (or "Bedlam"), opened in England throughout the eighteenth century and supplemented the system of boarding people with mental illness in licensed private madhouses or private homes. William Tuke, a Quaker who operated a private institution, developed the "moral therapy" that was to become so influential in the United States later on. Treating people with mental illness humanely and with dignity was revolutionary, as was the notion that mental illness was a disease that could be cured by scientific means.

In France at about this time, the philosophy of egalitarianism promoted by the French Revolution, as well as scientific thinking of the day, provided a rationale for physician Philippe Pinel to open the gates of two large institutions and remove the chains from mad men and women who were confined there with the poor. Pinel demonstrated that many inmates considered hopeless could be managed with a combination of kindness and firmness, and some even improved.

George III, the king of England at the time of the American Revolution, suffered from a form of mental illness, and was hospitalized several times. His care became a public issue when Parliament investigated his hospitalization. King George's physician claimed he could cure nine out of ten patients who had mental illness. Not to be outdone, other physicians made the same claims, producing "the cult of curability." Travelers carried this information along with Pinel's writings and news of Tuke's work from England to the United States, where eventually the information influenced the development of public policy.

The development of mental hospitals in the United States was similar to what happened in England. Colonists brought over the Elizabethan Poor Laws and established some large, undifferentiated almshouses. The colonists also relied on informal means of care for mental illness and some private mental hospitals were established in the eighteenth century. Key figures in America included Benjamin Rush, father of American psychiatry and signer of the Declaration of Independence, and Dorothea Dix, a nineteenth-century crusader for the release of people with mental illness from prisons. In 1830, Massachusetts built the publicly supported Worcester state hospital exclusively for the care of those with mental disorders. The Massachusetts legislature made this decision partly on the grounds that mental illness had been shown to be curable in England (the cult of curability) and in France (the work of Pinel). They hoped to save money by opening a hospital that could cure those with mental illness and remove their dependents from the welfare rolls.

Once created by state government, the mental hospital became embedded in our political system and political values influenced its subsequent development. For example, when the census of state hospitals declined in response to deinstitutionalization policies, it was difficult to close unneeded facilities because local communities depended on them economically. Legislators voted to keep hospitals open, often against the recommendations of state mental health commissioners. Today, ironically, when hospitals are closed, the facilities may be converted to prisons, thus undoing the work of Dorothea Dix who, in the mid-nineteenth century, campaigned for the construction of state hospitals for mental illness because those confined in prisons were treated so abysmally.

The decline of moral treatment. Worcester state hospital was designed architecturally to support the implementation of Tuke's and Pinel's moral therapy. It opened in 1833 with high hopes that patients could be cured quickly in the publicly funded hospital. Within a few years that ideology gave way to the professional belief that insanity was incurable. These changes in ideology, practice, and the fate of patients in institutions came about because the state mental hospital was now completely within the political system.

Politics changed ideology and practice. Proponents of moral treatment had sold the program to the legislature by overstating its effectiveness. A hospital discharging only 50 percent as cured instead of the expected 100 percent looked like a failure. Even if only a small percentage of those who were admitted failed to improve to the point they could be discharged, and if resources allocated to the hospital did not grow, inevitably the hospital would become swamped with chronic patients.

Although people who do not respond to treatment accumulate in every type of service, we make no real provision for them. As professionals who have absorbed medical model ideology, we act surprised and chagrined that failures occur at all. Professionals tend to blame the consumer, saying that he or she is not appropriate for the treatment rather than admitting that the treatment may be inadequate. The increasing number of chronic patients was an embarrassment to the developing profession of psychiatry. To conceal their presence, hospital superintendents literally manipulated their institutions' statistics to show better success rates. We will see in chapter 13 that the use of research and statistics in politically charged contexts is always vulnerable to the claim that advocates are at worst manipulating the data and at best overemphasizing information that supports the advocate's position. This problem emerged early in the history of attempts to apply scientific methods to public policy issues.

Because of the hospitals' reputations as places for the incurable, the dangerous, and the undesirable, including many Irish immigrants, middle-class people preferred to use private facilities if they could afford it. With the loss of middle-class patronage, the hospitals lost political support and the legislative will to appropriate funds declined.

By the 1870s, fiscal and managerial efficiency dominated practice in centralized state welfare bureaucracies. Cost and managerial efficiency became more important in evaluating hospitals than the quality of care.

Pliny Earle, a well-respected psychiatrist and hospital superintendent, concluded that insanity was incurable, an idea that came to dominate professional thinking. Even if a patient was adapting well with only residual symptoms, and might have coped adequately in the community, hospital care continued because the patient not been cured. Very large institutions housed a growing number of chronic patients and other social rejects. Few were discharged because of the theory that insanity was incurable. The large state hospital persisted as the major element of mental health care until well after World War II. A system of care that started out with high hopes had produced overcrowded "snake pits." It became the target of reform efforts that led to the community mental health approach.

There *were* some silver linings in this bleak picture of mental health care between 1850 and 1950. The major one, personified by Sigmund Freud, was the recognition of insanity as not so much a discrete condition as a continuum from psychosis through neurosis to mental health. This helped debunk the "us-them" mentality toward people with mental illness and led to modern psychotherapy. In Europe, this *second mental health revolution* focused on internal and unconscious psychoanalytic structures and processes. In the United States, the "mental hygiene movement" developed quite differently under the influence of Adolf Meyer, William James, and Clifford W. Beers (who wrote the 1908 book *A Mind That Found Itself* about his own wretched experience in an asylum; Rossi, 1969). Meyer foreshadowed much of community mental health in his writings on aftercare, prevention, and the need to create "community mental hygiene districts in which mental health personnel would coordinate the services of schools, playgrounds, churches, law enforcement agencies and other social agencies in an effort to prevent mental disorders and to foster sound mental health" (Rossi, 1969, p. 20). Meyer's viewpoint lost influence when psychiatry and social work came to be dominated by psychoanalytic theory (Levine and Levine, 1992).

Community Mental Health

The radical approach outlined in Kennedy's 1963 address has been called the *third revolution* in mental health for its expansion of services to early identification of social pathology and its victims (Hobbs, 1964). It resulted from several post–World War II developments.

Military psychiatry. During World War II, military psychiatrists demonstrated that with early treatment it was possible to restore a great many psychiatric casualties to full duty. The military claimed a high rate of cure (about 70%), in contrast to the very low rate of cure prevalent in civilian hospitals (5–20%). Community-based care in the new mental health centers was modeled conceptually after methods and approaches developed by the military.

The military idea that help should be located strategically to the stressful situation and provided as quickly as possible was a forerunner of the current concept of social support (Quick et al., 1992). In the military, psychologists, social workers and nurses had important roles in treatment in addition to psychiatrists, a consequence of "underpopulation" (see chapter 5). The idea grew that personnel in addition to psychiatrists could help treat mental illness, thus relieving the shortage of professional mental health workers uncovered in exposés of inadequate care in state hospitals. The military's success with crisis-oriented methods of intervention also sharply challenged the hopeless attitude toward mental illness that had prevailed since Pliny Earle's day.

Scientific developments. The concept of stress as a physiological disorder and the possibility that science could solve hitherto insoluble problems came into public consciousness after World War II. Hans Selye and others made progress in understanding the psychophysiology of stress. If soldiers could succumb to the stresses of military life and show symptoms of mental illness, then mental illness among civilians might also be a response to life stresses. The definition of a mental disorder expanded to include "normal" distress in reaction to "abnormal" situations such as combat. Later on we learned about the psychoactive drugs rauwolfia and Thorazine, which seemed to be able to relieve depression, anxiety, and other psychotic symptoms. Together with the public's belief, developed during World War II, in the power of science to produce, if not miracles then certainly wonders such as atomic power, radar, sulfa, and penicillin, the time seemed right to make an all-out attack on mental illness, now recognized as an important public health issue. With psychoactive drugs in use by the mid-1950s, many patients could be maintained outside of hospitals. However, if patients were to be maintained outside of hospitals, community-based services were necessary.

Mental health reaches the public agenda. Public action depends upon a problem achieving a prominent place on the public agenda. The prevalence of mental health–related problems (see chapter 1) was brought to public attention by World War II. A distressingly high proportion of the men called up for military service were rejected or, if accepted into service, discharged for neuropsychiatric reasons. This information was publicized through congressional hearings and the media. In addition, conditions in state hospitals were exceedingly poor. Exposed in the media, these conditions became political liabilities for state governors. The governors, claiming they did not have the financial resources to improve conditions in the hospitals nor to support training to meet the shortage of professional personnel, called for federal action.

Community mental health and the federal government. In our political system, mental health care and welfare programs were traditionally local and state responsibilities. After World War II, federal policies and funds dominated mental health care. The federal government had a role in mental health services since World War I when the Veterans Bureau served discharged veterans who suffered from "shell shock." After World War II, the Veterans Administration (VA) mounted a massive effort to provide mental health services for returning veterans in VA facilities but members of the civilian population, women (except for the few veterans), children, and the elderly were not eligible for such services. In the 1960s and later, new federal programs funding medical care (Medicaid, Medicare) and disability payments (SSI) were used to implement the deinstitutionalization policy.

Because mental illness was a prominent public health issue and because the government's partnership with science had been successful during World War II, postwar federal policy supported the development of a research and training capability in mental health. The National Institute of Mental Health (NIMH) was signed into law by President Harry S. Truman in 1946 to develop and support research and to produce trained clinical personnel in all of the mental health professions. By 1955 NIMH had shown considerable success in carrying out its mission.

Community Psychology Grows From Community Mental Health

In a political climate favorable to reform, we began thinking beyond the problems of the severely mentally ill and the state hospital system, and progressed to thought about prevention and alternative approaches to service delivery.

From state hospital to community mental health. The congressionally created Joint Commission on Mental Illness and Health (1955) was charged to develop a comprehensive mental health plan. The Joint Commission reported in 1960, just as Kennedy was about to take office, that current patterns of training and care could provide for only a tiny fraction of those in need of help (Albee, 1959) and was the stimulus for President Kennedy's address to Congress. Kennedy went far beyond the Commission's major recommendations for revitalizing the state hospital system. At that time, economists believed that economic growth depended on income redistribution and spending in the public sector to promote consumption of the goods and services produced by the private sector (Galbraith, 1998). The Community Mental Health Centers Act passed that same year (1963). It not only met a perceived mental health need, but spending on public services was in keeping with the economic policy of the day.

Criticism of conventional mental health practice. The community mental health thrust was based on more than optimism that a new approach would help. Hope lived side by side with frustration (see chapter 10). Critics asserted that mental hospitals created more problems than they solved (see Goffman, 1990). Aftercare facilities for adults released from mental hospitals were almost nonexistent, and institutions for the care of people with mental retardation were in scandalous condition (Sareyan, 1994). The new approach would solve these problems.

Szasz (1963) attacked the very concept of "mental illness," calling it a myth. He urged that we attend to the moral, legal, and social norms that produce our definitions of abnormal behavior, and determine what kind of person becomes a patient. His argument directed attention less to the patient's "illness" and more to the social conditions under which illness and patienthood were defined. Epidemiological studies consistently showed that emotional problems are more frequent and more severe in low-income populations, especially in communities marked by social and environmental disorganization (Leighton, Harding, Macklin, Macmillan, & Leighton, 1963; Srole, Langner, Michael, Opler, & Rennie, 1962).

The findings held true for children as well as adults. Children in low income populations had higher rates of premature birth, problems related to low birth weight, probable brain damage, childhood behavior disorders and learning problems (Knobloch & Pasamanick, 1961), and educational deficits (Coleman et al., 1966).

Moynihan (1965) pointed to a state of disorganization in lowerclass African American families that he believed would perpetuate social and psychological problems. Moynihan's critics attacked his report impolitely by calling it racist. Critics asserted that it failed to consider the effect of racial prejudice on family structure and neglected the strengths of matrifocal and extended family structures and of the 75 percent of African American families at that time that were twoparent households (Rainwater & Yancey, 1967). The Moynihan study may have stimulated African American scholars to redefine some of the research issues, enriching our understanding of black families and their needs (Moore, 1982; Zane, Sue, Castro, & George, 1982). On the other hand, criticism of the Moynihan study may have created barriers to studying problems in African American families. Leaders in the African American community are now expressing more concern about the issue of female-headed households (see also Wilson, 1987). This episode provides an excellent case study of the interplay among research, social values, and political considerations. Considered as a whole, data on class and race-related problems pointed to the need for social reform as well as better mental health care.

Critics questioned the fairness and the effectiveness of the existing mental health system of care. People from different social classes received different care (Hollingshead & Redlich, 1958). Critics also questioned the effectiveness of psychotherapy for adults and for children, as well as the efficiency of clinical practice with its high dropout rate (Tuckman & Lavell, 1959; Reiss & Brandt, 1965). These same concerns continue today (Bickman et al., 1995). The psychologist's testing functions also came under attack (Meehl, 1954).

The criticisms paved the way for a paradigm shift. Critics, citing sociological theories of deviance control, asserted that the mental health professions in general, and psychiatry in particular, contributed to the incidence of mental health problems by confirming and helping to enforce existing social norms (see chapter 6). By defining mental illness in isolation from social conditions, the profession distracted attention from social issues that were at the root of abnormal behavior in the first place. At a minimum, mental health professions needed to work more closely with the people staffing community agencies—schools, courts, welfare departments, churches, police departments—to encourage handling of problems by means other than referral to formal mental health agencies. This shift in perspective laid the groundwork for the later development of what came to be called community psychology, in contrast to community mental health.

The emphasis on prevention. Kennedy's bold new approach went beyond the reintegration of former psychiatric inpatients into the community. He called for the *prevention* of disorders and the promotion of positive mental health. Positive mental health meant more than the absence of symptoms; it included the state of well-being that enables an individual to pursue personal fulfillment. The notion of intervention with people who are well, before mental or social problems even begin, is called "primary prevention" (see chapter 8) and represents the *fourth revolution* in mental health. An important influence was Gerald Caplan's (1964) idea that mental health professionals might engage in social action before and during life crises. He outlined programs to identify and attenuate "hazardous circumstances" in the community and provide services to foster healthy coping. The implications of this general stress model will be examined in chapter 3.

Once we target positive mental health as a goal, we necessarily study and attempt to influence social institutions that contribute to the creation, perpetuation, or exacerbation of personal waste and misery, or that fail to support full development. In a sense, all of the soap opera that is life becomes the mental health professional's concern. He or she retains an interest in the distressed individual, but as a helper the professional now tries to influence families, schools, social agencies, courts, industrial organizations, and perhaps even the overall economic order. The role model changes from that of physician and healer to that of educator, social critic, reformer, and social planner.

The 1965 Swampscott, Massachusetts, Conference on the Education of Psychologists for Community Mental Health (Bennett et al., 1966) gave formal recognition to the emergence of a new and separate field of community psychology that needed appropriate training for its practitioners. The expansion in the scope of problems defined as mental health issues and the advocacy of social intervention by mental health workers were viewed by some articulate critics as a dangerous professional imperialism. Others worried that a separate community psychology would lose its influence with clinical psychology (Newbrough, 1967). Whatever the risks, the conscious creation of a new field had begun.

The Influence of Applied Social Psychology
and the War on Poverty

At the same time clinical psychology and mental health care were evolving, academic psychology was also changing with the political tenor of the times (Levine & Levine, 1992). During the economic depression and government expansion of the 1930s, social psychologists such as Kurt Lewin were heavily involved in field studies of important real-world issues, such as cooperation and competition in group dynamics and racial and religious prejudice (Lewin, 1946; Marrow, 1969). During World War II, many academics were involved in applied research in the armed forces. After the war, some of these researchers opted to create a laboratory science and retreated from applied work (Gergen, 1973). Lewin and others, however, continued the applied tradition of "action research" and formed the Society for the Psychological Study of Social Issues (Division 9 of the American Psychological Association) and its *Journal of Social Issues*. For example, Kenneth Clark, Stuart Cook, and Isidor Chein wrote the Social Science Statement on racial discrimination and the effects of school segregation that influenced the landmark 1954 U.S. Supreme Court decision *Brown* v. *Board of Education* (see chapter 11).

Three universities were particularly important in the development of a freestanding (nonclinical) community psychology. New York University, where Chein and Cook had pioneered the social psychology of racial and religious prejudice, created a graduate program in community psychology separate from social psychology (Lehmann, 1971). At the University of Kansas, Roger Barker (1968; see chapter 5) and colleagues created a new "ecological psychology" for the study of the environment of human behavior. The successor to that tradition is the KU Work Group of Steve Fawcett and colleagues (1995). At Peabody College, which later merged with Vanderbilt University, Nick Hobbs, J.R. Newbrough, Jack Glidewell, Phil Schoggen (who also worked with Barker at Kansas), William Rhodes, Paul Dokecki, and others borrowed ideas from Lewin and John Dewey to create a training model called "Transactional Ecological Psychology" that combined a community approach with more traditional areas of psychology (clinical, counseling, social, developmental; Hobbs, 1964; Newbrough, 1973). That program, now called Community Research and Action, combines community psychology and evaluation research with the interdisciplinary field of community development. There were several important community psychology programs in other universities (e.g., University of Texas under Ira Iscoe, University of Michigan [James G. Kelly and Richard Price], Michigan State University [George Fairweather]). In addition, the Laboratory for Community Psychiatry at Harvard under Gerald Caplan was an important training center. Many of its graduates became leaders in community research and community mental health centers. Unfortunately, the push to develop separate community psychology programs at other universities ran afoul of shrinking resources and increasing competition for those resources in the 1970s and 1980s. The competition blocked further development of free-standing community programs. However, partially in response to the NIMH policy of supporting training for community mental health, many clinical psychology programs included a community emphasis within clinical training.

The War on Poverty. President Kennedy was assassinated in 1963. His successor, Lyndon B. Johnson, came from a very different, more poverty-stricken part of the country, in rural, Depression-era Texas. Johnson supported the community mental health movement. He also initiated a war on poverty that created a great variety of programs designed to ameliorate problems of the poor. Office of Economic Opportunity (OEO) community action programs provided direct services, but they intended to influence existing service systems (e.g., welfare, medical care, schools, clinics, employment services, police, housing authorities) to improve services to poorer populations (Moynihan, 1969). Because of concerns about the effectiveness of expensive programs in the War on Poverty, and in community mental health, legislators appropriated funds for evaluation research. Many academic clinical and social psychologists and sociologists decided that their laboratory or "pure" research was irrelevant to the exciting social changes. Attracted by the opportunity for funding and for applying their skills, many undertook applied research. Encountering new field problems, some academics also began rethinking the limits of the laboratory research paradigm.

The War on Poverty had as a goal social change as well as the provision of direct assistance to the poor. It mandated the "maximum feasible participation" of those to be served by the programs, an idea that was translated into the concept of community control, which in turn led to a great deal of conflict (Moynihan, 1969). Community control as an ideology, challenging those in authority and seeking local empowerment, came to symbolize much more than making programs relevant to the people in the neighborhoods served. It included the empowerment of local citizens by giving them some power to influence how money was spent within the community mental health and antipoverty programs.

The climate of change encouraged experimentation in an effort to reach underserved and poorly served populations. Some mental health professionals became involved in the new community mental health center programs and in alternative service settings (e.g. Sarason, Levine, Goldenberg, Cherlin, & Bennett, 1966). Given attacks on the validity of conventional professional practice, the reform-minded rhetoric of the time, and the accumulating evidence that alternative personnel (e.g., paraprofessionals) and alternative services were viable, a great variety of programs emerged. Programs developed with and without the assistance of mental health professionals.

Activists, taking as their model the successful civil rights movement of the 1950s and 1960s, adopted similar ideologies, rhetoric, and strategies to achieve social and economic change. Their goals were not limited to material gains; they rejected the socially imposed view that one in need was a deservedly despised deviant. Activists and the social groups they created provided socially shared bases for maintaining self-esteem and encouraging social action to change one's situation (Ryan, 1976; Goldenberg, 1978). Activism in the social arena paralleled and was intertwined with the culturally profound antiwar movement and the sexual revolution, both of which entailed distrust of constituted authority and tradition.

The women's movement also contributed strongly to the challenge to unjust social norms. The women's movement developed parallel to community psychology, and with little contact, despite common goals, values, and conceptual similarities in theory and in critiques of existing research paradigms (Bond and Mulvey, 2000; Campbell & Wasco, 2000).

Many programs were directed toward relieving psychological misery and enhancing self-esteem. Some mental health professionals believed that almost any social action legitimately fell within the province of mental health. Empowering the powerless was worthwhile in and of itself in the quest for a more perfect democracy through the attainment of political, social, and economic equality (e.g., Cloward & Piven, 1971). It could also be justified as treatment for, and prevention of, a range of mental health problems that were direct consequences of psychological apathy and helplessness (Rappaport, 1977).

The need for new theory and concepts. The great expansion was confusing. Community psychology covered everything from "showing Szondi plates [a then popular projective technique] to ghetto residents in an inner city storefront, to engineering new communities" (Cowen, 1973, p. 423). The new thrust shot off in all directions at once, with little coherence and little conceptual clarity. Critics committed to traditional medical model practice looked askance at social activism. Those committed to "intrapsychic supremacy" (Levine, 1969)—that problems in living depend on people's internal psychological structures, which in turn dictate perceptions, feelings, and actions in everyday situations—viewed the activists as misguided romantics who had foolishly strayed from proper professional roles and activities, even though the settlement house movement of the late nineteenth and early twentieth centuries provided a tradition for social activism in social work (Levine and Levine, 1992) Community-oriented critics of traditional practice were equally firm in their convictions, but had little to offer by way of alternate theoretical conceptualizations.

Gerald Caplan's (1970) writings on consultation had become influential by this time. The theory of consultation, however, was simply an extension of clinical theory, and the practice was little different from the supervision of psychotherapy and perhaps not much more efficient. Consultation and education became a core service in community mental health centers and a major claimant on the imaginations, if not on the time, of professionals (D'Augelli, 1982). Consultation theory did not go very far in providing a guide to more general theory, strategy, or practice.

The new thrust developed along highly pragmatic lines (Cowen, Hightower, Pedro Carroll, & Work, 1996; see chapter 8). Levine (1973) justified novel activity on the basis of necessity, calling for a "responsible chutzpah," that is, doing the best one could even though the scientific base supporting novel activity was often thin. Academia offered little help.

Social psychologists, for the most part, had turned away from field studies in the real world, relying more on laboratory experiments on college students in contrived situations and settings, in the process sacrificing external validity and social relevance for internal validity (Gergen, 1973).

Behaviorism, while occasionally a stimulus for some community-oriented psychologists, was also limited as a source of theory. Operant psychology is based primarily on the laboratory study of single, mostly nonhuman organisms. (Would the field have been different if Skinner had put two rats in his box?) Although behavioral principles have been applied successfully in a variety of institutions, and in some community settings, the principles fail to address power relationships, abuses of authority in the control of rewards and punishment, or the goals and values of those institutions. Token economies and other behavioral strategies can have negative side-effects of inhibiting individual creativity and cultural diversity. Moreover as a "value free" perspective, extending behavioral "technology" to the community or institutional level could create a world of conformity and docility that would look more like Orwell's *1984* than Skinner's *Walden II*.

Psychometrics is another field with important lessons for community psychology. Intelligence and other psychological tests have long been used to characterize minority and immigrant populations as deficient, and contributed much to discrimination in employment and education. Some activists brought legal challenges against the use of tests on the grounds that they perpetuated discrimination.

For community psychologists, the implications are clear: The study of individual differences is often misused when drawing conclusions about groups. Fairness to individuals and disadvantaged groups should generally come before institutional or scientific interests. Scientists must remain alert to the misinterpretation and misapplication of their data. Research psychologists, like their more applied colleagues, have always been subject to the vicissitudes of social and political influence. Seymour Sarason, a leader in the movement toward acting on the basis of "responsible chutzpah" (Sarason, et al., 1966), was well aware of the theoretical and empirical problems facing psychologists. Sarason asserted that traditional psychology and other social sciences were not prepared to offer much to policymakers (Sarason, 1981b).

Arguing for more than relevance, Sarason (1981) urged we go beyond the dominant person-centered psychology to an approach that recognized history and social context to a greater degree. He said that the universe of alternatives in which problems are defined and solutions proposed can be severely constrained by cultural-theoretical blinders and narrow disciplinary perspectives. Because a university is divided into psychology, sociology, anthropology, economics, political science, law, philosophy, and English departments is no reason to believe that problems in the world are so divided. Unfortunately, those organizational divisions tend to compartmentalize knowledge in our minds as well.

Sarason argued that the social scientist's place and stake in the world is material. A problem doesn't just exist "out there." He said we should consider how the social scientist defines a problem, proposes solutions, and from which value positions. Better science is not enough, he argued. The nature of problem solving in social action is different from that in the physical sciences. Because social problems may be deeply rooted in the human condition, they may be intractable and will not yield to once-and-for-all solutions (Sarason, 1978).

We are developing theoretical perspectives and concepts that take us beyond individual psychology and beyond the limits imposed by psychology's reliance on experimental methods. Excursions into the community have opened our minds to new possibilities and pointed us in directions that may provide new insights into the human condition and the ability of the social sciences to illuminate that condition. We are now more aware than ever that we are inevitably dealing with matters of value and that action and research are inevitably intertwined with value considerations. Social scientists should not hide behind a false mantle of scientific or professional authority.

To summarize, community psychology emerged during a period of rapid social change. The field had a name, and to some extent an ideology, but it was unclear what community psychology encompassed, and what its methods, goals, or scientific theories were. Because one could justify so many diverse activities in the name of "community mental health," this concept appeared to have little real meaning and led to much soul-searching. A rough division emerged between rehabilitative and restorative efforts on the one hand and preventive-prophylactic efforts on the other (Cowen, 1973), a distinction others have called community mental health and community psychology, respectively (Rappaport, 1977). Much of what we call community psychology has had other roots than mental health (e.g., the women's movement; civil rights activism, Lewinian activism in social psychology) but the impetus for the development of the field for many psychologists came from the emphasis on prevention in President Kennedy's original proposal for community mental health centers.

The community movement had profound effects on the field of mental health and on our thinking about psychological issues. So many of community psychology's concepts and programs have been taken over in clinical settings that, in many areas, the community perspective has become the conventional wisdom! The question of community psychology's scientific foundations is important, and we return to it in coming chapters. In preparation for examining those issues, however, let us survey briefly the contemporary situation in community mental health.

Current Issues in Community Mental Health

The community movement starting with the 1963 Community Mental Health Centers (CMHC) Act had a far-reaching impact on mental health services. Community-based treatment required a change in the mix of services. In this section we discuss current mental health practice, including the development of community alternatives to inpatient care, the increasing significance of the consumer movement, mental health services for minority groups and other traditionally underserved populations, and mental health services for children.

Deinstitutionalization

The rate at which people with mental disorders were hospitalized in state psychiatric facilities went from 186 per 100,000 of population in 1969 to 33 per 100,000 in 1992 (Center for Mental Health Services, 1996), and the institutionalization of people with mental retardation also declined steeply during that period. These reductions in institutional populations fulfilled one goal of the CMHC program—to halve the institutional population within 10 years of the program's inception. The decline is only partly attributable to treatment philosophy. It also reflects changes in funding and reimbursement practices and changes in law that make it more difficult to hospitalize or retain people in hospital involuntarily (Levine, 1981; see chapter 4).

Not all commentators held a benign view of the deinstitutionalization movement (Scull, 1977). Critics also argued that CMHCs really didn't serve the most seriously mentally ill who were discharged from hospitals (Torrey et al., 1988). Providing adequate community-based services for formerly institutionalized people continues to be an important challenge (Shinn & Felton, 1981; Torrey, et al., 1988). Early in the deinstitutionalization process, patients were discharged from hospitals to single-room-occupancy hotels or to board-and-care homes. The level of care in many of these facilities was exceedingly poor. Elderly patients were simply discharged to nursing homes where, in too many instances, the care provided was scandalous. The scandals resulted in greater regulation. Conditions may have improved in recent years, but newspaper headlines continue to expose patient-care scandals in some of these facilities (e.g., Levy, 2002).

Deinstitutionalization policy created new underserved populations of vulnerable individuals, such as people with both mental illness and substance abuse problems. Many are younger people, disinclined to use the formal mental health system, who resist the appellation of "mental patient" (Johnson, Stiffman, Hadley-Ives, & Elze, 2001).

The state hospital provided a full array of services from the time of entrance to the patient's discharge or death. The community mental health system cannot readily supply the same range of services. A large number of the seriously mentally ill without adequate supports were unable to cope on their own and became homeless street people (see Box 2–1). Odd behavior in this group offers visible signs of the problems in deinstitutionalization policy.

Many former patients will not use the formal system of care. The poor living conditions of many former inpatients and problems in dealing with some consumers now living in the community have led family advocates to try to change the laws to permit involuntary hospitalization on broader grounds than dangerousness to self or others (see Special Issue of *Innovations and Research: Mental illness and the law*, 1993). Although some former patients (now often called "consumers") ac-

Box 2–1. Homelessness

At least several hundred thousand people in the United States are homeless at any given time (Breakey & Fischer, 1990). The increase in the homeless population starting in the early 1980s has been linked (unfairly) to deinstitutionalization. Estimates of the portion of homeless people who have mental or substance abuse problems vary widely from place to place and over time. Furthermore, homeless people are difficult to count, let alone diagnose accurately. The best guess may be that 15–30 percent of homeless people have mental illness, but a majority are thought to have drug and, particularly, alcohol disorders (with many having multiple disorders; Toro & Wall, 1991). Yet the fastest growing segment had no diagnosis other than incomes too low for their local housing market. An alarming portion of this latter group were single women with children, breaking the old stereotype of the single adult male "hobo" (Milburn & D'Ercole, 1991).

There are also a large number of runaway (or "throwaway") homeless youth, many of whom—both males and females—rely on prostitution to survive (Greene, Ennett, & Ringwalt, 1999; MacLean, Embry, & Cauce, 1999). Viewing homelessness from a stress and coping perspective is helpful, especially for runaway youth (see chapter 3).

The majority of homeless people are not so by choice, however. Even if we could cure all mental illness and addictions, people would still be homeless. Thus, it is misleading to think of homelessness as a mental health or deinstitutionalization problem, but rather a problem of economics, political will, government priorities that reduced or eliminated low-income housing programs and welfare payments, and real estate development that destroyed millions of low-income housing units (Shinn & Tsemberis, 1998). Homelessness is like a game of musical chairs in which there are simply too few affordable housing units. Those left standing when the music stops may have various individual or family vulnerability factors, or secondary causes of homelessness, such as mental illness, substance abuse, criminal history, spouse or child abuse and neglect, unemployment, or physical disability or disease. Yet the primary cause of homelessness is the loss of low-income housing units, especially in or near downtown areas, at a time when the need for them is rising. There are many root causes of this trend, including urban renewal policies of the past 50 years that demolished millions of low-income private and public housing units and replaced them with public buildings, freeways, open space, and luxury housing. Other affordable homes were upgraded via gentrification (middle- or upper-class people moving into poor neighborhoods), which drives up the cost, not only of those homes, but of all housing in the area. Government housing policies reducing the number of subsidized units was also to blame, especially during the 1980s. (Most people may assume that the vast majority of federal housing subsidies go to poor people. They would be surprised to learn that approximately two-thirds go to middle- and upper-class households in the form of tax deductions for mortgage interest and property taxes.) Development policies and market forces continue to favor middle- and upper-income home building, which along with increasing demand for housing due to population growth, higher construction costs, and low rental vacancy rates has made housing costs nationwide increase rapidly. Government policy suggests that households should pay 30 percent or less of their monthly income on housing and utilities. Yet it has become common for many to devote 50 percent *or more* of their income to housing, making it that much harder to afford everything else including the education and investment that could help lift them out of poverty.

From this broader perspective, it is clear that the vast and serious problem of homelessness is just the "tip of iceberg" of the many millions of people struggling with housing costs and problems (Wilson, 1987). Let us not forget that for every homeless person, there may be 100 more people living below the poverty line in substandard housing and leading hopeless lives. This in the wealthiest nation on earth!

The question of how best to respond to homelessness illustrates the difference between community and clinical psychology. The clinical response is to improve treatment and aftercare services for mentally ill and addicted individuals to reduce their vulnerability. Even if this were politically and economically feasible, which it has proved not to be, it ignores the root of the problem and thus would merely rearrange the players in the game of musical chairs. Nor is the solution just to build more shelters, which is the social policy equivalent to crisis intervention.

As will become clearer in the next two chapters, community psychology adopts a more ecological model in which the goal is to intervene at every stage of the stress process, not just the end, and every level, not just with individuals. Emergency shelter space is vital, but should include coordinated support services and connect to transitional and permanent housing (Shinn & Tsemberis, 1998). Even more important, to prevent homelessness, we must eliminate the root causes of both the affordable housing shortage (Shinn, 1992) and the environmental stressors that create or exacerbate individual vulnerabilities (Milburn & D'Ercole, 1991). The former requires action at all levels of government, from local protection of cheap single-room-occupancy apartments and requirements that new development include low- and moderate-income housing to state and regional planning to ensure that all cities and counties have affordable housing to federal support for safe public housing, adequate low-income private housing subsidies, and the creation of more living-wage jobs.

knowledge the need for involuntary hospitalization, and for involuntary medication, many still find the experience destructive and would prefer to avoid it. Many states have adopted involuntary outpatient commitment statutes that make it easier to rehospitalize a discharged person who refused medication or other care (Mulvey, Geller, & Roth, 1987)

In many cities "service ghettos" have been created in which persons who are sick, poor, old, mad, or bad are concentrated, almost as they were in the poorhouses of old. The slogan "problem creation through problem solution" is very apt.

Deinstitutionalization has had many positive effects (Shinn & Felton, 1981). Studies rather uniformly report that consumers feel more satisfied in community settings than in the hospital. Many who might have spent a lifetime in a hospital now have more freedom and live safely in the community, although their lifestyle may be restricted. Some have formed consumer self-help and advocacy groups, while others have themselves become trained providers of case management and other mental health services (Salzer, Blank, Rothbard, & Hadley, 2001). The positive consequences of deinstitutionalization might well be enhanced if we could solve some of the challenges to the service system (Lamb, 1984).

Care in the community. Since 1963 the proportion of inpatient care episodes to outpatient episodes has changed drastically. Thirty years ago, 75 percent of all patient care episodes (patient admitted and discharged in a year) took place in state and county mental hospitals. Today only 25 percent take place there. The change is reflected in data about where the 2,000,000 persons with diagnoses of serious mental disorders (schizophrenia or bipolar disorder) live. Only a small percentage live in state and county mental hospitals (Torrey et al., 1988).

Lengths of stay in mental hospitals have decreased drastically compared with 30 years ago. In 1969, the average length of stay in state and county mental hospitals was 421 days, and in 1978 it was 189 days. The average length of stay for psychiatric conditions in general hospitals is only eight days. These shorter stays have produced a "revolving-door" phenomenon. Some patients are in, out, and then in again (Kiesler, 2000).

A shortened length of stay reflects the community thrust of restoring the person's equilibrium as rapidly as possible and then returning him or her to the community. Considered alone, length-of-stay data do not tell us about the meaning of short stays to consumers and their families. If consumers improve as much in short stays as they do in longer ones, shorter stays have benefits for the consumer and for society. If consumers do not improve sufficiently to allow resumption of relatively peaceful and independent living, however, short stays may not be greeted with much enthusiasm, especially by families who felt relieved when hospitalization lifted a burden from their shoulders

(Hatfield, 1993). Short hospital stays underscore the necessity of after-care and of prepared environments, whether the consumer returns to the family or to some community residence.

Resources have not been adequately reallocated from state and county mental health budgets to community-based services (housing, income support, psychiatric and medical care) that are integrated and effective. Private sector for-profit psychiatric hospital chains take the eas-iest patients, keeping them as long as insurance covers their care. These chains compete with public sector agencies for the most qualified pro-fessional mental health workers, worsening the staffing problems of state hospitals and public sector community-based agencies (Torrey et al., 1988). With limited funds, states now "outsource" outpatient, day treat-ment, and residential services to private, nonprofit managed care enti-ties, with other public funds such as Medicaid used for short-term in-patient stays in community hospitals (Salzer et al., 2001).

In sum, over the past 30 years the health and mental health care systems in the United States have changed dramatically (Kiesler, 2000). With the community mental health system in an extended period of retrenchment, new community programs have not emerged (Heller, Jenkins, Steffen, & Swindle, 2000). Rates of hospitalization for many disorders have gone up as facilities, especially private ones, chase the higher reimbursements for inpatient care. Mental health centers are serving the same functions (psychotherapy and supportive care for the chronically ill) as private clinics and state mental hospitals. Whether community mental health can get back to its original goal of locally driven innovations in aftercare, consultation, education, research, eval-uation, and prevention remains to be seen (Heller et al., 2000).

Community Alternatives to Hospitalization

Over the years, psychosocial rehabilitation models, crisis and out-reach programs, intensive case management, and programs such as As-sertive Community Treatment (Stein & Test, 1985; Test, 1991; see Box 2–2) have superceded medical models of care that depended on the pa-

---

Box 2–2. *Assertive Community Supports*

An important development in the formal system of care has been the increasing use of case managers to coordinate an array of diverse services for people in need. In newer versions these providers work from one or two hours per week up to many hours per week with the same individuals, delivering services in the homes and other nat-ural settings where these consumers live. Below we describe two ex-amples: Assertive Community Treatment for people with serious mental illness, and the Homebuilders program for families in jeopardy of having their children placed outside the home.

Assertive Community Treatment (ACT), also known as Training in Community Living or the Madison Model, provides intensive support to individuals with severe mental illness (SMI) to prevent or reduce hospitalization and to increase quality of life in the community (Witheridge, 1990). ACT provides practical services focusing directly on basic living skills, medications, finances, housing, and advocacy for the client to obtain services from other providers. The ratio of staff to consumers is small (typically 1:10); staff members work as a team in an effort to increase consumer access to services (e.g., during evening and weekend hours) and to facilitate communication and support among staff (Stroul, 1986). Staff-consumer contacts occur almost exclusively in natural community settings rather than clinic offices. The staff works to keep consumers enrolled in the program. ACT promotes a mental health consumer's right to a fully integrated life in the community.

ACT has been used successfully in rural and inner-city communities (Bond, Witheridge, Dincin, & Wasmer, 1990; Witheridge & Dincin, 1985). It is well-suited to young adults with SMI (Stein & Test, 1985), who represent an especially challenging population (Iscoe & Harris, 1984). It has been used among homeless mentally ill individuals and mentally ill substance abusers (Olfson, 1990).

As for its results, ACT consistently reduces hospital use and therefore costs of service (e.g., Bond et al., 1990; Dincin, Wasmer, Witheridge, & Sobeck, 1993). Other desirable effects such as symptom reduction, improved social relationships, and subjective quality of life, have been less easy to substantiate through research (Olfson, 1990). Less costly than hospitalization, ACT is labor-intensive and thus relatively expensive compared with other forms of outpatient care. Lack of resources and resources maldistributed to hospitals rather than community programs limit its availability in many communities (Stein & Test, 1985; Torrey, 1990).

We may ask several questions about ACT. Are reductions in hospital use attributable simply to better compliance with medication under the intensive supports ACT provides? What is ACT's optimum place in cost-conscious systems of "managed care"? Is ACT best used as an intense support during episodes of crisis, with less formal consumer-driven supports readily available at other times? Could ACT be blended with principles of mutual help by enrolling mental health consumers as ACT staff (Toro, 1990)?

Homebuilders (Kinney, Haapala, & Booth, 1991) is another assertive support program. Other programs that use intensive family-based interventions to change the behavior of youths in their natural environments (e.g., Henggeler, Schoenwald, Borduin, Rowland, & Cunningham, 1998) have also reported some success.

tient coming voluntarily to an outpatient clinic for aftercare. These more intensive outpatient services are often supplemented by daycare programs or consumer organizations with their own clubhouses (See Special Issue on Clubhouses, *Psychosocial Rehabilitation Journal* [1992], 16, No. 2 October). Some clubhouses are staffed and operated by former patients (Chamberlin, 1990).

While the many examples of new services provide conceptual and research challenges to the mental health community, alternative services operating outside the formal mental health care system have also increased in number. Many cities now have shelters for the homeless, for battered women, and for runaway youths. There are treatment and residential facilities for substance abusers, peer counseling programs, and street worker projects. Facilities are staffed in whole or in part by people who themselves have suffered with the problem or who have a personal aptitude for the work instead of professional credentials. The staffs of alternative facilities believe they offer different services than do traditional mental health services and serve clients who would not use traditional services (Gordon & Curtin, 2000). Abortion clinics grew rapidly after *Roe* v. *Wade* (1973), and many offer counseling along with abortion services. In addition to protesting abortion clinics, some antiabortion groups offer counseling and assistance either in placing infants for adoption or in keeping them. Rape counseling programs have also developed, as have victim assistance programs. Descendants of community action programs, first established during the War on Poverty, still exist and provide neighborhood services, including counseling, training, advocacy for clients, and referral to other agencies.

Suicide prevention services developed during the 1960s and grew rapidly. Many now provide crisis services, broadly defined, using volunteers who are trained to staff telephone "hotlines" (Mishara & Daigle, 2001).

In some places church-affiliated or lay counseling centers have developed, staffed by volunteers trained in counseling methods and supervised by professionals. In recent years, faith-based services have proliferated; we will see more as President Bush's initiative to support faith-based services with federal dollars takes hold. Self-help groups also have proliferated (see chapter 9).

Our knowledge of alternative services is usually based on small-scale studies of programs that are probably unrepresentative, and the studies rarely include follow-ups. Who uses the services and who drops out? These questions remain for research if we are to understand which needs the community-based alternatives serve.

Outpatient psychotherapy. Outpatient psychotherapy providers have increased substantially (Torrey et al., 1988). Services are also provided by psychiatric nurses trained at the M.A. level, marriage and family counselors, and pastoral counselors and clergy trained in psychotherapy or counseling, as well as by unlicensed "psychotherapists" with diverse and sometimes dubious credentials. This increase in professional psychotherapy is consistent with the extensive needs identified by epidemiological surveys (chapter 1). The psychotherapy market may be oversaturated in some metropolitan areas, but the shortage is still severe in rural and less populated areas of the country.

Although many professional practitioners work in public clinics and agencies, a large number are in private practice. Insurance coverage for outpatient mental health services undergirded the growth of private practice. Managed care, limiting the number of visits, specifying treatment methods, and limiting the number of practitioners who may be reimbursed by insurance, is having profound effects on the field (Bickman et al., 1995). The service system may be less available to clients (Heflinger & Northrup, 2000; Sabin & Daniels, 2001) and practitioners have organized to do battle with managed care organizations. They argue that managed care is detrimental to patient care, and to the practitioners' livelihoods. Those who use outpatient services are not necessarily the severely mentally ill, and hospitalizations may not be avoided because of outpatient psychotherapy (Torrey et al., 1988).

Bureaucratic obstacles. The community movement has undoubtedly had a strong impact on how we approach problems, but change doesn't come easily (see chapter 10). Most mental health services provide primarily individual, group, and family therapy and psychotropic medications, and not always to those with the greatest need (Torrey et al., 1988). Furthermore, because most new services have developed piecemeal from pragmatic considerations, the result has been a crazy quilt pattern of funding and legislated eligibility requirements to receive services.

Before the community mental health centers program, 96 percent of funds for public mental health services came from state government. Twenty years later the federal government contributed 38 percent, local governments 9 percent, and state governments only 53 percent (Torrey et al., 1988). Program administrators must keep track of the different funding streams for treatment programs and the strings attached to each. Clinicians are also faced with keeping track of programs that help their clients individually—SSI, Social Security Disability, Medicaid, food stamps, state supplements, welfare, special housing programs, clothing allowances, and discounts for public transportation. Torrey et al. comment:

> Since the professionals themselves have difficulty keeping all these programs straight, it is little wonder that individuals with serious mental illness are usually overwhelmed with them all. (p. 13)

The diverse funding streams have resulted in a "fiscal shell game" as officials, sometimes working at cross-purposes, try to shift fiscal responsibility from one level of government to another. Torrey et al. (1988) claim that the fiscal shell game is now the driving force behind public mental health decision making, not patient care.

The basic distinction between public and private care has begun to break down as states and counties realign themselves and begin collaborating with private organizations in an effort to meet consumers' needs (Snowden, 1993). This trend may accelerate, given President Bush's policy to support faith-based services. Capitation systems, funded on the basis of eligible consumers rather than on fees for services, are adopted in theory to increase the efficiency and consumer-centeredness of services. Finally, managed care, where services may be allocated in fixed amounts and purchased at competitive prices in the open marketplace, gives an uneasy glimpse of how far we've come from the ad lib support based on mutual obligation that was once provided during the Middle Ages.

New developments. In considering the future, we cannot pay attention to program ideas alone. At every step, our thinking must take into account the political, social, and economic contexts of ideas and the programs they inspire. For example, political considerations and the conservative temper of the 1980s influenced the rhetoric and the allocation of funds for a "war on drugs" (Humphreys & Rappaport, 1993). We also need to consider alternatives to the medical model (see also Lorion & Ross, 1992). Kiesler (2000), moreover, arguing that medical model approaches are inherently flawed, concludes that unless alternative approaches to health policy in the provision of mental health care are devised, we can only expect more expensive and inappropriate care to emerge. If these ideas hold sway in the effort to reform health policy in the United States, the community approach will have continued significance in both mental health and substance abuse services.

This potential for still more diversity of service approaches challenges community psychology to articulate and test new concepts. This challenge was heightened by a renewed emphasis on preventive services attributable to the President's Commission on Mental Health (1978). In the absence of a viable theoretical paradigm, however, community psychology's response to the challenge of prevention may fail. (We review concepts of prevention and preventive programs in chapter 8.) We will identify some promising theoretical concepts generated by the community thrust in the next chapter. Before doing so, we will review the situation concerning services for racial and cultural minority groups and for children and adolescents.

Minorities and Other Underserved Groups

In 1978, the President's Commission on Mental Health identified rural populations and ethnic and racial minorities as unserved or underserved populations. Has the community thrust resulted in improved services to groups formerly less well served? There has probably been some increase in service utilization of mental health services by members of minority groups. Critics still raise questions about the appropriateness and usefulness of traditional medical model services to minority and ethnic populations, including African American, Native American, Hispanic or Latino, and the new Asian immigrants. Some members of these populations may come to use services, especially if the service providers adapt services to meet the needs and cultures of this diverse clientele. O'Sullivan et al. (1989) claim that utilization of services by minorities has improved substantially and attribute the improvement to changes in the pattern of service delivery:

> There were more ethnic-specific CMHCs located in their respective neighborhoods, more culturally unique and relevant treatment modalities being provided, and more ethnic and bilingual staff providing services. These developments were initiated within the ethnic communities and supported by local government. (p. 28)

From the viewpoint of some African American scholars, dealing with the many inequities in American society that may be related to the prevalence of mental health problems and stress in the African American population is a more important issue than utilization of mental health services may be: "What social changes are likely to promote the involvement and participation of black Americans as full and equal citizens?" (Moore, 1982, pp. 178–179). The question does not mean we should ignore service delivery issues, but that other matters should be addressed as well.

Children and Adolescents

Mental health problems of children and adolescents received far less attention than adult problems, despite evidence of need.

The extent of need. The prevalence of diagnosable disorders among children and adolescents under age 18 ranges from 5 to 23 percent (Namir & Weinstein, 1982). The variation in estimates stems from different methods and sampling procedures. The National Advisory Mental Health Council (1990) estimated that about 12 percent (or about 7.6 million) of the 63 million young people under age 18 have some mental disorders, with half of them severely handicapped because of them. The Institute of Medicine (1989), part of the National Research Council, speculated that the prevalence rate for all childhood disorders may fall between 17 and 22 percent but recommended adopting the more conservative estimate of 12 percent. The Surgeon General's (2001b) report settled on a prevalence rate of 10 percent.

Among the poorest inner-city populations the prevalence of disorder may be as high as 20 percent. A number of groups have higher rates than in the general population: children whose parents are mentally ill or substance abusers; children living in foster care; children with chronic medical illnesses; Native American children in some tribes with a high risk of suicide; children living on welfare; homeless children; children separated from parents for prolonged periods; children suffering physical or sexual abuse; orphans; and children in unstable families or families characterized by marital discord. Children with low birth weights, developmental delays, brain damage, early temperamental difficulties, or mental retardation also tend to have prevalence rates of psychopathology in excess of that found in the general population (Dykens, 2000; Institute of Medicine, 1989).

There are probably more than 2 million children and adolescents of school age who are not in school, many because they had been suspended or expelled for disciplinary reasons (Berg & Nursten, 1996). The 350,000–400,000 adolescents who have out-of-wedlock children each year and their children constitute another population at risk. The adolescents tend not to finish high school, and their children are at risk for school failure. These risk factors help us to identify characteristics of populations that should be targeted for services.

Services. Children's services have been chronically neglected. Existing services are neither sufficient in quantity to meet children's needs nor successful in reaching the populations at greatest risk.

Federal commissions and reports. In 1961 (Joint Commission on Mental Illness and Health), in 1969 (Joint Commission on the Mental Health of Children), in 1978 (President's Commission on Mental Health), in 1983 (federal Child and Adolescent Service System Program [see Friedman & Duchnowski, 1990]), and in 1990 (U.S. House of Representatives Select Committee on Children, Youth and Families) federal commissions and reports identified the same problems: children and adolescents were underserved. The prevalence of disorder among children and youth was high, but services did not reach those in greatest need. The youth in greatest need were from high-poverty and minority communities, children who had been abused or neglected, and those placed in foster care and residential treatment. Drug and alcohol abuse problems among the families affected children adversely, and added to the difficulty of successfully returning children placed out of their homes to their parents (Taussig, Clyman, & Landsverk, 2001). Children involved with the welfare, juvenile justice, and mental health systems were poorly served. Moreover, bureaucratic, patchwork, and uncoordinated services impeded care. There is evidence that these problems may only get worse under managed care (Bickman et al., 1995; Heflinger & Northrup, 2000). In January of 2001, the U.S. Surgeon General (2001b) issued a report on the mental health needs of children. The authors of this report could have saved a lot of work by simply cutting and pasting from the earlier reports. The problems described in the earlier reports continued unabated. The lack of progress reflects the complexity of our service systems, a complexity due in part to their embeddedness in the political system. The surgeon general issued a forward looking report, but a new president took office shortly after the report was issued. Perhaps his administration will follow up this time, but the history of services for children does not give us grounds for optimism.

The list in Table 2–1 does not include Aid to Families with Dependent Children (AFDC) now called TANF (Temporary Assistance for Needy Families) nor does it include funds made available through the Education of Handicapped Children Act designed to serve infants, toddlers, preschool children, and school-age children with educational and related handicaps (U.S. Office of Special Education and Rehabilitative Services, 1990).

The various acts and programs are administered either by different federal agencies or by different divisions within the same agency. Sometimes the acts provide for direct grants to service providers for demonstrations and related programs that, if successful, are supposed to be picked up by state or local funding sources, but rarely are. Sometimes funds are given to state mental health or social services or youth authorities to be used in accordance with federal regulations. It is lit-

Table 2–1
Federal Programs That Assist Children in Need

Abandoned Infants Assistance Act to help children and infants with AIDS (PL 100-505)

Adoption Assistance (Title IV-E, Social Security Act [SSA])

Adoption Opportunities (Title II, Child Abuse Prevention and Treatment Act [CAPTA])

Alcohol, Drug Abuse and Mental Health Block Grant, with 10 percent set aside for community-based mental health services for seriously emotionally disturbed children and youth (Title XIX, Part B, Public Health Service Act)

Child Abuse Challenge Grants to stimulate prevention-oriented programs (CAPTA)

Child Abuse Grants and Family Violence Grants (CAPTA)

Child Welfare (Title IV-B, SSA)

Foster Care and Independent Living (Title IV-E, SSA)

Runaway Youth Program (Title III, Juvenile Justice and Delinquency Prevention Act [JJDPA]); Juvenile Justice Program (JJDPA)

Social Services Block Grant (Title XX, SSA)

Temporary Child Care for Handicapped Children and Crisis Nurseries Act

tle wonder that critics complain of an ungainly, uncoordinated structure that delivers services inefficiently and ineffectively. The system is further complicated because some families have private insurance with diverse limitations, and others depend on public services with its rules for eligibility.

Despite the multitude of programs (or perhaps because of them), the problems in delivering services are so severe that the congressional report listed more than 80 lawsuits brought in 20 states asking the courts to order state child welfare, juvenile justice, mental health, or education authorities to live up to the requirements for service delivery that are written into law and for which the states received federal funds. A number of cases sought compensation for children who were maltreated or injured while in foster care or under the state's supervision.

Out-of-home placements. There are probably more than 450,000 children in foster care. Could the many out-of-home placements be avoided if other care were available? It is difficult to obtain accurate figures on the number of children and adolescents in need who actually receive services. Estimates range from one in three in need (Knitzer, 1984) to one in ten who receive mental health services (Namir & Weinstein, 1982; Richardson, Keller, Selby-Harrington, & Parrish, 1996). The U.S. Surgeon General (2001b) estimated that about one in five in need receive services. Increases in the admission of children and adolescents to institutions (Weithorn, 1988) may also reflect the lack of adequate or effective community services.

Managed care with its close examination of the need for psychiatric hospitalization may have done more to slow the trend toward placing adolescents in psychiatric hospitals than any other change in admission policies. Admissions to other residential treatment centers have also increased. Admissions to public and private facilities for those adjudicated juvenile delinquents has increased; there are now over 100,000 juveniles in public or private detention, correctional, and shelter facilities (U.S. Department of Justice, 1999). Because of legal changes allowing juveniles to be tried and punished as adults, many more are entering the adult prison system, one not noted for its high quality mental health services. While the majority of children and adolescents in need of services are not receiving them, as many as 40 percent of people of this age who are hospitalized are there merely because more suitable alternatives are not available. While many problems are identified early enough, appropriate services generally are not available to those previously identified as high-risk (see above) (Knitzer, 1984).

Alternative services. Are children inappropriately served in inpatient and residential settings? Most children improve while in residential facilities, but improvement at the point of discharge has little predictive value for adaptation in the community or for recidivism. Moreover, those who were admitted with milder forms of psychopathology do better after discharge from residential care than those with more severe pathology. Post-discharge care appears to be important for post-discharge adaptation (Levine, Toro, & Perkins, 1993). Taken together, these findings suggest that many who are placed in residential care could probably be maintained equally well if adequate community-based services were available. However, some will undoubtedly need residential care.

Unfortunately, our treatment technologies are not very powerful. Although more than 230 psychotherapeutic approaches were identified by the Institute of Medicine (1989) only a few have been subject to careful research. We now have some empirically validated treatment methods, but most of these have not been tested under field conditions. In any event, professionals providing routine services have been slow to adopt the newer approaches, even though existing research suggests that standard treatments yield only small effect sizes if any, and have high dropout rates. Medications show some promise, although many drugs in use have not been tested for safety and effectiveness with children. Pharmaceutical treatment for ADHD and related disorders is an exception, although many are concerned about the overuse of medication (Surgeon General, 2001b). Programs that focus on one aspect of a child's life (e.g., the family) may have only limited impact on school or interactions with peers in the community. In keeping with ecological principles developed in later chapters, how can we increase generalization and maintenance of gains across settings and over time? The social and political problems complicating the picture might be easier to overcome if our treatment technologies were more powerful.

There are some good examples of responsive service systems (Knitzer, 1984; Namir & Weinstein, 1982; Institute of Medicine, 1989; Surgeon General, 2001b). However there are barriers to extending the use of some effective programs. Services are delivered in alternative settings, using educational and rehabilitative as well as therapeutic modalities, and are staffed by traditional and nontraditional mental health personnel. In an age when funding is critical, and when insurance may not cover these types of "treatments," or even consultation services of mental health professionals, it is difficult to develop programs alternative to those offered in the medical model.

The Surgeon General (2001b) recommended more school-based approaches and more efforts to use local schools as neighborhood community centers providing child care and child-rearing aid to parents. However, funding problems, and interorganizational relationships receive scant attention. These school- and community-based programs do have potential value in preventing child abuse and neglect (U.S. Advisory Board on Child Abuse and Neglect, 1993). They appear to be

cost-effective as well as clinically effective, but they require cooperation between independent agencies. Unfortunately, the field is limited
by the fact that the medical model is still front and center in professional and policy thinking.

Integrating services in the community. New programs require cooperation among independent agencies. Political, social, and professional problems hamper the reform of children's services. Fragmented
services, children's lack of political clout, and cultural attitudes emphasizing family responsibility for children limit reform (Knitzer, 1984;
Namir & Weinstein, 1982).

A comprehensive program requires cooperation and collaboration
among diverse agencies responsible for child welfare, including school,
health, and mental health services. For example, problems of sexual and
physical abuse of children bring mental health workers into contact with
police, prosecutors, judges, lawyers, and social service agencies. The
problems of interagency cooperation are difficult but not impossible to
solve. A comprehensive plan for interagency cooperation requires coordination at the state and local levels and with local interagency planning groups. Financing coordinated outpatient services requires legal
and regulatory changes to ensure that agencies asked to provide certain services can actually be paid to provide them. Agencies need "flexible service dollars" to provide individualized care. "Blended funds"
from health, mental health, education, and social services should be
used flexibly to avoid the restrictions of existing programs that focus
on rigid diagnostic categories. Such an approach should probably include a case manager who will mediate between the family's needs and
the service system. The surgeon general made similar recommendations
(2001b), but will these be carried out? It remains to be seen whether our
political leaders will support new initiatives to solve problems that have
been brought to their attention for over 40 years now.

Policy changes. Mental health services alone are not enough. Family policies in general, and programs governing nutrition, health, prenatal care, day care, help for single-parent families, and family policies
all need reconsideration. Some very good studies of early childhood
education, such as the Head Start program, have demonstrated remarkable success in preventing educational disability and later social
disability (Hacsi, 2002; Zigler & Muenchow, 1992; see chapter 8). With
the exception of Head Start, however, large-scale programs holding out
the promise of prevention have not received favorable political attention in recent years. As Iscoe and Harris noted in 1984: "If the priorities of a nation are mirrored in its SCIs [social and community inter-
ventions], the welfare of children and youth are clearly not uppermost
in the minds and intentions of policymakers" (p. 354).

Continued cooperation between citizen advocates and professionals and among agencies will be necessary to move ahead in solving

critical problems and gaining new resources. If anything, the community perspective is even more important when we consider programs for persons from culturally diverse groups and programs for children and adolescents.

Summary

Community psychology is connected to many social and historical developments, both distant and recent. The public's obligation to provide for the needs of chronically dependent persons descends from laws enacted hundreds of years ago in Elizabethan England. By the mid-nineteenth century this responsibility was expressed in the form of the state mental hospital, the mainstay of mental health care in the United States for over 100 years. In the twentieth century, the Great Depression, World War II, the struggle for civil rights, and other events wrought great changes in American society, to a point where a contrasting ideological and scientific perspective such as community psychology could gain credence. Community psychology emerged from community mental health and applied social psychology in the ferment of the 1960s, and was in part a response to specific deficiencies in the traditional medical model of treatment for mental illness and partly an effort to expand psychology's purview to address social problems such as poverty and discrimination.

Community-based helping alternatives proliferated during the 1960s and 1970s as social changes continued. Despite disappointments with the power of interventions or the pace of change, the community approach has wrought considerable change in contemporary mental health practice. Community approaches now represent the conventional wisdom in such areas as long-term rehabilitation of people with chronic mental illness, programs for minorities and other underserved groups, and prevention of social problems in young children.

In the new millennium, community life for people at risk will be based less on a metaphor of "dependent care" and more on the idea of supporting "normal" living for members of diverse groups. More relevant than the nature of specific mental health services provided may be the question of what social changes are likely to promote the community involvement and participation of all vulnerable persons as full and equal citizens? In the next chapter we introduce several of community psychology's central concepts as we present a comprehensive framework useful in defining community psychology and distinguishing it from clinical psychology.

Note

1. The material in this section is based on Levine (1981) and sources cited in that book.

II

PERSPECTIVES IN COMMUNITY PSYCHOLOGY

3

A Conceptual Road Map of Community Psychology

The Dohrenwend Model

Because of its rapid development, community psychology lacked a well articulated, widely shared conceptual model, or set of theoretical principles that would help in making sense of the field's diversity and in guiding future development. The field recognized person-centered and environment-centered approaches. Some were engaged in clinical work, and yet were moving toward developing preventive interventions. The field needed a conceptual framework to bring some order for its practitioners.

In her presidential address to the Division of Community Psychology (later renamed The Society for Community Research and Action) of the American Psychological Association, Barbara Dohrenwend (1978) proposed a conceptual model to help answer two questions: "What do community psychologists do?" and "What is the difference between community psychology and clinical psychology?" These questions were pertinent because diffuse activities unified under the label *community psychology* implied differences with other fields sufficiently great to warrant a separate professional identity.

The Dohrenwend model (Figure 3–1) is helpful for several reasons. First, it is based on a hypothesized connection between psychopathology and psychosocial stress (the kinds of problems we described in chapter 1 as "the soap opera of life"). As presented, it is a heuristic conceptual framework, not a tightly specified path analysis or other complex statistical model. The emphasis on psychosocial stress helps us to think about problems in terms other than diagnosis and illness.

Second, it shows how certain interventions might be helpful and because the model includes a time dimension, it directs us to think about interventions that might be used *before* a person seeks treatment. We are not limited to thinking about what to do only after the client or patient shows up on the therapist's doorstep.

Third, it directs us to think about both person-centered and environment-centered issues within the same framework. That is, it directs us to consider mental health programs that create or strengthen the environmental resources available to persons at risk (upper row of boxes in Figure 3–1) as well as those that strengthen the individual resistance of people at risk (lower row of boxes). The Dohrenwend model was developed in a psychiatric-epidemiological context. However, the same general model can be used heuristically to guide interventions to improve the quality of life and well-being as well as to prevent disorder.

The field of community psychology had the very ambitious aim of reducing the prevalence of psychopathology in the population at large. Dohrenwend had a hypothesis about causation: The kind of life events discussed in chapter 1 create psychosocial stress, and under some circumstances can lead to psychopathology. The immediate emotional re-

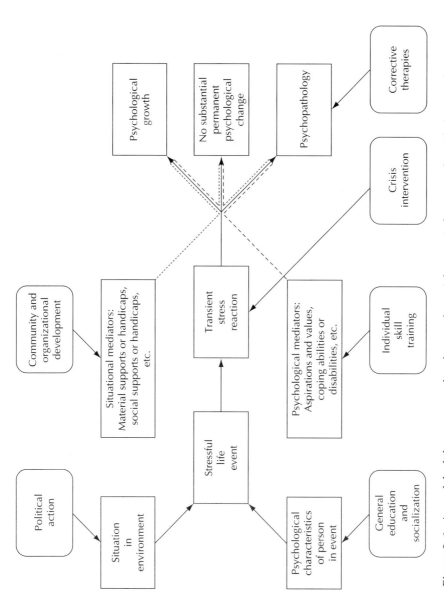

Figure 3–1. A model of the process whereby psychosocial stress induces psychopathology and some conceptions of how to counteract this process. (From Dohrenwend, 1978)

action to a stressful event is not pathological in and of itself. The aim is to understand the different points for and types of intervention that may undermine "the process whereby stress generates psychopathology" (Dohrenwend, 1978, p. 2).

Stressful Life Events

Under this model one looks at recent events in people's lives rather than at their early childhood experiences. Let us follow her argument:

> The process . . . starts with . . . recent events in the life of an individual rather than with distant childhood experiences. It describes an episode that is initiated by the occurrence of one or more stressful life events, and is terminated by psychological change, for good or ill, or by return to the psychological *status quo ante*. (pp. 2–3)

A stressful life event challenges the person's previous state of adaptation and requires a new adaptation. If you lose your job, get a divorce, or discover, as people at the Love Canal did, that your home is located near toxic chemicals that could seriously affect your family's health, you will have to do something different about your life. (Some have extended this idea to include everyday hassles as a form of stressful life events.)

In the psychopathological framework, a person's feelings of depression and anxiety in response to a stressful life event are often treated as symptoms of illness. In the Dohrenwend framework these feelings of anxiety and depression are temporary signs that one's current adaptation is being challenged and that the psychological means to cope and the social supports available to deal with one's current situation may be insufficient. (For more on stressful life events, see chapter 7.)

Person and Environment

Dohrenwend's model takes into account both person and environment, and allows us to focus on whichever aspect of a problem seems most salient: "Stressful life events vary in the extent to which they are determined by the environment or by psychological characteristics of the central person in the event" (p. 3). The model allows for the possibility "that an individual may take part in creating the very events that appear later to cause him to undergo psychological change" (p. 4). Thus, a stressful life event may be of the person's own making. A person could lose a job because a plant closes, but also because he drinks heavily, is having a bad time in a relationship and neglects his work, or because he has poor attitudes about coming to work on time every day. Whether the job is lost for personal or circumstantial reasons, however, the person faces the need to adapt to a new situation.

It is insufficient in this model to focus only on the person and to ignore all else, as the medical model of psychopathology leads us to do. The model doesn't exclude the possibility that biological vulnerability may contribute to the stress reactions. However, the outcomes may still depend on the processes suggested by the model.

Transient stress reactions are self-limiting. Regardless of the source of the stress response,

> a common characteristic of all of these forms of stress reaction is that they are inherently transient or self-limiting. . . . What follows after the immediate, transient stress reaction depends on the mediation of situational and psychological factors that define the context in which this reaction occurs. (p. 4)

Transient stress reactions include feelings of anxiety, depression, confusion, helplessness, or rage, and may include behaviors that resemble psychiatric symptoms; a person may develop headaches or muscle strain, may lose sleep, or seem very distracted. Usually these reactions are temporary, but should they persist for any length of time, such responses can themselves become troublesome as chronic reminders that one is feeling overwhelmed. Transient stress reactions are not considered psychopathological in and of themselves, however. In the normal course of events these reactions dissipate unless there is some reinforcement or secondary gain. For example, some claim that giving Supplemental Security Income (SSI; disability income) to persons with mental illness may help to perpetuate the symptoms that qualified these persons for disability support, thus insuring that they continue to receive payments indefinitely (see *National Alliance for the Mentally Ill,* 1993, p. 1). If symptoms get a person out of unpleasant circumstances or help to control the behavior of others, they may persist.

Situational and psychological mediators. By situational and psychological mediators, Dohrenwend is referring to resources a person may use coming from others in his or her support network, and to the psychological strengths and attitudes with which one copes with the demands of the stressful event. Both situational and psychological mediators of the stress-pathology relationship are important in Dohrenwend's model in determining the outcome:

> Other things being equal, an individual whose financial or other material resources are strained by the demands of a stressful life event is likely to have a worse outcome than a person with adequate material resources. Similarly, lack of social support is hypothesized to increase the likelihood

of a negative outcome . . . [Psychological] mediators . . . include "values"
. . . and "coping abilities." (p. 5)

(See chapter 7 for further discussion of these issues.)

Outcomes

Transient stress reactions and situational and psychological mediators interact in some complex fashion to produce one of three categories of outcomes; the person (a) may grow and change positively as
a result of mastering the experience, (b) may essentially return to some
state normal for that person, or (c) may develop psychopathology, defined by Dohrenwend as a persistent, apparently self-sustaining dysfunctional reaction. By that term she means the person is so affected
that negative emotions predominate and interfere with the enjoyment
of anything else, or functioning is so impaired that the person cannot
carry out the tasks expected given the person's age, gender, and general station in life. In other words, a waste of human potential results
when the reaction continues past the events that precipitated it.

The usefulness of that definition of psychopathology aside, the
model focuses attention on much more than the psychological and
emotional reaction of the individual person. (In chapter 7, we will contrast the concept of an acute neurotic reaction to the stressful life events
or crisis model.) The concept of psychosocial stress requires attention
to the individual's life circumstances and the resources—psychological, material, and social—available to meet the demands posed by
events and circumstances.

The model accounts for the possibility that maladaptive psychological mediators (e.g., low self-efficacy, inadequate problem-solving
skills, excessive "self-medication" using alcohol or drugs) may contribute to poorer outcomes, and that adverse elements in the person's
social environment can also contribute to poorer outcomes (e.g., conflict with someone who would ordinarily provide support). By following the three outcomes (the boxes at the far right of the model in
Figure 3–1) we see that the bulk of clinical efforts have been directed
toward providing treatment at the *end* point of the process, the outcome labeled psychopathology.

To summarize, Dohrenwend's model proposes that transient stress
reactions often follow the occurrence of a stressful event. These reactions point to an elevated risk for maladaptive behavior. Factors involving both the person and the environment affect whether a transient stress reaction occurs in response to a given event. If it does occur,
then various outcomes are possible depending on the strength and effectiveness of personal and situational mediators that are present.

In the remainder of this chapter we discuss selected ways in which
psychologists and others have intervened at various points specified

Box 3–1. Poverty, Unemployment, and Social Problems

Problems are interconnected and intertwined at every ecological level (see chapter 4). We will point out how the phenomena may be interpreted within the Dohrenwend framework. Race is less accepted as a valid concept from a biological viewpoint and more difficult to ascertain because of the large number of those of mixed parentage. In an "apartheid" age, "one drop of blood" was sufficient to classify a person as a member of a stigmatized minority. Today, that concept is meaningless. However, race discrimination and disadvantage still exist and so race is used as an imperfect proxy for a variety of socio-economic processes.

Stressful life events are not randomly distributed in the population. Rates of crime, welfare dependence, out-of-wedlock pregnancies, and unemployment are especially high in a segment of the African American population Wilson (1987) calls the "truly disadvantaged." We would be more precise if we talked about an "underclass" that exists to a greater or lesser extent in all ethnic groups rather than a racial group, but we don't have good measures of underclass. Demographers use statistics based on classification as African American because that information is widely available, but race should only be used as an indicator of bias and differential impact and need. When used as an *indicator* of social problems, racial classifications not only are inaccurate, they unfairly stereotype and stigmatize whole populations.

Race is a sensitive area, but that doesn't mean we should avoid discussion of the issues. Wilson (1987), a distinguished African American sociologist, said that in the 25 years since Moynihan's (1965) controversial book (see chapter 2) the problems of crime, poverty, out-of-wedlock births, and unemployment have increased. The uproar following publication of Moynihan's monograph did result in research and scholarship emphasizing the strengths of African American families, but Wilson believes that the criticism may have discouraged researchers and policymakers from giving race-related problems careful attention.

Applying Dohrenwend's model, we can interpret the data reviewed here in terms of changes in circumstances (environmental situation) that make stressful life events more or less likely, and that may contribute to growth or to maladaptation (far right, Figure 3–1). The quantity and type of stressful life events affecting an individual will produce transient stress reactions. In the absence of social and situation supports (top center, Figure 3–1), and positive psychological mediators (bottom center, Figure 3–1) adverse outcomes are more likely (bottom right, Figure 3–1). Conversely, when barriers to resources are removed, the population that benefits from the relief will thrive (see chapter 4).

Progress After Barriers Were Eliminated

African Americans as a group have benefited from policy changes that protected against discrimination in education, housing, employment, public accommodations, and voting. The number of African Americans in professional, managerial, and technical occupations increased rapidly from 1973 to 2001 (U.S. Bureau of the Census, 2002, Table 588). In 2001, 8.3 percent of those in managerial and professional specialties and 11.4 percent of those in technical, sales and administrative support positions were African American. The percent of African Americans earning more than $50,000 per year in constant 1990 dollars grew from 11.5 percent in 1970 to 19.8 percent in 1996. The median income of African Americans taken as a group, including many single-mother households with incomes below the poverty line, is substantially below that of the majority population. However, the income of married African American couples is now about 84 percent of that of the majority of married couples, a considerable improvement over the differential existing 20 years ago (Table 743). In 1973, 2.6 million African American families owned their own homes. By 1997, that had grown to 5.14 million. The rate of high school completion among African Americans increased from 31.4 percent in 1970 to 78.5 percent in 2000. The percent of college graduates among African Americans has increased from 4.4 percent to 16.5 percent (Table 208). These figures also reflect improvements both in social supports available to African Americans, and in the psychological mediators (education) to cope with challenges of adapting to a changing occupational world. To the degree that income and occupational status are correlated with better mental health and a higher quality of life the population that has benefited from supports or improved access to resources has also benefited psychologically.

Consequences of widening disparities within the African American community. The gap between upper- and lower-income African Americans has grown rapidly since 1965 (Henwood, 1995). The poorest fifth of the African American population has lost ground. That means many problems associated with race and poverty are concentrated in the underclass left behind by economic progress and increased opportunity for those previously denied opportunity.

As middle-class professionals and skilled workers improved their situations, many moved out of the ghettos where restrictive housing and mortgage-financing practices had kept them and into better homes in more desirable neighborhoods (Flippen, 2001; Taylor, 1990). Why is it desirable to move? For one, the rate of violent crime is much lower in suburban than in urban areas. For another, people believe suburban schools are better. By moving, the likelihood of experiencing stressful life events related to violence or to school failure is reduced.

When the African American middle class moves out, the number of people who have the clout and the know-how to demand better services from municipal officials is reduced. Public services may deteriorate in neighborhoods that lose middle-class population; churches and other sources of community stability may decline. Situation mediators providing resources for coping are lost, increasing vulnerability. Taylor (1990) described the extensive network of "churches, neighborhood block clubs, community-based organizations, cultural groups, youth centers, civil rights organizations, social clubs, formal and informal political organizations, and educational and research institutions" (p. 14) in the Buffalo, New York, African American community:

> They [the organizations] stand on the front-line in the struggle against racism and in the fight to improve the quality of life in the black community. They serve as action groups that mobilize people around community problems and that articulate the needs of the black community to city government. This organizational network represents one of black Buffalo's greatest assets. It has helped African-Americans stave off social catastrophes that have beset black communities in megacities. (Taylor, 1990, p. 14)

As the density of poorer people increases in a neighborhood, the likelihood that stressful life events will occur also increases; the lack of social supports and situation mediators, and the presence of environmental handicaps combine to increase the likelihood there will be adverse long-term effects for many people. The concentration in certain neighborhoods of those in poverty has increased in recent years (Taylor, 1990). The poor are less scattered. Those who could move out have done so, leaving a concentration of poorer people in particular neighborhoods. Although we have interpreted these data in terms used in the Dohrenwend model, the reader should also consider that similar data can be interpreted within the ecological analogy discussed in chapter 4.

Youth, crime and unemployment. The African American population is younger than the majority population. The median age for majority populations living in inner cities is 30.3 years; for the African American population, it is 23.9 (Wilson, 1987). The concentration of young people increases the likelihood that people in the area will experience stressful life events. Younger people commit more crimes and are more often the victims of crimes. The risk of crime is higher in African American neighborhoods. Victimization rates are higher among African American males and females than in the majority group.

Members of the "truly disadvantaged" are also arrested and convicted of crimes disproportionately to their numbers in the population (Wilson, 1987). Although African Americans are only 12 percent of the population, they constitute about 46 percent of the state prison population. Including federal prisons, local jails, and public residential treatment facilities, about 4 percent of the African American male population is incarcerated at any moment in time. These men are not employed, and upon leaving prison have histories that may close job opportunities for them. If convicted of a felony, they may lose the right to vote. These problems require political action to help create jobs, and to create situation mediators to assist those leaving prison with the challenge of readapting in the outside world.

Feminization of poverty. Twenty-two percent of all families with children under 18 are headed by single mothers (http://factfinder.census.gov). However, 61 percent of families below the poverty line and 45.6 percent of African American households are headed by single women, and in inner cities the figure is 60 percent. In 1970, 64 percent of the African American population was married; by 1991 only 43.6 percent was married. Moreover, 64.5 percent of births to African Americans are out-of-wedlock, with many infants born to teenagers. The rate of out-of-wedlock births to majority women has also increased sharply. Births to teenage mothers are events that seriously challenge the mothers' adaptation. If these are accompanied by other stresses they may result in drug use, in "crack babies," and in the neglect or abuse of children, especially as pressures increase on the mothers. The widespread nonpayment and underpayment of child support and alimony makes matters worse.

The welfare system is a situation mediator for many young mothers. Some become welfare dependent. These are the problems that Moynihan noted in 1965. Advocates of welfare reform argue that these situation supports should be considered negative in nature because they encourage out-of-wedlock births and welfare dependency. The full results of welfare reform, which took effect in the late 1990s, are not yet in. So far, in a period of low unemployment, welfare reform has resulted in fewer people on welfare and more former welfare clients in the workforce. Most still are living below the poverty line, however, which should draw lawmakers' attention to the more widespread problems of the working poor. These include a minimum wage that has decreased substantially since the 1970s in constant dollars, and the scarcity of affordable good quality child care and homes (see Box 2–1, chapter 2; for a review of welfare reform's impacts, see *Annals of the American Academy of Political and Social Science*, Sept., 2001 [vol. 577] and Julnes & Foster, 2001).

Job market changes. Marital status, out-of-wedlock children and crime rates are related to changes in the job market that create challenges to adaptation. Changes in the job market create circumstances in which stressful life events may arise for those who lose their jobs, or who do not have the educational or other qualifications to pursue the new jobs. The great migration north of African Americans after World War II resulted from the mechanization of agriculture and the development of pesticides that reduced the need for farm labor in the South. Stressful life events related to unemployment have always been greater among African Americans. In 1970, the White unemployment rate was 4.5 percent; the African American rate was 9.4 percent. In 2003, the White unemployment rate was 5.2 percent and the African American rate was 10.7 percent. Unemployment rates are particularly high among younger people. In 2003, 32.8 percent of African American youth between 16 and 19 were unemployed. The rate among majority youth was 13.6 percent (U.S. Department of Labor, Bureau of Labor Statistics, 2004).

Other aspects of the job market have also changed, creating situation-based challenges to adaptation. Well-paid manufacturing jobs have declined greatly. Today's work is information exchange. More people now process paper, or operate computer terminals. Employers require people with appropriate educational qualifications. The changed job market calls for people with different psychological mediators. People who have lost jobs require retraining. They may also need to develop appropriate psychological mediators. Older, displaced workers need situation resources to help develop those mediators—appropriate educational opportunities and income while attending school. Many may also need support to help develop more favorable psychological mediators—self-confidence about engaging in new learning, and optimism about succeeding in a new and challenging venture. (We describe the Michigan Jobs Project in this chapter and in chapter 8, on prevention.)

The male marriageable pool index (MMPI). Families provide important social support (see chapter 7). The unemployment rate has implications for family formation as well. Wilson (1987) developed the MMPI to illustrate the relationship between employment and family formation. The MMPI is the ratio of employed *civilian* males to women in the same age and ethnic grouping. Because of the large number who are unemployed, incarcerated, or dead due to street violence, the ratio of employed civilian African American males to African American females is quite unfavorable. Employment is presumably a minimum requirement for a desirable mate. The unfavorable MMPI, especially in the African American population helps make the high rate of single-mother households understandable. If a two-parent family provides better support for the spouses and for their children, then the unfavorable MMPI suggests that fewer in the African American population have the benefit of those supports. Moreover, to the degree that a stable marital relationship provides psychological and financial advantages for spouses and for their children, the lesser opportunity to develop that support system means that members of the population may be more vulnerable to stressful life events. Some are proposing interventions to encourage marriage to reduce the number of children living in single-parent households.

Policy implications. The concentration of young, poor, single-parent homes in high crime areas, with fewer middle-class people and social supports to promote stability, plus the demoralization and stigma associated with dependence on public welfare (negative support) means that fewer of those persons have the family and neighborhood resources to be able to take advantage of the opportunities that do exist. According to Wilson (1987), it is the truly disadvantaged group for which new solutions are necessary.

Wilson argues that in order to reduce political resistance to affirmative action, resources should be targeted to anyone who is truly disadvantaged irrespective of race to provide "equality of life chances." He would include anyone coming from a poverty background, a low-income family, anyone who grew up in inadequate housing, or whose cultural background and language may be different from that of the majority. These "handicaps" cause a failure of preparation and support. Without adequate preparation, the likelihood is low that persons from those backgrounds can take advantage of opportunities that are present.

Wilson sees a solution in an economic policy (upper right box in Figure 3–1) that would sharply reduce the unemployment rate. Wilson is in tune with the ecological perspective when he suggests that resources should be created and distributed to enhance adaptation.

Taylor (1990), who studied similar problems in the African American community in Buffalo, concluded:

> The key to developing a plan to attack the problem of the inner city is to conceive of the black community in geographic terms and to formulate a territorial based strategy for dealing with economic and social problems facing African-Americans. The strategic plan is to build a vibrant, economically prosperous, racially diverse, cross-class community where the middle-class, higher-paid workers, low-wage workers, and the poor and the underclass can live together in comfort and security. Logic says that if "bad neighborhoods" create an environment that makes the fight

against economic and social dislocations more difficult, "good neighbor-hoods" will make the fight easier. (p. 21)

The Dohrenwend framework allows us to see problems in a broader context than simply seeing the number in the population suffering from psychopathology. It also directs our attention to interventions other than treating individual deficiencies. We present a further discussion of these concepts in chapter 4, "The Ecological Analogy," and in our discussion of community development strategies for change in chapter 12.

by this model. Some interventions strive to limit the duration, intensity, or maladaptiveness of the transient stress reaction, while the purpose of others is to prevent a stressful event from even happening. The examples we review here are by no means exhaustive, and numerous others will be discussed or cited elsewhere in the book. In surveying these alternatives we will work backwards (in the model's hypothesized timeline) from the more treatment oriented elements on the right side of Figure 3–1 to the more preventive elements on the left.

Opportunities for Intervention Based on Dohrenwend's Model

Crisis Intervention

Dohrenwend's model suggests that it is not necessary to wait until the stress reaction has run its course and produced long-term pathology to provide help. What if help could be available during the acute stress reaction, that is, "crisis intervention" services? Dohrenwend has several criticisms of this strategy, however. Will enough people in need seek out the proffered help? Can crisis services be positioned to reach persons soon enough during acutely stressful episodes? Compared with the population that might be served, telephone crisis services tend not to be used very much, often drawing a large number of the same chronic callers. For example, in our unpublished study of stressful life events in college students, we found that less than 1 percent used a hotline when they experienced a stressful life event.

One evaluation of crisis services supported Dohrenwend's judgment that members of the population at risk might not use crisis services. Suicide prevention services provide an illustration of her point. Suicide prevention services may have an effect in reducing successful suicides among young white females. No statistically significant effect could be detected in other age and sex groups. Young white females are among the most frequent callers to crisis lines; however, the successful suicide rate is lowest in this age and sex group. Rates of completed suicide are 20 or more times higher among white males over age 65, and these men are not frequent callers to suicide prevention services (Miller, Coombs, Leeper, & Barton, 1984). The crisis hotline seems to reach the group at lowest risk, albeit with some success, and fails to reach the group at highest risk. Crisis hotlines clearly have a "marketing" problem. (The Dohrenwend model doesn't deal with this type of problem.)

These limitations of crisis hotlines should not close the question; other methods for delivering services at a time of crisis might prove more effective in reaching a target population. In natural disasters (hurricanes, floods, earthquakes) crisis teams are sent to the locations to be available for psychological "first-aid" to people who might have been overcome by their losses of property or lives of loved ones and to rescue workers who have to deal with maimed and burned bodies. These teams seem to benefit from debriefings with their leaders and members of their work groups in the period shortly after exposure to the dead (McCarroll, Ursano, Wright, & Fullerton, 1993). Support groups accessible to anyone in need, along with consistent and detailed information about coping shared community-wide by the media, have been credited with reducing the incidence of psychological casualties in response to disasters (see Gist & Stolz, 1982).

Reaching target populations. The life stress concept provides certain advantages in guiding the positioning of services (e.g., in relation to predictable, "milestone" events such as entering school, marriage, or taking a new job), and it suggests the possibility of prevention. However, recognizing that not everyone will use a particular service raises a number of questions: where, when, how, and to whom should a given service be offered? Developing a treatment technology to cope successfully with transient reactions is not the only concern.

We still need to learn how to "market" our services—to package, advertise, price, and sell—to different groups. A given service offered in a particular way will reach some in need, but characteristics of the service will likely result in a mismatch with the needs of others, effectively screening them out. For example, if there is no convenient public transportation to a program, people without automobiles are less likely to use the program. A university psychological services center located on a campus in the suburbs with very little public transportation will not attract many clients from the poorer parts of the city. For another example, rescue workers who deal with dead bodies prefer not to be debriefed by mental health workers but rather by experienced members of their work group and their leaders (McCarroll et al., 1993). We need to learn to tailor services, be they preventive or rehabilitative, or to empower individuals to take into account the characteristics of the target consumer. This problem, however, is not considered in the Dohrenwend model. We need other theoretical perspectives as well.

Intervention to Enhance Psychological Mediators

In theory, psychological mediators such as values or coping skills play an important role in determining the outcome of a transient stress reaction. Positive psychological mediators may aid in the adaptation required after exposure to a stressful life event. Just as there are negative situational supports, Dohrenwend's model makes provision for negative or handicapping psychological mediators as well. If one copes by abusing alcohol or drugs, throwing a temper tantrum, becoming highly dependent, or simply denying anything bad is happening and hoping it will just go away, the situation might well worsen. If you don't take care of business, so to speak, by the time you feel better you might have piled up so much you didn't do that you will be overwhelmed with new problems.

Dohrenwend notes that strengthening a person's psychological mediators may help the person "develop a high level of ability to face and solve complex social and emotional problems" (p. 8). One way of looking at these issues may involve early intervention to help children cope with emotional stresses or the challenges of growing up. The original child guidance clinics of the 1920s were based on a similar concept (Levine & Levine, 1992). Cowen's Primary Mental Health Project (Cowen et al., 1996) is an updated, school-based version of child guidance designed to help children who have already been identified as vulnerable in order to prevent the development of more serious problems later in life (see chapter 8).

In an approach that deviates still more from traditional helping services, Spivack and Shure (1974; Shure, 1997) were among the first to demonstrate that social adjustment may be enhanced by programs explicitly designed to teach social and interpersonal problem-solving skills—that is, psychological mediators. These programs are offered not only to children in difficulty or even only to those at high risk. Instead, the programs are designed to be integrated directly into the educational curriculum to help provide children with styles or means of coping with day by day problems, by teaching a child skills needed to master or to avoid interpersonal crises. Tens of thousands of schoolchildren all over the country are now regularly exposed to this type of program (Bruene-Butler, Hampson, Elias, Clabby, & Schuyler, 1997; Weissberg, Barton, & Shriver, 1997). Preschool programs designed to enhance children's abilities to adapt to elementary school are variants of this approach.

Some prevention programs are built on an analysis of the skills and attitudes one might use in dealing with problems should they arise

and then teaching these skills. The approach is similar in purpose to a
fire drill. We engage in fire drills so that we will have cognitive mediators to guide our actions when the emergency arises. By rehearsing
we are more likely to respond effectively if a fire ever does break out
instead of just panicking, or running and hurting others by trampling
them.

Sex education within the school curriculum is another example, although it has been little studied in the context of prevention. Sex education has among its aims the provision of greater knowledge and
healthier attitudes and values (psychological mediators) to help adolescents cope with sexuality and its demands. In theory, greater comfort with sexuality in childhood and youth has important ramifications
for each individual's interpersonal relationships and personal satisfaction throughout life.

People differ about what constitutes appropriate sex education.
Handing out condoms in schools to prevent disease and pregnancy is
highly controversial. Some believe sex education should emphasize abstinence as the best preventive. In addition to providing information
about sexual anatomy and physiology, sex education should emphasize moral values. These critics assert that the psychological mediators
taught in some contemporary sex education programs, for example,
encourage physical contact short of intercourse (a groping skill as a
coping skill) promote maladaptation (Whitehead, 1994). Preventive
programs such as sex education that influence the general education
and socialization of children and youth reach "back to the very origin
of the stress process and have, therefore, moved as far as possible from
the treatment of individual cases of psychopathology into the realm of
primary prevention" (Dohrenwend, 1978, p. 9).

As a final example, consider loss of a job (see also Box 3–1). This
event would precipitate a transient stress reaction in most people;
unemployment can in fact have immediate negative effects on mental health and well-being, including reduced self-esteem and increased
depression, anger, guilt, and boredom. However, as Dohrenwend's
model would hypothesize, people differ in the likelihood they will respond to unemployment in these ways. For example, unemployment
is more likely to elicit a transient stress response in middle-aged males
than in other groups, such as teenagers (Osipow & Fitzgerald, 1993).

Because financial strain is the single most stressful aspect of job
loss (Broman, Hamilton, & Hoffman, 2001), rapid reemployment at adequate pay offers the best short-term intervention goal. However, many
unemployed people lack the key psychological mediators of skills, confidence, and a positive or optimistic outlook when seeking reemployment (Kirk, 1995). Prompt intervention with recently unemployed people to help them find a job they will like may have especially valuable
preventive effects.

The Michigan Jobs Project (Caplan, Vinokur, Price, & van Ryn, 1989; Vinokur, Price, Caplan, van Ryn, & Curran, 1995) was a preventive intervention to combat the risk of poor mental health and low motivation to seek reemployment by providing job-seeking skills and supportive encouragement to the recently unemployed. Participants were randomly assigned to the training program or to a control condition that offered only a brief booklet of tips on job-seeking. Initial results found that those receiving the intervention program were more likely to have become reemployed at one-month and four-month follow-ups, and that people who became reemployed showed less anxiety, depression, and anger, and higher self-esteem, than those who did not. Within the intervention group, those who had not found reemployment were significantly less discouraged than were unemployed controls, suggesting an "inoculation" effect against future setbacks as one possible mediator provided by the intervention. By the 2.5-year follow-up, intervention participants as a group had found jobs of higher quality, and found them more quickly, than did controls (Vinokur, van Ryn, Gramlich, & Price, 1991). Further analyses showed that the intervention was especially effective at reducing the risk of later depression in participants who were initially at risk for depression (Caplan, Vinokur, & Price, 1997).

Several features make the Michigan Jobs Project a good illustration of a preventive intervention to strengthen psychological mediators. People with diagnosable mental illness were screened from the sample. Participants were essentially ordinary people experiencing acute job loss (four months or less) and facing the rapid onset of problems typically found in response to job loss. Staff delivering the program were not professionals. They provided not "treatment," but rather instruction, practice, and support in the use of cognitive and behavioral coping skills. These skills were designed for use in coping with future setbacks as well as current situations. The possibility of recurrent job loss in the future was fully recognized in the content of the intervention. Self-efficacy was the significant cognitive mediator of the intervention's effects on job-seeking behavior (van Ryn & Vinokur, 1992). Finally, as the Dohrenwend model would predict, the intervention succeeded in lowering the incidence of serious depressive symptoms in this risk group.

Intervention to Enhance Situational Mediators

The outcome of a transient stress reaction also depends on situation mediators, which means resources in the environment an individual can call upon when appraising the significance of a stressful life event. For most people, family and friends are their chief sources of social support (Rhodes, 1998; see chapter 7). For many people and many purposes, however, the resources of family and friends are insufficient. One may not be able to share everything with family members. For example, rescue workers who handled dead bodies couldn't discuss their work very well with spouses, many of whom just weren't able to listen to the gory details (McCarroll et al., 1993),

When social supports are insufficient, then situation moderators become more important. Public services are often necessary in lieu of family support. Levine (1982) points out that in the Love Canal emergency, blue-collar families simply did not have the financial resources to support a move away from the neighborhood threatened by toxic wastes. Government assistance, a form of situational mediator, was necessary. In many other problems, individual resources are insufficient, and collective resources are necessary. Some form of welfare (a situational mediator) is necessary for income maintenance for those who cannot provide for themselves. Unemployment insurance keeps many from despair when they lose their jobs. A women's shelter provides refuge to a woman trying to escape a batterer. Low-income loans after a flood or a hurricane are necessary to help businesses reopen and individuals to rebuild their lives.

Public services are supports that aid in coping (Thoits, 1986). In their absence community and organizational development efforts are needed to provide the necessary resources. As Kelly (1966) points out, one aim of the community movement is to produce the resources a community needs to cope with its problems. Thus when community-oriented mental health professionals help to develop respite care for families with retarded children, or help create a shelter for battered women, or a service to help widows with no recent work histories reenter the labor force, they are helping to create situational mediators. As we noted in the last chapter, Assertive Community Treatment teams provide support and coping assistance to people with serious mental illness and also work to strengthen directly the other supportive resources available to these persons. As a further example, increasing numbers of people at risk for maladaptive responses to bereavement, divorce, retirement, physical violence, and other life events now obtain some or all of the support they need from self-help groups (Hildingh, Fridlund, & Segesten, 1995; Jacobs & Goodman, 1989; see chapter 9).

Not all social support is helpful, however. The wrong type of support, or other aspects of the situation, may simply add to the person's handicap. In chapter 7 we will see that "negative" social support may be more important in creating distress following a stressful life event than is positive support in relieving the reaction. The availability of mediators, however, supplements and extends individual and family resources. In their absence, the outcomes of a stressful life event might be worse. Dohrenwend's model helps us see how such activity is comprehensible within a single conceptual framework.

Psychological Characteristics of the Person That Increase the Likelihood of a Stressful Life Event

In this section, we present several examples of sources of stressful life events that reflect individual vulnerabilities. These examples are not exhaustive, obviously, but they are meant to be illustrative.

Genetic or biological vulnerability. Some people may be more susceptible physiologically than others to the adverse effects of alcohol. Given the opportunity to drink at parties, such a person may be more vulnerable to consequences of drinking. Here is a built-in person limitation that enhances vulnerability to the maladaptive effects of drinking.

Having a parent with schizophrenia may increase genetic vulnerability to stress. A child from such a genetic background, facing normal stresses—demands of school, peer group rejection, developing sexuality, competitiveness—that another with less vulnerability might take in stride, may be more likely to experience a transient stress reaction that might persist. The Dohrenwend model asks us to consider whether some stresses can be avoided or whether we can help a potentially vulnerable child to develop psychological mediators or social supports that might help in coping with stressful life events.

The likelihood of being born prematurely or being a child with deficits that will affect later adjustment is increased due to poor prenatal care, poor nutrition, and the prenatal use of tobacco, drugs, and alcohol by the mother. Such children may develop poorer self-control or have learning deficits. When faced with school demands for discipline and learning, these children are more likely to fail and become discipline problems. With failure they bond less to school. They are more likely to engage in delinquent activity and to make a poorer social and economic adaptation in the future. In other words, some inborn characteristics that make it more difficult to adapt to the challenges of a school program lead to a succession of stressful life events. In the absence of supportive school programs or other alternatives, these life events may result in failure and in a poor future adaptation.

There may also be environmental causes for vulnerability in school. Some children exposed to lead may be less effective than others not so exposed. If there is anything to the belief that dioxin may cause learning difficulties (see Gibbs & CCHW, 1995), then our understanding of the etiology of some learning disorders will change. Long-range prevention programs will be directed toward reducing exposure to harmful substances in the environment.

Insufficient preparation for school. Factors in the child's general education and socialization may contribute to increased vulnerability. In the late nineteenth and early twentieth century when many of our great grandparents came to the United States, many did not speak English. They were required to go to schools where English was the required language and the use of foreign tongues was discouraged. People with foreign accents were often made to feel ashamed of themselves. In those days, in different cities, anywhere from 20 to 50 percent of the children were two or more years behind in school because they had failed and were repeating a grade (Levine & Levine, 1992). Children who are left back are likely to drop out of school as soon as they can; self-esteem may be impaired (Pagani, Tremblay, Vitaro, Boulerice & McDuff, 2001).

We have similar circumstances today, especially with Latinos and African Americans from homes where, for diverse reasons, children are not fully prepared to cope with school. If children do not respond to the usual school program, they are often identified as learning disabled or emotionally disturbed, and given special education (U.S. Department of Education, 1990). Even though some children are helped, for many there is stigma associated with labeling and placement into special education programs. The initial insufficient preparation for school makes failure more likely and future adaptation less favorable.

The Head Start program can be seen as providing psychological mediators, that is "coping" skills for school, and as a situation mediator that provides a great deal of support for parent and child in preparing for regular school (Weikart & Schweinhart, 1997; see chapter 8).

Alienation from family and community. Child-rearing practices and relationships with families may contribute to vulnerability in adolescence as well as in childhood. For whatever reason, some adolescents simply do not get along with their families, they lose ties to their families, they may say they never have fun with their families, and that their parent or parents do not know how they spend much of their time. Many of these adolescents lose interest in school and get poor grades. They tend not to be affiliated with a church group, and come to see the future rather pessimistically. Young people with these characteristics tend to become risk-takers; they hang out with other youth who share similar characteristics and are inclined to get into trouble. This pattern of alienation from family, school, church, and work, and affiliating with other youth who get into trouble, is associated with a higher rate of self-reported delinquency, drinking, drug use, and sexual activity (see Box 3–1). The probability of getting into difficulty in the community—being arrested, having an automobile accident involving drinking, or becoming pregnant—is increased by this pattern, and those stressful life events have important implications for later adaptation. Even though we can point to psychological mediators (e.g. attitudes toward school, risk-taking tendencies, etc.) that enhance vulnerability, efforts to increase youth bonding to school or to the community may help prevent the pattern of maladaptation.

Situations That Increase the Risk of Stressful Events

Some events can be so serious in themselves that for those who experience them, transient stress reactions (or worse) are almost inevitable, regardless of their psychological and supportive resources. Here we describe selected examples and comment on the roles available to psychologists for preventing distress related to such events.

Environmental threats. Most environmental stressors fall under one of three categories: strains of urban life, disasters, or ecological contamination (see Stokols, 1992, for alternative comprehensive frameworks). Living or working in cities and, increasingly, in suburbs can be stressful. One stressor that has been extensively researched is crowding, which is culturally and psychologically defined and is not the same as population density (Baum & Paulus, 1987). One need only contrast personal space norms to understand that crowding is experienced differently in Osaka, Japan, and Oskaloosa, Kansas. Other urban stressors include noise (Bronzaft, 2002), traffic (Appleyard, 1981), and physical disorder. Physical "incivilities," or symbols of disorder, include broken windows, graffiti, and deteriorated property and are consistently related to residents' level of fear, which in turn affects their mental health (Perkins & Taylor, 1996).

Environmental disasters (floods, earthquakes, hurricanes, fire), whether of natural or human causes, affect more than just life and property. Communities usually pull together in mutual aid following a disaster (Kaniasty, Norris, & Murrell, 1990). However, there are also stress-related impacts of disasters, crime, and other traumas (Norris & Thompson, 1995; Peek & Mileti, 2002), which disrupt people's emotional attachments to place and, depending on how individuals and communities respond, can have deep and lasting negative effects on both (Brown & Perkins, 1992; see chapter 5).

The third form of environmental stressor is contamination of homes, soil, water, or air, which can have individual emotional and community social effects similar to disasters (Baum & Fleming, 1993; Edelstein, 2001; Jacobs, Evans, Catalano, & Dooley, 1984) as well as serious health effects. The Love Canal crisis that created substantial stress for so many families was a function of the growth of the chemical industry, and inadequate awareness of how to dispose of the toxic byproducts of technology. The resulting damage included increases in the rates of miscarriage and of congenital malformations in infants, fears about the health of children and adults, community strife, and eventually, for many, relocation to new homes (Levine, 1982; see chapter 12). Since the Love Canal episode, many similar situations have come to public attention all over the country and around the world: Woburn, Massachusetts; Times Beach, Missouri; the Stringfellow Acid Pits in California; Tuscaloosa, Alabama; Bhopal, India; Three Mile Island, Pennsylvania; Chernobyl, Russia; atomic weapons testing in Nevada; PCB dairy farms in Michigan (Vyner, 1988); and the Legler community in Jackson, New Jersey (Edelstein, 2001).

The latest threat to life, health, property, and community is, of course, the threat of international and domestic terrorism. It shares certain features of each of the above categories (disorder, fear, disaster, panic, contamination). Like other environmental stressors, terrorists also threaten community trust and cohesion and so community psychologists must be prepared to address this new threat at more than just an individual or group level, but also at institutional, community, and national and international policy levels.

Psychological research on environmental stress typically focuses on individual-level (e.g., control, coping) and interpersonal (social support) mediators and effects (Anthony & Watkins, 2002; Evans & Cohen, 1987; see chapter 7). While these avenues have been fruitful, excessive attention to the emotional consequences of environmental threats may exacerbate perceptions that the public response is "irrational" (Wandersman & Hallman, 1993). Community psychology's emphasis on prevention draws us to changing the environment and not just of the individual, but at a larger scale (upper left box in Figure 3–1; Edelstein, 2001; Norris & Thompson, 1995; Shinn & Toohey, 2003; Stokols, 1992). Regulations governing safe disposal of toxic wastes, and governing how close such facilities can be placed to residences or to schools can decrease the probability that people will be exposed to conditions that threaten life, health, and psychological well-being.

One of the earliest and most consistent findings in the environmental stress literature is that the degree of personal (or even perceived) control one has in the situation can greatly moderate the stress-related impact (Evans & Cohen, 1987). A great way to gain and feel a sense of control is to engage in social and political action to promote laws and regulations that will also have a direct effect in preventing physical harm and psychological distress related to an environmental threat by reducing the probability that a stressful event affecting the community will arise at all (Wiesenfeld & Sanchez, 2002). Moreover, if people participating in community organizations share their problems, develop means for dealing with them, and teach each other, they are empowered (Rich, Edelstein, Hallman, & Wandersman, 1995) and develop psychological mediators to help deal with the current transient stress reaction and future ones as well (Stone & Levine, 1985). (For more on physical environmental influences, see chapter 5; for more on social action, see chapter 12.)

Divorce. Divorce is an event that transcends the problems of the individuals involved in the divorce. About half of marriages end in divorce, and many that do not involve significant distress and abuse (Vivian & O'Leary, 1990). Divorce is among the most stressful of life events as measured by the Holmes and Rahe type of scale. It is associated with increased use of psychological services, including hospitalization, increased use of alcohol, and increased risk of accidents, among other adverse consequences (Bloom & Hodges, 1988). The distress and increased risk for dysfunction may radiate to children and family members. Failure to receive adequate child support payments adds to psychological distress of custodial parents, and also to parents who have support obligations but wish to start new families. No-fault divorce laws have increased the likelihood that some women will experience stressful life events due to inadequate income. The plight of single, working mothers may be more acute because of the lack of affordable day care and other supports such as health insurance. These are situations in the environment that can best be corrected by political action to change certain features of the laws and to improve enforcement. On the individual level, groups such as Parents without Partners, and programs to prepare and to teach adaptation to problems post-divorce for adults and children provide important preventive services (Bloom & Hodges, 1988; Pillow, Sandler, Braver, Wolchik, & Gersten, 1991; Pedro-Carroll, 1997).

Although psychotherapy for marital distress is increasingly common, prevention programs appear to have more powerful long-term effects (Jacobson & Addis, 1993). Given the high probability of marital dissolution, it is possible that individual skill training undertaken before marriage, to help cope with the kind of issues that lead to divorce and separation and also the aftermath, would be reasonable preparation. Markman, Renick, Floyd, Stanley, and Clements (1993) report a longitudinal evaluation of a cognitive-behavioral program designed to improve communication and conflict-management skills in couples planning marriage. At the five-year follow-up couples who received the intervention showed better communication skills, and reported significantly less physical violence in their relationships than did control couples. Overall, while the rate of divorce was low after five years, it did not differ from that in the control group.

Unemployment. As we pointed out above, unemployment is a severe environmental stressor. The mental health risks of job loss are evident in a significant relationship between the onset of unemployment and later use of mental health services. Kiernan, Toro, Rappaport, and Seidman (1989) reviewed 19 studies published between 1973 and 1986 that used time-series methods to relate changes in unemployment rates to variables like admissions to mental hospitals, use of outpatient mental health facilities, suicide rates, and community surveys of depressed mood. These studies varied in their methods, some tracking changes on a month-by-month basis and some tracking annual changes over many years. Most (but not all) of these studies found that increased unemployment was associated with undesirable changes in behavior even though some sought to adapt by seeking mental health care.

To take these data seriously suggests that anything which increases employment or reduces unemployment, or, on the social support side of the model, anything which provides increased support such as unemployment insurance, could reduce the incidence of psychological disorder and the necessity for treatment. Thus, social and political action to influence government policies would be a valid form of "preventive intervention" to reduce the prevalence of mental disorder in the population. As social support, we have seen the development of support groups such as the Michigan Jobs Project for unemployed people to provide mutual assistance and encouragement in seeking new employment.

Exposure to violence. People exposed to violence experience stress. Violence is more prevalent in the lives of some people because of the neighborhoods they live in (see Box 3–1). When Garbarino, Kostelny, and Dubrow (1991) studied children and youth living in neighborhoods characterized by violence, they found that many showed signs of a post-traumatic stress disorder in response to witnessing shootings, stabbings, beatings, and experiencing the death of friends, peers, or family members.

Living in an area characterized by violence also increases the risk of pregnancy complications. Women living in neighborhoods in Santiago, Chile, that were characterized by a high rate of violence and confrontation between citizens and police suffered from high rates of pregnancy complications compared to women living in the same city but in neighborhoods without high levels of violence. "A fivefold increase in the risk of pregnancy complications was associated with living in high-violence versus low-violence neighborhoods, after adjustments were made for lack of social support and perception of neighborhood milieu" (Zapata, Rebolledo, Atalah, Newman, & King, 1992, p. 688). Even though the findings are correlational, the research workers used statistical techniques to rule out many confounding variables. These results may have some significance for pregnant mothers in neighborhoods that Garbarino et al. (1991) characterized as "war zones." Reducing people's exposure to violence raises issues not always thought of as part of a mental health professional's work, and we discuss some of these concerns in the next section.

Preventing Stressful Life Events

Dohrenwend's model includes political and social activism in the mental health professional's repertoire of methods for working to reduce psychopathology. Some preventive programs aim to eliminate the circumstances that produce stressful life events in the first place. Thus programs to develop housing, recreation, and employment opportunities may prevent life events related to inadequate housing, inactivity or extreme boredom, and unemployment (Shinn & Toohey, 2003). Good nutrition and prenatal care may reduce the incidence of low birth weight babies who prove to be at risk for several other disorders. Because the means necessary to attain such ends are political in nature, some have said that mental health professionals who wish to influence the political system should enter politics directly and run for office. One answer is that there are many means of influencing political action in addition to running for office. Harrington's (1962) book on poverty influenced John F. Kennedy's thinking about his political program and social objectives. President Clinton mentioned Wilson's (1987) *The Truly Disadvantaged* as the best discussion he had seen of the problems in our inner cities. President George W. Bush was influenced in his compassionate conservatism and toward faith-based programs by historian Marvin Olasky (1995). Social scientists work as advisors to government, and some testify before congressional committees regarding their research and its implications. Some may help empower local community groups by serving as experts in the service of local groups.

Thus there are many roles in addition to that of elected officeholder through which social scientists and mental health professionals may exercise influence within the political system. The settlement house workers at the turn of the twentieth century provided a living example for such activity. These early social workers were researchers, community organizers, lobbyists, and interpreters of the needs of poor immigrants to the middle class. Because of their knowledge, some were appointed to head governmental departments at state and federal levels. Later, some joined the Franklin D. Roosevelt administration and influenced many of its social policies. This tradition of social and political activism was forgotten because of the emphasis on individual psychology that permeated the social work field beginning in the 1920s (Levine & Levine, 1992).

Professor Edward Zigler is a good contemporary example of an academic political activist. He is a Yale faculty member and a clinical and developmental psychologist. He was part of a group that worked with President Lyndon Johnson to develop the Head Start program (Zigler & Muenchow, 1992). Zigler later took a leave from Yale University and worked for two years in Washington, DC, as the first head of the Office of Human Development. He has since headed Yale's Bush Center for policy studies in child welfare. He has been a vigorous advocate for Head Start and other child welfare programs. However, he grounds his policy positions in thorough analyses of the appropriate literature or other data bases.

Caveat. The space we have devoted to Dohrenwend's model should not be taken to indicate that we endorse all of its propositions. The various situational contributions to stress and recovery are not described in detail in this model. The model fits discrete life events much better than more chronic, enduring stresses, and is of limited help in understanding disorders having a strong biochemical base and an inexorable course over time. Such a course of illness may not be influenced very much by external factors, but the quality of life for the afflicted person and those around him or her may still be modified favorably by social support or enhanced coping techniques.

We believe the model helps us get our bearings by asking us to view problems in a more holistic light. It tells us we need to develop theories that take into account the "person in a situation." The words "holistic" and "embedded in a total context" are nothing more than truisms unless developed in greater detail.

Summary

The model proposed by Barbara Dohrenwend provides a useful framework for integrating the disparate activities of community psychology and more traditional interventions such as psychotherapy and crisis intervention. This model directs attention to the relationship between stress and behavior, including processes very early in the sequence of events leading to pathology or to recovery. This view raises a greater variety of options, based on either person-centered or environment-centered interventions, and particularly prominent in Dohrenwend's model are strategies aimed at prevention.

Dohrenwend's model is useful in several ways. It adds a time dimension to our thinking about intervening in problems. From this perspective the vast bulk of services following the medical model come into play at the end of a long sequence of events that culminate in what we are calling psychopathology. The Dohrenwend model directs our attention to earlier points in the sequence. The earlier in the sequence we intervene, whether to provide assistance at a point of crisis or to prepare individuals by enhancing psychological mediators, or to see that some supportive resources are available at convenient times and places for the person in difficulty, the more we are talking about prevention. If we can go back far enough in the sequence to actually do something to prevent the stressful life event from arising in the first place, we have something akin to what we will call primary prevention.

Moreover the Dohrenwend model is useful because it helps us respond to life-as-soap-opera types of events. Recall that in discussing the prevalence of diagnosed disorder in the population, we noted that you can also examine the prevalence of various stressful life events that many people face. If you keep thinking about "disorder" or disease in the medical model, you are more inclined to think about the cure of disease, and the undoing of psychopathology. A diagnosis in and of itself provides few clues to preventive intervention unless the etiology, or the set of causative factors that lead to the disorder, is clear (Institute of Medicine, 1989). Moreover, diagnosis has proven to be unreliable, especially for disorders of childhood (Kirk & Kutchins, 1992; U.S. Surgeon General, 2001b).

From the life events perspective you look at the circumstances in which different types of stressful life events arise and think about positioning helping resources at points when people experience transient stress reactions, or where possible before stressful life events even take place. We will discuss various strategies for prevention later in the text, but for now we simply ask you to think about how the different model alerts us to a much broader variety of helping and preventive strategies and guides us in using a much broader variety of helping persons or modalities for delivering help. A major advantage of the model is that it expands our thinking about the alternatives available across time, place, and approach.

As it stands, however, the Dohrenwend model is little more than a useful outline of a comprehensive field and its many activities. Considerably more theoretical detail is needed, as is empirical research. In the next four chapters we develop a number of theoretical and empirical details in preparation for a careful examination of prevention in mental health.

4

The Ecological Analogy

"Ecology" is a fundamental metaphor or analogy in community psychology, embodying both the structure of a scientific paradigm and a specific set of values (Moos, 2002). By an analogy or a metaphor, we mean that we draw on concepts developed in another field, environmental biology, and apply these to the subject matter of community psychology. We assume there are enough similarities between problems that concern community psychologists and those studied by biological ecologists so that we may try to use the concepts to illuminate problems of interest to us. Analogies are always imperfect. Nevertheless, the principles may still be useful in helping us to understand and to conceptualize problems of concern to community psychologists.

By scientific paradigm, we refer to the pattern of research in use in an area of inquiry. A new paradigm means that we ask different questions, make different observations, and generally apply different research methods than those used in the experimental paradigm favored by conventional psychological research. The ecological paradigm includes a set of fundamental beliefs. Among these is the belief that environments exert significant effects on human behavior, and that people can therefore explain and perhaps manage their behavior through greater understanding of specific environmental influences. A value held by many who adopt the ecological paradigm is that, to the extent that understanding of these influences is achieved, there is an obligation to apply the understanding in *actions* that improve people's lives.

When we act on the belief that environments exert significant effects, two further assumptions are involved. The first is that it is possible to change patterns of social and organizational relationships so that we can achieve programmatic, "wholesale" effects on the lives and adaptations of people, in contrast to the "retail" assistance provided to individuals when we use the medical model. On the other hand, this viewpoint does *not* say that anyone can become anything under ideal environmental circumstances. A person cannot become a tree, no matter the environment. If there are some inherent limitations due to biology (e.g., a person with mental retardation may have a damaged nervous system), changes in the environment may not compensate completely for that difference. However, two further points should be noted. First, even with certain limitations, different circumstances can still result in different adaptations, some more desirable than others. Second, this diversity among people in qualities or potentials is not necessarily a limitation or handicap to them or to society. Under the right conditions diversity can be a catalyst or resource for social development and change.

A second assumption is that if we are to achieve programmatic effects, it means introducing change at some broader level of social organization than just targeting an individual in need. Both assumptions mean that we need to know a lot more about the social environment, and we cannot find out what we need to know in the psychological laboratory. In the ecological perspective, we are directed to develop a greater variety of problem definitions and examine a greater variety of solutions, one or another of which will serve the needs of different segments of the population (Rappaport, 1981).

Implications of the ecological analogy for scientific work are also important. Any intervention in the social environment is predicated on a particular understanding of what that environment is like, that is, a point of view. From a scientific standpoint conceptualizing and measuring the environment of human behavior are relatively recent developments in psychology, and at present there is no single coherent and comprehensive theory. Several approaches offering a variety of heuristic constructs are regularly cited (e.g., Moos, 1973, 2002). In general, however, the empirical foundations of these conceptions are less thoroughly developed than are the theoretical proposals.

This chapter first presents the ecological analogy as a paradigm for thinking and research, and then outlines four fundamental ecological principles to guide the community psychologist. These principles will be illustrated by a number of examples. We also discuss principles of practice that follow from the ecological analogy, and the values inherent in the position.

Ecology as a Paradigm

Ecology is the field of environmental biology. The term ecology derives from the Greek noun *oikos,* meaning house. Ecology then is the study of "houses" within which organisms live or, more broadly, their environments. The modifier *social,* or human, is attached to indicate the specific interest in studying the environments in which people live.

In general, ecologists study units larger than individual organisms, including populations, communities, ecosystems, and the biosphere. A *population* is a group of similar individuals; *community* refers to the set of populations within a defined area. The community and the inanimate environment constitute the *ecosystem,* while *biosphere* refers to the larger inhabited environment. Although ecologists do not ignore the rest of biology by any means, they believe that explanatory concepts should be appropriate to the level of organization studied. While concepts from another level can be helpful in understanding the phenomena under study, the more reductionist concepts can never fully account for phenomena at other levels of organization. In Odum's (1971) words, "to understand a tree, it is necessary to study both the forest of which it is a part as well as the cells and tissues that are part of a tree" (p. 4).

In a different use of the concepts of ecology, Bronfenbrenner (1996) developed an ecological model to interpret research in child development. He identified five levels that were important in understanding child development: the *ontogenetic* or individual level of development (e.g., child's age, sex, temperament, etc.); the *microsystem*, or immediate social settings, such as the family (e.g., father-absent families; dysfunctional families), classroom, peer group, workplace, etc.; the *mesosystem*, or links between microsystems (e.g., parent-teacher conference or impact of work on home life); the *exosystem* or the community-environment level (e.g., medical, educational, recreational resources in the neighborhood to support family life) and the *macrosystem* or societal level of politics, economy, and culture (e.g., attitudes toward children, toward violence, etc.).[1]

Most community psychologists who use the language of ecology have not adopted this perspective completely, but rather find a useful analogy in its outline and general principles. In adopting the metaphor of ecology, proponents are trying to say both what they are for and what they are against. For example, they use the scientific language of ecology to assert that an individually oriented psychology is less than fully helpful in thinking about many problems, limits the range of options for intervention, and may distract attention from important issues. Proponents find ecological concepts attractive because they transcend individual psychology. Just as biological ecology directs attention to the intimate interrelationship between organisms and resources, the concept of the visible organism as a product of its built-in properties and its competitive adaptation to available or changing resources directs attention to more than the individual person.

A Paradigm Shift

Psychology is one of the few sciences that has no branch devoted to the observation of phenomena in their natural states. Psychology leaped from the armchair to the laboratory, omitting the study of people in natural settings.[2] As consequences of this leap, psychology's concepts are concerned with "inside" properties of organisms, and treat the outside as alien. The emphasis in our clinical heritage on the measurement of individual differences, and stable personality traits whose expression transcends situations, contributed to our tendency to ignore the natural environment. In the psychoanalytic perspective, which had such a strong influence on clinical theory and research, what mattered was the individual's perceptions, fantasies and emotional reactions based on those fantasies or perceptions. All that needed to be done or to be understood could be accomplished within the confines of the consulting room. The assumption in psychological testing that one could measure an individual's characteristics by a test administered in one set of circumstances, and then predict behavior in any number of other circumstances, reflects the assumption that differences in social environments do not matter very much. Even Kurt Lewin (1935), the field theorist who developed the formula B = f(P,E)—Behavior is a function of Person and Environment—and the concept of a life space which incorporates an external world, primarily examined the responses of single organisms to the inner-defined life space. However, an individual's behavior may make little sense when viewed in isolation. One would understand little about a baseball game by observing the behavior of the first baseman alone, since his or her actions have meaning only as part of the surrounding game. In adhering to the idea that knowledge is best obtained through the momentary experiment, moreover, psychological research lost a time perspective, and created the problem of ecological validity—that is, the questionable external validity or generalizability of its findings (Chow, 1987; Schmuckler, 2001).

The markedly different nature of scientific research from the ecological viewpoint is described well by Trickett, Kelly and Vincent (1985):

> Community research is an intervention into the ongoing flow of community life and should be approached as such. While community inquiry—like all research—is designed to generate knowledge, it also can serve as a primary vehicle for the development of a setting. By its very nature, it cannot help but have impact on the place where it occurs. (p. 284)

According to Trickett et al., research activities exemplify resource exchanges involving persons, settings, and events. The goal of research is to create products which benefit the community as a whole (i.e., not just the researcher or funding source). No distinction is made between setting and method. The method is part of the setting, and vice versa (see the principle of interdependence, below). All those who are affected by research, including community residents who serve as subjects, are considered formal participants in it. Wandersman and Florin (1990) have published a set of insightful articles on how citizens may be empowered through cooperation and partnership with research workers.

Because it is part of the community and is affected by the community, ecological research is much more flexible and improvisational than is laboratory research. Unplanned events and "side effects" are expected and are accounted for in the research design (Tebes & Kraemer, 1991). Research inevitably changes the community and its residents in important ways, and so the whole enterprise of research must be understood *longitudinally* (over time). All research is in fact longitudinal, regardless of the stated design in a particular case, since there is always a preexisting context of relationships among participants, and the research activity itself inevitably changes the subsequent nature of that context (e.g., for future research activities).

Box 4–1. Community Research From an Ecological Perspective

A project carried out over several years by Simon Singer, a sociologist and criminologist, and psychologist Murray Levine, illustrates many aspects of ecological research. The executive director of the Youth Board of Amherst, New York, Mr. Joseph Bachovchin, asked the Research Center for Children and Youth at SUNY-Buffalo to work with his agency to develop a needs assessment for planning purposes. The New York State Youth Board which provides funds to local agencies to support youth centers, recreational and other preventive services for young people, asked all of its local agencies to develop a plan for future services. The Amherst Youth Board agreed that a survey of youth problems, including delinquency and drug and alcohol use, would be appropriate for their needs. However, because this was to be a community-wide survey in three school districts, the first step taken by the Amherst Youth Board was to sponsor a community forum in cooperation with the parents' and teachers' organizations in each of the school districts. About 75 citizens including parents, some adolescents, community leaders, and people who work with youth attended. They were divided into groups to discuss specific problems they felt were of concern in the community.

Their concerns were recorded by the research team and became basic source material for developing the survey instruments used with both parents and high school youth. The research team also included questions of theoretical interest to enhance the likelihood that the survey would produce findings that could be published in the professional literature. This aspect of the survey reflected the interests of the university-based research center. Publication in professional journals is a matter of survival ("publish or perish") in a university setting.

The initial drafts of the survey instruments were reviewed by the citizen members of the agency's board of directors. They had been appointed by the town council to oversee all of the Youth Board's activities and programs. After the board members approved the drafts, the survey instruments were reviewed by representatives of the administration of each school district. The cooperation of the school districts was important in order to gain access to a list of names of students and parents (a sampling frame), to draw a random sample of students for the survey, and also to obtain the schools' mailing tapes to announce the study to parents. The school administrators also requested some modifications to see that their interests were adequately represented. Once the instrument was cleared in this way, the project was further reviewed by the SUNY-Buffalo Institutional Review Board for ethical propriety and to ensure that confidentiality was sufficiently safeguarded.

To take parental interests into account, the research team wrote to the parents of every high school student to let them know that a survey would be conducted, that if their son or daughter was chosen to participate it would be because that name was selected at random, and that no high school student would be allowed to take the survey without written parental permission. To encourage participation, the research team offered participants a coupon valid for a record or a tape at a local record store. The owner of the record store cooperated by providing the coupons at a wholesale price, reducing the costs of the survey to the Youth Board. Once the names were selected, parents and youth were again notified by mail and sent a parental permission slip. After they were returned, arrangements were made to administer the survey instrument in school, on noninstructional time. The survey was administered successfully, and even though the survey contained some sensitive questions, no one complained. In fact the Youth Board was widely praised for its concern for the community, and for its efforts to communicate what it was doing.

Once the survey was complete, the research team prepared a preliminary report and reviewed the results with the Youth Board and the executive director of the agency. After receiving their comments, questions, and suggestions for additional analyses, the research team prepared a second report. Once this report was cleared by the Youth Board, the research team presented the results formally to the Town Council, the legislative body responsible for receiving state funds for the Youth Board's programs, and this meeting was attended by members of the press. The report was summarized in the metropolitan daily, and in suburban newspapers, and a story featuring the executive director appeared on several of the local television news broadcasts. The study was also the subject of a favorable editorial in the metropolitan daily.

In the next several weeks, the report was fed back to citizen groups in open forums held in community centers and schools, and the executive director and the research team met with small groups of service providers, ministers, and youth workers to discuss the results of the study. Based on this information and feedback, the Youth Board made its plans for services for the next several years, a plan approved by its funding agency.

This process was repeated three years later. Community sentiment was sufficiently favorable that the second survey included questions about sexual activity, emotional distress, and suicidal inclinations. These topics were not included earlier because some citizen leaders and some school district representatives felt they were too sensitive. However, three years later, the concerns were still there, but sufficient trust had developed so that the second survey included these sensitive items. In keeping with national trends, the second survey showed a decline in alcohol and drug use over the three-year period. Although the decline could not be attributed specifically to Youth Board programs, it was certainly consistent with the goals of these programs.

The process continued. When the state legislature sought to reduce funds for Youth Board programs except to the most deprived communities, the results of the studies showing relatively high rates of delinquency and continued drug and alcohol use in this relatively affluent suburban community contributed to the legislative decision to continue funding for the program. The data have since been used by the Youth Board for planning purposes, and provided useful background data for community agencies who were themselves preparing grant applications for service programs. The Amherst School District, working in cooperation with the Youth Board, developed an application for a planning grant for a multi-service center to serve a neighborhood where scatter-site low-income housing brought many minority children and children for whom English was a second language into one school's catchment area. The data collected earlier supported the project application. The Amherst school district and the Youth Board, in cooperation with Levine and Singer, conducted a needs assessment. This study used census data, survey data from schoolchildren, open-ended interviews with students, parents, teachers, school officials, political leaders, low-income housing managers, and Youth Board authorities, and resulted in a report showing the need for a community center serving a particular area in town. The report also suggested that the community center might be built adjoining the school and use the school's gym, swimming pool, auditorium, and community room on weekends and after school hours. The report was presented to the School Board and to the town council. The town council voted an appropriation of $100,000 for services in that area, and authorized the Youth Board director to pursue other sources of funds for a community center. The report prepared by Levine and Singer was influential in the appropriation of funds, and various community members continued to refer to the report in public meetings even several years later.

In sum, ecological research methods are socially relevant and community- (as opposed to laboratory-) based, and involve community participation in all phases from planning to dissemination. Ideally, ecological methods include multiple sources of data, including both qualitative and quantitative measures, to cross-validate. Change over time is an important factor for testing causal relationships and because the ecology is never static, hence the importance of longitudinal designs measuring system dynamics at two or more points in time. To think ecologically is also to consider relationships at multiple levels: individuals, individuals relative to their group, and groups (e.g., organizations, communities). The definition or boundaries of communities chosen should be "ecologically valid" (e.g., neighborhood, not census tract; street block, not census block). Statistical procedures now permit the analysis of multiple levels simultaneously, which holds great promise for ecological community research (Perkins & Taylor, 1996; see entire special issue of the *American Journal of Community Psychology*, February, 1996, on ecological assessment methods).

Implications for the Research Enterprise

Compared to the relative ease of conducting a laboratory experiment, ecological research is "messy." It requires compromises and accommodations to the interests of persons other than the researchers. It is rare that one can establish a true random-assignment-of-subjects-to-conditions experiment in which challenges to internal validity and plausible rival hypotheses can be controlled or assessed. Furthermore, ecological psychologists typically rely on multiple measures, including unobtrusive techniques, to collect data in the field. These measures are designed to preserve the complexity of the phenomena under study, and to maximize generalizability in the sense that the research seeks to understand phenomena as they are found "in nature." Ecological investigators prefer this kind of ecological validity to the tight control and internal precision of the laboratory experiment. Because ecological research frequently has an applied orientation, it is necessary to study natural, unarranged patterns of social relationships. When we speak of ecologically valid research, we want the methods to produce knowledge that will be valid in the natural situation of interest. Finally, given the longitudinal character of ecological research, we do not strive to understand human behavior as the linear effect of some single, isolatable cause. This "noncausal" way of understanding behavior marks a sharp break with the dominant traditions and philosophies in psychology built on the testing of causal hypotheses.

Given these alternative methods and assumptions, we may speak of ecological psychology as a paradigm shift, or revolution, in the Kuhnian sense (Kuhn, 1996). However, community psychologists using ecological concepts continue to use the language of science, and in so doing confirm their endorsement of the values of science—objectivity, in the sense of requiring findings to be public and replicable, and empiricism, meaning that all concepts are open to modification in light of new evidence. Continuing identification with science is important in establishing certain boundaries for community psychology and ensuring that its intellectual products are not too discontinuous with other products of scientific endeavor. Identification with other sciences is important in another respect. Although the ecological critique of traditional individual psychology is intellectually grounded, it is also a political statement to the degree that it generates a basis for competing for resources necessary for the ecologist to thrive—research funds, jobs, and recognition within the community of science. In a sense, social ecologists can be viewed as a variant population competing for resources with existing populations in the same community.

The Youth Board example (Box 4–1) illustrates how the research process itself may alter phenomena in the natural setting. Value problems that arise in the course of field research are not easily resolved. However, we believe that cooperative arrangements in which the research is undertaken based on clear understandings and in accord with the varied interests of community populations is most likely to identify and come to terms with potentially conflicting values.

Given these many differences with the more familiar laboratory experiment, what standards of quality should we apply to ecological research? In particular, what implications follow from our assertion that the standards we strive to meet in the laboratory are less important for judging products in this new tradition? For one thing, we need standards of goodness if we are to assert entitlement to societal resources and to claim special status in society as professionals. If we relax our preference for control and internal precision, which standards replace those? Sarason (1976) struggled with this issue in trying to answer a student who asked how such research was anything more than "common sense." Sarason answered that such research was Everyman's common sense but, quoting the historian Carl Becker, was "more consciously and expertly applied." Levine (1980a, 1982) has suggested that it is self-conscious discipline which distinguishes the professional worker from the layman. Nonetheless, the standards of quality that are to be met if we or others are to rely on research findings emerging from such perspectives remain to be articulated. (See Levine, Reppucci, & Weinstein, 1990, for a discussion of epistemological considerations in community psychology.)

This issue of standards is not idle when viewed in relation to the competition for resources. To survive, a new population must have access to resources. One resource is a base within a university where research and scholarship may be conducted and the results disseminated by teaching. Standards for the goodness of research influence the award of grants and other funds, and publication in journals, and those in turn influence tenure and appointment decisions—in a word, survival. New journals may proliferate because the standards of excellence as well as the substance of new work differ from the traditional. In other words, the effects of a given change radiate. Where and how one may obtain funds for research, and where and how one might get work published strongly influence the thinking of researchers. Fortunately, the overall system does allow for diversity. A viable new population may find a niche and compete successfully for resources with other populations in the same community.

Principles of Ecology

James G. Kelly (1966) was an early proponent of the ecological analogy in community psychology. In the beginning of this chapter, we briefly defined four concepts Kelly employed. Here we will elaborate on the concepts of population, community, ecosystem, and biosphere. *Population* refers to a group of similar individuals, and for these purposes they are individuals with similar "interests." Populations can be defined by social interests—age, gender, ethnicity, race, social class—and often by roles such as police officer, mental health professional, legislator, parent, mental health consumer, etc. By *interests* we mean a concern about resources needed for survival, for carrying out the obligations of one's role, for growth and development, or for the fulfillment of one's potential. The term interest includes the need to be free of barriers or social "toxins" that interfere with obtaining resources, or that limit the growth and development of members of the population. Thus, access to jobs on an equal footing, or the equal commitment of money to education in different communities, are examples of concerns about essential resources. Issues like this are important because we believe there is strong evidence that the lack of resources places many members of the population in poverty at risk of disorder. Homelessness, for example, is an obvious condition that places many children at risk of severe disorder and a poor adaptation (Institute of Medicine, 1989).

By *community* we mean the populations sharing a defined area. For different purposes, the area that populations share will be different. Sometimes it will be a city, a county, a state, a neighborhood, a particular school or social organization, or in the case of school desegregation (see chapter 11) the entire nation. We cannot always be precise in specifying this unit of analysis, and it will differ for different purposes. The only constant is that any unit of analysis will always be composed of populations with differing, overlapping, and sometimes competing interests. Any effort to intervene or even to study a problem in a community must expect as a given to cope with the varied interests of members of different populations.

The *ecosystem* refers to the community *and* the inanimate environment. For some problems, we do need to know something about the inanimate environment. How much lead is in the air, and how will the ingestion of lead affect children's intellectual growth? What kind of housing is available? The architectural design of some high-rise public housing developments made it more difficult for residents to protect themselves against crime. The movement of jobs from the cities to the suburbs meant more unemployment among inner city residents, and eventually resulted in a high concentration of "the truly disadvantaged" in some neighborhoods adding to the problems of disorganization (Wilson, 1987; see Box 3–1). Traffic rush hours are part of the ecosystem. For example, commuters who regularly drove through high traffic congestion reported their general mood was poorer than those who had easier commutes. Perhaps because they had greater household and family responsibilities that made demands on their time, women were more sensitive than men (Novaco, Kliewer, & Broquet, 1991). In all these examples, the physical environment had important social effects. For our purposes, the ecosystem also includes social rules, customs, and laws that govern access to resources, that might limit people's opportunities, that might restrict freedom, or that protect individual rights. The *biosphere* includes the larger inhabited environment, or the whole planet. We have become familiar with worldwide environmental problems such as global warming, greenhouse effects, and the loss of protective ozone, each of which may have important behavioral effects. As a small example, we may limit our exposure to sunlight and buy and use protective sunscreens when we go to the beach. The analogue on the social level is large-scale movement of people due to changes in their own countries, for example, immigration of Latino and Asian populations to California. In 1970, about 80 percent of Californians were non-Hispanic whites. In 1992, this percentage declined to about 55 percent, and by the year 2020, the non-Hispanic white population will be about 40 percent (Data Reference Book prepared by Robert Page for the California Commission on the Future of the Courts, 1992; see also Rogler, 1994). The reaction against immigrants and affirmative action in California may well reflect the white majority's concerns about the changing composition of the population. Examining our own history, we know that immigrants often have severe problems in adapting to a new world with different language, customs, demands, and with limits on the social supports—schools, churches, community organizations—that are normally available to assist people through difficulties. In the absence of these resources, or if helping agencies do not adapt to the culture and needs of the immigrants, the helping agencies may become part of the problem.

Some changes have come about because we have a global economy with worldwide movement of capital. Multinational corporations take advantage of differentials in the price of labor and other costs of doing business and move industries to undeveloped countries. These changes often create new problems in the communities to which the industries move, and create problems here to the degree they result in plant closings and a loss of employment in our communities (Buss, 1992; Broman, Hamilton, & Hoffman, 1990). A great many steelworkers in Lackawanna, New York, lost well paying jobs in steel mills because of corporate decisions that it was more economical to build new plants elsewhere than to modernize in Lackawanna, or that corporate interests were better served by trading with Korea or Japan. When the worker in Lackawanna loses his job, he may start drinking more and perhaps abusing his spouse because his major source of pride and self-esteem is gone. He may be demoralized because he is angry and frightened about the future, and his plight can be directly attributed to global processes.

In a very influential article, Kelly (1966) articulated four principles, adapted from ecology, that he believed were useful in approaching problems in community intervention. These are *interdependence, cycling of resources, adaptation* and *succession*.

Interdependence

The first of these principles states that components within a social unit are *interdependent*. Changes in one component of an ecosystem will produce changes in other components of that system. For example, logging destroys trees and affects the habitat of other animals such as the spotted owl that may become extinct. As we explain later in this chapter, for example, the deinstitutionalization of patients from psychiatric hospitals had important effects on other systems besides mental health, such as justice and law enforcement.

Interdependence refers not only to the existence of mutual influence among community components but also to their dynamic interaction over time. In research, for example, the relationship between the investigator and the setting under study differentiates the community system in a particular way. Investigator and setting are assumed to have significant effects on one another during all stages of the research (Vincent & Trickett, 1983) as the Amherst Youth Board example (Box 4–1) showed. Furthermore, because the populations making up a community interact and exert mutual influences, any change can have reverberating effects, and we should expect the unexpected when it comes to the consequences of change.

Plant geneticists find they constantly have to adapt their techniques for creating insect-resistant plants, because the insect populations become toxin resistant over time due to selective breeding. They have to create plants with different toxins, or even provide nontoxic plants so susceptible populations will survive to breed with others slowing down the rate of development of toxin-resistant pests (McGaughey & Whalon, 1992).

Another example of dynamic mutual influence requiring solutions to problems caused by earlier solutions is affirmative action, which was designed to redress the underrepresentation of women, African Americans, and other groups in desirable work settings. Affirmative action programs succeeded in opening up opportunity for members of those populations by improving access to those resources. Members of the populations favored by the change in rules, the analogue to a change in the physical environment, could compete more favorably for resources after the barriers were removed. Because affirmative action changed the rules regarding competition for resources, those populations who believed they had lost out (e.g., white males) acted to change the rules again, to reduce the effects of affirmative action or even eliminate it. In other words, change on behalf of one population affected other populations, who then responded to restore their access to resources.

By definition, interdependent populations exercise mutual influence. Deinstitutionalization policy returned many people with serious mental illness to the community, and back on the streets many of them became very visible. This visibility, and the feeling of many citizens (e.g., as expressed in newspaper editorials) that the former inpatients were not properly cared for, led to a discussion of changing the rules again to either serve these people more aggressively or make it easier to rehospitalize them. Consumer groups, representing a different population, tried to change the system by organizing patient advocacy and consumer-run alternative services (Chamberlin, 1990). Some of their family members also organized to bring political pressure to improve services and to make it easier to rehospitalize persons in need. Mental health officials, as a population, were influenced by the actions of other populations (consumers and their families) to work together in changing the system of care.

More examples of the manifestation of mutual influence will be apparent when we examine prevention programs. Arguments now going on between parent groups, educators and others concerned with the spread of AIDS, teenage sexual activity, and pregnancy, also illustrate this mutual influence. Groups with different religious, political, and social interests are engaged in serious debate about sex education in schools and whether to issue condoms to high school students or to emphasize abstinence (Whitehead, 1994).

In Kelly's view, the principle of interdependence not only alerts us to the complexity of change, but also directs us to deal with the community as the unit of analysis for some interventions. It directs our attention to a different level of analysis than the internal characteristics of an individual patient. A further implication of interdependence, moreover, is that mental health professionals intervening in the community-oriented mode will adopt different roles, and work in different environments than where professionals are normally found (their usual niches). It is one thing to see patients in a clinic. It is quite another to consult with teachers in a classroom; still another to participate in a community-wide coordinating council or to become a partisan activist for change. Should effective coordination require additional legislative authority, for example, then mental health professionals must know how to operate in the appropriate political environments. The principle of interdependence warns us in general that we should attend to the relationships which comprise the community system, but it does not tell us precisely to what we should attend in any specific case.

Cycling of Resources

Kelly's second principle, referred to as the *cycling of resources*, suggests that the transfer of energy in a biological system reveals the individual components which comprise that system, and also their relationship to each other. A larger animal feeding on a smaller one, feeding on a plant, deriving energy from the sun, leaves fertilizer for the plant. Energy is transferred throughout the cycle; one creature's waste is another's raw material. An intervention represents a change in the way resources are cycled, and thus this principle concerns the way resources are created and defined as well as how they are distributed. Furthermore, Kelly states that before intervening to change the distribution of resources (e.g., creating a new service requiring funds), one ought to know how a community cycles resources on its own.

In a social system, the energy that is recycled may be people's time and effort or it may be in the form of money or other assets (see "*asset-based community development*" in chapter 12). Taxation results in income redistribution. Money goes from one source, the individual earner or the corporate taxpayer, to other sources. These may be the beneficiaries of Social Security income, unemployment insurance, disability payments, food stamps, or Medicaid. They may also be human service providers who receive appropriations for providing services.

Publicly funded programs that are based on new policies require a change in the way resources are cycled. Unless we assume unlimited resources, whenever we develop a new program, resources have to be taken from somewhere else. If public policymakers decide that we need a new service program, or new parks and playgrounds, and after-school programs to care for children of working parents, then resources have to be allocated and reallocated. The argument about faith-based services involves separation of church and state issues, but it also involves reallocation of resources to a new, competing group of service providers. The difficulties encountered in transferring resources from the psychiatric hospital to the community at large in support of deinstitutionalization policy provide a good example of an intervention or policy undertaken without full cognizance of how communities distribute resources.

Without sufficient resources, the effort to help can create problems. For example, in the 1970s we thought it was a good idea to have child abuse reporting laws. Professionals who worked with children were required to report to child protection authorities any suspicion that a child they were seeing professionally was being maltreated. Legislators thought that sponsoring child abuse reporting hotlines would be a manageable resource reallocation, making it possible to help children at low cost (Nelson, 1984). However, the child protection system was quickly swamped with calls. In 1998, hot lines received reports on 2.8 million children, and the child protection system is overwhelmed with cases. In fact, the U.S. Advisory Board on Child Abuse and Neglect

(1990) states the whole child protection system is in a state of crisis, as we described in chapter 1. In part the crisis came about because we do not have unlimited resources and we are unable or unwilling to allocate sufficient resources to implement policy-driven solutions to problems. When we consider the cycling and recycling of resources, those issues have to be taken into account. Innovations can lead to significant increases in the resources available to persons at risk. As we will see in chapter 9, for example, self-help groups represent significant innovations in the ecology of coping and support, in part because they are so much more efficient than professionals in their consumption of money and other resources.

Adaptation; Niche

Kelly's third principle is *adaptation*. No human environment is completely behavior-neutral: through the specific resources it provides, an environment effectively constrains some behaviors and facilitates others. Adaptation describes the process by which organisms vary their habits or characteristics to cope with available or changing resources. Consider the shape of a pine tree growing under different conditions. In a forest the tree may be straight and tall, its needles and branches bushy, while the same type of tree exposed to ocean winds on a Cape Cod sand dune will be scrubby, bent over, and close to the ground. Growing close to the low-oxygen line on a mountain, it will be shorter and have fewer needles. Without adaptation, changes in resources or the presence of toxins threaten survival.

Significant loss of resources is probably the most frequent trigger for adaptive responding. If one loses a job, unemployment insurance may help temporarily, but eventually it is necessary to find another job. If the new job doesn't pay as well, a family may have to move to a cheaper apartment or a less expensive home. Plans for children to attend an expensive private college may be replaced with a plan to send them to a less expensive state college. Some people may be demoralized by the change in status and lifestyle and employ less adaptive coping devices, drinking excessively or getting into marital arguments. Some may adopt entirely new lifestyles, and move to different parts of the country. In the previous chapter we noted that mental hospital admissions, suicides, and the overall level of pessimistic mood among people are all correlated with changes in the unemployment rate (Kiernan, Toro, Rappaport, & Seidman, 1989) . The point is that the loss of a significant resource requires a variety of adaptations. An increase in resources may also require adaptation. Because food is readily available, many people eat too much, feel they are overweight, and go on diets to lose weight. Authorities note that we have too many obese children and adults whose health is at risk because of the obesity.

Sometimes adaptation is triggered by the presence (or recognition) of toxins in the environment. Consider crime as a community toxin. Residential burglary, for example, provokes significant psychological distress and may seriously disrupt the victim's supportive attachment to home and neighborhood (Brown & Perkins, 1992). With respect to ecosystem variables, crime is perceived as a bigger problem by people living in neighborhoods marked by physical incivilities, such as litter, graffiti, and run-down or vacant buildings (Perkins, Meeks, & Taylor, 1992). People living in such an environment may act defensively in terms of when and where they move about and the number of locks on their outside doors. However, if the levels of residential satisfaction and neighboring are sufficient these same physical incivilities may serve as catalysts for increased participation in block organizations as an adaptive response (Perkins, Florin, Rich, Wandersman, & Chavis, 1990). Neighborhoods differ in rates of child abuse in part related to differences in good neighboring, even in the absence of socioeconomic differences. Parents and their children living in environments with high rates of violence learn to adapt by hiding in bathtubs when shooting breaks out, or by being sensitive to the appearance of teens or older youth who may begin to shoot at each other (Garbarino, 1995).

For some combinations of resource limits and toxins, adaptation may involve relinquishing attachments to specific places, which itself can pose serious challenges (Brown & Perkins, 1992). Some say that homeless people who live on the streets adapt in that manner because they don't have the rent for a room and believe the risk of being harmed in a shelter is greater than the risk of being harmed on the street. Living on the street is thus an adaptation to the available resources and to social toxins that stimulate avoidant behavior. Shinn and Tsemberis (1998) showed that a substantial majority of homeless people took advantage of new housing resources with minimal professional assistance when the housing was made accessible. The concept of adaptation directs us to look at more than the person and the diagnosis that can be applied to the person, although these may be important for some purposes. It directs us to look at the person's resources, or lack of them, and to recognize the toxins and other negative influences in the person's environment to understand the person's behavior.

Modern day professionals also adapt. When consumers who lived in the community refused to come to clinics for treatment, community mental health programs created outreach and crisis units which ventured out into the consumer's world. Professionals stopped insisting that consumers come to the clinic for appointments and started meeting them in restaurants for coffee, in the consumer's home, or in pool halls or other hangouts (see Box 2–2). Consumers are a resource for mental health professionals in the sense that funding depends upon serving a certain number of persons, and professionals' self-esteem depends in part upon doing a good job. The concept of adaptation leads us to try to understand the other person's condition of life, and to try to understand how that person's behavior reflects that condition of life.

The concept of adaptation is related to the concepts of *niche* and *niche breadth*. Niche refers to a habitat within which a given creature can survive. The broader the range of habitats within which creatures of the same type are found, the greater the niche breadth. Niche can also refer to the contribution a given population makes to the community. Humans, by virtue of their great ability to adapt behaviorally and culturally, are found at the north pole and at the equator, in oxygenless space and underwater. In that sense, humans may be said to have a wide niche breadth.

We can see that populations are not randomly scattered throughout the community. There are ethnic and racial concentrations in different neighborhoods, and also gender concentrations in different occupations. Women are often found in nursing or in elementary school teaching, but less often in mathematics, engineering, or construction. For years the formal barriers of legal segregation and discriminatory customs kept African Americans from living or working in many niches. When those formal barriers were removed, African Americans could enter certain occupations, use public accommodations, and be admitted to schools, colleges, universities, and professional schools formerly closed to them. They could also move into more neighborhoods. Many African Americans now live in integrated neighborhoods (Alba, Logan & Stults, 2000). In other words, their niche breadth widened. The expansion of niche breadth is a continuing goal of advocates for groups such as women, gays, and minority members. The argument about allowing gays into the military is essentially an argument about niche breadth.

Homeless people are more prevalent in some neighborhoods than others and in soup kitchens, missions, and shelters more than in a town's premier restaurants. Before deinstitutionalization, the most important niche in which persons with serious mental illness could be found was the mental hospital. Now their niche breadth is enlarged and mental health consumers are found in many different community settings.

Box 4–2. Behavior-Environment Congruence in Geel, Belgium

Geel, Belgium, is a community with a 700-year history as a religious shrine for mentally ill people. Although there is a psychiatric hospital located near Geel, hundreds of persons with chronic mental illness live as "boarders" with families in Geel who receive allowances for boarding these individuals (Roosens, 1979). Not everyone in town provides boarding. Most often it is working-class families and farm families who welcome the extra income. If boarders go to the movie theater in town, they are herded into the balcony rather than sitting among the patrons in the orchestra. Although boarders are free to move around town, they are found only in certain bars, and never in others. They sometimes attend church, but are not found in all churches in town. Boarders are rarely observed at town meetings about governance, nor are they part of community groups planning charitable affairs or other community projects. In other words, they are not randomly distributed among town settings but are found instead in certain niches.

Similarly, in the United States group living arrangements for persons with serious mental illness or mental retardation are not found just anywhere. Initially these homes were concentrated in neighborhoods where there was little community opposition. In Buffalo, New York, a great many group homes were initially established in the vicinity of a state hospital. However, so many former inpatients were wandering the streets and causing complaints from local businesses that a moratorium was declared on the placement of more homes in that area. Now laws generally allow the placing of homes in most communities, but opposition still arises in communities that are sufficiently stable so that the neighborhood can organize to protest against a home coming into the area (Levine, 1981).

Recognizing boarders' aspirations to be as normal as possible and the benefits that come from participating in community settings, townspeople have allowed boarders a reasonable degree of integration into everyday town life. Given many boarders' limitations, however, integration is most evident in settings that require only a few simple responses of participants (e.g., parades, church worship services). In general, integration is accomplished through "trial and error"—behavior that deviates from the accepted norms for that setting (e.g., playing a radio and pelting others in the audience with popcorn while at a movie theater) is tolerated up to a point, but sanctioned via correction or removal if it becomes too disruptive.

Given the uniformity of behavior expected within most settings, the Geel example illustrates why people find it so easy to attribute noticeable deviations in behavior to significant person-centered deficits such as mental illness, drunkenness, or mental retardation. This active, even coercive influence of particular environments on behavior is known as "behavior-environment congruence." The concept has important practical and theoretical implications for eliciting and maintaining specific changes in human behavior (Barker, 1968; Wicker, 1972; see also "behavior setting theory" in chapter 5).

The concept of niche leads us to think about the development of functional roles within a new social organization (niche) and the provision of resources appropriate for characteristics of the population occupying this niche. Thus some service systems employ former consumers, but adapt the jobs to take into account any residual limitations. We can also contemplate teaching adaptive skills so that a population's niche breadth can be enlarged. Consider persons with severe and persistent mental illness who have lived for many years in psychiatric hospitals, for example. Their behavioral characteristics to some extent reflect limited situational resources and adaptation to the custodial nature of hospital care. By training such individuals in skills of daily living and providing other resources (e.g., group homes, income under the Supplemental Security Income program), their niche breadth widens and the likelihood they will adapt to normal community life increases. Following discharge, moreover, persons with serious mental illness who live in communities giving them a wide niche (e.g., supportive arrangements for housing, employment, and recreation, plus a broad array of mental health services) are less likely to be rehospitalized. They are more likely to be employed, and to report higher well-being, than similar persons living in an otherwise comparable city providing a more limited niche (Beiser et al., 1985).

Many individuals labeled "mentally retarded" are impaired only with respect to their ability to cope with the intellectual demands of schools. Many were limited to the special class niche. Follow up studies indicate that at least within the upper ranges of mental retardation such individuals fare no worse occupationally and socially than other persons of similar social class background when they leave school (see Sarason & Doris, 1969, pp. 86–89; Bloch, 1984). (If the job market changes and requires skills that those with mental retardation have difficulty acquiring, this picture may change and the niches may become more limited; Katz, 1994.)

As another illustration, we note that the mobility of physically disabled people has been greatly improved by wheelchairs and other technological devices. Until well into the 1970s, however, the architecture of many buildings, including restroom facilities, made access by people in wheelchairs difficult or impossible. To a degree, one can say that the behavioral handicap of the person in the wheelchair is as much a function of the staircase or the curbstone as it is of the person's nonfunctional limbs. The concept in the American Disablity Act of requiring reasonable accommodations for employees with handicaps is an example of the principle of adaptation written into a law. Thus, following the passage of regulations requiring wheelchair access ramps and restroom modifications, the adaptation of such individuals to key community settings improved, and they appeared in more niches.

The concepts of niche and adaptation are useful because they teach us to think about alternatives, and the resources necessary to provide an alternative. They also help us accept differences among individuals and, if necessary, consider political solutions such as legal regulation to problems of poor person-environment fit.

Succession

Kelly's fourth principle is *succession*. Environments are not static; they change. A change in the environment may create conditions more favorable to one population and less favorable to another. Eventually a more favored population will squeeze out the others, or at least dominate a given area, or some new level of homeostasis will develop among populations sharing the same area. Thus, while interdependence teaches us to understand the community before trying to change it, succession implies that change, both natural and man-made, can contribute to our understanding in the first place.

The history of immigration to the United States provides some excellent examples of this principle. As the immigrants of an earlier day prospered, they moved out of poor neighborhoods into newer suburbs. The groups that later occupied this housing were moving up from what they had before. African Americans who moved to Chicago from unheated shacks with no running water in the rural, agricultural south found better quarters in the city tenements formerly occupied by other ethnic groups (Lemann, 1991). Urban ghettos developed over time, and when changes in civil rights laws opened new employment and housing opportunities for African Americans who had been denied them earlier, those who were able to take advantage of the opportunities moved out of the ghettos. These areas were left with high concentrations of poor, young people, who were more prone to crime and lacked both middle-class role models and peers who had the social clout and know-how to command services. Thus the ghetto areas became progressively worse for those who lived there and could not get out (Wilson, 1987).

The deinstitutionalization of persons with serious mental illness provides another illustration of succession in urban neighborhoods. Psychiatric ghettos take root more readily in transient neighborhoods where anonymity is widespread, other populations have little rootedness, and there is little formal organization in the neighborhood. Such ghettos developed where properties were not profitable for other use, as in the old residential hotels on Manhattan's upper west side. As property values increased and tax benefits were made available to developers, "gentrification" took place and these hotels were converted to condominiums. Many mental health consumers and welfare clients living in the hotels were evicted, sometimes ruthlessly, helping to create the troublesome phenomenon of homelessness. The economically and politically stronger middle class was better able to compete with the poor for housing niches.

Sometimes a neighborhood organization welcomes newcomers to the community because of resources the newcomers may bring. A YWCA residence with which we are familiar, dedicated to serving women but unable to attract young businesswomen as residents, opened its doors to women with serious mental illnesses. Its buildings were resources for these women, and their rental payments were resources to keep the building functioning and to pay for necessary staff. Convents in New York State, empty because of the declining number of persons entering religious life, were put to new use as group homes for retarded individuals deinstitutionalized under court order. Church organizations took in the deinstitutionalized persons, fulfilling the religious value of service, and received money for their care. Unused for their original purposes, convents became resources not only for the retarded living in them, but also for administrators charged with carrying out the deinstitutionalization order. The church, with a stake in providing service, often used its influence to restrain neighborhood resistance (competition from still other populations) to the invasion of the new population (Rothman, 1982).

In addition to alerting us to some issues of change, the principle of succession teaches that some resources otherwise discarded may be put to use by other populations. During much of the nineteenth century, railroad interests promoted the succession of Midwestern prairies by farming, industry, and other intensive development (Cronon, 1991). A hundred years later many Midwestern communities, now stuck with long stretches of abandoned railroad right-of-ways, have begun converting them to "linear parks" offering miles of uninterrupted hiking and biking trails for the recreational pursuits of twenty-first century citizens. Similarly, from the self-help perspective a "useless" individual, a drain on resources, becomes a therapeutic resource within the context of an organization such as Alcoholics Anonymous (see chapter 9). Self-help movements, able to use different resources than those which professionals require, are to a certain extent succeeding the population of professional service providers. The literature on how self-help organizations and mental health professionals can relate to each other may be taken as an example of the development of a new homeostasis between populations, based on the possibility of exchanging resources to meet mutual needs.

Box 4–3. The Boom in Hong Kong's Elderly Home Industry

An interesting illustration of Kelly's ecological principles and the analytic insights they offer is provided by Cheng (1993). Between 1981 and 1990 the city of Hong Kong showed a dramatic rise in the number of private, for-profit residential facilities for elderly people. This change was not entirely attributable simply to growth in the elderly population as a whole. Rather, it reflected sharp increases in the number of dependent elderly caused in part by decreased numbers of family caretakers (as more and more women took jobs outside the home) and increasing numbers of adults emigrating in advance of

Hong Kong's return to Chinese control. Over the same time period Hong Kong's publicly funded and regulated residential homes for dependent elderly grew at an inadequate rate, creating long waiting lists. Social security income, allocated to the elderly directly to enable them to remain independent or under family care, was exploited by entrepreneurs as a means of funding profitable new private homes. Cheng suggests that many of these unregulated homes may have been substandard in quality. Even so, there were good reasons not to close them, since doing so would reduce the affordable housing stock to the point that some elderly people would have no homes at all (Cheng & Chan, 2003).

Cheng used ecological principles to help explain why the rapid surge in numbers of dependent elderly had the effect that it did (i.e., an increase in private, for-profit residences). For example, following Kelly's principle of interdependence, specific changes in one arena (Hong Kong's political relationship with China) provoked changes in other spheres of life (widespread emigration that disrupted family support systems and sharply increased the number of dependent elderly lacking adequate support). The cycling of resources is evident in the way money injected into the system at one point (elderly persons living in their own homes) ended up fueling the expansion of a new kind of setting elsewhere in the community. Adaptation is shown in the behavior of entrepreneurs, who responded to rapid growth in demand for residential supports by creating profitable enterprises tied to guaranteed public commitments to social security funding. Adaptation is also illustrated in the rational selection of this private, for-profit housing option by many people facing challenging new circumstances and limited alternatives. Finally, succession is demonstrated in the process whereby the disappearance of family supports for elderly people due to emigration and to changes in the labor force, plus the slow response of public programs charged with meeting this need, created a social vacuum that rapidly came to be filled by a new kind of setting.

Cheng also points out how thinking ecologically helps us realize that solving the apparent problem of substandard homes is not simply a matter of enacting regulatory laws requiring private homes to meet certain rules, since other factors of importance would not be addressed directly by such laws and would continue to affect the situation, possibly making things worse. Costs resulting from regulation may shrink profit margins, causing private operators to quit the business and homelessness among the elderly to increase as an unintended consequence. Effective adaptations to changing conditions are more likely to evolve from the recognition that factors are interdependent and subject to modification by monetary and other resource considerations.

Mental Health and the Law

Kelly's principles of interdependence, cycling of resources, adaptation, and succession are well illustrated in the problem that Teplin (1983, 1984) called the criminalization of the mentally ill. As we noted, the inpatient census of state mental hospitals has declined dramatically since the 1950s. Whatever the merits of the argument that incarcerating people in "total" institutions was harmful, unnecessary, and expensive, the fact was that federal policies, reflected in reimbursement formulae, made it advantageous to shift consumers from in-hospital niches to other niches—that is, nursing homes, board and care homes, or other similar facilities. The consumer's adaptation to the community was to have been assisted by recycling resources in the form of supervised medication, day care, rehabilitation services, and outpatient psychotherapy. Those resources were not always forthcoming, however, nor were they forthcoming in forms many persons could use (Levine, 1981).

Levine (1981) described how litigation in the 1960s and 1970s, designed to correct abuses in the hospital system, led to a tightening of legal standards for involuntary commitment. To commit a person involuntarily to a mental facility for more than brief emergency care, it became necessary to show that the person was not just mentally ill but dangerous to himself or others, or unable to survive even with assistance from family or friends. In many states these judicially imposed restrictions were translated into statutory standards affecting everyone concerned with the problem of deviant behavior. The person at risk for involuntary hospitalization was entitled to a number of procedural due process protections to ensure that the commitment and loss of personal liberty occurred for good reason. It became more difficult to hospitalize someone involuntarily than it had been in years past. Relationships among the hospital as a resource, professional mental health workers as a population, and prospective consumers' families and other community agencies changed.

Although outpatient services have grown, it is not clear that those services have necessarily been directed to persons who formerly would have been served as inpatients. General hospital psychiatric services and outpatient clinics restrict the types of cases they believe are suitable for service in their facilities. A prospective consumer may be denied care because he or she doesn't have the financial resources and is not eligible for welfare or other insurance that will pay the costs of care. Other institutions may not have secure facilities to manage dangerous or suicidal persons. Teplin (1983, p. 60) reported that some mental hospitals will not accept a person who has any criminal charge pending, even if it is a minor one. Consumers can thus face barriers to gaining access to niches and the resources they contain.

These two sets of forces, mental health litigation and legislation regarding funding, made it more difficult to hospitalize people. The principle of interdependence would lead us to predict that policies which keep patients out of the hospital will influence the working environments of two important populations in the community—those working in the criminal justice system and in the mental health system. The families of consumers will also be affected, and services may be altered to reflect characteristics of consumers to whom the services are targeted. If these changes are potent, then we would expect to see evidence of adaptation by members of these populations, and also some change in the niches in which they are found.

Law as a Factor in the Ecological Analogy

We noted earlier that the ecosystem includes the social rules, customs, and laws that govern access to resources, limit opportunities, protect rights, or restrict freedom. Changes in legal rules are changes in the ecosystem. These changes have had extremely important effects on the mental health system, on deinstitutionalization policy, and on the provision of services in the community, and they have now brought lawyers and judges as populations into the picture. Members of the legal system are now interacting more actively with members of other populations concerned with the care of mental health consumers, including mental health professionals and, as we shall see, police and corrections personnel in jails and prisons.

The larger community within which we live has a legal system which operates by rules. The rules are designed to implement our highest values. Everyone in our society, at least after birth, is granted status as a person. The term "persons" includes children and adults, citizens and aliens, and the Fourteenth Amendment to the U.S. Constitution states basic protections for all persons:

> nor shall any State deprive any person of life, liberty, or property without due process of law; nor deny to any person within its jurisdiction the equal protection of the laws.

The Fourteenth Amendment preserves the rights and freedoms of individuals against the power of government to limit those rights and freedoms. Under the Fourteenth Amendment, every person is entitled to the equal protection of the laws. That means that even persons with DSM-IV diagnoses are persons under the law, and entitled to the same legal protections of their basic rights to life, liberty, and property that every other person has.

Due process of law refers to those procedures we recognize as necessary for the state to follow when the state acts to limit a person's rights. As a general rule, no right is absolute. All rights may be limited by state action if the state has sufficiently good reason and follows proper procedure. It is beyond our scope to deal with what constitutes due process under our Constitution. (The details of due process vary depending on the type of action and the interests at stake.) Suffice it to say that the state legislature must pass a law which authorizes involuntary commitment. The language of the law must be consistent with previous judicial interpretations of both the state's constitution and the U.S. Constitution. The law must also specify procedures that should be followed if a person is to be committed involuntarily. If the person who is to be involuntarily committed had a hearing in front of a judge, and the hearing was carried out fairly—the judge was neutral, the person had notice of why the hearing was held, was given an opportunity to be heard, to be represented by an attorney, and to cross examine witnesses against him or her—then due process was followed. If the person is committed involuntarily, we say that his or her liberty is restricted with due process of law. (Because of the nature of our federal system, with some functions reserved to the states, the precise form of the law will differ from state to state, although all laws must be written so that they meet constitutional requirements.)

Until the 1960s there was a general belief that psychiatry could help a great many people, that professionals were benign and helpful, and that government, and especially the courts, should not interfere with professional decisions. Involuntary treatment could be based on a professional judgment that a person needed treatment, with little court review of the order. Commitment could be for an unspecified time, and it was up to the hospital superintendent to decide when a person should be released. Patients in hospitals had very few civil rights. Patients had little privacy, and rights such as those to marry, to make contracts, to write letters, to visit with friends or relatives, or even to see an attorney were sharply limited. All of this, it was said, was being done for the patient's good.

Beginning in the 1960s and continuing into the 1970s, federal courts began to interpret individual constitutional rights to mean that a state could not involuntarily hospitalize someone solely because the person was diagnosed as having a mental illness, or some professional person said the person had a need for treatment. In addition to mental illness, the courts began to insist that the state show the person was dangerous to him- or herself or to others before involuntary commitment could be justified. The civil rights–oriented lawsuits were challenges to the professional and scientific authority of psychiatry, and to the state's right to curtail individual freedom so sharply. Psychiatrist Thomas Szasz (1974) also challenged the role of psychiatry in limiting patient civil rights and freedoms, calling it a form of tyranny (see chapter 6).

These new viewpoints led to legal challenges to professional authority and to lax commitment laws. One important challenge to the scientific authority of psychiatry came in *Baxtrom* v. *Herold* (1966). Baxtrom was in prison because he had been convicted of assault. He was transferred to a state institution used for the confinement of prisoners who became mentally ill while serving their time. When Baxtrom's time was up the authorities continued to hold him because they said he was mentally ill. Baxtrom brought suit requesting that he be released or committed to a civilian hospital for treatment.

When Baxtrom's case reached the U.S. Supreme Court, the Court said that Baxtrom could not be held arbitrarily, and was entitled to the same procedures used to commit anyone involuntarily. The Court ordered the same review for everyone else who had been confined under the same conditions, and one result was that a large number of prisoners in New York and other states were either released outright or transferred to civilian hospitals after a judicial hearing to determine the necessity for continued hospitalization.

In this situation people who had been convicted of committing crimes, and who were also allegedly mentally ill, were placed in less secure state hospitals or released to the community. Follow-up studies of those who were both mentally ill and "dangerous" showed that over a four-year period about 14 percent were known to have committed an act injurious to another person either while in a civilian state hospital or after release to the community. If we say that by history (based on diagnosis and history of conviction for a criminal offense) 100 percent were expected to act out, then the follow-up study showed that prediction was wrong in 86 percent of the cases, casting serious doubt on the professional expertise and authority of mental health professionals (Monahan, 1976; see also Teplin, Abram & McClelland, 1994).

The legal cases exposing abuses in legal process, and abusive situations within institutions, contributed to reform (see chapters 2 and 10). The legal rules changed the ecosystem by making it more difficult to hospitalize patients and to keep them there. Along with the changes in the way federal government reimbursed state governments for patient care, and for disability pensions (see chapter 2), psychiatric patients could no longer be restricted to the psychiatric hospital niche. Once patients occupy niches in the community in addition to hospitals, the principle of interdependence tells us that other populations in the community will also be affected.

Adapting to Legal Change

The police. The police represent another population in this community faced with the problem of adapting to changes in their work environment. Police act under a complex set of rules designed to protect citizens against the abuse of police power. Police can take into emergency custody people involved in a disturbance, but they cannot take a person into custody without having an arrest warrant, based on a complaint from someone that the person has done something wrong, or in the absence of a warrant, without witnessing the infraction themselves or having other probable cause to act.

In general, police have a great deal of authority to take into custody people who are overtly dangerous to themselves or others. Police are called to the scene of many disturbances, and generally speaking they cannot refuse to come when called. The police have authority to arrest someone who is committing a crime or disturbing the peace. They have less authority, however, to detain someone apparently unable to care for his or her own basic needs (and whose life or health is in danger for that reason), or someone who seems disoriented and confused but is sufficiently alert to decide that he or she does not wish to receive care. About 8 percent of all police encounters with citizens involve mentally ill persons (Teplin, 1984). As the ABA standards note, police must make an "on the spot" determination in such cases, weighing the state's interest in protecting an individual from harm against the individual's constitutionally based interest in being free to manage his or her own affairs. A moment's reflection on the inherent complexity of this decision helps to explain why police may be reluctant to become involved in noncriminal situations.

Both the availability of facilities in the community and the policies and attitudes of mental health workers affect police willingness to take someone into custody for mental health–related purposes. The ABA standards (chapter 7) cite research indicating that police become cynical about mental health services if the admission procedure is tedious or uncertain. On occasion the mental health worker may refuse admission to someone who later attempts suicide or engages in violence. A police officer might have to defer other important duties for several hours while waiting with a patient in an emergency room, only to have the admitting doctor decide the person doesn't meet the legal criteria for admission and should be back on the street. Such episodes may enter into folklore, not as the exceptional case but rather as the general rule, helping to shape police attitudes toward the use of mental health facilities as an alternative disposition in cases where the police have discretion in taking the person to a lockup or a hospital.

It is not that police view symptoms of mental disorder with indifference. Based on observations of police-citizen encounters, Teplin (1984; Abram & Teplin, 1991) found that if there was some indication of mental disorder, independent of the severity of the episode, the police were twice as likely to make an arrest as when such indication was absent. This is not just a bias against males feared to be dangerous. Over 80 percent of incarcerated women awaiting trial in Chicago had had a diagnosable mental illness (Teplin, Abram, & McClelland, 1996). Over 70 percent were substance abusers. Most prospective patients who come to police attention have probably committed at least a violation, if not a more serious crime. Even if the violation is disorderly conduct, once convicted the person can receive a jail sentence of up to

15 days. If the charge is sufficiently serious, the arraigning magistrate can set bail at a level the accused person may not be able to meet, requiring him or her to be held in custody until trial. If someone raises a good faith doubt as to the accused person's mental or emotional competence to stand trial, he or she may be held for an examination to determine competency or be admitted to a hospital for that purpose (ABA, Part IV; see *Jackson* v. *Indiana*, 1972). This combination of factors, including police preference for the criminal justice rather than mental health system, leads to the hypothesis that many people formerly confined to mental hospitals during an era of less rigid standards for admission and more rigid standards for discharge, now will be found in new niches: jails and prisons.

The National Alliance for the Mentally Ill (NAMI), a self-help and advocacy group (see chapter 9) comprised of family members of persons with mental illness and consumers of mental health services, released a 1992 report (National Alliance for the Mentally Ill Staff & Public Citizen's Health Research Group Staff, 1992) on the mentally ill and jails. They estimate that there are approximately 30,000 persons with mental illness in jails (generally pretrial lockups, or facilities where short-term sentences are served). The report claims there are more mentally ill persons in the Los Angeles County jail than in any psychiatric hospital in Los Angeles county. NAMI claims that although most seriously mentally ill individuals are charged criminally when arrested, most of the charges are for relatively trivial offenses that are more the manifestation of their mental illnesses than any intent to commit a criminal act. They also found that 29 percent of jail officials admitted that they held seriously mentally ill individuals who had no criminal charges levied against them.

If more disturbed persons are now found in jails and holding centers, and in prisons after sentencing on criminal charges, we are faced with a societal problem of reallocating or redistributing professional resources to new institutional settings. Arrest and jailing constitute a distinctively stressful experience, often triggering fear, anxiety, and depression. The suicide rate among inmates in county jails is 16 times greater than among adults of comparable age in the population at large. For youth held in adult jails, the rate is three to five times higher than the rate in the general population (Hayes, 1983). A heightened state of arousal may precipitate excited aggressive acts toward both custodial personnel and other prisoners, especially in individuals prone to such behavior. The NAMI report states that in 84 percent of jails, corrections officers receive either no training or less than three hours of training in dealing with the problems of mentally ill inmates. Custodial personnel in holding centers and short-term correctional facilities need training in the day-to-day management of disturbed persons and, if medication is used, to understand its nature and side effects (see ABA, Standard 7-2.8). It is difficult to answer the question of whether, as a result of deinstitutionalization policies, more people with mental and emotional disorders are being cared for now in the criminal justice system and in correctional facilities than was true before (Teplin, Abram, & McClelland, 1997). Certainly very disturbed individuals are being arrested, arraigned, and jailed. The 1992 NAMI survey found that 69 percent of jail officials reported they were seeing far more mentally ill individuals now compared with 10 years ago.

One hypothesis that seems to have solid support in the research literature is that formerly hospitalized persons have higher arrest rates than those without such histories (Teplin, 1983, p. 57). A NAMI study reported that 40 percent of mentally ill relatives of NAMI members had been arrested at least once. If police do prefer the criminal justice route, however, then there should now be more disturbed persons in jails (pre-sentencing holding facilities) than was formerly true. Although the epidemiology is difficult, Teplin reads the evidence to conclude that the jail has indeed become the poor person's mental health facility as a consequence of changes in the admission of persons to mental hospitals. It would indeed be ironic if that was the case, for Dorothea Dix's mid-nineteenth-century crusade to build mental hospitals was based in part on her observations that too many mentally ill people were being held in jails! (Levine, 1981, p. 24)

This excursion into the complex interrelationships among systems and the rules which govern their operation should adequately illustrate the implications of interdependence when community change occurs. Change requires adaptations on the part of existing populations in the ecosystem, in this instance the police, mental health workers, jailors, and court personnel. We see that adaptation by some populations can force another population (persons with mental illness) into new niches (jails). Furthermore, such a change also requires reallocation of resources to populations and niches with mental health personnel more active in criminal justice niches. Erie County, New York, added a 50-bed infirmary to its jail to care for the mentally ill now in the facility.

None of these events can be understood in terms of individual psychopathology, nor from examining clinical treatment or diagnostic processes. An understanding of behaviors that enter into a determination of diagnosis under the categories of DSM-IV will not explain the decisions mental health workers make. Similarly, examining the formal rules under which they operate will not fully explain the behavior and attitudes of police in exercising discretion when arresting and charging persons they encounter. Moreover, Teplin's research required field study and an analysis of data that could not possibly have been generated in a laboratory. This complex example indicates that mental health workers cannot fully appreciate their own behavior and the behavior of their clients without stepping back and looking at the system of which they are a part. Very similar processes have been observed in the deinstitutionalization of persons with mental retardation. The concepts of ecology, crude as they may be when applied in this context, are useful because they direct our attention to important issues that affect us every day which we cannot understand without examining the larger system around us.

Box 4–4. Unforeseen Consequences of a Change in Child Protection Laws

The death of a child touches everyone deeply. We are especially outraged when we learn that the child protection system knew about a high risk case and wasn't able to protect the child from a brutal death, or when a judge returns to his or her family a child taken into foster care because of abuse, and the child is then injured or killed. These stories receive wide publicity, and prompt demands to punish officials and change the law.

Child protection workers try to keep children with their families, and judges try to return children to their families, because of the family preservation policy established in 1980 (PL 96-272). This preference for keeping children in their own homes and returning them quickly from the custody of social services was designed to reduce the rapidly growing number of foster home placements that occurred in response to a rising tide of reports of child abuse and neglect. The policy favoring custody in the family home came under attack as citizens and legislators reacted to the death of children reported in the media.

Ecological principles tell us that a change in any one part of a system will affect other parts, and that actors in the system will adapt to changes in the environment. The Joseph Wallace case in Chicago resulted in widespread publicity, calls for a judge to resign or be relieved of his duties, and calls for a child protection worker to be prosecuted criminally. As a result of the publicity, the law in Illinois changed, but as happens all too often, changes in laws that take place in an emotionally charged context are not well thought through and have unintended consequences.

Joseph Wallace was born while his mother was in a mental hospital. Her doctors did not believe his mother Amanda was able to care for him, and on their recommendation Joseph was placed in foster care. As the law required, social services worked with the mother to prepare her for taking care of her child. Amanda, who was never clearly psychotic, wanted her child back, and in fact the child was returned to her. After she had a second child, and was hospitalized again, both children were taken into temporary care. Amanda entered treatment, and once again social services worked with her so that she could have her children back. Amanda also hired a private attorney who argued her case. However, the workers helping her turned over rapidly, the judges and legal guardians appointed to represent Joseph's interests were all overburdened with cases, and the case records were kept in another court. The upshot was that no one really knew Amanda's history, and a judge returned her children to her. Two months later, Amanda was arrested and accused of killing her three-year-old son. She was convicted and later committed suicide while in prison.

The press is also an element in the community. Events such as the Joseph Wallace case may be viewed as a "resource" for the press. Depending on the position the press takes, its news columns and editorials may be a resource for some actors, and a toxin for others. In any event, a sustained story in the press creates turbulence in the environment, provoking new adaptations by other actors. The Joseph Wallace case inspired many stories, editorials, and influential newspaper columns. One columnist called for a judge's resignation. The public defender, who had not objected to returning Joseph to his mother, called for the criminal prosecution of the case worker because he believed she was derelict in not having assembled all the relevant information about Amanda. The social services department appointed a person to review what went wrong, and other investigations took place. The public defender argued that the culprit was the family preservation policy, which encouraged the unwarranted return of children to unfit parents. He called for a change in the law from the family preservation policy to a "child's best interest" standard. He felt that this approach would give the judge more discretion and would result in better placements. The state legislature changed the law in Illinois.

The change in law was based upon emotional outrage over a child's death, but the new policy was not well conceived. First, it was not the standard that was at fault, but rather the overburdened child protection system that imposed huge caseloads on child protection workers, lawyers, and judges. Second, the death of a child due to maltreatment remains a relatively rare event, with the incidence of deaths related to maltreatment estimated to be 1.94 per 100,000 of child population (McCurdy & Daro, 1993), and the change in law overlooked the problem of accurately predicting such low-frequency events. Knowing that child fatalities due to maltreatment are rare occurrences, simply on statistical grounds we can predict there will be a large number of inaccurate predictions. Thus, in trying to ensure the safety of a child, the decision maker will inevitably remove from their homes a great many children who could safely remain there, and will be unwilling to return home a great number who will end up in foster care for longer periods than necessary. The number of Illinois children in out-of-home placement grew from 29,542 in 1992 to 51,358 in 1997 (Mezey, 1998).

The ecological view tells us that actors will adapt to a new element in their environment, in this case a law that presumably offers greater discretion to the judge as decision maker. Judges are elected, and are sensitive to public opinion, and the primary purpose of child protection workers is insuring the safety of children. What new calculations in the mind of a judge or child protection worker result from the change in law? If either one allows a maltreated child to remain in the home and the child is harmed, they will come under great criticism, whether or not that is fair. However, anyone who recommends that the child be placed out of the home will not be subject to criticism. Similarly, if a judge or child protection worker recommends that a child in foster care be returned to the parent and the child is harmed, they will be criticized harshly, but if they recommend that the child remain in the foster home, there is little chance of criticism.

Although the research hasn't yet been done, it is predictable that the net result of a policy adopted in response to emotional pressure will be to recreate the situation that led to the development of the earlier policy it replaced. In the present example, the new law will increase pressure on an already overburdened foster care system to absorb still more children. Under pressure to provide for more children, social service officials will take less care in selecting, training, and supervising foster parents, with deleterious consequences for some children. Moreover, there is already considerable pressure on the child welfare system to find permanent adoptive homes for children when parental rights have been terminated and the children have been released for adoption. A change in federal law (Adoption and Safe Families Act, 1997) will add to the pressure. The new law required states to find adoptive homes for those children whose parental rights have been terminated and are in foster care, and made it easier to terminate parental rights. Although the change in policy may allow legislators to express moral disapproval of the system's previous mistakes, in the absence of committing adequate resources to permit proper care of children the ecological analogy gives us some confidence in predicting that a symbolic gesture without regard to resources may well end up making things worse.

It is easy to offer examples of concepts. Such an exercise should not be mistaken for solid evidence of the validity of the concepts nor of their utility in providing predictive guidelines. However, new concepts enable us to depart from conceptual ruts and to explore the universe of alternatives more thoroughly by encouraging us to roam over many different terrains in search of resources.

New concepts also ask us to view our research problems in a different way. The ecological viewpoint tells us that the behavior we observe may be at least in part an adaptation to a specific situation, and thus that the behavior we see in the clinic or the laboratory may work itself out in quite a different fashion in another setting.

The ecological perspective poses different questions: How do members of different populations adapt to their environments? When a deviant (variant) individual comes to our clinical attention, is that an isolated aberration, or are we perforce directed toward examining the environment to see what other populations share the same space, what nutrients are missing, what toxins are present that might be removed? In this perspective, each variant case represents a class of phenomena that challenges our current level of understanding.

Ecology and Values

The ecological perspective asks us to examine the researcher's (or intervenor's) social values and perspective as well as his or her methods and concepts. Textbook writers in community psychology clearly believe the field's purpose is to serve the underdog. (Redding, 2001, claims that this kind of liberal bias is characteristic of the social sciences.) This desire reflects compassion and a sense of social justice. Rappaport (1977) wrote that the professional work of community psychology is directed toward the implementation of "a more equitable, just and fair society."

Those aims are frankly political. Viewing mental health issues in terms of the redistribution of power and money provides congruence between those writers' scientific interests and their personal and political values, and is also congruent with community psychology's origins in the Kennedy-Johnson War on Poverty. When public resources were allocated for the benefit of the underdog, the social justice concept attracted many social scientists whose values resonated with that conception. They saw an opportunity to fulfill, in professional roles, their personal social and political values.

Environmental explanations for the causes of social misery were then prominent (see Levine & Levine, 1992). It was easy to accept the argument that poverty and the evils attendant upon poverty were associated with lack of opportunity and the failure of social agencies to serve those in the poverty group. According to this viewpoint, schools, welfare agencies, employers, landlords, and police acted in concert to deny or to minimize opportunity. Chronic mental illness was attributed, at least in part, to hospitals that were inadequate to their task of healing and structured in a manner designed to perpetuate maladaptation. Goffman (1961), calling hospitals "total institutions," saw patient behavior as not entirely the result of psychosis but instead an adaptation to life in the oppressive hospital. Szasz' (1974) attack on psychiatry as a threat to civil liberties added to the climate of the time. Championing social justice and the cause of the underdog could be accomplished through applications of science, and enabled social scientists to fulfill in professional roles the values they held as persons and citizens.

The ecological analogy is consistent with the values of democracy and equality, for it directs us to value diversity (Rappaport, 1977). It asserts that while populations may be different from each other in appearance, culturally speaking, they are not different when viewed as products of adaptation.

The concept of adaptation to available resources leads us to think not of inferior persons, but of persons whose characteristics must be understood in relation to the resources available in a niche, to the persons' ability to extend niche breadth by adapting, and to barriers to extending niche breadth due to competition from members of other populations. The ecological perspective stands in contrast to an hereditarian position which attributes variance in human behavior primarily to unchangeable genetic characteristics of individual organisms. Social ecology accepts that organismic characteristics set certain limits for development. Within those limits, however, the variance among organisms is strongly related to available resources and to necessary adaptations.

Just as a potted houseplant may be small while its brother in a tropical rain forest is huge, the ecological analogy suggests that the person in one setting, nurtured in one way and competing for resources, may be very different in another setting if nurtured differently, or if given different cultural tools for adaptation. The problems and limitations we face reside not in people but in the capacity of our imagination to envision and create new settings. Scientific principles thus blend with personal values in a political argument for resource redistribution, and with an ideology which at once does not blame the victim (Ryan, 1976) and expresses hope for a brighter future.

Ecology and Practice

The ecological analogy led Levine (1969) to propose five principles of practice in community psychology:

1. *A problem arises in a setting or in a situation; factors in the situation cause, trigger, exacerbate and/or maintain the problem.* This first principle indicates that we cannot direct our "diagnostic" efforts exclusively toward describing the characteristics of the individual person. We have to understand the characteristics of settings as well. We need to look for a lack of fit between persons and environments, for environmental "toxins," and for the possibility that with different resources in the set-

ting the individual's behavioral adaptation would be different. The principle also implies that we must leave our offices and learn to appreciate how problems are actually manifested in a given setting.

2. *A problem arises because the problem-resolving (i.e., adaptive) capacity of the social setting is blocked.* The ecological notion of interdependence implies that persons and settings function as parts of the same integrated system. A second principle implies that the adaptive capacity of people in a setting is limited in some ways by the nature of its social organization, or its access to resources. If we ask workers in any human service setting to describe problems they face in providing service to their clients, a number of problems will be described. If we then ask for solutions to the problems, a number of creative ones will be suggested. If we ask further why the solutions are not implemented, system problems will emerge. In effect, the principle states that a problem is that for which you do not have a solution. When you have a solution, adaptation will occur. Problems are thus understood differently using an ecological perspective. Because a problem requires adaptation, it is essentially an opportunity for short- and long-term change in the system.

3. *To be effective, help has to be located strategically to the manifestation of the problem.* The third principle also emphasizes the situational approach inherent in the ecological analogy. It suggests that we should alter our view of how help is to be delivered. Rather than send the person to help, the principle suggests we should bring help to the person, or more precisely to the setting in which the person is defined as a problem. The term "strategically" can have temporal as well as spatial referents, which helps us to think of *when* in the course of the development of a problem it would be useful to deliver assistance. The ecological analogy suggests that we examine environmental circumstances, while Dohrenwend's model (chapter 3) introduces the dimension of time. This principle suggests that the design of helping services should make use of both the spatial and the temporal dimensions of a problem.

Modern day crisis intervention programs for the seriously and persistently mentally ill operate on this principle (see Box 2–2 on Assertive Community Treatment). Henggeler et al. (1998) developed multisystemic therapy, a program built on ecological principles designed to serve delinquent and violent adolescents. The program includes family counseling, individual counseling, a group experience involving counseling and recreational activities, and consultation on a regular basis with social agency and school personnel. In other words, the intervention seeks to have a presence in each of the systems affecting the youth—home and family, neighborhood, and school. The various interventions support each other because the workers know what is happening in each setting where intervention occurs. Moreover, when the program ends, an aftercare arrangement may be developed that may include periodic family or group sessions, with the primary counselor continuously available to deal with periodic crises. Henggeler et al. (1998) demonstrated considerable validity for this approach in carefully controlled studies. He and his colleagues are now disseminating the approach in a number of sites nationally.

4. *The goals and values of the helping agent or service must be consistent with the goals and values of the setting.* Settings have both latent and manifest purposes. If the goals of change are consistent with the latent and manifest purposes of the setting, the change process will not stimulate resistance on those grounds. If the essential values of the change agent conflict with values in the setting then the agent can expect opposition, including efforts to block the change or to extrude the agent. For example, a change agent may be able to justify on mental health and prevention grounds a course on sex education and the art of love, including supervised laboratory experiences. However, no high school in the country would allow such a program because of the conflict in values and goals that would be introduced. A change agent proposing such a project would undoubtedly be extruded from the setting, if not worse.

Some argue that conflict is essential to change, and that conflict should be used consciously to induce change. That may be so. The error is in *not* anticipating conflict or in misunderstanding its basis. This principle calls attention to the issue.

The principle also requires the change agent to confront the potential conflict between his or her values and the values of those in a setting. Suppose, for example, that the Ku Klux Klan (KKK) wanted help in improving communications among their own members so that they could more efficiently carry out attempts to terrorize or to intimidate various minority groups. They approach a university center for help. Staff members might have the technical skills to help the KKK improve communication and develop as an organization. Should the center accept the assignment? Essentially the same problem is posed if the change agent is asked to help improve the adjustment of prisoners to an oppressive institution or schoolchildren to a rigid or sterile school program, or to help develop methods to uncover welfare mothers who may earn some extra money doing housework without reporting the income to the welfare worker. Change may be accomplished using knowledge and methods that appear to be value free, but not all changes are equally desirable, and a request for help in achieving change may force the change agent to confront his or her own values (Sarason, 1978).

5. *The form of help should have potential for being established on a systematic basis, using the natural resources of the setting, or through introducing resources which can become institutionalized as part of the setting.* The fifth principle suggests that one should strive to understand the nature of resources and how a community cycles its resources. The

principle implies that one would prefer introducing a change which endures, and continues to help resolve problems in a particular setting. Using the ideas of interdependence and succession is the key to achieving truly long-term preventive effects through programs. Head Start is a good example of programs which become permanent niches in their communities, so that parents and other citizens become full participants (see chapter 8).

These principles establish a framework for conceptualization and action in community psychology, and foreshadow a number of important issues to be taken up in the chapters that follow, including assessment, intervention, community change, and research.

Summary

Community psychology is founded on a point of view perhaps best represented by the ecological analogy. This analogy is explicit in its endorsement of certain values, and raises important implications regarding the conduct of scientific research. As a conceptual paradigm ecology deals with units larger than the single individual, emphasizes natural settings rather than laboratories or clinics as the most valid and appropriate locus of intervention and research, and conceptualizes research as an ongoing, longitudinal collaboration between the researcher and the residents and settings of the community.

Four principles are fundamental to the ecological perspective. The first holds that, because the people and settings within a community are interdependent, change occurs in a social system, not just an individual, and thus a variety of different problem definitions and solutions are possible in any situation. Second, community systems are defined by resource exchanges among persons and settings involving commodities such as time, money, and political power. Third, the behavior we observe in a particular individual always reflects a continuous process of adaptation between that individual, and his or her level of competence, and the environment, with the nature and range of competence it supports. Adaptation can be affected by changing the environment as well as changing the person. Fourth, change occurs naturally in a community, as well as by intentional design, and change represents an opportunity to redefine and reallocate resources in ways that facilitate adaptation by all populations in the community.

We offered an extended illustration of these principles in describing how the deinstitutionalization of mental health consumers from hospitals to community settings forced law enforcement and justice officials to work alongside mental health professionals in unexpected ways and with unanticipated results. All parties concerned were affected, including the consumers and their families. The generality of the principles was suggested by a second detailed illustration con-

cerning consequences which followed the adoption of a new law affecting the placement of children at risk for maltreatment. The chapter closed by summarizing the values embodied in the ecological analogy and presenting five principles of practice derived from the
metaphor of ecology.

We conclude on the point that the ultimate usefulness of the ecological analogy for theory, research, or intervention remains to be demonstrated. It is an analogy useful only at the most general level, and it
has not yet been employed in rigorous study, even within its own
terms. Not much has been done as yet in designing interventions using ecological principles, although some research (e.g., Kelly, 1979) has
been reported on issues relevant to general questions in this field. Other
conceptions and the research associated with them are examined in the
next chapter. Although in sum ecology remains largely a metaphor, it
is a metaphor which may yet open our minds to new approaches to a
variety of problems.

Notes

1. See also Belsky (1980) and National Research Council (1993) for a discussion of the use of these concepts to guide research on child maltreatment.

2. Psychology broke away from philosophy in the late nineteenth century
after the natural sciences had succeeded theology and the humanities as the
dominant populations in the university community. The victory was so complete that the ideology of science and its language were adopted by traditional
fields, even law (Auerbach, 1976). The justification for separating psychology
from philosophy was that its mission, methods, and needs for laboratory space
and scientific equipment differed from those in philosophy. By going into the
laboratory, and modeling their field on the physical sciences, psychologists
concentrated on the individual and failed to study the individual in context.

5

Five Psychological Conceptions of the Environment

In chapter 4 we concluded that the ecological perspective on human behavior has important theoretical and political implications for community psychologists. Kelly's (1966) four ecological principles and Levine's (1969) five principles of intervention, however, are more abstract than they are specific. The metaphor of ecology tells us to recognize and attend to context without directly helping us identify what the important contextual factors are. Scientific advances and effective practical applications require sharper conceptualization of the operational units making up human environments. In this chapter, we expand on the idea that people do not exist in a vacuum by presenting some of the specific characteristics of social and physical environments, or settings, that influence human behavior and well-being. We acknowledge individual differences in this chapter, but we also emphasize that the roles people fulfill and their relationships with others and with important settings in their life *are* their lives. It is one thing to know that an individual is extraverted. It is another to appreciate how roles and settings influence the expression of that individual characteristic. It is still another to think about how to create settings and roles that facilitate or impede the expression of specific characteristics.

What details are left out of the orientation provided in chapter 4? The ecological analogy leads us to examine the various environments in which people live, work, and play to better understand their behavior. It suggests that problems and their solutions be defined in situational terms. This implies a need to identify explicitly the specific characteristics of situations that are relevant to problems of adaptation. But *how* do you examine the environment? By what mechanisms do settings facilitate changes in behavior? By what processes does a person adapt to a setting (or vice versa)? Theoretical conceptions are needed that offer more detailed descriptions of these effects.

Our classification schemes for settings are crude. Labels such as "foster home" or "group home" tell us little about size, staffing, rehabilitative focus, or quality of care. They tell us little about the program or about how the program facilitates or impedes the development of helpful relationships between staff and resident. Such settings as schools (Sarason & Klaber, 1985) or Head Start preschools (Lubeck, DeVries, Nicholson, & Post, 1997) are not uniform by any means. If settings of a similar kind produce different outcomes for children, what characteristics of settings account for the difference? If we believe in the concept of a person-environment fit, then how can we characterize settings so that we can evaluate who would do better in one setting than in another? A given setting is also occupied by people who have different relationships to it. Leader, members, children, teachers, research workers, and so on, all have different roles, different objectives for participating, and very likely different views of what goes on in the setting. Settings also change over time. How can we understand, track, and evaluate changes in the characteristics of settings?

These questions are useful in setting the stage for a review of some current conceptions of the psychological environment. Moos (1973) identified six approaches to conceptualizing and assessing human environments, including "reinforcement consequences" (rewards and punishments; which we touched on briefly in chapter 2), organizational structure (which we will discuss in chapter 10), and group characteristics (e.g., race/ethnicity, income, education, age, health, aggregated into a profile of one's group or community). The present chapter focuses on the other three conceptions Moos identified, including his own "perceived social climate" of organizations approach, physical environmental influences, and Roger Barker's "behavior-setting theory," plus two other well-known theoretical perspectives: Theodore Sarbin's "role theory" and various *community* psychological concepts related to the sociological construct of "*social capital.*" First, we will review the three social theories, then influences of both the built and natural physical environment, concluding with behavior-setting theory, which theoretically attends to both the social and physical environment. Finally, the community lodge program developed by George W. Fairweather and associates is presented and used to illustrate the perspectives in practical terms.

Social Environmental Influences on Behavior and Well-Being

Perceived Social Climates

Henry Murray's seminal work on personality theory (Murray, 1938) presented a model of behavior based on relative degrees of fit between what he called individual *needs,* for example the need to achieve or to affiliate with others, and environmental *presses.* Presses refer to characteristics of a setting that make it more likely that satisfaction of a need will be facilitated or impeded. Considerable effort has gone into developing instruments that measure the individual personality needs identified by Murray. It remained to Moos and his associates (Moos, 1976), however, to develop a corresponding set of scales assessing the behavioral presses of key community environments.

Assumptions. The underlying assumptions of Moos's (1979) approach are that (1) we can think of environments as having "personalities," achievement-oriented, interpersonally supportive, or controlling, and (2) these setting personalities can be measured using the same methods used to assess the personalities of people. In Moos's approach one simply asks the participants in a given setting to respond "true" or "false" to a set of declarative statements describing what it is like to be in that setting. The responses of all participants are then averaged to obtain a single profile (generally presented in terms of standard scores) describing the "perceived social climate" of the setting. These measures are a way of objectifying the characteristic responses people make to that environment.

Recognizing that such quantitative information would be useful for a broad range of natural community settings, Moos and his colleagues have developed specific social climate scales for psychiatric wards, community-oriented programs, family environments, work settings, classrooms, residence halls, military organizations, correctional facilities, and sheltered care settings for the elderly.

Basic dimensions. Moos believes that the key psychological aspects of any human environment are represented in three dimensions in all perceived social climate measures: *relationship-oriented dimensions, personal-development dimensions,* and *system-maintenance and change dimensions.* The specific subscales, or dimensions of environmental press, vary somewhat in the instruments used to measure perceived social climate in a family, in a work setting, or in a psychiatric ward. In the Family Environment Scale, for example, the specific relationship dimensions include *cohesiveness* (e.g., "Family members really help and support one another") and *conflict* ("We fight a lot in our family"); the personal development dimensions include *independence* ("Family members almost always rely on themselves when a problem comes up") and *achievement* ("We feel it is important to be the best at whatever you do"), and the system dimensions are *organization* ("Activities in our family are pretty carefully planned") and *control* ("There is a strong emphasis on following rules in our family").

Construct validity. Considerable data have been accumulated on the construct validity of Moos' scales (see Moos, 1976, 1987). For example, occupants of settings high in relationship-oriented dimensions show high satisfaction and self-esteem, low anxiety, depression, and irritability (Moos, 1976), and low amounts of physical complaints (Moos & Van Dort, 1979). Members of settings high in personal-development dimensions have more positive attitudes and higher skill acquisition, but in some cases they also exhibit greater tension (Trickett & Moos, 1974). A complex stimulus such as a school classroom can have unwanted as well as wanted effects. In schools, high order and clarity on the systems and maintenance dimension are associated with high satisfaction, while high degrees on the control dimension are associated with dissatisfaction and other negative outcomes.

Applications. Moos's social-climate scales have several useful applications in community psychology. One of these is to clearly describe and compare settings. For example, although mutual help groups are believed by their advocates to serve some of the same functions as professionally led therapy groups, do these differ from each other? Toro, Rappaport, and Seidman (1987) compared profiles from Moos's Group Environment Scale for 33 mutual help groups in the GROW organization (see chapter 9) with those of 25 insight-oriented professionally led therapy groups serving the same general clientele. GROW groups were perceived as more structured, task-oriented, and cohesive than professionally led therapy groups, while the latter were more flexible and more tolerant of members expressing anger and other intense emotions. Clarifying such differences in focus between helping alternatives can assist our understanding and may facilitate more appropriate referrals.

As an example of classification, consider the increasing visibility and importance of sheltered care settings (nursing homes, congregate apartments) for the elderly. Because sheltered care settings differ in relevant social climate characteristics, Lemke and Moos (1987) developed the Sheltered Care Environment Scale as a practical, efficient method of assessing relationship-oriented, personal growth, and system maintenance and change dimensions in such settings. Timko and Moos (1991) cluster analyzed Sheltered Care Environment Scale profiles from a national sample of 235 nursing homes, residential care facilities, and congregate apartments, identifying six distinct types of social climate in these settings. Two types of climates were labeled "supportive," and differed primarily in how much resident influence existed; two other types of climates emphasized "conflict" (one allowed open conflict and one tended to suppress conflict). Figure 5–1 compares the profiles for

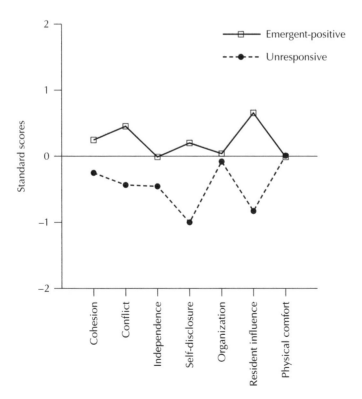

Figure 5–1. Mean Sheltered Care Environment profiles for emergent-positive and unresponsive facility clusters. (From Timko & Moos, 1991)

the remaining two types of settings, identified by Timko and Moos as "emergent-positive" and "unresponsive."

The climate in the emergent-positive settings is high in resident influence and emphasizes cohesion, conflict, and open disclosure of personal feelings. By comparison, the climate of unresponsive settings puts relatively little emphasis on resident influence, independence, and self-disclosure, and thus is low in responsiveness to residents' preferences. Emergent-positive and unresponsive facilities were both more likely to be nursing homes than less intensive kinds of care providers, did not differ in either typical size or nature of ownership, and were perceived by residents as average in degree of organization and physical comfort. However, residents in emergent-positive facilities scored higher on measures of well-being than did residents in unresponsive settings. These findings support the importance of factors such as resident self-direction. They also show the advantage of using comprehensive profiles rather than relying on single dimensions (such as physical comfort) to assess programs. It allows planners, administrators, and researchers of new programs or supportive interventions to test the effects of different psychological characteristics of the residential setting.

A second practical application of the perceived social climate approach is in evaluating the effects of consultation services or other setting interventions. A useful tactic at the outset of consultation, for example, is to have setting participants complete the relevant social climate scale twice, once as they currently perceive the setting and again as they would ideally like it to be. The two profiles can then be compared. Any disparities between them indicate characteristics of the psychological environment that deserve attention. Consultation sessions can then be devoted to discovering what influences the disparities and how change might be achieved. Later the scale can be readministered as a method of evaluating the outcome of consultation. If both real and ideal forms are again used, any remaining real-ideal discrepancies can form the basis for further consultation.

DeYoung (1977), for example, administered real and ideal forms of the Classroom Environment Scale (CES) to an undergraduate social science class. Discrepancies between the real and ideal profiles indicated that students wanted to be more involved in the class, experience more innovative teaching methods, and understand more clearly the organization of the course and the instructor's expectations. The next term DeYoung modified the course to include more individual contact with students, a more explicit grading policy, and group projects and other innovative forms of classroom participation by students. He readministered the real and ideal forms of the CES to evaluate the effect of the changes. Although the ideal climate did not change noticeably from one term to the next, students' perceptions of the actual classroom environment more closely resembled the ideal profile on each of the specific dimensions targeted for intervention. Furthermore, the changes during the second term were associated with greater student interest, participation, and attendance.

A third use of Moos's scales is in setting selection to maximize person-environment fit, for example, when deciding on a residential placement for someone with special needs. People who have serious mental illness represent a diverse population, but community-based group homes are not standardized by any means. Differences in size, structure, programming, and social climate may have significant implications for the levels and sources of stress and support experienced by people living in them.

Downs and Fox (1993) obtained responses to Moos's Community-Oriented Programs Environment Scale (COPES) from staff members at 49 diverse group homes for adults with mental illness. They used a statistical technique called cluster analysis to categorize the 49 homes into four groups on the basis of differences among the COPES profiles. On these measures, the first group, or cluster, of homes provided little support, structure, and staff involvement to individual residents, while those in the second cluster tended to be stimulating and goal-oriented for residents. Cluster 3 homes supported spontaneous expressions of feeling among residents without granting them a great deal of autonomy, and Cluster 4 homes were highly structured but did not provide programs for the personal development of residents.

Given these systematic variations among homes in social climates, choice of a group home placement might usefully be based on the fit likely between a prospective resident's needs and the social climates of available homes. For example, a goal-oriented person tolerant of high levels of stimulation would probably respond better to a Cluster 2 home than a Cluster 1 home, while an outspoken resident who had difficulty dealing with structure would adapt more easily to a Cluster 3 home than a Cluster 4 home. Similarly, a setting high on the personal development dimension might appeal to a young college student recovering from mental illness but might distress a much older person who wished to be left alone. Measurement using the COPES makes it possible to base a residential placement on the fit between a resident's personality and a home's social climate, as well as on relevant physical characteristics such as the home's size or location.

Use in planning and setting creation. Last, perceived social climate scales can be used in the planning and creation of new settings in the community. Those responsible for developing a new mental health center program, for example, could use the COPES to develop a shared conception of what the optimum social climate in the new setting would be. The ecological prescription that all points of view be represented in the data used to understand a setting could be addressed by obtaining separate profiles from line workers, supervisors, members of the administrative support staff, and other workers.

Settings can be designed to accomplish certain purposes by thinking through the desirable organization according to the COPES dimensions. If staff "burnout" is likely to be a problem, for example, a high degree of interpersonal support among staff members will be desirable. Regular meetings of a peer support group made up of program staff to enhance the relationship aspects of the setting might be planned for the program right from the start. Once the new program is under way, the COPES might then be readministered as a means of evaluating the social climate present in the setting and guiding adjustments in the program as necessary.

Practical advantages. Moos's perceived social climate concept has many practical applications. Its chief advantage over other approaches is probably the ease with which the relevant information can be collected and interpreted. However, to answer the items meaningfully, the respondents must have regular face-to-face contact, and the number of respondents must not be too large (no more than 20 to 25) in order to maximize member agreement about the group profile. Of course, the profiles generated by these instruments are not objective descriptions of the environment. They are subjectively *perceived* climates based on specific circumstances and events, respondents' roles or positions in the setting, and their personal beliefs and values (Lemke & Moos, 1987).

Setting taxonomies are being developed using this concept, although the focus thus far has been on types of settings such as psychiatric wards (Price & Moos, 1975), high school classrooms (Trickett, 1978), and special residential programs, instead of on the spatial and temporal distribution of setting climates as they occur in people's lives. In general, this view presents one of the clearest illustrations available of how psychologists can take seriously the need to assess and understand characteristics of key community environments as well as of the people inhabiting them. It assists people in "tuning in" to the social climates surrounding them (Moos, 1979). From an ecological perspective, it takes seriously the perceptions and experiences of rank-and-file participants in a setting or program and helps empower people to participate more widely in the process of community assessment and change.

Social Roles

The concept of a role provides another basis for defining the relationship between an individual person and his or her social environment. Roles relate to the functional significance of people in different contexts and thus may be more useful in diagnosing problems of adaptation and in designing interventions than concepts centered on individuals (Sarbin, 1970). Role theory is also a useful bridge between the discussion of the basic ecological analogy in community psychology and our analysis of labeling theory in the next chapter.

Sarbin introduces his version of role theory by arguing that *environment* is too vague a construct to be useful for community psychologists. The concept of *setting* is somewhat more defined, but lacks a social dimension. In Sarbin's view the environment is a set of differentiated "ecologies" within which people must correctly locate themselves to survive and to thrive. He identified four ecologies: *self-maintenance, social* (or the role system), *normative,* and *transcendental.*

Self-maintenance ecology. To survive as a biosocial organism, an individual must recognize the difference between friend and foe, between the edible and the poisonous, between potentially hostile and potentially benign circumstances. Upon encountering a new object or person, an individual quickly runs through such questions as: Should I run from, attack, or ignore this new object? Can I play with it, eat it, have sex with it, or make use of it in some other fashion? In addition to perceptual reality testing, social reality testing is also necessary. Are the social conditions appropriate for the activity I would like to select? Am I the appropriate person to engage in such activities in this situation? Incorrect answers to these questions result in dysfunctional conduct and could land the individual in a mental hospital, an institution for the retarded, or prison. Socially "correct" answers to these questions depend on one's socialization, education, and having the mental and moral capacity to accurately judge often ambiguous situations.

Social (role system) ecology. The second ecology is the social ecology or role system. The question to be answered is, "Who am I in relation to you, in this situation?" A man is king if others bow down and recognize his authority. If he calls himself king and others do not recognize his authority, under many circumstances he is considered a madman. Role relationships are reciprocal. Answers to the question, "Who am I in relation to you?" or the question asked by another, "Who are you?" define one's social identity (Turner, 1999). Failures (in terms of one's behavior) to answer these questions properly (that is, in accord with mutual expectations) lead to conflict and breakdown in social relationships. When Alfred Kinsey and his colleagues were interviewing thousands of Americans about their sex histories, one of Kinsey's interviewers appeared in a young psychology intern's office when the intern expected a psychotherapy client. This particular "client" turned the normal therapy relationship upside down by interrogating the therapist about intimate details of the therapist's sex life, an experience that reportedly sent this novice therapist screaming from the office!

Entrance into and recognition of appropriate roles also depend on opportunities. For example, social rules—gender, racial discrimination, or stigma—may prevent some individuals from entering some roles or from receiving acceptance in those roles. Changing social rules, by changing laws, by engaging in conflict and confrontation, or by changing incentives, can open up a greater variety of roles for those who were formerly denied them. In addition to examining the socialization of people for particular roles, Sarbin's position allows us to examine the opportunities for entering into given roles as well and to work to change those rules.

Normative ecology. The third ecology is the normative. Here one asks how *well* one is meeting the particular requirements of a given role. The answer, "Not too well" is often accompanied by low self-esteem, and the answer, "Pretty good" by a more positive sense of satisfaction. The answers to these questions are based partly on self-evaluations and partly on the feedback received from others. For example, even experienced college teachers sometimes feel, based on their own expectations or the behavior and attitudes shown by their students, that a course or a particular lecture is not going well. A perception that such difficulties are occurring more and more frequently may encourage the instructor to avoid that material or that course in the future, or in some cases may even cause the professor to consider retirement.

As shown in this last example, attributions for the "cause" of failure may vary. Under some circumstances, people engage in self-blame, and under others the cause of failure is seen to reside in factors beyond the individual's control. At one and the same time, an individual may believe that the cause of failure (or success) resides in his or her own efforts, while an external observer views the cause as situational in nature. The reverse may also be true, of course. We must recognize the implications of different perspectives, for the solution chosen will depend on how the problem is defined. How we perceive and value our accomplishments, or devalue ourselves for perceived failures, depends in part on the normative framework we adopt. It may also depend on the system of values we hold, and our system of values depends in substantial part upon our participation in social relationships with others who share those values. We shall see how those issues work themselves out when we examine self-help groups in chapter 9.

Transcendental ecology. Sarbin's fourth ecology, called transcendental ecology, consists of abstractions that give meaning to life. For some people, the important abstraction is the relationship to a deity. For others, it may be an existential issue: Given that death is inevitable, how am I spending my life? For still others at different ages, the question may be one of integrity, to use Erikson's (1950) term—the acceptance of one's life-style and the willingness to defend it against attack by others or by the vicissitudes of life. In other words, we need to achieve and maintain a sense of order, meaning, and continuity to our experiences. We gain that sense through a set of beliefs that help us come to terms with ourselves and with events in the world. As we shall see, one of the important outcomes of participating in a mutual assistance group is the development of a way of thinking about one's condition (that is, an ideology) and a concrete program for coping with everyday problems (e.g., a 12-step program). Such beliefs are best developed and maintained by our participation in social groups, and to be part of a group means one has a role within that group. One may be born into the role, as a family member, one may choose to participate in it, as a member of a political party, or one may earn a position within a group through accomplishment and effort.

Role dominance. People continuously strive to locate themselves within the four ecologies. Everyone has many roles, for example, and participates with many different social groups. Furthermore, the nature of most behavior in a social setting is much more a function of the given roles being performed than of the individuals performing them (Katz & Kahn, 1978). Over the sum of their behavior as members of a given psychology class, for example, individual students are much more alike than they are different; each will go through the complicated process of registering for the course within the time specified; buying the required books; reading and studying the various assignments; attending class meetings; and completing tests, papers, and any other requirements for the course (i.e., roles can involve multiple settings). The instructor's role has a similarly constraining effect on the nature and range of his or her behavior. The most efficient way to describe any person's behavior in the context of this course is thus based on the role he or she occupies, not the person's individual characteristics.

Roles are coercive in their influence on behavior, because people exert considerable behavioral effort to maintain their eligibility for certain roles (e.g., medical students and athletes spend long hours in training). Loss of roles is a serious threat to people, because most communities require their members to maintain stable role performance or run the risk of being labeled some sort of deviant. Minor criminal offenses such as loitering and vagrancy, and psychiatric diagnoses such as depression and mental retardation, are applied at least in part on the basis of the individual's failure to perform adequately a sufficient number of socially required roles.

In practice every adult is called on to perform many different roles, and not all of them are necessarily compatible. Roles conflict with each other when they limit the person's behavioral choices in a mutually exclusive way. For a woman who is strongly career oriented, for example, the birth of a first child, with its intense and anxiety-producing demands, can seriously divide her attention and lead to strongly mixed emotions. If performance of a given role limits choices in some cases, it also protects them in many others. People whose roles bring them substantial incomes, for example, can qualify for mortgages and loans to purchase homes and other expensive possessions, even when they have little or no money currently on hand.

One issue for the community psychologist is thus the availability of adequate numbers of roles (e.g., jobs) and settings in a community, given the number of people who live there. Beyond mere availability, however, the ecological perspective directs us to examine the degree of fit between the available roles and each individual's behavioral propensities, social aspirations, beliefs, and other role-related characteristics. Does a small college town have a sufficient number of suitable jobs for the professionally trained spouses of new faculty? Does an inner-city neighborhood have an adequate number of organized athletic programs for the interested young people there? Does a community have enough organized opportunities for newcomers to meet other residents and learn about the community?

Role importance. Not all roles have equal importance, either to the individual holding them or to others. Sarbin proposes that the relative contribution of different roles to an individual's social identity can be determined by examining each role along three dimensions: status, value, and involvement. *Status* refers to one's position in a social structure, for example, parent or child, student or instructor, army general or private, and so on. *Value* concerns the positive or negative evaluations attached to performance, or failure to perform, in a role. When you complete a course evaluation form, for example, you are "grading" the instructor just as he or she graded your work in the course. *Involvement* refers to the degree of participation in the role as measured both by time spent in it and by energy expended in performing it. For example, a police officer may always be on duty, carrying a firearm and obligated to arrest anyone he or she finds using an illegal drug. (A news story once told of a police captain who arrested his own daughter for drug dealing.)

Ascribed and achieved statuses. Sarbin further differentiated the status dimension into two types, ascribed and achieved. *Ascribed* statuses are those that are biosocial in nature. We enter those statuses with little contribution on our parts, and we can do little about changing them (e.g., age, sex, kinship, or race). *Achieved* statuses are those about which we have some degree of choice, often a great deal. For most people the most important achieved status is their occupation.

At a minimum, each individual is granted the status of a person, which entitles the individual to certain minimum rights no matter what his or her circumstances are. People in prisons or in mental hospitals, no matter how disturbed, are granted certain minimum rights regarding the way others may treat them. They can't be beaten, starved, or killed by official action. They should have minimum basic food and shelter. With achieved statuses, on the other hand, the individual is granted a great deal of power and social esteem. The president of the United States or the board chairperson of a major corporation exercises a great deal of power and receives much esteem from others.

Sarbin points out that we receive little positive valuation for minimally adequate performance in ascribed roles such as mother or father, male or female, for such performance is expected. To fail in such roles brings considerable social opprobrium, however. A neglectful mother may have her children taken away from her and under some circumstances may be prosecuted for criminal behavior. A good mother may be lucky to receive a Mother's Day card in some families. In contrast, no matter how poorly it is performed, an achieved role constitutes a basis for some esteem. Accepting a U. S. president's denigration of the accomplishments of his predecessor, for example, might lead us to consider the predecessor a complete failure in his role as president. Yet a former president receives many "perks" and is accorded the greatest respect when he arrives at a public gathering. The same is true for almost any occupation. Having had an occupational title earns some social points, almost no matter what else is true of your performance in that occupation. If you have a job, you are someone. If you don't and you should (i.e., you are not disabled, the beneficiary of a trust fund, or excused in some other fashion) you are considered a loafer or a bum. Sarbin also says that the degree of involvement will vary with the type of status. We are always involved in our ascribed statuses, whereas we can more easily step in and out of other statuses. However, we may have great difficulty escaping from some achieved roles, such as prisoner or "bag lady," even for brief periods.

Technological change may create complications when ascribed roles such as *sex* conflict with social roles such as *gender*. With the advent of sex reassignment surgery and treatment, we now have transsexuals who were born one sex but became another sex. Transsexuals assume the apearance and manners of the reassigned sex. Can we consider that they have now achieved a new gender? When a transsexual wishes to marry, and the law states that marriage is between one man and one woman, would such a person be considered a member of the birth sex (ascribed status) or a member of the reassigned sex (achieved status)? (See *Kantaras* v. *Kantaras*, 2003; see also pp. 216–17.)

Degraded social identity. Sarbin argues that persons with degraded social identities are those with few opportunities to enact roles that are entered by choice. The best such a person can hope for is to attain a neutral valued social identity if he or she meets all the expectations for whatever makes up his or her predominant ascribed status. In a sense, one can say that the best an individual with a degraded social identity can expect is to be ignored. The social relationships of persons with degraded social identities are often limited to those with similar identities, and in many cases their networks include a large proportion of persons who are paid to take care of them—doctors, nurses, social workers, jailers.

Sarbin's analysis is interesting, for it suggests additional avenues for assessment and intervention. To help persons with degraded social identities, for example, role theory suggests increasing the variety of roles and social relationships available to such persons and working to promote positive social esteem and value for all roles, including ascribed ones (e.g., "old" people). Behavior-setting theory (see below) offers useful methods for identifying roles and describing their behavioral content. Given that achieved roles are typically enacted as part of specific settings, the Johnny Appleseed approach to fostering the proliferation of new settings, which require leaders and members to staff them (described below in the section on behavior settings), offers one practical strategy for increasing the pool of achieved roles. Creating jobs, for example, even within sheltered settings, may be an important means of helping to undo a degraded social identity. For some persons (e.g., those with serious mental illness or retardation) who find the work or volunteer roles available to them in the community ambiguous or unsettling, individualized training and support can help clarify the obligations and behavioral expectations necessary to achieve and maintain these roles. Organizing support and advocacy groups or clubs, with roles such as president, secretary, or committee chairperson, also helps to upgrade social identities. Such clubs may even provide, if not a full ideology, at least a partial ideology to serve as a guide to behavioral conduct, to articulate some values, and to support the individual's self-esteem. Participation in self-help groups that admit to membership persons who are otherwise isolated helps to undo social degradation. Some people are able to find important positions of leadership in such organizations and can, to some extent, rebuild their social identities around participation in them (see chapter 9). All these efforts have as their goal an increase in the number of role choices available to community residents and a decrease in the amount of role conflict taking place.

Related concepts. Role theory implies a mechanism of role congruence in explaining how an individual's behavior, cognitions, and identity change and how these changes are maintained over time. Some recognition of the importance of person-environment fit (the need for available roles to match the individual's goals and values) is also present. However, Sarbin's conception makes little use of person-centered factors. It does not explain, for example (if the position stated by Alcoholics Anonymous is correct), why the alcohol abuser begins the process of recovery at the very moment he or she accepts what is otherwise an extremely ascribed and degraded role: that of alcoholic (see chapter 9).

Sarbin's use of roles is related to Seidman's (1990) concept of "social regularities," which are reciprocal relationships and interdependencies between settings, people, and outcomes that show consistent and predictable patterns over time. Social regularities, which Seidman considers fundamental to assessment and change in community psychology, extend the notion of a role in two important ways. First, a social regularity often encompasses more than one individual's relationship to a setting; it may relate settings to other settings and implicate broad power and resource inequalities, and it also includes the psychosocial outcomes that result. Second, the complexity and characteristic stability of these relationships over time explains why changing a community or even a setting can be so difficult.

Sarbin's role theory offers a conception complementary to those of Moos and the others in this chapter in defining a unit commensurate with the individual person that can also encompass many different settings at the community level. Both role theory and Seidman's social regularities leave unanswered the question of how a community psychologist participates directly in the creation of jobs and other achieved roles: in what types of roles and in which settings can the community psychologist participate in creating roles for others? The project described below offers one example.

Social Capital: Community Cognitions, Behaviors and Networks[1]

The concept of *social capital* grew out of the sociology of education (Bourdieu, 1985) but has spread to the rest of the social sciences. It has been defined as the norms of reciprocity and mutual trust ("bonding" relationships) in civil society that facilitate cooperative action ("bridging" relationships) among networks of citizens and institutions (Putnam, 2000). Although psychology has been much slower to embrace the term social capital, community psychologists have studied individual-level aspects of it extensively, but using other terminology. Social capital at the individual level consists of both informal, community-focused attitudes or cognitions (sense of community) and behaviors (neighboring), as well as cognitions (collective efficacy—or empowerment) and behaviors (citizen participation) relevant to the creation, maintenance, and efficacy of formally organized voluntary associations for direct action, advocacy, and community service (Perkins & Long, 2002). Psychological factors point to what motivates individuals to participate in particular settings and behaviors, how to maintain that participation, and how those motivations and behaviors interact with various setting and organizational characteristics to promote effective social capital.

Two of the first psychologists to study social capital measured it in terms of informal neighboring behaviors and formally organized community participation and leadership activity and found that social capital predicted the revitalization and upkeep of distressed inner-city housing (Saegert & Winkel, 1998). To those formal (bridging) and informal (bonding) *behaviors*, Perkins and Long (2002) added two *cognitive* components, both popular in community psychology: *Empowerment* is about the development of a sense of collective efficacy, or control over the institutions that affect one's life and community. *Sense of community* is an attitude of mutual trust and belonging with other members of one's group or locale. Adding the idea of formal and informal community "trust"—or a cognitive (perceptual and meaning-making) dimension—to formal and informal pro-social community behaviors results in a two-by-two framework for social capital at the individual, psychological level (see Figure 5–2). Each dimension of individual-level social capital is distinct but related to the others.

Psychological sense of community (informal-cognition cell of Figure 5–2) was defined by Sarason (1974) as "the sense that one was part of a readily available, mutually supportive network of relationships upon which one could depend and as a result of which one did not experience sustained feelings of loneliness that impel one to actions or to adopting a style of living masking anxiety and setting the stage for later more destructive anguish" (p. 1). McMillan and Chavis' (1986) four dimensions relate to three of the above four components of social capital: group membership and shared emotional connection (informal-cognition), mutual influence (collective efficacy), and fulfillment of needs (neighboring). Others have narrowed the definition of sense of community to social connections, mutual concerns, and community values (Perkins & Long, 2002) or offered a more dynamic perspective that captures community change in terms of shared history, common symbols, and ongoing development (Fisher & Sonn, 2002).

Sense of community has been studied by researchers in many different countries, including Australia (Fisher & Sonn, 2002), Canada (Pretty, 1990), Israel (Itzhaky & York, 2000), Italy (Prezza, Amici, Roberti, & Tedeschi, 2001), Taiwan (Li, 1998), the United Kingdom (Sampson, 1991), the United States, and Venezuela (Garcia, Giuliani, & Wiesenfeld, 1999). It is a widely valued indicator of quality of community life (Brodsky et al., 1999) and a consistent catalyst for both behavioral dimensions of social capital: organized participation and in-

	Cognition/Trust	Social Behavior
Informal	Sense of community	Neighboring
Formally Organized	Collective efficacy/ Empowerment	Citizen participation

Figure 5–2. Four Dimensions Of Individual-level Social Capital. (From Perkins & Long, 2002)

formal neighboring (Perkins & Long, 2002). Participation, in turn, may enhance sense of community (Hughey, Speer, & Peterson, 1999). Sense of community has also been linked with empowerment, in both the organizational (Speer, Jackson & Peterson, 2001) and neighborhood contexts (Perkins & Long, 2002).

Other correlates of sense of community include community satisfaction, local friendships, and informal social control (Perkins et al., 1990), residential social climate and well-being (Pretty, 1990), investment in one's home (Garcia et al., 1999), the physical condition of one's block (Perkins et al., 1990), more life satisfaction and less loneliness (Prezza et al., 2001) and fear of crime (Perkins et al., 1990). Environmental design researchers have studied the influence of common land (Li, 1998), green space (Kuo, Sullivan, Coley, & Brunson, 1998), and town planning (Plas & Lewis, 1996) on sense of community (see "Physical Environmental Influences," below). Recent research has examined adolescents' sense of community and found that the organization and activities of schools (Bateman, 2002), as well as places to congregate outside of school (Pretty, 2002), are critical factors in the development of sense of community, which may lead to lifelong commitments to community and service.

Collective efficacy (or *empowerment*; formal-cognition cell of Figure 5–2), or trust in the effectiveness of organized community action, has been an extremely influential concept in community psychology and beyond (see special issues related to empowerment of *Prevention in Human Services* in 1984 and *American Journal of Community Psychology* in 1990, 1994, and 1995). Empowerment has been defined as a process by which people gain control over their lives and their community (Rappaport, 1987) and gain a critical understanding of their environment (Zimmerman, Israel, Schulz, & Checkoway, 1992). It represents a new approach to social capital by focusing on the cognitive attributions and motivations that lead community members to engage professionals as collaborators rather than as authoritative experts.

Empowerment differs from other psychological concepts such as self-efficacy and internal locus of control by operating not only at the individual level, but also via empowering and empowered organizations and communities. Organizations that have been studied for their empowering ways include self-help groups, educational programs (Maton & Salem, 1995), religious congregations (Dokecki, Newbrough & O'Gorman, 2001) and other faith-based community action, service, and advocacy organizations (Speer & Hughey, 1995), substance abuse prevention (McMillan, Florin, Stevenson, Kerman, & Mitchell, 1995) and health promotion coalitions (Fawcett et al., 1995), environmental organizations (Rich et al., 1995), large companies (Spreitzer, 1995), community development organizations (Kroeker, 1995), school-based associations, citizen advisory boards of government agencies, youth sports and recreation groups, community crime prevention groups, resident associations (Perkins et al., 1996), and many other contexts.

Unfortunately, empowerment also became a vague and overused buzzword, especially at the state and national policy levels, where the ideology of empowerment has been widely applied, but with little attention to theory or research and with varied success (Perkins, 1995). At the local level, however, it is a natural construct to link with social capital as it focuses on how individual self-efficacy, confidence, competencies, and critical reflection relate to group and organization-level bridging via mutual respect, caring, participation, and resource exchange and acquisition, as well as community-level social change (Perkins & Zimmerman, 1995). In the same study in which social capital was found to improve the quality of inner-city, low-income housing (Saegert & Winkel, 1998), resident participation led to physical improvements, and those improvements, in turn, predicted empowerment and even voting behavior, at the group level (Saegert & Winkel, 1996). At the individual level, empowerment predicts participation, thus creating a mutually reinforcing change process.

Neighboring behavior (informal behavior cell of Figure 5–2) is the instrumental help we provide, or get from, other community members: for example, watching a neighbor's house or child, loaning some food or a tool, sharing information, and so on (Unger & Wandersman, 1985). Ordinary social interaction with one's neighbors—especially as it helps residents get better acquainted and discuss shared problems, thus encouraging more community involvement, either formally or informally—may also be considered a form of neighboring (Unger & Wandersman, 1985).

Despite the important role of neighboring to the quality of community life, it is the least researched of the social capital factors. However, what evidence exists is compelling. Unger and Wandersman (1983) found that neighboring facilitates forming block associations in that once a block is organized, association members engage in more social interaction. Neighboring is related to the level of community participation, sense of community and other bonding variables (communitarianism and community satisfaction [see below]; Perkins & Long, 2002). Perkins, Brown, & Taylor (1996) found that neighboring was, generally, the strongest single predictor of participation in community organizations in three cities, measured both simultaneously and one year later, at both the individual and block levels of analysis. Neighboring is especially important for the disenfranchised. Prezza et al. (2001) found that women and those with more children and less education rely more on neighboring relationships.

Referring back to the stress model in chapter 3, neighboring is a form of material and *social support* (see also chapter 7) and helps to explain the health/mental health benefits of both self-help/mutual aid groups (chapter 9) and a sense of community. Briggs (1998) found that adding just one steadily employed adult to a low-income minority adolescent's support network had dramatic effects on perceived access to job and school information/advice (social leverage). Thus, social capital is thought to serve at least three different kinds of social support functions: communal (shared expectations, values, or worldview; e.g., sense of community), instrumental (tangible or task-oriented assistance; e.g., neighboring), and informational support (access to new information and contacts). The fourth form of support, emotional, may also be involved, depending on the quality of one's relationships with community members.

Citizen participation in the same types of grassroots organizations listed above under collective efficacy constitutes the formal behavioral dimension of social capital in Figure 5–2. Sociologists and political scientists have studied participation but have generally concentrated on its demographics. Psychologists go beyond demographic differences by controlling for them while finding that participants in community councils, block, neighborhood, tenant or homeowner associations, and other local resident groups—individually and at the organizational and community level—enjoy more empowerment (Saegert & Winkel, 1996), sense of community (Perkins et al., 1996), neighboring (Unger & Wandersman, 1985), community satisfaction (Perkins et al., 1990), and other positive community attachments and organizational bridging activities (Perkins et al., 1996). These community organizations address a wide variety of local needs, from planning and traffic issues to park cleanups and community gardens to youth and recreation programs and block parties to crime prevention (see chapter 12).

Psychological antecedents to social capital. Just as social capital itself is psychological in nature, so too are the precursors to social capital largely psychological. These include a variety of other positive community-oriented cognitions, such as communitarianism, place attachment, community satisfaction, pride of place, and confidence in the future of one's community (Perkins & Long, 2002). Understanding the precursors to social capital can help us identify what may or may not help in mobilizing a particular community.

Communitarianism is the value placed on one's community and on working collectively to improve it. This term sounds very similar to sense of community. Yet, while communitarianism is empirically related to neighboring and collective efficacy, it is only marginally related to sense of community and participation (Perkins et al., 1990).

Other psychological antecedents to social capital relate to one's community as a physical place (see also "Physical Environmental Influences," below). *Place attachments* are emotional bonds, developed over time, to particular geographic spaces (Brown & Perkins, 1992). Through the related concepts of *place identity* (Twigger-Ross & Uzzell, 1996) and *community identity* (Puddifoot, 1995), these bonds are integral to how we see ourselves both as individuals and as a community. Place attachments help to resolve the inherent and paradoxical need for both stability and change in our lives and in our communities. Place attachments lead us to stay and protect what we cherish most in our communities and to invest time, energy, and money to improve that with which we are dissatisfied. From the ecological perspective of chapter 4, the interdependent effects are more than just physical. Politically, place attachment can lead the most disenfranchised members to participate in community change (Saegert & Winkel, 1996). Socially, it brings residents together directly or indirectly to address shared concerns (Brown & Perkins, 1992). Economically, where residents, through their history in, and attachments to, a place discover what is unique about their community, they can preserve or develop places and events that generate tourism and other business opportunities (see chapter 12).

Community satisfaction has been studied by psychologists (Hughey & Bardo, 1987) as well as by sociologists. It is related to all four individual-level dimensions of social capital, but is clearly a separate construct (Perkins & Long, 2002). For example, networking behaviors are motivated by both community bonds and perceived problems (Perkins et al., 1996). Those most aware and critical of local problems are often the most satisfied with their community as a place to live. If those problems are not solved, however, they may eventually lead to community dissatisfaction and disengagement.

Community confidence in the future of one's town or neighborhood is another antecedent to social capital, especially in older or rural areas that may be experiencing changes in local businesses or residential demography (income, tenure, racial composition). A lack of confidence may spell commercial and residential disinvestment and flight; it may explain why many urban policies and revitalization projects have failed. Confidence is significantly related to collective efficacy, neighboring, participation, sense of community (Perkins & Long, 2002), and resident decisions to move or stay (Varady, 1986).

Social capital at the community level: Ecology, institutions and networks. The above framework helps to distinguish key psychological differences in forms of social capital. For example, too much concern for cohesion, which is more a focus of the informal components of social capital than the formal ones, may undermine the ability to confront or engage in necessary conflict within and between groups, which would be disempowering. Most of psychology focuses too exclusively on individuals while most other social sciences tend to ignore important individual deviation from group norms. What marginalizes certain people? What makes others become leaders? What makes some of those successful and others not?

The ecological orientation (chapter 4) holds that analyzing *both* the powerful influences that groups and environments exert on collective behavior *and* how individuals vary within those collectives leads to a much more complete, nuanced, realistic, and useful understanding than does either level in isolation (van Uchelen, 2000). Thus social capital must be understood from a *multi-level perspective* that encompasses both the *individual* psychological and behavioral (micro-social) conceptions discussed above and institutional and community *network* (meso- and macro-social) conceptions. Social capital as a quality of groups, networks, settings, institutions, communities, and societies emphasizes the collective nature of the phenomena—the norms of reciprocity or the degree of social integration within and between settings.

Similar to sense of community and empowerment, social capital has received an explosion of interest among theorists, researchers, and policymakers. But the focus on trust, bonding, and attachment tends to obscure the institutional contexts that create, promote, and sustain connections within and across organizations and communities. Without the physical presence of the proper mix of institutions that are linked and provide opportunities for involvement, social capital may not even occur, let alone generate positive community change.

The writer most associated with the concept of social capital is political scientist Robert Putnam (2000), who observed that Americans are generally now "bowling alone" rather than in the leagues so popular in past generations. He was less concerned with the disappearance of recreational clubs, per se, than what he saw as the loss of the local institutional threads that bind together the social fabric of our communities and, ultimately, our society. His obituary for the American community may be exaggerated, but the importance of social capital to the functioning and quality of community life seems indisputable. Putnam (2000) concludes that involvement in local institutions, and the functioning of those institutions, are the most consistent predictors of citizen satisfaction.

Again from an ecological perspective, the existence of a diverse mix of institutions linked in ways that facilitate boundary spanning creates an environment that provides a rich base of behavioral niches—ones that promote adaptation and serve as settings for the promotion of social capital. What sociologists call mediating structures (small-scale community institutions) help "mediate" the wide gap between individuals and impersonal and unresponsive government and corporate institutions and are thus a key to empowerment.

They may also be the key to local economic development. A study of "entrepreneurial social infrastructure" in 718 rural communities in the United States found that the presence of active civic organizations was a precursor to successful economic activity (Flora, Sharp, Flora & Newlon, 1997). Viewed at the organizational and community levels of analysis, social capital becomes a more robust concept by linking human capital (e.g., opportunities for learning and skill development through organizational participation; chapter 10) to economic and political capital (DeFilippis, 2001; see chapter 12).

Bridging versus bonding. While both bonding (primarily through informal *gemeinschaft* relationships among neighbors) and bridging (via formal, instrumental *gesselschaft* relationships among individuals and community institutions; Tönnies, 1887/2001) are important, they are not equally so. Interpersonal bonding may be useful as a catalyst for participation and commitment, but network bridging opportunities that increase power, access, and learning may be even more important. It is possible to rely too heavily on bridging relationships with outside institutions, which can allow community ties to atrophy or even disempower community members if they do not participate. But an overemphasis on bonding, or developing and maintaining a sense of community, can inhibit a group from addressing controversial issues and necessary conflict (Hughey & Speer, 2002). Bonding *within* groups can even lead to insularity, alienation of outsiders, and inhibit bridging to other groups (Burt, 1999). It is through bridging relationships that larger-scale, "second order" change occurs. Bonding may help to support participation in organizations, but whether those organizations are empower*ing* and, themselves, empower*ed*, depends on their ability to bridge to other organizations and power structures.

Although social capital was originally conceived in relation to political and economic capital (Bourdieu, 1985), the current debate led by Putnam (2000) and, it must be acknowledged, the preceding psychological conceptions of social capital have tended to define it in purely social terms that provide little basis for large-scale or structural community change (DeFilippis, 2001). Community psychologists have a tremendous opportunity to contribute to the debate by melding psychological analyses of "micro" social capital with "meso" analyses of networks and "macro" analyses of institutional links to policy, power, and capital (Shinn & Toohey, 2003). One approach, proposed by Newbrough (1995), involves a "third position," synthesizing both individual freedom needs and collective societal needs, which emphasizes a more egalitarian "just community" and may provide a dialectical resolution to the dichotomy between gemeinschaft (bonding) and gesselschaft (bridging).

"Bringing it all home." At this point, the reader may well be wondering, "What do all these abstract social capital concepts actually mean and how might they be applied in real life?" Think of the neighborhood where you grew up. How did you feel about your home and neighborhood as a place to live (place attachment)? Did most people know each other and get along well (sense of community)? Did people ask each other for help when they needed it and was help provided (neighboring)? When a problem came up in the community, did people come together to get it solved (participation)? Do you think they had confidence in the community's future and in their own ability, together with the neighbors, to get things done to improve the neighborhood (collective efficacy/empowerment)? Did anyone rich, famous, or powerful live in the neighborhood or did any of the neighbors know someone with "loot" or "clout" (Ryan, 1976) well enough to ask them for help (network "bridging" ties)?

Now imagine you are living in that neighborhood, raising a family, and a nearby vacant lot is getting filled with weeds, litter, and a large heap of refuse. What could you and would you do about it? Your answer to *that* question will depend on your answers to the above questions. You might rely on your informal network of neighbors to help clean up the lot, but that may be only a temporary solution. So instead you contact your neighbors, not to do the clean up, but to get the word out and try to organize a more formal, collective response. What might that be? You could try to get the city or a local school, business, faith congregation, or community development organization to buy the lot and work with the neighborhood children, teens, and adults to turn it into a community garden or playground and maintain it.

As we will see in the next section, all your efforts may not be enough to bring your neighbors together unless they sense a real threat to the group and/or home territory. But choosing a local environmental problem like that one is often a great way to begin organizing your community because the issue is "winnable." Also, environmental problems tend to be widely and deeply felt because they are visible, or they are even scarier if they are not visible. Finally, local physical improvements allow participants to see the fruits of their labor every day and be reminded of their collective power.

Physical Environmental Influences on Behavior and Well-Being

A fourth psychological conception of the environment identified by Moos (1973) is the power of environmental design, geography, and climate to shape human behavior and well-being. Just as our physical surroundings are usually taken for granted, the subdiscipline of environmental psychology and the interdisciplinary field called "environment and behavior" have great, but undervalued and largely overlooked, relevance to community psychology. These fields go beyond the notion of "person-environment fit" discussed in chapter 4 to systematically examine the mutual *interactions* and *transactions* between people and their physical contexts (Altman & Rogoff, 1987). Most early research in environmental psychology focused on unconscious impacts of particular features (i.e., ergonomics, architectural design, city and regional planning) or conditions (e.g., crowding) of the built environment on individuals. More recently, conscious attitudes and behaviors (Geller, 2002) toward improvement and protection of all types of environments, planned and natural (Gifford, 2002), and at all levels—from the household products we use (Werner, 2003), to the design of one's house (Brown, Burton, & Sweaney, 1998) or condition of low-income housing (Saegert & Winkel, 1996) to schools and other neighborhood settings (Werner, Voce, Openshaw, & Simons, 2002) to global ecology (Bonnes & Bonaiuto, 2002)—are also being studied. This is even more compatible with community psychology than simply moving from intrapsychic or biological determinism to environmental determinism.

Environmental stress and health. One major area of theory and research is on environmental factors in stress, coping, and health and mental health outcomes. These generally fall under three broad categories, which were discussed in chapter 3: (1) urban stressors (noise, traffic, crime, physical signs of disorder); (2) contaminated homes, soil, water, or air; and (3) disasters (floods, earthquakes, hurricanes, fire). Stokols (1992) offers other, more comprehensive frameworks for cataloging the wide variety of environmental factors influencing physical health and illness, including geographic, architectural–technological, and sociocultural processes.

Territoriality. Another traditional area of environmental psychology with implications for community psychology has to do with how people regulate their *privacy* and *territoriality.* Altman (1975) notes that privacy regulation is a territorial boundary maintenance process of including or excluding certain people and behavior depending upon the situation. Thus, territorial behavior can be verbal, "body language," spatial/environmental (moving, decorating, personalizing one's room, home, or office), and cultural (e.g., whether children are taught to respect privacy).

Altman identified four dimensions of territory (duration, centrality to occupants' lives, types of markers, responses to "invasion") and three levels of territory: *Primary territories* (e.g., home, office) are those we spend the most time in, are very central to our lives, and ones we tend to decorate, personalize, and use barriers and markers in because we cannot move from them easily. *Secondary territories* (e.g., common ground shared by neighbors or a favorite frequented place for socializing or solitude—e.g., a pub, club, library, or church) are for short but regular usage; they are somewhat central to one's life; both physical and nonphysical markers may be used; and one can move in response to invasion. Secondary territories have ambiguous ownership and a mixture of public and private uses. The third level is *public territories* which are usually used for short periods and are not central to one's life. Mostly verbal and body language are used; if those are insufficient, one usually must move as physical markers are not an option.

Territorial behavior and environmental planning and design have important implications for crime control (Taylor, 2002), community cohesion (Brown & Werner, 1985), and as discussed in the last section, the development of community social capital (Perkins et al., 1996). Territorial regulation of conflict and order in communities has also been a major focus of theory and research in urban anthropology (Merry, 1987) and urban sociology (Suttles, 1968).

There is growing evidence that the physical design and condition of communities and buildings contribute significantly to the sense of community of their occupants (Nasar & Julian, 1995; see above concerning "sense of community" and "place attachment"). One example of this is the current popular movement in planning and architecture called New Urbanism (Brown & Cropper, 2001). Another example is the design of garden-style versus high-rise apartments in public housing (Taylor, 2002) and in congregant housing for elders (Zaff & Devlin, 1998). Green space also has a positive impact on sense of community (Kuo et al., 1998).

The physical environment may ordinarily remain more or less subconscious in our daily lives. Yet think about your favorite places now or from your childhood—those primary or secondary territories that provide so many valued memories and meanings (Brown & Perkins, 1992). How do they make you feel? How would you feel if they were developed or destroyed or both? What would you do to protect them? How should they be preserved, at what cost, who should decide, and how? Can preserving them actually lead to economic development and savings? These are just some of the important questions that community and environmental psychologists, planners, and developers address daily, and could address more effectively working together.

Community-environmental psychology. In the 1987 *Handbook of Environmental Psychology*, Holahan and Wandersman review the many areas of mutual interest between community and environmental psychology and offer a framework, not unlike the Dohrenwend model (Figure 3–1), that combines both subdisciplines in primary and secondary prevention research and intervention. The following year, two environmental psychologists, Irwin Altman and Carol Werner, were appointed as associate editors of the *American Journal of Community Psychology* and initiated a regular feature on ecological and environmental psychology. What is both disappointing and surprising is that the auspicious seeds for cross-fertilization sown fifteen years ago have born relatively little fruit.[2] Few scholars or students attend conferences in other than their primary field. Journal editors seem to impede publication of relevant and important work submitted by people outside the field. Most telling of all, research collaborations between community and environmental psychologists, instead of flourishing, are exceedingly rare.

What is needed is the development of a truly interdisciplinary field that integrates the psychological theory and experimental rigor of environmental psychology with the pragmatic, policy orientation of urban planning (Churchman, 2002) *and* the critical focus, values, and experience of community psychology and community development in engaging the community and conducting participatory action-research and program evaluations (see chapter 13). Despite some recent efforts toward interdisciplinary collaboration (Perkins et al., 2002) and a marriage that ought to be a natural fit, these four fields unfortunately remain merely "kissing cousins."

The Socio-Physical Environment: Behavior Settings

The fifth and final psychological conception of the environment we will discuss is at once the oldest and most forward looking. Fifty years ago, Roger Barker and his colleagues and students created a new approach to theory and research that came remarkably close to the systematic and integrated analysis of local sociophysical contexts we call for above. They called it "ecological psychology." While Moos conceives of the psychological environment much as a personality theorist does, Barker emphasized the physical and behavioral characteristics that are directly observable and objectively definable. Barker (1968) realized that most human behavior is not randomly distributed across space and time but instead occurs in consistent patterns of regularly scheduled activities he called "behavior settings." Everyday examples of such settings include school classrooms, stores, government offices, playgrounds, and even sidewalks.

For Barker, an important characteristic of every setting is the set of "standing" behavior patterns that define the nature and meaning of that setting regardless of its occupants (e.g., singing hymns in a church, sunbathing at the beach). In fact, the essence of any behavior setting is seen to reside in the relationship between these behaviors and characteristics of the setting's physical and temporal milieu (Barker, 1968; 1993). In most classrooms, for example, the chairs, desks, blackboards, and open spaces are uniquely constructed and arranged to facilitate performance of the standing behaviors in that setting—speaking, listening, sitting, and writing. Because people live their lives within settings, setting characteristics are important, whether we focus on the control of social problem behaviors, or the conditions under which people experience satisfaction in living.

Key assumptions. Behavior setting theory includes two key assumptions. First, the individuals who perform in a given setting are thought to be more or less interchangeable. Even a complete turnover in participants does not change the activities one would see in that setting. In Barker's conception, then, the psychological environment is defined independent of the people in it, which is not the case in Moos's approach.

Second, it is a key assumption that settings themselves generate the forces necessary for their own maintenance and survival (Schoggen, Barker, & Fox, 1989). Behavior settings are seen to possess "forces" that, in the interest of keeping the setting going (homeostasis), impel their occupants to perform the standing behavior patterns and conform to setting programs. In a church service, for example, the congregation stands or sits in unison at the appropriate times (e.g., for singing or prayer), as indicated by the organized ceremony of worship. In a classroom children do seat work and recite when called upon, while in gym class they play games organized in terms of specific programs of actions and rules. Even long-term patients in mental hospitals will eat when brought to a dining room.

Setting-motivation congruence. Part of the force resides in the confluence of participants' individual needs with specific experiences or products provided by the setting. The motivations of those attending a church service, for example, are typically congruent with the specific kinds of social and spiritual satisfactions such a setting provides. Similarly, the effectiveness of a school is partly based on the assumption that children are motivated to learn what the school is teaching. Problems can arise when a child is "unmotivated," that is, does not actively participate in the programs provided by school settings. Another kind of influence involves reducing or eliminating behavior that deviates from the program. A baby crying loudly during a wedding ceremony elicits prompt efforts by those nearby to quiet the child. A child who ignores assigned seat work to get up and wander about the classroom brings an admonishment from the teacher to rejoin the activity. A person who eats in a library will be asked to stop. Failure to conform may result in the ejection of a nonconforming occupant from the setting. The crying baby who cannot be quieted during a solemn ceremony will usually be ushered quickly away; a child who repeatedly refuses a teacher's direct admonition may find himself banished to the principal's office, suspended, or in an extreme case expelled from school (see Barker, 1968, pp. 167–185).

Underpopulation. People establish settings and the norms of behavior in settings. When we speak of settings, we assume human agency. The processes or mechanisms by which settings coercively influence participants' behavior are not well understood, although one kind of internal homeostatic mechanism operating within program circuits is thought to be the degree of "underpopulation" present (Schoggen et al, 1989). Underpopulation concerns the effects of various numbers of occupants in a setting relative to the optimal number for that setting; it grew out of Barker and Wright's (1970) behavior-setting survey of a town in Kansas (pseudonym "Midwest"). Barker and Schoggen (1973) subsequently extended the survey to a town in Yorkshire, England (pseudonym "Yoredale"). In 1953–1954, they identified 884 settings in the town of Midwest (population 830). Yoredale (population 1,310) contained only 758 settings. With more settings, the smaller number of people residing in Midwest of necessity participated more often and for longer lengths of time in the town's public activities. Barker and Schoggen also believed that because of the greater importance and responsibility given each resident of Midwest, social distinctions were less sharp than in Yoredale. Subsequent comparisons among small, "underpopulated" and larger, "overpopulated" high schools in Kansas showed that, on the average, students from small schools participated in more school settings, assumed more positions of responsibility, and expressed a greater "sense of obligation" to their schools than did students from large schools (Barker & Gump, 1972). Other research supported the predictions in churches of different sizes (Wicker, 1984) and in several laboratory-based experiments (e.g., Perkins, 1982; Wicker, 1984).

This dimension of underpopulation may provide new insights into how environments can be described and their effects on behavior understood. From Barker's viewpoint, for example, the relevant psychological characteristic of an organization or group residence is not number of members or residents but rather number per setting or activity (Perkins & Baker, 1991). The lower this ratio (i.e., the more underpopulated the settings are), the higher will be the average level of satisfaction reported by participants. We can think about deliberately creating underpopulated settings to widen the niche breadth (see previous chapter) of at-risk populations. People in underpopulated settings may welcome participation by a wider range of persons. Think of the differences in activities that a medic on a battlefield will undertake compared to ancillary medical personnel in fully staffed hospitals. The medic on the battlefield makes diagnoses, engages in minor surgical procedures, decides which medications to administer, and bandages wounds. The ancillary medical person in a hospital may be limited to taking pulse and temperatures. Someone else will take blood pressures. Still another person will distribute medications, and only a physician may remove the stitches after surgery. The large number of wounded on a battlefield compared to those available to help creates an underpopulated setting, and roles that might be maintained rigidly under other circumstances break down. Sarason, Carroll, Maton, Cohen, & Lorentz (1977) argue that in theory participants in underpopulated settings develop a sense of community. We apply this concept and other aspects of behavior-setting theory in our discussion of mutual help groups (chapter 9).

Limitations. Some observations are inconsistent with theoretical expectations derived from the concept of underpopulation. For some settings, fewer than the optimal number of occupants apparently does not produce greater satisfaction. Whyte (2001), for example, found that certain public settings in smaller communities (i.e., those considered more underpopulated by Barker) are generally less successful psychologically than similar settings in large cities. One solution might be for the smaller communities to "compress" or "concentrate" public spaces and the people in them to a much greater degree (p. 92)—that is, to make them more *over*populated. The physical arrangements are also important. Whyte's (2001) observations of urban plazas pointed to the importance of easy access, movable seating, good lighting, opportunities to eat and drink, and also the aesthetic value of trees and water (e.g., a fountain) for creating satisfied users. Successful community gathering places serve to foster participation by the largest number of different community groups, and provide unstructured, informal contact among people (i.e., visual and/or verbal, with no particular commitment to any strictly defined setting program), communication (e.g., news, gossip), social support, and ultimately the establishment and maintenance of a strong sense of community.

The importance of the number of participants may have more to do with the overall purpose of the setting for its occupants. Thus for some settings (e.g., parades, political conventions) whose purpose is to bring together large numbers of people, the optimal number of participants may be quite large, regardless of the number of different roles available. Consider that the purpose of a bar is to sell drinks. A lone person sitting at a bar is in an "underpopulated" setting. The person may nurse the drink for a long time. When the bar is filled (overpopulated), the customers will call for more drinks. Thus people fulfill the purpose of the setting more when it is crowded than when it is not. Obviously at least another dimension is necessary to understand how the over- or underpopulation concept predicts behavior.

Contributions to community psychology. Behavior-setting theory has made two fundamental contributions to community psychology. First, it provides an environmental "unit of analysis" for the description and assessment of human behavior on situational and community levels. Behavior settings are naturally occurring units in the environment—discrete, relatively stable, and "objective in the sense that they exist independent of anyone's perception of them" (Barker & Schoggen, 1973, p. 9). People live their lives in behavior settings (Wicker, 1984) and in this sense they are important to our understanding of what influences people's actions and feelings.

We can use behavior setting concepts to help us describe and understand how "livable" communities are for different populations. Neighborhoods make a difference in children's lives. For example, because of residential patterns (the distribution of housing settings in a community), middle-class African American families are more likely to live in closer proximity to poorer neighborhoods than middle-class white families. In consequence, middle-class African Americans may supervise their children more closely than white middle-class Americans who feel more comfortable in allowing their children to use neighborhood settings more freely.

Furthermore, although any individual setting may have only limited impact on a given person or community, Barker and Schoggen (1973) showed how settings can be aggregated systematically to make possible a systematic, comprehensive assessment of the specific behavioral opportunities provided in a given community. The settings available to particular subgroups, such as children, the elderly, and people with disabilities, can be compared with the specific behavioral needs of these groups (e.g., for health care, recreational opportunities) to provide sharper and more detailed assessments of how habitable a given community is for specific groups. Consider the effect on a community of the availability of jobs. If the number of employment settings is limited, young people and those with skills in demand elsewhere will leave. The number of employment settings will affect the age composition of the community, and related aspects of community life. Aggregates of communities and even larger units are also possible in theory, providing a basis for systems of social and behavioral accounting on a macroeconomic scale (Schoggen, Barker, & Fox, 1989).

Second, the behavior-setting theory concepts of behavior-environment congruence and underpopulation provide a way of thinking about how environmental settings may effect changes in behavior across different settings in the person's life (Levine & Perkins, 1980b). Because behavior is a property of settings as well as of people, it provides a basis for direct examinations of person-environment fit, including the process by which people acquire new behaviors when participating in new settings. For example, preschool children develop preventive "interpersonal cognitive problem solving skills" by actively participating in game-like settings where the specific behavior pattern emphasizes *how* to think, not *what* to think, in solving interpersonal problems (Spivack & Shure, 1993; see chapter 8). Similarly, the mechanism of underpopulation is exploited when mutual help groups are replicated in a target area using Zimmerman et al.'s (1991) "Johnny Appleseed" approach (i.e., convening the minimum number of participants required to fill necessary positions and let the benefits of underpopulation—flexible roles, sense of importance, and so on—accrue; see chapter 9).

Practical applications. Practical applications of the behavior-setting approach have focused on such problems as (1) assessing the range of therapeutic behavioral opportunities available to high-risk populations like persons with serious mental illness (Perkins & Baker, 1991; Perkins & Perry, 1985) and the residents of inner-city housing projects (Bechtel, 1977); (2) intervening to reduce problems of overcrowding in popular national parks (Wicker, 1984); (3) analyzing the psychological impact of declining populations on isolated rural towns (Norris-Baker, 1999); and (4) the functioning of different types of self-help groups (Luke, Rappaport, & Seidman, 1991). With respect to behavior settings for persons with mental illness, Perkins and Baker (1991) developed a simplified behavior-setting assessment procedure that they validated on large samples of supervised community residences and program activities for mental health consumers. Perkins and Baker then evaluated these settings in terms of their appropriateness for client needs, especially self-care skills and other functional competencies.

Barker's comprehensive community focus also helps us recognize important settings that may not be available to mental health consumers, such as paid employment or opportunities to live in housing that is fully integrated with that of nondisabled people. Like anyone else, people with special needs should have access to neighborhoods or work sites that include public gathering places (e.g., parks, public libraries, break areas) to facilitate their participation in community life and neighbors' or coworkers' awareness and acceptance of them.

"Least restrictive alternative." Behavior-setting theory helps us understand such concepts as the "most integrative," or least restrictive, setting, an important idea when considering the legal rights of people with disabilities. When a person's rights are restricted by law, the degree of restriction should be the least necessary to accomplish the legal purpose of restricting rights. It is helpful to be able to measure the degree of restriction in given settings. In practice, the determination of integrativeness rests on rather crude distinctions, such as living in the community rather than in an institution, or in one's own apartment rather than a supervised group home. A group home, however, while more integrative than a hospital, may still be rather "institutional" in the behavior patterns it requires of staff and residents (Mowbray, Greenfield, & Freddolino, 1992). An apartment may permit better integration but offer little stimulation or support. Behavior-setting theory allows for a more specific and substantive determination of behavioral integrativeness and focuses our attention on such questions as: What activities regularly occur in this residence? In this neighborhood? What desirable activities are missing? What do the people here learn? How do they have fun? Implicit in this view is the belief that, with the right resources, natural settings should offer sufficient supports to help people with special needs acquire and maintain the living and working skills needed for a satisfying life in the community.

Person-setting interaction and fit. One theme of this chapter, and the preceding one, is that preventive and therapeutic changes in individual behavior reflect processes of person-setting interaction and fit. What may prove fruitful for community psychology is to link persons and settings systematically using dimensions that are directly comparable to each other, such as the behavioral repertoire of the person and the set of standing behaviors required of that person by key community settings. Perkins and Perry (1985), for example, empirically derive several dimensions of behavioral "demandingness" for use in assessing the settings of a community residence for mental health consumers. (Among the high demand settings in this residence were playing bridge and holding a business meeting, while gardening and attending a speaker's lecture were relatively low demand settings.) When combined with similar information on behavioral capacities and skills of the residents themselves, such information allows psychologists to estimate the fit or lack of fit between residents and settings having significant implications for their long-term adaptation to community life.

Barker also overlooked characteristics of the setting program. A setting is not just "out there" in the environment; its program also resides inside the heads of its occupants (Schoggen, Barker, & Fox, 1989). Moreover, maladaptive behavior at work and in other public settings by persons with serious mental illness or retardation might be understood and dealt with in terms of incomplete or inappropriate cognitive scripts. To participate effectively, you have to know how and be motivated to do so. Some settings, for example, such as fast-food restaurants, have programs that are so straightforward or familiar that almost everyone behaves appropriately, while others, such as working efficiently with a complicated new computer system, would require considerably more preparation. Understanding the interaction of setting characteristics with the cognitive scripts or schemas held by occupants may help to shed light on the process of setting creation and change.

Behavior-setting research is evolving away from the study of entire communities toward more in-depth investigation of individual settings (Sommer & Wicker, 1991) such as mutual help groups, block organizations, and prevention programs. Latkin and colleagues (1994) studied patterns of illicit drug use in order to understand HIV risk behavior. One who uses illegal drugs has to inject them in some setting. They identified five primary settings in which illicit drugs are used: one's own residence, friends' residences, mother's residence, shooting galleries, and semi-public areas. Most injected in their own or in friends' homes. The behavior patterns were different in different settings. Once injection took place in the presence of others, the likelihood of high-risk behavior increased. The use of shared needles, unclean needles, and needles that were not disinfected before use was higher in shooting galleries and semi-public places. Setting demands were different, resulting in different levels of high-risk behavior. In some semi-public settings bleach or alcohol to clean needles was not as readily available. Norms of sharing may prevail in some settings affecting engagement in high-risk behavior. Behavior-setting theory leads to an alternative strategy for engaging in HIV preventive activities. For example, interventions that target social relationships among drug users may help in reducing high-risk behaviors.

Why do some settings thrive, while other, similar settings struggle and fail? Luke, Rappaport, and Seidman (1991) suggested that a better understanding of setting variations (which they termed "phenotypes") would increase behavior-setting theory's usefulness in answering such questions. To illustrate this point they showed how 13 different GROW mutual help groups (see chapter 9) varied significantly in the frequencies with which important behavior patterns occurred. This elaboration has the potential to enrich our functional understanding of settings to the point where effective community interventions (e.g., mutual help groups tailored specifically to currently underserved populations) can be developed and disseminated more reliably and efficiently.

Barker's work is ecological in its emphasis on the interdependence of environments and their human participants. It is also ecological in method (see chapter 4). Barker's example of nonintrusive, empirical, community-based research strongly influenced later community psychologists. Although its potential usefulness to community psychology is thus considerable, behavior-setting theory remains in need of further development (Perkins, Burns, Perry, & Nielsen, 1988). In particular, although behavior-setting theory addresses both the social and physical environment, it tends to emphasize the social (e.g., underpopulation) over the physical. Especially needed at this point are comprehensive ecological theories that simultaneously address the social, physical, economic, and political contexts of behavior at multiple levels of analysis (Shinn & Toohey, 2003; Wicker, 2002; see, e.g., "community development theory," chapter 12).

Box 5–1. The Fairweather Lodge

An excellent example of the application of social ecology to community intervention is the lodge program developed by Fairweather and his associates (Fairweather, 1980; Fairweather, Sanders, Maynard, & Cressler, 1969; Fairweather, Sanders & Tornatzky, 1974). Beginning as a "milieu treatment" program inside the walls of a psychiatric hospital, this intervention involved small, self-governing patient groups operating under an unusually limited degree of staff authority. Within the hospital this program was highly successful in helping patients recover from acute psychiatric episodes. The major difficulty encountered was that once patients were discharged from the program and away from the daily support of their peers, they had difficulty assuming or maintaining the kinds of roles and responsibilities that would help ensure their adaptation to the community.

Clinically, the traditional explanation for this kind of problem focuses on the characteristics of persons with chronic mental illness and attributes their failure to adapt to independent living to the behavioral deficits that are perceived to set them apart from other people. As we noted in chapter 4, however, adaptation is not a person-centered trait but a process of fit involving both person and environment. Maladaptive responses usually occur episodically over time (see Morell, Levine, & Perkins, 1982) and tend to involve certain situations more often than others. Fairweather's explanation for the poor adaptation shown by patients focuses on the community, particularly its intolerance of patients' psychotic symptomatology (e.g., delusions and hallucinations).

Table 5–1, taken from Fairweather et al. (1969), elaborates this explanation in some detail. The bottom row indicates the essential problem. Prior to Fairweather's development of the community lodge concept, the two psychiatric statuses available to individuals were "sick person," entailing supervised living in an institution with limited rights and duties, and "well person," requiring completely independent living with full adult rights and obligations.[3] The lightly supervised group work-living situation in the community, described in the right-center column, initially was not available to patients at release from the hospital.

Reasoning, much as Kelly did, that adaptation to the community needs to occur in the community instead of inside patients' heads, Fairweather worked with a group of consumers to develop a new kind of community setting. This "small-group" unit was designed to be a transitional step bridging the successful inpatient treatment program and the less receptive community settings outside. Its goal was to help the community assimilate diversity in the form of former hospital patients with serious mental illness. Fairweather draws an analogy between the lodge concept and the "melting pot" role attributed to ethnic ghettos—both were intended to be protective and tolerant of the in-group's characteristic behavioral idiosyncrasies, while at the same time providing an important and challenging interface with the larger society.

A guiding value of Fairweather's approach has been that any program that attempts to empower those with mental illness must aim to improve their social status so that they can control their own fate. The consumers themselves therefore decided who would be members of the lodge, and those chosen were assisted in developing small commercial enterprises (i.e., gardening and janitorial services). Mental health professionals designed the lodge program and initially took a great deal of responsibility for it. These professionals later reduced their participation to consulting roles and eventually turned over full responsibility for the operation of the residence and businesses to the residents.

Once they expressed a preference for the lodge lifestyle, how did prospective members prepare for its challenges? In Fairweather's

Table 5–1
Autonomy of Mental Patients' Social Status

	Dimension of Autonomy			Complete	
	None			Partially autonomous individual status	Autonomous individual status
Social situation	Supervised institutional situation mental hospital	Supervised community situations	Unsupervised community group situations	Counseling or psychotherapy	No treatment
	Closed locked ward / Open unlocked ward / Living situations (home care, day care centers, day hospitals)	Work situations (sheltered workshops) / Combination of work-living situations	Discharged former-patient-led group work-living situations—work in reference groups		
Status situation	Very limited adult rights and duties	Some adult rights and duties	Otherwise, full adult rights and duties	Otherwise, full adult rights and duties	Full adult rights and duties
Available social statuses	Sick person	Sick person	(Unavailable)	Well person	Well person

Source: Reprinted with permission from G. Fairweather et al., *Community Life for the Mentally Ill* (Chicago: Aldine), 1969.

189

original model, group support and skill acquisition were initiated inside the hospital prior to discharge. (Given the increased emphasis on community care in recent years, the lodge movement now includes "training" lodges where consumers who have spent little or no time together learn these preparatory skills; once in the community, members of the lodge continue to attend regular meetings designed to handle problems, review procedures, plan activities, and maintain the group-oriented focus of the lodge program. In doing this, lodge members were developing social capital.) Many positions of responsibility came with the residential and commercial operations of the lodge. Each of the two businesses had three levels of responsibility—crew chief, worker, and "marginal" worker—and support services at the lodge residence required a cook, dishwasher, housekeeper, medication distributor, bookkeeper, and truck driver. In what Fairweather (1980) describes as a "principle of substitution," every resident performing a given job was backed up and could be replaced by another resident with little or no notice.

Several principles of Barker's behavior-setting theory are clearly evident in the Fairweather lodge. For example, participation in the meetings, commercial activities, and other settings helped patients to recognize, model, and rehearse key behavioral skills necessary to community life. As Fairweather (1980) described it,

> Each member of the crew had a particular task; the usual composition of such a crew was a leader (crew chief), worker, and a marginal worker. It was the marginal worker whose work was constantly brought up to acceptable standards by the working example of the supervisor and the worker. Without the framework of the group and the supervision and help of the crew chief, the marginal worker often failed. (p. 29)

Lodge members thus carefully managed the setting programs. That this process sometimes operated differently here than in other settings is illustrated in another passage from Fairweather (1980).

> It is difficult, if not impossible, for individuals who have been hospitalized continuously to discard aberrant behaviors immediately upon entry into a community if, indeed, such behavior can be totally extinguished at all. The members of the subsystem must be tolerant of these behaviors. In the Lodge, for example, members often hallucinated while talking with other members within the confines of the Lodge itself. To take an extreme example of such tolerance, one member who openly hallucinated within the Lodge and on the way to work was informed by his crew chief upon arrival at the work site that no talking was permitted on the job. Usually he was silent during work hours, but upon entry into the truck for the trip back to the Lodge he began hallucinating again—an acceptable behavior to his peers. (p. 27)

Movement back and forth between jobs and levels of authority was used to assist a member in reaching the maximum level of participation he was capable of during a given period of time. Barker's principle of behavior-environment congruence, which focuses attention on the spatial and temporal regularities of behavior and not on the internal state of a specific performer (and assumes that individual performers are in fact interchangeable), was clearly a useful mechanism of therapeutic change here.

From Sarbin's viewpoint, the Fairweather lodge worked because it entailed roles other than that of "mental patient." Two key characteristics were that the new roles were (1) achieved instead of ascribed and (2) flexible in the degrees of involvement they entailed. Both of these characteristics served to increase the value or esteem given residents and enhance their social identities. Indeed, Fairweather believes that a key effect of the lodge intervention was the way it changed role expectations in both directions; people with serious mental illness earned new respect from their neighbors and customers as they worked in recognizable ways to earn a basic living, while members of the lodge (especially those assigned to prepare written bids for job contracts) learned much about what is expected of people who wish to be taken seriously in the world of competitive work.

Moos's interest would be drawn to the social group format of the lodge and to characteristics of the social climate that residents provided to one another on a day-to-day basis. From Fairweather's description, this climate appears high in such "relationship-oriented" dimensions as support, cohesiveness, and involvement and also in "personal development" dimensions such as autonomy and responsibility. Also consistent with Moos's conception, Fairweather suggests that the program not exceed a certain overall size to keep it on a human scale. The maximum size ever reached by the lodge was 33 members.

The lodge developed, and made better use of, human capital than did more traditional residential treatment facilities. Just as important, the social dynamics of the lodge can be viewed in social capital terms. Participants were engaged in a greater degree of collective self-governance both formally and informally, which may have led to greater group identity (sense of community), support (neighboring), and empowerment.

Other ecological factors may also have promoted the lodge's success. Socially and politically, the San Francisco Bay region, where the lodge was established, was much more liberal and tolerant of deviant behavior than most American communities. Economically, the area was wealthier than average, and during the 1960s it enjoyed very strong economic growth. Most fortuitous of all may have been the lodge's physical location. Its immediate neighborhood (which included a gas station and a rooming house of low-income transients) was heavily minority in makeup and very tolerant of deviants and low-status businesses (such as janitorial services). However, directly adjacent to this area, but clearly demarcated by a freeway, were very well-to-do neighborhoods (98% majority) that provided a strong demand for the lodge's janitorial services. With the freeway preserving important territorial boundaries, the very close proximity of the lodge to its high-income clientele aided its commercial success. At the level of building design, the lodge occupied a former motel with rooms laid out in a row, each with its own outside entrance, which allowed residents to come and go freely and thus develop more independence.

Fairweather did a careful experimental evaluation of the initial lodge program (Fairweather, 1980). Among the results were that over a 40-month follow-up period lodge members spent more time living in the community (rather than the hospital), and more time working, than did a control group that received traditional aftercare services. However, lodge members did not fare better than other consumers in their psychosocial adjustment and symptomatology, and many of those who left the lodge later became unemployed. Thus, compared with the hospital, the lodge was an economical source of support and gainful work, although it was not a cure for mental illness and was not really directed toward changing individuals per se. Instead, a setting was created that promoted some degree of social and vocational rehabilitation—if not for all, at least for many. Residents who were unable to adapt to the setting demands simply left or returned to the hospital.

Fairweather et al. (1974) also demonstrated that the lodge program could be replicated in other communities. In keeping with the experience that introducing change is not easy (see chapter 10), however, they reported that considerable effort was necessary to interest other hospitals in adopting their program. It may also be relevant that many consumers and providers have other options now, including publicly funded alternatives like Assertive Community Treatment (discussed in chapter 2) and programs that provide supported housing and employment.

If large institutions as settings have failed, and insufficiently planned deinstitutionalization also created many human problems, we may see the development of settings such as Fairweather's lodge or Zusman's Project Return (see chapter 7). These may be settings whose characteristics lay between hospitals and purely independent living. If we see such settings develop, environmental psychology, behavior setting, role theory, social capital, and social climate concepts may become important in planning and creating the settings so that we take into account the needs of both residents and staff.

Postscript: What Role Remains for Individual Differences?

The strong emphasis in this chapter on environmental influences on behavior may seem unsettling to some readers in light of the widely held assumption that personality traits and other individual characteristics are important precisely because they dominate behavioral responses across time and place. However, we emphasize that personality does not exist in a social vacuum. Personality characteristics are revealed in interaction in specific settings with other people while playing roles determined by the setting. Personality traits have received a great deal of attention, with some agreement among authorities that dimensions such as extroversion, conscientiousness, and negative affect (sometimes called "neuroticism") consistently account for differences among people (Goldberg, 1993), and may reflect genetic factors to a significant degree (Bouchard, 1994). It has also become increasingly apparent in recent years that biological factors play a significant role in the behavioral symptoms of major mental illnesses like schizophrenia and bipolar mood disorder (Torrey, Bowler, Taylor, & Gottesman, 1994).

How can our almost exclusive focus on settings in the present chapter be applied in light of these other influential views? Recall from our discussion of Dohrenwend's model (chapter 3) that individual characteristics of persons may increase or decrease the likelihood that a stressful event will happen and also the nature and success of the person's coping efforts in response to that event. What kinds of individual characteristics?

Mischel (1973) discussed two person-centered variables that help us anticipate the concepts of coping, support, and prevention, all discussed in later chapters. One of these Mischel calls "cognitive and behavioral construction competencies," which refers to differences in the efficiency with which people process information about the environment to come up with adaptive, effective coping responses to specific situations. Aside from the fact that the new settings and the responses they require may be unfamiliar, a person with serious mental illness may not automatically thrive when moved from an intense hospital-based program directly to the community if he or she has chronic difficulty in attending and responding to new stimuli or is heavily medicated. More generally, Mischel suggests that competence in cognitive and behavioral responding is related to such familiar constructs as intelligence, cognitive and social maturity, ego strength, and social and intellectual achievements. It thus points the way toward possible person-centered interventions that would build competence and foster positive mental health by explicitly facilitating the development of cognitive and behavioral competencies in high-risk individuals (see chapter 8).

A second relevant person-centered characteristic is one Mischel called "encoding strategies and personal constructs." These include ideological beliefs about oneself and the meaning of one's experiences. Such constructs have important implications for actions such as attributing blame for one's problems and evaluating the relative desirability of different solutions to problems (e.g., psychotherapy versus self-help). Changes in people's personal constructs or encoding strategies may help them maintain their adaptive responses across different situations precisely because this characteristic is generally so resistant to change. For example, Recovery, Inc., a self-help group for persons with chronic mental illness, encourages a belief by its members in their own individual power to make choices and to reject emotionally arousing stimuli. Members are taught to use a specific term, "spotting," to identify certain risky situations (e.g., "angry temper") and then to use a specific coping device (e.g., "deliberately smile") to deal with those situations. Last, personality factors influence a person's choice of situations, and these choices can have powerful feedback effects (Dickens & Flynn, 2001). For example, an introverted person who is uncomfortable in social relationships may seek out settings in which interpersonal interaction is minimized, and shrink into the corner if in a situation calling for much interpersonal exchange. One implication of environmentally oriented theories is that ideal communities provide a rich and varied set of opportunities from which a person can choose. In order to evaluate the opportunities, we need concepts and methods for assessing settings and their characteristics.

Once a community's richness of opportunities has been evaluated, self-determination requires that a person have opportunities to exert his or her preference and choice among those settings. Some years ago, for example, problems following the massive deinstitutionalization of people with serious mental illness led authorities to propose creating and funding a continuum of residential services, for example, running from hospital through nursing home and group home to supervised apartment and eventually independence, with consumers steadily moving through the continuum over time to increasingly less restrictive and more independent residences. There were two problems with this conception; first, it was not always the case that all steps in the continuum were actually available in a given community, and second, where it did exist the continuum did not foster movement and progress by consumers toward greater independence but rather functioned simply as a static array of alternative long-term placements (Geller & Fisher, 1993). Today, we try to start with the consumer and his or her aspirations and preferences, rather than with a hypothetically derived continuum or taxonomy of settings. That is, a diverse set of alternatives should be available, but consumers themselves choose where among these alternatives they wish to live, with the helping agency providing the supports needed for each consumer to succeed in the chosen residential situation (Carling, 1990).

With renewed interest in the influences of personality and biology on behavior, it is worth noting that the characteristics of persons and of settings are not independent (Dickens & Flynn, 2001) and the relevant perspective for community psychology is still the "person-in-context." Consideration of both person and situation opens up a much wider avenue of potential solutions to problems of adaptation, including environmentally facilitated changes alone, individual competence building alone, and strategies that unite both components in the pursuit of stable change, such as helping people with special needs recognize and select personally optimal environments (Levine & Perkins, 1980b). In summary, community psychologists believe that solutions should be divergent rather than convergent (Rappaport, 1981), with the kind of understanding of settings we developed in this chapter used to promote change and adaptation through individual choice and empowerment.

Summary

This chapter began by raising a number of potential limitations to the ecological metaphor in psychology. For example, what specific mechanisms of behavior change does this analogy provide? How are changes in behavior maintained over time? To what extent have taxonomies of environmental settings been developed, particularly with respect to the often overlooked spatial and temporal dimensions of behavior? What place is given by specific ecological concepts to individual differences in the expression of values, goals, and purposes using environmental settings? Moos's concept of perceived social climates, Sarbin's role theory, an array of social capital concepts, psychologically defined, interdisciplinary analysis of physical environmental influences on behavior, health, and well-being, and Barker's behavior-setting theory were reviewed in some detail as important theoretical systems community psychologists have used in developing answers to these questions.

Each of these concepts is essentially descriptive and ahistorical. The mechanism of behavior change each articulates is more intuitive than it is precise and complete. Moos's notion of fit between individual needs and environmental presses, for example, depends on a concrete behavioral prescription to achieve and maintain individual change. The complexity of environmental influences, which often produce unwanted as well as wanted effects, has not been fully examined using these concepts. Furthermore, the issues of how current environmental conditions came to be and what conditions are likely to follow them are not readily answerable. Relatively little research using these concepts has been longitudinal or otherwise focused on long-term changes.

We illustrated some of the ideas generated by these concepts in our discussion of Fairweather's community lodge program for persons with serious mental illness. Interpreted from the vantage of the five paradigms reviewed here, membership in the lodge community provided patients with a supportive network of relationships, gave them regular opportunities to rehearse adaptive behavioral responses to key community settings, and created respectable roles for them that helped to compensate for their erstwhile status as psychiatric inpatients. We closed the chapter by concluding that a place remains for individual differences in community psychology, especially when applied in helping empower individuals to recognize and control important aspects of their environment. Choices among settings made by individuals complement the conceptions discussed here, and suggest new ways of understanding how settings are created and why they fail.

In conclusion, the sociophysical context of behavior helps to define its nature. In so doing, it gives us an important perspective on individual and community change. There are limits to what an individual acting alone can do, however. Important restrictions can be imposed by others in the social context, as we will see in chapter 6.

Notes

1. This section is based on Perkins and Long (2002) and Perkins, Hughey, and Speer (2002); see also chapter 12.

2. Outside of a now-defunct community-environmental psychology program in Perth, Australia, there are no graduate training programs that explicitly combine the two areas, although the interdisciplinary programs in Environmental Psychology at City University of New York and Community Research and Action at Vanderbilt University probably come the closest.

3. The person in the mental hospital loses many rights associated with personal liberty when committed by a court. After discharge, the person in the community has all the rights that every other person has, including the right to refuse to participate in any aftercare program. The problem of treating people with serious mental illness in the community stems in part from their right to refuse treatment. Patients who are merely on a temporary furlough from the hospital can be rehospitalized readily, but those who are discharged have full liberty to decide for themselves about treatment. In some jurisdictions it is possible to "commit" a person to outpatient treatment, thus creating an intermediate legal status between those of sick person and well person. The roles are a function not only of custom but also of legal regulation.

6

Labeling Theory: An Alternative to the Illness Model

In chapters 4 and 5 we examined the idea that behavior is best understood not as a specific sign of health or disease but as the product of human adaptation to specific situations. The basic ecological analogy (see chapter 4), however, is rather abstract and thus difficult to use in specific predictive applications. The conceptions offered by Moos, Barker, and Sarbin (chapter 5) are more concrete and practical for many problems, but do not explicitly integrate a view of human individual differences into the perspective they provide on behavior. In the present chapter we examine a theoretical perspective that does make an effort to explain behavior in terms of a dynamic interaction between the person and his or her social context.

This perspective is known as "labeling theory." Developed during the 1960s, labeling theory was a product of new thinking about abnormal behavior and of criticism directed at traditional mental health diagnosis and treatment. An important tenet of labeling theory is that what gets formally diagnosed as psychopathology is not all the deviant behavior that occurs, but merely the behavior that is officially *noticed*. Whether a deviant episode is noticed or not is determined by factors other than the behavior itself, such as the individual's social identity and position, and the discretionary actions of professionals engaged in diagnostic and treatment activities. Like role congruence, labeling theory postulates a similar process in which other people actively interpret and respond to a person's behavior by imposing and maintaining the boundaries defined by a role.

Labeling theory was developed by sociologists; it is an interpersonal theory of deviance that places abnormal behavior in a social context and shows how a systems approach illuminates issues in mental health. In this theory, deviance is a property of an individual's actions and is also "in the eye of the beholder," beholders being all those who interact with the person who exhibits deviant behavior, including those who are in professional helping roles. The deviance perspective, as developed by sociologists Edwin Lemert, Howard Becker, and others (see Gove, 1980), was refined by Scheff (1966, 1984) into an elegant alternative to the illness model. Scheff's presentation of deviance theory in propositional form set the terms of debate for the decade following its appearance.

This chapter begins with a review of social and historical factors that attended the development of labeling theory and then presents its central concepts. We continue by examining the issue of stigma in abnormal behavior.

The Social Context for the Development of Labeling Theory

The labeling position took hold at a time when many people were seeking alternatives to the medical model. During the 1950s and 1960s the reality of terrible institutions became an impetus for reform. Goffman's (1961) widely acclaimed book, *Asylums,* argued persuasively that mental hospitals were inherently oppressive and acted to disable patients as much or more than did the conditions that brought them to the hospital in the first place. Parallel attacks on prisons, institutions for juveniles and for people with mental retardation, and even special class placement, emerged in that period. This attack on "oppressive social institutions" came during the same period as the Kennedy-Johnson reforms and at a time when the ideals of social justice and the plight of the underdog were moving our society to action. The labeling viewpoint fit well with the thrust toward deinstitutionalization and provided an intellectual rationale for that policy (e.g., Bachrach, 1983).

Szasz (1974), who vigorously attacked mental health professionals as "despots" who used coercive methods, worked independently of labeling theorists. He asserted that problematic behavior was not a medical illness based on known physical pathology, but instead was simply behavior that violated social, ethical, moral, and legal norms. Deviance was not an illness, but a social status created in response to our demands for social conformity. It is not too great a stretch to view discrimination on the basis of gender, race or sexual orientation in the same terms. If deviant behavior was defined by acts violating social norms, moreover, psychiatrists, and by implication other mental health professionals with formal responsibility for certifying that norms had been violated, were as much agents of social control as agents of healing (see also Morse, 1978; Morse, Roth, & Wettstein, 1991).

The position was popular because of several considerations—the general cultural disaffection of many in the 1960s, distrust of authority, and competition with psychiatry for dominance in service delivery. Psychologists, social workers, and others welcomed the assault on the medical model because it opened the mental health field to their fuller participation, and to newer thinking.

Principles of Labeling Theory

Labeling theory is designed to account for the presumed "amplification" of acts of *primary* deviance (violations of norms) into *secondary* or "career" deviance. Labeling theory seeks to answer this question: If deviant behavior is merely a norm violation, why do so many deviants become chronically and severely disabled, unable to assume other than ascribed roles? We can apply a similar conceptual analysis to understanding the careers of criminals, gays, and other stigmatized groups who may get locked into particular niches and lifestyles.

Primary and Secondary Deviance

Scheff, following other theorists of his school, differentiates primary and secondary deviance. *Primary deviance* is the specific act that violates one or more social norms. Labeling theory does not address the *cause* of the act of primary deviance in any explicit way. Primary deviance may originate from four sources—an organic deficit, psychological dynamics, external stress, or volitional acts in defiance of social rules. The theory implies that an intact person is capable of producing a much greater variety of behavior than we ordinarily believe, especially when we consider the labeling theory assumption that most pathological behavior is transitory in nature. In this view, less behavior is genuinely "abnormal" or "sick" than most of us believe. In the absence of public attention, the act of primary deviance is transitory, and if it goes unrecorded, that is the end of it.

Secondary deviance is a term applied to the role of a career deviant or chronic patient. Following an act of primary deviance, the single most important event in determining entrance into the role of career deviant is the societal response to the primary deviance. Depending on the class of rules broken, the individual will be referred to and processed by a specialized agency of social control (i.e., oriented to helping, punishing, containing, or isolating). People who have broken rules affecting property or who have harmed others "normally" are handled by the criminal justice system. Children who cannot function adequately in school may be characterized as having mental retardation and treated by the special education system, or they may be admitted to an institution.

Juveniles are treated differently, depending on their offense. Status offenses are acts that would not be criminal if committed by an adult (e.g., running away, incorrigibility, sexual activity, truancy) but that subject the juvenile to the court's jurisdiction. They are less serious in society's view than delinquent acts, which would be crimes if committed by adults. Juveniles who have committed delinquent acts are less often referred for psychiatric and social services than juveniles who commit status offenses. Status offenders are more likely to be referred to a social service agency under diversion programs, while juvenile delinquents receive probation or are sent to secure facilities (Murray, 1983; Handler & Satz, 1982). Now, for some serious crimes, juveniles are tried and punished as adults (Singer, 1996). Juveniles now have permanent criminal records that affect their later opportunities to obtain jobs or even to vote.

People who are processed through the psychiatric system have broken what Scheff calls "residual rules." These are the remaining social norms, so taken for granted that the violation of "goes-without-saying" assumptions regarding proper and decent conduct or the nature of social reality immediately leads to a perception of the individual as bizarre, strange, and perhaps frightening. Ordinarily we do not expect an individual to walk down the street smiling vacantly, gesticulating, talking to himself, apparently tuned to inner space (unless the person is carrying a Sony Walkman). Smiling at no one in particular, talking aloud to one's self, and gesticulating, with no one to receive the communication, are acts that so violate our assumptions about how people ought to act socially that we immediately question the person's sanity.

Because labeling theory postulates that residual rule-breaking is transitory, it assumes that a healthy person is capable of a great variety of behaviors and this variety is not necessarily abnormal. Moreover, what are taken as symptoms of mental illness can also be interpreted as violations of culturally particular norms. Thus interpreted, the "symptoms" should be studied by methods designed to analyze behavior in social contexts, as well as by methods suitable for the study of individual psychopathology.

The norm-violating behavior alone does not elicit the effort at social control, Scheff argues. Social control is exerted whenever a "socially unqualified person" engages in the norm-violating act. In this viewpoint, who is behaving where, when, and in whose presence are more important questions than what behavior was actually performed. A soldier on the battlefield killing an enemy is not committing murder, but one civilian shooting another is. A mime in a store window holds his body in an awkward position for a long time, completely unresponsive to those around him who may try to make him flinch or smile, but no one would consider him catatonic. A medium may talk to spirits or claim to be influenced by unearthly forces, yet is not considered to have paranoid schizophrenia. A patient in a psychiatric hospital claims she is possessed by a devil; yet the priest who tries to exorcise the devil will not be committed.[1] A person who isolates himself or herself, refuses to speak, practices self-flagellation, dresses in a strange costume, refuses to eat for long periods, keeps odd hours, arises at dawn, and goes to bed at a child's hour might well compel the anxious attention of friends or relatives—but not if that person belongs to a religious order. In short, the overt acts and expressed thoughts or feelings are not the only determinants of the outcome. The reactions of others to the actor are critical.[2]

In labeling theory the reactions of others may determine whether or not the individual enters into a career deviant role. In particular, the public labeling of the individual as mentally ill is critical. Labeling theory asserts that the individual is culturally prepared to accept a self-definition of mental illness, first because the individual can apply the label of "crazy" to his or her own behavior, and, second, because the definition of self as mentally ill is reinforced by powerful others in the hospital. Once the person is released, after having been in the role of "good patient," the stigma associated with the mental illness label will keep the person in the role of mental patient.

Murphy (1982), an anthropologist, advocates the illness model of deviance, especially for conditions such as schizophrenia. She notes that all groups have members who do not function normally and that some are considered crazy. The symptoms considered crazy are similar from one group to another. Murphy's observations suggest that labeling theory has distinct limits. In her view, entry into career deviance occurs for certain people without regard to the care they received.

Cultural Stereotypes and Labeling

In labeling theory, both the agent of social control and the rule breaker have to be able to recognize the manifestations of mental illness. Members of the public are one component of the agents of social control, but so are police and mental health workers. In labeling theory, the person who commits the rule-breaking act as a participant in the culture also has internally incorporated images of mental illness and may apply those images to him- or herself. These issues have led to a body of research to determine the public's stereotypes about mental illness.

We believe that the argument about stereotypes has been too narrowly conceived. Today a whole range of behaviors other than serious mental illness have fallen within the domain of the mental health professions. Mental health services have been used for purposes of social control of a wide range of behaviors for a long time. Alcohol and drug problems, sex offenses, and the behavior problems of juveniles were more and more treated as mental health problems than as criminal offenses. Responsibility for controlling and regulating a large variety of deviant behavior shifted from the criminal justice system to the mental health system.

Gove (1980, 1982) also argued that the increasing proportion of voluntary-to-involuntary admissions to mental hospitals and the fact that most referrals for service are voluntary in all types of mental health agencies are difficult for labeling theory to explain. However, Rogers (1993) found that approximately half of patients who admitted themselves to a psychiatric hospital felt coerced, and the psychiatrist was mentioned most often as the professional responsible for the coercion. Hoge, Lidz, Mulvey et al. (1993) and Lidz, Mulvey, Arnold, Bennett, & Kirsch, (1993) reported similar findings based on observations in an emergency room, and on an admissions service. Involuntary commitment may have changed in name only.

If people continue to define all kinds of problems in living as mental health problems (see Gordon, 1982), there may eventually result a normalization of many conditions and some degree of destigmatization. The argument about cultural stereotypes may be much more irrelevant today. The question should be the types of behavior and the conditions under which behavior patterns create sufficient social concern to elicit coerced intervention or the conditions under which people self-define as in need of mental health services.

When Is Residual Rule-Breaking Labeled?

Scheff states that most instances of residual rule-breaking are ignored, denied, or rationalized away. Lacking a societal reaction, these episodes do not lead to illness, but just fade away. Scheff's position assumes that illness does not exist unless the illness has social consequences. (This position is related to Bishop Berkeley's famous philosophical question about whether or not a tree falling in the forest makes a sound if no one hears it.) If most primary deviance is ignored, making the episode transitory, unrecorded, and of no particular social consequence, why in other cases does the same behavior lead to social control and public labeling? The outcome is essentially determined by five sets of variables (See Figure 6-1):

1. Irrespective of cause, the degree, amount, and visibility of the rule-breaking are determinants of whether or not there will be any public reaction and efforts at social control. As an extreme illustration, if an individual was capable of exhibiting crazy behavior but engaged in it only when alone, that behavior would never come to the attention of others, would pass, and would not be recorded as illness. Those who work with people who have chronic mental disabilities understand this principle when they encourage clients to suppress symptoms when in public. Thus patient members of Fairweather's community lodge (see chapter 5) were told they were not allowed to act crazy while interacting with customers of their janitorial and gardening service, and most were able to suppress norm-violating behavior (Fairweather et al., 1969). Patients were allowed to act crazy while at home in the lodge. This form of treatment recognizes that societal reaction has consequences for continued living in the community. In Scheff's view, to the degree that symptoms are "invisible," there is no illness. A "mole" who operated within the FBI for years was uncovered. The spy committed many illegal (and by definition deviant) acts, but it was only after the acts were discovered that he was subject to prosecution and labeled a traitor.

Many people suffer from anxiety, depression, strange thoughts, or bizarre, frightening, or embarrassing fantasies but are able to meet everyday responsibilities and conceal their symptoms from all but themselves. Their conditions may wax and wane without attracting the notice of others; without public notice, there is no illness.

The intensity, frequency, and duration of the rule-breaking episode may present primary conditions for the initiation of treatment and efforts at social control. Gove (1980, 1982) cited literature indicating that those who entered treatment have more severe symptoms than those who did not. Morrell, Levine, and Perkins (1982) reviewed the daily logs kept by staff in a proprietary home for adult mental patients located in a city neighborhood. Those patients who were later rehospitalized had many more episodes that brought the residents to the attention of staff as recorded in the log book than did comparable patients who were not rehospitalized. This difference in number of behavioral incidents was noticeable for many weeks before rehospitalization. Because both groups were chronically impaired, these data suggest that greater frequency and visibility of disturbed behavior is associated with rehospitalization and not just the episode of "rule breaking."

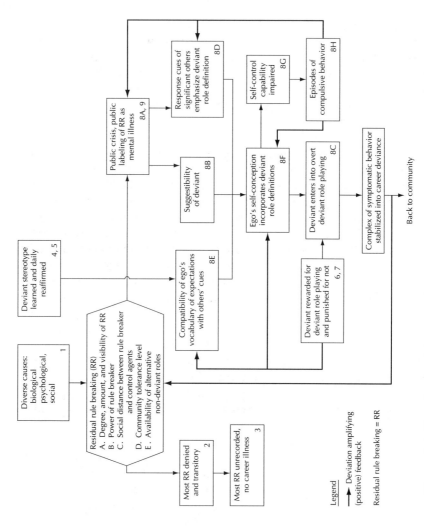

Figure 6-1. Flowchart-stabilization of deviance in a social system. (From Scheff, 1984)

Diverse causes: biological psychological, social 1

Residual rule breaking (RR)
A. Degree, amount, and visibility of RR
B. Power of rule breaker
C. Social distance between rule breaker and control agents
D. Community tolerance level
E. Availability of alternative non-deviant roles

Deviant stereotype learned and daily reaffirmed 4, 5

Most RR denied and transitory 2

Most RR unrecorded, no career illness 3

Public crisis, public labeling of RR as mental illness 8A, 9

Response cues of significant others emphasize deviant role definition 8D

Self-control capability impaired 8G

Episodes of compulsive behavior 8H

Suggestibility of deviant 8B

Compatibility of ego's vocabulary of expectations with others' cues 8E

Ego's self-conception incorporates deviant role definitions 8F

Deviant enters into overt deviant role playing 8C

Deviant rewarded for deviant role playing and punished for not 6, 7

Complex of symptomatic behavior stabilized into career deviance

Back to community

Legend
→ Deviation amplifying (positive) feedback

Residual rule breaking = RR

204

2. Scheff's second variable dealt with the power and social status of the rule breaker vis-à-vis the agent of social control. If the power differential favors the rule breaker, he or she may not be readily subject to social control. During his last days as president, Richard M. Nixon is said to have exhibited some bizarre behavior (Woodward & Bernstein, 1976). Although many expressed concern over the state of his mind, no one did anything to bring the president to the attention of a mental health professional. Taking another example closer to the everyday experience of people in the mental health field, we note that untold numbers of neophyte psychotherapists have been urged if not ordered by therapy supervisors to work out some personal problem interfering with therapy or supervision by entering treatment. Although any number of neophyte therapists may well have entertained serious doubts about the mental health of some of their supervisors, it is a rare student or intern who would have the courage to urge the supervisor to seek treatment. The student certainly could not order the supervisor to enter treatment and enforce the order with a threat of dismissal or a poor recommendation or letter of reference.

Former President Clinton pardoned two exceptionally wealthy men who were fugitives, avoiding a criminal indictment. After the pardon, they could no longer be prosecuted for their alleged criminal acts. The wealthy rule breakers avoided prosecution by their use of wealth to influence power. These and other pardons raised renewed questions about whether the justice system which labels criminals is different for wealthy, powerful, or well-connected people, than for the poor or even the ordinary citizen.

Looking at still another index of social power, Gove notes that people who occupy more central roles in families and who presumably have greater social power are hospitalized sooner than those occupying more peripheral roles. If a mother is unable to meet her obligations, the household soon falls apart, and others will seek help for her. If a grandmother wanders and is forgetful or incoherent, however, she may not be hospitalized for a much longer time after symptoms have been noted.

3. The social distance between the rule breaker and the agent of social control may also be a factor in determining whether the agent of social control will act in relation to an episode of primary deviance. Keil, Usui, & Busch (1983) found that people of higher socioeconomic status were better able to avoid rehospitalization for excessive drinking than those of lower status, even when drinking patterns were controlled. Consider the following example. A police officer seeing a drunk who is obviously a homeless street person may arrest the person or consider emergency hospitalization. The same officer seeing a disheveled but well-dressed drunk vomiting and staggering down the street may find a cab and send him home.

4. Scheff's fourth factor is the level of tolerance for deviance within

a community. A psychiatrist on an admitting service of a large urban receiving hospital reported a conversation with a newly arrived, itinerant, streetwise patient who desired to be admitted to the psychiatric facility in a city unfamiliar to him. The patient inquired seriously about what he had to do to be admitted—break a window or run down the street with his clothes off. In that particular city, the better choice would have been nudity. Yet in San Francisco's Golden Gate Park it would not have been unusual during the height of the "flower child" years of the 1960s to see an adult male, stark naked, happily listening to a concert in the park. That community's tolerance for personal oddity was much greater.

Citizens of Geel, Belgium, a haven for people with mental disorders for more than seven hundred years (Godemont, 1992; Roosens, 1979), has unusual tolerance for deviant behavior. The patients wander the streets freely and other citizens quietly but effectively engage anyone who is disruptive and stop the disruptiveness; everyone in the city accepts it as an obligation to work with patients. More overtly troubled and troublesome patients are returned to the hospital, of course, but the citizens of Geel accept a great deal of oddity without special notice. Geel is an important example; there are understood limits to the integration of people with deviant characteristics into the community. There can be great tolerance and substantial integration, but by no means is either tolerance or integration complete.

5. Scheff's fifth factor regarding the labeling of residual rule-breaking is the availability of alternative nondeviant roles. He describes several examples of primary deviance interpreted in such a fashion that the person's status was elevated. One example is the entrance into shamanship following a period of agitation (Murphy, 1964). A related example is that of religious prophets who report extraordinary extrasensory communications, but normalize that communication by putting it into a religious context. Such people sometimes emerge as respected members of a community. John Humphrey Noyes, founder of the religiously based Oneida Community, went through a "dark night of the soul" and emerged strengthened from the experience after his friends assisted him and continued to accept him as their spiritual leader (Levine & Bunker, 1975). A third example Scheff offers is of a woman who experienced hallucinations while in church at a time when her personal problems seemed overwhelming. Although she was startled by her hallucinations, her chance encounter with a stranger who identified herself as a psychic helped the woman to reinterpret her hallucinations as manifestations of psychic powers. The encounter led her into a career as a psychic.

The best known example of the creation of niches and roles as forms of treatment for people with mental disorders is the Fairweather et al. (1969) creation of roles for patients as managers of residential lodges and businesses (see chapter 5). In contemporary society, an alternative nondeviant role is often provided to those who participate in various self-help groups and become deeply involved as senior members or as more formal leaders. In these cases, it is necessary to have experienced the primary deviance (the alcoholism or the "nervous breakdown") and to have overcome it by active participation in the self-help group. Some adolescents in turmoil and feeling isolated because of their sexual orientation and identity can be helped by finding a place in a community of other gays. Although still considered deviant by the larger community, some adolescents find respite when accepted into such a group. Krizan (1982) described a small religious sect that evidently had success with some disturbed individuals who found personal havens and missions for themselves by joining the congregation and proselytizing for it. In these examples, people entered existing social organizations while under great stress. Whether prepared niches can be created as therapeutic devices for people who are experiencing great personal problems and who are acutely disturbed remains to be seen.

Diagnosis and Labeling Theory

The diagnostic process is an important element within labeling theory. After a person goes (or is brought by someone else) for care, a mental health professional uses a diagnostic process to certify whether or not the person has a disorder suitable for treatment in that particular facility. The U.S. Supreme Court based its decision in *Parham* v. *J. and J.R.* (1979) on the assumption that a child's personal rights when brought for hospitalization by a parent are sufficiently safeguarded by the integrity of the diagnostic process that additional safeguards of due process were unnecessary. However, we must still ask whether we can depend on the validity and integrity of the diagnostic process to identify and label only those who are ill and in need of care.

Scheff notes that the diagnostic process itself occurs within a social context that has implications for the outcome. In the cultural attitudes of physicians, it is more important to avoid failing to diagnose pathology when it exists than to avoid suspecting pathology when it doesn't exist. It is more harmful to miss a diagnosis and fail to institute treatment than to continue to observe and test in order to rule out pathology. The medical assumption that it does less harm to observe further than to miss illness may not be appropriate for mental illness, because the *social* costs for the prospective patient of hospitalization to diagnose mental illness are greater than the social costs of hospitalization for diagnosing physical illness. Admission to a hospital for laboratory tests and x-rays doesn't have the same implication for the person's social identity as admission to a psychiatric service.

Scheff believes that mental health professionals, by virtue of their positions in the social system providing care, are biased toward finding pathology and holding people for care. His argument is important for the "deviance amplification" position of labeling theory, in that any behavior pattern is potentially subject to labeling. Mental health professionals have to be able to differentiate between those whose problems are best characterized as manifestations of illness and those who have other problems in living. The use of psychiatric language and coerced hospitalization to control political dissidents and members of a religious group in China is a case in point. The psychiatrists insisted that the people who were hospitalized had paranoid schizophrenia. Scheff showed that in the commitment context, psychiatric interviews were often brief, legal hearings were often perfunctory, and the necessary evidence regarding the criteria for commitment, posing a danger to self or others, was often not clearly brought out in the record or the psychiatric testimony.

Scheff argued that the commitment system encourages findings of illness because mental health professionals who are not well paid for public work of this sort often increase their rates by reducing the amount of time they spend per case. Moreover, judges facing dispositions for troubled people brought to public attention also face possible political repercussions if they release someone who then harms him- or herself or others. They are therefore inclined to favor commitment. Judges may encourage mental health professionals in subtle and not so subtle fashion to produce findings supporting commitment. Ennis and Litwack (1974) note that mental health personnel are at risk for liability in a civil suit if they release someone who harms another (Beck, 1998), but they are far less likely to be found liable if they hold someone in a hospital for further treatment (but see *O'Connor* v. *Donaldson*, 1975).

In part, the issue is the reliability of psychiatric diagnosis. Spitzer and Williams (1982) agree that in the past such reliability left much to be desired. They claim that the situation improved substantially with the development of the *DSM-III* diagnostic system. However, Kirk and Kutchins (1992) claim that the reliability of the *DSM* system is no better than it was under the earlier system. Be that as it may, the weakness of psychiatric diagnosis and clinical methods has been exposed in many adversary hearings, such as the trial of would-be presidential assassin John Hinckley. The degree of reliability that may emerge in research tests of the diagnostic system may not hold for other contexts.

The diagnosis and degree of the patient's presenting condition are not the only (and may not even be the primary) considerations in the decision to hospitalize and thus to assign a diagnostic label for the record. Many other variables affect the decision to admit. On admission services, the family's desire for the individual to be hospitalized tends to be a stronger factor in the admission decision than is the clinician's judgment of degree of disorder, although some people who have unsuccessfully sought the hospitalization of a spouse or adult child may dispute that conclusion. Many factors beyond the patient's presenting condition influence admission decisions. These include insurance and managed care considerations, legal standards, fear of being manipulated by a patient, research needs for a certain kind of patient, or the need for certain cases for teaching or training purposes.

Those who are selected for labeling may have some social or clinical characteristics that make it easier for some labels to stick. Lindsay (1982) demonstrated that his research subjects could readily detect first-admission persons with schizophrenia from nonpatients when observing interviews on the topic of schooling, even when given false labels. Apparently, in some patients, disturbance is obvious.

However, the stringency of the decision-making process leaves much to be desired under ordinary working conditions, as Rosenhan's (1973) classic study demonstrates. Rosenhan showed that pseudopatients (researchers who presented themselves to a mental hospital admitting service as ill but who demonstrated only the most minimal symptoms) were readily admitted on their own application, and their deception went undetected. The diagnostic process is suffcently unreliable under ordinary working conditions that labels can readily be misapplied (Kirk and Kutchins, 1992). This body of evidence supports one component of the labeling theory model, although it by no means confirms the major proposition of labeling theory that anyone thus mislabeled could be made a career deviant.

Behavior Is Assimilated to the Label

Few rules govern observation and inference in the psychiatric setting. Many clinicians are unaware of the limits of inferences drawn from clinical observations (Dawes, 1994). Any behavior observed in the hospital may be readily interpreted in light of the initial diagnosis, or the patient's status as a patient. Patients are observed and diagnosed based on an important unstated assumption of the clinical enterprise stemming from the pervasive influence of Freudian thinking on clinical workers. In the Freudian system, surface appearances are distrusted and situational factors are discounted. The important factor is not what is apparent, but what lies underneath the apparent. Because there are no or few explicit rules relating observed behavior to the unobserved construct, anything can be related to anything else. One can accept the surface behavior or reinterpret it to fit whatever construct the worker has in mind. These issues can affect clinicians trying to meet their legal duty to report suspected child sexual abuse (Levine et al., 1995).

Observing psychiatric residents in training, Light (1982) notes that they were often bewildered by the intangible nature of psychiatric symptoms and complaints. He believes they were subject to doctrinaire instruction, with little review of the research literature to foster an appreciation of the weakness of the methods and theories they were being taught. He argues that the process of psychiatric interviewing leads to accentuating the neurotic characteristics of everyone concerned, including the psychiatric interviewer. Consequently, interviewers feel a need to distance and to differentiate themselves from patients. As a personal anecdote, when he worked in a mental hospital, Levine often found himself fingering the keys that differentiated him from the patients. These keys served as a security blanket. Light argues that all of the uncertainties lead to quick assimilation of the psychiatric culture, including uncritical use of diagnostic labels. We have no reason to believe that clinical psychologists or psychiatric social workers training in medical settings are any more immune to this culture than are psychiatric residents, but those who are trained behaviorally may be less subject to this bias.

Once a tentative diagnosis is developed, many aspects of patient behavior are assimilated to the diagnosis. Rosenhan (1973) reports that perfectly normal behavior of his pseudopatients was recorded as symptoms of disturbance. Psychiatric training, centering as it does on the classification of disorders into mutually exclusive categories and on the assumption that environmental circumstances do not matter very much, fails to sensitize practitioners to the situationally determined character of much behavior. Braginsky, Braginsky, and Ring (1969) demonstrated that patients can manipulate their presentation of themselves in psychiatric interviews depending on their goals.

Many studies have shown the limited predictability of clinical assessments to behavior in other settings including employment and adjustment in the community (Stack, Lannon, & Miley, 1983; Tuckman & Lavell, 1962). Even if the use of DSM-IV criteria results in more reliable application of clinical labels, we have no reason to believe that judgments predicated on those labels will have any greater validity. The mental health worldview simply does not take situational influences sufficiently into account, and so it is all too easy to assume that any behavior that is observed is related to pathology.

In labeling theory, staff within institutions assimilate patient behavior to patient diagnosis and find reasons why the patient is "sick." Patient complaints and objections are likely to be treated as manifestations of resistance or as part of the patient's illness. The patient's suggestibility during a period of crisis and the patient's distress at treatment in the hospital may lead to behavior that appears out of control both to the observer and to the patient.

A patient may refuse medication for any number of reasons, for example, including the fear that medication will produce untoward side effects. Yet hospital personnel may label the patient's resistance to taking medication "paranoid" and insist that the patient accept it. If the patient continues to refuse and loses his or her temper or cries when pressed, the patient may be considered to be hostile and aggressive or in a labile emotional state. The patient, noting the emotional behavior in himself or herself, may feel out of control. At that point, self-observation coupled with reinforcement from powerful others feeds into the formation of the person's identity as "sick."

Once the self is viewed as "sick," the next step is to accept the role of good patient and to play it out until discharge. During a hospital stay, much of a patient's life is regimented. Patients lose a great deal of autonomy and are encouraged to rely on the advice and direction of treating personnel. A "good" patient accepts the therapeutic regime without question. One who disputes the professional's view of his or her intentions, motives, feelings, or behavior is judged resistant. Rosenhan (1973) reports that a pseudopatient who was bored by the lack of activity in the hospital paced the dayroom. When questioned by a nurse, the pseudopatient said that he was bored. The nurse insisted that the pseudopatient was anxious and persisted in getting the pseudopatient to accept the "true" nature of his "symptom" of pacing. If the pseudopatient expressed annoyance at the nurse, in all likelihood he would have been characterized as resistant and hostile. If he accepted her interpretation of his state, he would have been characterized as having "gained insight" and thus improving. In other words, powerful social forces are at work to encourage the patient to accept and to internalize the hospital's and the professional's views of the patient's condition and capabilities.

Gove (1980) is willing to admit that in bygone days, chronicity may have been fostered in total institutions that kept patients for long periods. He believes the situation has changed drastically in recent decades, however. Given modern clinical practices, most patients are released relatively quickly, with little time for chronicity to set in. In addition, the removal of a patient from a stressful life setting has ameliorative effects in and of itself. The hospital experience provides a retreat during which the person may recover. Moreover, active therapy does help a great many individuals. Gove argues that far from keeping patients in the patient role, adequate treatment frees patients. He points out that in the absence of treatment, many deinstitutionalized patients quickly deteriorate.

In sum, methods of diagnosis and observation are not very precise. We do not have powerful theories and constructs that allow us to predict accurately to new circumstances (see chapter 5). We can too easily assume that once sick, always sick, or that everything we observe in a person reflects his or her sickness. Mental health personnel probably convey such attitudes to their patients, and to some degree patients tend to accept that view of themselves. Similar processes may affect prison inmates, or juveniles in institutions. Present-day conditions of treatment surely are not sufficient to produce the kind of chronic condition that is implied in the concept of a career deviant. Nonetheless, labeling theory's emphasis on the undesirable side effects of care should be taken seriously, if only to cause us to reexamine our attitudes and practices with an eye toward understanding their consequences and limitations. Not all that is done in the name of doing good in fact does good.

Stigma

The final factor aiding in the formation of a deviant career is the stigma attached to the role of mental patient or ex-mental patient (see Goffman, 1963). In Scheff's view, once the patient returns to the community, the stigma of having been a mental patient continues to follow him or her. Opportunities for employment may be affected, and, equally important, others will tend to interpret the individual's behavior in light of the history of mental illness. The person may also feel more uncomfortable knowing that his or her status is suspect, and his discomfort may leak, providing others with data to confirm their suspicions. It may be easier for the individual to be rehospitalized because he or she has never been fully rid of the taint to social identity. The stigma attached to mental illness serves to keep the released patient in the tainted role, thus creating the role of career deviant or chronic mental patient. The disagreement between Scheff and Gove revolves around the role of stigma in creating chronic disability. Labeling theory places a great deal of emphasis on this issue, while Gove claims that the primary determinant of any social reaction to a former mental patient is the person's current behavior.

In an earlier day, in addition to whatever informal social sanctions followed commitment, the individual was placed under a number of formal constraints. His or her liberty to engage in a great many activities was restricted. A committed mental patient, regardless of competence, might lose a driver's license, be unable to contract for goods and services, be disqualified from marrying, or be barred from military service. In recent times, the rights of people with disabilities have been better protected (Levy, Rubenstein, Ennis, & Friedman, 1996; Stefan, 2001). In addition to formal disabilities, occupational and social stigma also resulted. Former prisoners also carry such stigma. On the assumption that serving time as an adult is more stigmatizing than serving time as a juvenile, Howell (1996) showed that juveniles who were convicted as adults and who served prison sentences had worse recidivism rates than juveniles punished through the juvenile justice system. According to former patients and patient advocates, stigma is still a critical factor affecting the adaptation of former patients in the community.

In labeling theory, stigma helps to keep the person in the patient role. Significant others may interpret the individual's behavior in light of their knowledge of the person's history. Anger, dislikes, disagreements, moods, or failure to achieve may all be read as continued manifestations of disorder or as prodromal to another episode, even after a period of normality. Recall Rosenhan's (1973) report that the normal behavior of his pseudopatients was interpreted as pathological by nurses and attendants and recorded in case files as symptoms of disorder; pacing out of boredom was characterized as anxiety, note taking for purposes of research became compulsive writing. Even after discharge, the diagnosis was not changed, but the person continued to carry the label—Schizophrenia, Chronic Undifferentiated Type, in Remission. To use Goffman's (1963) term, the patient's social identity was "spoiled."

If we have any question concerning the power of stigmatization, we need only look at Senator Thomas Eagleton, who was forced to withdraw from candidacy for the vice presidency in the 1972 election campaign after it was revealed that he had been treated for a depressive disorder many years before. Even though he had functioned visibly and responsibly in positions of public leadership for many years following the episode, the stigma of mental disorder was sufficient to disqualify him from running for that office.

Not only public figures suffer. One of us was psychotherapist for a boy of about 14 who had been having more than the usual share of growing up difficulties. Several years later the young man joined the navy. He completed basic and specialist training successfully and performed competently in the navy. Despite the navy's experience with him over several years, when his promotion required an additional security clearance, a naval intelligence officer contacted his therapist wanting to know about the nature of problems for which the boy was treated several years earlier.

The ordinary person is also concerned about stigma. During the initial days of the Love Canal crisis blue-collar families actively avoided the eager mental health worker on the scene. They avoided the table labeled Mental Health, not because they were not under emotional strain but because they feared their neighbors' reactions if they openly accepted help. "I'm not crazy!" they would say (Gibbs, 1983).

Simple labeling may create a stigma. Law Professor Judy Scales-Trent is a very light-skinned African American who can easily pass for white. She recounts a number of incidents showing a change in attitude or behavior toward her after the other person learned she was African American (Scales-Trent, 1995).

Is stigma a potent factor in producing career deviants? One body of studies using surveys and questionnaires suggests that Americans have become more tolerant of mental illness over the years. The research procedure often makes use of vignettes portraying various types of disorders; it measures social distance in terms of a scale that asks questions such as: Would you accept such a person in your community? Would you work with such a person? Would you rent a room in your home to such a person? Would you want such a person to marry into your family?

Studies using these methods have reported very mixed results (So-call & Holtgraves, 1992). Most of the studies used two different methods of collecting data. In one group of studies, subjects completed paper-and-pencil social-distance scales using vignettes describing patients. The second group of studies employed face-to-face interviews and asked about a hypothetical mental patient. Researchers coming from medical backgrounds and institutions tended to use the face-to-face interview, using the hypothetical person with a mental disability as the stimulus, and found that public attitudes toward people with mental illness were improving. Social science researchers preferred to use self-response questionnaires and vignettes as the stimulus material. These studies consistently reported negative attitudes toward people with mental illness (Roessler, Salize, & Voges, 1995; Socall & Holtgraves, 1992). Results reporting the degree of optimism or pessimism attributed to the public may thus be a function of method and discipline of the investigator more than of the public's real attitude (Tebes, 1983).

At an attitudinal level, at least as measured by scales and self-report, the stigma attached to the person with a mental disability may have been reduced from the level of earlier times (Skinner, Berry, Griffith, & Byers, 1995). Public education campaigns to reduce the stigma of mental illness conducted by the American Psychiatric Association and the National Alliance for the Mentally Ill (see chapter 9) may be helping in this regard. We really know very little about the relationship between expressed attitudes and behavior. Public education on questions of mental illness may have influenced what people are willing to say on questionnaires, but it does not necessarily follow that people always act in complete consistency with those expressed attitudes.

Some studies, however, show that families of people with mental illness are more tolerant toward mentally ill people than is the general public. Nonetheless, family members do report concealing to some degree the family member's history of hospitalization for their own social comfort. A body of literature summarized in Tebes (1983) suggests that family members often reduce the frequency of their visits to mentally ill persons and that many are reluctant to accept the person back into the home. Distinguishing between rejection that results from stigma and rejection that results from the strain of dealing with a mentally ill person is difficult. Tebes believes the explanation that family members reject the mental patient because of the physical, economic, and psychological burdens of care is more plausible than the theory that rejection is based on stigma.

The situation of family members may differ from that of potential neighbors, employers, landlords, and others dealing with the person with mental illness. Many court cases have challenged zoning ordinances that exclude group homes for people with mental disabilities from residential neighborhoods. (The U.S. Supreme Court decided such a case in 1985: *City of Cleburne, Texas* v. *Cleburne Living Center*, 1985.) The existence of zoning ordinances reflects community attitudes. People fear being harmed or they fear property values will decrease. Both of those fears appear to be exaggerated.

In the case of people with mental retardation, studies show that the presence of a group home has little or no impact on neighborhood property values (Wiener, Anderson, & Nietupski, 1982). Studies also show that individuals with mental retardation living in group homes in the community have a far lower rate of contact with the police than do average citizens in that community (Uhl & Levine, 1990). When a group home is proposed for a neighborhood, there is often vocal community opposition, and plans to open some group homes may have been changed because of local opposition. If such a home does open, however, follow-up studies show that neighbors become positive or indifferent toward it after a while. We assume that if undesirable consequences had followed the opening of a group home, neighborhood opposition would have increased with time. The initial attitude thus appears to be prejudiced and based on stigma, not on the actual events that follow the opening of a group home.

Employers may stigmatize persons with a history of mental illness, making it difficult for the former patient to obtain employment. Brand and Claiborn (1976) sent four undergraduates and two graduate students to answer ads for job openings in retail sales. Each student participated in six interviews. In two they gave histories as former tuberculosis patients, in two they said they were former convicts, and in two they described themselves as former psychiatric patients. They were coached to dress and to act the same in each role. In the role of former tuberculosis patient, 75 percent received job offers. Those who said they were former convicts or former psychiatric patients drew job offers 58 percent of the time. These results indicate that although employers will hire former patients for some jobs, former patients are still at some handicap when being considered for employment. That this handicap is no worse than that facing former convicts does not change the conclusion. These were entry-level jobs. We don't know what would happen if the experiment were to be repeated with positions requiring more responsibility. Note also that Scheff's model should apply to any form of deviance.

Gebhard and Levine (1985) constructed resumés of people already employed and asked management students to say whether they would promote the people described to a more responsible position. The resumés were identical, except that in one the individual had lost time from work three years earlier due to a gall bladder operation; in the second, the person was described as having lost time from work due to alcoholism; in the third, the person was described as having lost time from work due to alcoholism and was a member of Alcoholics

Anonymous. The label of alcoholism significantly reduced the person's chances of being considered for promotion, even though the resumés all indicated very good job performance and no indication of alcohol problems over three years. The study was designed to test the hypothesis that membership in Alcoholics Anonymous would be destigmatizing. That hypothesis could not be confirmed.

Former patients are probably subject to labeling effects in social relationships. Page (1977, 1983) called landlords who had advertised the availability of rental units in the classified section of a daily newspaper. If the person calling identified himself as having had mental illness, the response from the landlord was immediately less positive. In one study, the simple fact that the caller stuttered was sufficient to reduce the number of positive responses to the call (a positive response being that the rental quarters were still available and the person was encouraged to make an appointment to see them). In other words, any deviant condition may be sufficiently stigmatizing to reduce opportunities for the person so stigmatized.

Tebes (1983) reviewed a large number of field and laboratory studies testing the effects of stigmatization. He concluded:

> The results from studies of labeling effects reveal that, in social interactions, both the perceptions and behaviors of persons carrying a mental disorder label and those responding to them are significantly affected by the pejorative impact of the label. This impact predisposes the labeled person to feel and be rejected by others. On the one hand, there is the situation where the non-labeled social participant is aware of the person's deviant history. In many such cases, the labeled person can expect social responses of rejection and/or avoidance especially if the labeled participant is male. On the other hand, if the former patient believes his deviant history is known to others in his immediate social situation, the problem is further compounded by the likelihood that he will act in a way which alienates those around him, thus predisposing him to rejection. Clearly, the former mental patient would do well to conceal his status if at all possible, a practice which, ironically in itself requires considerable social agility, as Goffman (1963) has described. (pp. 70–71)

The Use of Law to Reduce Stigma

Labeling in the context of deviance can result in stigma, and can contribute to the perpetuation of a deviant career. However, law can also be employed to reduce stigma and to "normalize" deviance by removing formal limitations otherwise imposed by law. Ogburn (1966) developed the concept of "cultural lag." He hypothesized that technological change results in maladaptation because aspects of the culture lag behind technological change. Eventually, the culture catches up with material change and a new equilibrium is reached.

Kantaras v. *Kantaras* (2003) is a case in point. Michael Kantaras is a female-to-male transsexual. He married Linda, adopted her child and they had a second child by artificial insemination. Linda and Michael became estranged after nine years of marriage. He fell in love with Sherry, and Linda sued for divorce and child custody. The case presented some unique issues. Florida law does not recognize same-sex marriages nor does it permit adoptions by same-sex couples. Despite his sex reassignment surgery, was Michael a woman and were the marriage and the adoption invalid?

After a long trial, Judge O'Brien issued an opinion saying the marriage and the adoption were valid because Michael, after sex reassignment surgery, was a man. Judge O'Brien said that although Michael was born a female, the law said nothing about when a man became a man, recognizing the sex reassignment surgery and treatment and expert medical and psychological testimony saying that Michael was a man. He also awarded custody of the two children to Michael because Linda had consistently interfered with Michael's visitation rights.

Michael was diagnosed as having a Gender Identity Disorder. Despite the diagnosis and the perception of many (e.g., members of Linda's family, her pastor) that transsexuals are deviants, the judge permitted the marriage and granted custody to Michael. Judge O'Brien said that the law must recognize scientific developments (e.g., sex reassignment surgery and hormone treatment) and accommodate the law to those developments. The court's decision thus removed formal disabilities (inability to marry and to adopt a child) from Michael's status.

Some Cautions

The usefulness and attractiveness of labeling theory as an analytic device do not imply that its every detail is accurate. Whatever the validity of its specific propositions, however, labeling theory is useful as an analytic device, provided one does not overlook the fact that the behavior of many who do come to the attention of some system of social control may indeed be difficult to tolerate, burdensome, repulsive, or dangerous. A flaw of labeling theory is that it feeds too neatly into an antiauthority stance in favor of any underdog. Nonetheless, the theory points out areas of interest for research, service, and prevention. As a model, it helps us pay attention to a broader set of variables than individual psychology includes.

Our first caution is that the labeling position in its strong version (i.e., that under given conditions, a person with a chronic disability can be created out of nothing more than the violation of a social norm) is almost certainly wrong, as Gove (1980, 1982) has diligently and persuasively shown. The reader, however, should take Scheff (1966, 1999) along with a full dose of Gove (1980, 1982), a proponent of the medical model and labeling theory's chief critic. The weaker version, that social disability (i.e., career deviance) based on an initial episode of rule-breaking may vary depending on treatment, is a more viable position (Killian & Killian, 1990). Even that version is unable to account for variations in outcomes after the initial deviant episode, however. Not all who are treated become chronic patients, and diagnosis does have some predictive significance for long-term outcomes. People diagnosed with schizophrenia, for example, are more likely to become chronic patients than those who receive diagnoses of depressive reactions. Since all patients are affected by the same diagnostic and treatment system, labeling theory must account for the fact that outcomes differ systematically by diagnostic category. We are learning more about the genetic and biochemical nature of some disorders. Those factors may account for the differences in outcome.

Outcomes also vary by initial symptom picture and diagnosis. Not all who are publicly labeled become career deviants, a fact that labeling theory does not explain. Moreover, other longitudinal studies have revealed perplexing problems for labeling theory. Robins (1974; Robins & Rutter, 1991) showed that antisocial behavior in childhood predicts antisocial behavior in adulthood among those who were treated (labeled) in a child guidance clinic. Yet most children with antisocial behavior patterns do not grow up into antisocial adults, whether or not they receive treatment. Moreover, those children who presented neurotic complaints and were treated (labeled) were no different at followup than untreated controls. Studies of these two categories of behavior show that outcome does vary by initial symptom picture, and labeling theory cannot account for that fact. Labeling theory is at best incomplete, and at worst wrong.

A second caution is also in order. Because labeling theory pays less attention to the behavior triggering the labeling process and more to the labeling process and its consequences, its adherents may well overlook the fact that difficult behavior does exist, and not only in the eyes of the beholder. Because labeling theory argues that the social reaction is critical does not mean that the behavior that triggers the labeling process is objectively harmless. Rule-breaking behavior can be difficult to bear, both for the person exhibiting it and for those around him or her. Such behavior may understandably elicit reactions of fear, anger, loathing, helplessness, or weariness.

Scheff's (1966/1999) exposition depicts deviance as a social status or role within the larger culture, but a role whose characteristics are closely related to the way in which mental hospitals and mental health professionals work. Perforce, labeling theory extended our vision to include among the variables of interest the individual's social position and the professional care system. Even if wrong in its details, and if it did nothing else, labeling theory made it more difficult for us to think about psychopathology in isolation from the social context and the system of care.

Summary

We have emphasized that labeling theory is to be valued more for the analytic perspective it offers than for the correctness of its details. However, a scientific conception that leads us to seek out observations that will test its propositions is valuable for that reason alone. Labeling theory has done exactly that. It has asked us to look at data that we would have overlooked had we adopted the perspective that psychopathology resides solely within an individual's skin.

Labeling theory encompasses individual differences in behavior. It does not say that any behavior or person is equally subject to labeling or to developing a deviant career. The theory does direct our attention to the social setting within which the particular behavior pattern is manifested, however, and asks us to look at the relationships among individuals in their roles, the agents of social control, and the therapeutic system. If we recall the ecological lessons of chapter 4, labeling theory alerts us to the consequences of diversity in status, values, and goals among different groups that happen to share the same community settings. It explains more thoroughly than did Sarbin's role theory how the behavior of others can limit one's opportunities in ways that cut across multiple situations and endure over time.

Labeling theory has something in common with the Dohrenwend position discussed in chapter 3 (and considered further in chapter 7). Both are systems theories emphasizing the context within which behavior is studied. Both viewpoints also emphasize the transient nature of the initial deviant episode. Labeling theory focuses on the undesirable and unanticipated effects of the existing treatment system, which might be understood as society's effort to supply social support to the individual in need. Dohrenwend's position calls attention to the positive effects of existing social and personal resources for helping when an individual is experiencing a stressful life event.

The reader should reflect on the similarities between the concepts of adaptation, crisis, coping, and social support and labeling theory. Primary deviance, for example, may be thought of as the initial emotional and behavioral reaction to a stressful life event. One may also draw a parallel between the social support available to a person and the system of care provided for mental health problems. In addition, one may consider how the societal reaction to an emotional response produced by acute stress (whether or not the person's problem comes to public attention) is influenced by psychological mediators the person uses as well as the social support that is available.

Last, when we propose alternative methods of providing assistance to the individual in distress, the reader should keep labeling theory in mind. Especially in its emphasis on the stigma associated with treatment under some conditions, labeling theory reminds us that interventions generally have multiple effects. It directs us to examine the possibility that the newer forms of assistance, designed to assist the processes of coping and adaptation following a stressful event, may also have unintended consequences. Having noted the complementary features of the Dohrenwend and labeling viewpoints, we turn now to an elaboration of the Dohrenwend discussion and some concepts and research associated with it.

Notes

1. We are indebted to attorney Sheila Graziano for this example drawn from her practice.

2. This position has something in common with Dohrenwend's model (see chapter 3). In neither Scheff's nor Dohrenwend's models does the stressful life event inevitably proceed to a pathological reaction.

7

Adaptation, Crisis, Coping, and Support

In chapter 3 we introduced Barbara Dohrenwend's (1978) useful perspective on stress and disorder as a more comprehensive model of mental health than that provided by traditional clinical conceptions, and one offering alternative solutions to mental health problems. The present chapter elaborates Dohrenwend's overall model. We begin by examining the concepts of adaptation and crisis in light of the traditional psychoanalytic conception of disorder, extend the idea of a psychological crisis to research on stressful life events, and then reevaluate the person-environment approach using what has come to be called the "vulnerability" model. This latter framework paves the way for a discussion of coping and social support.

One issue is how individuals avoid developing psychopathology or, more positively, how individuals move to restore psychological equilibrium, or even achieve psychological growth, as a result of exposure to and mastery of a stressful life event.

Adaptation

Dohrenwend (1978) defined the aim of community psychology as "undermining the process whereby stress generates psychopathology" (p. 2). A useful starting point in understanding this process is the concept of "adaptation." Adaptation refers to improvements in the fit between an individual's behavior and the specific demands and constraints of settings making up his or her environment. Adaptation is facilitated by widening the niche provided in the environment and/or increasing the behavioral competence of the resident person—that is, strengthening his or her opportunity to widen "niche breadth." Dohrenwend's model implies that change in the environment is an ongoing stimulus to behavior, and thus that any given state of adaptation is episodic and time limited, always subject to challenge by the next stressful event.

In addition to its meaning as the modification of one's behavior in response to altered conditions, adaptation has additional (dictionary) meanings that refer to conformity or adjustment. From a humanistic, "self-actualizing" perspective, the concept of adapting or adjusting oneself to external conditions can be anathema. If one sees the social environment as oppressive, then encouraging adaptation to it is to act as an agent of oppression. Should disadvantaged, poverty-stricken, stigmatized, and other relatively powerless groups play the game of adaptation to the social world as it is, or are their interests sometimes better served by methods that raise consciousness and demand change in the environment?

Raising this question may alert us to a problem that has no absolute solution, because it is impossible to think of a criterion of mental health that does not refer to a social order of some kind. There is no such thing as a social vacuum. Freud, for example, defined the normal, healthy person as one who can love, work, and play. These seem like individual goals, but as soon as one says love, work, or play, one is necessarily involved with other people in some kind of social order.

Although the term *social adaptation* seems to imply that individuals must adjust to a fixed social order and thus appears conservative, in fact every individual adapts to some social order. Furthermore, nothing in the concept precludes adapting by acting to change social conditions.

Social adaptations imply socially structured transactions between person and environment. A stressful event may threaten the availability of resources, disrupt ongoing transactions, and require an adaptive response. It is useful to use Sarbin's ecologies as a framework to illustrate that the range of possible disruptions is broad, and the adaptive change required may be quite significant. To survive as a biosocial organism in the "self-maintenance" ecology (see chapter 5), the individual must correctly identify objects and events and define him- or herself in relation to those objects and events; one must correctly identify one's own need for food, oxygen, shelter, and the like, and have the wherewithal to obtain those necessities. To have money, or purchasing power, is one form of attachment to the social order; in the absence of the means to participate in the exchange of goods and services, the individual is in serious difficulty. Health risks, for example, are linearly related to socioeconomic status. It is no surprise that you can expect to live a longer and healthier life if you have more money (Adler, et al., 1994).

Sarbin (1970) speaks also of the "social" ecology, where through a variety of social roles one achieves a sense of self-worth and belongingness. Failure to locate oneself correctly within the social ecology violates others' expectations and leads to corresponding efforts to have expectations fulfilled. You can claim to be royalty, but if no one bows before you, you can't fulfill the role. Moreover, if you claim the role without sufficient warrant, others may not only ignore you, they may also actively treat you as a deviant. People become attached to places—homes, neighborhoods, communities—where they have roles and expectations about how they and others should act. When those attachments or expectations are disrupted by a burglary, by moving to another residence, or by a disaster that destroys a community, attachments are disrupted and people experience distress (Brown and Perkins, 1992).

Failure and disappointment with oneself, or the reactions of others to oneself are critical to locating oneself within the "normative" ecology (i.e., to answering the question "How well am I doing?"). If the answer is "Not very well," the person may be forced to seek some other form of adaptation. Football coaches are good examples of this problem. The owner will fire the coach if he has a disappointing season.

Finally, the individual must locate himself or herself in what Sarbin calls the "transcendental" ecology, where the questions have to do with values. Each person needs a comprehensive system of meanings that help clarify current experience and help define ambiguity in events and relationships. When one's gods fail and a state of meaninglessness threatens, one is greatly troubled and may seek new sources of meaning or a new kind of adaptation. Think of the situation of a devoutly religious person who endures a crisis of faith, and may temporarily leave his or her church.

To summarize, adaptation can involve biological, social, self-referent, or value-laden dimensions. A given state of adaptation is also situation specific and temporary, not sweeping and permanent. It may be disrupted by new stressors and other changes in the external environment, so that periods of adaptation inevitably alternate with transient periods of disequilibrium. Some may be directed by disequilibrium toward greater achievement. An athlete may strive to break a record, or individually we try to exceed our "personal best." How can we conceptualize the disruptive state that signals the need for adaptation?

Crisis and Neurosis

Just as the individual deprived of oxygen or food experiences a physiological crisis or emergency, so too does the individual whose attachments, or locations in the several ecologies, are disrupted enter a state of crisis. Crisis is defined here as any rapid change or encounter that provides an individual with a "no-exit" challenge, no choice but to alter his or her conduct in some manner.

The concept of crisis was very influential in the development of community mental health and preventive modalities of care. Crisis theory began with Erich Lindemann's (1944) follow-up study of relatives of victims of a Boston nightclub fire. The Cocoanut Grove nightclub was very popular. It was particularly crowded on the night of November 28, 1942, when a fire broke out. There were only two exit doors and in the ensuing panic, 493 people died, many crushed by the crowd pressing toward the exits. Many more were burned, some severely. Emergency room facilities were overwhelmed. The best that could be done was to provide brief counseling not only for survivors but also for the friends, lovers, and relatives of those who died. Lindemann followed a large number of the relatives of those who died. He discovered that each survivor had to carry out "grief work" by detaching from the relationship with the deceased person, readapting to an environment no longer including the deceased, and then forming new attachments and relationships. Lindemann concluded that stressful events in the life cycle require adaptation. He didn't interpret the affective responses of the survivors as psychopathological but as a normal response to a situation that demanded a change in adaptation. This emphasis on adaptation to crisis was a shift from the dominant thinking in mental health at that time.

To understand fully the shift in orientation signaled by the crisis concept, contrast it with the psychoanalytic theory of neurosis. The person-centered model of psychoanalysis postulated that behavioral problems were the result of unresolved conflicts at earlier phases of development. These conflicts were repressed or otherwise defended against psychologically. If the underlying repressed impulse became too strong, the defense would fail, and repressed energy would return in the form of great anxiety, or secondarily as symptoms interpreted as an illness. The classical Freudian model recognizes as a precipitating event whatever it is that strengthens a drive or weakens a defense, and results in anxiety. The focus, however, is on the individual instead of on the precipitating event.

In crisis theory, change is viewed as a challenge to the previous state of adaptation, thus requiring a new adaptation. Consider the example of someone who attains a promotion at work. Accepting a new position of authority may call for new, yet to be learned, or unpracticed coping skills. Entering a position of authority also changes the individual's adaptation within a network of supportive relationships. After all, one can hardly get together with the boys to knock the boss when one *is* the boss. In crisis theory, any anxiety the person experiences is related to the challenge of the new adaptation.

The crisis concept is similar to that of "neurosis," except that crisis does not imply disease. The terms themselves express a difference in outlook. *Neurosis* comes from a Greek word meaning "sinew" or "tendon." The term also referred to the condition of an object, its strength, vigor, or energy—for example, a taut bowstring, or, in the vernacular, "strung out". By Freud's time neurosis meant a functional disorder of the nervous system, unaccompanied by organic change. In the medical model, the underlying concept of "nervous" means the nerves themselves are not functioning properly.

Crisis comes from a Greek root meaning "to decide." It describes a point in the course of a disease that is decisive for either recovery or death. More generally, the term means a critical turning point in the progress of some state of affairs in which a decisive change, for better or for worse, is imminent. The idea that change can be for the better and not just for the worse leads us to think and act differently; it implies a reserve of strength, a capacity to deal or cope with or master the distress. The crisis concept was important in drawing professional attention toward interventions to build strength and to the concept of resilience (Maton, Schellenbach, Leadbeater, & Solarz, 2004).

While neurosis is defined as a failure of the defenses, a crisis occurs when an individual faces seemingly insurmountable obstacles to important life goals and customary methods of resolving problems don't seem suitable. We may say the individual is dislocated in one of the four ecologies, or some vital attachments have been disrupted and a new response is required. Anyone can experience a state of crisis, not only those with some previous "fixation." A state of crisis should be expected whenever some external event requires a change in customary ways of dealing with a problem.

Crisis theorists (Parad & Parad, 1999; Slaikeu, 1984) postulated several essential features of a crisis. First is a stressful or hazardous event or events requiring change. The event presents a new problem, which the person may perceive as unsolvable in the present or the immediate future. Hazardous or stressful life events are classified as anticipated or unanticipated.

Unanticipated events refer to losses beyond the individual's control (e.g., death in the family, lost job, illness resulting in disability or disfigurement) or threats (e.g., physical disaster, assault, rape, or assault to one's personal integrity, as in the case of a woman in a concentration camp who had to make a choice between her life and her mother's life). Although unanticipated events are those whose timing cannot be predicted, in some cases (such as the death of a family member) the general class of events may be predictable.

Anticipated events generally refer to role transitions, changes in a way of life, new responsibilities, or the necessity to develop new social relationships. Entering school, getting married, retiring, becoming a parent, or moving to a new location are all examples. Because these events are predictable, we can devise preventive actions or position assistance so that it is available when and where it is needed.

A second characteristic of a crisis is that the new problem taxes the material, physical, or psychological resources of the individual, his or her family, or others in the individual's social support network. Bereavement, loss of a parent or a spouse, having a premature child born into the family, becoming a parent for the first time, or becoming the boss all require people to take action, experience new emotions, and make unfamiliar decisions. A crisis arises when one's methods of dealing with one's own emotions and the external problems are inadequate. A person in crisis may feel helpless, ineffective, anxious, fearful, and guilty, with the result that his or her behavior is less efficient than usual.

In the past, there was some controversy about what qualified as a crisis and how long the adverse reaction had to last, but present-day research workers seem to ignore that issue. Some said the crisis rarely lasted longer than six weeks, a number associated with crises in the Bible—Noah on the waters for 40 days, Christ in the desert for 40 days, Moses wandering for 40 years—and it also appears in the 40-week period of human gestation, the time normally required to create and deliver in a literal sense, a "new life."

Today, the concept of crisis seems to have been subsumed under the general notion of stress and stressful life events and at least on the surface it doesn't matter how long the episode lasts. With the recognition (appraisal) there is a problem, and with a rise in tension the individual initiates his or her habitual problem-solving responses, which can be as varied as depending on someone else to solve the problem, retreating, or actively seeking information or alternatives.

Tension dissipates once the problem is solved or if the individual can interpret the problem away ("It wasn't that important in my life so there is no real loss or threat"), or give up a goal (need resignation). If the problem-solving device used was a new one, the person can be said to have grown or developed new knowledge or skills and now can command additional personal resources for dealing with the world.

Box 7–1. Research on Stressful Life Events

Not all crises are resolved successfully. One hypothesis is that environmental factors and personal characteristics are both involved in adjusting to stressful events. Evidence has been accumulated among otherwise ordinary people undergoing situational crises showing a higher than expected incidence of disorders following highly traumatic experiences such as marital disruption (Bloom, Asher, & White, 1978) and economic distress (Kiernan, Toro, Rappaport, & Seidman, 1989; Dooley, Catalano, & Wilson, 1994). Large changes such as divorce or job loss, but also a series of smaller events in close succession, can overtax the individual's coping resources, threatening his or her physical or psychological well-being.

Stressful Life Events Scales

Subsequent investigators systematically pursued the idea that discrete, time-limited events requiring change or adaptation increase risk for a wide range of human disorders. An early list compiled by psychiatrists Thomas Holmes and Richard Rahe (1967), called the Schedule of Recent Experiences (SRE), contained 43 human events (e.g., marriage, change in residence, major personal injury, or illness). (We described the frequency in the population of many of these events in chapter 1.) An individual's life stress score was simply the number of events he or she reported experiencing during some recent interval of time (usually between 6 and 24 months). Holmes and Rahe soon recognized that some of these events (e.g., death of spouse) required considerably more change and adaptation than did others (e.g., vacation), and so was born the Social Readjustment Rating Scale (SRRS), which *weighted* each event for the amount of change or readjustment the event required (for the latest version, see Hobson et al., 1998). The estimate of total life stress experienced by a person thus became the sum of the weights, or "life-change units," for the events reported. Events representing both positive experiences (e.g., Christmas) and those that are clearly negative (e.g., fired from job) may make adaptive demands and thus produce stress. Initially, any change negative or positive was assumed to be stressful. However, research demonstrated that only negative life events, not positive ones, predicted later disorder, and positive life events did not offset the effects of negative events.

Despite their limitations, life events scales and hassle scales, measuring the stress of everyday life events (e.g., car breaks down; called into school because of child's misbehavior), have become standard survey measures of the amount of stress an individual is exposed to and have been used with many populations. The massive empirical literature leaves little doubt that a significant relationship exists between the cumulative experience of stress, as assessed by life events scales, and a host of adverse medical and psychological conditions (see Bloom, 1984, for a review).

Critical reviews, however, have pointed to the modest size of stress-disorder correlations (typically .30 or less, accounting for under 10% of variance; Rabkin & Streuning, 1976). Monroe and Steiner (1986) argue that because of overlap in language and meaning on life events or "hassles" scales and measures of disorder, the reported relationships may be partly artifactual. The appraisal and the subsequent response are also measured subjectively. A significant correlation between a hassles measure and a self-report of the experience of stress may be influenced by "negative affectivity." Negative affectivity refers to a style of responding to self-report scales with a readiness to appraise situations as traumatic.

Results of some studies may be method bound. French, Knox, & Gekoski, (1992) concluded: "when a relation between life events and health status measures in elderly samples is observed, much of it is due to health-related item confounding" (semantically similar items appear on the independent and dependent variable scales) (p. 249).

Confounding is not an issue in all studies. For example, Chilean women who lived in areas characterized by a great deal of social and political violence experienced more frequent pregnancy complications than women living in less disruptive areas, even when a variety of other social factors were controlled statistically. Stressful life events included the presence of armed forces and police, political arrests in the neighborhood, and knowledge that political prisoners were kidnapped, executed, and subjected to torture. In this instance, the independent and dependent variables were not affected by confounds (Zapata et al., 1992).

This debate notwithstanding, the degree of risk, for virtually all outcomes, as measured by life events scales appears to fall short of the expectation created by the early studies. Despite conceptual problems with the measures, the quantification of life events as a measure of stress was a methodological breakthrough in what was previously a qualitative area of study.

In Holmes and Rahe's work life events are nonspecific stimuli having no differential impacts. No significant role is played by the individual's cognitive appraisal of events or the degree of social support available to him or her. Their original idea now seems oversimplified, and an alternative approach emphasizes not life change per se but the psychological and emotional aspects of adapting to events.

Furthermore, any single life events list presents items that may or may not be relevant to a specific target population. Many Holmes and Rahe items (e.g., retirement from work, foreclosure on a mortgage or loan, son or daughter left home) would have little direct relevance for a population of college students, for whom the experience of many events *not* on that list (e.g., academic difficulties, relationship with parents) would more closely reflect their exposure to stress. Racism is a factor in the everyday lives of African Americans (Harrell, 2000), but such race-related life events and hassles are not represented on most scales. Investigators now tailor events lists for specific populations by asking representatives of the target group to nominate events based on what has happened to them or to people like them (Levine & Perkins, 1980a). Life events are not randomly distributed in the population. The events that impinge on males and females, or younger and older people, people of different racial or ethnic groups, or those of higher and lower status and power are quite different in nature and frequency.

Looking beyond stressful life events. Dohrenwend's general view that various personal and situational factors interact with characteristics of life events to produce stress and influence outcome is widely accepted (Perkins, 1982). A combination of temperament, coping styles, and social support apparently moderates the relationship between stressful life events and later adaptation. Luthar and Zigler (1991) reviewed the literature on children who were described as "resilient" or "stress-resistant" because they have adapted well even though they had serious stressors in their lives. Infant temperament, gender, humor, social problem-solving skills, a drive for academic achievement, a sense of personal control, and support from the family have been identified in various studies as characteristic of children considered resilient (See also Barbarin, Richter, & deWet (2001).

Vaillant and Davis (2000) followed a sample of 73 Caucasian inner-city residents with IQs less than 87 from the time they were 14 until they were 65. The low-IQ individuals completed less education and were more likely to have jobs as laborers, than a comparison

group with higher IQs. We would expect that people with lower social status and lower income would be more vulnerable to stressful
life events. However, as adults, about half of the low-IQ group had
good outcomes. They were no different from a comparison group
with higher IQs on a number of measures of adaptation. As the authors said, "low tested IQ is a terrible curse [during school years],
but IQ is not destiny." (p. 221). A combination of good marriages,
social skills, and emotional intelligence enabled members of this
group to attain decent incomes, to have positions of leadership in
their communities, and to have children who achieved in school. By
studying the lives of people who accomplished despite apparent vulnerabilities, we may learn how to help others adapt, and we might
learn not to overvalue predictions based on measurement of only
some of the critical variables.

How do resilient people thrive? The variables we mentioned are
all "person-centered" constructs and do not reveal just how resilient
individuals interpret stressors, use resources, or cope with specific
stressful events. In-depth interviews with urban, African American
single mothers considered resilient revealed many surprises in what
the mothers considered stressful, and what they could handle, or
avoid. Lack of money was a problem but some managed to work
things out anyway. For some the neighborhood they lived in was a
problem, but others managed to distance themselves and their children from the undesirable aspects of neighborhood life, and to feel
they were succeeding because they were transcending their environments (Brodsky, 1999). There is more to be learned from qualitative
research that digs more deeply than simply asking for a response on
a scale.

Mirowsky and Ross (1989) strongly criticize both the life events
and the "hassles" approaches to studying adaptation because these
methods focus attention on individuals and overlook the socioeconomic correlates of distress:

> both the idea of daily hassles and that of life change trivialize the social
> causes of psychological distress. . . . The link [to distress] is the undesir-
> able events, losses, failures, and ongoing stressors that flow from in-
> equality, inequity, and lack of opportunity. (p. 130)

An attack on those problems may require concerted social and political action, topics we take up in later chapters.

To summarize, measures of recent stressful events do not predict
with great accuracy a person's future level of well-being. Progress on
this problem will require a return to interest in the qualitative aspects of life stress, in the details of how events are experienced, and
in what people actually do to cope with specific stressors as in the
Brodsky (1999) study.

Vulnerability: An Integrative Perspective

Dohrenwend's model suggests three possible outcomes following a transient stress reaction: the person can return to the previous level of functioning, become a case of psychopathology, or resolve the experience and grow stronger. Furthermore, stress is ubiquitous in contemporary life (see chapter 1), yet clearly not everyone succumbs. While stressful events seem to increase a person's overall risk for disorder in a nonspecific way, no given external stressor is likely to be etiologically specific for any particular medical or psychological dysfunction.

A simple dichotomy between health and illness may be misleading. Individuals who at a particular moment are dysfunctional will eventually recover to a greater or lesser degree and for some period of time. Individuals who are currently healthy could conceivably become stressed to the point of succumbing to an episode of disorder. A study of children from abusive families who were characterized as resilient in the earlier school years, for example, found that these children were not necessarily high functioning in later adolescence. Those who were subject to chronic abuse in the family, and dysfunctional homes with major disruptions in the caretaking figures, were often not doing well in adolescence. (Herrenkohl, Herrenkohl, & Egolf, 1994).

Within the model, vulnerability is a function of exposure to stressors, the availability of coping devices, the availability of social support, and the individual's biological and other social characteristics. An increase in the level of stressors increases vulnerability, as would a loss of social support or the adoption of maladaptive coping devices such as increased use of alcohol or drugs.

It is useful to distinguish between an individual's degree of predisposition to disorder on the one hand and the onset and course of a given episode of disorder on the other. Stated another way, everyone is endowed with a specific degree of *vulnerability* to such episodes (somewhere from high to low) that under certain conditions will express itself in a time-limited crisis of adaptation. No one has zero vulnerability, and vulnerability represents the potential disorder, not the manifest disorder, or the symptoms. One's degree of vulnerability is determined partially by inborn or other "predisposing" factors such as genetic inheritance and prior coping competence, and may be offset by protective factors such as social support. An episode of disorder occurs when the degree of disequilibrium initiated by recent stressful experiences exceeds the threshold imposed by the individual's level of vulnerability.

Our bland phrase "recent stressful experiences" understates the complexity of some situations. Genetic factors may contribute substantially to the vulnerability faced by children of people with schizophrenia, but in addition the display of schizophrenic behavior in a mother or father may be chronically and unpredictably stressful. Vulnerability is intertwined with genetic predispositions over two generations, repetitive life stresses may stem from the parent's disorder and sometimes from inadequate or even harmful intervention into family life (Dunn, 1993; Grunebaum & Gammeltoft, 1993). The same may hold true for parental depression as a risk factor for a child's depression (Hammen, 1992).

This vulnerability perspective has advantages over the older person-centered view of psychopathology. Like Dohrenwend's model and the ecological analogy (chapter 4), it relates both person-centered and environmental factors to time-limited episodes of health and dysfunction. Even with a relatively stable degree of initial vulnerability, one's levels of acute stress and environmental support may fluctuate over time. In addition, while short-term improvement may result from a reduction in the level of external stress, more stable improvement may result from reduced vulnerability (e.g., the individual develops better coping skills, makes a permanent change in his or her environment, and so on). The model is consistent with the observation that with nearly everyone experiencing the soap opera that is life, most people do not develop diagnosable pathology. Finally, "vulnerability" is a less stigmatizing concept than "disease" (because everyone is vulnerable to some extent), yet is compatible with evidence for stable individual differences in the risk of illness. Those at greatest risk may share a high degree of vulnerability, not a uniform pattern of environmental experience.

We must still avoid oversimplification. Skaff, Finney, & Moos (1999) followed 515 men and women who had a drinking problem for one year. They found that over time, increased support and a decrease in the level of stressors (signs of reduced vulnerability) correlated with reduced drinking. However, support from friends was more important for women than for men. The vulnerability construct is useful, but we should keep in mind that the issues in nature may be far more complex than our simple models suggest.

Witnessed or directly experienced violence is a stressor. Witnessing violence increases vulnerability, and is correlated with an increase of symptoms of distress in children. With the unrest and social upheaval, children in South Africa were exposed to political violence, to familial violence and to violence in the community. Barbarin, Richter, and de Wet (2001), studied 625 Black South African children and their families when the children were six. They used as dependent variables a variety of measures of childrens' adjustment. Exposure to violence correlated with several measures of children's maladjustment although the type of violence mattered—violence in the community mattered the most for several measures of adaptation, and violence in the family affected only children's aggression. High levels of violence in the community affected the mother's level of distress. The correlations were statistically significant, but were not very strong.

The child's level of distress about these matters is likely to be mediated through how the family handles the issues, providing a barrier to the violence, and providing access to other resources and sources of support. Barbarin and colleagues note that even though one can establish support programs to prevent the adverse effects of violence, ultimately, the resolution of social and economic issues is of first importance. Prevention programs centered on the family, valuable as they can be, still may distract attention and effort away from social and political action to correct the core problems.

We now turn to a review of ideas and research on individual coping and social support, two important protective factors in Dohrenwend's model.

Coping

In theory, coping ability reduces vulnerability to stress (Dohrenwend, 1978). Coping can be defined as "cognitive and behavioral effort made to master, tolerate, or reduce demands that tax or exceed a person's resources" (Kessler, Price, & Wortman, 1985, p. 550). In this section we describe the general nature of coping and the evidence for important individual and situational differences in coping.

General Characteristics of Coping

The individual facing a stressful event has two problems. One is how to manage the internal stress: anxiety, tension, depression, anger, restlessness, difficulty in concentrating, sleeplessness and fatigue, and the associated thought content, self-doubt, and self-blame. Efforts to manage such feelings are called *emotion-focused* coping. The second problem is what specific action to take, and this response is called *problem-focused* coping. A third kind of response, *perception-focused* coping, uses altered cognitions to reduce the threatening nature of an event (Folkman & Lazarus, 1988; Thoits, 1986).

In the Dohrenwend model, having more adequate psychological mediators implies less vulnerability to stress. Coping devices are classified as psychological mediators. Risk-reduction may result from managing feelings, managing the situation, or altering an event's meaning. The wherewithal to manage effectively may come from resources in the person's support network. Given that both coping and interpersonal support may be emotion focused, problem focused, perception focused, or all three of these, Thoits (1986) proposes conceptualizing social support as the provision of coping assistance.

Strategies for the treatment or prevention of stress-related problems might then be organized along two dimensions: the nature of the individual's coping response (emotional, problem oriented, and/or cognitive), and the focus of intervention on either "psychological mediators" (e.g., through education) or "situational mediators" (e.g., by increasing support resources).

Phases. Initially, theory focused on a description of phases in responding to a stressor. Lazarus (1991) and Folkman (1984) originally defined two phases in the cognitive appraisal of stressors. The first phase included primary and secondary appraisal. *Primary appraisal* involves an individual judgment about whether the situation is harmful or potentially harmful. Some may find the situation potentially harmful, but also challenging. The person then engages in *secondary appraisal.* In secondary appraisal, the person decides whether he or she has the resources to cope, or can gain access to them. A person with resources or with access to resources is less vulnerable than someone without the resources. If the person does not feel he or she has the resources to deal with the situation, further strain follows. If the event-induced arousal is interpreted through self-statements as bad, wrong, sick, or a sign of weakness or incompetence, the person may not be up to coping and may worry about worrying, adding tension to the emotional mix.

Subsequent research focused on identifying just how people cope with specific stressors and on helping people to develop psychological mediators or methods for coping with specific stressors. This work reflects the crisis theory assumption that people have reserves of strength or that these can be created, thus reducing vulnerability.

General coping scales. Some have tried to characterize and measure general coping styles. They have developed self-report scales that ask people to say not how they coped with a particular stressor, but how they generally cope. Fleishman et al. (2000) studied factors that correlated with mood in HIV-positive participants in a large-scale study. They selected 40 items from various coping scales that appeared to be relevant to the situation of those with HIV infection. The scale was presented as a list of things that persons with HIV do in reaction to being infected with HIV; using a five-point scale, the respondents indicated how often in the previous four weeks they had engaged in each coping behavior.

These forty items produced six factors they labeled (1) positive coping (e.g., look on the bright side), (2) avoidant coping (wish you could change what happened), (3) cognitive avoidance (keep from worrying), (4) fatalistic acceptance (accept what happens), (5) social isolation (avoid others), and (6) seek information concerning HIV (learn more about HIV).

Elaborate regression analyses showed some relationships between the coping factors and mood states, but these were complex, and to some extent seemed to reflect a possible underlying variable of "negative affectivity." For example, optimism had a negative relationship with coping behaviors that had a negative affective tone, and a positive correlation with coping behaviors with a positive affective tone, such as taking positive action.

The diverse correlations may have been accidental, even though statistically significant, and in the absence of replication are probably not reliable. Studies using broadly abstract scales typically produce complex, sometimes inconsistent, and difficult to interpret results which do not seem to illuminate the coping process. Often, the analysis, the authors' attempt to make sense out of the results, is more insightful than anything that derives directly from the statistical results. The authors also note that the focus—coping with the state of being infected with HIV, was fairly general, while HIV infection produces a multiplicity of adaptive demands. Being infected with the HIV virus has implications for interpersonal and intimate relationships, for employment, for dealing with stigma, and for obtaining insurance and medical care. The authors note that respondents may have been thinking of different stressors when answering. The answers are thus unclear even if the respondents all understood the descriptions of the coping responses to refer to the same behaviors, a large assumption itself.

Box 7–2. Pollyanna and the Glad Game

Everyone knows the word Pollyanna, but few are aware of its origins. Pollyanna is the 11-year-old heroine of Eleanor Hodgman Porter's best-selling novel *Pollyanna* (1913). Pollyanna was an orphan who came to live with her Aunt Polly in a small Vermont town after her father died. Her father, an impoverished minister, had taught her to play the "Glad Game." The Glad Game is a forerunner of cognitive behavior therapy and positive psychology. The Glad Game refers to an effort a person makes to find something to feel glad about even in difficult situations. It is not so much a denial of the affect as it is a method of exercising voluntary control of the content of thought in an attempt to change mood by changing thoughts. The Glad Game seems very William Jamesian in its emphasis on the relationship between thought and affect. The Glad Game is also built on a form of "reciprocal inhibition." Pollyanna said that one cannot be fixed on the negative when searching for the positive. Pollyanna also teaches that it is important to persist in trying to find the thing to feel glad about, even when it is difficult. In that emphasis, Pollyanna is showing how persistence in the use of a coping device may be a precondition for the arousal of hope. In the prototypical example used by Pollyanna to teach others the Glad Game, Pollyanna related how she was bitterly disappointed when she wanted a doll, but the "missionary barrel," sent to ministers for their subsistence, contained only a child's crutch. Her father told her she could at lest feel glad that she didn't need the crutch. The Glad Game appears to be an all-purpose device for coping with emotions. In the book, Pollyanna taught others in her town to play the Glad Game and, in the author's vision, by transmitting the coping device, Pollyanna transformed her town.

Generalized coping scales and the classification systems they generate seem less informative than studies that identify how people cope with particular stressors. As a cognitive means of coping with emotions, education may help one to understand, identify, and tolerate a range of feelings and thus to prevent the secondary reaction to primary arousal. Some preventive efforts consist of little more than preparation and warning. If the dentist tells you that you will feel pain or the surgeon tells you that you will have a certain kind of discomfort following surgery, when the pain occurs later you tend not to worry about it because it was expected. Here discomfort is not a sign that something has gone wrong; it indicates that one's condition is "normal under the circumstances."

Simple preparation and warnings prior to surgery can have a measurable effect on the postsurgical course of recovery. One study, based on an extensive review of the literature, concluded that hospital patients who received information and emotional support in rather brief preoperative sessions had shorter lengths of hospital stay than untreated controls. The effect may be enhanced when the intervention is matched to the patient's coping style: patients who cope with stress by denial (under some circumstances a negative psychological mediator) may get little benefit from preoperative explanation and warning, while those who cope by seeking information and mastery derive more benefit from such preparation. In other words, even this simple attempt to improve coping may be affected by complex interactions. These interventions are inexpensive compared with the cost of a hospital day and are thus highly effective from a benefit/cost viewpoint (Mumford, Schlesinger, Glass, Patrick, & Cuerdon, 1998).

Keefe et al. (2000) evaluated six cognitive styles of coping in patients with painful osteoarthritis: diverting attention, reinterpreting pain sensation, ignoring pain sensations, coping self-statements (e.g., "I can do it"), praying or hoping, and "catastrophizing" (seeing events in the worst light). Controlling for participants' demographic background and medical condition, those who did not catastrophize, and who believed they could control or decrease their pain, reported less pain and less physical and psychological disability. Findings like these are encouraging, and the teaching of techniques to mediate stress-related feelings is an important area for research.

People facing certain stressors may benefit from coping responses specifically tailored to problems posed by those events. Telch and Telch (1986) developed a training program of cognitive, behavioral, and emotional coping skills to help patients adapt to cancer. Groups of patients learned relaxation and stress management, effective communication and assertiveness, problem solving and constructive thinking, the management of feelings, and the planning of pleasant activities. Behavioral components included homework, goal setting, self-monitoring, behavioral rehearsal and role-playing, and feedback and coaching.

After six weeks, patients in these coping-skills groups had improved significantly in their moods and self-efficacy and were having fewer problems related to their illness. They were superior in these outcomes to patients randomly assigned to loosely structured support groups. The support group intervention may also have been beneficial, however, since other patients randomly assigned to a no-treatment control group actually deteriorated on these measures over the same period and were significantly worse off than those in the support groups. Keep in mind that because coping-skills training also occurred in groups, it is possible that some form of mutual support was a significant component of that intervention as well.

Teaching coping skills can be effective with patients with diagnoses of schizophrenia. Leclerc, Lesage, Ricard, Leconte, & Cyr (2000) exposed 55 patients with diagnoses of schizophrenia to 24 one-hour group meetings over twelve weeks. The patient group had an average of 4.2 lifetime hospitalizations and 17.8 years of hospitalization. The disorders were serious and persistent. The sessions were built on the theory that fostering competence fosters self-esteem as well. The group members use paperwork, group discussion, role-playing, and prepared exercises to understand and learn the coping skills. Participants are encouraged with the group leader's guidance to see how the skills apply to everyday life. The participants are taught to identify symptoms, to identify stress and sources of stress, and to distinguish things that can be changed from those that can't. They are also taught to appraise resources, to review and select coping strategies for particular problems, and to evaluate results.

Participants were compared with a control group at the beginning and end of treatment and six months after treatment. Patients in the treatment group improved and maintained the improvement in self-esteem, and in a reduction in delusions. The control patients did not show statistically significant improvement on any of the dependent variables. One problem is that the improvement could not be related to change in the stress appraisal and coping scales. Another is that there were proportionately more women in the treated than in the control group. The results, though modest, are still interesting, because they demonstrate the potential for using a coping skills intervention to reduce deficits related to the schizophrenic disorder.

Others (Schwartz & Rogers, 1994) have reported similar positive results in teaching people to cope with continuing stressors such as multiple sclerosis (MS) where patients have functional losses and develop a great deal of uncertainty about themselves and their future. Similarly, Kirkby (1994) successfully used a coping skills treatment with women who identified themselves as having "serious premenstrual problems." These positive results of teaching specific coping skills to people who have enduring or repetitive problems are very promising. We will probably see more such specific efforts in the future.

The problem of arousing hope. Once the acute stress is under control, the second major task in a crisis is to take appropriate action to cope with the situation. If one is to take action, it has to imply the person believes that by taking action things can change for the better. Learned helplessness and hopelessness associated with suicide imply that the person believes nothing can change for the better. One coping task then is emotional; it involves the arousal of hope or a sense that one may indeed be able to do something about one's situation. After an initial psychotherapy interview clients often feel that something good may come of it—there is some hope that a desperate situation will be relieved. Consider as an example a woman with a new baby who moves to a new community and hasn't yet made any friends. Her husband is busy in a new and demanding job and doesn't have much time or energy to help at home. Finances are tight, and they can't afford household help. Their families live far away and cannot be counted on too much, for there are often petty squabbles when mother and daughter or son and mother-in-law are together for too long a time. One day the woman's husband disappoints her badly, and she considers leaving him to go home to her mother. She is greatly distressed, crying one moment and raging the next, and can't get over the episode, remaining tense and depressed. Finally she calls a therapist who helps her work out a plan of action. After a few days she calls back to report that she is following through, and now says that she is *hopeful* something good will happen. That feeling of hope represents an important aspect of her belief that she will be able to deal with her circumstances.

It is probably also true that people in neighborhoods seemingly faced with overcoming environmental threats, or drug dealing, or gang activity, may feel hopeless that anything can change. However, just meeting with others, and gaining strength from joining with others in a common cause can arouse hope that things can be different. Hope can motivate further action. The fact that hope is aroused may be an important value of organizing social action campaigns because these may overcome demoralization (see chapter 12, on social action, for a further discussion of these issues).

We know very little about hope. In his encyclopedic work on emotions, Lazarus (1991, p. 282) says: "Far less has been written about hope . . . than about other emotions . . . [H]ope is so important in the psychological economy of people as antidote to despair." Under what circumstances is hope aroused? Does it require some support from another person? Can hope be generated from within by recalling other occasions when one has succeeded in overcoming adversity? Is the ability to generate hope an indication that one has been strengthened by overcoming a prior adversity? Is the emotion of hope a necessary part of determination?

One hypothesis about hope derives from Pollyanna (see Box 7–2), who acknowledged that it is sometimes difficult to find something to feel glad about in some very difficult situations. However, she emphasized that it adds to the game if it is hard to find something to feel glad about. She recommends persisting in seeking for the glad solution. If one persists in seeking a solution, a solution will eventually emerge. Is that the essence of hope—the belief that a solution will eventually emerge? If so, the willingness to persist in seeking solutions may well be a cognitive mediator that is teachable, and that might serve to maintain morale under difficult circumstances.

Are there comparable motives such as a desire for revenge or a desire to prove something to another that can stimulate effort to overcome adversity? The latter motives may be less praiseworthy, but they nonetheless can be quite powerful. Many survivors of Nazi concentration camps managed to develop a transcendent goal—to tell the world about the experience or to finish some unfinished work—that aided them in coping with extreme adversity and helped them to avoid surrendering to seemingly insurmountable difficulties (Frankl, 1992). Some studies of resilient children note that the determination to be different from one's parent, and an overriding goal of achieving something can be important in overcoming severe adversity (Dunn, 1993; Herrenkohl, et al., 1994). Because much of our knowledge of personality derives from the study of persons who may be said to have succumbed to difficulty, we know all too little about those who have mastered difficulty and have become stronger for it.

Resilience. One line of study centers on the construct of resilience. Some have studied children who have backgrounds of poverty, broken homes, or exposure to violence and yet who seem to have adapted well. The Barbarin et al. (2001) study of South African children exposed to violence showed that those characterized by their mothers as having more resilience had a better adaptation despite exposure to violence. Children who showed academic motivation also seemed to do better psychologically.

In studies of resilience, the criterion measures vary from study to study. There may be children who do well in school, who are well regarded by their peers, who score within normal limits on anxiety or depression scales, and who do not get in trouble in the community. However, these criterion variables do not correlate strongly with each other, so there is resilience within domains. In the Barbarin, Richert, & deWet (2001) study, the criterion measures showed correlations with each other ranging from −.12 to .56. The median correlation among the six outcome measures was .183. Acosta (1998) reported similar levels of intercorrelation among her criterion measures of children's adaptation. In addition, the "predictors" of the criterion variables are different depending on which one we focus on (Acosta, 1998). It is therefore difficult to speak of resilience in general or to identify factors related to resilience in general. In addition, children who are resilient at one point in their lives may succumb at another point when faced with different challenges, or with continuing stressors. A good adaptation as a school-age youth doesn't guarantee a good adaptation as an adolescent.

Treating resilience as an individual difference variable or as a personality trait doesn't help us to understand what resilient individuals do and think when faced with a specific stressor. If resilience is a function of having a loving parent, preventive interventions are more difficult to develop. Is it more useful for prevention, intervention, or for understanding to ask what individuals we characterize as resilient do when faced with a challenge, and can what they do be taught?

Problem-focused coping. Coming to terms with a crisis is in part an emotional task. One must somehow modulate the feelings that preoccupy attention and focus on what to do next. Solving the problem requires additional thought and action. Consider a widow in her late forties or early fifties with grown children, who is not yet eligible for a Social Security pension, has only minimum resources from her husband's insurance for financial support, and has not been in the labor market for 20 or 25 years. She can expect to live another 30 or more years. In addition to living with the complex emotion of grief following the loss of her husband, the widow faces the problem of supporting herself. She may have little experience in managing finances or investments and now has to decide what to do about what money she does have. She has to assess her own resources, her assets on the job market. She may take an entry-level job with other workers much younger. She may have to find opportunities for training or education. Having decided on a program, she may then have new experiences of studying, taking (and worrying about) examinations, and relating in an unaccustomed role again with people much younger than herself. She may have to make new friends, especially if she finds herself uncomfortable as a single person among friends who are married couples. She may have to cope with problems of dating, should she decide she wants to develop an intimate relationship. There are many other problems, including how to maintain or repair the house if she continues to live in it or how to find and manage workers who will do the work. Beyond home and social relationships, she has to decide how to spend her time. Similar problems confront widowers and divorced men and women. Little wonder, when we review all of the adaptations that are necessary, that the death of a spouse and divorce are heavily weighted on life-events scales.

The widow's situation can be conceptualized in problem-solving terms: she must examine each problem, develop alternative strategies for solving it, assess the resources each solution requires, and then risk failure by acting in uncertain and unfamiliar territory. Psychologists have developed techniques and approaches to problem solving that, when taught to people, become psychological mediators (Spivack & Shure, 1985, 1993). Whenever a person has taken new risks, engaged in new experiences, or mastered some new approach to living, he or she may be said to have grown psychologically. The crisis model directs us to work to enhance the individual's ability to solve problems. If the technique is taught before the problem arises, we have a preventive approach where the psychological mediator, the problem-solving approach, is made available in advance of the crisis.

Stages in Crisis Resolution

The crisis model postulates stages in the resolution of crises. These stages change over time and mean that the best way of dealing with one stage may be different than the best way of dealing with another. Angel, Hjern, & Ingleby (2001) studied 99 school-age Bosnian children living in Sweden. The children had been exposed to fighting. They were forced to leave their homes in an atmosphere of fear and heightened uncertainty (ethnic cleansing). Families lost most of their possessions, and they were required to adapt in a strange culture. Many of the children had symptoms including hypervigilance, fears, and war-related dreams. Bosnian children, compared to Swedish children, more frequently experienced sad moods. Contrary to Western professional views, the data showed that children whose parents did not talk with them about their traumatic experiences had fewer symptoms of disorder than the children of parents who did talk with them. If the stressors the children had experienced were relatively minor, then talking about them helped. If the stressors were strong, children's problems seemed to be made worse by talking about them. Working through problems may be useful at some stages of distress, but if the cultural norm of the group is to try to forget the bad history, then persistently drawing attention to it may interfere with adaptation. It is possible that at some later point in the process of overcoming and working out a new adaptation, sharing distress may be helpful.

Kubler-Ross (1969) made an important contribution to the field of death and dying by specifying the stages a person goes through in coming to terms with death. Lindemann (1944) had earlier specified stages in working through loss, based on the reactions of people grieving over family members lost in a fire. Other crises may also have stages in their resolution. These stages are important to understand because the types of coping and support appropriate at one stage may not be appropriate at another stage.

Women who have been raped seem to go through three stages (Burgess & Holmstrom, 1979). The first is simply getting through the trauma, fear, shame, and related concerns. The second phase includes efforts to return to normal and to control or minimize the significance of the event for one's life. In the third phase, occurring weeks or sometimes months later, the experience returns to conscious attention, and the individual is once again faced with integrating and resolving it. This phase is often marked by depressive feelings or anxiety (Kilpatrick, Veronen, & Resick, 1979). In this last phase, the person works to integrate the experience into the self. The view of self as one who was once assaulted, violated, and subjected to sexual abuse has to be incorporated or assimilated within the general self-concept. Rape counselors encourage their clients to think of themselves not as victims, but as survivors.

Even though self-blame may reflect the interjection of cultural values, or may reflect experiences with insensitive police, prosecutors, medical personnel, relatives, lovers, or friends, nonetheless, many blame themselves: "I shouldn't have been out at night alone," "I shouldn't have been hitchhiking," "I shouldn't have gone to his apartment," or "I should have screamed louder or fought harder." The truth of the matter is subordinated to the process of self-blame (Morrow & Sorell, 1989). There may be some adaptive value to this self-blame, in that the person might be saying, "If I had something to do with causing the event, perhaps I can prevent a repetition in the future." Women who had a greater sense of personal control had lower rates of depression and symptoms of post-traumatic distress six months after the rape than those with a poorer sense of personal control, suggesting the adaptive advantage of the psychological mediator of the sense of personal control (Regehr, Cadell, & Jansen, 1999).

At a later time, to master the experience, a survivor might become involved in social or political action to offer escort services or rape crisis services, and to seek greater police protection, more vigorous prosecution, or more sensitive handling of people injured by a rape. Such efforts might also work to change culturally determined attitudes of some males that place a woman at risk simply because she is female.

Anger may be among the complex emotions a woman who was raped might experience. In the earlier phases, the woman may have suppressed or denied the anger, viewing the rape impersonally as a social fault. In the third phase, however, her anger can become more personalized and in a sense more real: "That SOB! He used me! I could kill him!" Such feelings of rage after the event need to be worked through. We have not considered the complications a rape introduces into relationships with lovers or husbands and the often frustrating if not humiliating encounters with the legal process (Silverman, 1992; Burgess & Holmstrom, 1979). Different types of coping and different supports may be called for depending on whether the problem is with intimates, acquaintances, or officials, and when in the course of recovering, the problem arises.

Reliving the experience may not occur with all challenges to adaptation and may be more likely when the strongest emotions of fear, rage, and guilt are engaged. However, characterizing the emotional experience as a phase in the restorative process rather than as a symptom of illness recasts the experience as a transient emotional state appropriate to the kind of event one has been through. The emotions and thoughts need not be interpreted as manifestations of a neurotic illness but as something more like the postsurgical discomfort one had been warned about. Moreover, the problem of adaptation may be different in different phases of the crisis. The person may need something different at each point. But with appropriate coping, it may be easier to live through the experience and even turn it to personal advantage.

Converting Traumas to "Strens"

Any life event may have positive or negative effects. Negative aspects are nearly always apparent almost immediately, while positive effects may take some time to emerge. Not everyone is able to benefit in a positive way from stress. What accounts for this difference? In the vulnerability perspective, the notion of protective factors enables us to shift the focus from personal and situational processes that damage a person's mental health to those that strengthen it. Here the question is not what accounts for disorder in response to stress, but what accounts for strength?

Finkel (Finkel & Jacobsen, 1977) had people describe significant life experiences that strengthened their personalities (which he called "strens") or that were traumas, harmful for personal development. Unexpectedly, many people spontaneously described *three* kinds of experiences: negative events, positive events, and events that started out as negative but later became positive in their overall effect. Finkel called these latter experiences trauma-stren conversions. They began with a sudden insight or "flash" that enabled the person to reinterpret the traumatic event in a more positive light. The previous debilitating construction produced by the event was replaced by a new construction that emphasized the individual's ability to cope, adapt, and learn from the trauma. Conversion was not simply a defensive distortion of the experience, since the person fully acknowledged feelings of pain, regret, and anger during the initial period of trauma. Only in hindsight was the event construed to have had positive value.

From a preventive standpoint, achieving a conversion may represent a "protective factor" that helps to reduce the negative impact of subsequent life events, and perhaps the risk of stress-related psychopathology as well (Finkel & Jacobsen, 1977).

What are the psychological correlates of converting stressful life experiences? About 4 percent of college students experience a parent's death during a given academic year. Parental death is among the most stressful of student life events (Levine & Perkins, 1980a), yet from 4 to 22 months following a parent's death about half of students convert the severe stress into positive change (Tebes & Perkins, 1984). What is the specific nature of a life-event conversion? Can we learn to facilitate trauma-stren conversions in individuals who would fail to do so on their own as a method for the primary prevention of stress-related problems? (Compare to the Pollyanna Glad Game in Box 7–2.)

While not a conversion, Taylor, Kemeny, Reed, Bower, & Gruenewald (2000) described a process of self-enhancement by means of social comparisons that allowed the person experiencing a stressful life event to feel better off than someone else. Taylor et al. illustrated the concepts in her study of women adapting to breast cancer. Women who make positive adaptations to breast cancer spontaneously use what Taylor et al. called "beneficial illusions." (Pollyanna described a similar process as a technique for feeling glad even if distressed.) Beneficial illusions are not denials; they are constructions of reality that permit one to function with a degree of optimism and a sense of control over events. Do these cognitive mechanisms help our understanding of the potential in stressful experiences for enhancing growth and self-esteem under difficult circumstances?

In contrast to an emphasis on trait-like psychological mediators (e.g., Kobasa, 1979), strategies for effective coping may be situation-specific instead of global. By examining how people actually do cope in particular circumstances, we may be able to "package" the coping approaches and teach them to others to enhance resilience. Not all coping responses are equally effective across all life situations; responses that are effective in resolving marital conflict, for example, are not necessarily successful at work (Pearlin & Schooler, 1978). That no single coping response is found to be universally effective suggests that we should be as careful in describing the specific stressful situation as in delineating successful or unsuccessful coping strategies.

Folkman and Lazarus (1980) attempted to answer directly the question of how consistently people use specific coping behaviors across a sample of everyday situations. Middle-aged men and women reported the specific thoughts and actions they used in coping with recent stressful events. Both problem-focused and emotion-focused coping were used extensively; contrary to cultural stereotype, women did not use emotion-focused coping more than men. The situation and how the event was appraised were the strongest determinants of the coping response. Work-related events, where an effective concrete response was often possible, elicited more problem-focused coping. Health-related problems, which may offer fewer opportunities for constructive action, were more likely to elicit emotion-focused coping. Lazarus (1991) and Folkman (2001) now call on researchers to pay more attention to the nature of the stressor than they have in the past. Their results support Dohrenwend's (1978) idea that the relationship between the person's individual appraisal of an event and its situational context determines the coping response.

Even when people are coping with similar problems their experiences and circumstances may dictate different coping efforts. Components of a group program designed to assist family caregivers of frail elderly patients in coping with their situations were differentially effective with spouses of the frail elderly patient and with middle-aged children. The spouses made less use of information about what to do because most knew what to do. They made more use of advice to take care of themselves, and find support in the form of approval and praise from others for their often heroic efforts. On the other hand, middle-aged relatives responsible for care needed more information about what to do and how to find resources (Labrecque, Peak, & Toseland, 1992).

Coping and Religion

Few researchers have examined "natural" coping by ordinary people in response to commonplace events. The use of religion in coping in particular has been neglected. Religious coping may be characterized as a form of emotional coping, but that abstraction fails as a description of what people actually do nor does it include the full social and cultural context within which religious coping takes place. Millions participate in organized religious services and consider themselves religious people. Millions rely on their religious beliefs to bring them through crises or other troubles. Trust in God, praying, confessing sins, or finding a lesson from God in the life event are examples of religious coping.

One's religiousness can affect the likelihood of experiencing some adverse events. Stress will be reduced if the person develops a healthier lifestyle, and on religious grounds doesn't use drugs or engage in extramarital affairs. Religious beliefs may affect one's appraisal of those events that do occur, and the choice of coping strategies. Religious communities can also be significant sources of social support. Religious beliefs and methods of coping would appear to have important implications for mental health and for the prevention of psychological problems (Pargament & Maton, 2000).

Important questions remain. To what extent are variations in coping strategies (direct action, cognitive reappraisal, etc.) consistently associated with a particular outcome achieved in response to a stressful event? Because coping and appraisal probably exert a reciprocal influence on each other over time, longitudinal studies examining the dynamic aspects of coping also need to be done. As we come to understand the coping process better, we may learn how to teach coping skills in a timely fashion to prevent crises and maladaptations.

Social Support

In the Dohrenwend model, the second major set of variables affecting the outcome of stressful life events is social support. Social support is a component of vulnerability. In theory, people who lack in social support are more vulnerable than those who are able to count on social support to help them through life's difficulties. At an individual level, Thoits (1986) thinks of social support as a source of coping assistance. As we shall see, the concept of social support is complex. Operationally it refers to several different constructs. It will be necessary to review the several definitions and measures separately because they seem to have different implications for well-being.

Social integration and health. Social integration, in contrast to social support (which has a number of meanings and measures—see below), is defined as the participation in a broad range of social relationships (Brissette, Cohen, & Seeman, 2000). Isolated individuals, by definition not part of a social network, may be highly vulnerable for that reason alone. One of the strongest penalties is to expel a person from the group through exile, excommunication, or "shunning," that is, treating a person as if the person was dead. Isolation and loneliness may be lethal (Blazer, 1982; House, Landis, & Umberson, 1988; Wong et al., 2001).

There is now substantial correlational evidence that social integration, but not necessarily other measures of social support, is related to health, longevity, and well-being in conditions as diverse as survival of breast cancer, resistance to the common cold, and heart attacks (Cohen, Gottlieb, & Underwood, 2000). A 50-year study of cardiac disease in a close-knit supportive community revealed that when the social cohesiveness of the community eroded, rates of cardiac disease increased (Egolf, Lasker, Wolf, & Potvin, 1992). Social integration is also critical for dealing with life's stresses. We will return to a more detailed examination of these issues below.

Theory and Research Concerning Social Support

A person enters a state of crisis when adaptation is threatened *and* he or she lacks the immediate resources to cope. Some coping resources may come from the person's social network (Thoits, 1986). In this section, we will develop some of the complexities of the issues. We will show that support is a dynamic concept with many dimensions. These dimensions may change over time and with changes in circumstances. This complexity may present problems for the measurement of support and its effects. Consider the following. (To make the example clear, think of the likelihood of receiving help from a random group of strangers.) A young woman goes to another city with a man she does not know very well. Far from home, he suddenly and unexpectedly tells her he is tired of their relationship, and he leaves her there alone. She is shocked, frightened, and too ashamed to call home. Fortunately, she remembers an old friend of the family who lives nearby. This person takes her in, allows her to stay, and asks no unwanted questions until she is able to make plans to return home. She was part of a network of relationships whose social norms were such that she could call on those in her network for help.

An individual in crisis may require material resources, emotional support, and guidance. As a second example, suppose a college woman becomes pregnant, decides to terminate the pregnancy, and does not have the money to pay for an abortion. She tells friends in her residence hall of her plight. She too was in a social network and could call on those in the network for assistance. They raise the money from among their friends, arrange for the abortion at a clinic, arrange for her to stay in another city with a college friend while she recovers from the abortion, and then have other friends meet her at the airport in her home city and take her to her parents' home. They continue to value her as a person, and can listen to her, or help her plan what to do. They are her confidantes in a difficult situation. The involvement of her social network might be the same if she decided to continue the pregnancy to term.

Both women obtained something they needed from their respective social networks. How typical is this? In the examples, the women felt free to ask for help and judged correctly who could provide assistance. Feeling free to ask and judging correctly who would provide assistance may be thought of as skills necessary to use social support. At the opposite pole, an individual may feel so guilty, have so little self-esteem, or for darker reasons feel so hopeless that he or she may not use available support. People embedded in a close and supportive social network have committed suicide despite the best efforts of friends, relatives, and professional therapists. Their difficulties in using support may reflect a maladaptive coping style that reduces their ability to see or to generate alternatives (Reinecke & DuBois, 2001).

In the examples, those asked were willing to help. Sometimes a person's needs are so great, and he or she has "gone to the well" so often, that the well turns up dry. Some people may be isolated precisely because they have exhausted others' goodwill and other interpersonal "credits." Under circumstances of chronic stress, support can erode, and that erosion can add to the distress of all concerned (Tebes, 1983). But situations change. Although the spouses of those with mental illness generally take care of them, if there is a divorce, responsibility for care may shift back to the parents. Similarly, as parents age, siblings may take more of a role, and as the patient ages, adult children may assume primary responsibility (Johnson, 2000). Even among those who give help willingly over a long period of time, new concerns arise. Parents of retarded or mentally ill individuals also worry about what will happen to their adult children as the parents "age out." "We are getting on in age, and there will be no one to look after our mentally ill son." "My son is terrified of what will happen to him when I die. So am I." "I hope and pray that one day there will be special housing" (Grosser & Vine, 1991, p. 288). Issues of support can't be understood in isolation from consideration of stages in the life course.

We have been speaking about support in family or in other friendship networks. The social networks of people with serious mental illness often consist of workers in agencies—case managers, vocational counselors, welfare workers, or police officers (Holmes-Eber & Riger, 1990). In sharp contrast, most other people can look to spouses, lovers, family, and friends, or they can afford to hire private sector professional helpers—doctors, lawyers, or tax accountants—whose help is not stigmatizing. Both those who use a social network of public helpers and those who use a private and personal network must possess certain skills and qualifications (again think of going to a random stranger for help) to gain access to the network's resources (Cronkite, Moos, Twohey, Cohen, & Swindle, 1998). Those who rely on a public network may need to have "bureaucratic competence," while those who rely on their families and the private marketplace utilize other skills. They also count on a norm of giving and receiving help in certain social relationships. We should not confuse the skills necessary to function in one network with those necessary to function in another. It is one thing to be a good client and another to be a good friend. However, programs that assist formerly hospitalized psychiatric patients to develop skills in using community resources and in gaining employment resulted in better relationships with family and others (Pilisuk, 2001). The effects of their successful changes radiated. The former patients came to believe there were more people whom they could count on for assistance (perceived support), and their vulnerability was thus reduced. The necessary skills may be teachable.

Effects of giving support. Giving support is as important to understand as receiving support. We have very little information about the effects of giving support in the long term on the one who gives support. Women who had cared for frail elderly spouses for a long time apparently needed support for themselves to take time off, to take care of their own needs, and to receive recognition for what they had been doing. Younger women who were just beginning to care for frail elderly relatives had more need for information about resources, and about what to do in specific circumstances than they had for emotional support (Labrecque, Peak, & Toseland, 1992).

Just as we should think about teaching skills of seeking and using support, we should also think about providing support to those who are giving support, especially when dealing with chronic problems. Grandparents often take on custodial care of grandchildren when child protective services removes custody of a child from a mother who is afflicted with substance abuse problems. The grandparent, who may not have the energy to keep up with a young child, may suffer from poor health, and depression, and may have a limited support network.

Children coming from deprived or dysfunctional backgrounds may have special needs, which add to the stress of caring for them (Burnette, 1999). We should consider the needs of providers of support, as well as those of the person in need of assistance.

"Negative support." In the examples, the individuals from whom help was sought did things that were helpful. Some people in a network of relationships might not be helpful and if approached would either not provide the support required or act in such a way as to make the problem worse. The supportive aspects of interpersonal relationships and the conflictual or burdensome aspects are important to measure for they have different implications for well-being (Wills & Shinar, 2000). As an example, middle-aged adults who were caring for their elderly parents were often deeply disappointed at not receiving the support of someone from whom support was expected; this made the total experience more stressful. The person providing the care struggled with feelings of anger and disappointment as well as with providing the care (Perrotta, 1982).

Sometimes well-meaning but inappropriate support can compound a problem by creating sources of distress in a supportive network. For example, in trying to protect a grandmother from the knowledge that her beloved granddaughter had committed suicide, other relatives told her nothing until she arrived in the city where the funeral was to be held. The grandmother was emotionally devastated, had no opportunity to prepare herself for the loss, and was quite angry with those who failed to respect her by telling her what had happened. Often people say well-meaning, but clumsy things to those who have experienced losses, creating distance, or anger at worst, or leaving the recipient with a feeling that the other is simply insincere.

Negative interactions within a support network correlate significantly with increased psychological distress and diminished well-being. These harmful relationships tend to be correlated more strongly with distress than positive network interactions alleviate distress (Finch, Okun, Barrera, Zautra, & Reich, 1989; Schuster, Kessler, & Aseltine, 1990; Wills & Shinar, 2000). Rape victims often must deal with unsupportive behaviors from people in their network. Davis, Brickman, and Baker (1991) studied post-rape adjustment among young women. They found that positive support from a significant other ("encouraged me to see a doctor," "took over some of my responsibilities temporarily") was outweighed by unsupportive behaviors ("has indicated I should have fought back more during the crime," "has criticized me for not being more careful"), thus making adaptation more difficult.

Distress in the family network after divorce can be a problem. Luepnitz (1991) found that children in divorced families were more maladjusted when their divorced parents continued to be in conflict. Children in divorcing families who get less positive support from family adults and other adults are more vulnerable to the stresses of divorce and have poorer adjustments than those with better support (Wolchik, Ruehlman, Braver, & Sandler, 1989).

Distress in the family network may have negative repercussions for other problems as well. D'Augelli and Hershberger (1993) found that suicidal ideation and depression in gay and lesbian youth were associated with fears about the reactions of parents and others in their social network to the discovery of their sexual orientation.

Feuds and splintering in voluntary associations and in community action groups, where people normally expect to support each other, can be highly debilitating. Members committed to a cause may spend more time and energy fighting with other factions within their own group than they do with the external "enemy." This kind of "in-fighting" can result in the demise of the action group.

Negative support research. The literature on negative support suffers from the same difficulties as other research that relies on generalized scales. Each research team defines and measures negative stress differently. In one study respondents were asked about whether spouse and friends "get on the respondents' nerves" (Antonucci, Lansford, & Akiyama, 2001). Reinhardt (2001) used two items. She counted the "number of network members who sometimes make you angry or upset" and the "number of network members who you sometimes make angry or upset." Rook (2001) used a diary method to identify and count negative exchanges. These included asking whether "someone had upset them, argued with them, behaved in an unkind manner toward them, refused to provide help in response to a request for assistance, made them angry or hurt their feelings or whether they had been stuck spending time with someone they do not enjoy." (Rook, 2001, p. 89) Swindle, Heller, Alexander, Allen, and Wyman (2001) used still another measure of negative support or negative transactions. Their measure included "encourages avoidance, discourages independence, withheld support/disappointment, esteem denigration, and criticism/conflict" (p. 102). This team also tried to measure specific negative transactions in relation to specific stressors, and also measured whether the respondent had a "global negative perceived network."

Each team has its own reasons for selecting its measure of negative support, but none ever establish the equivalence of the several measures. Teams rarely measure whether the different types of negative interaction are indeed equal in their effects on well-being. The measures are also employed in relation to different stressors, different time periods, and different populations (e.g., older adults, middle-age adults caring for elderly parents, visually impaired adults, African American women, etc.). Because the field is so fractionated, it is difficult to get beyond the simple statements that negative support is correlated with negative outcomes (most of the time), but that positive support does not overcome negative support. Rook (2001) developed some data in support of the "asymmetrical crossover model—specifically, one in which the effects of negative exchanges are so potent they spill across affective domains" (p. 94). In other words, having a bad interaction can spoil one's mood, and having a good interaction may not overcome that bad mood. However, others have not designed their studies so this hypothesis can be examined. Progress in this field is retarded by the lack of standardization and the lack of statements of a problem in such terms that it can be answered with any precision. Many of the studies show complex patterns of intercorrelations. Effect sizes involving 2 percent of the variance may be said to support a hypothesis, and unexpected correlations are ignored or interpreted away, but rarely have any implication for the theory which generated the research in the first place.

Complexities in the social support construct. Aside from the need to study negative support, social support is more than unconditional positive regard. In the past, its measurement in large-scale surveys tended to be oversimplified. More recent research has resulted in more differentiated concepts and in measurement that attempts to capture the complexity. Nonetheless, we have a long way to go before the concepts and measurements are standardized and we can truly examine results that truly replicate. It is not enough that researchers use the same words—social support—they need to use the same constructs and the same measurements as well (see Cohen, Gottlieb, & Underwood, 2000).

Janis (1983) identified three sets of support variables in a therapeutic relationship to aid in stopping smoking or losing weight. The first set was building referent power, by which he meant that the helping person becomes a significant other, one whose approval or disapproval exerts influence on the client. (Not everyone's support has the same weight for every problem, but measurement of support often does not take the differences in weight into account.) The second set referred to the use of referent power to enhance the client's commitment to change by rewarding actions that promote the desired goals and expressing *mild disapproval* of actions contrary to these goals. The opinion of the other person won't matter unless there is a relationship in which it matters. The third set is techniques designed to help the client shift from other-directed to self-directed approval. This aspect is less important for our purposes here than understanding how a relationship is created in which support can be given and be received.

If we take the therapist as a model for an effective supportive relationship, an effective therapist does more than just listen empathically. Successful treatment requires unconditional acceptance as a form of support most of the time. Once established, however, referent power is used to express mild criticism when the client departs from the agreed course of action. The role of effective criticism in a supportive relationship is not well developed in the support literature. (See the discussion of Caplan's description of social support below.) The words, actions, and feelings that constitute support can differ depending on the person, the problem, and circumstances, something that most scales measuring social support do not take into account (see Box 7–3).

Box 7–3. Coping and Support in the Context of Culture

William Dressler (1991) has studied the stress/coping/social support model in the context of history, culture, and social structure. Dressler studied the distribution of symptoms of "depression" or "demoralization" and social supports in an African American community in the rural South. He took as a starting point the profound effects of the civil rights movement in American society in terms of race relations and social stratification and differentiation in the African American community.

The civil rights movement created a more differentiated socioeconomic structure in the African American community. With the lifting of formal legal barriers to participation in American life, and with the enforcement of antidiscrimination legislation, many more African Americans achieved higher occupational statuses and incomes. At the same time, the difference between the top and bottom of the socioeconomic scale within the African American community grew larger (Wilson, 1987). Dressler hypothesized that the meaning of social supports and of stressors, or threats to an individual's social and personal identity, would differ by class and by history.

The older generation grew up within a rigid segregation system, which limited opportunity for education or employment. As viewed from the outside, segregation created a relatively homogeneous socioeconomic community. There was a small middle and upper class, but most people had low-paid, low-prestige, low-skilled jobs, and had little chance for advancement. For most, the extended family, others who were "near kin," and the church, provided the important sources of support. People developed their social identities (e.g., father, worker, churchgoer, or a "good person") as the culture and social structure allowed; within this framework people looked to others for help when it was needed to cope with life's vicissitudes. In this community, stressors were those that threatened the person's social identity or that threatened the links to others.

The older generation worked for and saw the changes wrought by the civil rights movement. Their efforts resulted in an historic achievement that rightly made many feel proud. However, for most of the older generation, the changes in opportunity to advance economically and socially came too late. For this group, the stressors may continue to be those that threaten one's linkages to the community or one's social identity. Moreover, the sources of support may continue to be those provided by the extended family and by the church. The younger generation did not experience the rigid limitations of segregation and had greater opportunities (albeit still limited by racism) for education, employment, and social and economic advancement. These greater opportunities encouraged younger people to identify with the larger American culture and adopt for themselves the standards of success and social interaction prevalent in the larger culture. However, the desire to obtain the possessions that reflect a successful material lifestyle (car, clothes, home, furnishings, vacations) may be discrepant with one's economic circumstances.

The better-off younger person, who has obtained an education, a job, and a spouse, has an achieved identity in several roles and is now concerned with locating him- or herself in the normative ecology. Using Sarbin's terminology, "How well am I doing in the several achieved roles?" is the pertinent question. Stressors that affect a person's sense of control and mastery may be more likely to affect the more successful younger person. In other words, the younger, less well-off person is concerned about entering or keeping roles, while the better-off younger person is concerned with performing well in his or her roles.

For younger people compared to older people, non-kin support will be more important than kin support in ameliorating distress related to stressors. He argues, as does Thoits (1986), that support is best provided by someone who shares the same values and goals and understands the problems from firsthand experience. Support may be better accepted or it may be more useful when it comes from someone with whom the younger person can identify.

Dressler tested these propositions by administering a survey to a randomly selected sample of adults in the community. A sampling of some of the quantitative results illustrates the power of his conceptual scheme. The analysis showed different risk factors for depression depending on the respondent's age and economic class. For example, unemployment was unrelated to depression among those over 40 who were in a higher economic class. Unemployment was related to depression among those who were 40 or older but in a lower economic class. In contrast, depression was more closely related to problems in the marital relationship, problems with children, stresses on the job, and concerns about retirement among those better off economically than it was among those less well-off in the same age group.

The importance of this work is in the interactions showing that the variables related to depression, and the degree of their effect in buffering the effects of stressors, were different in defined social groups. This study tells us we must elaborate our models of the stress/coping/social support field to an order of complexity, which takes into account the nature of a community, its stratification, and the culture of the people. It also tells us that our methods need to be adapted to the nature of the problem in a specific community and with regard to the historical flow of events affecting people in that community.

Social support and the model of a family. We need a model of support that is multidimensional and specifies the complexity of what constitutes support. One such model is Gerald Caplan's (1976) concept of the family as a prototypic model of social support. Caplan did not assert that *every* family functions supportively, but that an *idealized* family fulfills several functions for its members. First, the family collects and disseminates information about the world. Just as parents share their knowledge of the outside world with children, providing the basis for learning, even if vicariously, about various roles one might play in the world (parent, worker, etc.), so too, people in supportive relationships share information with each other about characteristics of the world. Self-help groups disseminate information for members who suffer with a disease, or they share information about the service system and how to negotiate it. Information receipt is one of the components in many scales measuring social support (see below).

Second, the family serves as a feedback and guidance system to help its members understand their reactions to others and the reactions of others to them. Caplan notes how family members almost ritually discuss with each other the day's events. During these discussions family members help each other evaluate the significance of others' reactions and evaluate the family member's behavior in relation to the family's beliefs and values. This aspect is not directly represented on social support scales, although having someone who listens as a confidante is.

Third, Caplan notes that the family group is the major source for developing "the belief systems, value systems, and codes of behavior that determine an individual's understanding of the nature and meaning of the universe, of his place in it, and of the paths he should strive to travel in his life" (p. 23). These "encoding strategies and personal constructs" (see chapter 5), come from direct teaching within the family, from a deep—even if unverbalized—learning of the family's culture, and from the day-by-day living out of these values. By applying the tenets of the ideology to everyday problems, the ideology provides, as Caplan puts it, "prescriptions for wise conduct." Support groups or supportive persons may help to provide or articulate an ideology helpful with a particular problem. This component of support as the maintenance or the application of an ideology to present problem situations is not directly represented on social support scales.

A fourth family function is that of serving as a guide and mediator in problem solving. Family members share each other's problems, offer each other advice and guidance, assist in finding external sources of aid, and may even make arrangements for such assistance. It is in the nature of family life for members to assist each other in dealing with the emotional and cognitive difficulties attendant upon role changes—entering school, becoming an adult, getting married, becoming a parent, experiencing loss, and the subsequent change in status when a spouse dies or a divorce takes place. Older members have gone through the changes and serve as models or transmit experience. Moreover, certain ceremonies mark the role transitions and help make the changes less ambiguous. Families share both joys and sorrows. Emotional sustenance comes from the shared experiences. Thoits (1986) says that it is easier to accept assistance from one with whom the recipient can identify. Giving advice is represented on social support scales, but it is difficult within the measurement framework that has been used to deal with the relationship within which support is offered or received. As Stanton Coit, one of the originators of the settlement house movement of the late nineteenth century put it, "It is terrible when men draw together only in suffering; whereas those who have laughed and thought together, and joined in ideal aims, can so enter into one another's sorrow as to steal much of its bitterness away" (quoted in Levine & Levine, 1992, p. 61).

As a fifth function, family members provide material aid and concrete services to each other. Gifts, help with specific tasks, housing, financial aid, and dozens of other exchanges take place on a daily basis. This aspect of support is represented on social support scales.

As a sixth function, the family is a haven for rest and recuperation. One can go home and lick one's wounds from the day, knowing that in the idealized family others will understand the need for peace and quiet. One can relax and be one's self within the family. There is no need to conceal or to explain the problem to anyone. All understand because all have experienced similar needs and emotions. Some children of parents with schizophrenia described how they sought out "normal" families with whom they could just spend time, free from the strife and disorder that characterized their own homes. A refuge was an important supportive element (Dunn, 1993). This aspect of support is not directly represented on social support scales.

A seventh function of the family is to serve as a reference and control group. Family members are highly sensitive to each other's opinions about attitudes and behavior reflecting family values. As Caplan notes, family members are likely to be judgmental. Success in meeting the family's expectations is rewarded, and failing to live up to the family's expectations is punished in some fashion. Thus the family's standards are enforced, helping to maintain behavior in conformity with family standards. Whether or not the individual family member lives up to family ideals, he or she is still a family member and entitled to call on the family for assistance as a matter of right. This aspect of support is not directly represented on social support scales. To represent such disapproval as negative may miss the meaningfulness of criticism from people whom the recipient loves and respects for maintaining behavior and morale.

As an eighth function, the family provides the foundation for personal identity. As Caplan (1976) puts it, "During the frustration and confusion of struggling with an at-present insurmountable problem, most individuals feel weak and impotent and tend to forget their continuing strengths. At such times, their family reminds them of their past achievements and validates their pre-crisis self-image of competence and ability to stand firm" (p. 30). This function is not directly represented on social support scales.

As a ninth function, family members assist each other with the task of emotional mastery. Family members ideally offer love, affection, and comfort to a member in need. By their constancy of support, family members help to counter feelings of despair or helplessness, and thus kindle hope that the difficult situation will be resolved. Moreover, in a time of crisis family members shore up the sense of personal worth by continuing to treat the individual with love and respect and, if a loss is involved, by providing an alternative source of satisfaction. This aspect may be represented in social support scales in items asking about whether the person has one or more people who are considered intimates, but the simple question of whether one has an intimate is but a pale reflection of this aspect of Caplan's view of the family as a support system.

The set of functions that Caplan specifies for the family may be thought of as dimensions of support that can be evaluated when studying support networks. His model may lead us to a more sophisticated and complex understanding of support than we have managed to achieve so far. It is also useful in understanding self-help groups, as we will see in chapter 9.

Empirical research on social support. Reviews of the literature (Barrera, 2000; Cohen, Gottlieb, & Underwood, 2001) conclude that the presence of social support is generally associated with lower risk for psychological problems. People with depression, for example, receive less support than do normal individuals. In addition, normal people experiencing high levels of stress are apparently at lower risk for disorder if they enjoy high levels of support than if they do not (i.e., the so-called buffering hypothesis).

The hypothesized mechanism here is that lack of support in the face of acute stress engenders negative psychological states such as anxiety, helplessness, and depression. These psychological states in turn will affect physical health either by directly influencing susceptibility to disease (involving the neuroendocrine or immune systems), or by provoking certain behavioral responses (such as smoking, drinking, or failing to seek needed medical care) that actually increase risk of disease or mortality (Cohen & Wills, 1985).

An important question however is whether the amount of support and degree of health are related in a direct monotonic fashion (monotonic means that one variable increases smoothly and steadily as the other does across all of their respective values) or whether there is instead simply a "threshold" effect in which only those people who receive the least amount of support (those who are truly isolated) have a significantly elevated risk for disease or death.

As with coping, the relationship between high levels of support and successful adaptation to stressful circumstances goes two ways. Marital stability and a large circle of positive friendships may produce high self-esteem and competent coping, but these latter assets may also explain why a particular person is able to attract and maintain many supportive relationships (Monroe & Steiner, 1986).

Investigators differ in their conceptual and operational definitions of social support, making it difficult to compare the outcomes of different studies. For example, support has both quantitative and qualitative dimensions that are distinguishable empirically as well as conceptually and correlate only modestly with each other (Cohen & Wills, 1985). When studies report different results, it may be because the measures differ in detail even when they are called by the same or a similar name. Coping strategies, and types of social support that are useful may be differentially useful with different problems and at different times in the resolution of a problem (e.g., at different stages in the development and treatment of AIDS or with different outcomes of a pregnancy; Pakenham, Dadds, & Terry, 1994; Collins, Dunkel-Schetter, Lobel, & Scrimshaw, 1993). These complex relationships mean that we must develop a more complex theory of social support and coping that takes into account more of the context within which people are struggling with problems in living and within which they give and receive support.

Measures of social support. There are quantitative measures of social support that are called "structural" in contrast to measures that deal with the quality of support. Social support has been operationalized quantitatively as the *number of people* in the person's "network" (i.e., family and friends with whom the person is frequently in contact), the *frequency of contact* with members in the network, the *degree of demographic homogeneity of members* (how similar members of the network are to each other in terms of age, race, sex, social class, etc.), the number of people in the network who know each other, sometimes called the *"density"* of the network, and/or the *degree of reciprocity* in supportive transactions among members (i.e., as givers as well as receivers of support).

The measure of the number of network members and the frequency and variety of contacts is called social integration, in contrast to social support. As discussed above, that measure seems clearly related to well-being. But how does it work? One theory holds that people are involved in social relationships and develop their identities through the roles they have in different relationships and settings. These social roles and their effects on forming a personal identity provide a sense of purpose and provide many opportunities for positive and satisfying interactions that add up to well-being. Qualitatively, social support has been defined by the nature of the resources provided by one person to another, by the specific content of social interactions (e.g., emotionally warm vs. hostile and destructive), or by perceptions of whether network members are helpful in times of need. The literature on the effects of social support contained some consistencies of result, but also many puzzling, and sometimes contradictory, findings.

Barrera (1986) reconciled some diverse findings by differentiating among types, conceptual definitions, and measures of support, and the resulting patterns of correlation with various outcomes. Barrera noted the importance of findings involving *perceived support,* in contrast to *enacted or received support.* This latter development puts an interesting cast on the concept of support, since it implies that one's expectations about help from others are more important for managing stress than is the coping assistance actually received. It also opens up new questions, such as what factors affect the perceived adequacy of support? It also leads to the question of artifactual relationships. Do correlations between measures of social support and criterion measures of adaptation reflect a "real" effect, or are they based on something like response styles ("negative affectivity"), or overlapping meanings between dependent and independent variables? The problem of artifacts is not present when the dependent variable is measured completely independently of the measure of social support (e.g., teachers' ratings versus self-ratings, or objective measures of health such as infant birth weight). However, artifacts have not been evaluated for measures of social support in the way they have been for stressful life events measures.

Cohen and Wills (1985) concluded that support appeared to influence well-being through two processes: (1) structural embeddedness in a network of human relationships (i.e., social integration), which may engender feelings of stability and predictability regarding one's social world, and (2) provision of the specific resources required to cope effectively with stressful situations. The general model presented by Cohen and Wills (1985) is depicted in Figure 7–1. In this model, stress results when one appraises an event or situation as demanding a response that one is unable to make.

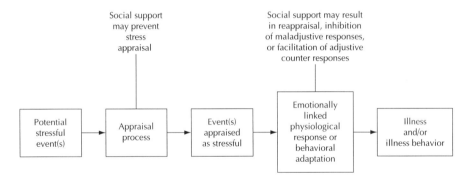

Figure 7–1. Social support and the buffering hypothesis. (From Cohen & Wills, 1985)

Support mitigates the effects of stress in either of two ways. First, the presence of social support may reduce the probability that the event will be appraised as stressful in the first place. That is, the threat implied by an event, such as changing jobs, is reduced or eliminated by the perception that others can and will provide the resources necessary to adapt to this change. A second possibility is that even if the event is appraised as stressful, perceived or enacted support may attenuate the stress reaction by offsetting the transient stress response (e.g., through restoring self-esteem), by directly facilitating healthy coping (e.g., through material assistance), or by influencing the individual's self-perceptions (e.g., regarding self-efficacy—"You can do it!") in a way which leads to more persistent coping efforts. This conceptual breakdown is helpful, but there are still analytic problems that need to be understood and worked into research. For example, enacted or received support may correlate negatively with well-being. The finding may mean that people who are in greater need because of illness or other distress receive more actual support (Wills & Shinar, 2000). If a researcher used received or enacted support measures as the indication of social support, the results may seem paradoxical.

New Directions in Research on Social Support

Our present understanding of social support, its power, and its limits are based largely on the results of correlational studies. In recent years, researchers and clinicians created or modified social networks as systematic interventions (Gottlieb, 2000, Eckenrode & Hamilton, 2000; Cutrona & Cole, 2000). Experimental methods can help determine whether supportive friendships can be established as protective factors for persons at risk, and whether such supplements actually enhance people's supportive resources and mental health. An experiment allows us to make "causal" statements about phenomena and perhaps to identify the critical aspects of a supportive relationship. An experiment by Heller, Thompson, Trueba, Hogg, & Vlachos-Weber (1991) raised a number of useful issues about social support.

Heller et al. (1991) arranged for regular telephone conversations between assigned pairs of isolated, low-income, elderly women. The women in one group carried on regular phone contacts with an assigned peer, while those in the other continued telephone contacts with research staff. They also had a control group that received no contacts over the same period of time. At the end of the study, measures of mental health and perceived friend support showed that the two intervention groups were not significantly different from each other, or from the control group. Given that the participants were all strangers to each other initially and all contact was by telephone, Heller et al. suggest that the intervention was too weak to establish significant new friendships. They speculate that a different intervention, such as one that increased the participation of these women in meaningful activities involving mutual interests and face-to-face contact, would have had more significant effects.

Heller et al. raised other useful questions. Are there substantive differences in the support coming from different sources (e.g., family member, friend, natural caregiver)? Heller et al. speculated that attention and support from family members, particularly adult children, may have been more important to the women in their study than was attention from friends. Having a role in the family and achieving self-esteem by performing this role cannot be duplicated in a friendship. Elderly persons may miss the satisfaction that comes from having their wisdom respected by younger people. Parents may also feel that they have sacrificed for their children and are disappointed when there is no reciprocity. These unmet expectations may not be resolved very easily by substitute activities, and sources of support may not be interchangeable.

In addition to the telephone friends Heller's group established, other studies employed home visitors, lay counselors, support groups, labor coaches, friendly companions, and network restructuring (Gottlieb, 2000). The aim in each instance is to provide a supportive person who will help the target person to cope, or perhaps to prevent isolation and demoralization. However, Gottlieb (2000) points out that such interventions need to be planned to take into account just what the need is. Gottlieb has developed a useful framework for selecting and designing interventions that goes well beyond the simple proposition that all support is necessarily good. For example, in some situations, the network is impoverished, drained, or conflictual. In such an instance, a friendly visitor for a person in a nursing home, or for a person with mental retardation residing in a community residence may be helpful. If the person considered at-risk already has a supportive network, another visitor may be a burden or simply ignored.

Sometimes, the existing social network is a problem and creating a new one is helpful. For example, a newly divorced person may have to develop a whole new network of relationships because of complexities in existing relationships created by the divorce as friends and relatives take sides. People trying to escape substance abuse may need to develop new networks in which the temptation to use substances is diminished. In the words of one member of Narcotics Anonymous, it is necessary to change one's playmates and one's playpen. Sometimes, members of the existing network may not have members with the experience or knowledge to assist the person in coping with a new challenge. For example, older women returning to school may need contact with others with experience in solving problems related to being an older student.

Eckenrode and Hamilton (2000) developed a framework for considering home visitation and mentoring programs. These are relationships that go beyond the medical model and are better seen as friendship, or a mentoring relationship with a teacher, a coach, or simply an older friend or relative. They review home visitation programs, including nineteenth-century "friendly visiting" home visits to families with newborns by community health nurses or paraprofessionals. Home visiting may focus not only on the child, but on the family as well. (For discussion of their effectiveness, see chapter 8.) In recent years, many programs have been experimenting with mentoring programs in which a person assumes the role of advisor, teacher, and friend or companion to another, particularly children and adolescents. The mentor may also be a role model for the youth. Eugene Lang, a wealthy philanthropist, offered to pay for the college education of every student in the sixth grade at a low-income school. Lang not only paid the tuition, but continued to take a personal interest in the youth, with apparently remarkable effects on the youths' long-range accomplishments (Eckenrode & Hamilton, 2000). Big Brother/Big Sister programs have been available for many years. There have been some systematic evaluations of these programs which showed that youth in the program, compared to controls, were less likely to begin using drugs or alcohol, had more positive attitudes toward school and their families and had much lower rates of skipping school. However, these programs require much attention and maintenance to be effective. The programs don't just happen (Eckenrode & Hamilton, 2000).

Some interventions seek to enlist the natural network to increase the opportunities for support. The New Zealand Family Group conference for juvenile delinquency and for child protection is one good example of the intervention (M. Levine, 2000). Under the law, a network consisting of nuclear family, extended family, friends, tribal officials (where appropriate), teachers, social workers, and religious leaders is activated by giving it responsibility for developing and carrying out a rehabilitation scheme for youngsters in difficulty with the law, or for families where there are child protection issues. Family therapy is a special case of work to enhance a natural support network.

Some have reported the use of influential leaders in the drug community or among those susceptible to AIDS to encourage the use of clean needles and syringes, or to provide information about HIV prevention. Intervening with one key network member (e.g., the spouse of an ill person) may have radiating effects in enlisting the supportive potential of a larger network. Some programs successfully sought to reduce school dropout rates by trying to strengthen youth ties to teachers and to weaken ties to other deviant youth, and by helping the youth to develop new friends in a class room (Cutrona & Cole, 2000). Sometimes network access can be improved by teaching one or more members how to seek assistance, or to teach network members what *not* to do.

In the past, the "unit" of intervention in the successful settlement houses of the nineteenth century was the multipurpose club. Youth became members of settlement house clubs that served for recreational, educational, and sometimes political purposes. They remained members over many years. Contemporary observers claimed that youth who were members of the club rarely were seen in juvenile court (Levine & Levine, 1992). The club may have served as a "moralnet" in which the opinions of people sharing common values and experiences mattered to each other (Naroll, 1983). Some have tried to create support groups within schools for children coping with problems such as neighborhood violence or divorce. Children in urban environments are often exposed to violence. Ceballo (2000) brought nine- to twelve-year-old children together in a psychoeducational format in a "club," not to discuss their own experiences with violence, but rather to focus on neighborhood violence. The purpose of the club is to discuss their neighborhoods, including both good and bad things. In addition to permitting sharing of perceptions, the facilitators also taught safety strategies and coping skills for dealing with neighborhood issues. No formal evaluation of the approach has been done, but the author claims participation enhanced the children's sense of control, and empathic connections with other children. Efforts to encourage block clubs put neighbors in more meaningful interaction with each other with increased potential for mutual assistance (Unger & Wandersman, 1983). Neighbors can act jointly to influence city government to keep the streets clean and in good repair, to act against homes in violation of housing codes, to beautify the neighborhood, to pressure officials to act against "crack houses" in a neighborhood, and to do other things such as clean up graffiti that contribute to the perception of a safe environment (see "social capital" in chapter 5 and "community development" in chapter 12).

Theoretical advances. The specific nature of support may differ depending on whether we are speaking of the home setting or the work setting. It may differ again by problem. How much should the support fit with the needs elicited by the particular stressful event? Material aid may be the most useful form of support in response to a loss of income, but will informational support or self-esteem support be equally effective in maintaining well-being? The source also matters. It is one thing to obtain support from unemployment insurance ("deserved," "earned," "nonstigmatizing"), another to obtain it from welfare ("undeserved," "stigmatizing"), and still another from parents ("guilt producing," "obligations created"). The possibility that support is situation-specific and source-specific suggests that more than one aspect or component of support should be measured. Can we specify the circumstances in which each component is useful? We may add that there is probably a distinct advantage in studying these variables in relation to common stressors such as the death of a parent rather than to examine the concepts globally. We have much to learn at a phenomenon level before we leap to a higher order of generality. We are now getting more systematic analyses of the issues in support and theoretical concepts that may allow us to design supportive interventions for particular problems and purposes. For example, a small, dense network may be most helpful in the initial stages of bereavement, but in readapting or in finding a new job, it may be better to activate a large, loosely connected network. The chapters in Cohen, Gottlieb, and Underwood (2000) show considerable theoretical and conceptual advance in this field and provide a framework for thinking through social support interventions systematically.

Box 7–4. Support Interventions for People With Disabilities

In chapter 2 we noted that the deinstitutionalization movement put back into their communities large numbers of mentally ill and retarded persons. Because many of their families are unable to provide adequate care and support, several programs have been created in recent years to provide extra social support to people with special needs. We reviewed Assertive Community Treatment (ACT) in chapter 2. Here we describe programs of supported living, supported employment, and supported education, which form part of a movement known as Psychosocial Rehabilitation (Farkas & Anthony, 1989).

Supported living, or supported housing, involves normal, fully integrated living for people with special needs, including housing no different from that available to the general public (Carling, 1990). The major difference between consumers of supported housing services and other community residents is that the case manager or other service provider provides flexible support to consumers tailored to the individual needs. Case management may involve help locating appropriate choices of housing, advocacy, crisis intervention, and other services as needed, and can range in intensity from an occasional phone call up to full-time, live-in assistance during a time of intense crisis.

Supported employment concerns paid work that a person with special needs chooses and undertakes as part of a fully integrated, competitively obtained job (Bond, 1992). Here much of the support is provided by a "job coach," who assists to the extent necessary with all aspects of the consumer's work career from job development and interviewing, to help on the job site (a form of support that typically fades away within a few weeks), to advocacy and education of employers and coworkers to reduce stigma (see previous chapter), and advice about quitting or changing jobs.

Supported education helps disabled people pursue the social and career advantages of post-secondary education (Moxley, Mowbray, & Brown, 1993). Support services consist of helping the person at risk obtain information about a school and course offerings, contacting school-related services such as academic advising, obtaining financial aid, and coping with the stresses of school life.

Some programs offer all three kinds of supports. Rhoda Zusman is the founder and director of Operation Return in Tampa, Florida. Ms. Zusman operates a 24-unit apartment complex in connection with a community center for consumers who were former patients in the mental health system in Florida. Residents, all former patients, pay a subsidized rent that is sufficient to enable Project Return to maintain the mortgage on the property. The center offers courses in computer skills, prepares participants for general education high school diplomas, offers some college-level courses through a community college, operates a business (thrift shop), teaches arts and crafts, puts on art and craft shows, and exhibits and sells consumers' work. The center has a drama group that puts on plays.

There is a range of social affairs including a weekend recreational program, social events, field trips, parties, and community meetings. The center also engages in extensive fund-raising efforts that involve the community. Some of the paid employees are consumers, and the program makes use of many volunteers. The center services as many as a thousand consumers per month. Ms. Zusman has been instrumental in stimulating a statewide network of 35 centers and clubs, and she has been in demand as a consultant in several other states and foreign countries.

Two recent developments in these services include organized teams of support-providers and the recruiting and training of peers (that is, people with similar special needs) to fill the provider roles. Supportive services are provided in the actual settings where the people at risk live, work, or go to school. These supports assume that people with special needs are similar to other people in the adaptive challenges they face—where to live, how to get money—and in the best ways to meet those challenges: fully integrated, competitively obtained housing, work, or schooling. Successful adaptation will help to transform the person's identity from that summarized by a stigmatizing label like "mental patient" to one of neighbor, coworker, or college student.

To critics it may appear that social support from a paid staff is even more artificial and contrived than what was attempted in the Heller et al. (1991) study reviewed earlier. Advocates of the interventions described here acknowledge that the support they provide is not adequate by itself, and that it is always better to have and use family, friends, and other natural, spontaneous sources of support. However, for many people with disabilities such natural supports are inadequate or nonexistent. The question is not "Are program supports as good as natural supports?" but instead "Are program supports better than no support at all?" It may be useful to see these services as analogous to the Employee Assistance Programs (EAPs) that are increasingly available to nondisabled people. EAPs are designed to give workers at risk for maladaptive outcomes second chances and extra supports to improve their chances of coping successfully.

The support services described here are not panaceas. The typical homes or jobs of these consumers are modest or "entry-level," similar to those of other people with comparable incomes, education, or skills. As a result, average or above average home- or job-related stressors can be expected to complicate the consumers' coping efforts; such stressors include safety concerns, low pay, and lack of control. In addition, fully integrated residences and jobs may be widely dispersed throughout a community, hampering access to peer support from other consumers. Community psychologists can help address this by assisting in the development of self-help groups for consumers (see chapter 9).

Summary

The specific concepts of adaptation, crisis, coping, and support are very useful when we consider the daily "soap opera" affecting a significant number of Americans of all ages, in all walks of life. The concepts of crisis and vulnerability open up a wider range of possible interventions and allow us to consider the possibility that a large proportion of human misery can be alleviated, even though we do not yet know whether the most serious and disabling mental illnesses can be prevented in this fashion.

We reviewed the process of coping and the state of crisis that ensues when a person's state of adaptation is disrupted in the absence of psychological, social, or material resources to produce a new adaptive response. Nearly everyone is assumed to be at risk for such experiences. The ensuing affective state is not a sign of illness but a natural response to a specific set of circumstances. Dysphoric feelings are a signal that the individual is in a situation calling for some change in customary ways of dealing with demands or solving problems. The crisis concept directs us to separate the issues into the management of affect (emotion-focused coping) on the one hand and solving the problem (problem-focused coping) on the other. Affective education and the possibilities of learning to manage or modulate feelings and learning to solve problems more effectively are important both therapeutically and preventively.

There are two classes of crises, anticipated and unanticipated. We speak of anticipated changes when the network of relationships, the tasks to be accomplished, and the roles the individual occupies will change predictably. Crises following anticipated changes are situational-transitional in nature, or developmental. If changes are anticipated, we can devise preventive strategies. Preparation, rehearsal, anticipation of feelings, warnings, preparation of resources beforehand, or practice with techniques for dealing with new problems all may be helpful in meeting anticipated challenges. Sex education in high school, or training for parenting, might similarly prepare individuals for new relationships and new challenges. In addition to preparing the individual to cope when crises can be anticipated, help can also be positioned so as to be available when the event occurs, or soon afterward.

If general problem-solving skills exist, we can teach those skills as part of the regular school curriculum. As we learn how people handle problems on an everyday basis, we can translate that learning into curricula and methods for teaching everyone. Spivack and Shure (1993), in fact, did precisely that when they created a curriculum in interpersonal problem solving that could be employed by nursery school teachers with preschool children (see the following chapter).

The concept that crises have phases and that each phase is different is useful in devising helping strategies, because useful assistance may vary at different phases in the crisis. If people are able on their own to convert traumatic events into growth-promoting experiences, can assistance be provided in advance to help that process? Alternatively, the crisis stages may themselves be understandable as adaptive responses to specific situations.

Much of what we have said about managing feelings and solving problems involves "psychological mediators." Individuals call on members of social networks to obtain coping assistance, to find the psychological, social, or material resources useful in achieving a new state of adaptation. The individual's ability to find and to call on members of a social network may depend on that person's understanding of reciprocity in social relationships. It may also depend on having the social skills necessary to function in a social network. In this sense we have been discussing the interaction between psychological and situational mediators. While apparently separable at a conceptual level, they are in reality intimately intertwined (Folkman, 2001).

Research on natural coping by ordinary people places emphasis on action-oriented, problem-solving responses in dealing with stress. Of course, some people, under some conditions, by virtue of their experiences and their biological and psychological makeups, would find the types of interventions we point to here inadequate and insufficient to help them cope with their problems. Psychoanalyst Herbert Herskovitz used to distinguish between those clients who, he said, came by their problems "honestly" (i.e., they had sufficient adversity in their background to account for their present state) and those whose problems could not be readily understood by examining their histories. The crisis concept and associated interventions may be meaningful only for those who come by their problems honestly. Our theoretical doubts, however, and the broad gaps in our knowledge should not prevent us from experimenting with different approaches when a reasonably interesting theory points the way.

III

APPLICATIONS OF COMMUNITY PSYCHOLOGY

8

Prevention

The history of efforts to reduce the prevalence of mental and emotional problems in this country is largely one of treating problems in individuals after they have arisen. However, from time to time various authorities have argued that proactive, preventive efforts should be given more emphasis. The mental hygiene movement and the child guidance clinics in first part of the twentieth century are examples of earlier efforts with a preventive thrust (Levine & Levine, 1992; see chapter 2). Crisis theory as developed by Lindemann and others as early as the 1940s (see chapter 7) provided a beginning for contemporary thinking about prevention. In the years after World War II prevention was a focus of those who saw psychiatry as an instrument of social change (Grob, 1994), and the Joint Commission on Mental Illness and Health (1961) discussed the desirability, if not the necessity, for programs in prevention. Both the 1963 Community Mental Health Centers Act and the President's Commission on Mental Health (1978) highlighted prevention as a major strategy for dealing with mental health problems in the United States. More recently the Institute of Medicine (IOM) of the National Academy of Sciences summarized the prevention knowledge base (Mrazek & Haggerty, 1994). We refer to those ideas in this chapter.

Healthy People 2010 is a federal government policy document describing the present state of the U. S. population with respect to many preventable illnesses, including mental disorders. It notes the burdens of illness on economic productivity and health care resources, sets specific percentage change goals for preventive efforts, and suggests directions for those efforts. *Healthy People* reflects a federal interest emphasizing prevention that goes back to 1979 and the presidency of Jimmy Carter. Carter's initiative was expanded when Ronald Reagan took office in 1981, and even though many other initiatives in social services and mental health were soon sharply curtailed during the Reagan administration, policies promoting preventive interventions were preserved (Levine, 1981).

Those interested in pursuing prevention programs will find the document worth examining, although many of its specific proposals may be on hold given a political climate that discourages more "government interference" in the lives of individuals and protests the commitment of more money to anything that can be labeled a "social program" (see chapter 13). *Healthy People 2010* considers neither the problem of finding resources to achieve the percentage change objectives it recommends nor the time necessary. The embeddedness of prevention programs in our economic, political, and social structures is readily apparent, a point we emphasize throughout this book. The complexity of problems is no excuse for not trying to develop solutions, but understanding the complexity should give us pause for thought and a sense of humility about the time and resources necessary to achieve these objectives.[1]

A moment's reflection may suggest why prevention is appealing. One reason is certainly the "numbers" problem we examined in chapter 1. Given the way psychological problems have traditionally been defined, there are not now and presumably never will be enough trained professionals to meet the mental health needs of most communities. Prevention of mental disorders would also improve the efficiency of the health care system in the United States by reducing costs related to long-term disabilities and the inappropriate use of medical services to treat psychosocial problems (Mrazek & Haggerty, 1994).

A second impetus for prevention, mentioned in chapter 2, is dissatisfaction with the effectiveness of traditional helping interventions, especially under restricted policies of managed care and other limitations in the service system. Lack of eligibility for mental health services and other barriers keep many people in need from receiving treatment at all. For problems like antisocial personality disorder that resist the known forms of psychological treatment, prevention at a *prior* stage of individual development (e.g., prevention of conduct disorder in childhood) may be more promising than treatment (Mrazek & Haggerty, 1994). Later in this chapter we cite projections claiming that full implementation of current behavioral and psychological techniques for preventing HIV infection could prevent 29 million new HIV infections and many other sexually transmitted diseases by 2010 (Stover et al., 2002).

A third compelling impetus toward prevention is that prevention may be much more cost-effective than treatment. The Michigan Jobs Project (see chapter 3) was designed to prevent depression and anxiety in unemployed adults and enhance their motivation to seek new employment. A follow-up after two and a half years found that people who had received the intervention had higher rates of reemployment and earnings, fewer job changes, and reduced anxiety and depression compared to those who had been randomly assigned to a control condition. For the average person in the intervention condition the program cost $286 but generated more than $5,000 in additional earnings and more than $1,000 in additional federal and state tax revenue. The average participant's additional earnings were projected to reach $50,000 over the years remaining until his or her retirement (Vinokur, van Ryn, Gramlich, & Price, 1991). Large financial benefits have also been reported for a 25-year follow-up of Head Start participants (Barnett, 1993).

Even though prevention efforts have been relatively slow to take off among mental health professionals (Kleist, 1996), the idea is much more accepted today than it was 25 years ago. Despite our limited understanding and the uncertain, albeit growing, knowledge base, prevention efforts are being emphasized by research workers, clinicians, government, and by professional and advocacy organizations. Opportunities for participation in research and training in prevention are more available than in the past. In fact, every day, tens of thousands, if not hundreds of thousands, of children in schools are exposed to a variety of programs with a preventive thrust. Schools, desiring to address substance abuse problems, school violence (Peterson, Larson, & Skiba, 2001), bullying, and related social problems (O'Donnell, 2001) have welcomed prevention workers who come with programs that have had some field testing and some evidence of success (e.g., Primary Mental Health Project, below), into individual schools and into school districts. In addition to projects that are variants of competence building, James Comer's comprehensive school model and Ed Zigler's program for 21st Century schools have been adopted in many school districts. These are efforts to reform entire school organizations. The extent of these programs indeed represents progress in the field and an increasing sophistication about what needs to be done to develop, test, introduce, and maintain programs in the field. (See the three volumes on prevention edited by Weissberg, Gullotta, Hampton, Ryan, and Adams [1997a; 1997b] and by Albee and Gullotta [1997].)

Compared to clinical treatment, prevention continues to be underfunded because its benefits are less immediate and because it requires us to confront social, ethical, and political factors in defining the solutions to social problems (Albee, 1998; Conner, 1990; Levine, 1981). A strategy of prevention implies environmental explanations for the causes of psychological problems and a firm belief in the value of large-scale, active intervention using public resources over more passive efforts by smaller private interests (Albee, 1998). Implementing preventive programs may require professionals to take social and political action designed to achieve change. Although we have a historical precedent for an activist role in the settlement house movement (Levine & Levine, 1992), in times of social and economic conservatism most professionals want to avoid "biting the hand that feeds them" (Rappaport, 1992).

Basic Concepts in Prevention

The core idea of prevention is to take action beforehand to limit or avoid an undesirable consequence or state of affairs in the future. While the undesirable state of affairs does not necessarily have to be an illness, prevention concepts are rooted in the nineteenth-century public health movement. While the disease model is not fully applicable to the problems of living that occupy our attention, we will review concepts borrowed from it, and will also explain some recently proposed alternatives.

Two terms are important and we will define them again. The incidence (I) of a disorder is the number of new cases that arise in the population of interest during a specified interval of time, usually one year. Its prevalence (P) is the number of cases in existence at a specified point in time, and reflects both the incidence rate and the duration (D) of the disorder. Note that prevalence (P) will be reduced if incidence (I) is reduced; P will also be reduced if treatment reduces the duration (D) of an episode of disorder. The formula $P = I \times D$ summarizes the concepts.

Gerald Caplan (1964) introduced the distinctions among primary, secondary, and tertiary prevention strategies in mental health. Tertiary prevention does not reduce the prevalence of a disorder; tertiary efforts are directed toward ameliorating its long-term symptoms and preventing further ramifications. Supported living and supported employment programs help people with serious mental and physical disabilities live and work in fully integrated community settings. These opportunities help to reduce the social and psychological difficulties associated with chronic disability even though participants would still be counted as "cases" in an epidemiological survey.

Secondary prevention means reducing the prevalence and duration of a disorder typically through early case finding and prompt intervention. Crisis intervention (Roberts, 2000), juvenile delinquency diversion, employee assistance programs, and psychological screening of elementary school children (e.g., Cowen et al., 1996) are examples of secondary prevention efforts. Programs like these are "preventive" in the sense that P is reduced if a case is successfully treated early and the duration (D) of the disorder is shortened. The rate of new cases (incidence or I), presumably is not affected, however.

Finally, when an intervention actually reduces the incidence of a disorder (I), the program is referred to as primary prevention. By definition, after the primary prevention intervention, the program's targets must show no detectable signs of the disorder. Social support groups for the newly widowed to prevent depression or training in cognitive problem solving to prevent school failure are examples of primary prevention. The goal of such programs is to act before the manifestation of an undesirable end-state to prevent its appearance.

Public health concepts do not apply readily to the prevention of mental disorders (Mrazek & Haggerty, 1994). The "primary/secondary" distinction assumes a clear demarcation between states of health and states of incipient disorder. In mental health we typically lack valid definitions or signs for making such distinctions. Instead we emphasize a *continuum of risk* for disorder based on multiple factors. In addition, "secondary" connotes a less direct and perhaps less significant effort than one designated "primary," yet depending on the intervention's focus and cost-effectiveness this may not be the case. "Tertiary" efforts are preventive in an indirect fashion. They assist in the long-term support and rehabilitation of persons with special needs.

In light of these conceptual problems, prevention in mental health is developing its own language and concepts. In the current terminology, *indicated prevention* is an intervention with individuals who already possess detectable signs or biological markers of disorder even though they are not yet diagnosable. A man prone to depressed moods would not be diagnosable if his episodes were always brief (less than two weeks), for example, but the eventual likelihood of serious mood disorder may be such that medication or other interventions might be worth considering immediately as a way of reducing the risk of diagnosable disorder. Indicated prevention involves the identification (and thus the labeling) of specific individuals. It would not be appropriate unless a cost-effective intervention is available.

When the target person faces above average risk but as yet shows no indications of disorder, the program involves *selective prevention*. For example, a pregnant woman should avoid using alcohol and other drugs to prevent harm to her fetus. Although the targeted individuals are at elevated risk they do not yet show any indications of disorder, making the program equivalent to primary prevention. Deciding whether a given psychological or behavioral characteristic is better understood as a "marker" or a "risk factor" (and thus subject to indicated or selective prevention, respectively) is difficult (Mrazek & Haggerty, 1994).

An intervention provided to everyone without regard to relative risk is called *universal prevention*; an example is ads urging people not to start smoking. Universal prevention programs can reach large numbers of people, but since relatively few people are likely to be at imminent risk, these programs can be inefficient, and thus low in cost-effectiveness. If they are relatively inexpensive financially and carry few social costs compared to the costs of having even a few cases develop, intervention may still be worthwhile. Figure 8–1 locates these preven-

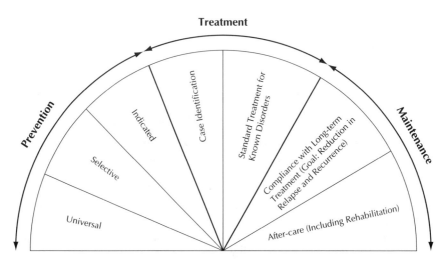

Figure 8–1. The mental health intervention spectrum for mental disorders. (From Mrazek & Haggerty, 1994)

tive activities on a spectrum of interventions for mental disorders. Aside from prevention, this spectrum includes active *treatment* for individuals who meet or approximate formal diagnostic criteria for mental disorder and *maintenance* strategies to support adaptation and coping and reduce the likelihood of relapse or deterioration.

Historically, indicated (or secondary) prevention has appealed to mental health professionals, even though it rests on certain assumptions and typically reveals some of the pitfalls of prevention efforts. We will describe an important example of indicated prevention and examine some of the issues it raises before reviewing examples of selective and universal prevention.

Indicated (Secondary) Prevention

The Primary Mental Health Project

The best known among indicated prevention programs in mental health is the Primary Mental Health Project (PMHP) conducted by Emory Cowen and his associates at the University of Rochester (Cowen, 1997; Cowen et al., 1996). PMHP began as an early detection and intervention program for children in the primary grades of a Rochester elementary school. PMHP demonstrated statistically significant success in predicting high versus low risk for later maladjustment in children as young as the first grade of elementary school; the effectiveness of its various intervention programs at reducing the degree of maladjustment shown by the high-risk children is more open to debate. Much of the voluminous literature on indicated prevention arising since Cowen's pioneering work shows more encouraging effects on outcomes. Perhaps we have learned to improve the interventions. For example, Durlak and Wells (1998) report a meta-analysis of 130 outcome studies of indicated prevention programs for children and adolescents who showed early signs of maladjustment. Similar to PMHP, the projects studied were mostly school-based and directed at children in elementary school. For programs using behavioral and cognitive-behavioral intervention techniques, Durlak and Wells found moderately strong effects involving both reduced problem behaviors and increased competencies. The average participant in one of these programs had a better outcome than did 70 percent of untreated control children. Effects like these are equivalent to those for psychotherapy with children who have established problems, and are stronger than those typically found for programs to prevent delinquency, alcohol use, and smoking in children. Particularly encouraging among Durlak and Wells' findings was that the children affected most positively included those with externalizing problems (aggression or disruptiveness). These are children who, if diagnosed later with conduct disorder, are often unresponsive to psychotherapy and other forms of help.

A key requirement of indicated and selective prevention strategies is accurate information about the risk of later disorder in populations targeted for preventive intervention. Accuracy of prediction can be judged in terms of the rates of two types of errors in classification, "false positives" and "false negatives." A false positive occurs when an individual is predicted to develop a disorder when in fact he or she will not. Conversely, a false negative represents the *failure* to predict later disorder in a case where the individual will eventually show it.

Mulvey and Cauffman (2001) offer an instructive example of the false positive problem when trying to predict school violence (see also Furlong, Morrison, Austin, Huh-Kim, & Skager, 2001). In the aftermath of such events as the shootings at Columbine High School in Colorado, schools felt pressured to develop and apply ways of identifying students likely to perpetrate further shootings. The first challenge schools face in such efforts is that millions of students attend school every day, yet less than 1 percent of homicides and suicides among school-age children occur on or around school grounds. The low incidence of homicidal violence in school settings makes it impossible to identify perpetrators in advance without a false positive rate that is many times the rate of correct identifications. Broadening the definition of violence to include bullying, fist-fighting, and other nonlethal aggression would reduce the false positive rate, but would also change significantly the nature of what is being predicted. A second challenge schools face is that at least some of the risks that contribute to school violence are not stable characteristics of individuals but rather transient situational factors. For example, there appears to be more risk at a larger school, and at schools where different student subgroups are socially isolated. Third, the risks and behaviors exhibited by adolescents fluctuate over time, and as a result the accuracy of classifications using established measures will also fluctuate over time. Finally, being identified as violence-prone is stigmatizing.

Mulvey and Cauffman conclude that the resources available for trying to prevent school violence are probably better invested in continuous risk management, where one determines the risk factors present in a given school or community and monitors them over time for changes. This approach is more likely to address situational factors (vs. labeling individuals). Rather than interventions that separate students (implying some are likely perpetrators) Mulvey and Cauffman suggest encouraging more communication and support among students and between students and teachers that will promote students' attachment to school. Others discuss zero tolerance for violence policies in schools, better school disciplinary policies, and the effectiveness of gun control legislation in reducing access to guns in schools (Redding & Shalf, 2001).

Box 8–1. *Preventing Child Maltreatment:*
          The Problem of False Positives

In chapter 4 we discussed the tragic death of Joseph Wallace, a three-year-old who was murdered by his mother. A judge had restored custody to this mother on the recommendation of a child protection worker and professional therapists who had presumably treated her. How does the problem of false positives hamper efforts to prevent such tragedies?

Recall that one estimate is that maltreatment-related child fatalities occur with an incidence of about 1.94 per 100,000 children. Several "risk factors" might be related to prevention. First, the vast majority (80–90 percent) of children who die because of maltreatment or neglect are under age five, and a high percentage of those are infants and children under age two. These very young children are also at the highest risk of receiving injuries severe enough to warrant hospitalization.

Second, the deaths are probably concentrated among low-income and ethnic minority families. Third, perhaps 75 percent of fatalities related to *physical* abuse involve a male (father, stepfather, boyfriend) acting alone, or together with (usually) the child's mother. Very few maltreatment deaths of very young children can be attributed to strangers. Almost all are committed by caretakers.

Fourth, our best estimate is that between one-third and one-half of maltreatment-related fatalities are related to neglect rather than abuse. Moreover, two-thirds of cases of fatalities were unknown to child protection services.

As we noted earlier with respect to school violence, it is difficult to predict low base rate events without making a large number of false positive errors unless the predictive instrument is perfect or near perfect (see Caldwell, Bogat, & Davidson, 1988). We will have to commit a great many resources to intervene in the lives of many people in order to reach a few who are identified correctly as potential child killers.

Can we improve our predictions over simply going with the base rate? K. Browne (1993) used a screening instrument completed by home health visitors who visited 14,252 children. About 7 percent, or 964 cases, were classified as high risk for abuse or neglect. All the families were followed for five years. At the end of that time, 106 of 14,252 cases, or 0.7 percent, had been officially reported for suspected or actual maltreatment. The screening instrument correctly identified 72 of the 106 (68%) maltreating cases, and *incorrectly* identified only 6 percent of the non-maltreating cases; however, the actual number of false positive errors (858 cases) was very large because of the low base rate of maltreatment. The screening instrument identified a rate of false positives that was ten times the actual rate (7% predicted versus 0.7% actual). These are cases of maltreatment and not of fatalities which are much rarer. Prediction could be improved by studying the 964 identified maltreating families more closely, using additional risk factors (K. Browne, 1993).

Implications for Prevention

Using data and theory, we can set some parameters for a program to prevent maltreatment fatalities. Targeting high-risk populations, even using a two-stage screening process (identifying those at high risk, and then studying the high-risk candidates more intensively to develop additional predictors), will not overcome the false positive problem. Even under a favorable two-stage screening scenario, we would still miss the false negatives. What of the political, cultural, financial, and psychological cost of intervening in a situation with a high false positive rate? How would the intervention be explained to the recipient in a way that would avoid the stigma of having the family or some family member labeled as a potential killer and the child labeled as a victim? Moreover, unless the high-risk parent voluntarily accepts services, under present law the state has no power to intervene coercively simply because of a predicted risk at some time in the indefinite future (Levine et al., 1995).

An individual-level preventive strategy is bound to be inefficient. We cannot depend on Child Protective Services to prevent all or even most child fatalities. Although cases known to CPS are at higher risk for child fatalities, the rate of fatalities is very low, and we would still have to deal with the false positive problem in an already overburdened system.

Home visiting for infants may prevent maltreatment fatalities because the children most at risk are infants and preschoolers. The home visitor can not only observe to prevent fatality, but provide other valued services and call for further intervention when it appears the family is in difficulty. Fatalities due to *neglect* occur as often as those due to *abuse* (Levine, Compaan, & Freeman, 1994). If neglect and abuse are qualitatively different phenomena, each with its own risk factors and dynamics, then a single program emphasizing either cannot be fully effective. More than one program is necessary.

For example, a high proportion of maltreatment-related fatalities result from shaken baby syndrome. A simple video warning all new mothers of the danger would be easy to develop and to use. If the video also were to contain information about coping when a baby won't stop crying, it would be useful generally, inexpensive, and culturally unobjectionable. In addition, many children each year are injured severely by hot water and require intensive medical care, sometimes lasting over many years. A simple governor that shuts off tap water when it gets too hot can prevent many of the burns (U.S. Advisory Board on Child Abuse and Neglect, 1995).

A more difficult prevention problem is posed by the finding that perhaps 75 percent of abuse-related deaths involve a man. What kind of prevention program can teach a mother how to deal with a potentially abusing man (Levine, Compaan, & Freeman, 1994)?

Warnings about leaving infants alone may be useful, especially if reinforced by frequent reminders. Assuming that parents sometimes reach the limits of their tolerance, advance preparation such as finding a neighbor or a relative who will provide some respite for a parent might help. However, abusive or neglectful families may be socially isolated and/or live in neighborhoods where not much neighboring goes on (Reppucci, Woolard, & Fried, 1999), in which case that solution may be difficult to implement. Increasing the availability of affordable and well-run nurseries, day care, drop-in centers, and preschools would serve two purposes: It would prevent abuse and neglect by giving desperate parents a safe outlet. By bringing more young children into situations in which they can be observed, it also provides opportunities for identifying abused or neglected children.

No single approach will be uniformly successful in preventing fatalities. One message and one program are not enough. Multiple approaches based on an ecological understanding of the conditions under which maltreatment-related fatalities occur are necessary.

Limitations of Indicated Prevention in Mental Health

Indicated prevention requires both early detection and effective intervention. Problems with the accuracy of detection and the efficiency of early intervention raise important concerns about the cost-effectiveness of indicated prevention efforts in mental health. Screening procedures may rely on incomplete knowledge about risk factors and ignore compensating protective factors. Normal individuals may be mislabeled as cases of "incipient" pathology, and we may miss important early problems in others. We often do not understand the natural course of a disorder over time well enough to identify its incipient stage, yet the incipient stage, assuming there is one, is the crucial period for indicated prevention. What we think of as an incipient stage may actually be a normal variation in behavior. Is an adolescent whose mood swings from elation to boredom to sadness to anger showing early signs of an emotional disorder, or is it just adolescence? If the latter, then intervention may be wasted, or worse. On the other hand, by the time we are able to identify an "early" case the problem may already exist in a more entrenched and resistant stage, making effective intervention more difficult.

Because target group status is based on *probabilities* of future disorder that are less than 100 percent (and usually not known precisely),
the costs of being wrong in some number of individual cases cannot
be overlooked in evaluating the overall effectiveness of an indicated
prevention program. Many highly regarded prevention programs are
not intended to enhance the overall mental health of populations but
focus much more narrowly on preventing specific disorders like alcohol abuse or schizophrenia (Mrazek & Haggerty, 1994). However, a
specific disorder like schizophrenia may occur in only 1 percent of the
population, and controlling costs by minimizing the rate of false positives can be very difficult when the base rate of a disorder is less than
the rate of cases the identification procedure can reliably detect.

A similar problem arises with suicide. The rate of successful suicide
is 71.9 per 100,000 for males over 65. The rate for adolescents males is
19.4 per 100,000 (Garland & Zigler, 1993). The rate of suicide in those hospitalized for an attempt is about 2 percent in the year following hospitalization and 10 percent within ten years. No detection procedure would
improve the error rate (false positives plus false negatives) over simply
predicting that no one would ever commit suicide, and there would be
enormous financial, psychological, and social costs associated with hos-
pitalizing everyone we believed was at risk. Our inability to predict accurately creates important dilemmas, not only for prevention but for clinical decision making in contexts where predictions are important.

The social costs of false positives and false negatives depend on
the particular disorder. A person would presumably rather be told he
might have cancer when in fact he does not (i.e., be a false positive),
for example, than *not* be told he might have cancer when in fact he
does (false negative). Tests for the presence of cancer can be carried
out with little social cost to the individual; a missed diagnosis on the
other hand, may cause the person to lose the opportunity for effective
treatment. However, a diagnosis of mental illness carries with it stigma
and other disadvantages. The action of holding a person for further
study of mental illness carries with it social costs that are not present
with other medical diagnoses.

There are also several requirements if we are to justify indicated prevention. Few, if any, behavioral or pharmacological interventions are
universally effective; for disorders involving poor impulse control or violent antisocial behavior there may be no effective intervention program.
What if we can detect a serious disorder but can do nothing about it?
Do ethics require that we inform the person (or parent) and thereby increase anxiety even if we have no treatment to offer? Is it better to ignore the signs of incipient disorder and let nature take its course? One
justifiable option is intervention to reduce the *current risk* of later disorder. For example, we might work to improve the quality of peer relationships in adolescents at risk for schizophrenia and target peer relationship quality (rather than schizophrenia) as the primary outcome of

interest. Whether such a program is truly preventive, of course, remains an empirical question. We might not see a lower-than-expected rate of schizophrenia among treated individuals later in adulthood.

Even a highly effective intervention will have to meet two further requirements. First, because the *timing* of the intervention is crucial to indicated prevention (i.e., the target may show precursor features for only a limited time before more entrenched pathology sets in), the intervention must be aggressively delivered to reach enough cases to have a measurable effect on prevalence. Although some authorities assert that crisis intervention has a secondary preventive effect, such a program requires additional backup mental health services to be fully effective. In addition, the typically "passive" format of intervention (persons in need must locate the service provider, rather than vice versa) effectively keeps crisis intervention from having an impact on very many people. Fewer than 1 percent of college students in one study who experienced stressful life events ever used a hotline or a crisis service (Levine & Perkins, 1980a). Many indicated prevention efforts referring alcohol abusers to employee assistance programs are delivered too late in the development of the disorder to test the benefits postulated for early intervention.

Second, the intervention must be deliverable *economically* and in *quantity* if it is to produce a significant reduction in the prevalence of disorder. The limits of lengthy, costly one-to-one interventions should be obvious by now—there are simply too many potential cases in existence for any kind of 1:1 approach to deliver a cost-effective indicated prevention service. Bloom's (2000) assertion that brief one- or two-session psychotherapy has positive lasting effects is interesting in this context, but we have no evidence of its preventive efficacy. Indicated prevention suffers from some of the same conceptual and practical problems that limit the social utility of psychotherapy and other variants on the medical model (see chapter 1).

The reduction of misery is a valid humanitarian argument, and there are others, for making treatment readily available as soon as it becomes evident that someone is having difficulties. But the promise of a systematic decrease in the prevalence of disorder is not one of the stronger arguments. Selective and universal prevention strategies avoid some of these problems, as we will see in the next section.

Universal and Selective (Primary) Prevention

Historically, medical disorders have been brought under control by the pursuit of primary prevention strategies that reduced the number of cases arising in the first place. Public health has accomplished the primary prevention of physical diseases through such specific measures as the development of vaccines, and through nonspecific measures such as improved sanitation and purified drinking water. Reasoning by analogy, authorities on prevention in mental health suggested that extensive, lasting benefits might be expected from large-scale social system changes and improvements in the quality of life, even though such efforts are not specifically targeted at reducing the incidence of a specific disorder (Albee, 1998). However, the scope of possible targets and interventions is exceedingly broad.

"Prevention" is a very loosely defined construct. Cowen (1983) would restrict the term primary prevention to programs that (1) are directed at groups, not at individuals, who are (2) well, not disordered, and (3) receive an intervention that rests on a knowledge base sufficient to allow for specific evaluation of well-articulated specific goals. Albee, Faenza and Gullotta (1997) identify four technologies: education, social support, the enhancement of social competencies, and rebuilding communities that can be put into service in achieving the goals.

Useful proposals such as Cowen's do not take into account the problems inherent in prevention. Any deliberate intervention into the lives of normal, healthy people raises questions about priorities and values. Resources are not limitless; money spent on preventing future problems is by definition not available to help people already in difficulty. The counterargument asserts that diverting resources to prevention is worthwhile because of the potential for great savings in human misery and in dollars.

What of the values of privacy and freedom? Some problems involve voluntary individual choices (cancer caused by smoking, HIV infection from unsafe sexual practices). What business do we have trying to influence such choices and, when we do try, what precedents are we setting for trying to dictate other voluntary choices (Leichter, 1991)? How long would it be before any arbitrarily defined condition of "risk" could qualify a person for "preventive" correction? The following "high-risk" groups were targeted for preventive interventions in the 1880s: "children of the insane, isolated persons, dark-haired persons, and the idle rich" (Spaulding & Balch, 1983, p. 60). Assessments of risk can be influenced by social and political factors as much as by physiological and behavioral ones (see chapter 6). How far do we wish to go in abrogating individual freedom or privacy by intervening in people's lives in the name of public mental health?

Furthermore, since no intervention is risk-free, what we do may well have unintended negative consequences. That is, procedures we believe to be powerful enough to change permanently a person's behavior in one direction are presumably capable of having significant harmful effects as well. Consider the well-known Cambridge-Somerville Youth Study (CSYS), for example, in which boys at risk for delinquency were randomly chosen to receive regular family counseling, academic tutoring, and community-based activities like Boy Scouts for five years. After thirty years, those who had participated in the program were compared with controls who had not with respect to adult criminal behavior, mortality, disease, and vocational history. Most comparisons revealed no significant differences, but those differences that were significant all favored the control group. Men who had been chosen at random to participate in the CSYS thirty years earlier were significantly *more* likely to have (1) committed multiple crimes; (2) shown signs of alcoholism, serious mental illness, or heart disease; (3) died at a young age; or (4) worked in lower-status occupations (McCord, 1978, 1992).

The reasons for the apparent negative impact of the CSYS intervention are not clear. The choice and use of "supportive guidance" as the preventive intervention was based on professional judgments at that time instead of on solid empirical evidence that such help would provide an antidote to later antisocial behavior. Perhaps the labeling of the boys in the intervention group as delinquency-prone became a self-fulfilling prophecy. Perhaps the socially and economically disadvantaged boys in the intervention group became dependent on the support and attention the program provided, so that ending the program after five years had a negative effect on them. (Keep in mind that stopping a long-term program is itself another "intervention" in the lives of participants.)

Another example helps to make this last point. Schulz and Hanusa (1978) describe the results of a preventive intervention designed to counteract the isolation and loss of control that elderly people may experience while institutionalized. Groups of elderly people living in an institution received regular social visits from college students. In one condition the frequency and duration of the visits were under the elderly person's control, while in another the visits were not under the elderly person's control. Members of an additional control group received no visits. Immediately after the intervention, the residents who had controlled the visits they received were rated higher in health status and zest for life than were the other groups. By 42 months after the end of the intervention, however, this same group was significantly lower than the others on both dimensions, and more people in this group had died. If increasing the amount and degree of control over social contacts was a positive intervention, then abruptly ending this program appears to have been a potent negative intervention.

Iatrogenic (physician- or treatment-induced) effects have been recognized in psychotherapy for some time, and they are of even greater ethical concern in prevention. Psychotherapy clients have initiated help-seeking voluntarily; participants in prevention programs enter in a healthy condition and therefore stand to be worse off if the program is harmful. The specific risks and benefits of participating in a prevention program whose effects are presumed to endure for the rest of one's life are not always predictable. If we adopt a preventive intervention on a large scale, we risk magnifying any negative effects. Universal interventions for very low base-rate problems such as teen suicide are of questionable value if these interventions have any side effects at all—for example, if the curriculum is emotionally upsetting to some recipients—such interventions may do much more harm than good. Suicide prevention programs directed at adolescents have some potential to harm participants. Suicide rates may increase after television programs focusing on adolescent suicide or they may induce copy-cat episodes. After a prevention program, many youth classified as most at-risk "reported feeling more hopeless, less sure that mental health professionals would be of help, and more likely to identify suicide as a possible solution to a problem" (Compas, Connor & Wadsworth, 1997, p. 157). Even a successful intervention may not persist. Its effectiveness may fade with time. Spence, Sheffield and Donovan (2003) reported a successful intervention for adolescents at high risk for depression, but the results faded after 12 months. Clearly, participation in prevention programs should be voluntary and with fully informed consent, but is that possible with a universal intervention?

There are two major approaches to selective and universal (primary) prevention. First is a set of methods directed at strengthening the organism, using inoculation as a model. The second group of strategies is directed at changing the social environment; metaphorically, we may call that approach "cleaning out the swamps." A variant may be termed "accident prevention" (Peterson & Mori, 1985).

Risk and protective factors. We can't really afford to deliver interventions to everyone. Currently healthy individuals may have different relative risks (genetic, prenatal, developmental, and experiential variables) for disorders. Although the risk any randomly selected member of the population has for developing schizophrenia is about 1 percent, for example, this risk for the child of a person with schizophrenia is about 13 percent (Gottesman, 1991). Keeping in mind the false positive problem, programs to prevent schizophrenia could be delivered more efficiently if aimed selectively at these children than if administered to all children. Implementation of a prevention program can be difficult with this population. Parents with schizophrenia who have custody of their children are often not amenable to intervention. Some parents may deny their difficulties, may fail to cooperate, or may flee to avoid involvement, even when legal action is threatened (Grunebaum & Gammeltoft, 1993).

In a typical example, a cohort of individuals who are initially at risk (e.g., because all are children of persons with schizophrenia) is followed prospectively until the period of risk for the disorder has passed (age 50 or so). By that time those who will develop schizophrenia have done so; any factors differentiating them from those who do not develop schizophrenia provide a basis for improving estimates of risk.

These additional factors, above and beyond being the child of someone with schizophrenia, may suggest additional preventive interventions. If stress during adolescence compounds the risk of being the child of a person with schizophrenia, we can try to reduce the stress for those at risk or increase their ability to cope.

This "high-risk" design has its own difficulties. The cohort at risk does not necessarily split into two "clean" groups (cases versus normals) by the end of the risk period. Instead it can fragment into several subgroups (e.g., borderline cases, those with other kinds of disorders). Another complication is that the time interval of interest is very long. Primary prevention of schizophrenia means a reduction in the incidence of the disorder over the entire duration of the period of risk, until every member of the cohort is at least 45 or 50 years of age. The expanded time perspective complicates our problem. The significance of risk and intervention may change with maturation and development across the life span. The vulnerability model suggests there may be no person- or situation-oriented *early* intervention that has the power to overcome all possible future stressors or losses of support. There are also practical problems in evaluating preventive interventions when their effects must span a lengthy period of time (Heller, 1996).

Strategies aimed at high-risk individuals may nonetheless be very effective if the risk factors predict a high incidence of disorder among the identified population. They may be still more effective if research pinpoints specific points of vulnerability later in life that may yield to further timely intervention. But we cannot depend on a one-time, forever-effective intervention in psychology. Most problems have complex etiologies and are affected by many variables that change with time.

Prevention research and intervention is becoming more sophisticated. Interest in hypothesized "protective" factors arose following the observation that some children at-risk show resilience and develop normally. Protective factors are not just normal advantages like high socioeconomic status, but include specific resources and characteristics that modify the individual's responses to conditions of risk (Mrazek & Haggerty, 1994). Because a given factor (e.g., ability to delay gratification) can affect the likelihood of developing more than one disorder, and because many disorders have low base rates, prevention now focuses on reducing the incidence of disorders by intervening to moderate risk factors and/or strengthen protective factors (Coie et al., 1993).

Risk and protective factors present a challenge. There may be many factors, not all equally important. Some may be incidental correlates of disorder, while others may be causal in nature. Furthermore, most problems are associated with more than one risk factor, most risk factors are associated with more than one problem, and individuals can be exposed to risk factors in more than one way (Coie et al., 1993). Most important are risk factors that play a direct causal role in the disorder.

We should try to specify precisely the vulnerable group, the targeted risk and protective factors, and the expected outcomes. These requirements are easier to meet when we work with a well-validated theory of how the given intervention should change the targeted factors to produce the desired outcomes. In the absence of a solid theory, however, the risk and protective factors may be vague and nonspecific.

The increased risk for schizophrenia because one is the child of a parent with schizophrenia could be due to genetic factors, environmental factors, or the interaction of both. Children of parents with schizophrenia are at risk for other disorders besides schizophrenia. Growing up with a mother who has schizophrenia can be psychologically difficult, if not actually damaging to personality development (Dunn, 1993). The coefficient of prediction (efficiency of prediction) for any single risk factor is small. Eighty-nine percent of people who develop schizophrenia do not have a parent with schizophrenia; and 63 percent have no family history of schizophrenia at all (Gottesman, 1991). Moreover, Coie et al. (1993) cite evidence that 74 percent of the children of people with schizophrenia are entirely normal.

Developmental theory is a starting point for a theoretical analysis of risk and protective factors (Reppucci et al., 1999). The importance of a given risk factor to a given disorder is different at different ages and with cumulative risk exposure (Coie et al., 1993). Peer influences, for example, may be especially powerful in early adolescence and less significant at other times. One can pinpoint individuals about to enter a developmental period of heightened risk.

We can also consider alternative intervention goals. In many disorders (e.g., juvenile delinquency, alcohol abuse) later-onset cases tend to be less severe. An alternative to outright elimination of the disorder would be intervention to delay its onset in a highly vulnerable group. For example, postponing age at first intercourse is a central goal of sex education programs designed to reduce unwanted pregnancies and sexually transmitted diseases.

Multifactorial etiologies. The health problems for which effective treatment and prevention efforts have lagged (e.g., heart disease, cancer, the common cold, and mental illnesses) all can be characterized as having multiple rather than single causes. They all include behavioral factors (e.g., habits, lifestyles, coping responses) among the contributing causes. Multifactorial etiology may account for the observation that any single factor is usually not sufficient to produce a case of disorder. In some cases the symptomatic manifestation of a disorder can occur long after the individual risk factors are present and active. For example, many people exposed to HIV progress rapidly to AIDS. Others remain infected for years without showing symptoms, and some do not become infected at all.

The complexity of the interaction of multiple causes may explain why progress in treating and preventing these disorders is so slow. Few interventions deal directly with more than one risk factor. Few investigators can follow participants for the number of years required to demonstrate conclusively that prevention was achieved. Multifactorial etiologies may complicate our conceptual understanding of cause and effect. However, some part of the risk and the incidence of the disorder can be reduced by intervening in relation to one contributing etiological factor. In theory, reducing one risk to zero may also influence all those risk factors with which the eliminated risk would have had to interact to produce the adverse effect. We might reduce the incidence of serious child abuse by providing supportive respite care for overstressed parents. That won't reduce all child abuse, but it may have an effect on those episodes related to parental overstress.

Precipitating versus predisposing factors. The vulnerability concept (see chapter 7) distinguishes between predisposing and precipitating factors. *Predisposing* factors may be genetic in nature, or may reflect the individual's history and experiences. A predisposing factor for committing child abuse, for example, may be the person's experience of having been abused as a child (Rosenberg & Reppucci, 1985). *Precipitating* factors occur close to the point when an episode of disorder begins. Exposure to severe combat may be a precipitating factor in the development of a stress-trauma syndrome, for example; being isolated with a crying child for a long period of time may precipitate an episode of child abuse (Rosenberg & Reppucci, 1985). Stressful life events (see chapter 7) can be conceptualized as precipitating factors.

On the assumption that predisposing factors are discernible in children's lives and are more important than anything that happens later in life for the development of disorder, primary prevention efforts have been directed more at children than any other age group (Spaulding & Balch, 1983). It might prove more fruitful to focus instead on proximal, precipitating factors such as stressful life events.

The natural history of many psychological disorders is not well understood. Over time, there are discontinuities in behavior. Herrenkohl, Herrenkohl and Egolf (1994) followed children whom they had identified as "resilient" in elementary school. These were children who came from abusive backgrounds but who were doing well in elementary school. In adolescence, about a third of those previously high-functioning students had dropped out of high school. Those who had a poorer outcome had less support, and had been subject to more abuse after elementary school. However, some managed to survive, if not thrive, under similar circumstances; somehow they developed the ability to hope for a different future for themselves and to work toward it.

Ecological conceptions of behavior (chapters 4–6) and the vulnerability model (see chapter 7) teach us that an individual's vulnerability varies with circumstances throughout life. Primary prevention should be effective at later life stages—adolescence, middle age, or even old age—as well as during early childhood. Excessive emphasis on interventions in infancy and early childhood, in the absence of compelling evidence on their long-term benefits, may needlessly hamper the practice of prevention at other milestones.

A focus on precipitating factors (see chapter 3) directs us to think about reducing the occurrence of stressful life events (e.g., lowering unemployment) or creating resources that are well positioned in time and place to reduce vulnerability (e.g., Michigan Jobs Project). The stressful life-events model directs our attention to here-and-now events that are predictable and can be modified to prevent difficulties. We may also be able to prepare individuals to cope with such events.

Research on preventive interventions. Prevention research may be different from other psychological research. The Institute of Medicine (IOM) report (Mrazek & Haggerty, 1994) presents a framework called the "preventive intervention research cycle." The initial steps in this cycle include defining the disorder or problem to be prevented, gathering information concerning specific risk and protective factors associated with that disorder, and studying the existing literature regarding effective interventions for that problem. Only after understanding this context for the problem is it appropriate to design and conduct intervention studies. Initially these should take the form of pilot studies to refine the program, determine the magnitudes of its likely effects, and test the research instruments and procedures. Promising results at this stage justify large-scale field trials and, if the program's effectiveness is confirmed, its later dissemination to other sites. Throughout this process, the investigator should be working collaboratively with other stakeholders, including policymakers, community leaders, and representatives of the population targeted to receive the intervention.

The IOM model for prevention research is useful for its attention to basic and epidemiological research as well as to the literature on interventions. The model also requires that policymakers have a tolerance for experimentation and redesign. If an intervention doesn't produce its intended effects on the first effort, prevention researchers should have the leeway to make false starts and to learn from them. The first drug that was successful in treating syphilis was called 606 because its discoverer had tried 605 previous compounds unsuccessfully. Few prevention research programs have had the same opportunity to redesign interventions based on the results of experimental trials.

Prevention research also needs to be theoretically based. Psychological and behavioral problems are complex. The bare finding that an intervention group does better (or worse) than a control group may provide little insight into why this happened. Research should include process measures documenting that the intervention worked as planned and that can be used to disseminate it to other sites. (There is a dispute about whether intervention programs can or should be faithfully duplicated in each new setting or whether the intervention needs to be adapted for each new situation [see Elias, 1997], such as rural versus urban.) Having a solid theory behind the intervention presumably makes it easier to implement the essential aspect of a successful intervention in a new situation (Bauman, Stein, & Ireys, 1991).

The point(s) at which short-term and long-term outcomes are assessed is also determined by their theoretical relevance. Recall that Schulz and Hanusa (1978) found that the results three years after terminating their intervention with institutionalized elderly were the exact opposite of the results obtained when the study first ended. A program to prevent delinquency in adolescents by intervening with primary school children, for example, might initially look at whether those who received the intervention showed improved peer relationships and school performance. Some years later, it would be important to determine the incidence rates of delinquency in the intervention and nonintervention groups. A single post-intervention measurement is not sufficient when the goal is to change a child's overall life trajectory.

Promoting positive mental health. Methods for improving the health of people in general (e.g., improving nutrition and exercise) are directed toward producing a higher prevalence of generally healthy people. An analogous strategy in mental health is to increase the prevalence of positive mental health rather than reduce the prevalence of psychopathology (Albee, 1998; Cowen, 2000). The aim of such interventions is to increase the overall level of well-being and thus reduce the potential for undesirable outcomes. Improvements in prenatal care; dissemination of information regarding effective child rearing, neighborhood-based family life development centers; and the creation of mutual support systems are all methods we have mentioned.

The terrorist attack on the World Trade Center in New York City and on the Pentagon near Washington, DC, on September 11, 2001, with the loss of 3,000 lives, introduced a new, worldwide war on terrorism. We seek to prevent terrorism through enhancing homeland security (think of the costs of dealing with massive numbers of false positives) and through increased efforts by police and intelligence agencies to identify and to penetrate terrorist networks to prevent further attacks. However, in the long run a preventive effort aimed to increase the overall well-being of people in the lands that produce and support terrorist activity may be the most effective prevention approach. Dumas (2002), a political economist wrote: "The more that inclusive economic and political developments increase the economic well-being and political status of the wider group of which terrorists and their supporters feel they are a part, the more difficult it becomes for terrorists to recruit operatives and to find others who will support the terrorists' cause. It is in this sense, then, that economic and political development will in the long run help to dry up the pool of potential terrorists, as well as the wider public support on which they depend" (p. 10). Dumas believes that counter-terrorist approaches have to take into account aspects of the psychology of terrorists. He sees the psychological aspects as critical; interventions should therefore attack the psychological roots of the problem. " . . . [T]he crux of the problem lies in the economic and political marginalization, frustration, and humiliation of the group to which terrorists and their supporters feel connected. If so, then the approach to development likely to prove most effective against terrorism is one that both reaches out directly to the most marginalized, disaffected, and disadvantaged of those people, and also allows individuals a sense of empowerment, self-worth, dignity and respect. The most effective program is one that simultaneously addresses the challenges of both economic and political development" (p. 11; more on community development in chapter 12).

Historically, psychologists have shown little interest in trying to understand or promote positive mental health, and only recently has a nucleus of influential researchers established a movement known as "positive psychology" (Seligman, 2002). Within prevention it is still difficult to identify and measure outcomes of mental health promotion efforts and to estimate their specific costs and benefits. The superior clarity and substance of the existing literature on interventions to prevent specific physical disorders is only a matter of degree, however. Since individual factors make a person at risk for multiple disorders, there is still some reason to pursue overall increases in positive mental health at the same time we work to reduce the incidence of specific disorders.

What person-centered protective factors may be stable across situations and over time and may have some role in promoting positive mental health? Recall the discussion in chapter 5 concerning "cognitive and behavioral construction competencies" of the sort identified by Mischel (1973). In the following section we examine the theory and research on "teachable" protective factors in primary prevention in mental health.

Competence Building

By the early 1970s several streams of thought had come together to form a primary prevention strategy known as "competence building" (Cowen, 1973; Task Panel on Prevention, 1978). Its roots can be found in psychoanalytic, cognitive, behavioral, humanistic, developmental, and evolutionary perspectives on behavior (Masterpasqua, 1989). Ultimately, the zeitgeist of the 1960s supported competence building. As an intervention, it was based squarely on the then-popular assumption of the "plasticity" of intellectual and psychological structures (Hunt, 1968). Competence building is best exemplified by the Head Start program (reviewed later in this chapter).

The competence-building paradigm starts with a theoretically or empirically based assumption that high-risk individuals within a given population differ from low-risk individuals in the same population by their lack of some basic psychosocial skill or skills and that individuals who lack these competencies can acquire them under the right conditions. These skills are then taught directly to the groups at risk. In theory, their acquisition eliminates the fundamental discrepancy between the high-risk and low-risk members of the population, thus reducing or eliminating the added risk.

Spivack and Shure (1989, 1993; Shure, 1997) pioneered in developing competence-building programs as a preventive intervention. Their initial research showed that about half the inner-city children in day care and kindergarten displayed behavioral problems, including impatience, over-emotionality, aggression, or excessive shyness and fear. Studies of hundreds of four- and five-year-old children revealed that those with behavior problems were often distinguishable from those without by their lack of certain "interpersonal cognitive problem-solving" (ICPS) skills, including:

1. *Alternative thinking*: the ability to conceptualize alternative solutions to problems involving peers or adults.
2. *Consequential thinking*: the ability to foresee accurately the consequences of one's own actions.
3. *Causal thinking*: an appreciation of the role of antecedent events as causes of other events.
4. *Sensitivity*: an awareness of others' feelings and the interpersonal nature of problems.
5. *Means/ends thinking*: the ability to plan a course of action in pursuit of a goal, one that can involve several different steps.

The Spivack and Shure prevention program consists of some 40 or more "game" activities, each taking about 20 minutes, designed to be used by preschool teachers in regular preschool classrooms or by parents at home to teach preschoolers the following kinds of skills: (1) *understanding word concepts*, such as "not" or "same-different," which prepare children to understand the meaning of "*not* a good idea, try something *different*"; (2) *developing interpersonal skills*, such as listening, watching, and understanding the other person's feelings; and (3) *generating alternative solutions* to a problem situation, including conceptualizing the potential consequences of actions and analyzing the relationship between cause and effect.

The results of this brief, focused training program were quite positive. Nearly all children gained in measured ICPS skills; those rated initially as more maladjusted gained more than those who were better adjusted initially. Improvement in ICPS skills was related to behavioral improvement. The most important ICPS skills seemed to be alternative and consequential thinking. At a two-year follow-up assessment, training effects had been maintained; children who had received the program were rated as better adjusted than control children during the next two years of elementary school. In some of the studies, the later teachers who rated the children's adjustment were "blind" to the training the children received. The program's positive effects were not related to children's IQs or socioeconomic status, and mothers and teachers were about equally effective as trainers.

This program is useful not only as an illustration of the competence-building paradigm but also as a demonstration of how successful mental health interventions can be carried out in ordinary community settings by natural caregivers. The program has been widely disseminated; teachers and parents have been consistently positive about their experience with the ICPS intervention. Spivack and Shure and their colleagues went on to study ICPS skills and the response-specific preventive impact of ICPS training on violence, substance use, teen pregnancy, and suicide.

Research by other investigators indicates that the relationship between learning specific ICPS skills and reductions in psychopathology may not be so simple (Durlak, 1995). The positive impact of ICPS training is clearer for younger children than for children older than seven (Durlak & Wells, 1998), and the specific links between skills and outcomes may vary among children of different ages and different sociodemographic groups (Gesten et al., 1982).

Spivack and Shure (1989) caution that regular practice of the various ICPS skills through "dialoging" in problem situations as they arise is necessary to maintain the skills and preserve their link to adjustment. Additional training, or booster sessions, are also very helpful, not only because learned responses may fade over time but also because new situations and challenges continually arise.

Second-generation competence-building interventions. Spivack and Shure's ideas have been adapted for older schoolchildren. Schools are a key setting for prevention efforts because they maintain sustained, intensive contact with nearly all children throughout childhood and adolescence. School provides important cognitive, social, and interpersonal challenges, and the cognitive and social aspects of competence-building interventions make them very compatible with educational settings.

The most widely known school-based competence-building interventions have focused on normative transitions. One program (Improving Social Awareness–Social Problem Solving/ISA–SPS) for elementary schoolchildren is designed to facilitate their adjustment to middle school. The program teaches social decision making and problem solving in three phases: (1) readiness, which is focused on self-control, group participation, and social awareness; (2) instruction, which involves intensive work on means-ends thinking and other ICPS-inspired skills; and (3) application, which emphasizes guided use of the skills in new situations to promote maintenance and generalization (Elias et al., 1986).

Compared with control children (who had attended the target schools the year before ISA–SPS was implemented), middle school-children who received the intervention showed greater sensitivity to other's feelings, greater ability to analyze and understand interpersonal behaviors and situations, and more positive self-concepts. Intervention children were also rated as more adjusted by their teachers and were sought out for help more often by their peers than were control children. Children who lacked SPS skills were more likely to report intense stressors, suggesting that SPS skills mediated or were responsible for the positive effects of the intervention on overall adjustment (Elias et al., 1986). Follow-ups five and six years after the intervention found modest differences in academic achievement and psychological adjustment (especially the levels of depression, delinquency, and self-efficacy) that favored the intervention group (Elias et al., 1991).

Levine (1998) notes that because the comparison group in this study was a previous cohort of students from the target schools, not a random sample of students from the same population that received the ISA–SPS intervention, Elias and colleagues were able to change not only the SPS skills of individual students but also the social context of the target schools. It is much easier to use new skills when everyone else is familiar with them and accepts them as the appropriate way to resolve interpersonal problems. A truly randomized experiment, with students in the same classrooms arbitrarily divided into intervention and control participants, might fail to instill these critical social norms (Levine, 1998).

Another important milestone is the transition to high school. During mid-adolescence, with its increased stress and vulnerability, some students loosen their ties to school (Kazdin, 1993). At the same time, however, many young people acquire key coping skills that will help them adjust to the ever-increasing demands of school and young adult life. Reducing the number of students who drop out of school would lower the risk of substance abuse, unwanted childbirths, and conduct problems. Dropping out of school is usually not sudden, or unpredictable; changes in peer relationships and increasing alienation from school precede dropping out (Srebnik & Elias, 1993). Warning signs of impending drop out include declines in academic performance and increases in absenteeism and substance use. The most useful approach to preventing this would be to intervene during middle school, while most adolescents still have some attachment to school.

Competence can increase in ways other than through cognitive intervention with individuals. Aspects of the social and physical environment can be modified to promote growth-enhancing experiences and to avoid some potentially destructive life events. The STEP (School Transitional Environment Program) intervention is a one-year program designed to ease the transition from middle school to high school (Felner & Adan, 1988). Both personal and environmental characteristics can constitute risk factors for dropping out and other adverse outcomes whose probability of occurring is increased when risk factors are present. Personal factors include a history of frequent changes in schools, socioeconomic disadvantage, low family support for schooling, and membership in an ethnic minority. Environmental risk factors include a complex school environment with high student turnover, haphazard scheduling, and inattentiveness to student needs, as shown by the amount of time teachers take to get to know students individually.

The goals of STEP were to increase (1) the social support available to students undergoing such transitions, (2) students' access to information and their ability to use it effectively, (3) students' sense of accountability while reducing their sense of anonymity, and (4) teacher's familiarity with students. STEP works to increase these coping and support resources in two ways: by reducing the complexity of a school's environment by simplifying new students' schedules (e.g., by having a group of new students take most or all classes together in rooms that are located near each other) and by redefining the role of homeroom teachers to facilitate more active involvement with students (e.g., by having homeroom teachers provide students with some of the counseling and guidance support normally provided only by school guidance staff and contact students' families to develop a relationship when school begins, and later, whenever absences occur).

In contrast to ISA–SPS and other school-based programs, STEP does not use a new curriculum or other modification of instruction. It entails a strategic change in how settings are organized (Felner et al., 2001). STEP reduces the scale of the learning environment and simplifies the new student's task of forming a support network. In behavior-setting terms, the multiple settings that challenge a new student are organized in such a way that they have many elements in common, making it possible to learn the various setting programs more quickly and easily. Homeroom is a multi-purpose setting whose program includes built-in mechanisms for developing teacher-student relationships. In terms of Moos's social climate perspective, STEP is clearly directed at helping schools meet students' "relationship-oriented" needs (e.g., for social support) as well as those involving "personal development" for which schools are more traditionally responsible. By controlling the location of STEP classrooms within the building and movement of students through the building, the program also minimizes contact with older children who might exploit the younger ones.

After one year, students in a predominantly minority school who had been randomly assigned to STEP had higher grades, better attendance, and more stable self-concepts than did control students (Felner, Ginter, & Primavera, 1982). Several years later those who had been STEP students had only half the dropout rate of control students. Teachers also expressed satisfaction with the STEP program. The program was implemented at relatively little cost, since it entailed a reorganization of existing resources rather than allocation of new resources. Its positive effects were replicated in another setting: student well-being and teacher-rated adjustment were improved among students making the transition from elementary to junior high school (Felner et al., 1993).

James Comer and Edward Zigler have been creating and disseminating a model of schools which are embedded in their communities and organized to support the development of children from preschool through high school. Ideally, the school program lasts all day, provides year-round child care for younger children, and after school and vacation care for school-age children. The school program also includes other services for families, health and nutrition services, and links to child care for infants and toddlers. The school may provide back-up and training for child care providers working outside of support networks (Zigler & Finn-Stevenson, 1997; Comer, 1997). In some places, the program also integrates a social competence promotion program throughout the school (Felner et al., 2001; Weisberg, Barton & Shriver, 1997). These programs intend to change the entire atmosphere within the school and to integrate community members and parents. Economic recession and government budget deficits may have an effect in slowing down this approach when schools in some areas are hard put to keep class size down and keep from laying off teachers and other school personnel.

*Box 8–2. A Successful School Change Effort**

In 1992, the New York City Board of Education, in partnership with educational advocacy agencies, began restructuring large high schools by replacing them with smaller schools within the larger school campuses. The effort was undertaken in part based on research such as STEP and others that reported that smaller schools have "higher achievement, lower dropout rates, lower rates of violence and vandalism, more positive feelings about self and school, and more participation in school activities." (Darling-Hammond, Ancess, & Ort, 2002, pp. 639–640) (See chapter 5, discussion of Behavior

*The material in this box is based on Darling-Hammond, L., Ancess, J., and Ort, S. W. (2002).

Setting Theory). In the particular project, two large, comprehensive high schools were replaced with eleven small schools and with re-design of the large campuses. This project intended to produce a second generation of schools that were based on the essential program design of the successful schools but didn't depend on a strong, charismatic leader.

The project involved two of the more troubled high schools in the system, Julia Richman and James Madison. The schools served about 3,000 students each, and had a four-year graduation rate of 36.9 percent and 26.9 percent respectively. The youths served by the project schools were predominantly minority (90%+) and poor. About 70 percent were eligible for the free lunch program.

The reform consisted of developing a more "communitarian" school, by "creating small units within schools, keeping students together over multiple years, forming teaching teams, assuring common planning time for teachers, involving staff in schoolwide problem solving, involving parents, and fostering cooperative learning." (pp. 641–642.) The intention was to create small learning communities, common academic standards and performance-based assessment, rather than test-based assessment, a curriculum focused on inquiry and developing intellectual skills, small pupil loads to foster relationships between students and teachers, student and teacher choice of schools to ensure compatibility with the educational philosophy, and shared decision making. Teachers participated in selecting new teachers for the staffs of the small schools. The design was adapted from a successful design used in another school within the New York City system. The same team of teachers worked with 40 to 80 students from seventh to tenth grade, with longer class periods (90 minutes). The teachers were supported by technical assistance and mentoring from teachers who had experience with similar innovations.

Five years later, the drop-out rate had dropped substantially, 73 percent of the cohort entering the small schools had graduated from high school, and 80 to 100 percent of the graduating seniors were entering college, even though average SAT scores remained low. Intensive interviewing and observation of the schools confirmed they were successful in creating a more personalized, caring environment with strong relationships between faculty and students and with excitement about learning. The schools created norms conducive to achievement and intellectual development and opposed to disruption or violence in the school environment.

There was considerable institutional support for the reform, but the reforms are also threatened by obstacles stemming from the needs of the Board of Education to put more students in the programs, and to standardize other procedures in keeping with state regulations.

Whether the reforms will survive the new federal emphasis on annual testing with achievement tests, rather than rely on performance assessments, remains to be seen. The report by Darling-Hammond, Ancess, and Ort (2002) should be read carefully by anyone interested in the complexities of school reform (See chapter 10, "Problem of Change"), or who want to appreciate how structural changes can translate into a social climate that is apparently high in both relationship and achievement dimensions (see chapter 5). The article is also a good model for evaluation of a complex process using methods from any levels of observation and measurement. The project is a good example of a preventive effort with intervention at an organizational level rather than interventions targeted to individuals.

Conclusions regarding competence-building. We share the widespread enthusiasm for competence building as an approach to primary prevention. However, there are cautions. Although many high-quality programs devoted to building cognitive and behavioral competencies in young people have shown promising results, one-shot interventions are probably not sufficient to produce permanent reductions in risk for most who receive them. Programs that provide opportunities to rehearse and apply these skills in ecologically relevant situations are likely to have more lasting effects, as are those which change social norms for appropriate behavior in groups at risk (Levine, 1998). Because risks are ongoing, competence-building programs for children and adolescents should be included in comprehensive health education efforts for children from preschool through high school or beyond (Weissberg & Elias, 1993).

Furthermore, successful dissemination of innovative programs cannot be taken for granted. Elias (1997) provides a detailed conceptual approach to the widespread dissemination and implementation of prevention programs. It is a problem to adopt programs to local settings and needs, and yet remain faithful to the basic form and spirit with which the original program was developed and tested. It cannot be taken for granted that just because a program was tested in one site and a manual developed for its use that it will be implemented with potency in another site. The new context must have the same resources and motivation to support the program as did the original context. All programs depend on decisions made by the people who carry them out, and school systems have their own agendas. An ambitious new program will have to fit into the existing curriculum and values of a target school, and it will also require additional training and ongoing supervision of teachers and other participants. The team implementing the program also has to have a deep appreciation of the core theoretical concepts underlying the prevention program so that modifications to suit local conditions don't affect basics. In addition, those responsible for the new implementation must have a deep understanding of principles of learning (Elias, 1997). Resistance to change on an organizational and system basis can be expected (see chapter 10).

Thorough use of this competence-building paradigm will depend on a clearer definition of "competence." To what extent is competence a global, all-purpose "skill" or a type of cognitive and behavioral construction competency (see chapter 5; Mischel, 1973)?[2] To what extent might it be better conceptualized as a situation-specific skill? In practice it has been taken both ways. The Spivack and Shure (1993) method and Finkel's (Finkel & Jacobsen, 1977) concept of the "trauma-stren conversion" (see chapter 7) represent attempts to induce or to study widely generalizable and durable cognitive changes.

Much of the preventive work with stressful life events takes a more situation-specific approach (Bloom, 1992). This perspective is also illustrated in a study by Sarason and Sarason (1981), who found that training inner-city ninth graders in specific skills related to finding employment led not only to more and better problem-solving solutions in a test situation in the students who received this training, but also to better performance in actual job-seeking interviews. These results suggest that it may be more useful to train specific competencies to deal with particular events rather than concentrate on general skills. The demonstration that many findings using ICPS type of interventions are difficult to replicate suggests we need to examine issues of specificity and implementation more carefully (Durlak, 1995).

To the extent that competence turns out to involve a specific set of skills whose value varies from one risk group/outcome context to another, however, more work is clearly necessary to identify the specific skills in all of the relevant contexts. The generalizability of any one set may not be broad. From the ecological vantage point, the problem is one of adaptation (see also Trickett & Birman, 2000; Trickett et al., 1985). Adaptation is not just an individual feat, but an ongoing process of person-environment fit. Do the relevant ICPS skills differ, or even conflict with each other, in key settings such as school, home, workplace, or street? Conditions of adaptation change over time as well, and the relationship between an individual's ICPS performance in childhood and his or her psychological adjustment as an adult has yet to be established.

Both global and situation-specific skills may develop out of competence building. Global competencies may reduce the risk related to predisposing causes (e.g., poverty, constitutional vulnerability) while task-specific skills reduce the risks associated with precipitating causes (e.g., unemployment and other stressful life events). The competencies can in fact be learned. However, will the new skills be used after inevitable changes in time and situation? Will cognitive skills taught in a relatively low state of emotional arousal be available and effective in a state of high emotional arousal? More information is needed regarding the nature of behavior-environment continuities across time and place. One day we may wish to teach the ability to assess environments behaviorally and either modify them according to one's needs or select those that naturally provide the best fit (Levine & Perkins, 1980b). The work we described using Barker's behavior-setting concepts to evaluate person-environment fits for mental health consumers is a case in point.

As practiced, the approach of individual competence building intentionally or unintentionally engages in what some critics (e.g., Albee, 1995; Ryan, 1976) have called "blaming the victim;" the "problem" is ultimately seen to reside in the existence of specific individual differences between high-risk and low-risk individuals. The inevitable implication is that the only way to rectify the problem is to *change* the high-risk individuals to make them "normal," or acceptable. This leads ultimately to *blaming* the high-risk individual for the predicament. Iscoe (1974) and Rappaport (1981) point out that competence building at the community level escapes this moral and political dilemma to a significant degree.

To summarize, the competence building approach to primary prevention arose out of interest in whether acquiring and using certain cognitive behavioral skills improved psychological adaptation. The empirical literature on competence building, while encouraging overall, has nevertheless left us with a complicated picture. From an ecological vantage point, it is important to remember that behavioral skills are not solely the property of individual people but also attach to settings and their "programs" (see chapter 5). These vary over time and place. Still needed are conceptual advances that relate persons and situations in behavioral terms and therefore make it possible to develop competent settings and communities as well as competent individuals. In the next section we present a general environmental strategy relevant to prevention.

Prevention Through Stepwise Risk Reduction

A different approach to prevention is based on a metaphor of "accident prevention." An "accident" does not imply something random or unpredictable; accident prevention also does not depend on a disease concept. Rather, this approach applies to undesirable end-states, including mental or physical problems or lifestyle predicaments, for which there are specific known risks. Often these risks are of different kinds. Some may involve personal characteristics and other environmental conditions, and these may occur independently of each other. Vulnerability is partly a function of exposure to risks. The goal in the accident-prevention approach is to reduce the incidence of maladaptive episodes by reducing individual vulnerability or the degree of risk added by "traumatic accidents."

Risks may occur sequentially, an idea expressed in the distinction between proximal (near in time), or precipitating, and distal (removed in time), or predisposing. The sequential relationship can be depicted by a Markov chain. Any given outcome is the end result of a particular sequence of steps. Each step has a dichotomous alternative—"yes" or "no" answers to a specific question. One may prevent accidents, or the injury associated with accidents, in any number of ways. Using the accident-prevention model, we examine the sequence of events that precede the undesirable end-state. We may identify promising points of intervention anywhere along the chain. In this view, if an event earlier in the chain is prevented from occurring, then an event later in the chain is less likely to occur.

Consider unwed teenage pregnancy. Children born to teenagers are more likely to have physical and behavioral problems, and their mothers also face maladaptive outcomes. They are more likely to drop out of school, to become welfare dependent, and to suffer from depression. Pregnancy is not a disease; thinking of this complex social and psychological problem as a "disease" leaves only a few limited options available for preventing its occurrence—abstinence, contraception, or abortion. Taking the longitudinal view depicted in the Markov chain allows us to consider other possibilities as well.

The sequence of steps that can produce maladaptive behavior as a result of unwanted pregnancy is depicted in Table 8–1 using a Markov chain. Depending on the answer to each of a series of questions, the

Table 8–1
Markov Chain for Problems Associated With Teenage Pregnancy

High-Risk Condition	Low-Risk Condition
Chaste?	
↓ No	→ Yes
Contraception?	
↓ No	→ Yes
Morning after pill?	
↓ No	→ Yes
Pregnant?	
↓ Yes	→ No
Abortion?	
↓ No	→ Yes
Compensating abilities?	
↓ No	→ Yes
Poor adaptation	
School dropout	
Child abuse	

risk of poor adaptation is either high or low. Aside from the biological statuses of pregnancy and abortion, there are alternative behavioral responses concerning amount of sexual activity, use of contraception, use of "morning after" pills,[3] and compensating responses made after the child is born (such as placing the child for adoption or making some other arrangement that prevents the mother from dropping out of school and other high-risk conditions). The important point is that choosing *any* one of the alternatives leading to the low risk condition is sufficient to break the chain leading to poor adaptation. Prevention is the result of interventions that increase the number of teenagers who change their trajectory in the more adaptive direction at any point in the sequence. For example, Furstenberg, Moore, & Peterson (1985) show that 15- and 16-year-olds exposed to sex education delay their initiation of sexual activity. Byrne, Kelley, and Fisher (1993) discuss programs specifically designed to increase motivation for contraception and decrease situational factors that inhibit contraception.

To summarize, teenage pregnancy is complicated and difficult to control. It is not just one condition, but the culmination of social and behavioral events, not just biological ones. The stepwise risk-reduction approach uses the idea of multifactorial etiologies and proximal versus distal steps in the causal chain to increase the number of different opportunities for prevention. Some of these opportunities occur much earlier in time than the target condition itself. When delivered on a community-wide or milestone basis, for example, through sex education or through creating a social climate supporting abstinence, they have a potentially wide impact. Furthermore, in this view nearly everyone is subject to at least a slight degree of risk for most kinds of problems, because risk is a function of events and circumstances as well as of people. For example, some argue that marijuana is a "gateway" drug in the sense that users of heavier drugs began with marijuana and progressed to other substances. In theory, reducing or preventing marijuana use may break a sequence leading to a more pervasive substance abuse problem. This view is controversial because one can also say that any widespread practice that comes before drug use is a "gateway"—for example, tobacco, or mother's milk. The conceptual links in the chain need to be established before we can argue for an intervention to break a link in the chain. Universal prevention programs that assume everyone is at risk may be politically and socially acceptable and less stigmatizing than programs that focus on people who are singled out as already at high risk.

Preventing partner violence. Interpersonal violence offers another example of the usefulness of a Markov chain analysis of prevention alternatives.[4] The most frequent perpetrators of violence against adult women (injuries, rape, or murder) are their current or former male partners (Healthy People 2010), and children who witness partner violence are themselves more likely to be perpetrators or victims of violence as adults (Tomkins, Steinman, Kenning, Mohamed, & Afrank, 1992). In terms of risk factors for partner violence, early studies emphasized victim characteristics and psychiatric symptoms (A. Browne, 1993), while more recent work suggests that perpetrator characteristics are better predictors of violence than victim characteristics (Hotaling & Sugarman, 1986). However, Koss et al. (1994) argue that a focus on individual psychology alone will not effect large, permanent reductions in male violence against women. The Markov chain concept lets us think about alternatives to a person-centered approach. This view tells us to attend to proximal risks and to examine personal, situational, and community factors.

The risk of partner violence is higher when there is ongoing physical aggression in the home (e.g., corporal punishment of children), the woman is socially isolated and economically disadvantaged, a handgun is readily available, and/or alcohol is used to excess. These are all factors in the situation, and we could intervene preventively by teaching parenting skills and limited use of alcohol. Couples-oriented intervention may be helpful early in a relationship if partners are unable to handle conflict constructively (Holtzworth-Munroe et al., 1995). Couples who participated in a premarital communication and conflict-management program later reported significantly fewer instances of physical violence than did couples randomly assigned to a no-intervention control group (Markman, Renick, Floyd, Stanley, & Clements, 1993).

Partner violence is more likely to occur if the woman lacks knowledge of the available community resources (e.g., shelters), lacks skills sufficient to formulate a plan for responding to a threat of violence, and/or is pregnant. Women who are financially independent of their partners are more likely to leave an abusive relationship than those who are more financially dependent. Homicides among intimate partners have declined as resources to assist women in leaving abusive relationships have increased. Moreover, orders of protection, bringing the justice system into the picture, may have some benefits, as do specialized domestic violence courts (see Levine & Wallach, 2002, chapter 12). Information about community resources and other alternatives presented to women as part of routine prenatal classes could have a preventive effect to the degree that information and knowledge improve personal competence. Risk is higher when shelter and other services are not readily available in a community, so helping to create resources in a community can have a preventive effect (Reppucci et al., 1999).

Dramatic reductions in the incidence of partner violence may be difficult to achieve soon. The right to privacy inhibits many opportunities for research and intervention with high-risk couples. However, an accident prevention approach can still assist those working in a challenging area to identify additional causal steps in the chain, better understand the processes leading to different outcomes, and test the alternative interventions that result from this analysis.

Implications of an accident-prevention model. The paradigm of accident prevention directs our attention to different issues for research and for intervention more than does a disease model. Research using the accident model focuses on the conditions under which undesirable events occur, the factors that lead to those conditions, and the reaction to the undesirable event. An ecological analogy is highly appropriate in an accident prevention orientation.

An additional example may help in making the point. When parents with children divorce, a formal agreement is reached settling the custody of the children and the noncustodial parent's visitation rights. In most cases, the custody settlement is satisfactory, and problems that arise are resolved informally between the parties. In perhaps 10 percent of the cases, however, continuing conflict between the divorced spouses centers on their relationships with the children. The primary occasion for contact and for face-to-face conflict between divorced spouses occurs when one spouse arrives at the home of the other to pick up or to deliver a child for a visit. The reasons for the conflict are complex and need not detain us here, but they often result in the parents returning to court to seek modification or enforcement of the visitation order.

Stott, Gaier, and Thomas (1984) describe a program of court-ordered, supervised, neutral-site visitation conceived and funded as part of a delinquency-prevention program. The sponsors reasoned that intervention in disrupted families will reduce the "negativity and trauma" associated with the visit and therefore reduce the child's potential for future acting out. Supervised visitation was ordered by the court in families with multiple problems and long histories of involvement with the courts, social services, and mental health agencies.

After an interview, a schedule was established for weekly one- to two-hour visits at a neutral site. Both parents signed a contract specifying the conditions of visitation. The custodial parent dropped the child off at the neutral site and left the child with a worker. Fifteen minutes later, the noncustodial parent arrived to pick up the child, thus avoiding the opportunity for face-to-face conflict with the former spouse. The worker participated actively in the visit if there was reason to suspect abuse or if a parent exhibited poor parenting skills. Records were kept on each visit, and the worker sent recommendations for future visitation based on these reports to the referring court.

No formal evaluation of this program has been conducted. According to Stott et al. (1984), however, the program had "the enthusiastic support of the family court judges, who are relieved of many hours of counterproductive courtroom time with noncompliant parents" (p. 216). The program provided safe visits for parents and children, where in the past there were no visits or the visits were stressful. It provided an opportunity for the noncustodial parent to continue a relationship with the child, and it offered both parties the opportunity to document allegations that the other was breaking agreements concerning visitation. Some parents worked out satisfactory arrangements with each other, if only because the court-imposed visitation was inconvenient.

The intervention was independent of any measurement or evaluation of the personalities or any analysis of the relationship between the parents that resulted in the continuing conflict. The intervention depended on an analysis of the situation in which conflict emerged. The circumstances were modified to prevent overt conflict. Just as a safety seat prevents injury to a child in an accident, so this intervention reduced the sum total of overt conflict, and presumably the undesirable sequelae of the conflict as well. The accident-prevention model may have much to recommend it in preventing such phenomena as child abuse or driving while drunk. The success of Head Start in preventing social problems also yields to analysis with an event avoidance model (see Box 8–2).

Research on a variety of social problems undertaken from an ecological perspective may help us to define the chain of events leading to undesirable end-states and may offer us new and different strategies for intervention. Creation of the original Holmes and Rahe (1967) stressful life-events scale was stimulated by the observation that stressful life events occurred frequently in the histories of those treated for psychiatric disorder. An analysis built on the Markov chain concept may well demonstrate that many behavior patterns we now consider manifestations of illness might instead be understood as the outcome of a potentially breakable chain of events.

One complication is that the accident-prevention model may require its own approach to evaluation, for the primary initial goal is to control specified target behaviors, not final end-states. In addition, the history of overall improvements to health and longevity resulting from environmental modifications suggests that simply changing the environment (e.g., making condoms more readily available to sexually active young people) may not be very effective unless at the same time people are educated about the risk and protective factors involved (Kahn et al., 2002; Sagan, 1987) and norms supporting the use of condoms change. Both partners play a part (Levine, 1998). If we do not limit ourselves to the disease model, we may open other opportunities for prevention.

Box 8–3. *Head Start and Early Head Start:*
         An Experiment in Selective Prevention

Head Start, a federally funded program for preschool children, has
been called "the nation's most successful educational and social experiment" (Zigler & Muenchow, 1992, p. 244). It has clearly been the
most popular and enduring of the 1960s War on Poverty programs.
Head Start was based on a belief that more could be accomplished
by taking preventive action and attempting to affect very young children, rather than just dealing with youth and adults already en-
meshed in poverty.

Head Start's original goals were quite broad. They included (1)
improving the child's physical health, (2) fostering emotional and social development, (3) improving mental processes and skills; (4) raising positive expectations for the child in creating a climate of confidence for subsequent learning efforts; (5) increasing the child's
capacity to relate positively to family members and others; (6) developing a responsible attitude toward society; and (7) increasing the
sense of dignity and self-worth within the child and his or her family. Head Start serves children from any racial or ethnic background.
Eligibility is limited only by family income (Zigler & Styfco, 1993).
From the outset, sponsors of Head Start programs were given great
discretion in tailoring programs, which made it easier to obtain local
support but hampered the replicability of Head Start interventions.
As a result, Head Start was never a static intervention program but
an "evolving concept" (Zigler & Muenchow, 1992).

Initiated in 1966 on a crash basis because political leaders believed that continued political support for the overall anti-poverty
program required rapid results that were popular and visible, Head
Start grew, but with little direction. The Office of Economic Opportunity (OEO), the agency designated to carry out the War on Poverty,
required community participation and insisted on parental involvement. Parents were offered classes in child care; others took jobs as
teacher aides, cooks, or playground supervisors. Programs began in
public school buildings, in church basements, and in other makeshift
facilities. Issues regarding the qualifications of teachers, standards
for facilities, equipment, curriculum, and quality control soon arose.
As the price tag grew, moreover, and the riots of the late 1960s
struck many of our inner cities, demands for evaluation increased.

An early evaluation known as the Westinghouse study (Cicirelli,
1969) created a stir by reporting that no lasting effect of participation
in Head Start programs could be measured: IQs of Head Start children rose immediately following participation in the program, but
any differences in cognitive ability between children who had been

in the Head Start program and those who had not disappeared within three to four years after the children entered public schools. Nevertheless, Head Start has remained popular with the public, presidents, and Congress.

Why has Head Start survived? Many explanations exist. Its nationwide implementation and the deliberate involvement of parents helped politically in building a broad grassroots constituency. More relevant to our focus here is the possibility that professionals, sponsors, parents, and others connected to Head Start recognized the tangible benefits it provided to children, their families, and society.

Many investigations of Head Start and other preschool programs have now been undertaken, and include a number of reasonably well designed studies, many with follow-up evaluations. At some sites it was possible to mount true experiments, with random assignment of children to preschool programs. In other places quasi-experimental designs were used because ethical and field conditions made it difficult to initiate or to sustain random assignment studies. In order to overcome some of the limitations of field studies, social scientists conducting 12 longitudinal studies formed a Consortium for Longitudinal Studies to pool their data and subject it to the most rigorous analysis.

One of the best designed studies, and one which has had the greatest success in following all of the children in both the preschool educated and the non-preschool educated groups, was conducted in Ypsilanti, Michigan (Weikart & Schweinhart, 1997). Although not funded through Head Start, this project was superior in quality to most of the early Head Start programs and provides encouraging evidence for the kinds of outcomes that well funded preschool education can deliver (Hacsi, 2002). Called the Perry Preschool study, it was initiated between 1962 and 1967 and followed a cohort of 58 children who had preschool education and 65 who did not, to age 27. All the children came from a single pool of families who had indicated an interest in preschool education at the outset. All were African American, and all were from lower socioeconomic backgrounds as measured by parents' education, father's or single parent's occupation, and the ratio of rooms in the residence to number of family members. The children's IQs ranged from 60 to 90, and none showed evidence of organic damage. The groups were assigned randomly at the outset, and the research team ensured that there were no pretest differences between the two groups on critical variables so that any differences that emerged later would be apparently attributable to the differences in the groups' access to preschool education.

The Perry project and others like it (e.g. Darlington, Royce, Snipper, Murray, & Lazar, 1980) have consistently reported that the preschool experience results in improved performance on IQ tests in the early grades. The early increase in IQ score represents more than simply improved cognitive performance. It reflects greater ability to concentrate on school-like tasks and better ability to communicate verbally and to adapt more successfully to the demands imposed by adults and structured settings. Although the advantage in IQ scores disappears within two or three years (Darlington et al., 1980), teachers working with preschool-educated children consistently rate them as better adjusted and more mature than similar children who have not been exposed to preschool education.

One remarkable finding from the Perry project was the difference in the number of children from the two groups to be classified at some point as having mental retardation. Thirty-five percent of those without preschool education received such a classification, compared with only 15 percent of those with preschool education. Darlington et al. (1980) reported a similar finding in the large group of studies they analyzed. Whereas 45 percent of children without preschool education had spent some time in special classes, that was true for only 24 percent of the preschool-educated subjects across all the studies.

In the Perry project consistent superiority in performance on academic achievement tests was still apparent at age 14 for those who had been exposed to preschool education. The Perry project also reported higher high school grade-point averages for the preschool-educated group, and more favorable attitudes toward high school. Not surprisingly, a significantly higher number of the preschool group completed high school on time (66 percent vs. 45 percent) and went on to obtain post-secondary academic or vocational training. Perhaps as a consequence of their better performance in school, by age 19 subjects from the preschool group were more likely to be working and had higher median earnings than did their non-preschool-educated counterparts. In keeping with their greater academic and vocational success, fewer were receiving public assistance.

The effects of preschool education, such as greater bonding to the school setting as a result of better performance, also showed up in better performance in the community. Fewer of the preschool-educated group had ever been arrested as juveniles or as adults (31 percent vs. 51 percent), as indicated in records from the juvenile courts and state police. Forty percent of females in the preschool-educated group were married at age 27, compared with 8 percent of control females. Using standard methods of economic analysis, measuring short-term costs and benefits and projecting those to lifetime benefits, the Perry Project reported an economic benefit-to-cost ratio of 7.16 for one year of preschooling. The net projected saving to society was $25,000 per child: "The estimated present value of net benefit is positive for both taxpayers (especially potential crime victims) and program participants. No one loses; taxpayers and participants are both better off with early education than without it" (Berrueta-Clement, Schweinhart, Barnett, Epstein, & Weikart, 1984, p. 92).

Head Start and related programs made varying efforts to involve parents in the preschool as volunteers or in paid positions. The Perry preschool program included weekly home visits with the mothers. While helping parents to learn to teach their children was not essential to the success of the preschool programs (Lazar & Darlington, 1982), increased contact with preschool staff may have taught parents a great deal about schools and how they work, making these parents more sophisticated in interacting with school personnel, more adept in seeking educational advantages and opportunities for their children, and more alert to possible pernicious placements for their children. That the good outcomes described above may simply have resulted from increased sophistication about schools is not a failure, but an unexpected consequence, a beneficial side effect.

Because of Head Start eligibility requirements, the first children to participate in the program were selected from clearly disadvantaged groups, such as African Americans living in very poor rural and inner-city areas; most had below average IQs. Later Head Start programs recruited disadvantaged children from all ethnic and racial groups. The significant effects of preschool education on later life outcomes shown for these children may not be generalizable to children from different or more advantaged backgrounds. It is also apparent that Head Start children as a group do not fully catch up to middle-class children in their subsequent school achievement (Zigler & Muenchow, 1992).

Although no single program is sufficient to "vaccinate" children against all future problems, preschool education may indeed have considerable effectiveness as a preventive program for the misery that befalls some who fail to do well in school. Head Start's comprehensiveness and degree of family involvement, the development of important cognitive competencies, and the repeated successes experienced by preschool-educated children are responsible for their superior "social competence" later in life.

Recent efforts have focused on improving program quality and expanding eligibility for Head Start and related programs to include infants and toddlers (Administration on Children, Youth and Families, 2002), and elementary schoolchildren and low-income families above the poverty line (Zigler & Muenchow, 1992; Zigler & Styfco, 1993). Head Start's advocates see the program as much more than simply an educational boost. It is intended to help parents have an impact on other agencies as well as on the children. It would be useful to study the role Head Start might play in affecting other agencies with which participants must interact, such as those providing welfare assistance, health care, nutritional guidance, or dental care.

The No Child Left Behind education act of 2001 ties federal funds to states for education to the use of tests and publishing test results every year from grades three to eight. Now the testing program may be extended to preschool. The tests will measure how many letters and numbers children can recognize among other such skills. Proposed standards for example call for four year olds to recognize 10 letters at the end of a preschool year. Whether the testing program and any associated teaching programs will result in improvement or a degradation of preschool education because of the pressure to "teach to the test" remains to be seen (Steinberg, 2002; see "Texas Miracle" in Education in chapter 10.)

Early Head Start[5]

Building on the success and popularity of the Head Start program, in response to national concerns about infants and toddlers, and based on research showing that very early intervention is effective, in 1994 Congress mandated infant-toddler services within Head Start for low-income parents. The authorizing legislation required evaluations focused on the services that were being delivered and their impact on children and families. By 1996, 68 programs were funded. Today there are 664 Early Head Start programs serving about 55,000 children. Note that even though evaluations were required, the program expanded rapidly well before the studies were available. (In 2001, 905,235 children were enrolled in Head Start programs, at a cost of 6.2 billion dollars. Head Start has enrolled 20,302,000 children since its inception in 1965.[6])

In 1996, the Head Start program contracted with Mathematica Policy Research to conduct an intensive evaluation. They began by selecting 17 program sites. These sites agreed to recruit twice as many children as they could serve and randomly assign children to participation in Early Head Start programs. The random assignment was done centrally. The conditions for fully random assignment were not met. The program sites were not selected randomly. Generalization is limited to the programs that participated. Nonetheless, it seemed an ideal design for an evaluation. The study included 1,513 children in the Early Head Start group and 1,488 in the control group. Although there were program guidelines, each site could choose to offer a different mix of the approved services. Some offered center-based programs, others emphasized home visiting, and still others had a mixed program. Program quality, the degree of implementation of the program, and community characteristics also varied from site to site. Moreover, because of changing conditions, programs were modified during the period of the study. Participants at the different sites stayed for different lengths of time, and received different mixes and amounts of services. Despite random assignment to treatment and control status, the elaborate study demonstrates that context makes a difference. A research team has to pay careful attention to actual field conditions when evaluating program effects.

For one, the Personal Responsibility and Work Opportunity Reconciliation Act (welfare reform) went into effect at that time. In many states, even parents of very young children were required to go to work, or to seek work. They may have been less available for program activities. Many states expanded the opportunities for child care in response to the act, creating competition for well-trained staff. One consequence is that many children in the control sample might well have received services at other than the Early Head Start centers. Because many in the control sample received services elsewhere, the results are likely to be underestimated if compared to an untreated control.

Because the program mix was different at different sites, and because those in the control group did not receive the same services, there was somewhat greater attrition in the control than in the Early Head Start group. Attrition meant a departure from randomness, and required regression analyses to correct for the differences. In addition, characteristics of families differed by site and by type of program. For example, race and ethnicity of recipients differed by type of program (e.g., a higher percentage of Whites, 41%, were in home-based approaches and a higher percentage of Blacks, 37%, were in center-based programs; 62% of those in center-based programs were employed or in school, while that was true for only 40% of those in home-based programs). Moreover, Early Head Start is a voluntary program. The acceptance of services, the amount of services, and the duration of services differed within and across programs by the family's choice introducing a self-selection factor. Although most parents participated in some programs, the average duration was 21 months; about half left the program in less than 24 months. Staff rated fewer than half the families as consistently highly engaged. On average, those children who were in center-based programs were in care for about seven hours a week and those in home-based programs received much less care in the centers. However, almost all Early Head Start participants visited a doctor and 99 percent had an immunization.

It was necessary to use statistical adjustments to ascertain effects due to program participation. The utility of the statistical adjustments depends on their assumptions. Measures based on statistical adjustments using different assumptions did not show many differences from each other, but sometimes the different measures resulted in different outcomes and were discarded.

An important goal of Early Head Start is to improve the cognitive, social, and emotional development of participating children, in part through the medium of developing trusting relationships with adults, and better parent-child interaction. Despite the methodological problems in evaluating gains, at age three, children showed improved cognitive and language development and played more effectively with their parents. Parenting skills also improved. Early Head Start children at age three showed better language development on the Bayley Mental Development Index (91.4 mean) than control children (89.9 mean). The differences were statistically significant, but in absolute terms relatively small. An important finding was that fewer Early Head Start (27.3%) than control children (32.0%) scored one or more standard deviations below the mean. Similar statistically significant differences were shown on the Peabody Picture Vocabulary Test. There were also a number of small but statistically significant differences on measures of child social and emotional development including aggressive behavior on the Child Behavior Check List (Early Head Start mean = 10.6; control mean = 11.3) and measures of parent-child interaction.

Some of the impact on children may have been effected through change in parental behavior. For example, maternal supportiveness at age two was correlated with improved child scores on the Bayley at age three. However, even though the finding is consistent with program expectations, parents with more positive attitudes may also have children with better development independently of program participation. We also cannot rule out that the program itself trained children and parents on the criterion tests. The results might reflect criterion contamination. The program also showed some positive impact on various measures of parental self-sufficiency and on measures of fathering as well.

Although the changes are modest, some of the changes are associated with improved school performance and family functioning later on in life. The program can claim "positive impacts on outcomes for low-income families with infants and toddlers" (Administration on Children, Youth, and Families, 2002, p. xxv) and supports the preventive benefits of early intervention.

Prevention of HIV/AIDS

By 2002, over 800,000 Americans had been diagnosed with Acquired Immune Deficiency Syndrome (AIDS) following infection by its precursor, the human immunodeficiency virus (HIV), and nearly half a million Americans had died of AIDS (CDC, 2002). Worldwide, 20 million people had died of AIDS and 40 million were living with HIV and at risk to transmit the disease to others (Stover et al., 2002). Behavior change is the most effective strategy for lowering the incidence of HIV infection and would also help prevent the spread of other sexually transmitted diseases (STDs). Prevention programs based on changing behavior thus constitute an important opportunity for psychologists. Interventions to prevent HIV infection include media campaigns, outreach programs for commercial sex workers and gay men, small group educational and skill-building programs, harm-reduction efforts such as distributing free condoms and hypodermic needles, and social changes to promote new behavioral norms (Kelly & Kalichman, 2002; Stover et al., 2002). These programs, which are strongly theory-based, emphasize cognitive factors (knowledge and attitudes, motivation), risk-reducing skills such as condom use, relationship communication skills, peer support for low-risk behaviors, and social and political changes (e.g., to promote an infrastructure of treatment services for STDs and drug abuse, and clean needle exchanges).

Media campaigns. Media campaigns are universal, and designed to increase knowledge and understanding about AIDS, because all people are potentially at risk if they engage in unsafe behaviors. Universal targeting is cost-effective. Some media-driven programs, however, take a selective approach, targeting specific populations. Crawford et al. (1990) developed a media-based intervention designed to facilitate communication about HIV within urban families in which eighth grade students in Chicago schools were given copies of a newspaper supplement about AIDS and encouraged to watch a series of television news segments on AIDS. Children in the intervention group viewed more of the broadcasts, learned more about AIDS, and talked more with their parents about AIDS than did children in the control group.

Reaching minority communities. HIV education programs targeted to the African American community may have special problems (Miller, Klotz, & Eckholdt, 1998). The notorious Tuskegee syphilis study, which began in 1929 and continued until public disclosure of the study in 1972 forced its discontinuation, continues to have repercussions. In the Tuskegee study, 399 African American men who had contracted syphilis were followed to "end point" (autopsy). They were not given treatment. In fact, they were discouraged from obtaining treatment, even after penicillin became available, in order to protect the scientific purpose of the study, which was to determine what the "natural course" was of untreated syphilis. Members of the African American community believed that this study was evidence of a genocidal conspiracy by a white government against Blacks. Surveys of the African American community have shown that a third believed that AIDS is a form of genocide, 44 percent believed the government is not telling the truth about AIDS, and 34 percent believed that AIDS is caused by a laboratory-created virus. These attitudes have important implications for HIV education and preventive intervention programs in the African American community, in which the number of AIDS infections is growing rapidly (Thomas & Quinn, 1991). The rate of new AIDS cases is also increasing faster among Asians, Pacific Islanders, and other minority groups than among Whites and to be effective, prevention efforts must be collaboratively tailored to the specific cultural norms, values, and common language of different groups (Choi, Yep, & Kumekawa, 1998; Zimmerman, Ramirez-Valles, Suarez, de la Rosa, & Castro, 1997).

Small group interventions. Face-to-face interventions are often the most effective way to teach and promote the specific skills needed to reduce risk. The best of these interventions are conceptually based and specific to the target group of interest and increase risk-reducing information, motivation, and behavioral skills simultaneously (Fisher & Fisher, 1992). They are best used in the context of routine health, mental health, and drug treatment services because engaging participants in a multisession, stand-alone program is difficult.

Hobfoll, Jackson, Lavin, Johnson, & Schroder (2002) developed a culturally sensitive small group HIV prevention program that promoted "communal effectance" (use of mutual dependence and support from family and community) by single women ages 16 to 29. Delivered in six small group sessions that included interactive use of videotapes by live group leaders, the intervention involved imagery, cognitive rehearsal, role-playing, and skills in assertiveness and negotiation with sexual partners. Role-play situations were drawn directly from participants' current experiences. Women randomly assigned to receive the HIV-focused intervention later reported more safe-sex behavior and purchased more condoms than did women who received a community effectance intervention focused on general health promotion. Among women who had had a previous STD, those in the HIV prevention condition were found to have a lower incidence of subsequent STD infection at a six-month follow-up than those in the health promotion condition. Generalizability was shown in that women receiving the HIV intervention benefited whether they were African American (about half the sample) or European American, and whether or not they were pregnant. In addition to an effective use of videotape examples, this intervention capitalized on a group format and process based on cultural sensitivity, mutual support, and empowerment. In these respects the intervention resembles mutual help groups, our focus in the next chapter.

Outreach programs. Small group interventions are labor-intensive and require aggressive outreach. Some high-risk individuals (e.g., runaways, prostitutes, transient residents of public housing projects, intravenous drug users who are not in treatment and their sexual partners) are hard to reach; others are unresponsive or hostile to intervention efforts. HIV prevention programs can be combined with other outreach efforts towards such groups. Rotheram-Borus, Koopman, Haignere, & Davies (1991) provided a high-intensity intervention to adolescent runaways at a New York City shelter. The intervention provided general HIV knowledge, coping skills to use in high-risk situations, access to health and mental health services, and efforts to reduce attitudinal obstacles to safe-sex behaviors in this population. Adolescents who received the intervention showed less high-risk sexual behavior at three- and six-month follow-ups. The number of sessions may be important. Those adolescents who had 15 or more sessions of intervention reduced risky behavior more than those who had fewer than 15 sessions.

Zimmerman and colleagues (1997) evaluated an empowerment-oriented HIV prevention project in which the Mexican gay male participants, who controlled the design and implementation of the intervention, showed significant improvements in HIV/AIDS knowledge and preventive behavior, and created community-level change.

Miller, Klotz, and Eckholdt (1998) evaluated an HIV prevention program based on diffusion of innovation and social influence theories with male prostitutes and patrons of "hustler" bars. The program aimed to encourage safer sexual and IV drug norms by training natural "opinion leaders" to endorse those behaviors to their peers. The intervention significantly reduced unprotected intercourse and oral sex in this group, although results varied by bar and race. White and Latino men engaged in less unprotected sex while there was no effect on African Americans.

HIV and the accident prevention model. HIV infection rates can be high even in people who have adequate knowledge about HIV and risky behaviors. The accident-prevention model suggests additional points for intervention. Besides information, individuals must recognize that their risk is almost entirely determined by their own behavioral choices. They need effective skills (e.g., managing relationships, substituting safe behaviors for risky ones), the motivation to use these skills under challenging conditions (temptation by sex or drugs), practice, and the adoption of new norms that both support low-risk behavior and sanction unhealthy behavior (Coates, 1990).

In an accident-prevention approach relevant to most young people, we would recognize that intimacy develops in sequential stages. Fostering delays in the onset of each stage reduces risk. One option for teens is to wait until later in adolescence to begin dating, and after that to delay physical intimacy. Later on, the adolescent would lower risk by postponing sex, by having sex only if precautions are taken, and remaining sexually monogamous.

Regarding IV drug abuse, sharing of used needles is more likely in some settings than in others, suggesting that behavior-setting theory (chapter 5) might help to explain the ways in which settings raise or lower the likelihood of risky behavior by participants. Latkin et al. (1994) found that needles were less likely to be shared and more likely to be bleached when the setting for use was a user's own home than in any of three other settings: a friend's home, a "shooting gallery" (a site where injection equipment is available for rent), or another semi-public space (e.g., an abandoned building). Setting programs outside the home are social experiences that include sharing needles as a norm. In some of these settings bleach is always available and used, while in others it is not. While in their own homes users are alone or feel less bound by social obligations to share needles. For intravenous drug users, HIV prevention from an accident-prevention perspective can also include treatment to reduce or stop IV drug use, providing means for and training in the adoption of safe methods, and education to prevent the initiation of direct injection of drugs in the first place, all of which have had some success (Des Jarlais, Friedman, & Casriel, 1990).

Changing social norms. The scope of HIV infection and the practical limitations of formal programs suggest that efforts built upon informal supports and resources will be critical. There is evidence that new norms supporting low-risk behavior can be established for sex (Catania et al., 1991; Ekstrand & Coates, 1990; adolescent abortions and live births have declined in recent years, indicating a change in sexual behavior among teens; Levine, 1998) and for IV drug use (Des Jarlais et al., 1990).

Peer educators have been used as positive role models to deliver credible messages and skills. Sikkema et al. (2000) reduced HIV risk among low-income minority women using a community-based intervention in public housing projects. Local opinion leaders conducted neighborhood-based risk-reduction workshops developed with input from community residents, and used supportive community events to help residents develop risk-reduction skills and new social norms to reinforce changes in behavior. Women in the intervention group were less likely to have unprotected intercourse and more likely to use condoms than were women in matched housing projects with no intervention program.

A consortium of researchers funded by the Centers for Disease Control (CDC; CDC AIDS Community Demonstration Projects Research Group, 1999) used a community-level intervention to change behavioral practices and norms among active injection drug users and their sexual partners, commercial sex workers, men who have sex with men, and people living in census tracts with a high prevalence of STDs. Trained, indigenous residents of five urban communities across the United States distributed behavior change materials and reinforced their use by at-risk peers in their immediate communities. The materials included condoms, bleach kits, and brief stories about actual people from those communities who were changing their HIV-related risk behaviors. Over a three-year period more than 15,000 interviews of residents in these communities and five matched communities used as controls found that in the intervention communities: (1) more than half of those interviewed reported having talked with an intervention worker or having received intervention materials, (2) significantly higher proportions of people reported condom use with primary and other sexual partners than in the control communities, and (3) among individuals interviewed more than once over time, significantly higher proportions in the intervention communities than the control communities were carrying condoms at the time they were interviewed.

A key aspect of this study was the participation of community volunteers, since the target groups included many persons who were unlikely to participate in facility-based prevention programs. These participants delivered a sustained, credible, culturally tailored message to people who were their own neighbors and peers. This strategy illustrates the ecological principle that even socially and economically disenfranchised communities have strengths and untapped resources that can be developed to make the entire community safer.

Structural and political changes. A number of the studies cited so far included free distribution of condoms to sexually active people at risk. Similarly, using a clean needle when taking drugs prevents the transmission of HIV as well as hepatitis and other blood-borne diseases. Stover et al. (2002) estimate that programs promoting the free exchange of sterile needles for used ones could reduce needle-sharing among addicts by 60 percent in high-risk countries outside the United States.

Experiments in Europe demonstrated that providing clean needles to drug addicts can reduce the incidence of HIV and hepatitis infections and does not result in an increase in drug users. An attempt to introduce a similar program in New York City, however, failed when politicians objected that the program would imply official approval of the use of drugs and would increase drug use. Politicizing needle exchange programs undercuts their effectiveness (Lichtenstein, 1996). HIV infection and its prevention are not simply technical matters but instead have moral dimensions that are critical for program implementation. Prevention programs cannot be divorced from the social, political, and moral context in which they are to be implemented (Anderson, 1991).

Multiple approaches are necessary. The enormity of the HIV epidemic suggests that multiple approaches to individual change (i.e., media-based, skill-oriented, and norm-focused), combined with policy and environmental modifications, will be necessary to achieve the largest and most lasting effects (Choi et al., 1998). Basic risk factors are similar across differences in gender, ethnicity, and other groupings, but the nature of optimally effective prevention programs may not be (Reppucci et al., 1999). Different groups vary widely in their expectations and conventions regarding sexual and drug-related behaviors, their access to information and other resources, and their trust in authorities who offer help.

We need to know more about "protective" factors such as the cognitive and social variables that influence motivation to change, the effects of providing opportunities to change (e.g., making condoms or clean needles readily available), the acquisition and use of skills, and support for change (Kelly, Murphy, Sikkema, & Kalichman, 1993; Kelly & Kalichman, 2002). In addition, we need to identify the critical ingredients of effective interventions and concentrate more of our effort on urban, poor, minority populations that face increasing risk. More programs are needed aimed at families, as are programs for use in normative settings like schools and worksites. We also need an adequate infrastructure of risk-reducing services (e.g., treatment programs, distributions of condoms and other devices to control sexually transmitted diseases, bleach sterilization kits, HIV antibody testing, job programs). For all of these reasons, collaborative studies involving investigators and representatives of the indigenous community are important. On the plus side, what is learned about sexual behavior will have implications for efforts to reduce unwanted pregnancy and control sexually transmitted diseases.

Prevention is a community issue. Risky behaviors are an individual matter. The necessary scale of change makes HIV prevention a community issue, as does the association of HIV risk with social disenfranchisement. Community psychology reminds us that in addition to individual competence-building efforts provided by education, the social context (e.g., family stability and support, peer group norms) is an important aspect of effecting and maintaining change (Shinn & Toohey, 2003). Given the increasing prevalence of HIV among ethnic minority populations and women, maximizing the involvement and participation of individuals at risk, community leaders, and community-based organizations is especially important. Thomas and Quinn (1991) described how prevention researchers coped with the distrust left by the legacy of the Tuskegee experiment by contracting with African American organizations to provide HIV education.

In addition, HIV prevention programs may not adequately consider women's realities. The effectiveness of HIV prevention interventions depends on the sexual relationship context. Because safer-sex behaviors challenge trust within nominally monogamous relationships, behavior change is less likely in these relationships than in encounters with new partners. Yet not all established sexual relationships are 100 percent monogamous. Traditional masculine ideology, sex role behavior, and differences in power and status may affect women's ability to take steps to reduce risk. Increasing the social and economic power of women, and prevention methods controlled by women, will help in the long run (Amaro, 1995). Thus far, the epidemiological research necessary to guide prevention has been stymied by political difficulties of doing research on sexual behavior and IV drug use (e.g., needle exchange behavior) and also by prejudice against gay men and intravenous drug users.

With adolescents, programs focused explicitly on sexual and drug use behavior are more effective than information-only programs, especially in younger children before they begin experimenting with high-risk behaviors. Yet these interventions are most likely to be resisted by families and communities. Just as with other community interventions, efforts to prevent HIV infection are inseparable from the social and political context in which they occur.

To summarize, the evidence (e.g., NIMH, 1999) is now in hand to implement HIV prevention programs in community settings. Preventive interventions need to include not just at-risk individuals who are currently free of infection but also individuals infected with HIV to help them avoid infecting others (Kelly & Kalichman, 2002). Reducing HIV transmission in developing countries will require not just education and norm-based support for new behaviors but also improved and expanded health care infrastructure. Prevention is most promising when it changes communities in a sustained way that involves services and other resources, policies, and social structures. These efforts will have to continue for decades to come, since HIV is well entrenched and future generations will remain at risk.

Thus, we will need to develop and maintain political commitment for HIV prevention at all levels of society. Projections such as those of Stover et al. (2002) that 29 million new cases of HIV infection are preventable worldwide by 2010, assume an expenditure of several billion dollars (approximately $1,000 per case prevented). Community psychology is well positioned for this effort because of its focus on social and community-level changes and outcomes (e.g., community-wide access to health care and other resources), empowerment, reducing stigma, supportive networks, and because of its attention to culturally sensitive program implementation.

Schools as a Locus of Prevention

Schools provide efficient public access to virtually all children and so are, in many ways, the easiest and most natural context for prevention efforts (Durlak, 1995). Of the 177 primary prevention studies reviewed by Durlak and Wells (1998), 129 (73%) were school-based. Schools are one of the few places where in-person (as opposed to media-based) milestone and other universal prevention is even feasible (see

"Competence Building," above). In schools, nearly all adolescents can be reached before they initiate high-risk sexual and drug-related behaviors.

School-based prevention programs have successfully increased AIDS-related knowledge and coping skills while reducing risky behaviors among urban minority youth in New York City (Walter & Vaughn, 1993) and Mississippi (St. Lawrence et al., 1995). In the long run, however, lapses in safe behavior are frequent (Kelly et al., 1991), and here (in contrast to smoking) a single lapse can prove fatal.

Intervention through schools, especially on matters involving sex, can pose political challenges. Current federal policy is to support abstinence education only. A fuller sex education program (e.g., distributing condoms) may be successful, but success may not be enough to stem community opposition when the program threatens local mores (Koo, Dunteman, George, Green, & Vincent, 1994).

School-based substance abuse prevention programs have become extremely popular, especially since the federal Anti-Drug Abuse Acts of 1986 and 1988. We do not feature them in this chapter, however, because their overall effectiveness has been seriously challenged (Gorman, 1998). The most widely known and implemented program, Drug Abuse Resistance Education (D.A.R.E.), shows no lasting effects (Clayton, Cattarello & Johnstone, 1996) and there is even concern that information-based programs may do more harm than good. Advocates for school-based drug prevention point to the decline of adolescent drug use from 1980 to 1992 as evidence for the policy's effectiveness; but the decline started years *before* the policies were implemented and in fact teen drug use increased again through the mid-1990s when federal spending on drug prevention was at its peak (Gorman, 1998). The most interesting aspect of school-based drug prevention therefore is why consistently negative to negligible research evidence has had no impact on policy-making (Gorman, 1998). Perhaps doing something easy to do, even if ineffective, is a way of warding off community pressures to deal with a problem.

Schools have many responsibilities. They cannot be expected to overcome all the other neighborhood, family, and peer-group risks that many students face. Normative change requires multiple, redundant messages coming from many sources, and repeated over time. Think of what was involved in changing Americans' smoking habits, or their diet and exercise habits as they affect heart disease.

Community-Based Health Promotion

A more promising role for schools in prevention and health promotion may be as a conduit for using children, teachers, volunteers, and local businesses and government in family- and neighborhood-based service-learning projects focusing on public education and environmental and behavioral change. For example, in response to the obesity and cancer epidemics in the United States, the "Bringing it Home" demonstration project involved lower-income, African American fourth graders learning in school about a healthy diet; then taking videotapes and other informational materials home to share with their parents; with systematic follow-up communications from project staff to parents. Parents of children in the randomly assigned intervention schools consumed significantly more fruits, juice, and vegetables, and on average weighed less postintervention, than did the control group (Davis et al., in press). More widespread diffusion of such programs that rely on grant-supported staff will likely require greater involvement of school staff and volunteers (e.g., local college students, businesses, or nonprofit organizations; see Elias, 1997).

A wide variety of community-based approaches to increasing physical activity have also been found to be effective, including informational interventions (e.g., "point-of-decision" prompts to encourage stair use and community-wide campaigns), school-based physical education, social support in community settings, and environmental interventions (creation of, or enhanced access to, places for exercise) combined with informational outreach (Kahn et al., 2002).

Daniel Stokols (1992, 1996), an environmental psychologist, has used social ecology theory to create a more community-oriented framework for promoting, not only individual health, but the establishment and maintainance of *healthy environments*. Increasing community participation has been a prominent goal of policy and research in health care and promotion for decades (Checkoway, 1981). Only more recently have many community psychologists moved into research on community partnerships for health promotion and substance abuse prevention (Altman, 1995; Fawcett et al., 1995; McMillan et al., 1995; Ribisl & Humphreys, 1998; Wandersman, Goodman, & Butterfoss, 1997; Zimmerman et al., 1997; see also chapter 12). The marked increase of interest may be due in part to funding opportunities for research on health issues.

Approximately 70 percent of people infected with HIV worldwide live in Africa. President George W. Bush proposed $15 billion of funding for HIV prevention and intervention programs on the African continent (SIECUS, 2003). At this writing it is not clear how successful this effort will be, but it clearly acknowledges the seriousness of the threat posed by the AIDS epidemic and the risk faced by all countries given the ease of international travel and the endemic nature of HIV in the most hard-hit countries. It also suggests that the United States recognizes a responsibility to invest public resources in efforts to reduce the impact of a massive global problem while there is still time to make a difference.

Summary

The metaphors of ecology and vulnerability have led to preventive approaches to behavioral problems. The practice of prevention poses difficult procedural and ethical questions; prevention programs require us to take responsibility in advance for the occurrence of conditions we do not fully understand and to adopt a much more extended outlook on the ultimate success of our efforts.

One intuitively appealing approach, defined as secondary or indicated prevention, involves the early identification and prompt treatment of incipient behavioral maladjustment in individuals. Problems exist with both the accuracy of identification and the treatment procedures currently used in secondary prevention, and efforts to prevent problems like domestic violence in people who have already committed such acts have not been very successful. Primary prevention, whose goal is to reduce the incidence of long-term problems, has attracted an extensive following in community psychology. However, its current popularity and appeal is also reason for caution; programs have been launched where there is no evidence for their effectiveness, and without adequate provision for evaluation (Weissberg & Elias, 1993). For now, authorities emphasize reducing risks and enhancing protective factors and urge the collection of more longitudinal data on such factors across the life span, as well as an increase in the number of experimental studies testing direct causal hypotheses (Mrazek & Haggerty, 1994).

Prevention research is becoming more sophisticated in methodology as well as conceptualization. Prevention stretches the time horizon for change, and the most successful prevention programs are those that attempt not just to impart information or new behaviors but to alter life trajectories. They change not only individuals but also their social contexts—families, schools, and community settings. Prevention of social or behavioral problems should not be likened to a one-shot inoculation. Promoting a change in life trajectory requires ongoing support and further skills as new settings and developmental stages are encountered. This makes it difficult to identify the key processes that account for preventive effects in a global intervention like ICPS training, for example, because motivation, skills, and support are all probably important. Programs that work need dissemination and continued evaluation so that the advantages of widespread reductions in incidence and prevalence are realized. Because prevention programs work to lower statistical risk of future difficulties instead of ameliorating present suffering, their benefits can seem abstract and the concrete cost-benefit advantages claimed for prevention need to be documented where possible.

To maintain our ethical footing, we should remember that prevention is value-driven and subject to analysis from multiple perspectives. Prevention efforts consume resources of the people and settings they involve, and those conducting the intervention should include all who are affected in the planning, implementation, and evaluation of programs. What values are represented in the intervention program and its goals? How do these values mesh with those of other participants? Are outcomes and other effects of the program (including unintended effects) being measured from the relevant perspectives? How has the program altered the settings in which it occurred?

We examined two generic strategies for primary prevention. One, known as competence-building, focuses on helping individuals at risk learn specific skills associated with successful adaptations to key settings. We described effective examples of such programs for preschool and middle-school children. The other, which we have termed accident-prevention, uses multiple strategies of active behavior change (increasing condom use, for example) and passive protection (mandatory use of seat belts) to decrease the likelihood of negative outcomes. We also examined the widely discussed Head Start program, which has had an encouraging preventive impact on the school and community adaptations of disadvantaged children over a respectably long time frame. Finally, there is increasing recognition of the important relationship between psychological and physical health and well-being, and we closed this chapter by reviewing programs to prevent HIV/AIDS and drug abuse and to promote healthy lifestyles.

The field of prevention has seen significant changes in recent decades. The examples discussed in this chapter illustrate current activities in prevention; future activities may change as the field evolves. Prevention is not a panacea for life's problems, and even very dedicated efforts are unlikely to eliminate problems or even affect in the same way every person who is targeted. Many people at risk also have access to important informal resources, and in the next chapter we look closely at a very different alternative for coping with problems—the self-help group.

Notes

1. Seymour Sarason tells the story of what happened when the late Claude Pepper went to heaven. The longtime senator and congressperson from Florida was a hardy and vigorous advocate of health care programs. He took the opportunity to request an audience with God, and when granted his wish, said he had one question he wished the good Lord would answer. That question was whether we would ever achieve health care reform. God pondered a moment and then said, "Yes, but not in My lifetime."

2. As an example, the "Glad Game" (see chapter 7) is an all purpose cognitive mediator that might be used to cope with a variety of emotional problems, just as prayer or the ideology of a self-help group may also have a place in the coping armamentarium of some people.

3. "Morning after" pills are apparently safe and effective, and reduce pregnancy rates by 74 percent when used after unprotected intercourse. This simple, safe method is not widely used because doctors don't prescribe the pills for that purpose, pharmaceutical companies don't market the pills aggressively for that purpose (Have you ever seen a TV ad for the pill used that way?), and many women don't know about their use (Trussel, Koenig, Ellerston, & Stewart, 1997). Based on a nationally representative survey of 10,683 women seeking abortion services in a 12-month period in 2000–2001, Jones, Darrach, and Henshaw (2002) estimate that 51,000 abortions were avoided by use of the morning after pill. This decrease accounts for about 25 percent of the decrease in abortions over that same 12-month period. That the morning after pill is currently not available over the counter is another example of political influence over scientific and medical decisions (see chapter 13).

4. Similar issues are involved in preventing assaultive violence among young African American men (Hammond & Yung, 1993).

5. This section is based on information found in Administration on Children, Youth, and Families (2002).

6. Administration on Children, Youth and Families, 2002 Fact Sheet. http:/www/acf/hhs/gov/programs/hsb/research/factsheets/02_hsfs.htm

9

Self-Help Groups

One important response to the "soap opera" of life is the voluntary self-help organization. Self-help groups date back to antiquity. Currently, they are among the fastest growing forms of assistance, adding substantially to community resources. Any newspaper reader can find regular announcements of self-help or support group meetings. Some prefer the term mutual assistance group, and many, following the Alcoholics Anonymous (AA) model are called 12-step programs.

Self-help groups are of interest to community psychology because they are an important indigenous resource within the private, non-professional segment of the community, and they address the current trend toward greater consumer choice and empowerment (Levy, 2000; see chapter 12). Some self-help groups may also serve a clientele different from the young, attractive, verbal, intelligent, successful individual considered the ideal candidate for traditional psychotherapy. One survey, for example, found that the average member of major self-help groups like AA or Parents Without Partners is middle-aged and a homemaker or blue-collar worker, typically with a high school education (Knight, Wollert, Levy, Frame, & Padgett, 1980). However, groups differ in the members they attract. According to data on their respective Web sites, two-thirds of the members of Cocaine Anonymous (CA) are males while 85 percent of the members of Al-Anon, a group for those related to alcoholics, are female. Almost 90 percent of the members of CA are between the ages of 18 and 44, while the average age of Al-Anon members is 51. It is difficult to generalize. Problems in living are not distributed randomly in the population, but are likely concentrated among certain populations. For example, there are AA groups for those who are hard of hearing. Local groups of the same organization may draw people of different socioeconomic, racial, or cultural backgrounds. Because people can attend most self-help groups without charge, the resource is open to people who do not have insurance, or the money to pay fees for service.

Not only are self-help groups important community resources, they are understandable using the same principles we have used in explaining other interventions. In this chapter, we first describe the phenomenon of the self-help group as a source of help, and then consider the dynamics of self-help groups, including theoretical explanations for how they seem to facilitate adaptation by vulnerable people. The chapter closes with a discussion of how community psychologists can directly assist individuals at risk by helping to create tailor-made self-help groups. We begin by examining the tremendous growth of self-help groups in recent years.

Growth of Self-Help Groups

As covered in chapter 5, "social capital" is a popular concept for describing social networks involving norms of reciprocity and trustworthiness (Putnam, 2000). This concept is similar to social support (chapter 7) and what Naroll (1983) called "moralnets," or face-to-face connections among people whose opinions matter to each other. Putnam (2000) amassed a large amount of data from diverse sources to show that, particularly in the last quarter of the twentieth century, there has been a decline in social capital manifested by declining membership in all sorts of organizations, including church attendance, political participation, and even in ordinary neighboring. Putnam (2000) recognizes that the growth of the self-help movement is counter to the general trend of declining participation in other community organizations. The decline in social capital that Putnam identified may well be related to the growth of self-help organizations.

The number of self-help groups of all kinds grew rapidly. Alcoholics Anonymous (AA) had about 50 groups in 1942; there are now more than 50,000 groups with over 1 million members in the United States alone. It has nearly 100,000 members in Canada, and over 800,000 members in countries other than the United States or Canada. There has been an incredible proliferation of groups modeled on AA using 12-step programs to help members cope with a great many different problems—Narcotics Anonymous, Cocaine Anonymous, Emotions Anonymous, Overeaters Anonymous, and Sexaholics Anonymous are just a few. Putnam (2000) says there are about 130 analogues of AA. Al-Anon and Alateen are groups for those who have a family member coping with alcoholism. Al-Anon now has 14,529 groups in the United States and 27,103 groups in 115 countries. Al-Anon claims nearly 200,000 members in the United States alone. Alateen, a group serving teenagers in families with alcoholics, has nearly 1,600 groups in the United States and nearly 2,700 groups worldwide. Adult Children of Alcoholics is another offshoot of AA.

Parents Anonymous began in 1969 with one group and two members. It now claims 2,200 groups and a presence in every state. (Parents Anonymous differs from most other groups modeled on AA. Most do not seek outside funds. PA does receive funds from state and local agencies such as the United Way. PA also uses trained facilitators along with parents as group leaders.)

Parents Without Partners began with two women in 1957. Twenty-five people came to the initial meeting. Today, Parents without Partners claims over 50,000 members in more than 400 clubs. Recovery, Inc., began with one group led by psychiatrist Abraham Low. It now has 700 weekly meetings in the United States and in other countries as well. Founded in 1980, Tough Love has about 1,000 groups worldwide today. A sampling of some of the names of self-help organizations provides a view of the range of problems for which the groups are solutions: Unwed Parents and Grandparents, Partners and Friends of Incest Survivors, Parents and Friends of Gays and Lesbians (PFLAG), Recovery from Mormonism (for those who lost their faith), and Christians in Recovery, a group for Christians who suffered from anxiety, depression, and related problems. Many groups are formed for people with specific diseases or conditions—e.g., CHADD, Children and Adults with Attention Deficit Disorders.

The national picture. Katz (1993) estimates there are currently 500,000 to 750,000 groups in the United States, with 10 to 15 million members. Jacobs and Goodman (1989) estimated 6.25 million self-help group members in 1987. Putnam (2000) cites data from surveys to the effect that 2 percent of the adult population is currently active in some support or self-help group, and another estimate that 3 percent of all adults had used a support group or a self-help group at some time in their lives (lifetime prevalence).

Regardless of these different estimates, so many self-help organizations exist today that a National Self-Help Clearinghouse has been formed to disseminate information about the activities of existing groups, the formation of new groups, publications, research findings, funding sources, and ideas and methods for starting new groups (White & Madara, 2002; Meissen, Gleason, & Embree, 1991). In their directory, White and Madara (2002) list almost 1,100 national and independent self-help groups, international networks, and Internet-based support groups focusing on an immense array of problems, including addictions, abuse, bereavement, mental and physical illness (including over 375 rare diseases), disabilities, parenting, and many other stressful life situations. Members of self-help groups often cite growth in the number of groups as indicative of their need and effectiveness. In recognition of the growth, the U.S. surgeon general organized a conference in the mid-1980s on self-help, basically endorsing their usefulness in the health field (Petrakis, 1988).

Many of the leaders of "mental health and consumers and survivors" organizations held a summit meeting in 1999 in Portland, Oregon. This group has taken on an action agenda. For example, they protested the surgeon general's characterization of electroconvulsive therapy (ECT) as "safe and effective" (The Key, 1999). Other community groups are also moving toward forming coalitions (Butterfoss, Goodman, & Wandersman, 1993).

The National Self-Help Clearinghouse listing does not include "right to life" groups such as Operation Rescue and its local affiliates, local pro-choice organizations, nor the thousands of grassroots activist environmental groups that Lois Gibbs' Center for Health, Environment and Justice claims to have contacted or assisted. Many national organizations concerned with the environment are not, strictly speaking, membership organizations with active chapters. They tend to be advocacy organizations run by professionals who receive financial support from a large number of people (Putnam, 2000). The growth of these types of organizations with people in face-to-face contact and involved in causes of deep significance to them, certainly a form of organization that enhances social capital, is contrary to the general trend of disengagement that Putnam described as characteristic of American society in the last quarter of the twentieth century.

   Historical antecedents. Self-help is not a new phenomenon on the American scene (Lee & Swenson, 1994). When Alexis De Tocqueville visited the United States in 1831, he noted: "Americans of all ages, all conditions and dispositions, constantly form associations . . . of a thousand . . . kinds—religious, moral, serious, futile, enormous or diminutive. . . . If it be proposed to inculcate some truth or foster some feeling by the encouragement of a great example, they form a society" (De Tocqueville, [1835] 1956, p. 198). De Tocqueville believed that associations were peculiarly American, a function of a democratic social order.

   In 1902, Kropotkin (1972) argued that cooperation is a basic survival mechanism for human beings. He provided many examples throughout history of spontaneously developed cooperative enterprises and associations for purposes of greater mutual protection and productivity. In medieval days, for example, members banded together in guilds to regulate their trade. Guild members constituted a brotherhood. Each was responsible not only for maintaining standards for the trade but also for providing fraternal benefits to the membership— aid in the event of illness, aid to widows and orphans, celebrations of births and marriages. Anticipating today's sociobiologists, Kropotkin argued that a social instinct leads people to help each other: "There is the gist of human psychology. Unless men are maddened in the battlefields, they cannot stand it to hear appeals for help, and not to respond to them. . . . The sophisms of the brain cannot resist the mutual aid feeling, because this feeling has been nurtured by thousands of years of pre-human life in societies" (Kropotkin, 1972, p. 234).

Contemporary Reasons for Growth

   People have always organized in response to mutual need, be it out of some social instinct, as Kropotkin argued, or as the manifestation of rational coping capacities (Hurvitz, 1976). If people organize in new ways to fulfill social need, existing means of providing support in time of need have evidently proven insufficient.

   For our purposes, we can most usefully link the recent spurt of growth of self-help to changes that reflect problems in existing social organizations and the means for providing mutual assistance. Growth in self-help or mutual assistance may reflect changes in other more traditional groups that might at one time have fulfilled human needs. In chapter 1 we discussed recent changes in the family with an increase in the number of single-parent households. American society is also very mobile. A large number of people change their addresses each year, many moving long distances and loosening their ties with family and old friends, which forces them to readapt in the sense of making new ties and becoming a part of new social networks. Geographic mobility puts distinct pressures on the nuclear family, and increasing numbers of working mothers may add to that pressure even as their working alleviates economic difficulties.

A large number of people live alone and may be unable to call upon friends or family for assistance. In still other cases, the resources of friends and family may not be sufficient to aid the individual in coping with problems in living that are foreign to ordinary experience. Both Naroll (1983) and Putnam (2000) demonstrated that, internationally, decline in "primary groups" (face-to-face normative reference groups) are associated with a variety of measures of social and personal malaise.

Medical model and reciprocity. We have already discussed several deficiencies in the medical model of service delivery. Another deficiency of the medical model will become apparent when we examine Kropotkin's view of charity. Writing from an anarchist viewpoint, Kropotkin (1972) argued that the existence of a centralized state interfered with the mutual assistance that would develop spontaneously in the absence of a state. He extended his argument to organized charitable enterprises as well.

> [W]hile early Christianity, like all other religions, was an appeal to the broadly human feelings of mutual aid and sympathy, the Christian church has aided the State in wrecking all standing institutions of mutual aid and support which were anterior to it, or developed outside of it; and, instead of the *mutual aid* which every savage considers as due to his kinsman, it has preached *charity* which bears a character of inspiration from above, and accordingly implies a certain superiority of the giver upon the receiver. (p. 238)

We need not accept Kropotkin's view regarding the role of the church. Drawing an analogy between organized charity and professional services, however, we can argue that the medical model is essentially a "trickle-down" model of assistance. Whatever its other merits, this model limits the possibilities for reciprocity and mutual assistance based on experience with the particular problem in living. Its very professionalism, certainly a strength for many purposes, nonetheless implies the superiority of the giver to the receiver and does not allow for reciprocity in their relationship.

We need not repeat other criticisms of the medical model here, but it is important to reemphasize one. Although a professional may have a great deal to offer, he or she usually does not know in great detail what it means to live with a particular problem, nor how one copes with it on a day-to-day basis. Our therapeutic philosophies and approaches tell us not to make our clients dependent and not to respond to the plea, "Tell me what to do!" Clients live with the problem of coping on a day-by-day basis, however, and most therapists do not focus on those day-by-day coping techniques. Professional therapists often do not transmit practical, gut-level, tried-and-true methods for handling problems. To the degree that all wisdom is seen to reside in the professional, there is a loss of the wisdom that comes from learning to cope on a day-by-day basis. The self-help model addresses that deficiency.

Anyone who reads the daily paper is also aware of serious and growing problems regarding the cost of physical or mental health care. Insurance companies, wary of the potential high cost of mental health services and the interminability of some mental health treatments, have imposed limits on both inpatient and outpatient care. If health care reform restricts insurance reimbursement for psychotherapy services, then we may expect still further growth in self-help organizations and membership.

For those who pay for care directly, the costs of extended treatment are prohibitive for all but the wealthiest. Public agencies with sliding-fee scales take into account the ability to pay, but even these fees can add up to considerable amounts. Moreover, most therapists would agree that it is difficult to show an even exchange—that for any unit of fee, a corresponding unit of progress is made. Payment of a fee does not make for an even exchange, nor does it undo the social inequality and lack of reciprocity in the relationship between the client and the professional. Self-help groups do permit equality and reciprocity among members.

Self-help groups provide services indefinitely to substantial numbers of people at very low cost. A telephone survey we did asking self-help groups in the Buffalo metropolitan area about the typical turnout at meetings revealed that as many as 1,000 people a month were being served for little more than coffee money. One thousand people a month was roughly comparable to the caseload of Buffalo's largest mental health center at that time, whose professional mental health services cost millions of dollars per year.

People who attend self-help groups are probably not a representative sample of those in need. Those who responded to our survey estimated that more than two-thirds of the participants in most of the organizations are female. It is also our impression that the vast bulk of participants are white, and there are relatively few examples of interracial groups. Emrick (1987) suggests that other self-selection factors are also important. AA members, for example, may be more sociable and affiliative than the average person. In addition, they may have more severe drinking problems and experience more guilt about their drinking than do alcohol abusers who are not AA members.

There is another interesting variation from the medical model: Where more than one chapter of a given self-help group exists, a prospective member can "shop around" among them, facilitating an ecological process of mutual selection that acknowledges the diversity among people and has as its goal the improvement of person-setting fit. We have no data on this point but would strongly conjecture that tolerance of such "shopping around" by prospective clients is not nearly so great among professionals. Some patients undoubtedly change therapists from time to time. Is it always a matter of "resistance," or can such changes be viewed as an attempt by the client to improve person-environment fit?

Types of Self-Help Groups

So far we have been discussing self-help as if all groups were similar in aims and methods to psychotherapy. Hurvitz (1976), in fact, termed these organizations "peer psychotherapy" groups. In common with psychotherapy, their aim is to assist the individual in coping with the emotions and the dilemmas generated by problems in living. The locus of pathology is within the individual, and the individual is assisted in making a better adaptation to self and to the world.

Sagarin (1969) pointed out that there are two general types of self-help groups. In one,

> individuals seek to reduce their deviant behavior and in this way escape from deviance. . . . Such groups paint deviants as worthwhile individuals, souls to be saved; but they view the deviance itself as immoral, sinful and self-defeating. . . . The second type of deviant group, consist[s] of those who are seeking to modify the definition of their conditions as deviant. . . . These groups seek to change the public attitude toward their particular deviance. . . . Groups seeking to change social attitudes thumb their noses at society in order to foster pride in the deviant. (p. 21)

Change the person. AA is an example of the first type of self-help group. Its aim is to help members overcome a drinking problem through mutual assistance. AA teaches that for *alcoholics* drinking is self-defeating. AA is not a temperance organization—it takes no position about the drinking of others who are not alcoholics, and it takes no public position on legislation related to drinking. It neither favors nor opposes legislation to raise the drinking age or to introduce stiffer penalties against drunk driving. It makes no effort to create sympathy for the alcoholic or to reduce stigmatization or discrimination directed against former alcoholics. It has no interest in changing society's views of alcoholics, except perhaps in furthering the conception that alcoholism is a disease. Even then it does not speak out as an organization, nor does it allow individual members to speak on such issues in the name of the group.

Change society. Notable examples of the second type of self-help organization would be any of the organizations comprising the civil

rights movement. The civil rights movement utilized political and social action and adopted a litigation strategy to help create opportunities for African Americans and for other minorities and to instill self-
esteem. It also served as a model for other oppressed (read "deviant")
groups to improve their lives by working to change society's view of
and actions toward members of those groups. Milner (1987) described
how the mental patients' rights movement (Chamberlin, 1990) used the
civil rights movement as a model in working for change through litigation, legislation, and direct social action. Women's consciousness-
raising[1] groups of the 1970s also modeled themselves on the civil rights
movement. They were concerned not only about helping individual
women to adapt in a changing social world, but also in changing the
larger society's views and treatment of women.

Another case in point is the gay rights movement. Gay activism
started in 1969 with a famous incident at the Stonewall bar in Green-
wich Village in New York when a group of gays resisted arrest for
nothing more than being in a gay bar. The incident triggered a week-
long riot, and was a defining episode. Since then, gay groups have been
active in attempting to change not homosexuals, except perhaps to instill pride in being gay, but aspects of the larger society (Duberman,
1993). To gay groups, homosexuality is simply an inherent identity and
should not be subject to social, economic, or criminal penalties. Gay
groups lobby and work for changes in laws that affect their members.
They seek to be included in antidiscrimination legislation, and they
pursue changes in sodomy laws attaching criminal penalties to sexual
acts between consenting adults. Gays do not wish to be barred from
having custody of children simply because of their sexual orientations.
Some gays want states to legalize gay marriages and would like to have
partners covered under their health insurance plans and other employment benefits.

Over the years, gay groups have been sufficiently active and persuasive to have homosexuality eliminated as an official psychiatric illness or deviation. All that remains in the current American Psychiatric
Association *Diagnostic and Statistical Manual*, 4th edition (*DSM-IV*) is
brief mention of "persistent and marked distress about sexual orientation" as a possible basis for diagnosing a "Sexual Disorder Not Otherwise Specified" (p. 538). This revision in diagnostic practice was the
result of social and political action to change the definition of deviance
and the world's view of the deviant individual. Other groups have
since organized to protest the inclusion of certain conditions in the
DSM, for example, on the grounds that labeling a condition can be prej-
udicial to the interests of women, or that failing to include abortion as
a possible trauma for the diagnosis of Post-Traumatic Stress Disorder
favors the pro-choice position on abortion (Kirk & Kutchins, 1992).

Parents and Friends of Lesbians and Gays (PFLAG) have mounted
an educational program to promote greater tolerance of gay youth in

schools. Gay youth suffer from discrimination, bullying, and isolation. Gay youth are at risk for suicide and for running away among other problems and the harsh social environment of schools contributes to their difficulties.

None of these goals is achievable simply by helping individuals to cope better with problems in living defined as individual problems. These changes require concerted group action to alter society's views of and actions toward a group commonly defined as deviant and subject to the burdens carried by deviants.

This general idea of social and political action to better the lives of certain people suffering with some handicap or feeling some grievance has powered the formation of a large number of groups. Some groups have aims as narrow as raising money to stimulate public interest or research on a given disease. Others form spontaneously in relation to a specific problem. The Love Canal Homeowners Association formed in 1978 when homeowners living in the neighborhood of a hidden toxic chemical waste dump site believed they were not getting fair treatment from the state agencies designated to deal with their problem. The homeowners organized and kept fighting for several years, taking their case to the public and in other ways continually making their demands known to public officials. They were successful in seeing their demands met, and in the process raised public consciousness regarding the problems of toxic wastes (Gibbs, 1998; A. Levine, 1982). Their organization also served to alleviate the sense of helplessness experienced by many who felt caught in a severe problem in living that taxed family and community resources (Gibbs, 1998; Stone & Levine, 1985–1986).

The Nature of Self-Help Groups

We have not yet defined self-help groups in any formal sense. This is difficult to do with great precision because we would like to include many different types of organizations, and many of them have mixed characteristics. Sagarin's twofold classification is insufficient to cover the variety of groups that have sufficient characteristics in common to be treated as related phenomena. Many authorities have attempted descriptions and classifications of self-help, but no single attempt seems fully satisfactory (Levy, 1976, 2000). We offer our own grouping simply to show the range of different types, and their goals for their members. For convenience of exposition, we list five types of self-help groups.

Disqualified from normal. One type involves people whose state or condition leads to some disqualification from being "normal." Members of these groups exhibit behavior or have characteristics that subject them to social isolation, stigmatization, scorn, pity, or social punishment. Although the concept of a degraded social identity (Sarbin, 1970) applies more or less here, we cannot say that all such people are necessarily limited to ascribed roles. Examples of those with behavioral characteristics that disqualify them from being "normal" are: mentally ill people, alcohol abusers, ex-convicts, gamblers, drug addicts, and gays. Examples of people with physical characteristics or illnesses subjecting the individual to disqualification are: little people (dwarfs), cancer patients, people with colostomies or other physical disabilities (see Hinrichsen, Revenson, & Shinn, 1985), or the obese, and people who are elderly (Stangor & Crandall, 2000). Although not at fault, people falling into this category are nonetheless subject to varying degrees of social disapprobation and social disqualification. Some are subjected to forms of social discrimination that limit opportunity and may affect self-esteem. African Americans, women, and gays are people subject to discriminatory treatment.

Relatives of those with stigmatizing conditions. The second type of self-help group is made up of people related to persons with stigmatizing conditions, who themselves may be subject to some secondary stigma or who suffer consequences because of the problems presented by the person related to them. Spouses and children of alcoholics, gamblers, or relatives of people with mental illness (Grosser & Vine, 1991) fall into this category, as do children who are charged with the care of elderly relatives. Parents of people with mental retardation, learning disabilities, or autism have much to cope with, as do those in serious conflict with their adolescent children who seek the assistance of the courts to help control their children (York & York, 1987).

Socially isolating conditions. A third type of group includes people with common problems that may not be stigmatizing but that do tend to be socially isolating. Other people who do not have the problem may not understand the individual's or the family's situation. Examples of these are groups for widows (Lieberman, 1989), groups for single parents such as Parents Without Partners, parents of diabetic children or parents of children with cancer (Chesler & Chesney, 1995).

Mutual assistance. A fourth type are groups organized along ethnic, religious, or racial lines for mutual assistance. These include fraternal organizations that provide education, recreation, cultural preservation, insurance, prepaid medical care, and similar services. Many of these organizations developed among immigrant groups, and many originated as burial societies (Howe & Libo, 2000). These organizations were very important in the Jewish community, and such groups made important contributions to the survival of African Americans. Jack and Jill is a social club formed in 1938 for African American families to provide their children with teas, cotillions, and pool parties because they were excluded from white organizations who provided those amenities. Formerly an elitist African American society, now Jack and Jill is being used by African American families who live in predominately white neighborhoods to give their children experience with African Americans. They feel their children are becoming alienated from their black heritage and even uncomfortable with black people and children (Edwards, 2001).

Quasi-political organizations. A fifth type is organized along quasi-political lines for the preservation of specific interests. These include taxpayers' groups seeking to limit taxation, civic organizations designed to preserve the character of neighborhoods, and organizations concerned with community development. Groups such as these may form whenever a common problem arises. The Love Canal Homeowners Association is an example of a spontaneously appearing organization. Groups opposed to abortion and groups in favor of choice in reproductive matters, are additional examples of this type. Men's groups have now organized in response to the women's movement (see *The Liberator*, 1994).

Mixed types. This classification system is difficult to apply because there are rarely pure forms of any one type, and most groups fit in more than one category such as African Americans in the preceding listing. Take as an example a relatively new group showing many mixed characteristics. Equal Rights for Fathers is a group of noncustodial parents dealing with the aftermath of divorce. Members are primarily male, but they include new wives or girlfriends and grandparents who wish to maintain ties with grandchildren following a divorce. Equal Rights for Fathers has political aims as well as self-help aims and believes that the legal system is biased against men. Fathers Rights Metro (New York), a related group, filed a class action lawsuit against the New York Department of Social Services and the New York Office of Court Administration, claiming that men are the victims of gender-biased discrimination by social services and in the Family Court (*The Liberator*, 1994). Chapters of this type of group successfully lobbied to have infant changing stations included in the men's rooms in airports to allow men to care for their infants and young children while traveling.

Members of this group also feel stigmatized because some in the public look on them as merely seeking to avoid paying child support. Others feel stigmatized because they feel that their masculinity is questioned when they assert their love for their children and their desire to have or to share custody. Members favor a legal presumption for joint custody. They agree that men should meet their obligations to pay child support, but argue that the courts do not show nearly the same vigor in protecting visitation rights as they do in enforcing support orders. Members engage in public information campaigns (broadcasts on public access TV channels, letters to the editor, Father's Day events designed to capture media attention, etc.). The members share information about the legal system, organize to influence legislation, attempt to educate judges and lawyers, help each other understand what to look for in an attorney, and share information about how to use the time they have with their children effectively. They conduct rap sessions to help each other come to terms with their circumstances and their feelings and attitudes about themselves, their ex-spouses, the legal system, and many other problems that require adaptation and for which little or no assistance is otherwise available. Members sometimes assist each other outside of the group meetings, and some core members often find themselves intervening in personal crises of other members. Similar functions were served by the women's consciousness-raising groups that grew rapidly in the late 1960s and early 1970s (Levine & Perkins, 1987).

Dynamics of Self-Help Groups

Describing self-help in theoretical terms may help us understand how self-help works to assist members in adapting. Galanter (1990) compares self-help to charismatic religious groups and to cults. He identifies many of the same features in charismatic and other self-help groups that have profound effects on thinking and behavior of their members. Groups such as the Unification Church and Hare Krishna are examples. Here we will briefly discuss some common features of the lives of those who participate in self-help groups. Later we will see how aspects of the programs and activities of self-help groups help its members to cope with common recurring problems and situations.

Departure from normative ideal. Prospective members of a self-help organization struggle with a problem in living or a life circumstance that departs from some normative ideal. The condition the person has or the situation the person is faced with is simply "not good" in cultural terms. The problem or circumstance will not disappear rapidly no matter what remedies are sought, and as a result the individual faces the problem of adapting over a considerable period of time. Because the core problem represents a departure from a normative ideal, the individual tends to engage in a process of self-isolation in perceiving himself or herself as having failed, as abnormal, or as a hapless victim of uncontrollable forces or of fate.

Feelings of isolation. Most important, because the problem is interpreted as a departure from a normative ideal, the individual feels alone, as if his or her problems and feelings and experiences are unique. This feeling of isolation may exist even if the individual is part of a network that may be supportive in many other respects. The person's difficulties are often exacerbated because the ordinary agencies of assistance have proved insufficient, inadequate, or even punitive.

Difficulty in developing philosophy of life and coping strategies. As a consequence of isolation and the inadequacies of helping agencies, the individual will not have developed a philosophy for viewing the problem, nor had the opportunity to learn, directly or vicariously, useful strategies for coping with the myriad everyday issues related to the core problem. Faced with the difficulty in developing a philosophy of life, and in learning coping strategies from others, the individual struggles on his or her own, without being able to develop a clear direction. We will call this philosophy of life with associated coping strategies an ideology.

Self-Help and the Model of a Family

What does participation in a self-help group provide that reduces the vulnerability and/or acute stress affecting a person at risk? Like any significant social support system, a self-help group can profitably be compared with the model of an ideal family to theorize about what a self-help group provides for its members. We assume in this discussion that groups contain more and less experienced members. This conceptualization provides a lens through which we can view and interpret the activities of self-help groups. Recall from our discussion of social support that Caplan depicts the ideal family as fulfilling several functions for its members.

Disseminate information. Just as older members of the family collect and disseminate information about the world, providing models for younger members to emulate, so more experienced members of the self-help group provide information about their mutual plight, and serve as models for less experienced members.

For example, women's consciousness-raising groups of the 1970s worked out ways of thinking about problems such as sharing homemaking and child care responsibilities with husbands, working out the norms of living with partners when not married, or dealing with discrimination in the workplace. Women in groups shared their experiences and their solutions. Eventually members who had been in the movement longer and who seemed to have thought through issues became role models for others who knew they were struggling but did not know how to think about their situations (Levine & Perkins, 1987). Members of groups share information about doctors, lawyers, social service agencies, and, depending on the problem, how to deal with bureaucratic agencies affecting their lives. Members of the National Alliance for the Mentally Ill (NAMI) tell each other about the newest medications and their side effects.

Feedback and guidance. Self-help groups may also serve as a feedback and guidance system to help members understand their reactions to others and others' reactions to them. Consciousness-raising groups included assigned discussion topics ranging from dress to relationships, assertiveness, and women's lack of self-confidence. In discussing the various topics and in reflecting on their experiences, group members provided a way of interpreting their experiences and a basis for thinking of new ways of responding to others. Members of NAMI may teach their family members with disabilities to understand the reactions of "normals" who respond to some of their symptoms and other atypical characteristics. Some pass on ways of coping with their difficulties in social interactions by explaining to others that they (the persons with mental illness) may sometimes be internally absorbed, for example.

"Prescriptions for wise conduct." Self-help groups provide a philosophy of life, an outlook on the problem condition. Through repeated discussion of concrete situations with other members, the group's philosophy or ideology comes to serve an organizing function in the lives of self-help group members. By applying the tenets of the ideology to everyday problems, the ideology provides, as Caplan puts it, "prescriptions for wise conduct." Women's consciousness-raising groups provided reinforcement for behavior consistent with the groups' objectives and the elimination of undesirable behavior. The groups' ideology promoted action to modify the social environment, and provided a rationale, encouragement, and specific methods consistent with ideology for dealing with commonplace problems. Members of local NAMI groups share experiences, develop a way of looking at mental illness, and engage in political and social action. Importantly, they reject the idea that family relationships "cause" mental illness.

Sharing and mutual assistance. Family members share each other's problems, offer each other advice and guidance, assist in finding external sources of aid, and even make arrangements for such assistance. Much analogous learning occurs in self-help groups. Members of the groups share happy occasions as well as problems. In some groups members celebrate birthdays, job promotions, and other successful life changes. Think of yourself in the position of having good news and no one to share the good news with. In many self-help groups members also extend concrete services and material aid to each other. For example, women in pro-life as well as those in pro-choice groups see each other socially. During crises members of women's consciousness-raising groups provided assistance, such as baby-sitting, or allowing a member to move in temporarily after a woman decided to seek a divorce and needed a place to stay.

Haven for rest and recuperation. As a haven for rest and recuperation, the self-help group provides a place where members can be themselves and be assured of understanding and acceptance. There is no need to conceal or to explain the problem to anyone. All understand because all have experienced similar needs and emotions. In many ways, the self-help group also becomes the reference group for its members. For example, in one women's consciousness-raising group, members expressed concern that their bodies did not live up to fashion magazine ideals. Members literally bared their breasts to the group, each woman confessing the feeling that her breasts were inadequate but receiving reassurance from the other members that her breasts were perfectly adequate. With other problems such as reactions to the hospitalization of a family member, because others in the group have "been there," there is no need to explain or to justify.

Develop and maintain self-esteem. Members feel good when they live up to the codes of the self-help group and presumably feel bad when they fail to live up to its standards. The desire to have the approbation and support of fellow group members motivates the individual to live up to the group's standards. Just as in a family, however, failure to conquer the core problem does not lead to banishment. The sinner, so to speak, may always return to the fold and be welcomed, if not honored, for being willing to try again. In any successful self-help group, members identify with each other and develop a sense of trust and community that promotes belongingness and fellowship, often extending beyond the boundaries of the group.

Enhance personal identity. A foundation for personal identity beyond the identity as a "deviant" is established within self-help groups as members share their current problems. In fact, because members are both givers and receivers of help, with the roles changing from moment to moment, sharing of weakness contributes positively to self and to others. An individual member may find himself or herself of value to another simply by sharing a failure. By being of value to another, one's sense of competence and worthwhileness may be enhanced.

Emotional mastery. Finally, sharing problems and feelings within a family enables members to assist each other with the task of emotional mastery. Sharing problems and feelings within a self-help group comes to fulfill similar functions. For some, participation in the self-help group can become critical, not only for the assistance provided in achieving emotional mastery but also because the individual comes to feel like an integral part of a larger social group. In Naroll's (1983) terms, participation in a mutual help group may result in an improved condition because of participation in a protective and restorative "moralnet."

How Self-Help Groups Work

While Caplan's model of the ideal family helps us speculate about the important characteristics of self-help groups, psychological research and thinking have expanded our understanding considerably in the past few years. We can identify six aspects of self-help that serve its members' interests. These aspects of self-help constitute a testable theory of self-help groups. Self-help groups (1) promote the psychological sense of community; (2) provide an ideology that serves as a philosophical antidote; (3) provide an opportunity for confession, catharsis, and mutual criticism; (4) provide role models; (5) teach effective coping strategies for day-to-day problems; and (6) provide a network of social relationships.

Psychological sense of community (see chapter 5). Bringing together people who face a common dilemma overcomes the problem of aloneness or self-isolation. Another way of putting this is that self-help groups promote the psychological sense of community. Discovering that others experience the same problem and feel the same way helps make the personal crisis a social experience. In Sagarin's terms, the odd man is in. For example, gay youth who feel isolated and fearful about coming out can find each other nowadays by using the Internet. One said: "When you see people around the world writing the same things, you get the feeling you are not alone, . . . You may be no closer than the modem, but you go, 'Oh my God, that's exactly how I feel'." (Gabriel, 1995). The person may come to feel less "abnormal" and therefore less separated from society.

Moreover, in those instances where members feel their grievances may be attributed to existing social conditions, the personal becomes not only the social but also the political. Members no longer feel isolated, and the group's ideology provides a program of action for living with and overcoming the core problem. Feeling less isolated and more bonded with others, members will interpret their own conditions differently and may be ready to act, sometimes to change themselves and sometimes to change the world. Some groups encourage members to try to change the world, or the world's view of their circumstances. That approach was certainly true of many women's consciousness-raising groups, civil rights, and gay groups whose aims have included social change as well as personal change.

Ideologies as philosophical (cognitive) antidotes. Self-help groups have more or less articulated ideologies that serve as philosophical or cognitive antidotes to give meaning to the particular life circumstance that represents a departure from the normative ideal. The dictionary defines ideology as "a system of ideas concerning phenomena, especially those of social life; the manner of thinking characteristic of a class or an individual." Ideologies are based on values that are shared among people and may be used to interpret daily life. An ideology may also be associated with a program of action in keeping with the ideology. Ideologies contribute to a sense of personal identity by defining what an individual should believe, which reduces ambiguity and uncertainty about the world and provides a basis for making choices in everyday life. Many of the articles in the *Liberator* (1994), a newsletter representing aspects of the men's movement, are articulations of a male ideology, developed perhaps in response to the success of the women's movement. The masthead of the newsletter says: "Our definition of men's liberation is freedom *to be* (not from being) men." The articles teach men how to think about themselves and about problems they face as men in a changing world.

Just as every religious group has a body of sacred writings, so many self-help groups have bodies of literature that define the group's beliefs and approach to the common problem. AA's "Twelve Steps" and "Big Book" are primary examples of such core sacred writings. Some groups may not have as precisely delineated a set of beliefs as does AA, but generally speaking such a set of beliefs is identifiable even if not fully detailed. Weiss (1987) describes how he developed an ideology for Mothers Against Drunk Driving (MADD) in the form of a therapeutic manual for families who had lost a child to a drunk driver.

Antze (1976) developed a remarkably useful hypothesis about the role of ideologies in self-help. He states that a group's teachings are its very essence and that social scientists have neglected the role of specific self-help group teachings because some seem contradictory. A group such as AA urges its members to give their problems up to a higher power, arguing that members are powerless to control their situations. On the other hand, a group such as Recovery, Inc., a self-help organization for "nervous people," teaches that members can overcome their problems through an exercise of will power. How can both teachings be correct?

Antze resolved this dilemma by arguing that self-help organizations are specialized. Within this specialization of problem, "It may be possible for a group's ideology to function more precisely, working as a 'cognitive antidote' to basic features of a condition shared by everyone who joins" (p. 327). Given the nature of social organization, anyone having the particular problem is in a:

> socially standardized situation. . . . No matter how an individual comes to a given problem, once he arrives he is very much in the same boat with his fellow victims. He comes to cope with life in a similar fashion; he comes to think of himself and others in similar ways; he faces identical problems in trying to change. . . . The ideologies of peer therapy groups may be seen as extremely shrewd and insightful attacks on the most harm-

ful of these standardized implications. If they have therapeutic value, it is because each manages to break some link in the chain of events maintaining a condition and to provide viable defenses against its renewal. (pp. 328–329)

As examples Antze uses the difference in the core problems of alcoholics and of "nervous" persons such as the members of Recovery, Inc. According to Antze, the core problem of the alcoholic is:

he exaggerates his own authorship in the events of his life. Sober or drunk, he tends to perceive his world as fashioned mainly by his own acts; somehow he always finds himself at center stage. . . . This group of attitudes adds up to *unrealistic volition.* . . . Problem drinkers have an unusually high need to assert power over people and situations. . . . The alcoholic also feels himself to be sole author of his failures. . . . *To absorb the AA message is to see oneself as much less the author of events in life, the active fighter and doer, and much more as a person with the wisdom to accept limitations and wait for things to come.* (pp. 331–332)

Members of Recovery, Inc., are mental health consumers with complaints of "nervousness." Most experience symptoms that are essentially "ego alien." In the face of an episode of depression or a panic attack, the person feels he or she is not himself or herself. The symptom appears to come from outside the person, and he or she feels powerless in the face of it. The ideology of Recovery, Inc., emphasizes the belief that symptoms, no matter how troublesome, are basically within the individual's mind and are therefore capable of being controlled. Members of Recovery, Inc., learn that the one critical faculty, the "Will," can always be utilized to overcome the ego-alien symptom. Recovery, Inc., emphasizes taking specific actions, no matter how small, to exert will against the symptom (Low, 1997); although "the ideologies of AA and Recovery represent mirror images of one another . . . their opposition is explained by an equally marked opposition in the phenomenology of the problems they treat" (Antze, 1976, p. 337).

Another example of ideology as antidote is provided by NAMI groups, whose primary members are families of people with serious mental illness. As a cognitive antidote to problems its members face, the NAMI ideology includes: "(a) belief that family members of a person with mental illness are not pathogenic and dysfunctional themselves, but instead are normal individuals attempting to cope with abnormal events or circumstances; (b) a belief in a biological etiology for schizophrenia and other severe mental illness, plus a rejection of psychogenic theories placing blame on parents and family members; and (c) a belief that clients and family members share with professionals the responsibility for improving services for those with severe mental illness" (Levine, Toro, & Perkins, 1993, p. 540).

Culture and special language. Self-help groups develop cultures and specialized languages that help to implement the ideology. Recovery, Inc.'s special language includes procedures for identifying the onset of symptoms (e.g., "spotting" an "angry temper") and taking action to limit the effect of the symptoms (e.g. "swapping thoughts" and "commanding the muscles to relax"). This language is practiced in ritualistic fashion at each meeting, where members are called on to present experiences where they used the Recovery method to overcome a problem. Other members contribute to the analysis of the experience using the Recovery language. Conceptual tags tied to concrete experiences are thus developed, and the members may take these tags away and use them every day on a minute-by-minute basis.

Al-Anon, an organization for family members of people with alcoholism, follows AA's methods closely. Al-Anon has also developed its own ideas, such as "loving detachment," in which the spouse of the alcoholic is taught to love the alcoholic but not to protect him or her from the consequences of excessive drinking. Al-Anon also teaches its members to "live one day at a time" and to "learn to let go," meaning that the spouse must learn to live his or her own life, and cannot do anything to control the alcoholic's drinking. These slogans are applied as members discuss their experiences in the group. They take on generalized meaning and may then be used to help the individual decide what to do, if not how to feel, about everyday problems related to the alcoholic spouse and perhaps other problems in living as well. This process can be compared with the way religious sermons use passages from the Bible to show how biblical wisdom can be applied to problems in contemporary life.

Some hypotheses. Several testable propositions follow from this viewpoint. A member's commitment and understanding of the group's ideology should increase with the duration of his or her membership. Newer members should have a lesser appreciation of the ideology, and will use its tenets less often in solving problems in living, than veteran members. Using the ideology to help solve other everyday problems will result in reduced feelings of hopelessness, increased feelings of self-efficacy, and improved self-esteem.

Data from members of NAMI and of Recovery, Inc., offer support for these propositions. NAMI members who are more involved in their groups and more accepting of the NAMI ideology report reduced feelings of stigma, guilt, and personal responsibility, and more comfortable interactions with a mentally ill child (Medvene & Krauss, 1989). Similarly, Galanter (1988) found that the longer a person with mental illness was involved in Recovery, Inc., the better was his or her mental health and the less need he or she had for medication and other professional services. Other studies have reported similar results (see a review by Kurtz, 1990). Of course these results may reflect some self-selection. Those who remained in the groups for longer periods of time may have been stronger persons to begin with, or may have found the group, its members, and procedures more compatible than those who do not stay. Nevertheless, the findings are consistent with theory, and to the degree that adoption of the ideology correlates with positive coping, the theory's prediction is satisfied.

Confession, catharsis, and mutual criticism. Many groups have a ritualistic format that includes elements of confession, catharsis, and criticism. A sense of group solidarity is developed as members share their feelings and experiences. Members are encouraged to speak of their failures and their problems, experiences that may be associated with lowered self-esteem and guilt. The descriptions of women's consciousness-raising groups provide many examples of confessing personal inadequacies and dilemmas, including honest descriptions of dissatisfaction with sexual relationships, or guilt at devoting time to intellectual or professional development instead of to children or husband. By sharing these experiences with others who have "been there," members essentially unload unwanted baggage and find forgiveness.

Thoits (1986) hypothesizes that people will accept advice or sympathy more readily from someone with whom they can identify. Speaking with and listening to someone who "has been there" may be more relieving than speaking to someone who can only say "I think I know how you feel." Gay youth who used the Internet gay bulletin board seemed to accept counsel from those in similar circumstances where they might not accept help from another source (Gabriel, 1995).

The atmosphere in self-help groups is generally more supportive than that in professionally led therapy groups (Toro et al, 1988). Observers of substance abuse self-help groups reported that they saw flexible, sophisticated, and sensitive group management practices (Woff, Toumbourou, Herlihy, Hamilton, & Wales, 1996). As the feeling of solidarity develops, members feel free to confront each other. This mutual criticism (Levine & Bunker, 1975) is a form of deviance control; it is also a method for enhancing self-esteem. If one lives up to the ideals of the group, by definition one has become a better person. During this experience of sharing, moreover, the group helps the individual learn to use its teachings to overcome the problem. Group members learn "prescriptions for wise conduct" and actions in keeping with those ideas. Recovery, Inc. teaches that one only needs to be "average," and does not need to be perfect or a superachiever in order to have self-esteem. By adopting that aspect of the ideology, a member can avoid the self-derogation that comes from failing to achieve unattainable goals. Members of consciousness-raising groups helped each other to relax their self-imposed demands to be superwomen and to stop trying to excel at the roles of wife, mother, and wage earner to the point of exhaustion.

Role models. Members provide role models for each other. Self-help groups create places and roles for individuals. Those who strive to fulfill the groups' teachings and have been more successful at it become role models for others. Because no formal distinctions exist among members, a new member can easily identify with a more experienced member and say, "If she can overcome this problem, so can I." Even though a given individual may not be able to overcome his or her own problems, for example, that individual understands the difficulty of coping with the problem and is aware of mistakes a person is likely to make. Thus in many instances he or she may be able to give another member the benefit of vicarious learning. Something that might have been a matter of shame is transformed into an experience of value for a fellow group member. Lois Gibbs serves as a role model for hundreds of people threatened by toxic waste and other pollution problems; she habitually uses examples from her own experiences, including mistakes and her feelings to instruct others and to relate to them.

"Helper-therapy principle." The roles of help-giver and help-receiver are thoroughly interchangeable. Because each member is living with a chronic problem, each will encounter difficulty at one time or another. Even the most successful of members may turn to other members of the group for emotional sustenance or support or for help in solving some new dilemma. Any implication of "inferior" and "superior" positions is reduced because any member may play either role from time to time. Maton (1988) found that those members of self-help groups who both gave and received support had lower levels of depression and higher self-esteem than did those who just received assistance.

Reissman (1965) developed an idea he called the "helper-therapy" principle. It means that the most effective way to learn is to teach, and that people who help others may be those who are helped the most (Roberts et al., 1999). Although not done in a self-help context, research by Li (1989) found that Chinese children randomly selected to teach younger children in preparation for entering the Red Guard, a highly desirable youth group in China, learned public speaking, gained in confidence, and improved their grades in Chinese more than did a control group that lacked the experience of teaching. The effectiveness of this principle can be derived from role theory in that a person playing a role will strive to meet the requirements of that role.

> In effect, as a helper the individual displays mastery over the afflicting condition—plays the role of a nonaddict, for example—and thereby acquires the appropriate skills, attitudes, behaviors and mental set. Having modeled this for others, the individual may see him or herself as behaving in a new way and may, in effect, take on the new role as his or her own. (Gartner & Reissman, 1977, p. 103)

Some persons become active leaders in self-help organizations and actually build new identities and lifestyles around the membership role. Some women who participated in consciousness-raising groups and political activities associated with the women's movement subsequently changed their dress, their appearance, their demeanor, the language they used, the people with whom they interacted, their activities, and their goals. Members of AA or Al-Anon who engage in 12th step work by becoming speakers to other groups illustrate the point. A person who was in deep difficulty gains esteem from others by revealing his history in an effort to bring the message to others. A leader in the fathers' rights movement told about how his family had learned to share him with the group because he was called on so much by other members. The family recognized that his role within the group was important for his identity.

Coping strategies. By sharing day-by-day experiences, members discover and share proven coping devices. Because the individuals are in a "standardized situation," their problems generally recur, and the solutions that one member passes on to another are pertinent for their respective circumstances. Professionals may not have the opportunity to observe these concrete, everyday coping strategies and would not record them in research. In self-help groups, culturally acquired wisdom is transmitted in an oral rather than a written tradition.

Al-Anon members teach each other not to lie to the spouse's boss to "cover up" for a spouse who misses work due to a hangover. The member learns to protect her own integrity and learns that her behavior is enabling the spouse's drinking. She can then act without interpreting the action as a "betrayal" of her love for the spouse. Members of the group encourage each other to experiment with new solutions, support each other through any failures, and rejoice even at members' small successes. Members of Recovery, Inc., encourage their members to use their special language to remind them of specific actions they can take when in distress outside the group. Members of the Love Canal Homeowners Association often had to deal with the media. They learned how to get their major points across to journalists in a few minutes, or even seconds by practicing and critiquing each other.

Social relationships. Members provide a network of friends and social relationships not readily available otherwise to the person struggling with social disqualification or with adaptive demands that others who do not share the problem may fail to understand. Because their social network is enlarged, members gain access to more resources. Members celebrate happy occasions with each other, socialize, have parties, and provide companionship. Salem, Seidman and Rappaport (1988) reported that GROW provided its members with an entire social network. Humphreys and Noke (1997) followed 2,337 veterans who had been admitted to an inpatient substance abuse program. Some of these men had contact with a 12-step program. On follow-up after one year, 84.4 percent had had at least some minimal involvement with 12-step activities; 17.3 percent had gone to 20 or more meetings in the previous three months. In a complex structural equation modeling procedure, greater post-treatment involvement with 12-step programs correlated with a larger number of close friends, and an increase in the number of 12-step friends. Post-treatment 12-step involvement correlated with having friendship networks with more close friends, more frequent contact with friends, and contact with friends who did not support substance use. Involvement with others who also participated in 12-step activities correlated with greater abstinence from the use of drugs or alcohol. Fewer friends in their network used alcohol or drugs than among those who had little or no 12-step activity. It appears that those who participate in 12-step activities replace non-12-step friends with 12-step friends with increased possibilities for constructive influences and for access to resources.

In some groups members may go further and provide concrete help to each other. For example, Reach is a self-help group for relatives of people with mental illness. It is sponsored by the Buffalo and Erie County chapter of the National Association for Mental Health. Its members provide respite care for each other; a member who needs a short vacation or rest period may ask another member, experienced in handling the problems of mental illness, to look after the ill family member. Members will reciprocate and provide here-and-now assistance for each other. Many groups, AA for example, and weight-loss groups provide new members with sponsors who may be called at any time, day or night, for assistance. Help is delivered when and where it is needed, "on call" so to speak, in the situation where the problem arises.

Self-Help and Ecological Concepts

As we noted in introducing this chapter, self-help groups are also understandable using the ecological principles and conceptions discussed in earlier chapters. Self-help groups represent a broadly applicable mode of intervention, for example, yet they address the ecological fact of diversity among people and their needs by providing relatively precise ideological antidotes that can be tailored to any vulnerable condition. In this respect self-help groups illustrate a point we made about social support in chapter 7: the specific resources a supportive network provides may be more important to its effectiveness than the size of the group or how it is structured.

Ecological setting. Self-help groups are also understandable as ecological settings that improve the degree of behavioral adaptation to the community by improving person-environment fit. In the ideology of self-help groups, improved adaptation follows from concrete, practical changes in behavior. Members of Narcotics Anonymous recognize that former companions provide temptations to use drugs again. They recommend that the recovering addict change his or her "playpen and playmates." Such concrete behaviors can be understood as joint properties of people and settings. We earlier characterized vulnerability as poor fit between the individual's behavioral repertoire and the demands of settings in his or her life (the outcome of which is alcohol abuse, feelings of oppression, withdrawal and isolation, and so on). Participation in new settings enlarges the individual's behavioral repertoire and expands the community niches available to that person, increasing his or her niche breadth. Consumer members of some self-help groups are invited to be members of advisory councils for government agencies. Others may testify at public hearings. Members of Al-Anon are encouraged to care for themselves by seeking jobs, or taking advantage of recreational opportunities.

Psychosocial climate and relationship. Two ecological principles of practice are relevant. By what specific mechanisms does participation in a self-help group produce behavior change? How is change maintained? For specific theoretical answers to these questions, recall the five psychological conceptions of the environment that were examined in chapter 5. In Moos' psychosocial climate conception, for example, one important dimension of a setting is its relationship-oriented qualities. Because membership in most groups is relatively open-ended (the only requirement for membership in AA, for example, is a desire to stop drinking), self-help groups are high in their support and acceptance of participants (Toro, Rappaport, & Seidman, 1987). Support and acceptance serve to reduce self-ostracization and to increase the psychological sense of community among members. Relationship-oriented aspects of the climate are also enhanced by a strengthened and expanded network of friendships involving reversible roles, sponsorship, and other activities or contacts outside the meetings.

Psychosocial climate and personal development. A second important psychosocial dimension is the degree to which a setting fosters participants' personal development. Important responsibilities, such as those implied by sponsorship and by Reissman's helper-therapy principle, would strengthen the personal development dimensions of a self-help group's climate. Clear differences would likely exist among groups on specific personal development dimensions, however, reflecting the different directions that personal development ideally takes in different groups (e.g., the importance of taking willful control of one's life in Recovery, Inc., versus acquiring the serenity to accept what one cannot change in AA). Those in groups such as Al-Anon often emphasize how members can come from all walks of life, all socioeconomic and educational backgrounds, and so on, yet within the group they still experience a strong sense of equality and mutual understanding. Moos would explain this by suggesting that the social climate defines the group experience and accounts for its effects, not the specific members as individuals.

Self-help and role theory. In terms of Sarbin's role theory, self-help groups help to structure the various ecologies surrounding the vulnerable individual. In the social ecology, a self-help group provides an egalitarian network of peer relationships that reduces isolation and helps to relieve the ambiguity and uncertainty imposed by the real world. Members of a self-help group also respect the individual and help him or her to gain self-respect. The group's ideology also provides a sense of meaningful integrity to the individual's transcendental needs. In cases where other group members provide material aid outside of group meetings, such as a place to stay, they enhance even the individual's self-maintenance ecology.

Generally speaking, membership in a self-help group provides important new roles for a person otherwise disqualified by some form of stigma. These roles sidestep the negative aspects of the individual's vulnerable condition and instead offer opportunities for responsibility and leadership that are flexible and open-ended in the degrees of involvement they require. Although these factors improve the individual's self-perceptions, the effects of this role enhancement on the public identities of self-help group members are unclear, because membership is usually a private (and often even anonymous) matter.

Self-help as social capital. Self-help groups serve as a common form of social capital at a community and societal level, where they provide a safety net for people not being adequately served by either their informal network or a costly and overburdened social and health-care services sector (Putnam, 2000). These groups also serve as ideal examples at the individual and organizational levels as they provide people in crisis an opportunity to *do* something constructive (participation), a sense of community (see above), a sense of personal and group efficacy or empowerment (Maton & Salem, 1995), and mutual assistance (neighboring). A study of a support group for parents of children affected directly or indirectly by HIV infection found that important themes in the success of the group included continued and increasing participation of members, empowerment, group cohesion, and mutual support (Melvin & Appleby, 1995). Each of these social capital factors helped members deal with the various complex changes and losses associated with the disease.

Self-help and the physical environment. Melvin and Appleby (1995) also found that provision of a safe and secure meeting place and a space and supervision for child care during meetings were essential to the success of the group. Location of meetings and available transportation to them are also important to the viability of any group. The larger connection to the physical environment is that the many citizen groups that have formed in response to contamination, as in Love Canal (chapters 3 and 13), or other environmental threats can be viewed as a form of self-help. Like other kinds of groups, they provide support and information in a time of stress and confusion. They tend to be suspicious of "experts" who use technical language and other professionals and are all about individual, group, and community empowerment (Rich et al., 1995).

Self-help groups as behavior settings. In Barker's conception of behavior settings, self-help groups are important community resources in the form of alternative settings the individual can use in structuring his or her time. That is, to a certain extent group meetings compete with other settings for the person's time, and the standing patterns of behavior they enforce (through the principle of behavior-environment congruence) are risk-reducing in their incompatibility with the maladaptive responses made previously. When a member first begins the AA program, he or she may attend meetings every night in the week, and sometimes during the day as well. The person lives out some portion of his or her life in a new setting.

As behavior settings, moreover, self-help groups instill the specific coping devices and other adaptive responses necessary to cope successfully with the core problem. Recall Barker's description of the person-environment circuits that define all settings. First, goal circuits represent the member's motivation to change (e.g., to stop drinking). The ritualistic procedures in meetings constitute the program circuits. These include confession ("Hi, my name is Jane and I'm an alcoholic"), catharsis ("Here's my story"), and acceptance (applause, handshakes, and hugs). Processes such as confrontation serve a corrective, "deviation-countering" function that may or may not be present in other settings in the person's life. The chronic nature of the problem situation provides multiple opportunities for learning, rehearsing, and generalizing the new behavioral responses required to improve the vulnerable individual's fit with key community settings.

Unless the individual's repertoire of responses is permanently changed, however, the recurring nature of most problems increases the chance of relapse into the old maladaptive ways. Clinical treatment, being expensive and thus short-term, often must be repeated, leading to the "revolving-door" syndrome whereby clients must frequently return for another round of care. Self-help groups, on the other hand, are stable, enduring communities—they are permanent fixtures in the community habitat. Thus, while maladaptation is chronic and recurrent, so are the meetings of self-help groups.

One limitation of self-help groups is that as settings they are bounded in time and space. The existence of a group on paper or in the telephone book does not mean it is actually available to everyone in need. Given the huge numbers of people at risk implied by the view of life as a soap opera, multiple-setting occasions may be needed weekly in many communities. In this connection, Zimmerman et al. (1991) illustrate how behavior-setting principles can be used to explain the successful proliferation of GROW groups among people with mental illness. Rather than waiting to start a new group when some existing group had grown too large, GROW organizers exploited contacts with professionals, educational workshops, and media publicity to establish fledgling groups well in advance of much demand from potential members. One result was that these new groups were very "underpopulated" as behavior settings (see chapter 5), and the resulting pressure on members to occupy more than one role (e.g., help-giver as well as help-receiver) increased the salience and importance of each individual member and helped to ensure members' commitment to the continuation of their group.

Are Self-Help Groups Effective?

It is difficult to evaluate the effectiveness of self-help. For the most part we rely on the testimonials of those who are members. Self-help groups are difficult to study because the membership tends to be shifting and because some self-help groups have little interest in cooperating with research on themselves. Members of self-help groups see themselves as there to help each other with similar problems, not to be research subjects. Leaders point to their personal growth and the growth of the movement as adequate evidence of their effectiveness. We rarely hear about the dropouts from self-help organizations or about their failures. Few if any substantial studies have researched comparable populations served by self-help groups and by professional helpers, so we cannot say one mode of treatment is more or less effective than another.

Given there are difficult methodological and field problems, a large number of uncontrolled studies have yielded positive results on a variety of criteria. Studies comparing professional help with self-help have generally found that self-help group members improve, and other than occasional studies finding that professional care was superior there is little difference between self-help outcomes and professional outcomes (Levine, Toro, & Perkins, 1993). Based on a review of the self-help evaluative literature, Kurtz (1990) concluded that "most involved members report greater life satisfaction, shorter hospital stays if rehospitalized, less dependence on professionals, raised self-esteem and improved attitudes [toward life]" (p.110). However, she notes that no one has clearly demonstrated using standardized instruments that self-help membership results in the removal of symptoms. She cautions professionals who refer clients not to expect too much of the group.

The GROW organization, which originated in Australia and uses a modified AA model, received an extensive evaluation when it was established in Illinois. Systematic studies by Rappaport, Seidman, Toro, and their colleagues and students find that the more a member attends GROW meetings, the more positive change the member shows. More-over, members who attend more frequently also develop more effec-tive coping strategies. Members who attended GROW meetings for at least nine months had a greater number of social relationships, more occupational success, and better mental health functioning than did those who attended for fewer months. Compared to a matched sam-ple of persons with similar psychiatric histories, GROW members were less likely to be rehospitalized. A similar evaluation of GROW has been done in Australia (Young, 1992), and studies of related groups like Re-covery, Inc., show comparable results (Galanter, 1988).

As with any heterogeneous group, however, people with mental illness present a diverse spectrum of needs, and any given group is un-likely to meet the needs of all members (Young & Williams, 1988). While GROW apparently helps those who participate, a dropout rate of about 25 percent after the first meeting indicates selection bias and suggests that a select group whose characteristics are not well under-stood may benefit the most (Levine, Toro, & Perkins, 1993). On the other hand, the dropout rate from self-help groups is probably not ter-ribly different than the dropout rate in psychotherapy.

Professional assistance and self-help. Self-help group members who have had experience with professional helping services frequently assert they get something different from the self-help group than from professional helpers (Videka-Sherman & Lieberman, 1985). For some that difference is striking. Some are willing to assert that professional assistance was no help at all and sometimes even made them feel guilty about having the problem for which they sought help. Others, how-ever, assert that they valued the opportunity to work problems through on an individual basis with professional assistance.

Many women who were in consciousness-raising groups were also in psychotherapy. Based on responses to a survey instrument, women in consciousness-raising groups were dissatisfied with their lives. On standardized scales of depression, anxiety and other psychological symptoms, they appeared more distressed than a control sample of women who were not in groups. However, they were less distressed than women in outpatient treatment (Videka-Sherman & Lieberman, 1985). Some with more distress who are in self-help groups may need professional assistance. Members of Recovery, Inc., who often take pre-scribed medication, are encouraged to respect their doctors' authority and to comply with professional advice.

We need not take a black-and-white view of the situation, seeing one form of help as all good and another as all bad or one as necessarily superior to the other. Ideally we should examine each form carefully to see what each can learn from the other about the therapeutic change process. Some professionals believe that the federal mandate to include patients and their families and representatives of self-help groups on the planning councils of mental health centers results in the professionals learning how to make their services more responsive to the needs of their clients (Segal, Silverman, & Temkin, 1993).

AA and Recovery From Alcoholism

Alcoholism is a devastating disorder affecting tens of millions of Americans (see chapter 1). The costs to society include expenditure for health care and the medical consequences of alcoholism ($18.8 billion), and over 100,000 deaths attributable to alcohol. In addition to the associated loss of lifetime earnings ($31.3 billion), experts estimate that lost productivity (work not performed, lost earnings, etc.) cost an additional $68 billion dollars. Alcohol is involved in many motor vehicle crashes. The costs are estimated to be $24.7 billion, not counting treatment for injuries. Alcohol is involved in many crimes. Costs of alcohol-related criminal activity, which include reduced earnings while in prison, criminal victimization (lost work, damaged property, and lifetime earnings of homicide victims), and the costs of the criminal justice system, amount to $19.7 billion. In 1995, an expert group estimated that alcohol abuse cost society $166.5 billion (Harwood, Fountain & Livermore, 1998).

The scope and severity of these problems make alcoholism a major challenge to all help-giving professions. Many professionals freely admit that in the area of alcoholism the effectiveness of their services leaves much to be desired. Perhaps as a result, AA groups are frequently welcomed into hospitals and prisons to recruit members. Although alcoholism is correctly perceived as a relatively intransigent problem, the probability of stable recovery following any given episode of alcoholism is apparently only minimally improved by formal treatment (Vaillant, 1995).

The vaillant study. Perhaps the best illustration of this phenomenon comes from the large-scale follow-up studies undertaken by Vaillant (1995). Vaillant's data comprised two large cohorts of initially normal males, one upper middle class (N 5 204) and one working class (N 5 456), each of which was followed prospectively from the late 1930s until 1980. Comprehensive and sophisticated measures were taken regarding the incidence of alcoholism and other behavioral characteristics in these samples, and the prospective longitudinal research design enabled Vaillant to untangle specific temporal sequences among many often-related events (for example, the frequent relationship breakups that occurred among alcoholic subjects were more often found to be a consequence of prior heavy drinking than its cause).

Conditions for change. Conditions found directly to precede stable recovery from alcoholism involved the following specific changes in lifestyle and/or circumstances: (1) development of a *substitute dependency,* such as candy, tranquilizers, heavy smoking, or compulsive work or hobbies; (2) new *constraints* on drinking, either external (e.g., close supervision from a spouse, employer, or judge), or internal (e.g., threats to health, use of Antabuse); (3) increased involvement in religion, or some analogous spiritual or ideological experience (such an experience typically helped the alcoholic replace feelings of defeat, worthlessness, helplessness, and guilt with renewed hope, self-esteem, and a powerful new belief system that enabled him to swear off his old maladaptive lifestyle for a new one); and (4) focused *social support,* often in the form of a new (or renewed) love relationship (e.g., with a spouse or other family member, or another recovering alcoholic).

Participation in AA. Many in Vaillant's samples changed their lives and recovered from alcoholism more or less on their own. Given the specific changes required, however, it is not surprising that the single most effective intervention for alcoholism was AA (see also Johnson, 1996). Although it is certainly no panacea, AA does embody all of the natural recovery processes to an extent no contemporary treatment program can. AA facilitates fundamental changes in the alcoholic's belief system, provides an unambiguous conception of the disorder (the disease theory) that is meaningful to him or her, and gives a sense of hope in the possibility of recovery. Thus the alcoholic's previous faith in alcohol as the most dependable source of gratification is turned into the "curse" of alcohol as the cause of all life's pain, and this new attitude is strongly enforced through adherence to total abstinence as the only acknowledged path to recovery.

Opportunity to identify. The fellowship and support provided by other AA members, both during the actual meetings and when needed at other times and places, are powerful reinforcers in the life of the isolated alcoholic and induce strong tendencies to affiliate and identify.

Identification is easier with other recovering alcoholics than with a professional therapist both because of the obvious similarities among those recovering from the same problem and because of the way psychotherapy is structured asymmetrically (i.e., so that personal disclosure and motivation to change flow only from client to therapist, while effective help and support are assumed to flow only from therapist to client). The social support provided by AA's more reversible roles is clearly expressed in this enthusiastic testimonial from one of Vaillant's upper-middle-class alcoholics:

> Most alcoholics, I believe, grow up in a glass isolation booth which they build for themselves to separate themselves from other people. . . . AA shows us how to dissolve the glass walls around us and realize that there are other people out there, good loving people. . . . I love the AA meetings and love being able to call people up when I feel tense. Occasionally, someone calls me for help and that makes me feel good. I get much more out of this than I got from decades of psychiatry. My relationship with a psychiatrist always seemed to be distressingly cold. I hated the huge bills. For $50 an hour, one doctor kept assuring me that I was nutty to worry about money, and at the time I couldn't keep up my life insurance. I wish there were some form of Alcoholics Anonymous for troubled people who don't drink. We old drunks are lucky. (p. 208, 1983 edition)

Ready availability. AA reaches an estimated 1,162,000 alcoholics in the United States, many more than all hospitals, clinics, and physicians combined (772,578 in all forms of treatment; U.S. Bureau of Census, 1997, Table 219). Over 50,000 AA groups exist in this country, and in a large city it would be rare not to find a group meeting at almost any hour on any day of the week, making AA much more accessible than formal treatment for alcoholism. This ready availability was important to those of Vaillant's subjects who were already flirting with sobriety for one reason or another (e.g., a health problem, love relationship) and who were able to take advantage of AA's accessibility to help cement the changes in behavior they were already trying to make.

Extended participation. Another important explanation for why AA is more effective than formal treatment is that the duration of participation in AA is generally much longer; it lasts months, years, or even a lifetime as opposed to a few weeks. For example, 53 percent of Al-Anon members have been in the program for more than five years, and 32 percent over 10 years (Al-Anon 1999; http://www.al-anon.org/surveyx.html). One consequence is that the whole meaning of one's relationship to AA is different; one "visits" a treatment clinic, and one "belongs" to AA. The lasting impact of AA's communally shared rituals, performed again and again over months or years of participation, is understandable from Barker's ecological conception, since in that view maintaining continuities in an individual's behavior over time is simply a matter of maintaining continuity in the specific settings he or she participates in. Although structuring one's time by frequent attendance at AA meetings may become a new "addiction" substituting for time previously spent with alcohol, the risks associated with active alcoholism presumably far outweigh those involved in addiction to AA.

Church as the model for AA. The very question of an addiction to AA reflects the assumptions of the medical model. Operating with the medical model, we feel we ought to be able to cure and discharge the client so that he or she can stand alone, without "crutches." These expectations partly reflect our concern about the cost of treatment and the value that should be returned. AA may reflect another model entirely. We would think it ludicrous if a patient remained in psychoanalysis for an entire adult lifetime, but we might think it admirable if another person remained a member of a church and participated in its activities for an adult lifetime. AA in its underlying model more resembles a church or a fraternal order than it does group therapy. Galanter (1990, 1999) characterizes AA as a charismatic healing group. He recognizes that while AA has features in common with charismatic religious sects, or even some cults, it is also differentiated from religious sects along a number of dimensions. AA members relate to the organization because of their common drinking problem. AA doesn't make demands on how a member should live his or her life, except to abstain from alcohol. AA's target is the drinking behavior of its members; it has no interest in proselytizing to transform the beliefs of others.

Low cost. We noted in chapter 4 that self-help groups recycle resources more efficiently than do professionally directed programs. Joining AA, for example, involves little cost. It is no burden on health insurance. The member makes voluntary donations and can go to a meeting for little more than coffee money and perhaps the occasional purchase of AA literature. The question of lifetime reliance on AA or enduring membership in other similar groups can only be examined in relation to the assumptions that led us to raise the questions in the first place. Are we concerned about lifelong membership because, under medical model assumptions, a healing technology should simply heal and then allow a person to get on with his or her life? If so, we may need to reexamine that assumption when viewed from a societal perspective.

These characteristics make AA a clear illustration of the ecological principle that interventions should take a form that can be maintained as a natural part of the community (see chapter 4). That is, AA begins with a natural resource, indigenous residents of the community, and defines their involvement as participation in a setting entailing nominal cost over an indefinite length of time. Although the most serious conditions of risk are episodic, the members' basic need for this setting is continuously present, and many in the vulnerable population thus recognize the value of maintaining a relationship with AA similar to the one with their church or fraternal society.

A Controlled Experiment

Al-Anon, an offshoot of AA, is a self-help group for spouses or other relatives of alcoholics who are not alcoholic themselves. Al-Anon operates much as AA does. Gillick (1977) conducted a controlled experiment in which wives of patients hospitalized for alcoholism at a VA hospital were randomly assigned to attend an Al-Anon group for six weeks or to do nothing different during that time. More than two-thirds of the spouses of alcoholics attended six or more Al-Anon meetings over the six-week period of the study. Gillick used the Community Adaptation Scale, a 217-item, self-administered measure that evaluates a person's community activities in a number of different spheres: work, family, personal, civic, commercial, professional services (see Roen & Burnes, 1968). Gillick used the scale because research on the wives of alcoholics had indicated that they were frequently socially isolated.

After six weeks the group that had attended Al-Anon meetings showed a number of changes compared to the control group. Spouses who attended Al-Anon reported better and more frequent interaction with family and friends, and an overall positive change in community adaptation. The control group showed deterioration on some of the scales over the same period. On post-test interviews, 14 of the 15 Al-Anon attenders rated the experience *very helpful* or *extremely helpful*, and all 15 were able to describe some benefit from attending meetings. Most often they expressed themselves in terms reflecting Al-Anon's ideology: "I liked the idea of living one day at a time and learning to let go." "It made me realize there is practically nothing I can do to stop his drinking once he starts." All but two of the 15 spouses said they planned to continue attending Al-Anon meetings. These short-term results are similar to those claimed for Al-Anon by its long-term members. This controlled experiment demonstrated systematic benefits from attending the groups beyond those resulting simply from the passage of time and treatment of the alcoholic spouse in the hospital.

Cooperation with professional services. Vaillant concludes that at present natural healing processes involved in recovery from alcoholism seem to be far more significant than what formal treatment can provide. About half of alcoholics do recover eventually, and the power of natural healing has long been used by physicians in the treatment of wounds and other conditions where zealous intervention can do more harm than good. Because apparently *no amount* of formal treatment increases the likelihood of permanent recovery from alcoholism beyond that contributed by natural healing, the most useful role for formal treatment at present is not to pursue increasingly intensive and costly services for a limited number of individual clients, but to facilitate the natural healing process in as many alcoholics as possible.

Vaillant's own program, for example, the Cambridge and Somerville Program for Alcohol Rehabilitation (CASPAR), is a comprehensive community-based system set up to lower the incidence and prevalence of alcohol problems by providing an array of medical services, support groups, halfway houses, and educational programs. In a typical year CASPAR receives 20,000 outpatient visits, conducts 2,500 detoxifications, and adds 1,000 new alcoholic clients to its rolls, all at a cost of only about $1 million (Vaillant, 1995). In keeping with the preceding conclusions, the primary long-term goal of CASPAR is to involve alcoholics with AA.

Reversing roles. A potentially important role for existing alcoholism treatment services thus exists if such efforts are applied as part of a comprehensive effort to reduce incidence and prevalence across the entire community. Gillick's study also showed that professionals can cooperate with self-help programs by making referrals and encouraging their clients to participate. Fifty-one percent of Al-Anon members were referred by professionals. Reasoning from the helper-therapy principle, Gartner and Reissman (1977) suggest that one way of overcoming the "numbers problem" in providing help (see chapter 1) is by finding ways to:

> transform recipients of help into new dispensers of help, thus reversing their roles, and to structure the situation so that recipients of help will be placed in roles requiring the giving of assistance. The helper-therapy principle operates, of course, in all kinds of peer help situations, in peer counseling in schools, children teaching children or mutual help groups. Therefore, all situations involving human service should be restructured to allow the principle to operate more fully. (p. 106)

Vaillant's research took place before the widespread use of other substances began to complicate treatment for alcoholism. In 1995, fully 46 percent of 1,008,626 clients in alcohol and drug abuse treatment units had both alcohol and substance abuse problems (U.S. Bureau of the Census, 1997, Table 219). How the existence of a dual diagnosis will complicate the effectiveness of all treatment modalities, including self-help, remains to be seen.

Starting Self-Help Groups

The issue of what relationship should exist between professionals and self-help groups has become an important focus of discussion.

Surprisingly, many self-help groups and certainly support groups of all kinds, are established with professional assistance. Self-help groups now provide information on their Web sites about how to start new self-help groups. Professionals work to create or maintain self-help as one reliable alternative for a particular group at risk. Each chapter of Parents Anonymous, for example, has its own professional sponsor to facilitate the group's functioning. Another option is for professionals simply to stimulate the formation of a group, thereafter leaving its operation largely or entirely in the hands of the members.

The active involvement of professionals can change the character of the group. Professionally led parent groups did not exhibit shared control with members, and used a medical model of service delivery. They engaged in little outreach for example (Cherniss & Cherniss, 1987). Toro et al. (1988) also reported that the group atmosphere was different under professional leadership when compared with member-led groups. Segal et al. (1993) believe that consumer-led groups and agencies enhance empowerment of the members, and help to overcome stigma. Professionally led agencies may inadvertently support a view that consumers are limited in their abilities to govern themselves. With the exception of AA, survival rates for groups formed with professional assistance are not necessarily higher than for independently established groups, but professionals seem to play an important part in establishing new groups (Leventhal, Maton, & Madara, 1988; Galanter, 1990).

Advocacy Groups

The National Alliance for the Mentally Ill (NAMI) was formed to support the families of people with mental illness and engage in political and social action to affect the mental health system (Levine, Toro, & Perkins, 1993). NAMI arose in response to the deinsitutionalization movement of the 1960s and 70s, which greatly increased the burden of care placed on the families of mentally ill people, and in response to the movement to have consumers on mental health center boards. Increased consumer and citizen involvement put people with common problems in touch with each other, and in 1979 NAMI was founded with 284 members. By 1989, it had 1,050 chapters in all states, with an overall membership of 130,000. In addition to providing mutual support, NAMI has been successful in advocating for better local services (crisis intervention, respite care), lobbying for Social Security Disability Income and insurance coverage for individuals with severe mental illness, and expanding legal grounds for the involuntary commitment of persons with mental illness. (The latter goal is not advocated by members of the patients' rights movement, which sees the mental health system as oppressive.)

NAMI has worked to reduce the cost of the drug Clozapine, a medication effective with some patients who do not respond to other treatment. NAMI is powerful politically and has influenced the approach to schizophrenia taken by the National Institute of Mental Health in its grant programs. In addition, it has its own research foundation that awards about $1 million per year for research in keeping with its biologically based view of mental illness. The group has also been active in combating the effects of stigma, and has worked actively to influence professional training and professionals' views of family members.

Professionals take no leadership positions in NAMI or in its local chapters unless they have mentally ill relatives. Professionals are involved as consultants or as members of professional advisory groups. The majority of members are relatives of those with mental illnesses, although some current or former patients are also active. Local chapters act as support groups for members, who may share common experiences or organize activities that assist members in coping. For example, some members who have been estranged from children suffering with a mental illness miss celebrating holidays such as Christmas with their children. A local NAMI chapter organized Christmas parties for children with disabilities or mental illness, and members participated by hosting parties and giving the children gifts, helping in some small way to make up for a void in their own lives.

Local groups, however, are also organized for grassroots advocacy, and attempt to influence state and local officials to improve services. Family members have diverging views from those of mental health officials about which services are most needed. NAMI members (93%) believed that community-based residences certified by the Office of Mental Health were the most desirable living arrangements. Only 21 percent of their mentally ill relatives were living in such a facility (Grosser & Vine, 1991).

Members also receive current scientific information about mental illness, medications, rehabilitation services, and alternative ways to understand severe mental illness. They also receive authoritative information about insurance practices. We have already described components of the NAMI ideology, and members absorb that ideology through meetings and literature.

Despite these successes, some limitations should be noted. NAMI's current membership consists primarily of white, upper-middle-class, well-educated parents of mentally ill adults. The organization is attempting to broaden its base, but it may be difficult to overcome social, economic, and cultural barriers. Sometimes the interests of members who have themselves been hospitalized with mental illness conflict with the interests of parents. A case in point is the organization's emphasis on making involuntary hospitalization less difficult. Parents who worry about their adult children living on the streets or decompensating want the system to be more responsive to their needs and perspectives, making it easier to hospitalize. The adult children themselves, the consumers who have had bad experiences with involuntary hospitalization prefer to retain due process safeguards that make it more difficult to commit people involuntarily and preserve consumers' right to request discharge from the hospital.

For another good example of the formation and evolution of an advocacy group, see Levine (1981) on the Love Canal Homeowners' Association and Gibbs (1998) for an insider's perspective on the LCHA and the Center for Health, Environment and Justice.

The Internet as a self-help resource. The Internet and the wide-spread availability of home computers will eventually affect our lives in unforeseeable ways. We already read about office workstations in the home, and "telecommuting." These developments will affect where we live as well as the way we live and work. Professionals, seeing the Internet as a new resource to enhance practice and to reach people free of the strictures of managed care are developing on-line therapy services. These services may include information about conditions, questionnaires to evaluate one's need for service, and the development of a plan to deal with the problem (Rabasca, 2000).

The self-help movement has taken to the Internet. Almost every large self-help group has a Web site with information about the group, the location and times of meetings, and information about how to start a new group. Some of the groups also sponsor e-mail lists, and chatrooms where members can communicate outside of meetings.

Gabriel (1995) described bulletin board "chat rooms" and multimedia sites where gay youth can communicate with each other. The Internet is a safe place to express one's concerns about coming out (publicly acknowledging one's homosexuality), a serious problem for gay youth (D'Augelli & Hershberger, 1993). One young man who came out on the Internet received 100 encouraging e-mail messages, some telling how they coped with the problem of telling their parents. He used these coping devices to finally come out to his mother. The Internet may be particularly important for people living in smaller places: "Does anyone else feel like you're the only gay guy on the planet, or at least in Arlington, Texas?" A 15-year-old gay living in Montana can communicate without revealing himself to those around who not only are unsympathetic but may reject him or worse. The Internet can also serve as a crisis hotline. One gay teenager logged onto a chat channel and revealed that he had been date raped, but was too fearful to tell his parents or the police. The distraught youth appeared to be on the verge of suicide, but an hour and a half later, he calmed down. He logged on the next day to say he was all right.

Some are concerned that the Internet may be used to influence youngsters to become gay, or as a vehicle for older gays to prey on younger ones. Current legislation designed to control obscene and pornographic communications on the Internet may have an effect on how the medium can be used. It also remains to be seen whether face-to-face contact is essential for the helping process.

Nonetheless, this new medium is just beginning. Chat rooms on the Internet inside and outside the context of self-help groups may offer people the opportunity to experiment with different identities. John Suler says: "The Web is a safe place to try out different roles, voices and identities. It's sort of like training wheels for the self you want to bring out in real life" (quoted in Murray, 2000, p. 17). Its revolutionary potential is great but psychologists are split on whether or under what conditions trying out new selves on the Internet can be helpful or harmful. Some are concerned that the Internet may not be enhancing interpersonal connections so much as creating greater social isolation. Moreover, the growing capacity to create "virtual environments" in which people can interact "face-to-face" may result in still greater changes in the future (Clay, 2000).

Should self-help research workers monitor and evaluate the psychological effects of participating on-line in intimate discussion or even in trying out new selves? Will research create new ethical problems of informed consent? People "lurk" (i.e., tune in but don't actively participate) on networks. Can research workers also "lurk" without telling others what they are doing? Obviously, this new medium will raise its own problems in the future, but its potential is also very exciting. Many years ago, Jacob Moreno who created psychodrama envisioned community psychodramas occurring on the stage in huge theaters with an audience of thousands. Perhaps the Internet and the communications revolution will bring his vision to fulfillment on a scale he never dreamed about.

Summary

Over roughly the same period of time that community psychology has existed, the number and use of self-help groups has increased tremendously. The many examples now in existence suggest that self-help groups serve a range of important needs. One advantage they have over professional care is that self-help groups are generally indigenous community resources offering help to vulnerable individuals at little or no cost.

We identified five types of self-help groups, each serving one or more of the following populations: (1) people whose social identities disqualify them from being normal because of a defect in conduct or physical appearance; (2) people who are related to or otherwise involved with those in the first group, and who themselves experience increased stress or a restricted range of available coping options; (3) people who are isolated by some social circumstance, such as divorce or widowhood; (4) individuals organized for mutual assistance along ethnic, racial, or religious lines; and (5) people organized on a more purely political basis who seek to preserve certain special interests.

From a conceptual vantage point, self-help groups provide a supportive, relationship-oriented social climate that reduces isolation and self-ostracization and promotes a better psychological sense of community. They also function as behavior settings that instill practical, tried-and-true coping techniques through repetitive rehearsal of ritualistic programs and procedures. New roles are provided, allowing members to achieve important opportunities and responsibilities, and all roles are reversible and interchangeable. Most interestingly, perhaps, self-help groups apply specific cognitive antidotes to members' problems, tailored precisely to the maladaptive thoughts making that particular condition of vulnerability so disruptive and distressing. Self-help groups are important and our increasing conceptual understanding of them may enable us to create self-help alternatives that do not yet exist.

Note

1. The 1987 edition of this book had a chapter on women's consciousness-raising groups of the 1970s. Because the material was dated, and in the interests of space, we eliminated that chapter and incorporated examples in this revised chapter on self-help. The interested reader should consult the earlier edition.

10

The Problem of Change

In the 1960s, mental health workers, social activists, lawyers, judges, administrators, social scientists, and others who attempted to introduce new programs or to foster change in existing service agencies often encountered system problems (Bennis, 1966). It became apparent very quickly that the "compulsive personality" of the bureaucrat and symptoms of anxiety in those faced with impending change were inadequate to account for problems or inspire solutions.

Having an insufficient grasp of system problems, we failed to appreciate the complexities of social organizations and lacked the conceptual tools needed to understand the problems, estimate the resources necessary for change, or comprehend the time scale of change. Despite problems, many efforts were productive and contributed to a theoretical and practical understanding of change (Zigler & Styfco, 2000). This chapter focuses on issues in introducing planned change.

Earlier chapters in this book have discussed numerous examples of planned attempts at community change, including Fairweather's lodges for persons with serious mental illness (chapter 5) and Head Start programs for disadvantaged preschool children (chapter 8). Another important example from the chapter on prevention was Rochester's Primary Mental Health Project (PMHP), led by Emory Cowen (Cowen, et al., 1996). In summarizing PMHP's early history, and with the benefit of a decade's experience, they were able to say:

> The preceding section is essentially an insider's clinical account of some of the vexing moment-to-moment problems and rooting difficulties associated with implementing a new program in new settings. How true it is, to quote Robbie Burns, that "The best laid schemes o' mice and men gang aft a-gley." Establishing a program is not just a matter of developing a good idea or a sound plan. (p. 97)

If everything is connected to everything else (the principle of interdependence), any attempt at planned change is necessarily influenced by the existing social context. Any social organization that endures has structures and means to ensure continuity despite environmental vicissitudes. The corporation, for example, has a life that exceeds the life of any human being involved with it. It continues to own property even after individual stockholders die. Its contracts bind it no matter who is the chief executive. It cannot be made to disappear easily.

The same structures and means that provide for the continuity of a social organization will also create resistance to change. In principle, the issues are no different when we consider a single agency or the "community" of agencies.

From an ecological perspective, problems of change that arise when a new program or organization is introduced into a community are similar to those that arise when attempts are made to change an existing organization. Change stimulates resistance, although resistance does not necessarily mean that change will be stopped. Anything new that survives will be changed itself by the context, and the context in turn will make some accommodations.

Although these principles seem self-evident now, it took us all a long time to learn them. Experiences in the 1960s and 1970s helped us to conceptualize the problem of change. We face similar problems when, for example, we wish to implement a successful prevention program into other settings (see chapter 8). Although the tasks of changing existing organizations and of creating new programs involve similar concepts, we will discuss them separately.

The Creation of New Settings

In a major creative contribution to the literature on social organizations, Sarason (1972) identified some core issues in the creation of settings. Claiming that more new settings had been created in the decade of the 1960s than in the entire previous history of the human race,[1] he noted that little thought was devoted to how settings are created. Thus, when new settings turned out to be little different from those they had replaced, participants often believed that it was the vision motivating the new setting that failed. Sarason's work is dedicated to understanding and avoiding issues implicit in the saying, "The more things change, the more they remain the same."

Sarason (1972) defined a setting as "any instance in which two or more people come together in new relationships over a sustained period of time in order to achieve certain goals" (p. 1). His concepts are applicable to settings as diverse as marriage (probably the most frequent new setting) and revolution, or the creation of a new society. His central interest, however, is in the creation of new human service settings.

When two or more people agree on the need for a new setting different from the familiar ones, their agreement is based on verbal abstractions reflecting their experiences or their vision of the new setting. Agreement on abstract values and strong motivation to succeed are insufficient to guarantee agreement on specific actions that express the abstract values; differences cannot be completely avoided. Sarason describes a common fantasy of participants that a point will be reached when all major goals are accomplished and all conflicts are resolved. This fantasy interferes with coming to terms with the reality that problems and conflicts will always arise.

Agreement on abstract values, strong motivation to succeed, and the fantasy of a problem-free future lead to the neglect of critical issues. Drawing on the experience of the U. S. Constitutional Convention of 1787, he argues that setting creation requires explicit rules by which participants agree to be governed. Some means to resolve the inevitable problems are necessary. If the expectation is that problems will inevitably arise, then settings need to include problem-sensing and problem-resolving devices.

The concept of a universe of alternatives—the recognition that for any problem there is always a range of potential solutions—implies an openness and a social climate conducive to the generation of potential solutions, some of which challenge assumptions that are so much a part of us that we rarely question them. The aim is not to question for its own sake, but to allow for the generation of solutions appropriate to the new setting and its context.

Contexts include history; Sarason calls this "the before the beginning" (1972, chap. 2). Settings are not created in vacuums. Something goes on before the creation of the setting. Because inevitably the pool of resources is always limited, new settings are always in competition with existing settings for shares of that limited pool. There is frequently ideological competition. The very creation of the new contains an implicit criticism of the old. Creators of new settings often say explicitly that existing settings are not performing well and that a new setting will perform better. Competition for resources and the ideological critique guarantee if not active conflict with existing settings, then a disinclination on the part of existing agencies to be helpful or supportive of the new (see Graziano, 1969, 1974).

By taking into account the mutual interests of the major players and by recognizing a problem that affects all, it is possible to develop a setting with mutual cooperation and without rancor. Erie County, New York, recently developed a "one-stop shopping" advocacy center for sexually abused children and their parents. The center uses mental health workers, medical personnel, child protective services workers, and representatives from the police and prosecutor's offices. Recognizing a mutual interest in serving children and their families, all the departments worked to design a center to meet their needs as well as those of the families. The project emerged out of an experience where major actors identified beforehand the problems the advocacy center was meant to solve. In that sense, the project's designers "confronted history."

In creating a setting, it is always necessary to confront history. The new setting always develops in a preexisting context of structured relationships that include histories and visions of the future that must be understood and taken into account. Given this history of structured relationships, setting creators have to consider how the context may move the new setting away from the values or concepts the setting creators intended to implement.

Sarason focuses carefully on the setting leader in the beginning context, but not on the leader's personality. The creation-of-settings game is so structured that while leaders may deal with the issues differently, all will confront the same dilemmas; for example, the pressure to open the setting according to a timetable while still establishing and negotiating relationships with other leaders and subordinates may result in compromises and undesired changes in the new setting.

Sarason analogizes joining a new setting to entering a relationship based on romantic love. The leader puts the best face on the new venture in order to attract the most desirable people. A new person, often leaving a disappointing situation, is prepared to see only the beauty and to overlook the warts. As Sarason (1972) says, "Time and again I have observed the leader and his core group enter into what is to be an enduring relationship grounded in (if not suffused with) enthusiasm, good will and a problem-free view of their future relationships" (p. 76).

The issues that inevitably lead to differences are predictable. Academics are expected to publish, for example, and all of the differences that can emerge in such a situation—authorship order, share of royalties, ownership of the data, and responsibility for writing and interpreting data—are guaranteed to crop up. Goodwill cannot supplant explicit understandings when active conflict occurs (Fairweather & Tornatzky, 1977).

Predictable problems also occur between the leader and the members of the core group and among members of the core group, as their relationships to the total enterprise differentiate and as members' relationships to the leader change. Such problems are rarely anticipated or discussed, partly because of the tendency for the relationship to begin in an atmosphere of romantic love and partly because we do not have theoretical conceptions that warn us to confront problems before they arise.

Sarason (1972) challenges a core assumption when he asks: "For whom does a setting exist?" He is not satisfied with the obvious answer—that it exists to serve its clients. A service setting should be concerned with its clients' welfare and with "the professional and personal growth and change of its members, and the ways in which their mutuality can enhance this growth and change" (p. 86). He says that clients are better served when the setting provides for the personal development of all its members, including its staff, because burnout and these other consequences may be averted:

> rigidity in function, insularity from changes in the larger society, increased competitiveness for resources within and among settings, decreasing satisfaction in work with a concomitant increase in the need for professional status and money, and the steady loss of the sense of community within the setting. (1972, pp. 124–125)

For Sarason (1974), maintaining the psychological sense of community among staff has a high priority.

At some point, leaders and others become aware that resources are not unlimited. How should the leader convey the limitation on resources to others? Will core group members compete for resources to promote the growth of their departments? Competition for resources will bring out differences in values as each subgroup justifies its call on resources and its version of how things should be done. The choices when allocating resources, including personnel, are critical; values are illuminated in the choices and in their consequences. Bypassing value questions helps to defeat the purposes of a setting.

Sarason (1972) summarizes the dilemmas of the leadership position:

> Whereas at the beginning he could dream, savor possibilities, indulge the joys of new-found status and power, and see the future as cloudless, he now knows that he has become (or must become) a "realist," that he has become *dependent* on those whom he has attracted, that the surrounding world tends to be indifferent or demanding, or hostile to his setting, that the problems of today and tomorrow crowd out the future, that there are no isolated problems but rather that everything is potentially related to everything else, and that there is in him a tension between what is and what may be and between his needs and ideas and those of others. (pp. 214–215)

Hargrove and Glidewell (1990) present narratives of administrators in public human service agencies that reflect many of the issues Sarason discusses. Many of Sarason's criteria for the success or failure of alternative settings—such as the influence of the larger social and historical context, the role of leadership, and anticipation of, and planning for predictable problems of new settings—have been confirmed by Cherniss and Deegan (2000).

Sarason's ideas are complex, subtle, and not easy to summarize. He analyzes commonly recurring dilemmas and the dynamics of creating settings. Such issues will be faced by anyone involved in creating settings, a task he views as having more kinship with the work of an artist than with that of an engineer. The issues can be sketched but not blueprinted. His concepts are useful; the dilemmas they address are recognizable and replicable because of the common structure of the problem of creating a new setting. Goldenberg's (1971) book *Build Me a Mountain* described the Residential Youth Center (RYC), a setting created by following Sarason's concepts.

Box 10–1. The Residential Youth Center (RYC)

Ira Goldenberg was a member of the Yale Psychoeducational Clinic (Sarason, Levine, Goldenberg, Cherlin, & Bennett, 1966), an organization whose activities under Sarason's leadership generated some of the firsthand experiences for Sarason's ideas. Goldenberg was a consultant to the work crew foremen and forewomen of New Haven's pioneer anti-poverty agency, Community Progress, Inc. (CPI).

Work crews had been in existence for about two years when the federal government announced the Job Corps program, and CPI workers selected urban young people for vocational and educational training in rural Job Corps camps. Many of the New Haven Job Corps participants maintained contact with their work crew forepersons. After a few months, Goldenberg and a group of forepersons visited their former charges at a Job Corps camp. Disappointed by what they observed, they returned to New Haven with the thought that if they had had the opportunity to set up a Job Corps program, they would have done it better.

The relationship of their new venture to CPI, the successful anti-poverty program that had sponsored the work crews, added credibility. Goldenberg's proposal for an urban Job Corps received a hostile reception from Job Corps officials who saw it as an ideological competitor and a criticism of their program. He received funding from the Labor Department.

Other aspects of the "before the beginning" had to be confronted. Once the program was funded, the RYC core group engaged in a two-month planning process. They wanted to find a building suitable for a residence for the participants. CPI officials, then in the process of expanding, were thinking of leasing a large office building. To help cover leasing costs, they wanted RYC to remodel several floors of the office building. RYC planners wanted a more homelike setting in a real neighborhood. Fortunately CPI's demand was dropped, but it provides an example of prehistory affecting a developing program.

Additional prehistory problems emerged. The funding agency, eager to see results, wanted Goldenberg to open quickly before the completion of planning, training, and other preparations. Although he was able to resist, the process did move more quickly. Goldenberg also described problems in relating to existing agencies. The local community mental health center was willing to accept referrals, but would not accommodate its services to the RYC clients' cultural characteristics (e.g., the lower importance they placed on punctuality in keeping appointments). Although the mental health center was located at the edge of New Haven's African American ghetto, the psychological distance between the center and the RYC participants was great. Goldenberg also wanted an understanding with the local police. The police were interested in the program, but because many of the participants had had run-ins with the law, a police official proposed placing an undercover agent on the staff or among the residents. Goldenberg declined the offer. Sarason's "before the beginning" phase is richly illustrated by these experiences. The new setting opened in a context that may have shaped it in directions not envisioned or desired by the setting's planners.

To enhance the sense of community (see Sarason, 1974), Goldenberg proposed a horizontal organizational structure instead of the more familiar pyramidal one (see Riggio, 1990). The horizontal structure and a matrix organization that diffused responsibility also provided the staff the opportunities to develop themselves using skills important to them, no matter their job description, thus providing them with a great deal of satisfaction, as matrix organizations usually do (Riggio, 1990).

To provide for internal self-reflection, self-correction, and an open atmosphere, the core group initiated "sensitivity training" during the planning phase. It also conducted regular group sensitivity sessions in which any staff member was free to bring up any problem concerning the group, specific individuals, or the RYC. Special sensitivity sessions, scheduled at six-month intervals to review where RYC had been and where it was going, were used to work through periodic "crises." These practices resemble the "Quality Circle" model adopted by some American industries based on practices observed in Japanese factories (Riggio, 1990; see "Organizational Change" below) and the mutual criticism of a nineteenth-century religious commune (Levine & Bunker, 1975). The open atmosphere also helped to reduce the leader's isolation.

The ethos of participation extended to the center's young people. A house council had responsibility for generating house rules and recreational, educational, and community service programs. The furnishings were built by residents in a woodworking class under the direction of a work crew foreperson. Residents' family members, using materials and instructions provided by the RYC, sewed curtains and other decorations. Some rooms in the house would not pass muster in most public institutions. One room (including the ceiling) was painted in a high gloss black with a collage of *Playboy* centerfolds covering most of the ceiling. The room was striking in appearance and reflected its occupant's individuality.

The first residents were recruited from among the most difficult adolescents served in CPI's neighborhood outreach centers. The six-month evaluation revealed considerable success in helping residents to maintain employment and educational placements, change their attitudes, and reduce their contact with the police. Because RYC residents and controls were not assigned at random—the most difficult were selected for treatment—the improved outcomes over time are subject to the technical criticism of regression to the mean. That is, because the worst were selected, there was no place for them to go but up. In addition, no long-term follow-up was ever reported so it is impossible to determine the program's long-term effectiveness.

Change in Existing Settings

Pressman and Wildavsky (1984) note that if a change requires positive action by 10 independent actors, the a priori probability that everything will go right and the change be implemented is $1/2^{10}$, or one chance in 1,024! Not much can be left to chance, but how can we think about this problem?

Systems Theory

Open-systems theory can be applied to the analysis of change in human service organizations (Kelly, Ryan, Altman, & Stelzner, 2000). Human service organizations may be viewed as open systems engaging in resource exchanges with their environments. A psychiatric center receives public funds, takes in people in need, helps to solve a community problem, and presumably returns productive citizens to the community. An open system retains some of the resources it receives for its maintenance and growth. Systems that are highly reactive to variations in the exchange process may direct a considerable portion of their resources toward enhancing the exchange. Publicly supported human service organizations obtain resources only indirectly from exchanges, however, and therefore they have greater potential for converting resources to the organization's benefit—that is, to use resources to enhance working conditions and rewards for employees rather than to benefit patients. For example, staff members in a specialized child protection team spent 40 percent of their time in paperwork, 29 percent in consultation with colleagues, 20 percent in consultation with other agency staff, and only 11 percent with families (Crittenden, 1992). Ideally there should be no conflict; in practice there is tension between an organization's needs and those of the people it serves. Organizations may not respond readily to the environment because resources do not depend on a direct exchange.

An open system is dependent on its environment for a number of factors: (1) the acquisition of "materials" (e.g., clients); (2) capital (annual program and capital budget allocations); (3) production factors (e.g., services technology, trained employees); (4) labor (e.g., hiring of sufficient personnel with adequate skills, education, or aptitude); (5) output disposal (release of clients back to a receptive community). The terminology, although useful, is geared to industrial production and inexact when applied to human service organizations.

Open systems respond to "turbulence," by which system theorists mean a change in the relationship between the organization and one or more of the factors on which it depends. Fairweather et al. (1974) noted that little change occurs in mental hospitals without some form of outside intervention. If the turbulence is created by some other agency to which an organization is linked and on whom it is highly dependent (e.g., a legislature that controls its funds), the organization must adapt to the turbulence.

In today's mental health world, turbulence arises from the demands of advocacy groups, from the media, or from a legislator with a special agenda. Sometimes the demand for change comes from a lawsuit against an institution for violating patient rights (Miller & Iscoe, 1990). The adaptation may be positive in that the organization changes to meet the new demand, or it may freeze and fail to adapt. Whether an organization adapts or freezes in relation to environmental turbulence is in turn a function of other variables such as available resources, knowledge, and leadership.

First- and Second-Order Change

Watzlawick, Weakland, and Fisch (1974) note two general classes of change. In one, called first-order change, only a portion of the system (e.g., personnel, clients, or tools) is affected; most of the system remains intact. Second-order change is change in the system itself—that is, in the relationships among the component parts and sometimes a change in the basic goals, structure, or processes of the institution. A simple example of first-order change would be to add something new without taking anything else away, although adding on still entails complications. For example, an additional faculty member requires office and laboratory space and adds to the demand for services and supplies. It is also possible to effect change by stopping a program entirely by eliminating its budget. Taking away something may seem straightforward, but the changes can have serious ramifications. Michigan eliminated its general assistance (welfare) program, saving money, but the change affected former recipients of the aid who were forced to double up in housing, use shelters, or live on the streets when they lost rent money.

Second-order change requiring reorganization or reallocation of resources or functions is more complicated. If any social organization is to continue, it must have structures that ensure its continuity despite environmental vicissitudes. Structures that provide for organizational continuity also create resistance to change.

Change from "welfare" to "workfare" is simple in concept but very complex in implementation (Lynn, 1990). The designers of workfare intended radical change in the welfare system. The changes succeeded to the extent that the number of welfare recipients has declined sharply. However, the full effect, both positive (increased self-esteem due to loss of stigma) and negative (e.g., inability to support children with increased neglect and placement out of the home) is yet to be assessed.

Simple change, even for an ostensibly good purpose, can provoke unexpected and sometimes powerful resistance. Proposals to exchange dirty needles for clean ones have been controversial. Data supporting the effectiveness of needle exchanges in curbing the spread of AIDS and hepatitis did not settle the moral and political conflict about taking public actions that seemed to approve drug use (Lawlor, 1990; Anderson, 1991).

Organizational Change, Development, and Learning

Change occurs at different levels, from building skills in individuals to prevent problems from occurring or worsening (chapter 8) and forming supportive self-help groups (chapter 9) to engaging in community and societal-level change efforts (chapters 12 and 11, respectively). The present chapter concentrates mainly on organizational, institutional, and setting-level interventions. Most of the theory and action strategies for organizational change come from other areas of psychology (e.g., industrial and organizational) and from outside of psychology (e.g., business management and public administration). Much of it is based more on the practical experience of organizational consultants and managers than on scientific research. Yet there are valuable ideas in this literature for community psychologists about how to effect changes in any kind of organization, not just large corporations, and in the people who work in, or are affected by them (Shinn & Perkins, 2000).

Job stress. Work has always been stressful, but in recent decades community and organizational psychologists and other researchers have studied sources of, and solutions to, job and workplace stress and "burnout" (see chapters 3 and 7; Cherniss, 1980; Shinn, Rosario, Mørch, & Chestnut, 1984). Risk factors for job-related stress include risky occupations, such as law enforcement, the "glass ceiling" and other forms of job discrimination or harassment, a competitive corporate culture, negative social climate, poor fit of employee skills and job, physical or chemical agents (e.g., "sick building syndrome"), new technology (e.g., repetitive motion syndrome, carpal tunnel syndrome, working all day on a computer), social and economic change (e.g., layoffs), and corporate restructuring.

The effects of job stress on workers and their families include psychological disorders (e.g., depression and anxiety), post-traumatic stress and cumulative strain, dysfunctional relations with family and friends, violence, and a host of health problems, including substance abuse/chemical dependency, cardiovascular disease, and immune system problems. The effects of job stress on the organization include higher absenteeism, turnover, health care costs, worker compensation, and lower productivity.

Programs for preventing or reducing job-related stress include job redesign, occupational safety and health programs, stress management, health and fitness promotion, employee assistance programs (EAPs), management/employee training, family leave, work team support, and flexible work hours (Shinn, Wong, Simko, & Ortiz-Torres, 1989).

Many of the problems in human service organizations stem from the fact that their structure is typically based on the large-scale, bureaucratic corporations. The advent of industrialized mass production had several negative effects on the workplace and the quality of work life (and the same things occurred in service organizations; Toch & Grant, 1982). As Upton Sinclair and other reformers revealed, working conditions were often deplorably unhealthy, inhumane, and depressing. The emphasis on bottom-line productivity and efficiency led to greater regimentation and authoritarianism and so workers' needs and concerns were ignored, ironically even on issues of production. As external rewards—wages and benefits—replaced internal rewards of pride in workmanship, the intrinsic motivation for work—its meaning and creativity—was lost, which led to widespread alienation and burnout. A caste system of different jobs and levels having very different prestige and power made workers even more cynical. In the human services especially, peer protection codes are based on principles of social support, but are so anti-management, anti-evaluation, and anti-outsiders that they create "pluralistic ignorance" and a custodial subculture.

Organization Development (OD) is a profession and field of action-research that was created to deal with these kinds of problems. There are many types of OD interventions, including adult education workshops, organizational consultation (analysis and recommendations regarding organization processes), mediation between conflicting parties, data (e.g., survey-guided) feedback, and problem identification, diagnosis, and solution generation and implementation, based on Kurt Lewin's theory of "action research."

OD has been used in both the public and private sector for facilitating change in people (e.g., work styles, values, skills) and in organizational cultures, processes, and structures (Burke, 1994). It emphasizes workers' morale, satisfaction, participation, and, especially, work climate. Some OD approaches focus on decreasing layers of supervision in the organizational chart and pushing decision making lower in the hierarchy ("participatory workplace democracy"), but they rarely involve grassroots organizing (e.g., union contract negotiation) or true worker empowerment (see below), let alone result in second-order change in the basic goals, structure, or processes of the organization in any major or lasting way.

Instead, OD generally focuses on "job enrichment," or improving communication and the social and psychological aspects of work. An enriched job is one that offers (1) adequate psychological as well as physical space (i.e., supervisors not breathing down your neck), (2) opportunities for meaningful feedback (it is also possible to get too much space and too little supervision), (3) opportunities to learn on the job and be challenged, (4) not too much and not too little variety, (5) help and respect from fellow workers, (6) a sense that one's own work is meaningful and contributes to one's community (sense of mission), (7) a desirable future with new possibilities (not "dead end"), (8) a sense that the job uses the abilities that the worker has to offer, (9) a sense of control over goal setting and over the paths to reach those goals (sense of ownership), (10) respect for oneself and one's coworkers, (11) important new knowledge and lines of communication, and (12) group support for solving problems (Toch & Grant, 1982).

Even these nonstructural changes would be no small feat in most organizations, however. Walton (1977) identified seven common problems that limit the success of innovative programs in organizations. These include (1) inconsistencies in the initial design that lead to confusion about the key elements of the project, (2) loss of management support, (3) premature turnover of leaders or consultants directly associated with the project, (4) stress and crisis in the firm that lead to more authoritarian management, (5) tension in the innovative unit's relations with other groups in the firm (e.g., staff in other units, supervisors, labor unions), (6) excessive publicity about the innovative unit which leads to jealousy in other units and disappointment as the innovation turns out to be less effective than initially claimed, and (7) inadequate diffusion of the results to other parts of the organization, which isolates the original experiment and its leaders.

According to Burke (1994), OD requires that the organization respond to an actual and perceived need for change on the part of the client, involve the client in the planning and implementation of the change, and lead to change in the organization's culture. Organizational "culture" refers to the unique rules of behavior to which members must conform, how authority exercises power, prevailing values, rewards and how they are dispensed, and communication patterns. Echoing Walton's seven organizational problems, Burke (1994) summarizes these seven characteristics of innovative and effective organizations—they (1) are less hierarchical in structure and "network" more to get work done and to communicate, (2) involve organizational members in decisions they are expected to implement, (3) are more people-oriented, (4) are flexible in how work is done, allowing as much autonomy as possible, (5) actively encourage innovation by all members, (6) facilitate information flow both inside and outside of the organization, and (7) provide development opportunities and activities for members.

Organizational empowerment (see chapter 5). Accomplishing most OD goals requires enhancing control and decision-making authority of staff, volunteers, and clients, and thus involves empowerment (Klein, Hamilton, McCaffrey, & Stecher, 2000). Maton and Salem (1995) analyzed a religious fellowship, a mutual help organization for persons with mental illness, and an education program for urban African Americans. They identified four key empowering organizational characteristics of each setting: (1) motivating and challenging positive group belief systems, (2) meaningful opportunity role structures which capitalize on members' different strengths, (3) an array of economic and social supports, and (4) organizationally and interpersonally talented leaders. Second-order (structurally transformative) change may be impossible without effective empowerment strategies at *both* the individual and organizational levels (Zimmerman, 2000). By the same token, community-level change requires empowerment at the individual, organizational, and community levels (see chapter 12; Speer, Hughey, Gensheimer, & Adams-Leavitt, 1995).

Learning organizations. Organizations develop through stages just as humans do and in both cases, learning is key to development. If organizations are only as effective as the human capital (skills, knowledge) they contain and how that capital is used, the challenge becomes how to restructure learning and decision-making opportunities to lead to transformative, second-order change. The idea of learning organizations derives from the fields of organizational behavior and organizational development and has been the basis for interventions that have been shown to positively affect group and organizational communication, culture, job satisfaction, and performance (Argyris, 1993). A "learning organization" helps staff and volunteers engage in critical analysis of (1) the organization's demonstrated goals and values (not just its mission statement), (2) the power relationships implicit in decision-making practices, (3) the interdependent role of participant stakeholders and organizations as part of a complex, community-wide (or larger) system, and (4) how to work toward fundamental change of all the above. According to Marsick, Bitterman, & van der Veen (2000), among other characteristics, learning organizations include an emphasis on knowledge generation and sharing, systems thinking, greater participation and accountability by a larger percentage of employees, and a culture and structure of rapid communication and learning. Marsick identifies several core learning organization practices: creating continuous learning opportunities, promoting inquiry and dialogue, encouraging collaboration and team learning, creating systems to capture and share learning, including feedback loops across the system, empowering people toward a collective vision, connecting the organization to its environment, and providing strategic leadership for learning. In sum, organizational learning is enhanced through opportunities for critical reflection, team work collaboration, and fast and effective communication.

Youth organizations (see also Box 10–1).[2] Schools and other organizations that work with and serve young people can become more effective contexts for learning and development by making intentional efforts to become learning organizations (Evans & Bess, 2003). In addition, those that include young people in organizational planning and development may enhance both the learning in the organization and its overall effectiveness. Youth organizations do not always facilitate critical reflection, open communication, or team learning. For many reasons (funding, quality of leadership, staff turnover), these organizations are wading in the waters of lower stages of development, unable to reflect on their own processes. For youth organizations and schools to become models of learning organizations so as to better facilitate the development of young citizens, leaders and upper-level managers need help in their own personal and professional development. A dual focus on an organization's development and that of the leader may impact organizational culture, and ultimately the development of a learning organization. The development of adults who respect differences, value justice, fairness, and community, and take active roles in society requires that organizations where people spend their hours be contexts for learning and positive development. This can be especially important for the development of young people who unfortunately spend too much time in contexts that are not learning environments and where they are not valued as resources and contributors to the success of the organization. Paying attention to the culture of the systems that young people are in as well as the quality of leadership in those systems may help them develop the skills and character of young citizens.

Production and Satisfaction Goals

Change goals may be classified into two types—production and satisfaction. Production goals are related to the manifest purpose of the setting. Achievement test scores, arrest and conviction rates, recidivist rates, patients released from a hospital, or doctoral students graduated from a Ph.D. program are all examples of items of production. In systems theory, items of production are exchanged for resources, but in human service organizations the relationship between items of production and resources is not clear-cut. Administrators have attempted to sharpen this relationship by tying budgets to units of production through contractual arrangements that call for so many client contact hours, or for so many patients discharged from a hospital within a given period of time.[3]

Employees, clients, and other actors exchanging with a human service organization all have satisfaction goals. The satisfaction of members of one group is not necessarily positively correlated with the satisfaction of members of other groups. Production measures and satisfaction measures tend to be orthogonal. It is possible to envision every combination of production achievement and satisfaction level. Workers may be very productive, turning out many items, and still be dissatisfied. They work too hard, are underpaid, or other working conditions are inadequate. A mental hospital may increase "production" by reducing its census, but if the patients still need assistance when discharged to the community, the work has simply been shifted elsewhere. Thus the achievement of a production goal, halving the population of state mental hospitals, was not greeted with universal acclaim.

Satisfaction goals are more important than we usually acknowledge. Some policies persist even where there is evidence that the policy is harmful. Despite 70 or more years of research showing that it does no good and may do harm to leave children back in school (Levine & Graziano, 1972), from time to time educators back a get-tough nonpromotion policy. Social promotion solutions are unsatisfying to teachers and some citizens who believe that children will not work unless threatened with nonpromotion. Proposals for retaining children in grade rarely include any program for educating them differently to avoid the failure that occurred the first time. They contain no means for dealing with the blow to self-esteem and the stigma of being retained in grade.

Creating the perception that a program is doing good things is a variant of satisfaction. Cowen et al. (1975) pointed out that a decision to allocate funds is not determined by scientific evidence of a program's effectiveness, but by the satisfaction of constituencies willing to lobby for it. The satisfied audiences can vary; for a state welfare commissioner, it might be the state's governor or a powerful state legislator (Lynn, 1990).

The Social Context of Change

A program targeted for change always functions in a social context defined by the sets of positions and roles within the organization and by the institutions and constituencies (e.g., parents of schoolchildren) making up the external environment (Sarason, 1996). These groups are sometimes called "stakeholders." A change may require modification of the relationships among members or groups within the human-service agency, and among and between members of external groups.

Members of role groups stand to gain or to lose when a change is proposed or implemented. Potential losers will oppose change, either actively or passively, but they may not have the power to defeat or to retard the change significantly. Potential gainers will support the change.

The set of interests can be categorized in different ways and with many subclassifications. For the sake of exposition, we reduce the sets of interests to seven:

1. Energy (money, work time, amount of work).
2. Power (including status or influence).
3. Culture (beliefs, norms, values).
4. Competence (ability and satisfaction in carrying out work tasks).
5. Relationships (generally, satisfactions in social interaction deriving from work relationships).

6. Legal and administrative considerations.

7. Information and communication (knowing what's going on).

We will illustrate each of these dimensions before looking at case studies of change in human-service organizations.

1. *Energy.* Workers expend characteristic levels of energy on the job. The amounts of work, time, money, and other benefits are interrelated variables. If a program change requires increased hours or energy output, and there is neither a compensating increase in money or other benefits nor a decrease in hours, employees will oppose change. The New York City More Effective Schools program was vigorously supported by the teachers union in part because it provided additional free periods for teachers and teacher aides to assist with classroom work, despite evidence that the expensive program had not improved pupil academic achievement (Levine & Graziano, 1972). Researchers have taken budgeted funds to pay teachers for their time after teachers resisted participating in uncompensated research.

There is an optimal range for the amount of work someone does; changes that require either a marked increase or a marked decrease in work will elicit resistance. A change that removes most functions from a position, even though the person continued to receive full pay, will prove distressing. Most people like to feel they are earning their money. Some may not work hard, or may take extended coffee or rest room breaks, but the illusion of working is maintained. If a person doesn't have enough work the feeling of being a worthwhile member of society is undermined.

2. *Power.* Power is the ability to issue and enforce a command concerning the use of resources. Power is exercised in the control of resources (physical space, materials, supplies), personnel (hire, fire, promote, or determine duties), or territory (e.g., admission to an institution). Power is generally correlated with status in a social organization, and with the expectation of receiving respect or deference from those of lower status. Role incumbents relate to programs and to each other through the exercise of power. An incumbent whose power is increased by a given change will favor that change, while one whose power is decreased will oppose it.

Powerlessness and efforts to overcome feelings of helplessness and alienation through the sharing of power and the problems of accommodating to power are well documented (Moynihan, 1969). Power struggles and problems stemming from the fragmentation of local, state, federal, and private sector agencies resulted in delays and difficulties in implementing the Community Mental Health Centers Act (Levine, 1981). Crittenden (1992) describes similar phenomena after a specialized child protection team changed its practices in ways that affected other agencies, the courts, and its funding agency.

Jacobs (1980) notes that prison guards felt they lost power when courts allowed inmates to bring suits against prisons. Similarly, hospital personnel lose power to patients when courts recognize a patient's right to refuse treatment. Increasing power for some actors has salutary effects in the change process. Goldenberg's RYC program substantially increased the power of line workers, resulting in great support for the program by employees. In some hospital wards, a similar process occurred when a ward changed to a therapeutic community with shared power and greater role diffusion (activities shared by those in different roles) (Colarelli & Siegel, 1966).

3. *Culture*. The term "culture" is a convenient shorthand for the set of beliefs, ideologies, values, and norms characteristic of a given group. These concepts imply behavior in social relationships. There are rewards for meeting social expectations and sanctions for failing to meet them. Belief systems or ideologies are especially important in institutional change (see Crittenden, 1992).

A change may challenge ideologies. Court orders for change supporting prisoners' rights changed good-guy/bad-guy roles within prisons; whereas guards had thought of themselves as performing a necessary and valuable service, the courts were saying, in the eyes of the guards, that they were oppressors preventing inmates from exercising legitimate constitutional rights (Jacobs, 1980). The *O'Connor* v. *Donaldson* (1975) decision implied that psychiatrists who retain patients who are psychiatrically "sick" but whose behavior does not meet legal standards of dangerousness, are not engaging in good psychiatric practice but violating patient rights. Miller and Iscoe (1990) also observed that employees of mental hospitals were distressed by court findings in lawsuits against institutions that the employees had not cared sufficiently well for their patients.

Strong commitments to forms of practice (norms) stem from training, cultural conditioning, direct experience, and the need to believe that what is done is right and good. We can appreciate the reaction of physicians told by Semmelweiss that they carried germs on their hands, causing the deaths of mothers whose deliveries they had attended. Can we be less sympathetic with the schoolteacher's reaction of rage to Kozol's (1985) accusations in *Death at an Early Age*, or to mental health workers decrying the destructiveness of Rosenhan's (1973) demonstration that admitting personnel cannot detect pseudopatients? Psychotherapists, told by critics (e.g., Dawes, 1994) that they do little good, charge high fees, accept for treatment easy, middle-class clients, and could be replaced with paraprofessionals who can do whatever it is they do with a few weeks of training, cannot be expected to react to such propositions by thanking the critic for providing enlightenment. When a practice to which an individual has a deep commitment is challenged, one cannot expect that individual to say gratefully, "Thank you very much for telling me I have been destroying my clients all these years. I never thought about it that way before and I am now ready to do everything you say."

Not all resistance is irrational by any means. Sometimes there may be good and sufficient reason to maintain incumbents' views of what their role and professional status require. We have to understand what the demand for change means in their contexts and from their perspectives.

All groups relating to a program have beliefs or theories that are as powerful for those who hold them as mental health theories are for the mental health worker. The concepts always reflect the data incompletely, but they often have empirical referents, just as there are some empirical referents for concepts held by professional mental health workers.

In one case, parents of children with mental retardation who were told their children would be moved from an acceptable institution to an open, community-based group home reacted with anger. They opposed the policy, despite the beliefs of mental health workers that the children would be better off (Miller & Iscoe, 1990). Deinstitutionalization was partly justified by labeling theory (see chapter 6). Proponents claimed that patients in mental hospitals behaved the way they did because of their labels and the institutional regime. Proponents also predicted that the patients would change greatly if the environment changed. Those propositions were not believable to others with knowledge of the severe disabilities of patients with severe and persistent disorders.

Priorities in the change agent's value system will not necessarily match the value priorities of other concerned groups. Mental health personnel sometimes assume the primacy of mental health values, failing to realize that others may value alternative behaviors and outcomes more. "He may be happier in school, but he is still two years behind in his reading level." "You can't reward bad kids by giving them special treatment, because it is unfair to good kids." "You shouldn't use a reward system that rewards children for doing what they should be doing anyway. That's bribery." "Democratic decision making and participation are all very well, but the result is disrespect for authority." Those familiar statements all reflect value hierarchies. Methods of ascertaining and measuring hierarchies of values are not well developed, but change agents are sometimes insensitive to the issue.

4. *Competence.* Probably the single most important piece of information about an individual in American society is his or her occupational title. Occupation is central to personal identity and to social existence. Beyond the financial and social rewards of an occupation, the mastery and exercise of occupational skills is critical for self-esteem and for individual well-being. The peak experience (Maslow, 1998) often arises during the exercise of occupational skills. One enjoys doing what one does well. Change may require that an employee no longer exercise skills that provide personal gratification.

A change in program requiring that individuals learn new skills or fulfill new functions may be more threatening to an established worker than to a novice. Crittenden (1992) staffed an innovative child protection team with young, less experienced, but more enthusiastic personnel because experienced professionals refused to participate. Inequalities in a social order are rationalized on the grounds that differential experience and training justify differences in status and related perquisites of office; when individuals having different statuses in the same organization are required to engage in new learning, there is no guarantee that the competence-based order that emerges will match the status order of the original organization.

Learning new skills can be difficult. Conditioned by years of educational experience, we may expect that learning will be painful, that we will be vulnerable to evaluation, and that our self-esteem will be diminished. For all these reasons, the "old dog" may not want to learn new tricks.

In order to institute change, not only must persons exercise new competencies; the social organization must support the exercise of these new competencies. For example, teachers trained in methods of life-space interviewing did not use these methods because of insufficient support from their principals and other teachers in the school who had not been similarly trained. Poythress (1978) demonstrated that he could train attorneys to cross-examine psychiatric expert witnesses, but few attorneys used the methods in the courtroom during commitment hearings claiming that judges were not interested in vigorous advocacy during routine hearings.

To change an ongoing service requires us to define required new competencies, assess whether the target populations of the change effort possess those competencies, evaluate the amount of time and training necessary to acquire new competencies (Fairweather et al., 1974), and consider changes in social organization that may be required if the new competencies are to be utilized at all. The problem of change may create a problem of person-environment fit, not only for the clients of a program, but also for the employees who will carry out the new program.

5. *Work relationships.* Social relationships on the job can be a great source of satisfaction and a great source of distress. People's emotional states are highly dependent on the state of office politics and rivalries at work. For those who do not have the opportunity or the ambition to be promoted, social relationships on the job are critically important (Kanter, 1993).

A change that requires people to give up attachments to coworkers or to places may well be difficult. Program changes may require concomitant change between supervisors and supervisors, supervisors and agencies, workers and supervisors, workers and workers, workers and clients, workers and agency, and many other permutations and combinations. A change that may be exciting for one person may disrupt many relationships for another. An analysis of relationships that may be affected should probably be undertaken as part of any change effort, taking into account that the change may be a positive factor, as when a relationship filled with conflict is ended by the change.

6. *Legal and administrative considerations.* Stability in a social organization depends in part on regulations with the force of law and on contractual agreements, as well as on shared expectations.

Examples abound. Laws may restrict or mandate actions. For example, in a mental hospital, only nurses or those attendants who have completed a course of training may pass out medications. Problems arise in treatment relationships when clients who may be accused of sexual abuse are referred for treatment; a psychotherapist may be under a duty to maintain confidentiality, but other laws mandate that he or she violate confidentiality in reporting any suspicion of child maltreatment. In some cases union contracts may restrict the degree of freedom to change; a prison superintendent who wanted to institute a weekend recreation program found that he had to change tours of duty of several of his officers; and restrictions in the union contract required prolonged negotiation before he could achieve his aim.

Regulations may be protective and provide a means through which a change effort is carried out. The systematically better conditions in veterans mental hospitals than in state mental hospitals may be the result of careful regulation of standards of patient care and the enforcement of those standards. In the Wuori case (discussed later in this chapter; Levine, 1986), reforms achieved through litigation were made permanent when they were written into state statutes and regulations.

Legal or administrative rules and structures may represent barriers to change, or they may be seen as challenges to be met and overcome by risk-taking leaders willing to "bend but not break" the rules to facilitate program implementation (Levine, 1980b; Sarason, 1982b). A bureaucratic structure may be an impediment and seem unnecessary, but it is ignored only at the peril of the change effort. Problems that arise because of formal rule-based constraints cannot be ignored.

7. *Information and communication.* Information has psychological importance. People use information to maintain, plan, or reorient their activities or to satisfy curiosity. People exchange information and opinions on matters of mutual interest, and those "in the know" participate with a sense of belonging. Information in advance of actions prevents surprises and may prevent actors from taking action at cross-purposes with each other. Moreover, providing information and explanation in advance is a way of extending deference to people's positions and to them as individuals. Not knowing about events may result in a loss of prestige to those who feel they should know about events affecting their domains.

Advance knowledge may facilitate change. However, advance knowledge may also serve to give opposition time to organize. From the point of view of the change agent, sometimes a fait accompli is preferable. The issue of whether or not to inform neighbors may be prominent when an agency wishes to open a group home in the community (Zippay, 1997). One school of thought states that neighbors should be brought into the planning in order to win support for a group home (Miller & Iscoe, 1990). Goldenberg (1971) tells how he made an effort to meet with some concerned citizens and made an attempt to include them in the planning process.

Advance knowledge can lead to active opposition (Wenocur & Belcher, 1990). A local zoning ordinance in Texas required that a group home for retarded adolescents obtain a permit before it could open, while a nursing home for the elderly, or a group home for delinquent youngsters did not need one. The U.S. Supreme Court agreed with the group home operator that the decision denying the permit was prejudiced against those with mental retardation (*City of Cleburne, Texas* v. *Cleburne Living Center, Inc.*, 1985). Opposition to group homes once they open is not usually prolonged, but no one knows how many group homes were not opened because of community opposition (Miller & Iscoe, 1990).

In sum, a change in any program occurs in a context consisting of social groups relating to programs and to each other through seven groups of interests. Members of the groups evaluate the change by examining the way the proposed changes might affect their interests, and each role representative arrives at a position opposed to or in favor of the change based on a weighing or balancing of those sets of interests. Groups that on balance gain from the changes will support them; groups that on balance lose from the changes will oppose. The opposition may or may not have the power to block change. Forces in the social context always pull back toward the status quo, however, and a change effort has to recognize that pull, for it may well result in some modification of the planned change. We have no precise measures of the strength of the existing interests or of their relative weights; the schema we have described is a loose set of guidelines for looking at a problem of change. Within each class of variables it is possible to have a large number of separate dimensions. Given Pressman and Wildavsky's (1984) concept that change must touch a large number of "switches," and all "switches" have to be lined up properly, the wonder is not that change efforts fail, but that successful change takes place at all. We now turn to an examination of some successful change efforts.

Case Studies of Change in Existing Settings

Changing a State Mental Hospital

In the space of four years the Harlem Valley Psychiatric Center in New York changed from a predominantly custodial institution to a modern psychiatric center (Levine, 1980b). Under the leadership of its director, Yoosuf Haveliwala, its census was reduced rapidly, and it developed an elaborate network of outpatient and aftercare services. The change was accomplished with a declining budget by reallocating, not adding, resources. Its patients were served as well as the state of the art permitted. The changes were accomplished following recognizable methods.

On July 1, 1974, the hospital had a census of 2,652 patients, of which 1,826 (69%) were inpatients averaging 19.5 years of hospitalization. The rest were outpatients. Most full-time staff were assigned to inpatient care. A few part-time clinics provided aftercare services. The hospital's orientation was custodial. Staff members had little sense of mission except to keep patients reasonably clean and involved in routine occupational and recreational programs. There was nothing to attract well-trained, ambitious professional personnel. Hospital staff did no research and received only perfunctory in-service training. The community was not involved in its programs, and the hospital had no active public relations program.

By 1977, the Joint Commission on the Accreditation of Hospitals (JCAH) renewed the hospital's accreditation with praise for its progress, for its programs, and for a medical records system it said was a model. The hospital census was reduced to 590 inpatients, and it carried 2,478 outpatients on its rolls. Thirty separate services were located in seven communities offering programs such as individual, group, and family therapy, day care, day hospitalization, crisis intervention, housing and sheltered living, sheltered workshops and work placement, advocacy services to link clients with other community agencies, and outreach including home visits. Hospital admissions had dropped from about 1,000 in 1974 to about 350 in 1977. A vigorous recruiting program attracted physicians and other mental health professionals, and an extensive in-service education program for professionals and paraprofessionals was in place. Eight psychology interns and 20 students from other disciplines were in training or were doing fieldwork at the hospital.

An extensive new monitoring and evaluation system was a key instrument in the change effort. The monitoring devices produced quantitative data on the status of patients and on the quality of service rendered patients. In addition, the hospital developed an epidemiological unit used to assess the needs for care within its catchment area, and new program development was based on its data. The hospital developed a small research department to conduct clinical studies with funds from government agencies and drug companies. Staff members participated in national and international professional meetings.

Haveliwala took over as director in July of 1974, but there was a "before the beginning." The hospital census had already started to decline in response to New York's deinstitutionalization policy, and its existence was threatened because a rural hospital was not needed.

(Harlem Valley eventually closed as a psychiatric hospital.) The community depended heavily on the institution, however, and would have suffered economically had it closed in 1974.

Haveliwala was among the first generation of state psychiatric center directors formally trained in concepts and practices of community mental health, and had clear plans. He quickly announced his intention to continue to place patients in the community, but each patient would be placed in accordance with the patient's needs, and excellent care would be provided. He also said that a deinstitutionalization program accompanied by community-based services would preserve jobs. He thus provided the institution with an ideology to rationalize change. Haveliwala reduced the hospital's executive committee (EC) from 50 to 14 members and changed its composition to give much more representation to the unit chiefs rather than to central staff.

Given civil service and union restrictions, Haveliwala had little power to hire and fire at will. He therefore used peer pressure. The EC became a deliberative and decision-making body, as well as a public forum to review each unit chief's success and failure in meeting objectives. Each unit chief consulted with staff and developed a target number of patients for placement in appropriate settings. These targets were discussed in the EC and agreed to by the director. Once objectives were assigned, unit chiefs were responsible for meeting them. A similar approach, called management by objectives, is found in industry (Riggio, 1990).

The program evaluation department produced reports showing each unit's success in meeting targets, and these reports were distributed to all EC members. Some unit chiefs met or exceeded their goals, while others failed, but failure was public, putting competitive pressure on the leaders and their units to meet standards. All of the other monitoring devices were used in exactly the same way. Unit chiefs had to explain publicly the reasons for success or failure. The director allocated resources and rewards on the basis of performance. Although workloads and pressure increased, these were offset by rewards, including the prospect of promotion.

Haveliwala's program assumed that resources should precede the patient into the community. He provided the resources and more by creatively bending rules, although he was always careful not to break the rules, thus taking into account the legal and administrative structure of the institution. Thus, he temporarily overcrowded a few wards to a slight degree, closing a few other wards and releasing the personnel that had staffed the now closed wards to establish community programs. Using a situational theory, he maintained that rehabilitation begins in the community. He argued that preparation for discharge did not predict patient tenure in the community; participation in aftercare programs did. Consequently, he developed resources in the community and devoted little effort to preparing patients to leave the hospital.

Harlem Valley's evaluation research, and our own efforts to review its programs, showed that 72 percent of discharged patients were still in the community one year after discharge. That record is quite good compared to other programs. Patients were by and large content with their community placements, and we could find little evidence that current community placements were substandard. The outpatient centers maintained contact with almost all inpatients who were discharged, at least for the first few months.

It is striking how little the "state of the art" in downsizing a state mental hospital has changed in the two decades since the Harlem Valley experiment. An adequate quantity and quality of community-based services, such as assertive community treatment (see chapter 2) and supported living (see chapter 7) is clearly necessary, as is a mechanism for shifting resources from the state-run facility to community settings, some of which may be privately managed. Perhaps the biggest difference between contemporary practice and the Harlem Valley story is that today admission to or discharge from a state hospital is often controlled not by the hospital staff but by a community provider (e.g., mental health center), which must actively manage its use of the hospital to stay within a fixed number of bed-days per year (see, e.g., Rapp & Moore, 1995).

A case study cannot pin down causal factors. In this instance, change followed a design using recognizable tools and methods understandable within a systems and social organization perspective. The consistent application of certain principles produced predictable results.[4]

Court-Ordered Change in Caring for Persons With Mental Retardation

In the 1970s, public interest lawyers along with advocacy organizations sued some institutions (mental hospitals, institutions for people with mental retardation, prisons) in the federal courts, alleging that they provided a substandard level of care (Chayes, 1976). These highly complex suits brought to the surface the political structure within which human services are embedded and raised issues around the separation of powers (legislative, executive, judicial), and the nature of federalism (state-federal relationships). In the early suits, the violations of standards of care were so egregious that issues of liability (who was responsible) were rarely important. Once the defendant state agencies lost the suits, they were ordered to remedy the problems, and the courts retained jurisdiction to oversee implementation of the remedies. The cases continued for years; one of the first cases, *Wyatt* v. *Stickney*, was brought in 1972 and was finally closed in December 2003 when the judge ruled that the state had met its "obligations under a 2000 settlement to provide necessary services, primarily in the community, and to treat clients with dignity" (Rawls, 2003).

The 1975 case of *Wuori* v. *Zitnay cont'd sub nom Wuori* v. *Concannon* (Levine, 1986)[5] was an unusually successful case. The court gave up active supervision within a relatively few years after finding substantial, if not full, compliance with an expensive, complex, and highly detailed consent decree calling for the improvement of an institution for people with mental retardation and the creation of community facilities and programming. The case was a class action on behalf of Martti Wuori, a resident of the Pineland Center in Maine, and all others similarly situated, filed by Neville Woodruff, a public interest lawyer. The complaint specified many substandard conditions at Pineland and many instances of poor treatment of residents.

Shortly afterwards, George Zitnay was appointed commissioner of mental health and corrections in Maine. He and Kevin Concannon, then director of the Bureau of Mental Retardation, worked with the plaintiff's attorney to develop a remediation plan. After spending two years developing plans to improve the institution, they came up with a comprehensive remediation plan with the assistance of the Mental Health Law Project, a Washington-based public interest law firm. At Zitnay's and Concannon's recommendation, the state agreed to the plan. U.S. District Court Judge Edward T. Gignoux, a highly respected jurist, entered the plan as the judgment of the court in July 1978.

The plan called for far-reaching changes in the institution and the development of community-based facilities and programming. It included several hundred specifications covering just about every aspect of living and habilitation (treatment) in the institution and in community programs and called for the appointment of a special master, a court-appointed official whose job is to monitor the implementation of the order and to recommend necessary steps to achieve compliance with the decree (Nathan, 1979; D. Levine, 1984).

David Gregory, a law professor with experience in civil rights litigation but none in the care of the retarded, was appointed master for a period of two years. Initially, he thought the monitoring task was straightforward, but he quickly became aware of organizational and political complexities. When the new governor did not reappoint Zitnay to the state commissioner post, he resumed the position as director of Pineland and worked closely with Gregory to use the court order to help him improve Pineland. By exercising firm and creative leadership and using the court order to back him when needed, Zitnay quickly managed to turn a backward institution into one that could be shown with pride to any visitor. Even the most disabled residents were clean and well dressed. The living quarters were personalized and attractive. An enthusiastic staff was deployed in creative ways. Good ratios of personnel to residents supported active programming.

At the end of Gregory's two-year tenure, the court order had not yet been fully implemented, and Gregory recommended that the court retain jurisdiction. Lincoln Clark replaced Gregory as special master.

Clark concentrated on the Pineland Center first because it was close to compliance with the court order. When a consultant affirmed that the institution was in substantial compliance, Clark recommended that the institution be discharged from the court's supervision. It took two more years to fulfill the community plan.

A combination of mediation and pressure stemming from Clark's reports (which received a lot of attention in the press) moved the state system along. By 1983, Clark's independent consultants issued reports agreeing either that the standards had been met or that working mechanisms had been created to ensure that the remaining standards would be met. The plaintiff's attorney agreed that progress had been made but insisted that permanent and independent monitoring devices be put into place. A consumer's advisory board was given full access to all programs and records related to the care of residents. The board was authorized to hear complaints about any aspect of client care. The state also agreed to public hearings and annual, independent compliance reviews that would be announced publicly, with specific notice given to advocacy organizations. The auditor's reports would be made public; if they called for corrective action, the commissioner of mental health and mental retardation had to develop and publish a plan for correction.

The monitoring process was put in place. Public hearings to identify problems in the service system, the first step in the reviewing process, took place. The Consumer Advisory Board reorganized itself to handle the work of monitoring compliance with the court order, appointing about 130 "correspondents" to act as friends to those who had no families or who had been abandoned. These correspondents were organized into smaller groups reporting to a coordinator. The correspondents provided "eyes" on the system, seeing to it that the people they befriended received appropriate care.

Remarkable changes took place. The court's order supplied the blueprint and the leverage for change, and skillful and firm leadership, making use of the opportunity provided by the lawsuit and the court's decree, led to substantial improvement and modernization of the system of care. During litigation and during the implementation phase, Maine changed many of its laws governing the care of people with mental retardation to bring its facilities into compliance with decree requirements, thus making the changes permanent as a matter of state law. Even though the court eventually stopped its active supervision, the program appeared to be firmly in place. The Consumer Advisory Board continued its monitoring with federal court support (*Consumer Advisory Board* v. *Glover*, 1993). The decree continued to provide leverage for advocates to keep the reforms intact.

Litigation was successful in this case in achieving the goals of improving the system. Miller and Iscoe (1990), writing from the viewpoint of defendants in institutional reform suits, have a somewhat more jaundiced view of court-ordered change. They argue that some activists' hypercriticism is destructive. Miller and Iscoe say that a minor industry of well paid, self-serving advocates and special masters has developed and note that if the advocates didn't find anything wrong in the care provided by institutions, they would go out of business.

Planned Change on a Statewide Level:
The Texas Educational Miracle

President George W. Bush, who is committed to educational reform, signed into federal law the No Child Left Behind Act of 2001. The Act is intended to produce planned change in the educational system nationally. According to the Department of Education, now headed by a Texas educator, Secretary Rod Paige,

> the new law will change the culture of America's schools so that they define their success in terms of student achievement and invest in the achievement of every child. The act is based on four basic principles: stronger accountability for results, increased flexibility and local control, expanded options for parents, and an emphasis on teaching methods that have been proven to work. (U.S. Department of Education, n.d.)

A key element of the law and in the reform of education in Texas is that states are directed to create statewide standards for what each child should know. Progress is to be assessed by tests constructed to measure how well each child and each school is meeting the state's standards. The tests are to be given to every child in grades three through eight every year. The test results are to be published on a school-by-school basis as the measure of accountability. In theory, published test results will give the public, politicians responsible for funding the schools, school administrators and teachers, and parents feedback to assess educational progress. Based on the assessment, educators will act to improve test scores by providing resources to help those schools and children to improve if they do not meet the standards.

Elements in the 2001 Education Act are based on the experience in Texas education over a period of years, beginning in 1984 with a Select Committee on Public Education (SCOPE) headed by Ross Perot. (Perot is a billionaire businessman who ran unsuccessfully for the U.S. presidency as an independent third-party candidate in 1992 and in 1996.) Texas had long been at the bottom of the rank of states in its provision for education. At that time, its major industries, oil and agriculture, were suffering. Texas leaders believed that it was necessary to improve the schools in order to be competitive in the coming high technological age. Perot, a business executive, pressed for the adoption of measures that would result in tightly managed school organizations and measurable results. He believed in the efficacy of management methods. He also believed it would help to sell increased funding for teachers and for the schools if politicians could promise results (Mc-Neil, 2000).

Texas school reform underwent several iterations but an important element was the use of annual achievement tests. (McAdams, 2000; Mc-Neil, 2000). By the 1990s, Texas was hailed as a leader in the national accountability movement and its program was held up as a model for other states to follow. The Texas miracle was widely publicized (Haney, 2000), and was a factor in the 2000 presidential election. Candidate George Bush advocated the Texas model of testing as a key to his program of educational reform. The 2001 federal education law makes federal aid to education contingent on states adopting the law's provisions, and President Bush has proposed extending testing programs to Head Start (Zremski, 2002). The Texas educational miracle provides us with a good case study of the process of planned change and its intended and unintended consequences.

The evidence for the Texas miracle is based in part on improvements on a standardized academic achievement test, the Texas Assessment of Academic Skills (TAAS). The test was mandated by the state legislature and introduced into the schools in the 1990–1991 school year. It is a criterion-referenced test designed to measure the skills specified in the statewide educational standards adopted as part of the reform effort. The test measures progress in reading, math, and writing. Scores are reported in terms of the percentages of students who pass each of the tests, and who pass all three tests. The state sets the passing score; 70 percent of the items on each test must be answered correctly for the student to pass. In addition, for upper-grade students, the tests involve "high stakes." Texas students can't graduate high school unless they pass the tests, no matter their classroom grades (Haney, 2000).

McAdams (2000, Table 15.1, p. 253), a historian who was a member of the Houston school board during the period of reform, presents some test data showing the effects of the reforms. The average percentage of students in grades three through eight and in tenth grade who passed all three tests increased from 40 percent in 1994 to 66 percent in 1998. The percent of Black and Hispanic students who passed all three tests increased from 29 percent to 55 percent and from 35 percent to 59 percent, respectively, from 1994 to 1998. In 1998, 85 percent of white students passed all three tests (Haney, 2000). The improvement is remarkable, but it has not been without its critics.

The change process involved more than testing children annually and publishing the results school by school. The Texas Education Agency (TEA) put into place a statewide curriculum and experimented with a variety of ways of measuring and evaluating teacher performance. These experiments were based on the theory that the state's educational problem was not attributable to inadequate resources but to inadequate supervision and insufficient management controls over teaching (McNeil, 2000). Two other reforms affecting teachers were introduced as well. New teachers no longer received permanent appointments after a probationary period, but were put on renewable contracts, with renewal based on performance. The administrative process for dismissing teachers for cause was modified to make it easier to dismiss a teacher. Increments in teacher pay were based in large part on each school's performance on the TAAS, giving all teachers an incentive to work to improve student performance (McAdams, 2000).

The Houston school district also went to "private sector contracts" for administrators and principals, tying their positions and increments in their pay to their school's performance, largely measured by increments in annual test scores.

> Tenure for principals . . . has been replaced by a "performance contract." Principals no longer have tenure, but work under a two-year contract. Contract renewal, building assignment, and annual salary bonuses are, under the terms of the performance contract, contingent on the passing rate in each principal's school . . . the principal becomes the building-level compliance officer for teaching to the TAAS. (McNeil, 2000, p. 233)

Rod Paige, then superintendent of the Houston schools, used his authority a number of times to terminate principals and other administrators. In the words of McAdams, "the loss of job security has significantly sharpened their focus on student performance" (McAdams, 2000, p. 252). Principals began working on "better curriculum alignment," or tying classroom teaching to the state curriculum, which in turn was tied to the TAAS.

Haney (2000) questioned the validity of the reported changes. He argued that some proportion of the gains in test scores may be related to factors such as changing the definition of low-scoring special education students to exclude their scores from the report of results, changing levels of difficulty in subsequent versions of the tests, and on occasion outright cheating by teachers or principals. The TAAS is scored centrally, but teachers administer the annual tests in their own schools. Different forms are prepared each year, but the content of the questions is similar from year to year (Klein, Hamilton, McCaffrey, & Stecher, 2000). Haney did not believe that artifacts accounted for all of the impressive increase in test scores. He raised the rival hypothesis that the scores were inflated "due to extensive preparation for this test" (Part 7, p. 14).

To test the hypothesis, Haney examined Texas student performance on other standardized tests. If the students had indeed gained academic skills, these would manifest themselves in comparable performance on other tests. He compared Texas student performance over time to national norms on the SAT. Haney concluded that results on the SAT failed to confirm gains for upper-grade Texas students found on the TAAS. If there were real educational gains in academic skills, they were not reflected in the SAT scores.

Haney's conclusion that gains did not generalize to other tests was supported by a Rand study (Klein, Hamilton, McCaffrey, & Stecher, 2000) that examined results for Texas students on the National Assessment of Educational Progress (NAEP) tests. Texas students showed gains from 1992 to 1996, but so did students in other school districts nationally. The Texas gains on the NAEP were substantially smaller than gains on the TAAS, raising questions about what Texas students had actually learned.

Haney also evaluated the state's data on dropouts. He concluded the TEA's method of measuring dropouts was substantially faulty. The TEA claimed that 14.7 percent of a cohort of students dropped out between seventh and twelfth grade, and that the dropout rate fell dramatically over a ten-year period. Haney examined two other independent sources of data on school dropouts using somewhat different methods of calculating the dropout rate. These two studies showed higher dropout rates than the TEA claimed. On his measure, whites averaged about a 25 percent dropout rate while minority students averaged close to 50 percent, and the rates grew somewhat worse after introduction of the TAAS (Part 5). Based on evidence from a study by the state's auditor, the TEA estimates covered only about half the dropouts. The rules for defining dropouts changed over time. The TEA relied on district reports of dropouts while using dropout rates as a key factor in the system of rating districts. Haney also alleged fraud in district reporting. Many types of school "leavers" are not counted as dropouts. For example, a student who leaves school because of an inability to pass the tenth grade TAAS but who pursues a high school equivalency program to obtain a general education diploma is not counted as a dropout. Haney wrote: "It is clear that the TEA has been playing a Texas-sized shell game on the matter of counting dropouts" (Part 7, p. 11). Phelps (2000) argues that Haney's analysis was faulty, and that he was selective in the comparison periods he used.

The Rand team reviewing test scores recommended "audit testing" to validate test gains. They raised several issues: "(1) students being coached to develop skills that are unique to the specific type of questions that are asked on the statewide exam (i.e., as distinct from what is generally meant by reading, math, or the other subjects tests); (2) narrowing the curriculum to improve scores on the state exam at the expense of other important subjects and skills not tested" (Klein, Hamilton, McCaffrey, & Stecher, 2000, p. 13).

Phelps (2000), an advisor to President George Bush on education, was highly critical of the Rand report and also of Haney's work. Phelps suggested the Rand report was deliberately released in time to affect the presidential election. He believed the Rand group misinterpreted the NAEP results for Texas compared to those for the nation. He also discounted the finding that TAAS gains were so much larger than NAEP gains on the grounds that the tests were different. He also defends "teaching to the test." "Teaching to the test is a problem only when students are tested on material they have not been taught" (p. 7). Phelps did not address the concern that the skills learned when teachers teach to the test may not generalize.

McNeil (2000) and McNeil and Valenzuela (2000) conducted extensive observational studies in Texas high schools. Their original interest was in observing innovative programs in magnet schools, but over the course of their observations their interests shifted. They observed that teachers in what they regarded as superior, innovative schools were being pressured to give up creative teaching methods to teach to the test. One observer estimated that teachers were spending eight to ten hours a week in test preparation drills, and that principals, whose pay increments depended on test score increases, were exerting pressure for them to spend even more time in test preparation (Weisman, 2000). The educational process was affected:

> substantial class time is spent practicing bubbling in answers and learning to recognize "distractor" (obviously incorrect) answers. Students are drilled on such strategies as the one in [a] pep rally cheer . . . if you see you have answered "b" three times in a row, you know ("no, no, no") that at least one of those answers is likely to be wrong. . . . The basis for such advice comes from the publishers of test-prep materials, many of whom send consultants into schools—for a substantial price—to help plan pep rallies, to train teachers to use the TAAS-prep kits, and to ease the substitution of their TAAS-prep materials for the curriculum in classrooms where teachers stubbornly resist. (McNeil, 2000, p. 235)

McNeil (2000) concluded that principals were spending more and more of their instructional budgets on test preparation materials and on consultants. Especially in poor and minority schools, principals diverted the school's resources "into materials, activities, conferences, staff development days, consultants and packages aimed at prep for the state test rather than at high academic quality" (p. 244). District superintendents used their meetings with principals and their communications with them to consider TAAS issues. The rising test scores justified using more TAAS-prep materials, and substituting test-based programs for the regular curriculum. Some principals begin test preparation teaching in September and continued until March, after the TAAS test (p. 238). Teachers who wanted to focus on a broader curriculum had to squeeze it in from March to the end of the school year.

McNeil (2000) asks whether the use of test prep materials year after year in place of the curriculum and other teaching methods has other educational consequences. Some teachers believe that the emphasis on test prep materials for learning may undermine a student's ability to read sustained passages or longer literature. Students are taught to read short, unrelated passages and to select an answer in multiple-choice format from a list of answers. Some claim students may not even read the passages, but simply scan to find some key phrases that appear in the set of responses and select those. Students may not learn to read for meaning, but simply to find a particular answer. Even though test scores go up, students may be nonreaders. Some teachers told McNeil that:

> few can use reading for assignments in literature, science or history classes; few of them choose to read; few of them can make meaning of literature or connect writing and discussing to reading. (p. 237)

A similar problem arises with the teaching of writing. Students are taught on a daily basis to write "the persuasive essay" consisting of five paragraphs with five sentences in each paragraph. The TAAS writing test is based on the persuasive essay. According to McNeil (p. 239), it didn't matter what students actually wrote. It was the form that mattered because that is how the test is scored. Allegedly, those who score the test count indentations to see that there are five paragraphs, and count sentences, but pay less attention to what is actually written. Mathematics teaching suffered as well. Students were encouraged to guess at the correct answer from among five choices without working the problem through. They didn't have to explain their answers nor were they encouraged to work out the reasons behind selecting an answer. McNeil (2000) also claims that teaching of subjects not tested has suffered. For example, some science teachers said they suspended the teaching of science to concentrate on TAAS-tested math.

McNeil (2000) claims that the negative effects of "teaching to the test" are even more profound in schools with high proportions of minority students, who tend to score low on tests. Principals and teachers directed to raise test scores spend even more time teaching to the test there than in other schools. In schools with a high percentage of higher socioeconomic status students who normally score well, there is less emphasis on teaching to the test and the curriculum is more enriched. Teachers are able to use more varied teaching methods: "extended reading assignments, analytical writing, research papers, role play . . . student-led discussions, speaking activities, oral histories, multimedia activities, science experiments, library hours" (p. 246). McNeil also argues that the emphasis on test results and on teacher accountability takes attention away from deficits and inequalities of resources in different schools.

Opponents of the Texas policy were attacked; teachers who voiced opposition were accused of "being against minority students' chance to get high scores" (McNeil, 2000, p. 237). Secretary of Education Paige said: "Anyone who opposes annual testing of children is an apologist for a broken system of education that dismisses certain children and classes of children as unteachable" (U.S. Department of Education, n.d., p. 3).

The U.S. Department of Education (n.d.) answered the arguments against testing by publishing a list of "testing myths" and "realities." According to this statement (http://www.ed.gov/ncbl/accountability/ ayp/testingforresults.html), testing is an integral part of teaching and test results help teachers and parents to know what children need. Annual tests are analogized to annual physical examinations. The statement denies that "testing narrows the curriculum by rewarding test taking skills" and emphasizes that "Tests geared to rigorous state standards provide a measure of student knowledge and skills. If the academic standards are truly rigorous, student learning will be as well." The statement denies that testing promotes teaching to the test, but it states "Testing is part of teaching and learning. Gifted and inspiring teachers use tests to motivate students as well as to assess their learning. Effective teachers recognize the value of testing and know how to employ testing in instruction." "Effective teachers assess their students in various ways during the school year. As they do this, they not only monitor student achievement but also help to ensure that their students will excel on annual tests."

The statement goes on to argue that testing will benefit minority students because it "will make it impossible to ignore achievement gaps when they exist." The statement says that "where testing systems are now in place, low income and minority students are indeed excelling. A recent study reports there are more than 4,500 high-poverty and high-minority schools nationwide that scored in the top one-third on the state tests." The report argues that students dropout because they are frustrated by not being able to learn, and that testing will identify those students early and get for them the services they need to succeed.

The Department of Education report says nothing about the necessity of providing adequate resources to ensure that each child will receive what he or she needs to succeed. McNeil (2000) reviews the history of accountability in Texas and shows that educational change and accountability were sold on the basis that they would help improve the climate for allocating more resources to education. However, she also describes how accountability measures were put into place, but when economic circumstances and budgetary exigencies resulted in a shortfall of promised resources, accountability measures were left in place.

One problem is that tests are taken uncritically as a "gold standard." The validity of tests themselves as measures of learning is not examined. If increments in test scores are due to intensive "teaching to the test," do increments in scores continue to have significance as an index of mastery? Some argue that students exposed to the new intensive teaching are learning more than they did under less rigorously managed systems, but that assertion depends on the validity of the test score as a measure of learning.

This case study of change reminds us of the late Don Campbell's law, which we paraphrase here: Whenever resource allocation depends on an arbitrary quantitative index, one of two results is likely to occur:

Either the index gets corrupted (e.g., cheating, making the test easier) or the process to produce the index number gets corrupted (intensive teaching to the test to the relative exclusion of other education methods). In this case, we see evidence of both results.

The emphasis on testing also takes testing out of the context of other changes that promoted alignment of the curriculum and teaching methods with state standards and the state tests. We have briefly described some other changes that took place (e.g., performance contracts for principals and other administrators, and term contracts for new teachers). Will testing have the same effects on schools in the absence of these changes? Moreover, the idea that one can induce changes in performance by introducing annual testing omits consideration of the complex context of education.

The context includes the political system and its dependence on allocation of tax money collected from citizens who can vote on school budgets and on proposed increments in tax rates. Many groups exercise influence, including elected boards of education, superintendents with career interests, business leaders concerned about school taxes and the quality of schools, community activists, parents, older citizens without children in the schools concerned about property taxes, teachers unions, mayors and state governors, and local as well as state level legislatures and state level education authorities. The politics of ethnic conflict in the United States is also a factor, as is the trend toward privatization (McNeil, 2000). McAdams (2000) provides a detailed and frank description of the dynamics of change that play out over a period of years. As we have tried to emphasize, producing change is more complex that it appears, and we should be concerned about intended as well as unintended consequences of any planned change.

The change process reveals how much the service system is embedded in our political and governmental system. The disciplines and practices of law, political science, sociology, economics, psychology, medicine, rehabilitation, education, organization and management, mediation and negotiation evaluation research, and public relations are needed to understand and to produce change.

Summary

If we are to modify existing helping services and implement new program concepts, we must create or modify social organizations to deliver the new services. The principles that guide planned change, be it the creation of a new setting or the modification of an existing service organization, were forged out of difficult experiences in which change failed or failed to fulfill some part of its important purposes. These principles help us to understand common problems encountered in creating new settings or changing existing settings.

The creation of new settings requires more than a good idea, agreement on abstract values, and strong motivation to succeed. We illustrated the issues in the creation of settings by showing how the Residential Youth Center was developed.

Change in existing organizations presents other problems. The most fundamental distinction is between first-order, or incremental, changes to just part of the system, and second-order, or transformative, change in the structure, purpose, or processes of the system as a whole. To deal with job stress and other problems, community and organizational psychologists have studied and adapted many management strategies for organizational change, including organization development, and learning organizations. Community psychology has been at the forefront of organizational empowerment research.

Every new program exists in a context consisting of social groups that relate to the program and to each other in relation to the program. We identified seven broad sets of interests: energy, power, culture, competence, relationships, legal and administrative considerations, and information and communication. Members of each of the social groups evaluate proposed changes by examining how the proposed change affects their interests. Groups that on balance will gain from the changes will support them. Those groups that on balance stand to lose will oppose the change. Forces in the social context tend to pull new programs or concepts back toward the status quo ante. Change efforts and change agents must recognize and overcome that pull.

We presented brief case studies of changes in a mental hospital and in a state's system for the care of the retarded. In the first case, change was brought about by skillful leadership. In the second case, skillful leaders used the power of a court to correct wrongs in the service system. We also examined issues raised by change in a state's educational system.

In the next chapter, we illustrate change brought about on a national scale by examining the racial desegregation of the schools. Once again we will see the interplay among law, social science, and the complexities of introducing widespread change.

Notes

1. Sarason was thinking of the large number of antipoverty programs, community mental health centers, Head Start programs, and the myriad of alternative service settings that emerged in the 1960s and early 1970s. The pace of creating settings continues today as new problems emerge or new issues capture our attention. Innumerable abortion clinics with attendant counseling facilities sprang up in the wake of *Roe* v. *Wade* protecting a woman's right to an abortion. Rape crisis centers, havens for battered women, and a large number of health maintenance organizations were also formed. Thousands of self-help organizations have been created in recent years; for example, many citizens' organizations opposed to burying toxic wastes in landfills near residential

neighborhoods and water supplies were formed after the Love Canal revelation raised the nation's consciousness and led to national and state efforts to identify toxic waste dump sites (Gibbs, 1998; A. Levine, 1982).

2. This section is based on Evans and Bess (2003).

3. Donald T. Campbell (personal communication), in discussing a critical problem in evaluation research, noted that whenever a program is evaluated by some more or less arbitrary criterion, and political or resource allocation consequences depend on the evaluation, one of two results obtain. Either the process becomes corrupted to produce the index or the index becomes corrupted. Thus if a school program is evaluated by achievement test results, the educational process may become corrupted by concentrating on teaching students to perform well on tests. In one notable example, an educational contractor who was to be paid on the basis of achievement test results spent time actually teaching students to do test items that later comprised the criterion.

The concept of index corruption is undoubtedly familiar to anyone who has ever responded to bureaucratic demands for figures. Many people can attest that the reliability of some of the figures offered is highly suspect. For example, in an academic department that was evaluated by administrators in part on the basis of faculty publication productivity, it was common practice to include items that were in press in one year and to count the same item again the following year when the piece had been published, effectively doubling output. No doubt readers can multiply the examples from their own experiences.

4. Shortly after the research for the case study of Harlem Valley was completed, Haveliwala left Harlem Valley and took over the directorship of another larger hospital within the state system. The problems and the task in the new situation were quite different. Haveliwala encountered great conflict with the state bureaucracy, which accused him of mismanagement. The facts on the public record are unclear, but eventually he resigned. Some believe he was forced out because he had publicly opposed some of the governor's and the commissioner's policies in a letter published in the *New York Times*. At any rate, the circumstances were different at his new post and it is not clear that he was able to adopt the same approach. The subsequent history indicates that methods must be adapted to the historical situation and to conditions as they exist. As Sarason (1981a) notes, psychology is peculiarly ahistorical and focused on contextless principles. The case study is warning that we can ignore history and contexts only at our peril when applying theoretical principles.

5. The research reported here was completed with support from the National Science Foundation Law and Social Science Program, Grant No. SES-8023954. This section is adapted from a longer report published elsewhere (Levine, 1986).

11

School Desegregation: A Societal-Level Intervention

The desegregation of American society is one of the more profound social changes of our time. We include a discussion of school desegregation in part because social scientists played an important, supportive role in the desegregation effort and in part because it is a good example of an intervention that affected the entire nation. Moreover, at the level of individual school districts and individual schools, responsible authorities had to institute a process to accommodate change initiated externally by court orders. By virtue of their applied research expertise in such methods as program evaluation, community psychologists are in a good position to inform the judicial process in the public interest (see Perkins, 1988, and the rest of that special issue of the *American Journal of Community Psychology* on Law and Community

Psychology). In periods of judicial conservatism, however, community psychologists may have more success working for change through the executive and legislative branches at all levels of government (Perkins, 1995).

Another important aspect from community psychology's perspective was that social scientists helped to create a body of knowledge and theory that attributed the plight of African American people in the United States not to their individual characteristics but to the environmental conditions under which they lived—segregation enforced by law. Black and White scholars, literary figures, and social activists developed coherent intellectual rationales to fight racial oppression. Later, especially with regard to the effort to desegregate the schools, social scientists provided important expert testimony in the courts regarding the detrimental psychological effects of segregation. Social scientists also provided theoretical propositions justifying desegregation remedies.

Although the desegregation of American society was propelled by many forces, it can be described as a massive, planned, societal level intervention whose purpose was to solve complex moral, social, economic, and psychological problems. Segregation of the races, a social practice enforced by the power of law, was built on an assumption held by the majority that African Americans were inherently inferior to Whites, and therefore that the interests of both races would be served by rigidly enforcing their separation. This assumption rationalized the exploitation of the African American minority who did not share it and who experienced segregation as oppression. Eventually a body of scholarly opinion developed to support the view that segregation was oppression and was the cause of social, economic, and psychological problems found among African Americans. Given that segregation was accepted as the cause of the evils associated with it, attacking the cause by getting rid of the formal barriers to full integration made sense.

The theory that segregation as a social and legal practice was the cause of diverse social, economic, and psychological consequences is a situationally oriented theory. The proposition that removing formal barriers to integration would undo the undesirable consequences is a corollary to the theory. The theory and the intervention were aimed not at changing people, but at changing conditions, with the assumption that changes in behavior, attitudes, and self-image would follow.

At the level of our schools, the specific remedy for the evils of segregation—to desegregate them—was based in part on a set of premises drawn from the psychological study of prejudice. Attempting to change a deeply engrained social pattern has revealed both that we know less than we thought we did and that the underlying phenomena are more complex than we thought.

Much has happened in the fifty years since *Brown* v. *Board of Education*, the landmark school desegregation case. Although racial segregation on the basis of law has been eliminated and efforts have been made to desegregate, or integrate the schools, powerful social forces have resulted in the resegregation of many schools because of residential patterns and U.S. Supreme Court decisions that limited the options for school desegregation (Orfield, 1993, 2001). In particular, the federal courts receptive to social science arguments about desegregation in years past, have been disinclined to recognize the concept of institutional racism or of social system contributions to segregation. The courts have been insisting that unless a plaintiff can show *intentional* efforts on the part of officials to maintain segregated schools, the courts will not intervene. The courts will not provide remedies for resegregation due to "private choices" (*Belk* v. *Charlotte Mecklenburg Board of Education*, 2001). Some critical race theorists believe that people challenging school segregation based on institutional racism should continue to bring those issues to the attention of the courts even though the arguments may not have legal weight (Gutierrez, 2001).

Out of frustration over continuing racial problems, some have begun to rethink the ideal of integration as a solution to racial problems. These changing views and political and intellectual backlash to busing (Ravitch, 2000) remind us that we are always functioning in a social and historical context. Solutions appropriate for one time and one set of circumstances may not be the preferred solutions in another historical period. Busing for integration was one solution. If schools become more segregated and the courts won't intervene where segregation is not the result of intentionally discriminatory acts by public officials, new solutions will be necessary. These will include community development and social action (see chapter 12) to see that schools in minority communities receive their fair share of resources. Judging from our past history, minority schools with their heavier need for social services and special education will not be supported adequately. Political efforts and litigation to make school financing more equitable will be increasingly necessary if we move toward increasingly segregated residential communities and schools (Swenson, 2000). Let us examine the history of segregation in the United States.

Slavery, Segregation, and the Constitution[1]

Slavery and race relations occupied our attention from the very beginning of our nation. The contradiction in values is clear between the ringing words of political freedom in the Declaration of Independence—"all men are create equal"—and the section of the original Constitution that counted slaves as three-fifths of a person for purposes of taxation and representation.[2] This contradiction was solved for many by viewing African Americans as less than fully human in intellectual, moral, and social characteristics.

Slavery was an issue at every step in the nation's growth before the Civil War. Whether a new state or territory entered the nation as a free or a slave state was a source of political and armed conflict. Eventually that conflict erupted in the Civil War. In the United States, African Americans were viewed and treated as inferior beings and had difficult lives. Slaves had few rights. They did not own their own bodies or labor. A master who killed a slave while disciplining him was not held accountable. In the notorious Dred Scott case, Chief Justice Taney of the U.S. Supreme Court wrote: "[the negro] had no rights which the white man was bound to respect." (*Scott* v. *Sanford,* 1856, p. 407). They were denied an education; segregation in public accommodations, churches, and schools was common throughout the non-slave states of the North. Before the Civil War, free African Americans were denied the right to vote or had their voting rights drastically restricted.

In 1865, after the Civil War, Lincoln's Emancipation Proclamation became a permanent part of our Constitution as the Thirteenth Amendment, banning involuntary servitude. The Thirteenth Amendment was not sufficient to protect the civil and political rights of newly freed African Americans, however. Many Southern states passed Black codes designed to restore slavery in fact if not in name. The Fourteenth Amendment in 1868 provided all persons, African American and White, with protections against state action that denied the equal protection of the law or that deprived any person of life, liberty, or property without due process of law. Although intended to protect newly freed slaves, the Fourteenth Amendment was written in much broader terms to reflect ideals of political freedom and social equality (tenBroek, 1965). The Fifteenth Amendment, protecting the right to vote, became a part of the Constitution in 1870.

For the next 30 years the promise of these amendments was undercut by violence and economic pressure against African Americans and by a U.S. Supreme Court that "interpreted away" the protections of the post–Civil War amendments.[3] Protection became a matter for state law. If the states saw fit to permit private discrimination, or if the states did not enforce their laws against violence, there was no protection. Lynching was a constant threat to African Americans.

In 1890, the Louisiana legislature passed a law calling for separate but equal accommodations for white and "colored" passengers on railroad trains. The phrase "separate but equal" was designed to meet the requirements of the equal-protection clause of the Fourteenth Amendment. The African American citizens of New Orleans, in cooperation with railroad officials who were not pleased with the prospect of having to add extra cars to their trains, tested the law. In 1892 Homer Adolph Plessy, who was seven-eighths Caucasian, boarded a train and refused to move to the segregated car (much as Rosa Parks refused to move to the back of the bus 70 years later). Arrested and fined, he appealed his conviction, and in 1896 his case reached the U.S. Supreme Court.

The Supreme Court then enunciated its notorious separate-but-equal doctrine. Holding that the equal-protection clause of the Fourteenth Amendment did not abolish all social distinctions and could not require that the races commingle "upon terms unsatisfactory to either," the Court went on to say:

> We consider the underlying fallacy of the plaintiff's argument to consist in the assumption that the enforced separation of the two races stamps the colored race with a badge of inferiority. If this be so, it is not by reason of anything found in the act, but solely because the colored race chooses to put that construction upon it. (*Plessy* v. *Ferguson*, 1896)

A dissent by Justice Harlan recognized the fallacy in the argument. The law was not passed to keep Whites out of African American railway carriages but to keep African Americans out of White cars. Moreover, Justice Harlan argued that the Constitution was "color-blind" and "neither knows or tolerates classes among citizens."

In later years the *Plessy* decision was used to support and to sustain discriminatory legislation affecting all American social institutions.[4] The Supreme Court had grounded its decision in *Plessy* on the social psychological proposition that stigma was not inherent in the action of forced segregation because the law itself contained no stigmatizing words. The problem, according to the Court, was in the perceptions of those who were the victims of discrimination. The Court's use of a social psychological proposition was to set the agenda for the next 58 years in the study of race relations. Because the *Plessy* Court used a social psychological concept, the proposition could be challenged with data to show that enforced separation *was* stigmatizing and harmful.

The NAACP and Its Litigative Strategy

The victory for school desegregation in *Brown* v. *Board of Education* (1954) represented the culmination of a planned self-help effort by a private community organization. The National Association for the Advancement of Colored People (NAACP) was formed in 1909, in the shadow of virulent and violent anti–African American sentiment. The organization had as its major aim protecting the rights of African Americans through social, political, and legal action (Hughes, 1962). It settled on litigation as the major means to pursue its aims. After 1929 the Howard University Law School became a center for research on civil rights law and many of the African American lawyers who carried the fight trained there, including late U.S. Supreme Court Justice Thurgood Marshall, the first African American to achieve that position.

The attack on school segregation began as early as 1929, and by

1935 more than 100 court cases had challenged the legality of school segregation. Direct challenges to segregated schools invariably lost in the courts, however. The administration of the laws, not desegregation itself, seemed a more promising legal target. Much less money was spent on schools serving African American children than on schools serving Whites, especially in the South.

By suing to obtain equal resources for separate schools, the NAACP leadership hoped that segregation would be brought down by the financial weight of maintaining two truly equal school systems.

Thurgood Marshall led the NAACP's legal battles from the late 1930s on. The postwar attack began at graduate and professional schools supported by tax money that excluded African Americans. With a group of African American lawyers centered at Howard University, and with a few White lawyers, Marshall successfully pursued the strategy of insisting upon separate-but-equal at the graduate and professional school levels.[5] These cases resulted in the admission of African American students to formerly all-white schools, since the alternative was to build equal facilities or close down all-white schools. The struggle against elementary school segregation was renewed in the years following World War II. NAACP legal briefs more and more stressed the stigmatizing and stultifying consequences of segregation. Although the Supreme Court struck down segregation barriers in the higher education cases, it had not confronted the argument that separate educational facilities were inherently unequal.

Marshall and the NAACP thought carefully about how to mount a direct litigative assault on the assumption that separate could be equal. Not only were the legal grounds uncertain; participation in the cases by African American plaintiffs was perilous both physically and financially. African Americans who brought the suits were threatened with violence, loss of jobs, loss of business, and revocation of bank loans. It was also perilous for African American civil rights lawyers to bring cases in the South, where there was a constant threat of physical violence, but they proceeded with heroic determination. Thurgood Marshall drove around back roads of Southern towns to collect depositions with a gun on the seat of his car. Kenneth Clark collected his data in the South with a threat of violence hovering in the background. The cultural belief that the low social and economic state of African Americans in society was attributable not to segregation but to inherent inferiority was at stake.

In the years after *Plessy* a "scientific literature" rationalized the belief in racial inferiority.[6] By the late 1920s other social scientists had developed the opposing position that the social environment was the primary cause of African Americans' failure to achieve. The growing social science literature on the effects of racism provided an intellectual rationale for the argument that segregated facilities were inherently unequal because segregation itself caused severe psychological damage.

Kenneth Clark, an African American social psychologist who had been an undergraduate at Howard and later became president of the American Psychological Association, had been experimenting with techniques to show that segregation resulted in impaired self-images in African American children. Marshall viewed Clark's studies (conducted in collaboration with Clark's wife, Mamie) as an excellent means of demonstrating that segregation damaged the self-esteem of African American children.

Cases challenging segregation itself as inherently unequal worked their way through lower courts to the Supreme Court. Clark and other social scientists testified in a number of these cases.[7] Testifying in *Brown v. Board of Education of Topeka* (1954), the social science expert Louisa P. Holt influenced the trial court's findings of fact on the ill effects of segregation, and these findings of fact were later cited by the Supreme Court in its decision. At the request of NAACP attorneys, a group of social scientists headed by Isidor Chein, Kenneth Clark, and Stuart Cook prepared a review of the evidence on segregation (now called the Social Science Statement) that was appended to the NAACP brief to the Supreme Court and noted in the *Brown* decision.

When the *Brown* decision was rendered in 1954, the importance of the psychological and sociological premises for the argument were apparent in Chief Justice Earl Warren's opinion for a unanimous Court:

> Segregation of white and colored children in public schools has a detrimental effect upon the colored children. The impact is greater when it has the sanction of law; for the policy of separating the races is usually interpreted as denoting the inferiority in the negro group. A sense of inferiority affects the motivation of the child to learn. Segregation with the sanction of law, therefore, has a tendency to [retard] the educational and mental development of negro children and to deprive them of some of the benefits they would receive in a racial[ly] integrated school system. Whatever may have been the extent of psychological knowledge at the time of *Plessy v. Ferguson*, this finding is amply supported by modern authority.

The court then cited the ample modern authority, listing social science studies by name and citing their authors in a now famous footnote 11,[8] thus directly contradicting the social psychological assertions made by the Court in *Plessy* and providing an important part of the rationale for overruling the 1896 decision.

Warren's opinion for a unanimous Court declared segregated schools unconstitutional, but the Court waited another year before issuing its word on remedies. The Court offered few guidelines to the federal district courts that were to oversee the implementation of remedies, urging only that the desegregation of the schools be accomplished "with all deliberate speed." The Court was appropriately cautious. No decision before had affected so many American families and communities directly and personally.

The two *Brown* decisions opposed a few words on paper against 200 years of history and custom. The words of the Supreme Court were law, however, and all of the federal government's power to enforce the law was behind the words. In 1957, when the governor of Arkansas used the National Guard to prevent African American children from entering White schools, President Dwight D. Eisenhower sent federal troops to protect the African American children's rights (Bickel, 1962). The show of force was not sufficient to end the legal skirmishing. Community after community adopted foot-dragging plans. Constance Baker Motley, an African American woman and then a recent graduate of Columbia University Law School, traveled throughout the South arguing cases for the NAACP to win desegregation orders in different communities. A real novelty at that time as an African American female lawyer arguing cases in Southern courtrooms, she braved hardship, insults, and threats. However, she was determined and regularly won her cases. She is now a federal court judge (Brenner, 1994).

In legal terms, desegregation meant that African American and White children and African American and White teachers and administrators should work side by side in unitary, racially mixed schools. The remedies—busing within districts, busing across school district lines, pairing schools, and affirmative action hiring—required a departure from the concept of neighborhood schools and from some hiring practices.[9] Busing was supported by a massive national study showing that African American students in integrated schools performed better than African American students in segregated schools, and that money spent on schools made little difference in performance (Coleman et al., 1966; Ravitch, 2000).

Not only Southern schools were segregated. African Americans in Northern urban areas also attended segregated schools, partly because of the increasing suburbanization of the nation after World War II and the increasing concentration of African Americans in the inner cities. Segregation in Northern schools was not only the result of the "succession" of one population by another (see chapter 4). In many cities, authorities had drawn school district lines or located new schools in such a way as to ensure segregated schools. In Cleveland, for example, 81 percent of schools were either all White or all Black. African American schools were overcrowded, while schools on the White side of town had space. New schools were sited in a way to encourage segregation (Ravitch, 2000). In 1973 the Supreme Court ruled in *Keyes* v. *Denver* that if a portion of a school system was segregated as a result of discriminatory practices by school authorities, a systemwide remedy could be imposed even if there was no other history of officially imposed segregation.

Where African American students constituted a majority or near majority of the school populations, integration could not be achieved without busing students across school district lines. The Court refused to authorize cross district busing, however, in the absence of evidence that school authorities in the affected suburban districts had acted to cause segregation in the urban district. The Court refused to recognize arguments that governments in suburban districts had contributed indirectly to segregated schools. Zoning requiring large, expensive houses or large lots, real estate sales practices of steering African Americans away from housing in White areas, discriminatory mortgage lending practices, and White hostility toward African Americans seeking to buy homes in White suburbs contributed to the concentration of African Americans in the inner cities. In other words, the Court refused to take into account institutional racism. The Court approved the plaintiff's request that resources be allocated to remedy educational deficits and to develop programs that facilitated integration within the urban school district (*Milliken* v. *Bradley*, 1974).

The *Milliken* decision limited the possibilities for desegregation to whatever could be accomplished within a given school district, and probably contributed to so-called White flight (the movement of White families out of the cities to avoid busing to integrate the schools). Busing undoubtedly contributed to a backlash against integration efforts and to the development of resistance to further efforts at integrating the schools (Ravitch, 2000; but see Orfield, 2001, who believed the effect of busing in contributing to White flight was less potent than others believed). Moreover, political leaders, sensing the resistance of large numbers of parents to busing programs, articulated those views and turned them into votes (Ravitch, 1983). Although some efforts to impose busing provoked violence (e.g., the Boston schools; Smith, 1978; Metcalf, 1983), in other communities busing and integration proceeded peacefully (Willie, 1984).

Court orders to desegregate affected school districts all over the country. Implementation was monitored by federal judges or special masters reporting to the judge who had issued the order. These cases continued for many years. Thirty years later, Clegg (2000) reported that there were about 450 cases in federal courts involving the federal government in some fashion. These cases intruded on local prerogatives. Critics claimed that federal judges "were running the schools," a complaint based on the traditional value that schools could be controlled locally. More recently, the Supreme Court authorized federal judges to relinquish jurisdiction over school desegregation cases when the judge found the school district to be "unitary," that is in substantial compliance with the court's desegregation order and when new segregation was caused by housing patterns rather than by actions of school officials or legislatures (D. Levine, 1993). These decisions, along with the decision eliminating busing across school district lines in Northern communities, have contributed to the resegregation of the schools (Orfield, 1993, 2001).

The *Brown* decision had a large effect in reducing segregation in schools after the 1970s, especially in the South. In 1954, before *Brown*, only .001 percent of African American students were in majority White schools in the South. By 1988 this had grown to 43.5 percent, although by 1998 it had declined to 32.7 percent. The suburban population became segregated as Whites moved into some neighborhoods and African Americans into others. Poorer African Americans were concentrated in the cities, a consequence of "private decisions" not subject to court intervention.

Most people are in favor of integrated communities, but both Whites and African Americans feel more comfortable when their own group is in the majority in the integrated neighborhood. Whites moved to White communities. Middle-class African Americans sought out middle-class African American communities, for the benefits of enjoying a sense of community, and in part because of the stresses of living in an integrated society (Cashin, 2001).

Increasing residential segregation due to population shifts has also made it more difficult to integrate schools racially. Orfield (2001) reported that in 26 of the largest urban school districts the percentage of White students ranged from 4 percent in Detroit and Washington, DC, to 42 percent in Albuquerque, New Mexico. The median percentage of White students in those school districts was about 12.2. In 1999, 70 percent of African Americans and 75.6 percent of Latinos were in schools that had between 50 and 100 percent minority students. In 1999, 36.5 percent of African Americans and 36.6 percent of Latinos were in schools that had between 90 and 100 percent minority students.

The changes are not only due to housing patterns and court decisions. The demographic makeup of the nation is changing. Latinos and Asians make up a larger proportion of the population in many parts of the country. Orfield sums up the trend:

> We will increasingly see entire metropolitan areas and states where there will be no majority group, or the majority group will be Latino or African American. This will be a new experience in American educational history. We will be facing either pluralism in schools on an unprecedented level, with millions of whites needing to adjust to minority status, or the possibility of very serious racial and ethnic polarization, reinforced by educational inequalities, with the possible exclusion of the majority of students from access to educational mobility. We will, in the process, be affecting the kinds of relationships and experiences that prepare people to function in highly multiracial civic life and workplaces. (Orfield, 2001, p. 20)

Disappointing experiences in desegregated schools, including ability-tracking that effectively resegregated integrated schools (Linehan, 2001), and the overrepresentation of African American children in special education classes (Stashenko, 1999; Simon, 1999) have led some African American leaders to rethink the values of integrated education (Hill, 1993). They question whether integration leading to assimilation into the majority culture is a worthwhile goal even if attainable. They argue that self-imposed instead of governmentally imposed separation, and an Afrocentric curriculum, have value for the development of identity in both male and female African Americans (Cummings, 1993). One problem however, is whether all-African American public schools will be able to command a fair share of public resources.

Social Science Theory and Integration

The social science testimony given in cases reaching the Supreme Court asserted that segregation was wrong and harmful and that desegregation would undo the harm. It offered little discussion of the specific problems of implementing remedies. Cook (1984), a coauthor of the Social Sciences Statement cited in *Brown*, noted that the legal issue in *Brown* (1954) dealt with the effects on children of lifelong de jure (by law) segregation and did not require a detailed discussion of remedies. Nonetheless, their testimony and position papers contained a set of implicit situational hypotheses.

Stephan (1978) reviewed the testimony and drew a causal model in which White prejudice toward African Americans led to low African American self-esteem and achievement, and African American prejudice toward Whites. In turn, the same factors looped back to stimulate and maintain White prejudice against African Americans. If enforced segregation, the institutional base for the loop, were to be interrupted, African American self-esteem and achievement should improve, African Americans should develop more positive attitudes toward Whites, and Whites would have more positive attitudes toward African Americans. Stephen's model implies rapid change but did not include time as a variable.

Stephan (1978) reviewed a large number of studies that tested hypotheses derived from the Social Science Statement. The results are generally equivocal with respect to improving interracial attitudes. An equal number of studies showed increases and decreases in African American prejudice toward Whites, and more studies show an increase in White prejudice toward African Americans than show a decrease.

The problems of integration transcend Black–White issues. White students, who were admitted to racially balance an elite school that was majority Asian, experienced the problems of being in the minority. Asian students stigmatized White students as relatively poorly qualified affirmative action admittees to this high-achieving, highly regarded high school. White students recognized their special status, but did not seem as distressed by it as one might expect. However, White students tended to self-segregate and formed an "All American Club" in response to clubs celebrating various Asian ethnicities (Chuang,

2001). These examples show the problem is complex. As the relative proportion of Hispanic and non-European immigrant groups grows, we will be faced with new issues. The focus on African Americans and Whites is insufficient in today's society.

Orfield (2001) reviewed more recent research which suggested that African American and White students learned to get along with each other, and felt more comfortable interacting with each other across racial lines in integrated settings later in life. However, the consequences of desegregation for school achievement are complex. According to Stephan's summary, African American students in integrated schools do somewhat better than African American students in segregated schools, and White achievement is not adversely affected in desegregated schools. Earlier studies showed that the achievement test score gap between younger African American and White children was decreasing. However, more recent studies suggest that as the level of school segregation increased, the achievement gap between African American and White youth also increased (Orfield, 2001).

Achievement test scores are not the only index of educational accomplishment. High school graduation rates increased among African Americans in integrated schools, although the rate has declined in recent years. African American youth in integrated schools opt to go to college more frequently than those in more segregated schools. Moreover, African American youth from integrated schools have better college grades, and they are more likely to gain entrance into prestigious law schools than students coming from more segregated schools (Orfield, 2001).

Could integrated schools be more successful? Since part of the challenge was to implement desegregation orders, to what extent was desegregation implemented in a systematic fashion? Gerard (1983) notes that the Social Science Statement specified several conditions under which real integration, and thus the posited effects, could take place. These included:

> (a) firm and consistent endorsement by those in authority; (b) the absence of competition among representatives of different racial groups; (c) the equivalence of positions and functions among all participants in the desegregated setting; and (d) interracial contacts of a type that permitted learning about one another as individuals. (p. 870)

The statement was drawn from existing knowledge about prejudice extended to the school situation (Cook, 1984). However, few of these conditions could be met in most places nor did most school authorities have the social engineering knowledge or the skills to make integration work.

Looking back, Gerard concludes that data were not available to warrant the confident predictions that were derived from the Social Science Statement and, moreover, that the social scientists were not fully cognizant of the contexts within which the abstract principles they had culled from the literature would have to be implemented. In effect, he claims that they were unfamiliar with the culture of the schools (see Sarason, 1982b).

Some (e.g., Cahn, 1955) argue that it is an error to rely on empirical outcomes to decide moral questions. Should we be able to argue that because all the postulated benefits of desegregation cannot be demonstrated empirically, we should again allow states to enforce segregation? Although certain benefits were implied for forced busing, if we did not integrate schools and did not integrate faculties, what else could we have done, in Justice William Brennan's words (*Green* v. *County*, 1968), to eliminate discrimination "root and branch"? Below, we will briefly examine a relatively successful school desegregation case.

Beyond busing. In hindsight, some observers argue that the premises behind desegregation were flawed. The simple placement of African Americans and Whites in the same buildings was insufficient; more profound changes were necessary to equalize the positions of African American and White children.

> Substantive change requires the following: an examination of disparate funding levels, a finding of de facto school desegregation [i.e., without the operation of law] as sufficient for an order desegregating suburban school systems, a diverse curriculum, an elimination of testing bias to the extent practicable, and the placement of decisions affecting minority children in the hands of minority parents. Racism is so much a part of the American fabric that every aspect of the school environment must be examined and re-examined to measures its effects on patterns of dominance and exclusion. (Hill, 1993, p. 723)

Some writers prescribe the conditions they believe will enhance the engagement of African American children in the classroom. These writers believe that subtle and not-so-subtle devaluation of African Americans in the larger society and in the classroom result in student disengagement from school and failure to learn. In keeping with the view that emphasizing children's deficits and providing remediation is a form of blaming the victim, Steele (1992) suggests that remedial programs may have the unintended consequence of increasing the African American student's sense of vulnerability, and argues that "wise" teaching—accepting that African American children can learn, creating a classroom atmosphere in which students are valued, and holding out demands for achievement—can be a powerful preventive to the disengagement that leads to failure and dropping out.

Kagan (1990) also believes that classroom settings can alienate students. For Kagan, and for Steele, the solutions require a reanalysis of the classroom as a setting that can "coerce" learning and engagement. They would agree with Sarason's (1990) analysis that no school reform can succeed unless it changes student-teacher relationships in the classroom. Steele and Kagan have more integrationist aims and do not believe that "wise" teaching can take place only in racially segregated settings. Kagan wants to reduce alienation by changing classroom practices. Steele (1992, p. 78) wants "to foster in our children a sense of hope and entitlement to mainstream American life and schooling. . . ." It is unlikely that successful lawsuits will be brought on the grounds that classrooms are not successful. However, in an attempt to remedy an unsatisfactory condition in education, community participation in the schools may lead us to a better educational program for all.

Successful Desegregation of the Schools—A Case Study[10]

The organizational changes necessary to support desegregation were not at the forefront of the consciousness of the federal judges who were overseeing desegregation efforts (Kirp & Babcock, 1981). With time, however, judges, plaintiffs, and school board officials did learn to cope with the problems of overseeing desegregation efforts. (See *Belk* v. *Charlotte Mecklenburg Board of Education*, 2001, for a history of the resistance to desegregation and the progress this Southern school board made over the years.) Critics of busing have emphasized the difficulties, including the moral questions and dilemmas of discriminating on the basis of race even to effect a remedy (e.g., Glazer, 1975), and whether the 1.75 billion dollars spent on desegregation could have been better spent (Ravitch, 2000). However, as Orfield (2001) has shown, in at least some cases desegregation efforts have produced overall improvements in the schools.

We now turn to a brief case history of successful school desegregation in Buffalo, New York. In 1976, federal district court Judge John T. Curtin found that Buffalo city school officials, the Common Council, and the mayor had acted to create or to perpetuate segregated schools. The school board had redistricted school zones to maintain segregated schools, allowed Whites to transfer out of integrated schools, stopped teaching Polish in a high school with many African American students (thus encouraging Whites to enroll in Polish classes in other high schools), placed a junior high school in a neighborhood that guaranteed it would be segregated, and fostered discriminatory policies affecting admission to desirable technical high schools. Moreover, a busing plan ordered by the commissioner of education after the 1964 complaint was found to be inadequate. The Common Council had tried to block a voluntary busing plan and through its fiscal control had refused to support a new building plan that might have relieved segregation.[11] The U.S. Supreme Court had held in *Keyes* (1973) that if any portion of a school system had been segregated as a result of the action of school officials, a system-wide desegregation remedy was in order. Once the city schools and the city administration had been found responsible for the degree of segregation that existed, it was necessary to prepare and implement a remedy. Because of inadequate previous plans, the judge insisted that if a comprehensive plan be adopted.

White and African American parents were angry. They resented the idea of busing for racial balance, and were concerned about their children's safety and their opportunities for a good education. By this time there was sufficient understanding of the problems of integration that school officials, led by school superintendent Eugene Reville, and the plaintiffs agreed to develop educational programs of high quality to make the schools attractive to parents, along with instituting business to achieve integration. Judge Curtin insisted that the integration plans be developed in consultation with the community. Associate Superintendent Joseph Murray, who had been a highly effective principal of a secondary school in a difficult neighborhood, played an important role in desegregation planning.

School officials arranged more than 40 open meetings with community groups. The school administrators decided not to use outside consultants who did not know the community. Instead, they sent teams of local African American and White educators and lawyers into neighborhoods, not only to meet with and inform parents that desegregation was going to take place, but also to let parents know this was an opportunity to improve the schools as well. Parents were outspoken and the meetings were often quite heated. With the cooperation of the ecumenical Buffalo Area Metropolitan Ministries, clergy were present when trouble was anticipated. In Buffalo, community leadership was unified behind the desegregation plan.

The meetings were intended to bring forward ideas for regional and citywide "magnet" schools, schools so special that students from all parts of the district were strongly attracted to them (i.e., as if by magnets) even if attending one meant riding a bus. The meetings were also intended to organize community groups that would contribute to the development of the desegregation plan. The emphasis on education and educational choice was presented to citizens as a means of avoiding forced busing. Eventually many of the meetings resulted in parent groups convening to develop constructive plans not only to improve the schools, but also to have schools that reflected diverse educational viewpoints.

The 22 regional magnet schools were located in integrated neighborhoods or in inner-city neighborhoods. They were designed to reflect neighborhood interest and to make the schools attractive to White and Black parents whose children would be bused to those schools to keep them integrated. The school programs were designed to attract parents to their educational philosophies. One school, for example, operated on Montessori principles. Another was highly structured and traditional. One former alternative school had been developed by

White parents and was now taken over by the school system but continued to operate on the same principles of informal and individualized instruction. Still another was located in a new open-plan building suitable for an open-education program. The schools were diverse in emphasis. One had Native American programming, while another emphasized education in English and Spanish. One school specialized in programs for gifted children, while another became a prekindergarten through eighth grade school stressing science in all grades. (The Charlotte Mecklenberg school district developed a similar array of schools with special offerings as part of their desegregation program.)

The magnet schools in Buffalo accepted children from all over the city. In addition to schools at the elementary level, three citywide magnet schools were developed at the high school level. These included an academy for visual and performing arts, a traditional high school, and City Honors, a school for academically talented youth. Junior high schools were replaced with kindergarten through eighth grade schools. At a later phase, early childhood education programs offering excellent care and education for preschool children accommodated the day care needs of many female-headed households. However, at that time, because the school district had been found responsible for segregating the schools, they could use race-conscious admission criteria to the magnet schools as a remedy in order to maintain racial balance in each of the schools.

Neighborhood leaders were identified. Some were given paid positions within the school programs they helped design. One grass roots leader, once among the most articulate opponents of busing, subsequently became an advocate of busing. Teams of African American and White parents were formed to be troubleshooters in schools that were to be integrated.

Judge Curtin made himself available on an informal basis to listen to people in the neighborhoods. He received at least his fair share of hate mail, but none of that deterred him in his course. Observers say that although he unequivocally supported the integration program, he also showed his willingness to listen to problems people were experiencing, giving people a feeling that communication was taking place and that plans were not simply being imposed on them from above.

Although they had relinquished some power over public education to the judge and the parents, school administrators became enthusiastic as they realized that the desegregation order now gave them leverage to obtain the financial resources necessary to improve the schools. The interests of parents and teachers were not ignored. Teachers were allowed to transfer between schools if the educational philosophy in the school clashed with their own. Parents were actively included in implementation plans. The school district placed ads in the newspapers and on television describing the merits of the plan. The press also maintained a favorable stance toward the integration program. School personnel kept Common Council members informed. It is to the credit of Buffalo politicians that no one overtly exploited feelings about integration for political advantage.

The community was involved at an early date. School superintendent Reville invited the Buffalo Area Metropolitan Ministries to provide support from the clergy for desegregation programs. In addition, a Citizens Commission on Desegregation was formed with representatives from a variety of constituencies. In 1978 another citizens' organization under the aegis of the Buffalo Area Metropolitan Ministries, Citizens for Quality Education (C4QE), was funded to assist community leadership in desegregating the school system. The organization was to work with the school system and the court primarily to develop and assist grassroots leadership.

C4QE set up a citywide advisory council with representatives from every school board district in the city. It included a representative from the mayor's office and from the school board. Most of the members were parent representatives. Eventually Lewis Sinatra, a former Buffalo teacher, became its executive director. The organization adopted a strategy of working with specific neighborhood projects and with a strategy of empowerment. C4QE told parents they had a right to be active and then assisted parents in working out their programs. C4QE did the staff work and research, but always stayed in the background when it came to any formal presentation to officials. The desegregation program in Buffalo has been hailed as a model (Winerip, 1985). Desegregation took place in peace and relative harmony. There was no significant change in the racial composition of the schools in the short run. The White population of the city did not flee but became highly supportive of its schools. Parental involvement and satisfaction with the schools increased. Student achievement scores increased overall, while curriculum options proliferated. Students and parents participated more in extracurricular school programs (see Baud, 1982).

One cannot say that Buffalo schools are without problems. They have many of the problems of urban school systems. Despite the continuing problems, the same legal mandate to desegregate that led to negative social and educational consequences elsewhere had a more positive impact in Buffalo. We cannot attribute the positive impact only to the approach taken to implement the program, but in examining the approach we observe that officials responsible for desegregation made sensible use of identifiable community processes to produce change that benefited the entire community.

After Desegregation

Forty years after *Brown*, hundreds of school desegregation cases were still open under the supervision of federal judges (Clegg, 2000). Many, including the U.S. Supreme Court, became uneasy at the length of time the cases were continuing and wanted to see control of the schools restored to local authorities. In 1976, the U.S. Supreme Court said that the supervising federal trial court judge had no authority to order annual changes in school district boundaries to maintain desegregated schools when the changes were due to population changes (*Pasadena Board of Education* v. *Spangler*, 1976). In subsequent cases, the Supreme Court said that cases could be closed when "vestiges of past discrimination have been eliminated to the extent practicable" (*Board of Education* v. *Dowell*, 1991). School districts could ask to be relieved of federal supervision if they had achieved "unitary status." They achieved unitary status when there were no vestiges of unlawful segregation in "student assignment, faculty assignment, facilities and resources, staff assignment and extracurricular activities" (*Freeman* v. *Pitts*, 1992, p. 492).

The Court did not consider equality of school achievement a factor. The Court concluded that differences in achievement were complexly determined and not provable "vestiges" of illegal discrimination. The Court was never explicit about what would demonstrate vestiges of past illegal discrimination in the present. Once we go past the relatively objective standards of pupil assignments, facilities, racial composition of the teaching staff, and similar quantitative indices, what could we measure and how could it be demonstrated that the measured discrepancy was caused by past, illegal discrimination? The question presents a difficult challenge for social scientists interested in desegregation.

These court decisions now allow school districts to return to neighborhood schools if they so choose, and if their reasons for doing so are not intentionally discriminatory. The magnet school programs remain in place in most communities, a permanent legacy of the desegregation effort. When school districts were still under court order to remedy past illegal discriminatory practices, they were able to use "race conscious remedies" to balance enrollment. Thus school district administrators could assign students to school programs based on race to maintain racial balance in school programs. That meant selecting some students for desirable programs based on a racial preference as well as other credentials.

Once school districts were declared unitary, it was as if the past was totally erased. School districts that had never been found to discriminate could not use race as a basis for student assignments to school even if they wanted voluntarily to undertake or maintain an integrated school system. Those districts that had discriminated in the past and were able to use racial preferences to desegregate schools could no longer use race as a standard for admitting or rejecting students from desirable magnet schools.

Some school districts continued to use race-conscious standards for admission to desirable magnet schools in order to maintain racial balance as a matter of policy. For example, in Buffalo the school district continued to use racial preferences for admission to two magnet schools, even after the judge in the case declared the school district "unitary." The next year, a White student claimed she was rejected from admission to City Honors even though her credentials were better than those of some minority students who were accepted. The school district, realizing they would very likely lose in court, changed the admission standards to rely more on test scores. As a result, fewer minority students were admitted to City Honors in the next year. Minority admissions fell from 52 percent of new admissions to 40 percent of new admissions in a city where minority students made up 60 percent of the school population. In a second competitive elementary school with a program for gifted children, minority admissions dropped from 57 percent to 34 percent (Heaney, 1998).

White students challenged race-conscious admission standards for a magnet school in Charlotte Mecklenberg schools as a violation of equal protection. Their challenge was part of a suit to get the Charlotte Mecklenberg schools declared unitary (*Belk* v. *Charlotte Mecklenburg Board of Education* (2001). The magnet school had a long waiting list of White students seeking admission, but to maintain racial balance the Board of Education refused to admit some White students even though there were places in the school. After the school district was declared unitary, more White children gained admission but the level of racial balance in the school was reduced.

Asian American students in the multiethnic school district of San Francisco challenged admission standards to elite Lowell High School. Chinese students claimed that to maintain racial balance admission standards at Lowell were higher for Asian students than for White students. They claimed that the higher admission standard for Chinese students was a form of "affirmative action" for Whites and thus was discriminatory (D. Levine, 2000). As a result of the challenges, Lowell High School changed its admission criteria to make the admission scores (tests and grade point average in junior high school) comparable for Chinese and for White students.

In 1999 the judge hearing the case challenging the desegregation plan in San Francisco abolished racial caps in the San Francisco schools (D. Levine, 2000). Chinese students benefited; under the new admission standards (weighting only grade point averages and test scores, and eliminating a "value added index which included race or ethnicity"), their enrollment rose from 40.0 percent in 1996 to 51.9 percent in 1999. White enrollment increased slightly under the new standards, from 17.5 percent to 19.8 percent. African American student enrollment declined from 6.3 percent to 3.8 percent; Latino enrollment declined from 12.2 percent to 4.5 percent and Filipino enrollment declined from 6.3 percent to 3.5 percent. African Americans and Latinos were a small percentage of the overall students, but in relative terms the decline was nearly one-half in the number of African American and Filipino students and two-thirds in the number of Latinos admitted (Chuang, 2001, p. 47). Minority youth might have felt even more isolated because of their reduced numbers in the school.

These experiences show that changes in race-based preferences have complex effects, especially in multiracial contexts. The problem is not limited simply to White and African American students. We also note that in each instance, although the proportion of minorities declined, the elite schools retained diversity. Whether the benefits to society of going to a "merit-based" system outweigh the losses due to smaller numbers of minority students being afforded an elite education remains to be seen. The recent U.S. Supreme Court decisions supporting the importance of diversity as an educational goal apply to colleges and law schools. Whether a similar argument can be made successfully at the high school or the elementary school level to support some form of action to increase diversity at specialized elementary and high schools remains to be seen (*Grutter* v. *Bollinger* 2003 U.S. Lexis 4800, 2003; *Gratz* v. *Bollinger* 2003 Lexis 4801, 2003).

Future Problems

As the income gap grows between wealthier Americans and poorer people, "private choices" for homes, neighborhoods, and private schools will lead to a growing separation of rich from poor. Given the preferences the African American middle class expresses for living in African American neighborhoods (Cashin 2001), segregation will increase. It is likely that other ethnic groups also express similar preferences for living in relatively homogeneous neighborhoods. In addition, the income gap between wealthier African American and poorer African Americans is also growing. That means the poorest segment of society will be even more isolated with all the ensuing consequences that Wilson (1987) described. Racially integrated suburban neighborhoods tend to be transient in nature because Whites as a general role don't move in, but African Americans do (Cashin, 2001). In addition, poorer African Americans tend to move into the older first ring suburbs. Wealthier African Americans who are concerned about lowered school standards, increase in crime, and in general poorer upkeep of homes by the poor (who may be renting from absentee landlords) move to suburbs farther out, or put their children into private schools.

Those factors contribute to increasing racial and social class isolation. They may also contribute to reduced political support from Whites for largely African American schools serving a poorer clientele with greater needs for expensive special education and social services. This problem of racial and class isolation may result in sharp differences in the adequacy of schools for poorer students with large consequences for the opportunity for quality education and the social mobility education can bring. Schools in poorer school districts may have less adequate physical facilities, fewer computers, and fewer advanced placement classes, a credential competitive colleges weight in their admission decisions.

In most states at present, school financing is based in part on local property taxes, and on state aid. School districts with a more valuable property base, which may include expensive shopping malls and other light industry or commercial real estate, can keep the property tax rate low and still provide handsomely for their schools. School districts with many tax exempt nonprofit, religious, or government properties and with less expensive homes must have higher tax rates to support their schools. Swenson (2000) cites some representative figures: "Baldwin Park [CA] citizens who paid a school tax of $5.48 per hundred of assessed valuation were able to spend less than half as much on education as Beverly Hills residents who were taxed only $2.38 per $100." In New York State schools in the poorest districts spent $7,000 per pupil while those in the wealthiest district spent $43,000 per pupil. (Swenson, 2000, n. 4, p. 1147).

In the past the U.S. Supreme Court said that education was not a fundamental right under the U.S. Constitution (*San Antonio Independent School District* v. *Rodriguez*, 1973) and refused to order school tax equalization under the Constitution as a matter of equal protection. Because an attack on unequal school finances on a national constitutional basis is foreclosed, advocates have been using state constitutions as a basis for suits seeking equal funding throughout a state. These suits have met with varying success (see Swenson, 2000). However, litigation is but one avenue for equalizing educational opportunities and facilities when we have segregated schools and neighborhoods. If some are rethinking the goals of integration, as Professor Thom Moore suggested to us, will community psychologists have a role in articulating new goals and paths to achieve those new goals? This sort of social action requires organization and resources to carry out. It can also require political organization to influence state legislatures to appropriate funds without court orders to equalize educational opportunity. Minorities cannot depend on the good will of the majority. It may require greater parental involvement. If the schools are to serve the needs of all children, then it will also require social action and community development to convince legislatures to do the right thing and to improve schools.

As David Levine, who represented Chinese children in San Francisco, wrote,

As the era of court-ordered school desegregation comes to a close in the coming years, and the more general affirmative action debate is played out, we must continue to think of new ways of achieving equity and fairness in different situations. (D. Levine, 2000, p. 143)

Here is a new arena and a new challenge for community psychology. We take up these types of approaches when we discuss community development and social action in chapter 12.

Summary

The history of efforts to desegregate the schools helps us to understand that the social problem of race relations goes back to the beginning of our nation. We have been struggling with the problem for 200 years and more, and only in the last 40 years have we approached an open society. The profound social changes that we have seen resulted from a concerted self-help effort. Social scientists participated by developing data and arguments that permitted an attack on the then-conventional wisdom, as embodied in law, that segregation not only was not harmful, but was positively beneficial. Social science research and writing established the harmful, oppressive nature of segregation enforced by law. Social science research and theory provided part of the rationale for the desegregation remedy.

Events have outrun our ability to control circumstances. The failures of desegregation can be attributed to our oversimplified understanding of the problems and to changes in employment and housing, related socioeconomic issues, and U.S. Supreme Court decisions that limited the available remedies. The schools may be more segregated today than they were 20 years ago. A large majority of African American and Latino students attend schools in which most of the students are members of minority groups and are poor. Students in schools with a large majority of poor families perform less well than minority students in more diverse schools. Even suburban schools in the North have high levels of segregation. Relatively few White students go to school with minority students and, because of housing patterns, minority students in suburban schools tend to be concentrated in a few schools (Orfield, 1993, 2001).

We have not yet learned to balance ethnic pride with mutual respect in a multicultural society. Although it is easy to decry the failures of integration, we cannot overlook the positive changes that have accrued. One of the authors recently had lunch with two young African American professionals in a hotel dining room in Florida. We were all at a professional conference. The conversation turned to the failures of the civil rights movement and the failure of integration. At one point, however, we all acknowledged that not too many years ago, an interracial group like ours would not have been seated together in a hotel dining room in a Southern state or in a border state. Our presence together was a visible reminder of the accomplishments of the civil rights movement, accomplishments not to be dismissed lightly.

Clearly, no single discipline's perspective is enough to help us understand a phenomenon as complex as school desegregation. We will have to take fuller cognizance of the complex historical, social, political, legal, and economic contexts within which we work and live.

One might argue, as Gerard (1983) does, that social scientists do not yet have enough to say and should stay out of public affairs until their disciplines are better developed. On the other hand, social scientists do have analytic methods and concepts, and bodies of knowledge with utility for real-world problems. Sarason (1974) issued a call for social scientists not only to engage in relevant research but also to undertake social action as a vehicle for research. In his view social science would be benefited by "messing in a sustained way with the realities of modern society" (p. 261). In his view social action research with an uncertain disciplinary base is justified when "one does the best one can and relies on the efforts and criticisms of others to do better the next time" (p. 267). In our view, neither social science nor society has suffered by the immersion of social scientists in desegregation efforts, and a strong argument can be made that both have benefited.

In the last two chapters we will deal further with the rationale for participation in social action, with the problems that arise when science is employed in a politicized context, and with the ethics of participation in social action and intervention in the community.

Notes

1. This chapter owes a great deal to Kluger's magnificent book, *Simple Justice* (1976).

2. Article I, Section 2. The Constitution contained two other provisions with respect to slavery. The importation of slaves could not be prohibited by Congress before 1808 (Article I, Section 9) and runaway slaves could be compelled to return, even if they went to free territory (Article IV, Section 2).

3. *Civil Rights Cases*, 109 U.S. 3 (1883); *U.S.* v. *Cruickshank* 92 U.S. 542 (1875).

4. The U.S. Supreme Court cited *Plessy* when it upheld the decision of a Mississippi school board to send a native-born Chinese girl to a segregated school. The court thus found that the state had the power to segregate its citizens (*Gong Lum* v. *Rice*, 275 U.S. 78, 1927).

5. *Sipuel* v. *Oklahoma State Board of Regents*, 332 U.S. 631 (1948); *McLaurin* v. *Oklahoma State Regents for Higher Education*, 337 U.S. 637 (1950); *Sweatt* v. *Painter*, 339 U.S. 629 (1950).

6. See Myrdal (1944, chap. 28, Vol. 2) for a discussion of this literature.

7. See *Briggs* v. *Elliott*, 347 U.S. 497 (1954); *Davis* v. *County School Board of Prince Edward County*, 347 U.S. 483 (1954); *Belton* v. *Gebhart*, 347 U.S. 483 (1954).

8. Since *Brown*, the courts at all levels have paid increasing attention to expert social science testimony in a wide variety of cases, although there are many problems to be resolved (see Levine & Howe, 1985; Monahan & Walker, 1986).

9. *Swann* v. *Charlotte-Mecklenburg Board of Education,* 402 U.S. 1 (1971). Prior to that time there had been a question as to whether a remedy that required a state to take into account race would itself be a form of discrimination. The Supreme Court said that to take race into account for purposes of fashioning a remedy was permissible.

10. The information in this section is based upon notes taken by Adeline Levine at public lectures given by superintendent Eugene Reville and associate superintendent Joseph Murray, lectures and an interview with Lewis Sinatra conducted by Murray Levine, and Winerip's *New York Times* article (1985).

11. *Arthur* v. *Nyquist,* 415 F. Supp. 904 (W.D. N.Y. 1976); see Seller (1979) for a history of ethnic groups and education in Buffalo.

12. In recent years City Honors has contributed three finalists to the Westinghouse Science Talent Search, bringing national recognition to the city and its schools.

12

Community Development and Social Action in Community Psychology

Chapter 11, on school desegregation, illustrated the complexity of community change and the need in many real-world settings for action to achieve change, even when our understanding of the process is incomplete. In this chapter, we develop further aspects of this theme in terms of the ecological analogy and other perspectives presented ear-

lier in the book. We focus on two primary modes of action that can relieve powerlessness and that address power disparities that contribute
to social problems. One mode is called community development, a
strategy that involves consensus and cooperation. The second is social
action, a strategy that calls for confrontation and conflict. Even though
we can identify two modes, there are no pure types. Most groups will
at various times engage in both strategies. People who try to change
aspects of the social world define problems as having their "cause" in
the social world, not in the psychological deficits of people suffering
from the problem. Their problem in adaptation is interpreted to result
from barriers to access to resources. We begin with issues of problem
definition.

The Politics of Problem Definition

Problem definition is basic to how we understand and try to solve problems, but our usual approach may be so grounded in the assumptions
of our worldview that we are not even aware of them. Our definitions
may restrict the universe of alternatives (Sarason, 1972; Levine &
Levine, 1992). For example, if we try to understand poverty by studying poor people, we will identify certain person-centered explanations
for this problem such as lack of education or skills, cultural deficits,
dysfunctional families, or "laziness", and we will try to correct those
flaws. If we define the problem in the context of the overall political
and economic system, however, we could just as easily understand
poverty by studying rich people. Our explanations would involve capitalism as a system, and solutions such as distributing wealth more eq-
uitably might be among our choices.

Humphreys and Rappaport (1993) point out the political and
power consequences of different ways of defining problems as they affect the federal government's role in mental illness and substance abuse
programs. They characterize the process of defining a problem as stak-
ing out a specific "claim" on the way that problem will be understood
and dealt with and cite the example of community mental health programs. Federal policy toward behavior disorders in the politically pro-
gressive 1960s focused on improving cities and the system of care.
Beginning in 1981 the much more conservative Reagan and Bush ad-
ministrations reallocated considerable federal money from community
treatment services to basic biomedical research on mental illness. As
cutbacks occurred in mental health programs, the Reagan administration substantially increased federal funding for programs that defined
substance abuse as a problem of defective individuals. This new claim
on the public's understanding of a widely acknowledged problem was
backed up with the individually targeted rhetoric of "Just say no" and
with sizable funding increases for law enforcement. Redefining the

drug problem as one brought about by criminals and defective or weak-willed individuals gave federal policymakers the opportunity to shape the federal role in dealing with disorders of behavior. The definition of drug problems as individual problems also had a substantial impact on federal research funding priorities and therefore on new research, and the new knowledge created that in turn affected solutions. Humphreys and Rappaport caution us to recognize our tendency to adopt a one-sided policy analysis because of our values and to combat this tendency by incorporating divergent perspectives into problem definitions right from the start—for example, the view that substance abuse is caused by *both* individual vulnerabilities and by social conditions that put people at risk.

Blaming the Victim

In most peoples' perception, wealth and power form the obvious metric of successful adaptation in our society. Wealth and power are finite and are not evenly distributed; some people are wealthier and more powerful than others. People, liberals and conservatives alike, who enjoy a disproportionate share of money and power naturally want to assume that they earned it all through individual talent and hard work. This logic makes them see those less fortunate as lazy and ignorant. All desserts, good or bad, are seen as just, and so they resist attempts to make the distribution more equitable. Because access to wealth and power and control of key community resources is restricted, those without access feel powerless, hopeless, and frustrated—emotions intimately connected to the prevalence of social problems and stressful life circumstances. Given that some degree of vulnerability is present in everyone, events and circumstances in the soap opera of life have more serious implications for those who lack resources. Because most Americans share common values, from time to time many advantaged people become appalled at the existence of poverty, crime, mental disorders, and other social problems, and insist that something be changed (Ryan, 1976).

In Ryan's words, one solution is to "blame the victim" by defining the problem in person-centered terms. Primary deviance might be attributed to biological malfunctions understood as "mental illness," which leads to labeling and delimiting the problem at the level of individuals. Thus a problem is contained in a way that does not threaten the existing distribution of power and wealth. Once the problem is defined as a pathological characteristic of certain individuals, the range of relevant solutions naturally becomes restricted to interventions that change those individuals. We can congratulate ourselves that we are a caring society, while at the same time we neatly avoid a definition of social problems in economic and political terms with different implications for change. Putting it simply, blaming the victim enables advantaged citizens to reconcile humanitarian values with their own self-interest.

When victims accept the definition of social problems in person-centered terms they reinforce the process of person blame and essentially end up blaming themselves for their predicament. As one example, before the Stonewall riot that initiated the gay rights movement, most gays accepted the then prevailing definition of their conditions as a form of deviance based on a psychiatric disorder. As a result, many were submissive and concealed their identities rather than fight openly for their rights and for a definition of themselves as loving human beings who simply had a different sexual identity, as happened after Stonewall (Duberman, 1993).

Blaming the victim is inherent in clinical interventions that may simply encourage victims to feel less distressed about their circumstances. Some prevention programs implicitly blame the victim. Competence-building undertaken with "high-risk" individuals, for example, clearly involves changing these individuals and not the disadvantageous economic and political circumstances that typically surround them. It makes no difference that the alleged deficiency is social or cognitive, not genetic. Victim blaming thus becomes an inevitable by-product of professional activities not directed explicitly at changing circumstances or reallocating resources.

Victim blaming shows a lack of ecological thinking, or the ability to understand how much we are all affected by our environment at multiple levels. It is also antithetical to the strengths orientation community psychologists generally try to adopt. Both strengths and adversities must be examined from an ecological perspective, which places individuals, families, and communities in context. That context includes multiple systems, institutions, and environments that, interdependently, both affect people and are affected by them (see chapter 4).

Paradox and Empowerment

One rationale for political solutions to social problems is the limited validity of existing therapeutic and preventive interventions and the recognition that there may not be a perfect solution to many social problems (Sarason, 1978). Rappaport (1981) argued that, far from achieving absolute solutions to social problems, much of what community psychologists have learned leaves us confronting a set of paradoxes—seemingly self-contradictory viewpoints. One paradox, for example, is that professional "experts" with prestigious positions and impressive degrees are still able to learn much about certain behavioral problems from otherwise ordinary people who have managed to overcome these problems, such as members of Alcoholics Anonymous and other self-help groups. Who is really the expert in such cases? Either one can make a valid claim to this role, and therein lies the paradox.

Ideological differences can also lead to paradoxes. In the debate over whether people have "needs" or "rights," one issue is this: If people have "needs," they have *deficiencies*, the removal of which makes them "equal" by making them the same as others. If instead they have "rights" they have *strengths*, which if supported make them "equal" by allowing them to be different from others.

Another example of paradox arises from the realization that in trying to help people through identifying and treating "cases" of psychopathology, we may end up harming them through iatrogenic ("physician induced") influences such as labeling and its consequence, stigma. Rather than successfully helping people, traditional programs to treat or prevent psychological problems in individuals may represent a kind of paternalistic colonialism by professionals toward society's less powerful members (Rappaport, 1981).

To a large extent, mental health and other human service professionals in effect force the community to accept their goods and services. They hold prestigious jobs and command good salaries for themselves; community residents become dependents unable to determine for themselves how best to live and to attain their own goals. Is professional intervention then helpful to clients or is it harmful? Although apparently contradictory, these two perspectives both lead to valid observations, to potentially different definitions of problems, and to alternative solutions.

Recognition of the paradoxical nature of social problems and their attendant solutions leads to the conclusion that permanent solutions to social problems may not exist (Sarason, 1978); today's "solution" merely sows the seeds for tomorrow's problem, in the way that Moral Treatment, for example, the solution to a problem in its mid-nineteenth-century heyday, itself later became a problem in the form of large custodial mental hospitals (Levine, 1981). Rappaport raises the possibility that social problems, intertwined as they are with basic human differences that may ultimately be irreconcilable, are not "absolute" in nature and in solution but are *dialectical*—that is, they may best be understood when viewed from more than one perspective. Following Piaget's definition of objectivity, we should assume that phenomena appear different when they are viewed from different perspectives.

One implication of viewing a problem as dialectical is that the solutions should be many and diverse, having in common only that they entail decentralized control and empowerment of citizens at the local level. Decentralization and empowerment are high in Rappaport's value hierarchy. To empower people is to enhance their ability to control their own lives and means that professionals function more as collaborators than symbolic parents. In this view, professionals have something important to offer, but in a different relationship to their clients than that entailed in the medical model.

The paradoxical status of Head Start within the needs-versus-rights dialectic may be one reason why it has far outlived the rest of the War on Poverty. Head Start was both an educationally oriented prevention program for poverty-stricken preschoolers and a vehicle for empowering disadvantaged communities by creating jobs and fostering parents' sense of control over their lives and those of their children. It is a clear example of a multidimensional solution to poverty.

Many of these points are also evident in Cohen and Thompson's (1992) instructive analysis of homelessness among persons with serious and persistent mental illness. What causes homelessness in this population? Are they "crazy" and unable to function, or just poor? Are such people homeless as a direct and inevitable consequence of disabling cognitive or emotional deficits that render them unable to cope outside of institutions, or is their homelessness coincidental with the difficulty they as a vulnerable group, along with others who are not mentally ill—families in crisis, unemployed single parents, disadvantaged ethnic minorities—have had retaining a niche within the ever-decreasing supply of low-income housing?

Is the best solution to homelessness in people with mental illness one of funding mental health professionals to locate and engage these people in high-intensity psychiatric services, including reinstitutionalization, or would it be better for professionals and others to work collaboratively to improve access to safe, comfortable housing that is well integrated with that of nonmentally ill people, and in this way simply help to support peoples' own coping and problem-solving efforts?

Shinn and Tsemberis (1998) reported the results of a very large, long-term longitudinal study of homeless families. Five years after their initial contact with the researchers, 80 percent of the families were housed in their own apartments, on average for 35 months. The best predictor of long-term housing stability was the family's receipt of one of five forms of subsidized housing. The family's history of mental illness, substance abuse, or health problems did not affect stability of housing. Receipt of mental health and social services did not contribute to housing stability. Shinn and Tsemberis (1998) came to a radical conclusion:

> We claim that in many cases receipt of subsidized housing is sufficient to end homelessness for families. The additional value of specialized services in promoting stability is less clear. (Shinn and Tsemberis, 1998, p. 61)

Shinn and Tsemberis (1998) compared two models: In the linear continuum model the professional makes a diagnosis of the patient's needs and deficits and assigns the patient to the service the professional believes is appropriate. The second model emphasizes consumer preference and independent living. In the latter model, homeless people are offered subsidized services and empowered to select the services they consider appropriate. Where 62 percent of those treated in the linear continuum model dropped out of treatment within one month, 86 percent of those in the community preference model were still in stable housing four years later.

To summarize, in Rappaport's judgment community psychologists should clarify paradoxical definitions of social problems and facilitate the proliferation of multiple solutions to each problem. Recognition of paradoxes and the dialectical nature of problems allows one to see alternatives and exposes one's own basic assumptions to constructive criticism. Neither victim nor environment is blamed. Instead the focus is on creating settings that empower segments of a community to control their own resources rather than on solving problems in a once-and-for-all convergent sense.

Competent Communities

One implication of our analysis is that the community psychologist's job is to help to build competent communities through increased participation in decision making by those affected by the decisions. Although community participation has not always led to desirable results (Moynihan, 1969), in recent years problems of competition for control of funds and programs seem to have settled down. Many helpful community-based and community-controlled programs can be identified (Ladner, 2001).

Community competence building commits us to developing opportunities for self-determination by effecting change through social and political action. Strategies that pursue competence building at the community level can be broadly organized into two general approaches, called community development and social action, that differ significantly in their basic assumptions (Heller & Monahan, 1977). Community-development techniques assume that the community already has within it the knowledge, resources, and potential for organization and leadership to effect constructive community change through consensus. In contrast, social action assumes that resources are finite and distributed unequally, differences among various interests in the community are not easily reconcilable, and as a result the solutions to social problems are explicitly political in nature. Again, there are few pure forms. Organizations may adopt community development and social action strategies at different times.

Community Development

Community development is a process designed to create conditions of economic, social, political, and environmental progress with the active participation of the whole community and fullest possible

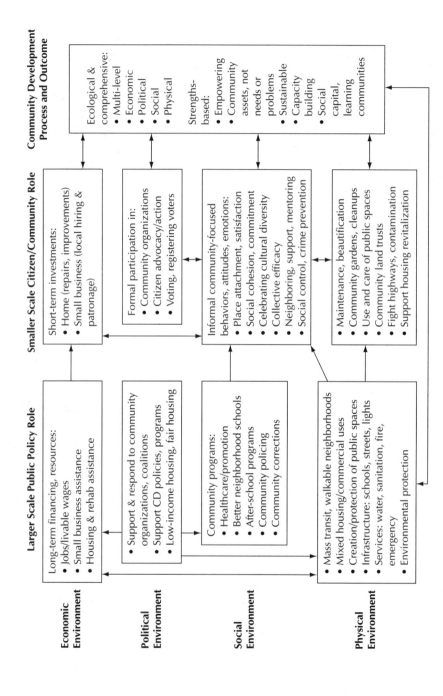

Figure 12-1. An Ecological Framework for Community Development. (From Perkins et al., 2004)

Community Development Process and Outcome

Ecological & comprehensive:
- Multi-level
- Economic
- Political
- Social
- Physical

Strengths-based:
- Empowering
- Community assets, not needs or problems
- Sustainable
- Capacity building
- Social capital, learning communities

Smaller Scale Citizen/Community Role

Short-term investments:
- Home (repairs, improvements)
- Small business (local hiring & patronage)

Formal participation in:
- Community organizations
- Citizen advocacy/action
- Voting, registering voters

Informal community-focused behaviors, attitudes, emotions:
- Place attachment, satisfaction
- Social cohesion, commitment
- Celebrating cultural diversity
- Collective efficacy
- Neighboring, support, mentoring
- Social control, crime prevention

- Maintenance, beautification
- Community gardens, cleanups
- Use and care of public spaces
- Community land trusts
- Fight highways, contamination
- Support housing revitalization

Larger Scale Public Policy Role

Long-term financing, resources:
- Jobs/livable wages
- Small business assistance
- Housing & rehab assistance

- Support & respond to community organizations, coalitions
- Support CD policies, programs
- Low-income housing, fair housing

Community programs:
- Healthcare/promotion
- Better neighborhood schools
- After-school programs
- Community policing
- Community corrections

- Mass transit, walkable neighborhoods
- Mixed housing/commercial uses
- Creation/protection of public spaces
- Infrastructure: schools, streets, lights
- Services: water, sanitation, fire, emergency
- Environmental protection

Economic Environment

Political Environment

Social Environment

Physical Environment

reliance on the community's initiative (see Figure 12–1; Perkins, Crim, Silberman, & Brown, 2004). It is based on the simple idea that the most direct way to improve community life is to create active community organizations, responsive local government, more or better housing, businesses, jobs, recreational facilities, clean and safe public spaces, and neighborliness. Community development consists of government policies, nonprofit and other nongovernmental organizations (NGOs), such as community development corporations (CDCs), citizen voluntary associations, and public-private partnerships.

There are three major types of community development by geographic location: urban and suburban residential neighborhood revitalization, large-scale downtown commercial and public space redevelopment, and rural community development in response to worldwide economic (farming) and infrastructure (housing, roads, schools, utilities, healthcare facilities) problems. There is also a fundamental difference between broad-based, grassroots (generally smaller scale) efforts organized from the bottom up and larger-scale development programs, planned and managed by government or international agencies too often from the top down with little input or control by the local people who are most affected.

Christenson, Fendley, and Robinson (1989) observed that government cutbacks, not only in the United States but around the globe, have put tremendous pressure on local governments and the private sector to meet local needs. They identify six keys to community development success: (1) having informed leaders with access to outside sources, (2) understanding the current economic system of the community in light of the changing world economy, (3) having public participation, (4) finding what is unique to a community (i.e., finding its niche in the local, state, and world economy), (5) being willing to be innovative, to accept alternatives, and (6) organizing and maximizing both human and financial capital.

Five strength-based community development concepts. In fact, the notion that "social capital" can compensate to some extent for a lack of economic capital has become one of several popular theories of grassroots community development. *Social capital* refers to the level of residents' integration into the community through informal networks and mutual trust, participation in civic and direct service organizations, and links among those organizations (Putnam, 2000; see chapter 5). Recently, community development researchers have emphasized the role of informal group learning processes in building social capital in communities and organizations (Falk & Kilpatrick, 2000). Social capital fits well with the ecological orientation of community psychology; in contrast with the older term "human capital," it focuses on the strengths related to interdependent social networks (not simply on individual strengths, such as education levels). One caveat, however: social capital alone is limited in what it can achieve without political, economic, and physical capital (Perkins, Hughey, & Speer, 2002).

A second concept, *sustainability*, refers to ecologically healthy development over time based on renewable community resources (Rao, 2000). Economic sustainability, or developing a local economy that can be maintained without regular infusions of outside capital or credit, was the original goal. More recently, sustainability has also taken on an environmental meaning, that is, developing means of production that do not contaminate the ecosystem or exhaust natural resources. The principle of sustainability can also be usefully applied to the political and social domains of community development (Perkins et al., 2004). Political sustainability is important at both the local and societal levels. At the local level, it means developing and maintaining active grassroots participation in community decision making. Political sustainability on a societal level implies that government development policies must be sustained by popular support and must survive changes of government. Social sustainability may be considered the degree to which communities develop and maintain social capital.

The third popular concept in community development is grassroots *empowerment*, or members of the community organizing to collectively influence the institutions and problems that affect them (Speer & Hughey, 1995; see above and chapter 5). Empowerment operates at many levels, from psychological to organizational to community (Perkins et al., 1996). At the psychological level, individuals develop a sense of self-efficacy, control, and self-worth based on the realization that they can contribute and make a difference. Organizationally, decisions are made, democratically or consensually, from the bottom up (see "Organizational Empowerment" in chapter 10). As community development efforts begin to show results, the community itself is empowered; it is seen by its members and others as headed in the right direction and not to be ignored (Saegert & Winkel, 1996). Internationally, empowerment has become a guiding principle for many community development organizations (Friedmann, 1992; Perkins, 1995). Empowerment is strengths-based in focusing on people's and communities' rights, abilities, assets, and resources more than on their needs or problems.

A fourth community development concept, *capacity building*, also operates at multiple levels as it refers to the development of individual skills and information, organizational resources, or the development of organizations and coalitions within an entire community (Perkins et al., 2004). Whereas social capital describes the community-wide resources and networks that make grassroots community development possible, capacity building is a resource development process applied to extant community development organizations. Both concepts are based on the notion that communities have indigenous human resources that can be developed and used to address community problems.

The fifth important, strengths-based idea is *asset-based community development* (Kretzmann & McKnight, 1993), which is an approach to mobilizing people and local organizations in order to identify, map, and develop a community's assets, as opposed to its needs or problems. Consistent with the broad, ecological definition of community development above and shown in Figure 12–1, assets are broadly defined and may be (a) physical (e.g., underutilized land that could become a community garden, park, or playground, or a building that could be used for public meetings or a daycare or recreation center), (b) social (cohesion, volunteers), (c) economic (consumers, entrepreneurs and workers, funding agencies), or (d) political (voters, advocates, local officials, community leaders).

Community development as prevention and self-help. Community development may have a preventive effect in reducing the probability that stressful life events will result from economic distress and community disorganization. Community development can also have a preventive effect by helping to create resources that promote positive adaptations, provide support, and reduce the demoralization that can itself create psychological and social problems.

An important assumption is that community change will be accomplished most effectively through participation of local citizens in goal determination and in action. The important themes in community development include democratic procedures, voluntary cooperation, self-help, development of indigenous leadership, and education. In order to engage in community development, it is necessary to cooperate with others who control resources. Neighborhoods with high concentrations of people who are "truly disadvantaged" (Wilson, 1987) might be appropriate targets for community development efforts, as are currently stable communities that are subject to succession by poorer groups with fewer resources. The actual units targeted for development can be any size, and in urban areas may be as small as individual blocks (Perkins et al., 1990).

Economic development, housing policies, and schools are important community development targets. Leaders work to create community centers and organizations that will help reduce isolation and create a "conspiracy among neighbors" to maintain community standards. From this perspective, maintaining community standards will help to limit crime, violence, drug traffic, child neglect and abuse, despair, and demoralization.

The community development approach assumes that people have potential and will respond to opportunity and that leadership will emerge. Just as crisis theory makes the assumption that people have reserves of coping strength, so this approach assumes that, given resources, people will take advantage of opportunities and participate in social organizations that create roles and settings in which their strengths can blossom. Some organizations and leaders work with disadvantaged youth and with gangs to provide role models and alternatives to illegal activity. They include the youth in community development activities and in business enterprises by providing jobs and training (Ladner, 2001).

The impetus for the community development corporation came from the late Robert Kennedy's concerns about the urban riots of the mid- and late 1960s. Kennedy, then a U.S. senator from New York, visited local neighborhoods to try to understand what had gone wrong with the War on Poverty. The people he spoke with objected to being studied and wanted concrete assistance such as a supermarket or a shopping plaza. In 1966, Kennedy, and his fellow senator from New York Jacob Javits successfully amended the antipoverty act to provide for community development projects. The Ford Foundation also contributed through its "gray areas" project. The general movement was founded on the ideas of community participation, and the organizing tactics developed by Alinsky (1971) were useful. Local churches participated, and a combination of private and public funds helped the agency to develop and grow.

Peirce and Steinbach (1987) describe a number of CDCs, some of which operate in the most hopeless-appearing neighborhoods. In the mid-1980s there were an estimated 3,000–5,000 CDCs in the United States, located in many states and in rural as well as urban areas. Most had developed during the previous 25 years. CDCs vary in size and in resources but tend to have certain features in common. They operate in distressed city neighborhoods or in rural communities and tend to serve geographically defined low-income target areas. The people who live in that ecosystem niche control the CDC. According to Peirce and Steinbach (1987), CDCs are now the most important suppliers of low-income housing in the country and have a range of other business and service provision activities. Although CDCs serve all ethnic groups, some of the most successful ones serve the African American community, and we will concentrate on those agencies.

Community organizations in the African American community. CDCs did not appear full grown out of thin air; there was a "before the beginning" (Sarason, 1972). Many CDCs in African American communities developed in cooperation with churches and other nonprofit organizations. For example, Taylor (1990) points out that a great strength of the African American community in Buffalo, New York, is the number (about 600) and diversity of its social organizations—churches, neighborhood block clubs, cultural groups, youth centers, civil rights organizations, social clubs, fraternal organizations, and formal and informal political organizations. These organizations often provide the base from which CDCs develop. Because members of the majority are generally unaware of the important role such organizations have always played in the life of the African American community, we will discuss some of them briefly.

The church. The church is the African American community's oldest institution, brought into existence by racism that would not permit integrated churches. The church has been a key to Blacks' survival, an institution within which African American people gain sustenance, grow, and develop. The majority of well-known and effective African American leaders, including Martin Luther King, Jr., and Jesse Jackson, emerged from the churches, which provided a niche, a setting, and roles for people who were otherwise blocked from access to resources. A former slave could become president of a congregation, a trustee, deacon, or preacher who could speak with authority to his community, and many times to the majority community as well. These achieved roles all were a source of enhanced self-esteem and leadership experience; they also enabled people to learn organizational skills.

A number of the new urban leaders Ladner (2001) described were pastors in churches in African American neighborhoods. The Ten Points Coalition in Boston, which was credited with sharply reducing gun violence in their neighborhoods, began with a group of ministers in African American churches who were appalled when gang violence reached into one of their churches. They started by walking the streets to reach out to gang youth. They cooperated with a Boston police department initiative to vigorously prosecute crime, but also provided a diversion service for many youth who would otherwise have been prosecuted. Eugene Rivers, a minister, led the program to stabilize communities. The program, affiliated with the Azusa Christian Community and the Ella Baker House, a latter day settlement house, emphasized the idea of personal and community responsibility and community participation. Minister Rivers argued against the "culture of victimization." The Baker House offered Outward Bound programs, a summer Freedom School, and a music camp.

The African American church was and is important in unifying its community. It created settings in which people of different social statuses could come to know each other and provided for the social and recreational needs of church members through its many activities (Pattillo McCoy, 1998). The organization of African American churches gave members of the community experience in community development activities; building a church required people to pool resources to buy land or buildings and to construct church buildings (Davis & Nelson, 1980).

Mutual aid organizations. African American churches often developed mutual aid associations and benevolent societies to provide assistance for the sick or disabled, the widows, and fatherless families. African American women's clubs were another important force in community development (Carson, 1993). Some mutual aid organizations that began in the eighteenth and nineteenth centuries developed into insurance companies serving the African American community. Some of these organizations, struggling as they were with the virulent forces of racism that limited access to resources (and sometimes with internal rivalries), didn't always fulfill their promise, but others did.

In the early twentieth century, the National Negro Business League, the National Association for the Advancement of Colored People (NAACP), and the Urban League were organized (Davis & Nelson, 1980). Movements with community development components arose as needs changed. Marcus Garvey promoted a self-help mutual assistance orientation that included the creation of cooperative economic initiatives in his Universal Negro Improvement Association. Father Divine's Peace Mission Movement had as many as 2 million members and owned rental income property, small businesses such as grocery stores, barber shops, produce stands, dry cleaning and tailoring shops, and furriers, and operated hotels and boarding houses. Since the 1930s the Nation of Islam has operated a network of business enterprises. In addition to civil rights organizations, the Opportunities Industrialization Center (OIC) and Reverend Jesse Jackson's Operation PUSH continue the tradition of mutual aid and economic development (Davis & Nelson, 1980). African American philanthropic activities remain an important force within the community for stability, direction, problem solving, and individual growth (Carson, 1993).

Ladner (2001) argues that the new urban leaders in predominantly African American communities often had their start in civil rights organizations, and later participated in antipoverty programs developed during the Kennedy–Johnson War on Poverty. When funds for antipoverty programs dried up, leaders with organizational experience, management know-how, a track record, and new programming ideas developed new agencies with local funds or with private foundation funds.

Elected officials. Community development requires political support, and for most of its existence the African American community was powerless because so many of its members were barred from voting. The Voting Rights Act of 1964 reduced many of the barriers, however. While there was a negligible number of elected African American officials before passage of this act, by 1988 there were 6,793 Black officials at all levels of government, twice the number in 1980 (Fisher, 1992). By January of 2000, the number of African American elected officials had grown to over 9,000 (Ladner, 2001). The presence of elected officials and the voting power demonstrated by the African American community also increased access to resources for community development projects.

Leadership. The leadership of the new CDCs comes from a wide variety of backgrounds and many different ethnic groups. A great many CDC leaders are women. Some have little professional preparation for their positions, some are former welfare recipients, while others have outstanding academic credentials and experience.

Ladner (2001) described a number of African American urban leaders, men and women who have dedicated their lives to improving the conditions of African American people and their neighborhoods. Kent Amos, a college graduate and former combat officer in Vietnam, was a vice president of the Xerox Corporation before he left his position to devote all of his time to working with youth. He began by taking many into his own home, including some who were very violent, to create "families" for them. His work grew and he established Urban Family Institutes to provide parent training, adult training, Kids Houses, and schools. The goal of his programs is to "enable families to become healthy, stable and independent—and committed to staying in their old communities, and rebuilding them instead of fleeing to the suburbs" (Ladner, 2001, p. 23).

Not all urban leaders were African American. In 1958, Marvin Caplan (1999), a self-described White liberal and civil rights activist, created Neighbors, Inc. He lived in Washington, DC, at a time when many neighborhoods were changing. The exclusively White population was succeeded by an influx of African Americans in racially integrated neighborhoods, and then the neighborhoods became largely African American. In the years before fair-housing laws, some real estate agencies engaged in "block busting." After an African American family moved in, those real estate agencies would encourage White homeowners to sell before the neighborhood "tipped." The homeowners would sell at low prices to speculators who would then resell to African American families at much higher prices. Caplan worked with his African American and White neighbors to encourage Whites not to move and to encourage some White families to move into the neighborhood in order to maintain its integrated character.

To encourage neighborhood stability, Neighbors, Inc., worked to develop an image of the neighborhood as an interesting, exciting place to live. It used community members' talents to enrich the school program and to develop a children's chorus, an annual art and book fair, and an annual house and garden tour of the neighborhood. They organized door to door Christmas caroling, a tutoring program, and an integrated Girl Scout troop, which was unusual at that time. They corrected neighborhood nuisances and encouraged better policing. They had some success, but eventually the neighborhood became 63 percent African American and the local public schools became almost 90 percent African American. Caplan and his family continued to live in the neighborhood. Because their children were fearful and said they were picked on because they were White, the Caplans transferred their children into another school that served middle-class neighborhoods, but not without conflict in the family and much personal anguish. As Ladner (2001) reported for her new urban leaders, commitment to the cause has powerful effects, both positive and negative, on personal and family life.

Paul Adams, an African American educator, was president of an independent school in Chicago. He raised funds to buy a parochial school the Catholic diocese was going to close, and reopened it as a private school, Providence–Saint Mel. The school now has about 700 mostly African American students. The school program requires parental involvement in student education. Adams and his board of directors organized a community development corporation. They built 26 rental townhouses in the school's neighborhood and are remodeling a building into condominiums. The corporation runs a McDonald's restaurant in the neighborhood and employs students.

CDCs and the ecological analogy. CDCs and similar programs provide excellent examples of the ecological principles discussed in chapter 4 and the setting and role concepts presented in chapter 5. First, CDCs provide organizational niches and roles within which people can attain achieved statuses. When a CDC employs people, or helps them gain access to better housing through "sweat equity," it is providing resources for improved adaptation. When communities improve and people acquire a stake in them, the new niches facilitate personal development, growth, and satisfaction. People who earn better housing through participation in a community effort may also experience improved self-esteem as a result of perceiving (correctly) that they have done well. The programs also provide job training, work experience, and opportunities for advancement. With new resources and a stake in the community, residents have the energy to maintain a desirable lifestyle for themselves and their children. None of these results required efforts to change the personal characteristics of people in the neighborhood. Change in personal morale and satisfaction in living resulted from changes in the neighborhood, in its resources and in its opportunities, not from professional help to change personal traits and feelings.

Community effects. Peirce and Steinbach (1987) describe the impact of the Bedford-Stuyvesant Restoration Corporation on the neighborhood:

> The Bedford-Stuyvesant Restoration Corporation symbolizes the first, grand era of community development corporations. Into Brooklyn's five-mile-square Bed-Stuy section—with 450,000 people the nation's second largest black community—plagued by housing decay, school dropout,

junkies, and muggers, comes a flood of investment dollars. Not for the typical poverty-program social services, but for hard investment, a new "business" approach to community development. The federal government and the Ford Foundation pour millions into the Bed-Stuy CDC. Banks and corporations pitch in; IBM opens a major plant in the neighborhood.

Visit Bed-Stuy twenty years later and there's pride, not depression, the sights and sounds of an energetic place. There's a Restoration Plaza Commercial Center, a visible central core the community never had before. Within the center are stores and offices, restaurants, two commercial banks, a supermarket, an ice skating rink, the Billie Holiday Theater. The CDC has produced or renovated more than 1,600 units of housing, restored the exteriors of 4,200 homes on 150 blocks, provided mortgage assistance to 1,700 homeowners and loans and technical assistance to 130 local businesses. Some 16,000 jobs have been created. Some summers, the CDC has hired as many as 1,500 young men and women—up on ladders and scaffolds, decked out in hard hats and tee-shirts, refurbishing as many as ten blocks of brownstones in a season.

True, social pathologies have not disappeared: now they crop up in such new forms as teenage pregnancies and the drug "crack." Unemployment is still a grave problem. Graffiti stains even some of the CDC's proud new structures. But Bed-Stuy has more: a new middle class. Young professionals have purchased brownstones, deciding to remain or return, becoming vital role models for their community. From restoring housing, then building a commercial core, Restoration has proceeded to the restoration of lives and the re-creation of a viable community. (p. 19)

Kent Amos, who works in Washington, DC, describes the accomplishments of the community development approach in similar terms:

Our task is to transform rundown neighborhoods into revitalized neighborhoods. We have new windows where boards used to be. We have new fencing where no fencing used to be. We have paint where peeling used to be. We have clean walls where graffiti used to be. . . . We have hope where despair used to be. We have dreams where nightmares used to be. We have children engaged with adults where children used to scare adults. We have generational involvement. All of that can come together by having belief in one another as fellow human beings. (Kent Amos, quoted in Ladner, 2001, p. 15)

CDCs have not solved all the problems, and some have failed. In a few cases they were mismanaged, and in some scandals occurred. There are important limits to what a CDC can accomplish. Developing successful businesses and other enterprises is not easy and requires at least a core of experienced and trained personnel. Some CDCs have managed to build good housing, but because of union rules and other limits the construction jobs did not always stay in the community.

Some enterprises, such as those that provide child care, serve an important community need. Like social service agencies, child care centers may contribute a great deal to community life. But child care work is not well-paid and offers few benefits to employees and limited opportunity for advancement. Pitegoff (1993) advises such enterprises to develop closer ties with corporations who value what CDCs and similar agencies have to offer, thus providing access to a variety of resources and reducing dependence on government funding.

Subsequent generations of CDCs have become more sophisticated in their approaches and have developed support networks of organizations. Many of the programs Ladner (2001) described offered improved educational opportunities, after school enrichment, parent training, and the development of housing and other businesses. The CDC movement has really just begun to bring "the opportunities of the American economic system to peoples and neighborhoods long excluded" (Center for the Future of Children, 1992, p. 85).

Social Action

Social action is a strategy used by community groups that do not perceive the government, business leaders, or others who are "in charge" as responsive to their concerns. The members of aggrieved community groups may experience both anger and anxiety, depending on the threat to their interests. Not only is social action often effective, even when used as a last resort, there is evidence that the elation and social support that often come with participating in protests and demonstrations may actually be good for your physical and mental health (Drury, 2002). Change tactics in the social action approach include conflict, confrontation, and direct action. Saul Alinsky (1971) articulated the "rules" of social action, including mass organizing and the use of pressure tactics to influence those who control resources to share them with those who perceive themselves in need. The sit-ins used by civil rights groups in the 1960s and 1970s to attack racially segregated facilities, the bus boycott initiated by Rosa Parks, who was tired of being told she had to sit at the back of the bus, and boycotts used to pressure retail organizations to open up jobs to members of minority groups became models for other organizations. Antiabortion groups that use pressure tactics against abortion clinics, against women seeking abortions, and against doctors and other employees of clinics are a current example. Alinsky, however, was opposed to the use of violence and would not have condoned violence such as the shooting of physicians who perform abortions or the fire bombings and vandalism against clinics that have characterized the antiabortion movement. In Alinsky's view, the fundamental tactic is not violence but the exertion of social and political pressure on those who control the resources needed by the aggrieved group.

Social action that empowers people is an ideologically compelling approach to community change. To demonstrate how such an approach actually works, we present as an example the community response to the disaster at the Love Canal in upper New York State. The Love Canal episode served as an example for groups in many other communities in the United States (Roberts & Toffolon-Weiss, 2001; Mertig, Dunlap, & Morrison, 2001) and even in other countries (e.g., Brazil) facing environmental hazards and conflict with corporations, industry, and government.

An Example of Social Action:
The Love Canal Homeowners Association[1]

The Love Canal Homeowners Association (LCHA) developed spontaneously in response to a community crisis, the discovery that an abandoned toxic waste dump site was leaking into a residential neighborhood and imperiling the health of residents living nearby. Residents of the affected area had complained from time to time of yawning holes filled with dark, evil-smelling matter on the 16-acre site adjoining their property, and even of foul-smelling materials seeping into their yards and basements, but local officials took no action. Although an elementary school building was located on the filled-in dump site and hundreds of houses surrounded it, little notice was taken of the complaints until 1976. That year, in the course of an investigation of chemical contaminants in Lake Ontario fish, the Love Canal disposal site came to the attention of a local city employee who alerted U.S. Congressman John LaFalce, who in turn prevailed on the Environmental Protection Agency (EPA) to investigate the situation.

In 1978 the investigation of the disposal site expanded to involve several state and federal agencies, and local news coverage increased. At first, Lois Gibbs, then a 25-year-old high school–educated mother of two children, paid only passing attention to the reports. She lived several blocks away from the dump site and didn't even consider that her life was affected. Shortly after her son started kindergarten at the school built on top of the Love Canal, however, he developed allergies and kidney and neurological symptoms. Gibbs then put two and two together. The more she read, the more she became concerned that chemical contamination of the school property might be responsible. School officials, however, denied her request to transfer her son to a different school. They would not acknowledge that the school might be dangerous.

During the summer of 1978, as Gibbs went door to door to ask her neighbors to sign a petition to close the school, she became aware of a large number of illnesses in her neighborhood. By now she was heavily involved, and drove to the state capitol to attend a meeting where the health commissioner announced that pregnant women and young children should move out of the area.

Gibbs and her companions drove home despondent, only to find the streets in their neighborhood filled with people who had heard the announcement on television or over the radio. There was no Health Department representative or other official in the area to talk with the frightened, angry people who felt their health and the lives of their children were threatened, as well as the value of their homes. Some in the crowd were burning symbolic mortgages and talking of taking drastic action.

Because Lois Gibbs had met many neighborhood people when she was circulating her petition, she was pushed up to the front of the crowd, given a microphone attached to a homemade public-address system, and asked to tell what had happened in Albany. Gibbs, self-described as painfully shy, had never addressed an audience before, but she took the microphone and tried to give the people some hope. That evening, plans were announced for a homeowners' group. Within a few days the Love Canal Homeowners Association was organized.

Because this was the first example of toxic wastes affecting a residential neighborhood, it was highly publicized. Then-governor Hugh Carey announced that the state would buy the houses immediately adjacent to the Love Canal site and those across the street from it. The remaining homeowners were given vague promises that investigations would continue. Gibbs quickly concluded that politicians were not so much interested in what she had to say as they were in giving the appearance that citizens were being allowed to participate in decisions affecting their lives. She also decided that the only way the remaining residents' interests would be taken into consideration was if they remained active, pressed their concerns on officials, and rallied public support through the media.

One night, while sitting in her kitchen pondering her next moves, Gibbs hit on the idea of putting pins on a street map to identify the houses where she knew that people had health problems. When she did that, using her own notes, it seemed that the pins took on a pattern. Illnesses appeared to follow the paths that had been identified by longtime residents as underground drainage ditches running off the canal into neighborhoods several blocks away. Gibbs concluded that the underground ditches, called swales, could have provided a preferred path for migration of the chemical leachate. Excited by what she had found, she took her map to biologist Beverly Paigen.

Paigen, who risked conflict with the New York State Health Department, her employer, trained the Love Canal homemakers to conduct a systematic telephone health survey of the residents in the area. When the survey results were mapped, a concentration of illnesses did appear in what came to be known as "historically wet areas" in the neighborhood. Paigen took her results to Health Department officials, who discounted the research publicly because it was done by "house-wives." However, the publicity generated by this home survey forced the Health Department to review its own data. A few months late, in February 1979, the Health Department announced that indeed there was an increased risk of miscarriages in the formerly wet underground drainage areas, and that it would be best if pregnant women and children under age two who were living on those streets left the area at state expense, at least until the corrective work to cap the canal was completed.

This solution was unsatisfactory to the remaining residents, because it implied that the hazard to unborn children was not a hazard to everyone. Another implication was that it was not safe for young couples to conceive while living in the area. Property values had plummeted by then, and people could neither sell nor afford to leave their houses, which often constituted the bulk of their life savings. Gibbs led the homeowners in a series of actions designed to keep their cause in the newspapers and thus to keep it alive. In addition to general education efforts, speeches to any audience that would listen, and letters to congressional representatives and state legislators, the group's more dramatic actions included marches and demonstrations in the Niagara Falls area, taking a child's coffin to Albany to be delivered to the governor, and burning effigies of the governor and the health commissioner. Each of these events received media attention. Gibbs made trips to Albany and to Washington in an effort to persuade state and federal officials to pay attention to the Love Canal situation. The officials repeatedly told her there was no definitive evidence of danger that would warrant moving more people.

The homeowners kept up the pressure as much as they could, and the situation continued to draw media attention. Residents continued to confront governmental officials whenever they could. One day when Governor Carey visited Buffalo, a Love Canal resident confronted him on the street and managed to get a statement from him that the state would indeed purchase more houses. A bill went before the state legislature to authorize the use of some existing funds to help buy out the rest of the neighborhood.

Meanwhile, to prepare for an impending lawsuit against the Hooker Chemical Company, which had dumped the toxic chemicals into the canal, the Environmental Protection Agency (EPA) conducted a small pilot study of chromosome damage among Love Canal residents. This study was done without recruiting and testing a different group to serve as controls, because the EPA did not wish to spend the money to do a thorough study at that time. In May 1980 tentative findings from this study indicating chromosome damage in residents were leaked to the press. The story made headlines, and soon the area was overrun with television and newspaper reporters from all over the world. The EPA announced that it would assist in the evacuation of residents based on these new data but swiftly backed away from that position, apparently because of pressure from the federal Office of Management and Budget, which was concerned that a precedent was being set for the purchase of houses in "normal" disasters such as floods or tornadoes by the actions being taken in this new and un- precedented type of disaster. The inconsistencies frightened and en- raged residents, who found themselves learning of matters affecting their health and their families' health from newspaper headlines.

As word spread that the White House had changed its position on evacuating the neighborhood, distressed residents gathered on the lawn in front of the LCHA office. Someone poured gasoline in the form of the letters "EPA" on a lawn across the street and ignited it. Other residents, who in every other way were law-abiding middle-class cit- izens, stopped cars in the street and in one case began rocking a car, threatening to turn it over. By midafternoon Gibbs managed to reach two EPA officials who were in town. They agreed to come to the LCHA office to speak with residents. About 100 people were gathered on the lawn when the EPA officials entered the office. Lois Gibbs and several others told the two men they couldn't leave because it wasn't safe for them to go outside into the crowd.

Concerned about protecting federal officials, early in the evening the FBI called and told the group that they had two minutes to re- lease the "hostages." That threat led to the immediate release of the EPA officials, who were escorted through the angry crowd by the police. The residents' point had been made forcefully and was front- page news.

The solution did not emerge immediately. Residents were told that the government was still studying the problem. The 1980 presidential primary campaign was under way, and it was by no means certain that President Jimmy Carter would be renominated or that he would win the primary in New York. Subsequent events took place against this political backdrop. Gibbs and many of the other Love Canal residents who had been told they had chromosome damage were invited to ap- pear on Phil Donahue's television talk show. Love Canal residents also went to New York City to picket the Democratic nominating conven- tion in the hope of embarrassing the president. In September Gibbs was interviewed on the *Good Morning America* television show, where she blamed Carter for his failure to offer federal help in the crisis. Two weeks later, an announcement came that New York State and the fed- eral government had concluded an agreement to purchase the re- maining houses and relocate the residents. President Carter came to Niagara Falls to make the announcement himself. Eventually all of the residents who wished to sell their homes and move out did so. The LCHA had achieved its major goal. It had fought the state and federal government successfully for two years and had finally convinced the government to take action.

Comment. The Love Canal story is important for several reasons. First, it brought the problem of toxic waste disposal to national consciousness. The Love Canal citizens fought for themselves, but by their fight they called attention to the critical national problem of toxic waste disposal. Their efforts resulted in the issuance of long-delayed regulations to implement some existing environmental laws, as well as federal legislation creating a "Superfund" to clean up abandoned toxic waste sites. The Love Canal story has been an inspiration for thousands of citizen groups that have sprung up to protest landfills too close to homes or schools or that threaten to contaminate water supplies (Mertig, Dunlap, & Morrison, 2001).

Industry and some local governments are concerned that more stringent regulation will increase the costs of waste disposal. Local industries often use their economic, political, and scientific resources to fight citizen groups. Some corporations used their power to conceal the dangers of toxic wastes from local residents even though the corporations were fully aware of the dangers (Grunwald, 2001). Some industry groups have helped to organize their own citizen groups consisting of people concerned that environmental regulation would cost their communities jobs (Mertig et al., 2001). There is still argument about the scientific data and about their significance for decision making in a politicized environment (see Box 12–1). Nonetheless, citizens are making their weight felt in decisions affecting their communities (Roberts & Toffolon-Weiss, 2001).

Second, Lois Gibbs' personal story demonstrates that ordinary citizens can uncover extraordinary abilities during a crisis and can emerge much strengthened. From a shy housewife, concerned primarily with her own home and family, she became a folk heroine and national figure who dealt with governors, senators, journalists, and governmental officials as an equal. She founded and now heads the Center for Health, Environment, and Justice, a Washington, DC–based nonprofit corporation, supported largely by private foundation funds, that provides organizing help to local groups faced with toxic waste emergencies in their communities. Roberts and Toffolon-Weiss (2001) described four cases in Louisiana in which ordinary citizens in local communities organized to block the development of hazardous industries, or to demand clean up of contaminated sites. Many women who became involved in grassroots organizations were "completely transformed from complacent housewives with innocent beliefs in the efficacy of government and industry, and no prior experience in political participation, into sophisticated and empowered (and sometimes regional or national) leaders" (Mertig, et al., 2001, p. 471).

**Box 12–1. Center for Health, Environment, and
Justice and the Environmental Justice Movement**

After residents of New York's Love Canal were relocated, Lois Gibbs
moved her family to the Washington, DC, area. By this time, she was
nationally known and had received thousands of communications
asking for help from people facing situations similar to Love Canal.
She decided to develop an organization to assist grassroots groups
struggling with problems of hazardous waste dumps, incinerators,
and related threats to their safety and well-being. The Center for
Health, Environment, and Justice (CHEJ) grew out of that vision.
Aided by her contacts with citizen advocates like Ralph Nader,
Gibbs obtained private foundation support for her work. CHEJ has
some income from memberships, subscriptions, and sales of its publications, but it accepts no money from government or from industries whose products contribute to pollution.

Now 20 years old, CHEJ remains true to its original purpose of
helping grassroots organizations with their struggles. It provides
technical scientific information, organizing assistance, advice about
how to find and use lawyers and technical experts, and leadership
training to local groups facing hazardous waste problems. CHEJ organizers, including Lois Gibbs, accept invitations to participate in local struggles. Gibbs speaks at meetings; more important, CHEJ organizers use such opportunities to energize and strengthen local
groups and to encourage coalitions in local areas. CHEJ does not testify in Congress for or against particular legislation.

A number of similar centers have been organized, particularly in
the South, where the environmental justice movement drew attention
to the disproportionate impact on predominantly African American
communities of toxic waste facilities and unregulated or poorly regulated production of hazardous chemicals and wastes (Bullard, 1990;
Wright, Bryant & Bullard, 1994). In October 1991 grassroots leaders
came together in a People of Color Leadership Summit, which developed principles of environmental justice and included a demand "to
participate as equal partners in every phase of decision-making, including needs assessment, planning, implementation, enforcement
and evaluation" (quoted in Roberts & Toffolon-Weiss, 2001, p. 57).

The summit led to the development of African American–led
centers that function similarly to CHEJ. Beverly Wright, a Ph.D. sociologist, directs the Deep South Center for Environmental Justice at
Xavier University in New Orleans. Robert Bullard, another Ph.D. sociologist and a pioneer in the movement for environmental justice,
directs the Environmental Justice Research Center at Clark Atlanta
University in Atlanta, Georgia. These centers also work with community groups. They assist organizing efforts, train community

members to take social action, help the groups do research on particular community problems, and either testify themselves or prepare community members to testify at regulatory hearings or when plants seek permits and public hearings are required.

Dioxin

CHEJ's projects have included a national campaign against dioxin, which is among the most toxic of chemicals (Gibbs & CCHW, 1995). The discussion of dioxin leads to controversy because it touches so many interests. It is used in the manufacture and disposal of waste products of many widely used plastics, pesticides, and paper. Dioxin does not degrade easily and enters the food chain, where it is stored in body fat. Dioxin is toxic because it interferes with chemical signals and hormones affecting normal cell growth and regulation. Epidemiological studies and studies with animals have shown that the relative risks of various cancers and other disorders are higher in individuals exposed to dioxin than in those with minimal exposure (Gibbs & CCHW, 1995).

Economic, social, and scientific complications. Given all of these dire effects, why aren't we making every effort to ban dioxin, remove it from the environment, and prevent its creation in industrial processes and in incinerators? Banning dioxin and related chemicals would have significant economic and social consequences. Dioxin production is important to many industries—plastics, pesticides, and paper—and to waste disposal through incineration. Ironically, medical waste incinerators are among the major sources producing and releasing dioxin into the environment.

Banning dioxin would require manufacturers and medical facilities to make costly changes in their methods. The economic principle of externalities predicts that if "costs" can be placed on someone else's shoulders, the costs will be passed on. One way to stop this externalizing of costs is to create a countervailing force. The threat of a lawsuit is one such countervailing force, and community action is another, especially when community action leads politicians to pass laws that limit pollution in manufacturing or in waste disposal. For community action to be effective, activists need to develop technical and legal knowledge as well as engage in imaginative demonstrations.

Because of these important economic and social consequences, those who produce and dispose of waste, and the EPA which regulates these processes, are reluctant to adopt costly changes unless there is clear evidence that dioxin poses a serious health risk to a great many people. We are really dealing with a version of the Type

I/Type II error problem in statistical inference. When we emphasize avoiding a Type I error and say we will reject the null hypothesis only when the result is significant at the .05 level, we are saying we will not accept a finding unless it would not have arisen by chance more often than five times in a hundred, the familiar .05 standard. In so doing we are also supporting the status quo. Government and industry say the status quo—that is, existing procedures for handling dioxin—should not change until we are absolutely sure that harm has occurred or will certainly occur in the very near future. People who are concerned about their welfare and their children's welfare, on the other hand, want to avoid the Type II error of failing to recognize a genuine toxic effect of dioxin amid the "noise" of normal biochemical fluctuations and measurement error; they argue that if there is any chance of harm they should be protected against it.

Risk and benefit/cost analyses have been proposed to resolve these competing interests. The results of such analyses, determining how much it will cost to reduce exposure and how many additional cases of illness will be avoided for each increment in cost, are only as good as the assumptions the analysts make, however, and some assumptions favoring one course of action over another may be hidden or not readily apparent to affected citizens. Gibbs (1994) challenges the basic assumptions that a reliable threshold of damage can be determined, that regulation can control the release of damaging substances in the environment to less than dangerous levels, and that scientists will recognize the early signs of unanticipated effects in time to stop them. She argues that accepting risk analysis as an approach to solutions distracts attention from the real problem, which is that we are producing too much waste in the first place, and undermines the search for alternatives that would eliminate the waste itself. Her argument represents a different definition of the problem that leads to a different solution.

Dioxin research has been plagued with controversy and has affected litigation. Activists have to learn to cope with scientific language or they need to learn to work with sympathetic scientists who understand the technical problems. Companies worked hard in using science to support their position that dioxin was not as toxic as others had claimed and that its harmful effects did not warrant banning or even very strict regulation (Grunwald, 2001).

Activism and science. EPA officials are engaged in reassessing the scientific literature and have held hearings around the country to help determine what level of dioxin exposure is safe and what kind of regulations are appropriate. At the same time, a panel of outside scientists has criticized some of EPA's conclusions about dioxin (Stone, 1995), and release of the final report has been substantially delayed. CHEJ has pressed EPA to release the dioxin report and it has worked to expose conflicts of interest among panel members and consultants who are working on the conclusions of the report (Planin, 2001). For example, CHEJ brought a number of women to an EPA hearing wearing pillows under their skirts to simulate pregnancy. The women carried signs calling for panelists to reveal their conflicts of interest. (There has been a general trend for scientific journals to require scientists who publish in standard peer-reviewed journals to reveal any conflict of interest—for example, chemical or tobacco industry sponsorship of research, or ongoing paid consultancies.)

This controversy teaches several lessons about the uses and misuses of science. People who live close to dump sites, incinerators, or other sources of dioxin pollution often face government science experts, company scientists, and public relations professionals who argue that there is nothing to fear or no evidence of danger. When company officials, scientists, or government representatives say there is no evidence of danger they may mean that a single study (perhaps a flawed or biased one) showed no evidence of risk, or they may mean that no studies have even been done (A. Levine, 1982, chapter 6). Like the Love Canal residents, people, sometimes advised by scientists sympathetic to their cause, quickly become sensitive to dissembling on the part of authorities. When technical issues are involved, as they so often are, community groups need scientific experts who understand their perspective and on whom they can rely for accurate information. Having one's own trusted consultant partially reintroduces the adversarial structure of scientific research (Levine, 1974).

Many citizens who formerly believed that companies and government officials would do the right thing if they only knew the truth have been disillusioned. They have come to appreciate that truth is difficult to come by and authority figures cannot necessarily be trusted, that decisions are affected not only by science but also by political and financial considerations. When people in affected communities realize that they are not playing on a level field with corporate officials (Grunwald, 2000), they may resort to legal, political, or social action to attain their ends.

Gibbs and Citizens Clearinghouse for Hazardous Waste (1995) have written a book summarizing and evaluating the evidence that dioxin is harmful and calling for action. Some chapters teach community residents how to organize and how to obtain information about dioxin sources. The book also has tips for attending public meetings and writing letters to government and corporate officials, and for confrontational "actions" designed to capture media attention and keep the issue in the forefront of public attention.

Because the dioxin campaign touches so many key interests, it is a useful example to illustrate the complexity of community action and the impossibility of conceptualizing or understanding problems from a single perspective. As with most social movements, the environmental justice movement depends on coalitions of different groups and interests that often make strange bedfellows and are difficult to hold together. Major constituencies of the movement include poor White and minority communities, workers in toxic industries, academics, professional lobbyists, and activists who are often labeled "tree huggers." Splits and contradictions within the movement, based in part on competition for funding, are common. Movements are frequently harmed more by fighting among factions than by actions of the external foe.

Another critical lesson of social movements is that "once-and-for-all" success is virtually never achieved (at least not without addressing underlying political and economic causes of social and environmental problems) and persistence and anticipation of unintended consequences are required. Pellow (2002) chronicled an environmental justice campaign he participated in for six years that successfully closed a solid waste incinerator that had been spewing toxic gases into a low-income, African American section of Chicago. The community leaders also hoped that the recycling plant that replaced the incinerator would provide desperately needed jobs for local residents, which it did. What Pellow and the leaders did not anticipate, however, is that the low-pay jobs—sorting tons of garbage, including infectious medical waste and hazardous household waste—would mean replacing one form of "environmental racism" with another. Pellow argues that the environmental justice movement must look beyond simplistic questions of where waste sites are being located to also deal with thornier and more widespread environmental hazards in all sorts of workplaces and in homes. These tend to be discriminatory socioeconomic class issues even more than race issues.

The Love Canal Homeowners Association is an example of a spontaneous organization that developed out of a community crisis and gave people a means of taking vigorous action on their own behalf. It is all the more interesting as an illustration of how traditional, nonpolitical working- and middle-class citizens can take increasingly radical action as their frustration grows. Families in the area were clearly subjected to considerable stress for a prolonged period of time, as were families in other communities when members became active in community struggles (Roberts & Toffolon-Weiss, 2001). For many families the LCHA provided a means of social support and a sense of community that enabled them to cope over time with the stressful life events that followed their discovery of the problem (Stone & Levine, 1985–1986; Roberts & Tof-folon-Weiss, 2001). The fact that the story had national significance is a positive side effect of the efforts of community activists. They were concerned with saving themselves, but in struggling in their own interest they contributed to the well-being of all of us.

The Superfund legislation providing funds for cleaning the worst sites was one product of their efforts. In November 2001 the EPA ordered General Electric (GE) to spend $460 million to dredge PCBs (a toxic industrial coolant used in electrical equipment) it had dumped over many years in the Hudson River in New York and New Jersey. Lawsuits based on the dumping of hazardous wastes continue. Many suits have revealed that companies were often quite aware of the toxic nature of the substances they released into the environment but consciously intended to continue their practices, conceal what they were doing or their knowledge of the dangers, and/or minimize their compliance with regulations limiting the release of toxics into the environment (Grunwald, 2001; Moyers, 2001).

Summary

An important theme developed in the later chapters of this book is that even though community change is complex and incompletely understood, this is not an excuse for inaction. The starting point for action to accomplish change, as we emphasized in this chapter, is the step of problem definition. Traditional clinical approaches to problem definition are sometimes said to "blame the victim"—that is, conceptualize the problem as a person-centered characteristic of those individuals who are suffering the most. This approach can create paradoxes, situations in which two or more contradictory interpretations, implying radically different ways of understanding a given problem, both lead to logically convincing and empirically valid solutions—for example, do those at risk need special interventions whose sole purpose is to make them behave in the same way others do, or do they instead deserve additional resources sufficient to guarantee their right to behave differently from others?

Community psychology's ecological approach to problem definition assumes that more than one point of view on an issue can be legitimate and that problem definitions and solutions are divergent rather than singular. The ecological metaphor enables us to consider the definition of problems and solutions in terms of situations and systems instead of in terms of individuals. It enlarges the scope of potential directions for change, which helps to resolve paradoxes. An intervention such as Head Start, for example, addresses the serious cognitive and nutritional needs of individual children while at the same time providing employment opportunities to their disadvantaged parents as a fundamental economic right.

Community psychology also assumes that the essential path to change and adaptation is empowerment, in the form of increased access to resources for those at risk. One such resource involves *social organization* (e.g., increased involvement and participation in defining problems and decision making), and another is *information*, including substantive knowledge regarding the strategies and resources necessary for adaptation (Pilisuk, McAllister, & Rothman, 1996). For the community psychologist, identifying paradoxes and developing strategies of empowerment also have the salutary effect of placing in a constructively self-critical light his or her own place in the ecological context surrounding a problem.

Community psychology honors a tradition of action outside the established professional system in the service of individual and community adaptation. In this chapter we discussed two approaches to community-level intervention. Community development involves identifying and finding new ways to use indigenous resources to improve the social, physical, economic, and political environment of the community, and emphasizes concepts of social capital, sustainability, empowerment, capacity building, and asset mapping and development. Social action forces a definition (or redefinition) of the problem in terms of an unfair allocation of resources, making the solution one of redistributing those resources.

Many of these points were illustrated by the examples of the Love Canal Homeowners Association and a successor organization, the Center for Health, Environment, and Justice. In this case, as in many situations in the soap opera of life, a serious community problem came to be defined in terms of situational circumstances instead of individual weaknesses and was ultimately dealt with ecologically through organization and more direct access to public resources, including media publicity.

In the final chapter we will continue to examine the interplay between science, politics and ethics in community intervention.

Notes

1. The material in this section is drawn largely from A. Levine (1982) and Gibbs (1998).

2. The Love Canal was a short waterway used for recreation for about 40 years until 1942, when the Hooker Chemical Company began to dump chemical wastes there. In 1953, when the canal was completely filled, Hooker sold the site for one dollar to the Niagara Falls School Board. The school board needed land for a new school to accommodate the growing population of that area. The deed of sale included a disclaimer that the Hooker Company would be free of responsibility for any injuries or death or damage to property resulting from the chemical waste buried on the site. Deeds of sale to the buyers of modest, low-priced houses adjacent to the attractive new school contained no such warning, of course, and citizens didn't dream that government officials would allow a school and houses to be built in such a dangerous location.

13

Science, Ethics, and the Future of Community Psychology

In previous chapters we have seen how social science research contributed to the development of the school desegregation decision and later became important in the Love Canal controversy. We also observed that political problems can plague scientific research, even when technology is capable of great precision of measurement. In the first part of this chapter we explore further the relationships among science, politics, ethics, and the social context. We will introduce a model based on the premise that every cultural artifact is a compromise product of its social surroundings, provide examples of the influence of context on science applied to the solution of social problems, and then review ethical problems that arise when doing community work.

Just as community psychology has a past, so it will have a future. In the second half of this chapter we raise some issues of concern for the direction of the field that have been expressed by the current generation of leadership and indeed by community psychologists in other countries around the world. We raise these issues here because the generation of students entering the field will likely have to cope with the problems community psychologists have identified today. These include making interdisciplinary study real, a clearer focus on issues of power, and the potential that exists in a more global view of community psychology, including taking into account the perspectives of many thoughtful and articulate scholars who work in other countries around the world.

Ecology and Science

Community psychologists are committed to the belief that applications of scientific approaches to social and psychological problems can contribute to the solution of those problems and to our knowledge of ourselves and our social world. Community psychologists participate in generating the research that defines social problems, and they participate in implementing and evaluating interventions built on that knowledge. The model of a "value free" science never fit "pure science," and it is incorrect when we consider the application of scientific approaches to the solution of social problems. Every cultural artifact, in this case scientific research, is a compromise product of its social surroundings. We make this point because the social surroundings of the pure science that most of us learn are different from the social surroundings of science in applied contexts.

A simple model illustrates the point. Films and novels are artistic forms that are shaped in contexts including artists, financial sponsors, publishers, critics, and audiences (Huaco, 1965). Analogous roles influence social science research. In pure research the researchers, funding agencies, journal editors, publishers, critics, and audience all tend to be social scientists who share a common frame of reference. When the research has implications for social issues, however, the surrounding roles are filled with people who have different assumptions and different values from those of scientists (see Gardner & Wilcox, 1993). Aside from academic social scientists, the actors may include employees of government agencies, private industry executives, political figures, citizens affected by the particular action, and critics and supporters of a particular position. If a social program is involved, those who are employed in the program also have stakes in it (Levine & Levine, 1977).

We are also a rational society. We are unable to say we want something just because we want it and instead must argue on our own behalf by referring to empirical evidence. A political view of this debate sees science as the language of discourse, with the prizes the resources that will be redistributed. Scientific studies were used on all sides of the Love Canal conflict and are central to the current controversy over dioxin.

Pauly (1994) describes how scientific research played a role in the debate over the Eighteenth Amendment, which prohibited "the manufacture, sale, or transportation of intoxicating liquors." As part of this debate, Prohibition supporters commissioned an elaborate series of experiments by psychologist Walter Miles that found consistent decrements in performance following consumption of low-alcohol beer. This work was used to justify the Eighteenth Amendment's prohibition of all forms of alcoholic beverage.

The Great Depression later wrought significant changes in the social and political context. Political figures supported the repeal of Prohibition, arguing that legalization would help the struggling economy and reduce the social and economic burden of coping with organized crime. The United States Brewers' Association funded another university researcher to replicate Miles' work. However, this researcher modified Miles' procedures to include a more demographically diverse sample of subjects, lower doses of alcohol, and briefer test trials of subjects' performance. One consequence of these modifications was much greater variation among subjects in their performance, whether drinking or not. Furthermore, this researcher adopted a more stringent criterion than had Miles for testing the statistical significance of differences in performance before and after drinking ($p \leq .01$).

Generally speaking, the interests of companies producing risky products (e.g., liquor, tobacco, toxic wastes) are served when the available evidence supports the "null hypothesis" of no differences in risk across levels of exposure. Toxic effects that are small-to-moderate in size, no matter how reliable, lack credence if the standards for rejecting the null hypothesis require a rigorous level of proof. Given the greater variance within the drinking and nondrinking conditions and the more stringent statistical criterion, it is not surprising the second researcher concluded that performance was not significantly different whether subjects had consumed a little alcohol or no alcohol. Although his study was funded by brewers' interests, the researcher claimed these findings spoke for themselves and were completely objective. His work helped to set the stage for the repeal of the Eighteenth Amendment.

One way of using science to advance political aims is to oversimplify the value-laden nature of issues, reducing complex decisions to a seemingly objective choice between "good" or "bad" alternatives. For example, Ong and Glantz (2001) describe how tobacco companies made a concerted effort to create standards of scientific rigor so stringent that many epidemiological findings would be hard pressed to satisfy them.

Specifically, the tobacco companies used their considerable resources to organize groups of reputable scientists, both in Europe and the United States, to establish and maintain exacting standards of "sound science" in all areas of epidemiological research. Studies reporting effects below these stringent standards (which would include most of the evidence for the effects of global warming, air pollution, second-hand tobacco smoke, and other environmental hazards) would thereafter be labeled "junk science" not worthy of public support. The tobacco companies' role in this effort was not at first recognized, because the campaign's appeal to "sound science" had plausibility, was articulated by reputable scientists in appropriate scientific forums, and because the focus was on epidemiological practices in general, not just research directly related to tobacco.

As these examples and others in this chapter illustrate, the ground rules of science are not applied in a vacuum. Scientific work is done in a context of competing interests and the scientific process is intrinsically adversarial (Levine, 1974). How a problem gets defined, and who defines it, determines what gets studied, what data are collected, and how they are interpreted. The process of obtaining knowledge and the resulting policies flowing from the interpretation of the knowledge are all influenced by more than the scientific quest for truth.

Experimental design. Details of experimental design can favor one side of a scientific debate over another by making it easier or more difficult to detect effects. The fact that in many situations it is impossible or unfeasible to assign subjects to alternative conditions at random presents such an opportunity. The research team from the New York Health Department that studied miscarriages among women living at Love Canal used as a basis for comparison an existing report of miscarriage rates calculated as part of a study whose subjects were women who had previously borne a defective child. This miscarriage rate was based on the women's self-reports. In determining the rate among Love Canal women, however, the Health Department accepted a case of miscarriage only if it had been verified in medical records. The comparison of self-report rates with physician-verified rates biased the study in the direction of minimizing the miscarriage effect among the exposed women. The rate in the Love Canal was so still high that the difference was statistically significant, but Health Department officials and others were able to say that the rate of miscarriage among Love Canal women was "only" one and one-half times the control rate when, if compared with a proper control sample, it might actually have been three or four times the control rate (A. Levine, 1982).

Type I and Type II errors. Other issues that we take for granted in research also have important implications when decision making is involved. In pure science we generally try to avoid the "Type I" error, that is, rejecting the null hypothesis when it should not be rejected. In simple terms, this means avoiding the conclusion that the evidence shows that something has happened when it has not actually happened. In the alcohol example, when the investigator funded by brewery interests changed the standard for rejecting the null hypothesis from .05 to .01, he made it less likely that the results would demonstrate that something had happened. Of course, in avoiding the Type I error by changing the decision standard, an arbitrary matter in any event, this researcher also made it *more* likely he would commit a "Type II" error, mistakenly concluding nothing had happened when in fact there had been an effect. He therefore concluded that low doses of alcohol had no effects on behavior when in fact they probably did.

In the Love Canal situation much of the dispute between health department scientists and citizens concerned a tradeoff between Type I and Type II errors. Health Department officials, concerned that a decision that the area was unhealthy would result in costly relocation of many people, wanted to avoid the Type I error. They adopted the usual scientific standard, demanding strong evidence before they concluded that there was an inordinate amount of illness in the area. On the other hand, residents wanted to avoid the Type II error. They took the position that if there was any chance of danger they should be moved out of harm's way, whether or not compelling proof of the danger was present. Whereas a journal editor might want data indicating an increase in fetal morbidity and mortality significant at the .05 level before publishing an article, a pregnant woman would more likely be interested in being relieved of anxiety over the possibility that her baby might be harmed, regardless of whether there was absolute proof that the chemicals buried in the Love Canal were the cause of the harm.

In this case the adoption of the usual scientific decision standard proved to be very favorable to the government's position that it wanted to avoid wholesale buyouts of homes. The Love Canal residents, eager to have the government buy their homes, were very suspicious of the state health department's "neutrality," a position unfavorable to the residents who wished to avoid any avoidable risk (A. Levine, 1982).

The written report. An evaluation report and its interpretation may also reflect systematic biases of the investigators or of their sponsors. In the Gary, Indiana, education plan of 1914–18, an administrator who wrote a descriptive report based on a site visit to a school was forced by members of the school board to rewrite the report so that it came out more favorable to the program under review (Levine & Levine, 1977). While the assertion of naked power in the writing of a report may be unusual, authors of research reports, particularly evaluation reports, probably do take into consideration the positions and sensibilities of their audiences and patrons. In 2002 and 2003, the Environmental Protection Agency censored excerpts on the dangers of global warming from two separate, ostensibly scientific environmental reports in order to be consistent with the political views of the Bush White House (Revkin & Seelye, 2003). Similar charges were leveled with regard to "objective" intelligence reports used to justify the 2003 war in Iraq.

The integrity of a scientific effort is not guaranteed by the names and scientific reputations of the participants. We have all heard of instances in which reputable senior researchers had their names on papers that proved to be fraudulent. In many laboratories, the senior scientist is named as a coauthor even if he or she had very little to do with the research. Senior people are also subject to a variety of powerful nonscientific influences. In the Love Canal situation, the governor of New York appointed a commission of highly reputable medical scientists to review all research done up to that time on the Love Canal. All but one of the five participants in this commission were administrators in medical facilities regulated by the New York Department of Health. (Among its other powers, the Health Department sets reimbursement rates for hospital beds, decides how much is allotted in the rates for teaching costs, and approves certificates for building or remodeling medical facilities, including laboratories.) Although we have no "smoking gun" showing that commission participants were directly influenced by such considerations, the appearance of a potential conflict of interest leads one to look with skepticism on their conclusions that there was no evidence of major systemic disorders present among residents of the Love Canal area (A. Levine, 1982).

The timing of the release of reports is still another matter. In the Gary school situation, there is some reason to believe that the release of a negative report was delayed until after a mayoral election in order not to embarrass the incumbent mayor, who had supported the program (Levine & Levine, 1977). We have already seen how a leaked report in the Love Canal situation led to turmoil that resulted in the eventual relocation of the citizens. If the report had not been leaked, the results might have been buried; if officially released, the results might have been accompanied by criticism carefully designed to mute their effect.

Impact on those affected by the research. Research results may have effects on the researcher. Beverly Paigen's employers subjected her to harassment for her work with Love Canal residents. She eventually left New York State for employment elsewhere (A. Levine, 1982). In the Gary school situation, the office of the researcher who issued the negative findings was subject to reprisal by school board officials. The school administrator who took responsibility for implementing the Gary program in New York had difficulty gaining reappointment to his position, apparently in retaliation for his participation in the Gary experiment (Levine & Levine, 1977).

Research can also have direct and indirect effects on those who are the subjects of the research. In the early 1900s a body of scholarly opinion developed that purported to show the inherent inferiority of African Americans. That research was used to support segregationist practices and to justify the low social status of African Americans in the United States. It required another body of scholarly opinion to assert the opposite position in order to rally efforts to attack segregation. Arthur Jensen's (1969) assertions that most of the variance in intelligence is due to heredity and that the learning styles of Blacks and Whites are fundamentally different were used politically to justify cutting off aid to education. In human terms, consider the impact on children and youth's motivation to achieve and on their self-esteem when they learn that scientific studies show they are less intelligent or less well able to learn (Steele, 1992).

Research bias. Because the stakes are high, the actors diverse, and the points of potential influence many, we should recognize that the error is not in having "biased" research but in believing that research can ever be completely unbiased. The closed character of the logical system underlying our concepts of research design may be inappropriate when applied to practical arguments about the real world (Toulmin, 1958). The social context modifies and influences the research procedures, the inferential process, the report, the participants, and the varied uses to which research may be put. Donald Campbell identified and discussed many of the problems in evaluation research and suggested many creative "social inventions" designed to cope with these problems (Campbell, 1969, 1979). It is an important problem in evaluation research that we do not have a self-critical scientific community who critique and replicate each other's work. Too often, a single study might be commissioned, and that study constitutes the sole body of evidence for a political decision about resource allocation.

We need to recognize in this field that we are as much concerned with fairness as with accuracy and that any approach to research has to be deemed fair by those it affects. We also need to recognize that, given even the best of intentions, many research efforts yield ambiguous or disputable results and that, in the end, decisions are often made on the basis of power, politics, and related values, despite any wishes we may have as social scientists that decisions be grounded entirely on hard evidence.

Political values shape the discovery, organization, and interpretation of scientific "facts" just as other details of the cultural context do, in that investigators' political views influence what problems they choose to study, the methods they select, and the kinds of results they obtain. Does a preponderance of liberal views among community psychologists increase the likelihood of distortion, inaccuracy, or incompleteness in the knowledge that community psychology contributes to society? Redding (2001) argues that an underrepresentation of politically conservative views in policy-relevant fields like community psychology hampers broad advances in scientific understanding and in policy development and application. He further warns that the ideological dominance of liberal views in these disciplines is self-perpetuating, engendering bias in the selection and training of graduate students and in the peer review of articles and grant proposals, and that psychology's liberal bias also hurts its credibility with policymakers. For example, because policymakers (e.g., members of Congress) always expect there to be at least two sides to every issue, they become suspicious when organized psychology (e.g., the American Psychological Association) consistently presents only the more liberal side on issues like gun control or affirmative action.

However, as we stress throughout this book, social problems are complex and multidimensional. Many different values, agendas, historical precedents, and other contextual factors influence how communities cope with and solve problems, and Redding's dichotomizing of political input into "liberal" or "conservative" seems oversimplified. Moreover, his characterization of community psychology as responsive to liberal values, even if accurate, is not necessarily the shortcoming Redding makes it out to be. Because business, government, and taxpayer interests are often conservative or centrist in orientation, the liberal (community-oriented) process of eliciting and shaping contrasting perspectives from all stakeholders provides a suitably broad representation of views when problems are defined and solutions are proposed and evaluated. Finally, to a greater degree than most other stakeholders, community psychologists adopt and modify their positions on the basis of scientific evidence. All students learn the ground rules for obtaining and interpreting such evidence, authors and grant writers all have access to these same strategies and principles, and policymakers have ample opportunity to consider the role that scientific evidence should play in the decisions they make. Thus, while a value-free community psychology is impossible, a discipline that pursues its objectives using scientific evidence makes valuable contributions to stakeholders on all sides of the political spectrum.

The Ethics of Community Intervention

Clinical psychologists have an ethical code that largely defines proper relationships between professionals and clients, and between professionals and the public (American Psychological Association, 2002). The professionally trained individual who lays claim to the mantle of science and enters the difficult field of social intervention has no such guidelines but does have special problems. One question is simply: "Who asked you?" By what authority does a community psychologist or any other social scientist try to influence other people's lives? In the medical model, a client seeks out a professional who offers a defined treatment under specific terms. In the community model, the development of policies and the allocation of resources are political questions. Elected officials or their appointees decide the policies they will pursue, and these may be shaped by advice from social scientists.

When a professional person enters this field and claims some special knowledge or expertise, what obligations does this person have to the community at large and to his or her professional discipline? Is it enough simply to report data? Does the professional person have an obligation to acknowledge openly his or her own values? After all, data depend on how the question was framed initially and on what interpretations were made.

O'Neill (1989) provides a case study in which a psychologist's slanting of her interpretation of data to support a sponsor's agenda had unintended consequences. The psychologist was working with a women's group that wanted to expand a battered women's transition house. The group needed data to convince the government officials who would be funding the project that the expansion was economically viable, and invited the psychologist to conduct a needs assessment to determine how many people, with what needs, might use such an expanded center. Because it was not feasible to do a random sampling survey, the community psychologist sought information from key informants, people with experience who might be able to offer reasonable estimates. The information was ambiguous. If taken from any single source, the number of physically battered women in that community was too small to justify the expansion. If the psychologist assumed there was no overlap in the cases described by key informants, however, then the number did justify the project. Despite her reservations about the numbers and about assuming that every identified woman would use the service, she concluded there was probably enough need to justify the cost.

The center was funded, but very few clients came and it was seriously underused. Eventually, the center was filled, but few of the clients were physically battered. The center's staff had redefined "battering" to include "emotional battering," and many of the clients were women who had separated from their husbands. The psychologist knew that the funders' intent was to serve physically battered women, and she knew that the staff had concealed the change in objective from the funders, reporting only the large number of women and children who used the service and collecting the per diem stipend from the funders to operate the service.

The psychologist was faced with a dilemma. What was her responsibility in the situation? She spoke to the center's administrator, who justified the actions by saying that the house was performing a valuable service and without the funds couldn't be kept open. If it closed, the few physically battered women who did use it would have no place to go. The psychologist thus fulfilled one ethical duty by calling the attention of responsible people to the unethical conduct. But the administrator hadn't responded. Did the psychologist have an ethical duty to go further and inform the founders of what was going on? O'Neill didn't say but went on to discuss the ethical principles that might govern the situation. Things are never simple when it is necessary to balance competing values of loyalty to the funder, to the client, and to the people in need.

What if a community psychologist disagrees with positions held by consultees or accepts an assignment while hiding a professional agenda to move an agency to another position or pursues a personal agenda about whom should be served, how, and by whom (O'Neill, 1989; Heller, 1989)? Given the limits of knowledge, what obligation does the professional have to be forthcoming about the limits of expertise in a given field or about the limits of knowledge for decision making? Does the professional person have a right to "invade" institutions in order to study them or change them, sometimes surreptitiously (Heller, 1989)? What if the mode of intervening in the institutions is experimental and unproved?

One answer is that all such interventions ought to be undertaken collaboratively, in the interests of all those who participate in the particular setting. Such a simple answer fails to recognize the diverse constituencies and the conflicting interests that are usually represented in any setting. None of the complex issues originating in the context of community intervention is well understood. Ethical discussion is still rare. (For welcome exceptions see O'Neill's, 1989, case vignettes, responses by other psychologists in that same issue, Serrano-Garcia, 1994, and Dokecki, 1996).

We have saved formal consideration of the ethical implications of community intervention until this point so that we could base our discussion of ethics on a comprehensive understanding of community psychology concepts and practices. Our discussion relies heavily on Bermant, Kelman, and Warwick (1978) and on O'Neill (1989) and commentary on his paper. Certain characteristics peculiar to community interventions create different problems from those that obtain in clinical interventions. Professional ethical codes are written in general terms and do not always offer precise guidelines for specific situations. Moreover, professional ethical guidelines such as those promulgated by the American Psychological Association (2002) are directed to defining and protecting the fiduciary relationship between a professional and a client and may not have much to say about complex contexts in which the professional's contract and obligations are unclear or may shift as circumstances change.

Bermant, Kelman, and Warwick (1978) say that important ethical considerations affect several aspects of community intervention. Implicit in this discussion is the question of whether the professional accepts an invitation to intervene. Each invitation and each issue must be judged against the psychologist's personal and professional values, although the issues may not become clear until a consulting relationship is well along. The psychologist is then faced with an ethical and personal decision about how to proceed when his or her initial assumptions have not been borne out and the interests of the client may be adversely affected by the psychologist's subsequent actions. Should the psychologist become a whistle-blower when he or she observes problems in a setting?

The first decision in an intervention is the choice of *goals*, or specifically what we choose to change—individuals or relationships among elements of society. The choice is by no means obvious or routine. Scientists must be able to recognize and question their own ideologies and paradigms to be in a position to contribute to solving large-scale problems and to communicate those goals to those who might be most affected.

A second issue is our definition of *targets*—the "victims" themselves, or some other point of entry into the problem (visible need doesn't always provide the most effective point of intervention). We have previously pointed to the dilemma posed by the potential stigmatization of persons recruited for primary or secondary prevention programs. The important ethical questions, however, are whether the cumulative damage to the individual's mental health from labeling outweighs the benefit of the preventive intervention itself and who is to make that decision?

A third issue is the means of *intervention* we choose: What desirable effects does it have? What undesirable or side effects? Will participation be compulsory or voluntary? What if we have reason to believe at the outset that the community interventions will at best have a weak effect? In seeking informed consent under those circumstances, can we describe direct or indirect benefits of participation, especially in contrast to any risks subjects face such as loss of privacy or potential labeling? Given the doubtful empirical status of any cause-and-effect hypothesis in community intervention, any expectation of direct benefit given to participants might be equivalent to false advertising (Campbell & Kimmel, 1985). How can we participate responsibly when we can't confidently predict the results of our efforts? Is there a place for "responsible chutzpah," a place for trying to solve a problem in the absence of reliable data?

A final issue is our assessment of *consequences*. Our choice of outcome variables and measures will define the nature of our results, including the unanticipated consequences. The principle of interdependence tells us that what we do may well have radiating effects. As a matter of ethics, we should always be alert to the possibility of unintended negative as well as positive consequences and to our responsibilities should these arise. Some long-term longitudinal studies of preventive interventions have shown adverse effects as a likely outcome for some participants even when there are also direct positive effects (Campbell & Kimmel, 1985). Such effects, even if iatrogenic, provide important information about the processes underlying our interventions. They will never even be observed, however, unless investigators are conceptually and methodologically prepared to observe them and feel ethically obligated to search for them.

How do the activities we described in this chapter and the ethical position outlined here differ from those of the ordinary "good citizen" participating in his or her community? In part, the answer is that they do not differ, and so here we confront yet another paradox of professional activity. Every citizen has the obligation to remain informed about whatever affects the community. The professional community psychologist has the obligation to learn about the community from many vantage points and to disseminate that knowledge in many community forums. In doing our best to promote understanding from many different perspectives, perhaps we can contribute to the development and maintenance of the sense of community that is so important to all of us. Sarason (1976) reminds us that the community psychologist necessarily views problems and solutions from a specific position in time and in social space, but his or her actions should be "more consciously and expertly applied" (p. 328) than are those of "Mr. Everyman." The community psychologist thus has a responsibility to conform to the ethics and the best practices of his or her professional discipline that is different from the responsibility of the ordinary citizen, and in the end we are left with the reassuring if still somewhat paradoxical conclusion that the community psychologist is both similar to *and* different from every other member of the community.

Interdisciplinary Community Psychology

The inherent interdisciplinary nature of the phenomena of concern to community psychology was clear at the Swampscott Conference in 1965 (see chapter 2) and by the 1971 national training conference in Austin, Texas[1], community psychologists defined the field as being

> concerned with participating in planning for social change; with organizing and implementing planned changes; with designing and conducting programs of service to provide for the human needs generated by social changes; and with the development of community resources and process to deal with the future implications of social changes. It was recognized that these are activities that involve the efforts of persons from several different fields, and that community psychologists should give a high priority to cooperation and collaboration with the community and with other disciplines . . . (C)onference participants . . . generated three major topics that would provide the focus for a body of knowledge in community psychology:

1. Analyses of social processes. This topic includes discussion of knowledge of past and current social institutions, social movements, and the interaction between economic, social, and political processes . . .
2. Study of interactions in a specific social system . . .
3. Design of social interventions. . . . (Mann, 1978, pp. 18–19)

In 1978, Barbara Dohrenwend published the elaborated stress model as a guiding framework for community psychology (see chapter 3). Although stress would seem to be a highly individualistic, even clinical perspective on social problems, the appeal of that model is that it encompasses not only late-stage corrective therapies and crisis intervention, but also system-level preventive interventions—such as general education, community and organizational development, and political action—strategies that absolutely require an interdisciplinary approach to theory, research, and implementation. In 1988, the Society for Community Research and Action (SCRA) was created, partly to provide community psychologists in the United States some institutional independence from the American Psychological Association[2] and partly to encourage the interdisciplinary development of the field.

How have community psychologists responded to 40 years of efforts to define the field as interdisciplinary and challenge its members to make that definition a reality? In terms of the three major topics identified at the Austin Conference, we have been fairly good at studying interactions in specific social systems and designing and evaluating social interventions. Yet psychologists have always done those things. It is our ability to analyze social institutions and movements and the interaction between economic, social, and political processes, which will make us truly interdisciplinary. Thus far, we would have to conclude that, while community psychologists frequently pay lip service to interdisciplinary work, they have engaged in it only in limited ways.

Ever so gradually, however, the field is beginning to change. In 1998, then-SCRA-President Kenneth Maton organized a "summit meeting" of professional association leaders from other disciplines and branches of psychology, which led to a SCRA Interdisciplinary Initiative Task Force and in 2003 an Interdisciplinary Committee. Maton surveyed 51 community psychologists and found that on average each considered over two other disciplines and/or professional organizations important to his or her research or intervention work (Maton, 1999). Most remarkable for such a small sample was the diversity of disciplines and organizations cited. Most branches of psychology have ties to at least one or two other relevant fields (e.g., biopsychology, law and clinical psychology, industrial psychology and business management, developmental psychology and gerontology). Community psychologists have connections to every social science and virtually all of the professions. The most frequently mentioned disciplines in the survey were public health, developmental psychology, education, sociology, anthropology, political science, policy/public affairs, evaluation, and social work. A number of community psychologists have also studied law.

Nearly all of those surveyed agreed that it would be beneficial for community psychology or SCRA to develop enhanced linkages with other disciplines and organizations. Some of the other organizations community psychologists belong to are the American Public Health Association, American Evaluation Association, Society for Research in Child Development, Society for the Psychological Study of Social Issues, Society for Prevention Research, Society of Public Health Education, Community Development Society, Urban Affairs Association, Environmental Design Research Association, American Orthopsychiatric Association, Society for Applied Anthropology, and National Association of School Psychologists. SCRA now has official liaisons to many of these organizations and to other Divisions of APA.

The SCRA Interdisciplinary Initiative included several joint projects, including an effort to increase recruitment of minorities into community studies or community action in any discipline, jointly organized conference sessions, at least one cosponsored conference, and an edited book on strengths-oriented policy research in human development and community psychology (Maton et al., 2004). Other activities are just in the discussion stage, such as publishing special issues of research journals on topics of mutual interest, and making joint policy statements.

Many community psychologists serve on editorial boards or even as editors of interdisciplinary journals; a long overdue step would be to include more nonpsychologists on the boards of community psychology journals. Similarly, community psychologists attend conferences sponsored by all of the above organizations, but few nonpsychologists ever attend community psychology conferences. Thus, what interdisciplinary work we do represents a centrifugal force, or a one-way street, with very little centripetal activity in return, outside of the ideas we bring into the field from other disciplines.

To begin to address these limitations, a conference on interdisciplinary community research, featuring nationally recognized psychologists and nonpsychologists engaged in collaborative research, occurred in May 2004, at Vanderbilt University. With the understanding that community psychology's interdisciplinary rhetoric has thus far exceeded the reality, the emphasis of this conference was not on research results but on the problems and processes of conducting effective interdisciplinary collaborations.

Ecological and Psychopolitical Validity

The preceding section argues that, while community psychology has always been interdisciplinary, it should become even more so to help the field to develop and avoid intellectual stagnation. The argument for greater interdisciplinary collaboration can be based on an even more important and pressing cause. The world's greatest problems—poverty, disease, hunger, violence, war, oppression, environmental contamination, resource depletion, and all the soap opera problems of chapter 1—have as root causes, solutions, or both, complex political, economic, environmental, and sociocultural issues. If community psychology is to contribute anything useful to addressing those problems, we must think more ecologically, act more politically, and actively engage the various disciplines that understand those issues, or at least their particular piece of those issues, including political science, economics, sociology, anthropology, public health, law, urban planning, community development, and others.

A comprehensive model for analyzing stages and levels of well-being across four ecological domains.[3] Prilleltensky (in press) calls for psychologists to be concerned not only with scientific validity but also "psycho-political validity," which he defines as the degree to which psychological research addresses issues of power, oppression, and liberation, and the degree to which interventions move beyond mere amelioration toward structural change. Prilleltensky's argument is important as a general critique and vision for community psychology. Like all general visions, however, it requires careful consideration of the specific ecological contexts of each problem at different levels of analysis and intervention, and of how change occurs over time, in order to make the vision practical. Sometimes, holding out too grand a vision may demoralize individuals who are working at a less comprehensive level to achieve "small wins" (Weick, 1984). We need to have a grander vision, but the field also needs to support those who are doing its everyday work.

Figure 13–1 is a comprehensive framework that attempts to expand and begin to contextualize, or specify, Prilleltensky's vision for community psychology into each of those three dimensions. Ecological validity holds that levels of analysis must be made clear and specific. As shown in the vertical axis of Figure 13–1, first is the level of individual behaviors, emotions, cognitions, and beliefs, and interpersonal microsystem relationships (Bronfenbrenner, 1996). At the mesosystem level are groups, voluntary associations, and other local organizations and networks. At the macrosystem or "collective" level are communities, institutions, and social structures.

From left to right in Figure 13–1, it is possible to think of oppression, liberation, and wellness as stages on a temporal dimension, or at least that is the goal. The oppressed become liberated which leads to social, material, physical, and spiritual wellness. However we should also keep in mind African psychiatrist Franz Fanon's keen insight, that the dream of the oppressed is not to become the liberated, but to be-

Oppression (state):   Liberation/Empowerment (process):   Wellness (outcome):

Domain of Environment:
Political:
Socio-cultural:
Economic:
Physical:

Level of Analysis/Intervention:

	PHYSICAL / ECONOMIC / SOCIAL / POLITICAL (Oppression)	PHYSICAL / ECONOMIC / SOCIAL / POLITICAL (Liberation/Empowerment) / CAPITAL
Macro/Collective/ Structural/Community	Examines political & economic structures in society that threaten environmental wellness in both man-made & natural environments. Seeks understanding of both oppressed populations & reactive actions of policymakers & stakeholders	Examines collective social action, community organizing and network theories. Compares movements and techniques and seeks to understand community processes and societal policies that lead to attainment of popular environmental goals.	Seeks understanding of macro-level environmental variables that affect human wellness. Scrutinizes planning, development, & design policies, as well as preservation regulations for optimal promotion of community wellness.
Meso/Organizational/ Group/Relational	Examines organizations that violate standards of environmental justice for workers and communities. Generates knowledge about group/relational inequities in environmental wellness.	Studies both change in organizations creating environmental risks & organizational learning, decision making, & development in groups and institutions addressing environmental oppression & justice.	Identifies/promotes participatory organizational opportunities & methods of reducing environmental threats and enhancing environmental wellness.
Micro/Individual/ Personal/Psychological (emotional, cognitive, behavioral, spiritual):	Studies the relationship between setting-level environmental features and conditions and individual powerlessness, helplessness, internalized oppression, guilt, and physical and mental disorders.	Studies behavioral practices and beliefs on the part of individuals that affect their immediate environment. Focuses on environmental & political consciousness, activism, leadership, & self-efficacy.	Studies the relationship between environmental variables and personal wellness. Identifies dynamics promoting self-determination, pride, empowerment, health, personal growth, meaning and spirituality.

Figure 13–1. Comprehensive Framework for Ecologically and Psychopolitically Valid Community Action-Research. (From Christens & Perkins, in press)

come the oppressor. We need to balance an idealistic view with practical, hardheaded understanding of how things are in developing our grand view.

Regardless of how common that is, or whether a degree of wellness is required before the hard work of liberation can occur, change over time is an important ecological dimension that may be informed by various human, organizational, and community developmental theories.

The environmental domains (depth dimension of Figure 13–1) imply a critical need for truly interdisciplinary research to adequately understand the sociocultural (psychology, sociology, and anthropology), physical (environmental planning and design research, engineering, environmental branches of psychology, sociology, economics, etc.), economic, and political ecologies. A step in the right direction is to read and adapt the literature of other relevant fields, but that is not enough. Real progress is not likely to be made until more scholars from the various disciplines collaborate closely and begin to develop new fields that are fully interdisciplinary. (In our own experience, it is easier and more successful to approach a colleague in another discipline on an individual basis for advice about an undertaking, or to offer to collaborate. The problems arise when we attempt to incorporate an institutional framework—how will teaching credit be divided, how will grant overhead be allocated to different departments or academic divisions, what additional permissions are necessary from department chairpersons or deans? Similar problems arise if we try to work across professional organizational lines. These problems are more difficult than the problems of adapting different paradigms, and understanding similarities and differences in theoretical languages in a collaboration, although those issues are far from trivial.)

By focusing systematically on issues of power across the different domains, levels, and stages of development, certain questions naturally arise.[4] They are difficult questions, often overlooked by psychologists, but are more likely to lead to solutions that address root causes rather than merely blame the victim (Ryan, 1976). Questions related to oppression include: Who are the players and what are the power relations at each level of analysis? What exchanges of labor, resources, and coercion take place among the various players? What are the consequences of these power relations for each player or group? Questions related to liberation or empowerment include: What strategies are being implemented at each level of analysis to change the oppressive power relations? What factors help or hinder those strategies and change processes? What conditions enable people and groups to resist or block the development of consciousness and empowerment? What specific tactics are used? Questions related to the desired outcome of wellness include: What is the ideal outcome of the liberation/empowerment process envisioned by each player, group, and community?

Applications of Community Psychology

What "small wins" are achievable in a short time under existing conditions that will sustain the necessary commitment to reach the ideal outcome? What are the actual outcomes of the strategies and tactics employed? How long did the effects last? Were power relations changed at each level? How do you explain the outcomes? Although not often addressed in explicit power terms, many of these questions are familiar to community psychologists who conduct evaluation research and so using this framework may only require a slight shift in orientation.

One problem that crops up frequently is the ability of community psychologists to maintain the commitment to the applications of scientific approaches to social and psychological problems. The data don't always come out the way we would like, or the way activists who are our collaborators would like. Others are not interested in objectivity. A lawyer who was involved in litigation said to one of us: "make sure the survey comes out the right way." That request may be perfectly all right within the adversary model of the law, but it is a request to violate scientific standards of practice. Community psychologists working in activist settings, and especially when committed to a certain ideology, may find it difficult to maintain the "scientific" approach, and may find themselves subject to pressures both from within themselves because of their commitment, and from without to argue a position irrespective of data. This dilemma is not solved by having your heart in the right place.

Box 13–1. Applying the Ecological-Psychopolitical Model to One Domain: The Physical Environment

The physical environment, although often taken for granted and overlooked, provides an example of how the different environmental domains depicted in Figure 13–1 interact with the phenomena of interest to community psychologists (see chapter 5). The nine boxes visible in Figure 13–1 illustrate ways in which environment and behavior theories, physical-environmental prevention and intervention efforts, and environmental empowerment movements may apply to Prilleltensky's oppression, liberation, and wellness concerns at different levels of analysis. Similar to economic, sociocultural, and (obviously) political domains, physical environments are often the expression of power issues and relationships at the personal, relational, and collective levels. Identifying relevant issues and areas of inquiry at each level, and how they may relate across levels and domains, helps community psychologists and other social scientists find specific research questions and interventions on which to collaborate.

At the personal level, many individuals are oppressed by environmental degradation. More research is needed on the relationship between setting-level environmental features and conditions, and individuals' internalized helplessness and physical and mental disorders. At the same time, individual positive, liberating environmental behaviors (e.g., recycling, conservation, transit use, consumer decision making) and beliefs/cognitions (e.g., locus of control) must also be better understood and facilitated (Geller, 2002; Werner, 2003). Environmental psychology also studies the relationship between physical setting characteristics and behavior, health, and wellness. What is needed is more attention to environmental conditions conducive to self-determination, pride, empowerment, personal growth, and meaning.

At the organizational level, the idea of environmental oppression includes organizations that violate standards of environmental justice for workers and communities resulting in inequities in environmental wellness. Liberation at this level would include improving practices and decisions both in organizations that create environmental risks and ones addressing environmental oppression and justice. Among other strategies, this would entail the development of grassroots organizations, such as the Love Canal Homeowners Association and other neighborhood groups and advocacy organizations, to reduce environmental threats and enhance environmental wellness.

At the collective level, environmental justice addresses societal factors that lead to environmental oppression in both man-made and natural environments. Collective liberation is based on community organizing, action, empowerment, and political change (see chapters 11 and 12). The goal of collective environmental wellness leads one to consider community and societal-level planning, development, and design policies, as well as preservation regulations that affect community wellness.

Community Psychology Around the Globe

The view of community psychology we have presented in this book is admittedly narrow in at least one sense—it concentrates mainly on the history of, and recent developments in, the field *in the United States*. A full presentation of how the field has developed in other parts of the world would take several more textbooks. Indeed, community psychology textbooks have been written in Great Britain (Orford, 1992), Australia (Thomas & Veno, 1992), South Africa (Seedat & Duncan, 2001), and Canada and Australia (Nelson & Prilleltensky, in press). And those are just the ones in English!

Wingenfeld and Newbrough (2000) provide an excellent, concise outline of the origins, conceptualization, current status of training, research, and practice, and future prospects of community psychology internationally. In addition to the countries above, they review community psychology in New Zealand, Italy, Germany, Poland, Israel, Puerto Rico, Venezuela, Mexico, Cuba, and South Africa, and briefly touch on its presence in several other countries. Others have reviewed community psychology in other Latin American countries (Wiesenfeld, 1998), in Asia (Levine, 1989), and periodic issues of *The Community Psychologist* (SCRA newsletter) have been devoted to international community psychology.

The growth of community psychology internationally is very important for the field's development, both in the United States and in every other country where it has gained a toehold. Wingenfeld and Newbrough (2000) show that the development of community psychology in the United States provided a model and helped launch the field in many other countries, especially in North America and the Caribbean Basin. Over the past 15 years, however, community psychologists in those countries—as well as in Europe, Asia, Australia, and New Zealand, which have always been a bit more independent (Francescato & Tomai, 2001)—have developed very different ideas about community theories and research methods. Community psychologists in the United States have much to learn from them. For example, due to the longer, and in some ways continuing, experience of colonialism in Latin America, community psychologists (Serrano-García, 1984) and educators (Freire, 1970) in that region have developed a much more critical sense of oppression and political consciousness.

Similarly, American community psychologists may think of themselves as egalitarian, but community-oriented psychology in Europe and elsewhere is much more collectivist and egalitarian and less focused on freedom, autonomy, and other individualistic definitions of wellness (Francescato & Tomai, 2001). In general, community psychology outside the United States tends to be more theoretical and less practical (e.g., not quite as heavy an emphasis on program evaluation research). Community researchers in other countries are likely to adopt a Postmodern, anti-Positivist view of science and conduct more qualitative than quantitative studies. There are, of course, many exceptions to these generalizations.

Similar to the argument above that to grow the field must become more interdisciplinary, the internationalization of community psychology has led to a tremendous diversity of new ideas, methods, and intervention strategies tested in very different contexts around the globe. All we need now is more direct, cross-cultural comparisons of community theories and actions in order to see how different political and cultural contexts affect the same problems and solutions. The

Ecological-Psychopolitical Model described above is one framework that an international group of community psychologists from the United States, Australia, and Latin America (with other countries likely to join) are developing to explore and compare issues of community power, oppression, liberation or empowerment, and wellness in their home countries.

Summary

Scientific research serves values, and community research is inevitably a compromise product of its social and political context. Values influence what research topics are chosen, how questions get defined, what is measured, and the ground rules for subjecting empirical effects to statistical evaluation, interpretation, and presentation. We illustrated these points with examples showing how the social context of an investigation modifies and influences the methodological procedures, the inferential process, the report, the participants, and the varied uses to which research may be put. With decisions often made on the basis of power, politics, and related values, community psychology's emphasis is on identifying and articulating the perspectives of all stakeholders and promoting a process of fairness.

Value issues lead to ethical considerations. From a community perspective the ethical choices are many: whether the professional chooses to intervene, his or her choices among the many possible goals, targets of change, and means of intervening, and the adequacy of efforts to determine all of the resulting consequences (including those that were unexpected).

Community psychology's multiple levels of analysis (from individual coping to broad societal change) make an interdisciplinary perspective essential. Although the visibility and contributions of interdisciplinary work have to date been limited, tangible efforts to organize and make explicit community psychology's interdisciplinary potential are under way. One result has been a better understanding of how different ecological and societal levels of action lead to a more systematic consideration of power, money, and other resources, and thus inevitably to a direct and explicit focus on the politics of intervention and change. These processes are discussed formally in a model proposed by Prilleltensky, and were illustrated in this chapter by an examination of the effects of the physical environment from a community psychology perspective.

We concluded the chapter by acknowledging that despite our almost exclusive attention to work in the United States, community psychology is very much alive and well in other parts of the world. International scholars have put their own stamp on community psychology, especially with respect to the impact of political consciousness and collectivist values. The future looks promising, with international relationships generating a tremendous diversity of new ideas, methods, and intervention strategies along with new opportunities for cross-cultural comparisons of community theories and interventions.

In the beginning of the book, we described the aims of community psychologists. It is worth repeating those here:

> . . . it [is] their mission to help create or change service organizations and other institutions and agencies to become more effective in achieving the goals of providing humane, effective care and less stigmatizing services to those in need, and of enhancing human growth and development.

We all have those duties as participants in a community, as citizens, and as professionals.

Notes

1. This was the second of three conferences on training in community psychology held in Austin. The others were in 1967 and 1975 (Iscoe, Bloom, & Spielberger, 1977).

2. The membership of Division 27 (Community Psychology) of APA created SCRA as a parallel, independent entity.

3. This section is based on a paper by Brian D. Christens and Douglas D. Perkins (in press).

4. We thank Isaac Prilleltensky and Adrian Fisher for suggesting many of these questions. For a classic game theory analysis of community power, see Long (1958).

References

Abram, K. M., & Teplin, L. A. (1991). Co-occurring disorders among mentally ill jail detainees: Implications for public policy. *American Psychologist, 46*(10), 1036–1045.

Academy of Leisure Sciences. (n.d.). White Paper #3: Leisure: The new center of the economy? http://www.cas.ualberta.ca/elj/als/alswp3.html

Acierno, R., Brady, K., Gray, M., Kilpatrick, D. G., Resnick, H., & Best, C. L. (2002). Psychopathology following interpersonal violence: A comparison of risk factors in older and younger adults. *Journal of Clinical Geropsychology, 8*(1), 13–23.

Acosta, O. M. (1998). Resilience among Latin-American children and adolescents: An examination of individual and family variables as moderators of stress. Dissertation: State University of New York, Buffalo, NY.

Acs, G., and Loprest, P. (2001). The status of TANF leavers in the District of Columbia: Final report. Washington, DC: Urban Institute. http://www.wkap.nl/journalhome.htm/ 1079-9362

Addams, J. (1910). *Twenty years at Hull House.* New York: Macmillan.

Adler, N. E., Boyce, T., Chesney, M. A., Cohen, S., Folkman, S., Kahn, R. L., & Syme, S. L. (1994). Socioeconomic status and health: The challenge of the gradient. *American Psychologist, 49,* 15–24.

Administration on Children, Youth and Families. (2002). *Making a difference in the lives of infants and toddlers and their families: The impacts of Early Head Start, 1.* Final Technical Report.

Adoption and Safe Families Act, PL 105-89 (1997).

AFSCME. (2002). http://www.afscme.org/pol-leg/opendo2.htm

Alan Guttmacher Institute. (1999). Facts in brief. Teen sex and pregnancy. http://www.agi-usa.org/pubs/tb_teen_sex.html

Alba, R. D., Logan, J. R., & Stults, B. J. (2000). How segregated are middle-class African Americans? *Social Problems, 47*(4), 543–558.

Albee, B. W. (1995). Ann and me. *The Journal of Primary Prevention, 15,* 331–349.

Albee, G. W. (1959). *Mental health manpower trends.* New York: Basic Books.

Albee, G. W. (1998). The politics of primary prevention. *Journal of Primary Prevention, 19*(2), 117–127.

Albee, G. W., Faenza, M. M., & Gullotta, T. P. (1997). Introduction. In Albee, G. W., & Gullotta, T. P. (Eds.), *Primary prevention works* (pp xi–xiv). Thousand Oaks, CA: Sage.

Albee, G. W., & Gullotta, T. P. (Eds.). (1997). *Primary prevention works.* Thousand Oaks, CA: Sage.

Alinsky, S. (1971). *Rules for radicals.* New York: Vantage Press.

Altman, D. (1995). Sustaining interventions in community systems: On the relationship between researchers and communities. *Health Psychology, 14,* 526–536.

Altman, I. (1975). *The environment and social behavior: Privacy, personal space, territory and crowding.* Monterey: Brooks/Cole.

Altman, I., & Rogoff, B. (1987). World views in psychology: Trait, interactional, organismic, and transactional perspectives. In D. Stokols & I. Altman (Eds.), *Handbook of environmental psychology* (pp. 1–40). New York: Wiley.

Amaro, H. (1995). Love, sex, and power. Considering women's realities in HIV prevention. *American Psychologist, 50,* 437–447.

American Academy of Pediatrics. (2000). Reducing the number of deaths and injuries from residential firs (RE9952). *Pediatrics, 105*(6), 1355–1357.

American Bankruptcy Institute. (2003). ABI World. http://www/abiworld.org.stats/1980annual.html

American Psychological Association. (2002). Ethical principles of psychologists and code of conduct. *American Psychologist, 57,* 1060–1073.

American Public Health Association. (1991). Large percent of Americans exposed to alcoholism in the family. *Nation's Health, 11,* 1–24.

Anderson, W. (1991). The New York needle trial: The politics of public health in the age of AIDS. *American Journal of Public Health, 81,* 1506–1517.

Angel, B., Hjern, A., & Ingleby, D. (2001). Effects of war and organized violence on children: A study of Bosnian refugees in Sweden. *American Journal of Orthopsychiatry, 71*(1), 4–15.

Annals of the American Academy of Political and Social Science, 577. (2001, September). (Whole issue).

Anthony, K. H., & Watkins, N. J. (2002). Exploring pathology: Relationships between clinical and environmental psychology. In R. B. Bechtel & A. Churchman (Eds.), *Handbook of environmental psychology* (pp. 129–146). New York: John Wiley & Sons.

Antonucci, T. C., Lansford, J. E., & Akiyama, H. (2001). Impact of positive and negative aspects of marital relationships and friendships on well-being of older adults. *Applied Developmental Science, 5*(2), 68–75.

Antze, P. (1976). The role of ideologies in peer psychotherapy organizations: Some theoretical considerations and three case studies. *Journal of Applied Behavioral Science, 12,* 323–346.

Appleyard, D. (1981). *Livable streets, protected neighborhoods.* Los Angeles: University of California Press.

Aral, S. O., VanderPlate, C., & Magder, L. (1988). Recurrent genital herpes: What helps adjustment? *Sexually Transmitted Diseases, 15*(3), 164–166.

Argyris, C. (1993). *Knowledge for action: A guide to overcoming barriers to organizational change.* San Francisco: Jossey-Bass.

Arthur v. Nyquist 415 F. Supp. 904 (W. D. N. Y. 1976).

Auerbach, J. S. (1976). *Unequal justice.* New York: Oxford University Press.

Ault, A. (2002). New Mexico first to let psychologists give meds. Reuters, March 7, 2002.

Bachrach, L. L. (1983). *Deinstitutionalization.* San Francisco: Jossey-Bass.

Barbarin, O. A., Richter, L., & deWet, T. (2001). Exposure to violence, coping resources, and psychological adjustment of South African children. *American Journal of Orthopsychiatry, 72*(1), 16–25.

Barker, R. G. (1968). *Ecological psychology: Concepts and methods for studying the environment of human behavior.* Stanford, CA: Stanford University Press.

Barker, R. G. (1993). *Habitats, environments, and human behavior* (2nd ed.). San Francisco: Jossey-Bass.

Barker, R. G., & Gump, P. V. (1972). *Big school, small school: High school size and student behavior* (2nd ed.). Stanford, CA: Stanford University Press.

Barker, R. G., & Schoggen, P. (1973). *Qualities of community life: Methods of measuring environment and behavior applied to an American and an English town.* San Francisco: Jossey-Bass.

Barker, R. G., & Wright, H. F. (1970). *Midwest and its children. The psychological ecology of an American Town* (2d ed.). Evanston, IL: Row Peterson.

Barnett, W. S. (1993). Benefit-cost analysis of preschool education: Findings from a 25-year follow-up. *American Journal of Orthopsychiatry, 63,* 500–508.

Barrera, M., Jr. (1986). Distinctions between social support concepts, measures and models. *American Journal of Community Psychology, 14,* 413–445.

Barrera, M., Jr. (2000). Social support research in community psychology. In J. Rappaport & E. Seidman (Eds.), *Handbook of community psychology* (pp. 215–245). New York: Kluwer Academic/Plenum.

Bateman, H. V. (2002). Sense of community in the school: listening to students' voices.

In A. Fisher, C. Sonn, & B. Bishop (Eds.), *Psychological sense of community: Research, applications, and implications* pp. 161–179. New York: Plenum.

Baud, R. K. (Ed.). (1982). *Parent power: A handbook for Buffalo public school parents.* Buffalo, NY: Citizens for Quality Education.

Baum, A., & Fleming, I. (1993). Implications of psychological research on stress and technological accidents. *American Psychologist, 48*(6), 665–672.

Baum, A., & Paulus, P. B. (1987). Crowding. In D. Stokols & I. Altman (Eds.), *Handbook of environmental psychology* (pp. 533–570). New York: Wiley.

Baum, S., & Saunders, D. (1998). Life after debt: Summary results of the National Student Loan Survey. In *Student Loan Debt: Problems and Prospects* (pp. 77–96). Proceedings from a National Symposium sponsored by Sally Mae Education Institute, Reston, VA.; Institute for Higher Education Policy, Washington, DC; Education Resources Institute, Boston, MA.

Bauman, L. J., Stein, R. E. K., & Ireys, H. T. (1991). Reinventing fidelity: the transfer of social technology among settings. *American Journal of Community Psychology, 19,* 619–639.

Baxtrom v. Herald 383 U. S. 107 (1966).

Bazelon Center. (2003). Landmark mental disability law suit ends after 33 years. http://www.bazelon.org/newsroom/12-15-03wyatt.htm

Bechtel, R. B. (1977). *Enclosing behavior.* Stroudsburg, PA: Dowden, Hutchinson & Ross.

Beck, J. C. (1998). Legal and ethical duties of the clinician treating a patient who is liable to be impulsively violent. *Behavioral Sciences and the Law, 16*(3), 375–389.

Becker, M., Stiles, P. G., & Schonfeld, L. (2002). Mental health service use, and cost of care for older adults in assisted living facilities: Implications for public policy. *Journal of Behavioral Health Services and Research, 29,* 91–98.

Beers, C. W. (1933). *A mind that found itself.* (originally published in 1908). New York: Doubleday Doran.

Beiser, M., Shore, J. H., Peters, R., & Tatum, E. (1985). Does community care for the mentally ill make a difference? A tale of two cities. *American Journal of Psychiatry, 142,* 1047–1052.

Belk v. Charlotte Mecklenburg Board of Education 269 F.3rd 305 (4th Cir 2001).

Belsky, J. (1980). Child maltreatment: An ecological integration. *American Psychologist, 35,* 320–335.

Belton v. Gebhart 347 U.S. 483 (1954).

Bennett, C. C., Anderson, L. S., Cooper, S., Hassol, L., Klein, D. C., & Rosenblum, G. (1966). Community psychology. A report on the Boston Conference on the Education of Psychologists for Community Mental Health. Boston: Department of Psychology, Boston University.

Bennis, W. G. (1966). *Changing organizations.* New York: McGraw Hill.

Berg, I., & Nursten, J. (Eds.). (1996). *Unwillingly to school* (4th ed.). London: Gaskell.

Bermant, G., Kelman, H. C., & Warwick, D. P. (1978). *The ethics of social intervention.* New York: Halstead Press.

Berrueta-Clement, J. R., Schweinhart, L. J., Barnett, W. S., Epstein, A. S., & Weikart, D. P. (1984). *Changed lives. The effects of the Perry preschool program on youths through age 19.* Ypsilanti, MI: The High/Scope Press.

Bickel, A. M. (1962). *The least dangerous branch: The Supreme Court at the bar of politics.* Indianapolis: Bobbs-Merrill.

Bickman, L., Guthrie, P. R., Foster, E. M., Lambert, E. W., Summerfelt, W. T., Breda, C., & Heflinger, C. A. (1995). *Managed care in mental health: The Fort Bragg Experiment.* New York: Plenum Press.

Blazer, D. G. (1982). Social support and mortality in an elderly community population. *American Journal of Epidemiology, 115,* 684–694.

Bloch, A. (1984). Twenty-year follow-up of pupils in a special class for the mentally retarded: A study of a complete school community. *American Journal of Orthopsychiatry, 54,* 436–443.

Bloom, B. L. (1984). *Community mental health. a general introduction.* 2nd Ed. Monterey, CA: Brooks/Cole.

Bloom, B. L. (1992). Stressful life event theory and the prevention of psychopathology.

In M. Kessler & S. E. Goldston (Eds.), *The present and future of prevention: In honor of George W. Albee* (pp. 115–124). Newbury Park: Sage.

Bloom, B. L. (2000). Planned short-term psychotherapies. In C. R. Snyder & R. E. Ingram (Eds.), *Handbook of psychological change: Psychotherapy processes & practices for the 21st century* (pp. 429–454). New York: Wiley.

Bloom, B. L., Asher, S. J., & White, S. W. (1978). Marital disruption as a stressor: A review and analysis. *Psychological Bulletin, 85*, 867–894.

Bloom, B. L., & Hodges, W. F. (1988). The Colorado separation and divorce program: A preventive intervention for newly separated persons. In R. H. Price, E. L. Cowen, R. P. Lorion, & Ramos-McKay, J. *14 Ounces of prevention.* Washington, DC: American Psychological Association.

Board of Education v. Dowell 498 U. S. 237 (1991).

Bond, G. R. (1992). Vocational rehabilitation. In R. Liberman (Ed.), *Handbook of psychiatric rehabilitation* (pp. 244–275). New York: MacMillan.

Bond, G. R., Witheridge, T. F., Dincin, J., & Wasmer, D. (1990). Assertive community treatment for frequent users of psychiatric hospitals in a large city: A controlled study. *American Journal of Community Psychology, 18*, 865–891.

Bond, M. A., & Mulvey, A. (2000). A history of women and feminist perspectives in community psychology. *American Journal of Community Psychology, 28*(5), 599–630.

Bonnes, M., & Bonaiuto, M. (2002). Environmental psychology: From spatial-physical environment to sustainable development. In R. B. Bechtel, & A. Churchman (Eds.), *Handbook of environmental psychology* (pp. 28–54). New York: John Wiley & Sons.

Bouchard, T. J. (1994). Genes, environment, and personality. *Science, 264*, 1700–1701.

Bourdieu, P. (1985). The forms of capital. Pp. 241–258 in J. Richardson (Ed.), *Handbook of theory and research for the sociology of education.* New York: Greenwood.

Braginsky, B. M., Braginsky, D. D., & Ring, K. (1969). *The mental hospital as a last resort.* New York: Holt, Rhinehart & Winston.

Brand, R. S. Jr., & Claiborn, W. L. (1976). Two studies of coparative stigma: Employer attitudes and practices toward rehabilitated convicts, mental and tuberculosis patients. *Community Mental Health Journal, 12*, 168–175.

Breakey, W. R., & Fischer, P. J. (1990). Homelessness: The extent of the problem. *Journal of Social Issues, 46*(4), 31–47.

Brenner, M. (1994). Judge Motley's verdict. *The New Yorker*, May 16, 1994, 65–71.

Breslau, N., & Prabucki, K. (1987). Siblings of disabled children: Effects of chronic stress in the family. *Archives of General Psychiatry, 44*, 1040–1046.

Briggs v. Elliott 347 U. S. 497 (1954).

Briggs, X. S. (1998). Brown kids in white suburbs: Housing mobility and the many faces of social capital. *Housing Policy Debate, 9*, 177–221.

Brissette, I., Cohen, S., & Seeman, T. E. (2000). Measuring social integration and social networks. In S. Cohen, L. G. Underwood and B. H. Gottlieb (Eds.), *Social support: Measurement and intervention* (pp. 53–85). New York: Oxford.

Brodsky, A. E. (1999). "Making it.": The components and process of resilience among urban African-American single mothers. *American Journal of Orthopsychiatry, 69*(2), 148–160.

Brodsky, A. E., O'Campo, P. J., & Aronson, R. E. (1999). PSOC in community context: Multi-level correlates of a measure of psychological sense of community in low-income, urban neighborhoods. *Journal of Community Psychology, 27*, 659–679.

Broman, C. L., Hamilton, V. L., & Hoffman, W. S. (1990). Unemployment and its effect on families: Evidence from a plant closing study. *American Journal of Community Psychology, 18*, 643–659.

Broman, C. L., Hamilton, V. L., & Hoffman, W. S. (2001). *Stress and distress among the unemployed: Hard times and vulnerable people.* New York: Kluwer Academic/Plenum.

Bronfenbrenner, U. (1996). *The ecology of human development: Experiments by nature and design.* Cambridge, MA: Harvard University Press.

Bronzaft, A. L. (2002). Noise pollution: A hazard to physical and mental well-being. In R. B. Bechtel & A. Churchman (Eds.), *Handbook of environmental psychology* (pp. 499–510). New York: John Wiley & Sons.

Brown v. Board of Education of Topeka 349 U. S. 294 (1955).

Brown v. Board of Education, 347 U. S. 483 (1954).

Brown, B. B., Burton, J. R., & Sweaney, A. (1998). Neighbors, households, and front porches: New urbanish community tool or mere nostalgia? *Environment and Behavior, 30,* 579–600.

Brown, B. B., & Cropper, V.L. (2001). New urban and standard suburban subdivisions: Evaluating psychological and social goals. *Journal of the American Planning Association, 67,* 402–419.

Brown, B. B., & Perkins, D. D. (1992). Disruptions in place attachment. In I. Altman & S. Low (Eds.), *Place attachment* (pp. 279–304). New York: Plenum.

Brown, B. B., & Werner, C. M. (1985). Social cohesiveness, territoriality and holiday decorations: The influence of cul-de-sacs. *Environment and Behavior, 17,* 539–565.

Browne, A. (1993). Violence against women by male partners: Prevalence, outcomes, and policy implications. *American Psychologist, 48,* 1077–1087.

Browne, K. (1993). Home visitation and child abuse: The British experience. *The ASPA Advisor, 6,* 11–12, 28–31.

Bruene-Butler, L., Hampson, J., Elias, M. J., Clabby, J. F., & Schuyler, T. (1997). In. G. W. Albee and T. P. Gullotta (Eds.), *Primary prevention works* (Ch. 11, pp. 239–267). Thousand Oaks, CA: Sage.

Bullard, R. (1990). *Dumping in Dixie.* Boulder, CO: Westview Press.

Bureau of Justice Statistics. (1998). *Alcohol and crime.* Washington, DC: U. S. Department of Justice.

Bureau of Labor Statistics (2000–2001). Occupational Outlook Handbook. http://www.bls.gov

Bureau of Labor Statistics (2001). Report on the American labor force, 2001. Washington, DC: U. S. Department of Labor, Bureau of Labor Statistics.

Bureau of Labor Statistics. (2003). http://www.bls.gov

Burgess, A. W., & Holmstrom, L. L. (1979). Rape: Sexual disruption and recovery. *American Journal of Orthopsychiatry, 49,* 648–657.

Burke, W. W. (1994). *Organization development: A process of learning and changing.* Reading, MA: Addison-Wesley.

Burnette, D. (1999). Physical and emotional well-being of custodial grandparents in Latino families. *American Journal of Orthopsychiatry, 69*(3), 305–318.

Burt, R. S. (1999). The social capital of opinion leaders. *Annals of the American Academy of Political and Social Sciences 566,* 37–64.

Buss, T. F. (1992). *Mass unemployment: Plant closings and community mental health.* Beverly Hills, CA: Sage.

Butterfoss, F. D., Goodman, R. M., & Wandersman, A. (1993). Community coalitions for prevention and health promotion. *Health Education Research. Theory and Practice, 8,* 315–330.

Byrne, D., Kelley, K., & Fisher, W. A. (1993). Unwanted teenage pregnancies: Incidence, interpretation, and intervention. *Applied and Preventive Psychology, 2,* 101–113.

Cahn, E. (1955). Jurisprudence. *NYU Law Review, 30,* 150–169.

Caldwell, R. A., Bogat, G. A., & Davidson, W. S. II. (1988). The assessment of child abuse potential and the prevention of child abuse and neglect: A policy analysis. *American Journal of Community Psychology, 16,* 608–624.

Campbell, D. T. (1969). Reforms as experiments. *American Psychologist, 24,* 409–429.

Campbell, D. T. (1979). Assessing the impact of planned social change. *Evaluation and Program Planning, 2,* 67–90.

Campbell, D. T., & Kimmel, H. (1985). Guiding preventive intervention research centers for research validity. Unpublished manuscript, Department of Social Relations, Lehigh University, Bethlehem, PA.

Campbell, R., & Wasco, S. M. (2000). Feminist approaches to social science: Epistemological and methodological tenets. *American Journal of Community Psychology, 28*(6), 773–791.

Capizzano, J., Tout, K., & Adams, G. (2000). *Child care patterns of school-age children with employed mothers.* Washington, DC: The Urban Institute.

Caplan, G. (1964). *Principles of preventive psychiatry.* New York: Basic Books.

Caplan, G. (1970). *The theory and practice of mental health consultation.* New York: Basic Books.

Caplan, G. (1976). The family as a support system. In G. Caplan & M. Killilea (Eds.), *Support systems and mutual help*. New York: Grune & Stratton.

Caplan, M. (1999). *Farther along: A civil rights memoir*. Baton Rouge, LA: Louisiana State University.

Caplan, R. D., Vinokur, A. D., & Price, R. H. (1997). From job loss to reemployment: Field experiments in prevention-focused coping. In. G. W. Albee and T. P. Gullotta (Eds.), *Primary prevention works*. (Ch. 15, pp. 341–379). Thousand Oaks, CA: Sage.

Caplan, R. D., Vinokur, A. D., Price, R. H., & van Ryn, M. (1989). Job seeking, reemployment, and mental health: A randomized field experiment in coping with job loss. *Journal of Applied Psychology, 74,* 759–769.

Carling, P. J. (1990). Major mental illness, housing, and supports: The promise of community integration. *American Psychologist, 45,* 969–975.

Carson, E. D. (1993). *A hand up. Black philanthropy and self-help in America*. Washington, DC: Joint Center for Political and Economic Studies Press.

Cashin, S. D. (2001). Middle-class black suburbs and the state of integration: A post-integrationist vision for metropolitan America. *Cornell Law Review, 86,* 729–776.

Cassidy, L., Meadows, J., Catalan, J., & Barton, S. (1997). Are reported stress and coping style associated with frequent recurrence of genital herpes? *Genitourinary Medicine, 73*(4), 263–266.

Catania, J. A., Coates, T. J., Stall, R., Bye, L. Kegeles, S. M., Capell, F., Henne, J., McKusick, L., Morin, S., Turner, H. (1991). Changes in condom use among homosexual men in San Francisco. *Health Psychology, 10*(3), 190–199.

Ceballo, R. (2000). The neighborhood club: A supportive intervention group for children exposed to urban violence. *American Journal of Orthopsychiatry, 70*(3), 401–407.

Center for Health, Environment, and Justice. (2002). *Creating safe learning zones: Invisible threats, visible actions*. Falls Church, VA: author.

Center for Mental Health Services and National Institute of Mental Health. Mental Health, United States, 1996. Manderscheid, R. W., & Sonnenschein, M. A. (Eds). DHHS Pub. No. (SMA) 96-3098. Washington, DC: U. S. Government Printing Office, 1996.

Center for the Future of Children. (1992). *The future of children. School linked services, 2*(1) (Whole Issue).

Centers for Disease Control. (1999). Achievements in public health, 1900–1999: Healthier mothers and babies. *MMWR Weekly, 48*(38), 849–858.

Centers for Disease Control. (2001a). National overview of sexually transmitted diseases, 2000. http://www.cdc.gov/std/stats/2000NatOverview.htm

Centers for Disease Control. (2001b). National Vital Statistics Reports, December 28, 2001.

Centers for Disease Control and Prevention. HIV/AIDS Surveillance Report, 2002, 14. http://www.cdc.gov/hiv/stats/hasrlink.htm

Chamberlin, J. (1990). The ex-patient's movement: Where we've been and where we're going. *The Journal of Mind and Behavior, 11,* 323–336.

Chayes, A. (1976). The role of the judge in public law litigation. *Harvard Law Review, 89,* 1281–1316.

Checkoway, B. (1981). *Citizens and health care: Participation and planning for social change*. Elmsford, NY: Pergamon.

Chen, E., Matthews, K. A., & Boyce, W. T. (2002). Socioeconomic differences in children's health: How and why do these relationships change with age? *Psychological Bulletin, 128*(2), 295–329.

Cheng, S. -T. (1993). The social context of Hong Kong's booming elderly home industry. *American Journal of Community Psychology, 21,* 449–467.

Cheng, S. -T., & Chan, A. C. M. (2003). An ecological model of industrial regulation: Nursing homes for the elderly in Hong Kong. *Law and Policy,25*(4), 403–423.

Cherniss, C. (1980). *Professional burnout in human service organizations*. New York: Praeger.

Cherniss, C., & Cherniss, D. S. (1987). Professional involvement in self-help groups for parents of high risk newborns. *American Journal of Community Psychology, 15,* 435–444.

Cherniss, C., & Deegan, G. (2000). The creation of alternative settings. In J. Rappaport, & E. Seidman (Eds.), *Handbook of community psychology*. New York: Kluwer Academic/ Plenum Publishers.

Chesler, M. A., & Chesney, B. K. (1995). *Cancer and self-help: Bridging the troubled waters of childhood illness*. Madison, WI: University of Wisconsin Press.

Choi, K. H., Yep, G. A., & Kumekawa, E. (1998). HIV prevention among Asian and Pacific islander American men who have sex with men: A critical review of theoretical models and directions for future research. *AIDS Education and Prevention, 10* (Suppl 3), 19–30.

Chow, S. L. (1987). Science, ecological validity and experimentation. *Journal for the Theory of Social Behaviour, 17*(2), 181–194.

Christens, B., & Perkins, D. D. (in press). Interdisciplinary, multilevel action—research to enhance ecological and psychopolitical validity. *Journal of Community Psychology.*

Christenson, J. A., Fendley, K., & Robinson, J. W., Jr. (1989). Community development. In J. A. Christenson & J.W. Robinson, Jr. (Eds.), *Community development in perspective.* Ames: IA State University Press (pp. 1–25).

Chuang, D. K. (2001). Power, merit and the imitations (sic) of the black white binary in the affirmative action debate: The case of Asian Americans at Whitney High School. *Asian Law Journal, 8,* 31–70.

Churchman, A. (2002). Environmental psychology and urban planning: Where can the twain meet? In R. B. Bechtel & A. Churchman (Eds.), *Handbook of environmental psychology* (pp. 191–200). New York: John Wiley.

Cicirelli, V. G. (1969). *The impact of Head Start: An evaluation of the effects of Head Start on children's cognitive and affective development.* Washington, DC: National Bureau of Standards, Institute for Applied Technology.

City of Cleburne, Texas v. Cleburen Living Center, 473 U. S. 432 (1985).

Civil Rights Cases, 109 U. S. 3 (1883).

Clay, R. A. (2000). Linking up online. *Monitor on Psychology, 31*(4), 20–23.

Clayton, R. R., Cattarello, A. M., & Johnstone, B. M. (1996). The effectiveness of Drug Abuse Resistance Education (Project D.A.R.E.): 5-year follow-up results. *Preventive Medicine, 25,* 307–318.

Clegg, R. (2000, May 29). Gavels down. *New Jersey Law Journal.*

Clingempeel, W. G., & Reppucci, N. D. (1982). Joint custody after divorce: Major issues and goals for research. *Psychological Bulletin, 91,* 102–127.

Cloward, R., & Piven, F. F. (1971). *Regulating the poor: The function of public welfare in America.* New York: Random House.

Coates, T. J. (1990). Strategies for modifying sexual behavior for primary and secondary prevention of HIV disease. *Journal of Consulting and Clinical Psychology, 58,* 57–69.

Cohen, C. I., & Thompson, K. S. (1992). Homeless mentally ill, mentally ill homeless? *American Journal of Psychiatry, 149,* 816–823.

Cohen, S. Gottlieb, B. H., & Underwood, L. G. (2000). Social relationships and health. In S. Cohen, L. G. Underwood, and B. H., Gottlieb (Eds.), *Social support measurement and intervention* (pp. 3–25). New York: Oxford University Press.

Cohen, S., Gottlieb, B. H., & Underwood, L. G. (2001). Social relationships and health: Challenges for measurement and intervention. *Advances in Mind Body Medicine, 17*(2), 129–141.

Cohen, S., & Wills, T. A. (1985). Stress, social support, and the buffering hypothesis. *Psychological Bulletin, 98,* 310–357.

Coie, J. D., Watt, N. F., West, S. G., Hawkins, J. D., Asarnow, J. R., Markman, H. J., et al. (1993). The science of prevention: A conceptual framework and some directions for a national research program. *American Psychologist, 48,* 1013–1022.

Colarelli, N . J., & Siegel, S. M. (1966). Ward H. *An adventure in innovation.* Princeton, NJ: Van Nostrand.

Coleman, J. S., Campbell, E. Q., Hobson, C. J., McPartland, J., Mood, A. M., Weinfeld, F. D., & York, R. L. (1966). *Equality of educational opportunity.* Washington, DC: U.S. Government Printing Office.

Collins, N. L., Dunkel-Schetter, C., Lobel, M., & Scrimshaw, S. C. M. (1993). Social support in pregnancy: Psychosocial correlates of birth outcomes and postpartum depression. *Journal of Personality and Social Psychology, 65,* 1243–1258.

Comer, J. P. (1997). *Waiting for a miracle.* NY: Plume.

Compas, B. A., Connor, J., & Wadsworth, M. (1997). Prevention of depression. In R. P. Weisberg, T. P. Gullotta, R. L. Hampton, B. A. Ryan, & G. R. Adams, (Eds.), *Enhancing children's wellness* (pp. 129–174). Thousand Oaks, CA: Sage.

Comptroller General of the United States. (1977). Report to Congress. Returning the mentally disabled to the community: Government needs to do more. Washington, DC: Author.

Consumer Advisory Board v. Glover 989 F. 2d 65 (First Cir. 1993).

Cook, R. L., Pollock, N. K., Rao, A. K., & Clark, D. B. (2002). Increased prevalence of herpes simplex virus type 2 among adolescent women with alcohol use disorders. *Journal of Adolescent Health, 30*(3), 169–174.

Cook, S. W. (1984). The 1954 Social Science statement and school desegregation: a reply to Gerard. *American Psychologist, 39,* 819–832.

Cowen, E. L. (1973). Social and community interventions. *Annual Review of Psychology, 24,* 423–472.

Cowen, E. L. (1982). Help is where you find it: Four informal helping groups. *American Psychologist, 37,* 385–395.

Cowen, E. L. (1983). Primary prevention in mental health: Past, present, and future (pp. 11–25). In R. Felner, et al. (Eds.), *Preventive psychology.* New York: Plenum.

Cowen, E. L. (1997). Schools and the enhancement of children's wellness: Some opportunities and some limiting factors. In R. P. Weissberg & T. P. Gullotta (Eds.), *Healthy children 2010: Establishing preventive services* (pp. 97–123). Thousand Oaks, CA: Sage.

Cowen, E. L. (2000). Community psychology and routes to psychological wellness. In J. Rappaport & E. Seidman (Eds.), *Handbook of community psychology* (pp. 79–99). New York: Kluwer Academic/Plenum.

Cowen, E. L., Hightower, A. D., Pedro Carroll, J. L., & Work, W. C. (1996). *School-based prevention for children at risk: The Primary Mental Health Project.* Washington DC: American Psychological Association.

Cowen, E. L., Trost, M. A., Izzo, L. D., Lorion, R. P., Dorr, D., & Isaacson, R. V. (1975). *New ways in school mental health.* New York: Human Sciences Press.

Coyne, J. C., Kessler, R. S., Tal, M. Turnbull, J., Wortman, C. B., & Greden, J. F. (1987). Living with a depressed person. *Journal of Consulting and Clinical Psychology, 55,* 347–352.

Coyne, J. C., Thompson, R., & Palmer, S. C. (2002). Marital quality, coping with conflict, marital complaints, and affection in couples with a depressed wife. *Journal of Family Psychology, 16*(1), 26–37.

Crawford, I., Jason, L. A., Riordan, N., Kaufman, J., Salina, D., Sawalski, L., et al. (1990). A multimedia-based approach to increasing communication and the level of AIDS knowledge within families. *Journal of Community Psychology, 18*(4), 361–373.

Crittenden, P. M. (1992). The social ecology of treatment: Case study of a service system for maltreated children. *American Journal of Orthopsychiatry, 62,* 22–34.

Cronkite, R. C., Moos, R. H., Twohey, J., Cohen, C., & Swindle, R., Jr. (1998). Life circumstances and personal resources as predictors of the ten-year course of depression. *American Journal of Community Psychology, 26*(2), 255–280.

Cronon, W. (1991). *Nature's metropolis: Chicago and the great west.* New York: Norton.

Crouter, A. C., & McHale, S. M. (1993). Temporal rhythms in family life: Seasonal variation in the relation between family work and family processes. *Developmental Psychology, 29,* 198–205.

Cummings, R. (1993). All-male black schools: Equal protection, the new separatism and Brown v. Board of Education. *Hastings Constitutional Law Quarterly, 20,* 752–782.

Cutrona, C. E., & Cole, V. (2000). Optimizing support in the natural network. In Cohen, Underwood, & Gottlieb (Eds.), *Social support measurement and intervention* (pp. 278–308). New York: Oxford University Press.

Darling-Hammond, L., Ancess, J., & Ort, S. W. (2002). Reinventing high school: Outcomes of the coalition campus schools project. *American Educational Research Journal, 39*(3), 639–673.

Darlington, R. B., Royce, J. M., Snipper, A. S., Murray, H. W., & Lazar, I. (1980). Preschool programs and later school competence of children from low-income families. *Science, 208,* 202–204.

D'Augelli, A.R. (1982). Historical synthesis of consultation and education. In D. R. Ritter (Ed.), *Consultation, education and prevention in community mental health.* Springfield, IL: Charles C. Thomas.

D'Augelli, A. R., & Hershberger, S. L. (1993). Lesbian, gay, and bisexual youth in community settings: Personal challenges and mental health problems. *American Journal of Community Psychology, 21,* 421–448.

Davis v. County School Board of Prince Edward County 347 U. S. 483 (1954).

Davis, L. G., & Nelson, W. E. (1980). The politics of black self-help in the United States: A historical overview. In L. S. Yearwood (Ed.), *Black organizations: Issues on survival techniques: A historical overview* (pp. 37–50). Lanham, MD: University Press of America.

Davis, M., Baranowski, T., Hughes, M., Warneke, C., deMoor, C., Baranowski, J., Cullen, K., & Mullis, R. (in press). Using children as change agents to increase fruit and vegetable consumption among lower-income African American parents: Outcome results of the Bringing It Home program. *Preventive Medicine.*

Davis, R. C., Brickman, E., & Baker, T. (1991). Supportive and unsupportive responses of others to rape victims: Effects on concurrent victim adjustment. *American Journal of Community Psychology, 19,* 443–451.

Dawes, R. M. (1994). *House of cards: Psychology and psychotherapy built on myth.* New York: Free Press.

DeFilippis, J. (2001). The myth of social capital in community development. *Housing Policy Debate, 12,* 781–806.

DeGrazia, S. (1962). *Of time, work and leisure.* New York: Twentieth Century Fund.

Des Jarlais, D. C., Friedman, S. R., & Casriel, C. (1990). Target groups for preventing AIDS among intravenous drug users: 2. The "hard" data studies. *Journal of Consulting and Clinical Psychology, 58,* 50–56.

De Tocqueville, A. ([1835] 1956). *Democracy in America.* New York: Mentor Books.

DeYoung, A. (1977). Classroom climate and class success: A case study at the university level. *Journal of Educational Research, 70,* 252–257.

Dickens, W. R., & Flynn, J. R. (2001). Heritability estimates versus large environmental effects: The IQ paradox resolved. *Psychological Review, 108,* 346–369.

Dincin, J., Wasmer, D., Witheridge, T. F., & Sobeck, L. (1993). Impact of assertive community treatment on the use of state hospital inpatient bed-days. *Hospital and Community Psychiatry, 44*(9), 833–838.

Doctor's Guide, 1997. Two-thirds of psychiatric hospitals transfer patients for economic reasons. http://www.palgroup.com/dg/4d30s.htm

Dohrenwend, B. P., & Dohrenwend, B. S. (1969). *Social status and psychological disorder.* New York: Wiley.

Dohrenwend, B., P., Levav, I., Shrout, P. E., Schwartz, S., Naveh, G., Link, B. G., et al. (1992). Socioeconomic status and psychiatric disorders: The causation-selection issue. *Science, 255,* 946–952.

Dohrenwend, B. S. (1978). Social stress and community psychology. *American Journal of Community Psychology, 6,* 1–14.

Dokecki, P. (1996). *The tragi-comic professional: Basic considerations for ethical reflective-generative practice.* Pittsburgh, PA: Duquesne University Press.

Dokecki, P. R., Newbrough, J. R. & O'Gorman, R. T. (2001). Toward a community-oriented action research framework for spirituality: Community psychological and theological perspectives. *Journal of Community Psychology, 29,* 497–518.

Dooley, D., Catalano, R., & Wilson, G. (1994). Depression and unemployment: Panel findings from the epidemiological catchment area study. *American Journal of Community Psychology, 22,* 745–765

Downs, M. W., & Fox, J. C. (1993). Social environments of adult homes. *Community Mental Health Journal, 29,* 15–23.

Dressler, W. W. (1991). *Stress and adaptation in the context of culture.* Albany, NY: State University of New York Press.

Drury, J. (2002). Protesting may be good for your health. http://www.reutershealth.com/archive/2002/12/23/eline/links/20021223elin022.

Duberman, M. (1993). *Stonewall.* New York: Dutton.

Du Bois, W. E. B. (1903). *The souls of black folk.* Chicago: McClung.

Dumas, L. J. (2002). Is development an effective way to fight terrorism? *Philosophy and Public Policy Quarterly, 22*(4), 7–12.

Dunn, B. (1993). Growing up with a psychotic mother: A retrospective study. *American Journal of Orthopsychiatry, 63,* 177–189.

Durlak, J. A. (1995). *School-based prevention programs for children and adolescents.* Newbury Park, CA: Sage.

Durlak, J. A., & Wells, A. M. (1998). Evaluation of indicated preventive intervention (secondary prevention) mental health programs for children and adolescents. *American Journal of Community Psychology, 26,* 775–802.

Dykens, E. M. (2000). Psychopathology in children with intellectual disability. *Journal of Child Psychology and Psychiatry and Allied Disciplines, 41*(4), 407–417.

Eckenrode, J. H., & Hamilton, S. (2000). One-to-one support interventions. In Cohen, Underwood, & Gottlieb (Eds.), *Social support measurement and intervention* (pp. 246–277). New York: Oxford University Press.

Edelstein, M. R. (1988). *Contaminated communities. The social and psychological impacts of residential toxic exposure.* Boulder, CO: Westview.

Edelstein, M. R. (2001). *Contaminated communities: Psychosocial impacts from the contamination of home and place* (2nd ed.). Boulder, CO: Westview Press.

Edwards, T. M. (2001). A twist on Jack and Jill: Blacks turn to an old social club for a new reason. *Time,* July 2, 2001, p. 53.

Egolf, B., Lasker, J., Wolf, S., & Potvin, L. (1992). The Roseto effect: A fifty-year comparison of mortality rates. *American Journal of Public Health, 82,* 1089–1092.

Ekstrand, M. L., & Coates, T. J. (1990). Maintenance of safer sexual behaviors and predictors of risky sex: The San Francisco Men's Health study. *American Journal of Public Health, 80,* 973–977.

Elias, M. J. (1997). Reinterpreting dissemination of prevention programs as widespread implementation with effectiveness and fidelity. In R. P. Weisberg, T. P. Gullotta, R. L. Hampton, B. A. Ryan, & G. R. Adams (Eds.), *Establishing preventive services* (pp. 253–289). Thousand Oaks, CA: Sage.

Elias, M. J., Gara, M. A., Schuyler, T. F., et al. (1991). The promotion of social competence: Longitudinal study of a preventive school-based program. *American Journal of Orthopsychiatry, 61,* 409–417.

Elias, M. J., Gara, M., Ubriaco, M., Rothbaum, P. A., Clabby, J. F., & Schuyler, T. (1986). Impact of a preventive social problem solving intervention on children's coping with middle school stressors. *American Journal of Community Psychology, 14,* 259–275.

Elrod, L. D. (2001). Reforming the system to protect children in high conflict custody cases. *William Mitchell Law Review, 28,* 495–549.

Emery, R. E. (1982). Interparental conflict and the children of discord and divorce. *Psychological Bulletin, 92,* 310–330.

Emrick, C. D. (1987). Alcoholics Anonymous: Affiliation processes and effectiveness as treatment. *Alcoholism: Clinical and Experimental Research 11,* 416–442.

Ennis, B. J., & Litwack, T. R. (1974). Psychiatry and the presumption of expertise: Flipping coins in the courtroom. *California Law Review, 62,* 693–752.

Erikson, E. H. (1950). *Childhood and society.* New York: Norton.

Evans, G. W., & Cohen, S. (1987). Environmental stress. In D. Stokols & I. Altman (Eds.), *Handbook of environmental psychology: Volume 2* (pp. 571–610). New York: Wiley.

Evans, S., & Bess, K. (2003). Preliminary content analyses: Youth and neighborhood service organizations. Presented in symposium on learning communities and learning organizations at the Biennial Conference of the Society for Community Research and Action, Las Vegas, New Mexico.

Fairweather, G. W. (1980). *The Fairweather Lodge: A twenty-five year retrospective.* Chicago: Aldine.

Fairweather, G. W., Sanders, D. H., Maynard, H., & Cressler, D. L. (1969). *Community life for the mentally ill.* Chicago: Aldine.

Fairweather, G. W., Sanders, D. H., & Tornatzky, L. G. (1974). *Creating change in mental health organizations.* New York: Pergamon.

Fairweather, G. W., & Tornatzky, L. G. (1977). *Experimental methods for social policy research.* New York: Pergamon Press.

Falk, I., & Kilpatrick, S. (2000). What is social capital? A study of interaction in a rural community. *Sociologia Ruralis, 40,* 87–110.

Farkas, M. D., & Anthony, W. A. (1989). *Psychiatric rehabilitation programs: Putting theory into practice.* Baltimore: Johns Hopkins University Press.

Fawcett, S. B., Paine-Andrews, A. L., Francisco, V. T., Schultz, J. A., Richter, K. P., Lewis, R. K., Williams, E. L., Harris, K. J., Berkley, J. Y., Fisher, J. L., & Lopez, C. M. (1995). Using empowerment theory in collaborative partnerships for community health and development. *American Journal of Community Psychology 23*, 677–697.

Felner, R. D., & Adan, A. M. (1988). The School Transitional Environment Project: An ecological intervention and evaluation (pp. 111–122). In R. H. Price, E. L. Cowen, R. P. Lorion, & J. Ramos-McKay. *14 ounces of prevention: A casebook for practitioners.* Washington, DC: American Psychological Association.

Felner, R. D., Favazza, A., Shim, M., Brand, S., Gu, K., & Noonan, N. (2001). Whole school improvement and restructuring as prevention and promotion: Lessons from STEP and the Project on High Performance Learning Communities. *Journal of School Psychology, 39*(2), 177–202.

Felner, R. D., Ginter, M., & Primavera, J. (1982). Primary prevention during school transitions: Social support and environmental structure. *American Journal of Community Psychology, 10*, 277–290.

FEMA (2002, February 4). *Federal/state disaster assistance tops $1 billion.* Press release.

Fields, J., & Casper, L. M. (2001). America's families and living arrangements. Current population reports. Washington, DC: U.S. Census Bureau. (P20-537).

Finch, J. F., Okun, M. A., Barrera, M. Jr., Zautra, A. I., & Reich, J. W. (1989). Positive and negative social ties among older adults: Measurement models and the prediction of psychological distress and well-being. *American Journal of Community Psychology, 17*, 585–605.

Finkel, N. J., & Jacobsen, C. A. (1977). Significant life experiences in an adult sample. *American Journal of Community Psychology, 5*, 165–177.

Finkelhor, D. (1990). Early and long-term effects of child sexual abuse: An update. *Professional Psychology: Research and Practice, 21*(5), 325–330.

Finkelhor, D., & Dziuba-Leatherman, J. (1994). Victimization of children. *American Psychologist, 49*, 173–183.

Finkelhor, D., & Hashima, P. Y. (2001). The victimization of children and youth. A comprehensive overview. In S. White (Ed.), *Handbook of youth and justice* (Chapter 4, pp. 49–78). NY: Kluwer Academic/Plenum.

Fisher, A. T., & Sonn, C. C. (2002). Psychological sense of community in Australia and the challenges of change. *Journal of Community Psychology 30*, 597–610.

Fisher, G. M. (1992). *Social Security Bulletin, 55*(4), 43–46.

Fisher, J. D., & Fisher, W. A. (1992). Changing AIDS-risk behavior. *Psychological Bulletin, 111*, 455–474.

Fleishman, J. A., Sherbourne, C. D., Crystal, S., Collins, R. L., Marshall, G. N., Kelly, M., Bozzette, S. A., Shapiro, M. F., & Hayes, R. D. (2000). Coping, conflictual social interactions, social support, and mood among HIV-infected persons. *American Journal of Community Psychology, 28*, 421–453.

Flippen, C. A. (2001). Racial and ethnic inequality in homeownership and housing equity. *Sociological Quarterly, 42*(2), 121–149. URL: http://www.ucpress.edu/journals/tsq/

Flora, J. L., Sharp, J., Flora, C., & Newlon, B. (1997). Entrepreneurial social infrastructure and locally initiated economic development in the non-metropolitan United States. *Sociological Quarterly 38*, 623–645.

Folkman, S. (1984). Personal control and stress and coping processes: A theoretical analysis. *Journal of Personality and Social Psychology, 46*, 839–852.

Folkman, S. (2001). Revised coping theory and the process of bereavement. In M. S. Stroebe & R. O. Hansson (Eds.), *Handbook of bereavement research: Consequences, coping, and care* (pp. 563–584). Washington, DC: American Psychological Association.

Folkman, S., & Lazarus, R. S. (1980). An analysis of coping in a middle aged sample. *Journal of Health and Social Behavior, 21*, 219–239.

Folkman, S., & Lazarus, R. S. (1988). Coping as a mediator of emotion. *Journal of Personality and Social Psychology, 54*, 466–475.

Francescato, D., & Tomai, M. (2001). Community psychology: should there be a European perspective? *Journal of Community and Applied Social Psychology, 11*(5), 371–380.

Frankl, V. E. (1992). *Man's search for meaning: An introduction to logotherapy* (4th ed.). Boston: Beacon Press.

Freeman v. Pitts 503 U.S. 467 (1992).

French, S. L., Knox, V. J., & Gekoski, W. L. (1992). Confounding as a problem in relating life events to health status in elderly individuals. *American Journal of Community Psychology, 20,* 243–252.

Friedman, R. M., & Duchnowski, A. J. (1990). Service trends in the children's mental health system: Implications for the training of psychologists. In R. R. Magrab and P. Wohlford (Eds.), *Improving psychological services for children and adolescents with severe mental disorders: Clinical training in psychology.* Washington, DC: American Psychological Association.

Friedmann, J. (1992). *Empowerment: The politics of alternative development.* Cambridge, MA: Blackwell.

Fuchs, V. R. (1968). *The service economy.* New York: National Bureau of Economic Research.

Furlong, M., Morrison, G. M., Austin, G., Huh-Kim, J., & Skager, R. (2001). Using student risk factors in school violence surveillance reports: Illustrative examples for enhanced policy formation, implementation and evaluation. *Law & Policy, 23*(3), 271–295).

Furstenberg, F. F., Jr., Moore, K. A. & Peterson, J. L. (1985). Sex education and sexual experience among adolescents. *American Journal of Public Health, 75,* 1331–1332.

Gabriel, T. (1995). Some on-line discoveries give gay youth a path to themselves. *New York Times,* July 2, 1995, A-1, 16.

Galanter, M. (1988). Zealous self-help groups as adjuncts to psychiatric treatment: A study of Recovery, Inc. *American Journal of Psychiatry, 145,* 1248–1253.

Galanter, M. (1990). Cults and zealous self-help movements: A psychiatric perspective. *American Journal of Psychiatry, 147,* 543–551.

Galanter, M. (1999). *Cults: Faith, healing, and coercion* (2nd ed.). New York: Oxford University Press.

Galbraith, J. K. (1998). *The affluent society* (40th anniversary ed.). Boston: Houghton Mifflin.

Garbarino, J., Kostelny, K., & Dubrow, N. (1991). *No place to be a child: Growing up in a war zone.* Lexington, MA: Lexington Books.

Garbarino, J. (1995). *Raising children in a socially toxic environment.* San Francisco: Jossey-Bass.

Garcia, I., Giuliani, F., & Wiesenfeld, E. (1999). Community and sense of community: The case of an urban barrio in Caracas. *Journal of Community Psychology, 27,* 727–740.

Gardner, W., & Wilcox, B. L. (1993). Political intervention in scientific peer review: Research on adolescent sexual behavior. *American Psychologist, 48,* 972–983.

Garfinkel, I., McLanahan, S. S., Meyer, D. R., & Seltzer, J. A. (Eds.). (1998). *Fathers under fire: The revolution in child support enforcement.* New York: Russell Sage.

Garland, A. F., & Zigler, E. (1993). Adolescent suicide prevention: Current research and social policy implications. *American Psychologist, 48,* 169–182.

Gartner, A., & Reissman, F. (1977). Self-help in the human services. San Francisco: Jossey-Bass.

Gebhard, C., & Levine, M. (1985). Does membership in Alcoholics Anonymous reduce the stigma of alcoholism? Paper presented at the annual meeting of the Eastern Psychological Association, Boston, MA, March 22, 1985.

Geller, E. S. (2002). The challenge of increasing proenvironmental behavior. In R. B. Bechtel & A. Churchman (Eds.), *Handbook of environmental psychology* (pp. 525–540). New York: John Wiley & Sons.

Geller, J. L., & Fisher, W. H. (1993). The linear continuum of transitional residences: Debunking the myth. *American Journal of Psychiatry, 150,* 1070–1076.

Gerard, H. B. (1983). School desegregaton: The social science role. *American Psychologist, 38,* 869–877.

Gergen, K. J. (1973). Social psychology as history. *Journal of personality and social psychology, 26,* 309–320.

Gesten, E. L., Rains, M. H., Rapkin, B. D., Weissberg, R. P., de Apocada, R. F., Cowen, E. L., & Bowen, R. (1982). Training children in social problem-solving competencies: A first and second look. *American Journal of Community Psychology, 10,* 95–115.

Giannarelli, L., & Barsimantov, J. (2000). *Child care expenses of America's families.* Washington, DC: The Urban Institute.

Gibbs, L. (1994). Risk assessments from a community perspective. *Environmental Impact Assessment Review, 14*, 327–335.

Gibbs, L., & Citizens Clearinghouse for Hazardous Waste (now the Center for Health, Environment and Justice). (1995). *Dying from dioxin. A citizen's guide to reclaiming our health and rebuilding democracy.* Boston, MA: South End Press.

Gibbs, L. M. (1998). *Love Canal: The story continues.* Gabriola Island, B.C.: Stony Creek, CT.

Gibbs, L. M. (1983). Community response to an emergency situation: Psychological destruction and the Love Canal. *American Journal of Community Psychology, 11*, 116–125.

Gifford, R. (2002). Making a difference: Some ways environmental psychology has improved the world. In R. B. Bechtel & A. Churchman (Eds.), *Handbook of environmental psychology* (pp. 323–334). New York: John Wiley & Sons.

Gillick, J. (1977). Al-Anon: A self-help group for co-alcoholics. Unpublished doctoral dissertation, Department of Psychology, State University of New York at Buffalo.

Giordano, J., & Giordano, G. P. (1976). Ethnicity and community mental health. *Community Mental Health Review, 1*, No. 3.

Gist, R., & Stolz, S. (1982). Mental health promotion and the media: Community response to the Kansas City hotel disaster. *American Psychologist, 37*, 1136–1139.

Glazer, N. (1975). *Affirmative discrimination: Ethnic inequality and public policy.* New York: Basic Books.

Godemont, M. (1992). 600 years of family care in Geel, Belgium: 600 years of familiarity with madness in town life. *Community Alternatives: International Journal of Family Care, 4*(2), 155–168.

Goffman, E. (1961). *Asylums.* New York: Doubleday.

Goffman, E. (1963). *Stigma.* Englewood Cliffs, NJ: Prentice-Hall.

Goffman, E. (1990). *Asylums: Essays on the social situation of mental patients and other inmates.* New York: Doubleday.

Goldberg, L. R. (1993). The structure of phenotypic personality traits. *American Psychologist, 48*, 26–34.

Goldenberg, I. I. (1971). *Build me a mountain. Youth, poverty and the creation of new settings.* Cambridge, MA: MIT Press.

Goldenberg, I. I. (1978). *Oppression and social intervention.* Chicago: Nelson-Hall.

Gong Lum v. Rice 275 U. S. 78 (1927).

Gordon, J. S., & Curtin, S. (2000). *Comprehensive cancer care: Integrating alternative, complementary, and conventional therapies.* Cambridge, MA: Perseus.

Gordon, M. (1982). Attitudes toward mental illness held by two disadvantaged inner city ethnic groups. Unpublished doctoral dissertation, Department of Psychology, SUNY at Buffalo.

Gorman, D. M. (1998). The irrelevance of evidence in the development of school-based drug prevention policy, 1986–1996. *Evaluation Review, 22*, 118–146.

Gottesman, I. I. (1991). *Schizophrenia genesis.* New York: Freeman.

Gottlieb, B. H. (2000). Selecting and planning interventions. In Cohen, Underwood, & Gottlieb (Eds.), *Social support measurement and intervention* (pp. 195–220). New York: Oxford University Press.

Gove, W. R. (Ed.). (1980). *The labelling of deviance* (2nd ed.). Beverly Hills, CA: Sage.

Gove, W. R. (Ed.). (1982). *Deviance and mental illness.* Beverly Hills, CA: Sage.

Gratz v. Bollinger 539 U. S. 244 (2003).

Graziano, A. M. (1969). Clinical innovation and the mental health power structure: A social case history. *American Psychologist, 24*, 10–18.

Graziano, A. M. (1974). *Child without tomorrow.* New York: Pergamon Press.

Graziano, A. M. (1977). Parents as behavior therapists. *Progress in Behavior Modification, 4*, 251–298.

Green v. County School Board, 391, U. S. 430 (1968).

Green, J., & Kocsis A. (1997). Psychological factors in recurrent genital herpes. *Genitourinary medicine, 73*(4), 253–258.

Greene, J. M., Ennett, S. T., & Ringwalt, C. L. (1999). Prevalence and correlates of survival sex among runaway and homeless youth. *American Journal of Public Health, 89*, 1406–1409.

Grob, G. N. (1994). *The mad among us: A history of the care of America's mentally ill.* New York: The Free Press.

Grosser, R. C. , & Vine, P. (1991). Families as advocates for the mentally ill: A survey of characteristics and service needs. *American Journal of Orthopsychiatry, 61,* 282–290.

Grunebaum, L., & Gammeltoft, M. (1993). Young children of schizophrenic mothers: Difficulties of intervention. *American Journal of Orthopsychiatry, 63,* 16–27.

Grunwald, M. (2001). Monsanto hid decades of pollution. *Washington Post,* Dec. 31, 2001. http://www.washingtonpost.com/wp-dyn/articles/A46648-2001Dec31.html

Grutter v. Bollinger 124 S. Ct. 35 (2003).

Gutierrez, G. S. (2001). Taking account of another race: Reframing Asian-American challenges to race-conscious admissions in public schools. *Cornell Law Review, 86,* 1283–1333.

Hacker, A. (2000). The case against kids. *New York Review of Books, 47*(19) Nov. 30, 2000, 12–16.

Hacsi, T. A. (2002). *Children as pawns: The politics of educational reform.* Cambridge, MA: Harvard University Press.

Hammen, C. (1992). Life events and depression: The plot thickens. *American Journal of Community Psychology, 20,* 179–193.

Hammond, W. R. & Yung, B. (1993). Psychology's role in the public health response to assaultive violence among young African-American men. *American Psychologist, 48,* 142–154.

Handler, J. F., & Satz, J. (Eds.). (1982). *Neither angels nor thieves: Studies in deinstitutionalization of status offenders.* Washington, DC: National Academy Press.

Haney, W. The myth of the Texas miracle in education. *Education Policy Analysis Archives, 8*(41). http://olam.ed.asu.edu/epaa/v8n41.

Hargrove, E. C., & Glidewell, J. C. (1990). *Impossible jobs in public management.* Lawrence, KS: University Press of Kansas.

Harrell, S. P. (2000). A multi-dimensional conceptualization of racism-related stress: Implications for the well-being of people of color. *American Journal of Orthopsychiatry, 70*(1), 42–57.

Harrington, M. (1962). *The other America: Poverty in the United States.* New York: Macmillan.

Harrison, P. M., & Karberg, J. C. (2003). Prison and jail inmates at midyear 2002. *Bureau of Justice Statistics Bulletin.* NCJ 198877.

Harwood, H., Fountain, D., & Livermore, G. (1998). The economic costs of alcohol and drug abuse in the United States, 1992. Washington, DC: National Institute on Drug Abuse (NIH Publication Number 98-4327). http://www.nida.nih.gov/Economic-Costs/Intro.html

Haskins, R., Sawhill, I., & Weaver, K. (2001). *Welfare reform: An overview of effects to date.* Washington, DC: The Brookings Institute.

Hatfield, A. (1993). Involuntary commitment: A consumer perspective. *Innovations & Research, 2,* 43–46.

Hayes, L. M. (1983). And darkness closes in . . . A national study of jail suicides. *Criminal Justice and Behavior, 10,* 461–484.

Healthy People 2010: http://www.health.gov/healthypeople/Document/pdf/Volume2/15Injury.pdf

Heaney, J. (1998). Life after quotas. *Buffalo News,* August 31, A-1,4.

Hecker, D. E. (2001). Occupational employment projections to 2010. *Monthly Labor Review,* November 2001.

Heflinger, C. A., & Northrup, D. (2000). What happens when capitated behavioral health comes to town? The transition from Fort Bragg Demonstration to a capitated managed behavioral health contract. *Journal of Behavioral Health Services and Research 27*(4), 390–405.

Heller, K. (1989). Ethical dilemmas in community intervention. *American Journal of Community Psychology, 17,* 367–378.

Heller, K. (1996). Coming of age of prevention science: Comments on the 1994 National Institute of Mental Health–Institute of Medicine prevention reports. *American Psychologist, 51,* 1123–1127.

Heller, K., Jenkins, R. A., Steffen, A. M., & Swindle, R. W., Jr. (2000). Prospects for a viable community mental health system: Reconciling ideology, professional traditions, and political reality. In J. Rappaport & E. Seidman (Eds.), *Handbook of community psychology* (pp. 445–470). New York: Kluwer Academic/Plenum.

Heller, K., & Monahan, J. (1977). *Psychology and community change.* Homewood, IL: Dorsey Press.

Heller, K., Thompson, M. G., Trueba, P. E., Hogg, J. R., & Vlachos-Weber, I. (1991). Peer support dyads for elderly women: Was this the wrong intervention? *American Journal of Community Psychology, 19,* 53–74.

Henggeler, S. W., Schoenwald, S. K., Borduin, C. M., Rowland, M. D., & Cunningham, P. B. (1998). *Multisystemic treatment of antisocial behavior in children and adolescents.* New York: Guilford.

Henwood, D. (1995). Race and money. http://www.panix.com/-dhenwood /Race-and-money.html

Herrenkohl, E. C., Herrenkohl, R. C., & Egolf, B. (1994). Resilient early school-age children from maltreating homes: Outcomes in late adolescence. *American Journal of Orthopsychiatry, 64,* 301–309.

Hildingh, C., Fridlund, B., & Segesten, K. (1995). Social support in self-help groups, as experienced by persons having coronary heart disease and their next of kin. *International Journal of Nursing Studies, 32*(3), 224–232. http://www.elsevier.com/inca/publications/store/2/6/6/

Hill, D. D. (1993). Afrocentric movements in education: examining equity, culture, and power relations in the public schools. *Hastings Constitutional Law Quarterly, 20,* 681–724.

Hilts, P. J. (1992). Mentally ill jailed on no charges, survey says. *New York Times,* Thursday, September 10, 1992, A–18.

Hinrichsen, G. A., Revenson, T. A., & Shinn, M. (1985). Does self-help help? An empirical investigation of scoliosis peer support groups. *Journal of Social Issues, 41,* 65–87.

Hobbs, N. (1964). Mental health's third revolution. *American Journal of Orthopsychiatry, 34,* 822–833.

Hobfoll, S. E., Jackson, A. P., Lavin, J., Johnson, R. J., & Schroder, K. E. E. (2002). Effects and generalizability of communally oriented HIV-AIDS prevention versus general health promotion groups for single, inner-city women in urban clinics. *Journal of Consulting and Clinical Psychology, 70*(4), 950–960.

Hobson, C. J., Kamen, J., Szostek, J., Nethercut, C. M., Tiedmann, J. W., & Wojnarowicz, S. (1998). Stressful life events: A revision and update of the Social Readjustment Rating Scale. *International Journal of Stress Management, 5*(1), 1–23.

Hoge, S. K., Lidz, C., Mulvey, E., Roth, L., Bennett, N., Siminoff, L., Arnold, R., & Monahan, J. (1993). Patient, family, and staff perceptions of coercion in mental hospital admission: An exploratory study. *Behavioral Sciences and the Law, 11,* 281–293.

Holahan, C. J., & Wandersman, A. (1987). The community psychology perspective in environmental psychology. In D. Stokols & I. Altman (Eds.), *Handbook of Environmental psychology: Vol. 1* (pp. 827–861). New York: Wiley.

Hollingshead, A. B., & Redlich, F. C. (1958). *Social class and mental illness.* New York: Wiley.

Holmes, T. H., & Rahe, R. H. (1967). The Social Readjustment Rating Scale. *Journal of Psychosomatic Research, 11,* 213–218.

Holmes-Eber, P., & Riger, S. (1990). Hospitalization and the composition of mental patients' social networks. *Schizophrenia Bulletin, 16,* 157–164.

Holtzworth-Munroe, A., Markman, H., O'Leary, K. D., Neidig, P., Leber, D., Heyman, R. D., Hulbert, D., & Smutzler, N. (1995). The need for marital violence prevention efforts: A behavioral-cognitive secondary prevention program for engaged and newly married couples. *Applied & Preventive Psychology, 4,* 77–88.

Horan, S., Kang, G., Levine, M., Duax, C., Luntz, B., & Tasca, C. (1993). Empirical studies on foster care: Review and assessment. *Journal of Sociology and Social Welfare, 20,* 131–154.

Hotaling, G. T., & Sugarman, D. B. (1986). An analysis of risk markers in husband to wife violence: The current state of knowledge. *Violence and Victims, 1,* 101–124.

House, J. S., Landis, K. R., & Umberson, D. (1988). Social relationships and health. *Science, 241,* 540–545.

Howe, I., & Libo, K. (2000). *World of our fathers: The journey of the East European Jews to America and the life they found and made there.* London: Phoenix.

Howell, J. C. (1996). Juvenile transfers to the criminal justice system: State of the art. *Law & Policy, 18,* 17–60.

Huaco, G. (1965). *The sociology of film art.* New York: Basic Books.

Hudnall, C. E. (2001). "Grand" parents to get help. *AARP,* November 2001, 9–13.

Hughes, L. (1962). *Fight for freedom: The story of the NAACP.* New York: W. W. Norton.

Hughey, J., & Speer, P. W. (2002). Community, sense of community, and networks. In A. T. Fisher, C. C. Sonn, & B. J. Bishop (Eds.), *Psychological sense of community: Research, applications, and implications* (pp. 69–84). New York: KluwerAcademic/Plenum.

Hughey, J., Speer, P. W., & Peterson, N. A. (1999). Sense of community in community organizations: Structure and evidence of validity. *Journal of Community Psychology, 27,* 97–113.

Hughey, J. B., & Bardo, J. W. (1987). Social psychology dimensions of community satisfaction and quality of life: Some obtained relations. *Psychological Reports, 61,* 239–246.

Humphreys, K., & Noke, J. M. (1997). The influence of posttreatment mutual help group participation on the friendship networks of substance abuse patients. *American Journal of Community Psychology, 25*(1), 1–16.

Humphreys, K., & Rappaport, J. (1993). From the community mental health movement to the war on drugs: A study in the definition of social problems. *American Psychologist, 48,* 892–901.

Hunt, J. McV. (1968). Toward the prevention of incompetence. In J. Carter (Ed.), *Research contributions from psychology to community mental health.* New York: Behavioral Publications.

Hurvitz, N. (1976). The origins of the peer self-help psychotherapy group movement. *Journal of Applied Behavioral Science, 12,* 283–294.

Hyman, I. A. (1995). Corporal punishment, psychological mlatreatment, violence, and punitiveness in America: Research advocacy, and public policy. *Applied & Preventive Psychology, 4,* 113–140.

Innovations & Research. (1993). Special section: Mental illness and the law. *Innovations & Research, 2,* 3–54.

Institute of Medicine. (1989). *Research on children & adolescents with mental, behavioral & developmental disorders.* Washington, DC: National Academy Press.

Irvine, M. (2002). Abusing trust, parents dip into children's credit. *Buffalo News,* November 26, p.A4.

Iscoe, I. (1974). Community psychology and the competent community. *American Psychologist, 29,* 607–613.

Iscoe, I., Bloom, B. L., & Spielberger, C. D. (1977). *Community psychology in transition.* New York: Halsted Press.

Iscoe, I., & Harris, L. C. (1984). Social and community interventions. *Annual Review of Psychology, 35,* 333–360.

Itzhaky, H., & York, A. S. (2000). Sociopolitical control and empowerment: An extended replication. *Journal of Community Psychology, 28,* 407–415.

Jacob, H. (1989). Another look at no-fault divorce and the post-divorce finances of women. *Law & Society Review, 23,* 95–115.

Jacobs, J. B. (1980). The prisoners' rights movement and its impacts, 1960–1980. In N. Morris & M. Tonry. (Eds.), *Crime, and justice: An annual review of research.* Chicago: University of Chicago Press.

Jacobs, M. K., & Goodman, G. (1989). Psychology and self-help groups: Predictions on a partnership. *American Psychologist, 44,* 536–545.

Jacobs, S. J., Evans, G. W., Catalano, R., & Dooley, D. (1984). Air pollution and depressive symptomatology: Exploratory analyses of intervening psychological factors. *Population and Environment, 7*(4), 260–272.

Jacobson, N. S., & Addis, M. E. (1993). Research on couples and couple therapy: What do we know? Where are we going? *Journal of Consulting and Clinical Psychology, 61,* 85–93.

Janis, I. L. (1983). The role of social support in adherence to stressful life decisions. *American Psychologist, 38,* 143–160.

Jensen, A. R. (1969). How much can we boost I. Q. And scholastic achievement? *Harvard Educational Review, 39,* 1–123.

Johnson, E. (2000). Differences among families coping with serious mental illness: A qualitative analysis. *American Journal of Orthopsychiatry, 70*(1), 126–134.

Johnson, J. (1996). Addiction and recovery for individuals and society. In J. Chesworth (Ed.), *The ecology of health: Identifying issues and alternatives* (pp. 234–246). Thousand Oaks, CA: Sage.

Johnson, S. D., Stiffman, A., Hadley Ives, E., & Elze, D. (2001). An analysis of stressors and co-morbid mental health problems that contribute to youths' paths to substance-specific services. *Journal of Behavioral Health Services and Research, 28*(4), 412–426.

Joint Commission on Mental Illness and Health. (1961). *Action for mental health.* New York: Basic Books.

Joint Commission on the Mental Health of Children. (1969). *Crisis in child mental health: Challenge for the 1970's.* New York: Harper & Row.

Jones, R. K., Darrach, J. E., & Henshaw, S. K. (2002). Contraceptive use among U.S. women having abortions in 2000–2001. *Perspectives on Sexual and Reproductive Health, 34,* 294–303.

Julnes, G., & Foster, E. F. (2001). Outcomes of Welfare reform for families who leave TANF. *New Directions for Evaluation, 91(Fall)* (Whole issue).

Kadushin, A. (1980). *Child welfare services* (3rd ed.). New York: Macmillan.

Kagan, D. M. (1990). How schools alienate students at risk: A model for examining proximal classroom variables. *Educational Psychologist, 25,* 105–125.

Kahn, E. B., Ramsey, L. T., Brownson, R. C., Heath, G. W., Howze, E. H., Powell, K. E., Stone, E. J., Rajab, M. W., & Corso, P. (2002). The effectiveness of interventions to increase physical activity: A systematic review. *American Journal of Preventive Medicine,* 22(Suppl. 4), 73–106.

Kaniasty, K., Norris, F. H., & Murrell, S. A. (1990). Received and perceived social support following natural disaster. *Journal of Applied Social Psychology, 20,* 85–114.

Kantaras v. Kantaras (2003). Case No: 98-5375CA. Circuit Court of the Sixth Judicial Circuit, Pasco County, Florida.

Kanter, R. M. (1993). *Men and women of the corporation* (2nd ed.). New York: Basic Books.

Katz, A. H. (1993). *Self-help in America: A social movement perspective.* New York: Maxwell Macmillan International.

Katz, D., & Kahn, R. L. (1978). *The social psychology of organizations* (2d ed.). New York: Wiley.

Katz, S. (1994). Twenty years later: A follow-up study of graduates of two sheltered workshop programmes in Israel. *British Journal of Developmental Disabilities, 40*(78, Pt 1), 4–14.

Kazdin, A. E. (1993). Adolescent mental health: Prevention and treatment programs. *American Psychologist, 48,* 127–141.

Keefe, F. J., Lefebvre, J. C., Egert, J. R., Affleck, G., Sullivan, M. J., & Caldwell, D. S. (2000). The relationship of gender to pain, pain behavior and disability in osteoarthritis patients: The role of catastrophizing. *Pain, 87*(3), 325–334.

Keil, T. J., Usui, W. M., & Busch, J. A. (1983). Repeat admissions for perceived problem drinking: A social resources perpsective. *Journal of Studies on Alcohol, 44,* 95–108.

Kelly, J. A., & Kalichman, S. C. (2002). Behavioral research in HIV/AIDS primary and secondary prevention: Recent advances and future directions. *Journal of Consulting and Clinical Psychology, 70,* 626–639.

Kelly, J. A., Kalichman, S. C., Kauth, M. R., Kilgore, H. G., Hood, H. V., Campos, P. E., Rao, S. M., Brasfield, T. L., St. Lawrence, J. S. (1991). Situational factors associated with AIDS risk behavior lapses and coping strategies used by gay men who successfully avoid lapses. *American Journal of Public Health, 81*(10), 1335–1338.

Kelly, J. A., Murphy, D. A., Sikkema, K. J., & Kalichman, S. C. (1993). Psychological interventions to prevent HIV infection are urgently needed. *American Psychologist, 48,* 1023–1034.

Kelly, J. G. (1966). Ecological constraints on mental health services. *American Psychologist, 21,* 535–539.

Kelly, J. G. (1979). *Adolescent boys in high school: A psychological study of coping and adaptation.* Hillsdale, NJ: Erlbaum.

Kelly, J. G., Ryan, A. M., Altman, B. E., & Stelzner, S. P. (2000). Understanding and changing social systems: An ecological view. In J. Rappaport & E. Seidman (Eds.), *Handbook of community psychology* (pp. 133–159). New York: Kluwer Academic/Plenum.

Kennedy, J. F. (1963). Mental illness and mental retardation. Message from the President of the United States relative to mental illness and mental retardation. House of Representatives, 88th Congress, 1st Session, Document No. 58, February 5, 1963.

Kessler, R., Price, R. H., & Wortman, C. (1985). Social factors in psychopathology: Stress, social support, and coping processes. *Annual Review of Psychology, 36,* 531–572.

Keyes v. Denver School District, No. 1, 413 U. S. 189 (1973).

Kiernan, M., Toro, P. A., Rappaport, J., & Seidman, E. (1989). Economic predictors of mental health service utilization: A time series analysis. *American Journal of Community Psychology, 17,* 801–820.

Kiesler, C. A. (2000). National mental health issues. In C. R. Snyder & R. E. Ingram (Eds.), *Handbook of psychological change: Psychotherapy processes & practices for the 21st century* (pp. 681–688). New York: Wiley.

Killian, T. M., & Killian, L. T. (1990). Sociological investigations of mental illness: A review. *Hospital and Community Psychiatry, 41,* 902–911.

Kilpatrick, D. G., Veronen, J. J., & Resick, P. A. (1979). The aftermath of rape: Recent empirical findings. *American Journal of Orthopsychiatry, 49,* 658–669.

King, J. E. (1998). Student borrowing: Is there a crisis? In *Student Loan Debt Problems and Prospects* (pp. 1–14). Proceedings from a National Symposium sponsored by Sally Mae Education Institute, Reston, VA.; Institute for Higher Education Policy, Washington, DC; Education Resources Institute, Boston, MA.

Kinney, J., Haapala, D., & Booth, C. (1991). *Keeping families together: The Homebuilders Model.* Hawthorne, NY: Aldine de Gruyter.

Kirk, M. O. (1995). When surviving just isn't enough when seeking reemployment. *New York Times,* Sunday, June 25, 1995, Sec. 3, p. 11.

Kirk, S. A., & Kutchins, H. (1992). *The selling of DSM: The rhetoric of science in psychiatry.* Hawthorne, NY: Aldine de Gruyter.

Kirkby, R. J. (1994). Changes in premenstrual symptoms and irrational thinking following cognitive-behavioral coping skills training. *Journal of Consulting and Clinical Psychology, 62,* 1026–1032.

Kirp, D. L., & Babcock, G. (1981). Judge and company: Court-appointed masters, school desegregation, and insitutional reform. *Alabama Law Review, 32,* 313–397.

Klaus, P. A. (1994). The costs of crime to victims. Crime Data Brief. Washington, DC: Department of Justice.

Klein, S. P., Hamilton, L. S., McCaffrey, D. F., & Stecher, B. M. (2000). What do test scores in Texas tell us? Rand Corporation Issue Paper. http://www.rand.org/publications/IP/IP202

Kleist, D. M. (1996). *Counselor educators' explanations for a disparity between a philosophy of prevention in mental health and prevention training and practice in counselor education.* Southern Illinois University, Carbondale, IL.

Kluger, R. (1976). *Simple justice.* New York: Knopf.

Knight, B., Wollert, R. W., Levy, L. H., Frame, C. L., & Padgett, V. P. (1980). Self-help groups: The members' perspectives. *American Journal of Community Psychology, 8,* 53–65.

Knitzer, J. (1984). Mental health services to children and adolescents: A national view of public policies. *American Psychologist, 39,* 905–911.

Knobloch, H., & Pasamanick, B. (1961). Some thoughts on the inheritance of intelligence. *American Journal of Orthopsychiatry, 31,* 454–73.

Kobasa, S. C. (1979). Stressful life events, personality, and health: An inquiry into hardiness. *Journal of Personality and Social Psychology, 37,* 1–11.

Koo, H. P., Dunteman, G. H., George, C., Green, Y., & Vincent, M. (1994). Reducing adolescent pregnancy through a school- and community-based intervention: Denmark, SC revisited. *Family Planning Perspectives, 26,* 206–211, 217.

Koss, M. P., Goodman, L. A., Browne, A., Fitzgerald, L. F., Keita, G. P., & Russo, N. F. (1994). *No safe haven: Male violence against women at home, at work, and in the community.* Washington, DC: American Psychological Association.

Kozol, J. (1985). *Death at an early age: The destruction of the hearts and minds of Negro children in the Boston public schools.* New York: New American Library.

Kretzmann, J. P., & McKnight, J. L. (1993). *Building communities from the inside out: A path toward finding and mobilizing a community's assets.* Chicago: ACTA.

Krizan, L. (1982). A descriptive study of the Niagara Falls Christian Fellowship from a social intervention perspective. Unpublished manuscript, Department of Psychology, SUNY Buffalo, Buffalo, NY.

Kroeker, C. J. (1995). Individual, organizational, and societal empowerment: A study of the processes in a Nicaraguan agricultural cooperative. *American Journal of Community Psychology, 23,* 749–764.

Kropotkin, P. (1972). *Mutual aid. A factor of evolution.* New York: New York University Press (originally published 1902).

Kubler-Ross, E. (1969). *On death and dying.* New York: Macmillan.

Kuhn, T. S. (1996). *The structure of scientific revolutions* (3rd ed.). Chicago, IL: University of Chicago Press.

Kuo, F. E., Sullivan, W. C., Coley, R. L., & Brunson, L. (1998). Fertile ground for community: Inner-city neighborhood common spaces. *American Journal of Community Psychology, 26*(6), 823–851.

Kurtz, L. F. (1990). The self-help movement: Review of the past decade of research. *Social Work with Groups, 13,* 101–115.

Labrecque, M. S., Peak, T., & Toseland, R. W. (1992). Long-term effectiveness of a group program for caregivers of frail elderly veterans. *American Journal of Orthopsychiatry, 62,* 575–588.

Ladner, J. (2001). *The new urban leaders.* Washington, DC: Brookings Institution Press.

Lamb, H. R. (Ed.). (1984). *The homeless mentally ill.* Washington, DC: American Psychiatric Association.

Latkin, C., Mandell, W., Vlahov, D., Oziemkowska, M., Knowlton, A, & Celentano, D. (1994). My place, your place, and no place: Behavior settings as a risk factor for HIV-related injection practices of drug users in Baltimore, Maryland. *American Journal of Community Psychology, 22*(3), 415–430.

Lawless, R. A. (2001). The relationship between nonbusiness bankruptcy filings and various basic measures of consumer debt. Version 1.1. http://www.law.missouri.edu/lawless/bus_bkr/body_filings.htm

Lawlor, E. F. (1990). When a possible job becomes impossible: Politics, public health and the management of the AIDS epidemic. In E. C. Hargrove &J. C. Glidewell (Eds.), *Impossible jobs in public management.* Lawrence KS: University Press of Kansas.

Lazar, I., & Darlington, R. B. (1982). *Lasting effects of early education: A report from the Consortium for Longitudinal Studies.* Chicago: University of Chicago Press.

Lazarus, R. S. (1991). *Emotion and adaptation.* New York: Oxford University Press.

Leclerc, C., Lesage, A. D., Ricard, N., Lecombe, T. , & Cyr, M. (2000). Assessment of a new rehabilitative coping skills module for persons with schizophrenia. *American Journal of Orthopsychiatry, 70*(3), 380–388.

Lee, C. M., & Hunsley, J. (2001). Empirically informed consultation to parents concerning the effects of separation and divorce on their children. *Cognitive and Behavioral Practice, 8*(1), 85–96.

Lee, J. A. B., & Swenson, C. R. (1994). The concept of mutual aid. In A. Gitterman & L. Shulman (Eds.), *Mutual aid groups, vulnerable populations, and the life cycle* (2nd ed.; pp. 413–429). New York: Columbia University Press.

Lehmann, S. (1971). Community and psychology and community psychology. *American Psychologist, 26,* 554–560.

Leichter, H. M. (1991). *Free to be foolish: Politics and health promotion in the United States and Great Britain.* Princeton, NJ: Princeton University Press.

Leighton, D. C., Harding, J. S., Macklin, D. B., Macmillan, A. M., & Leighton, A. H. (1963). *The character of danger: Psychiatric symptoms in selected communities.* New York: Basic Books.

Lemann, N. (1991). *The promised land. The great black migration and how it changed America.* New York: Alfred A. Knopf.

Lemke, S., & Moos, R. H. (1987). Measuring the social climate of congregate residences for older people: Sheltered Care Environment Scale. *Psychology and Aging, 2,* 20–29.

Leventhal, G. S., Maton, K. I., & Madara, E. J. (1988). Systematic organizational support for self-help groups. *American Journal of Orthopsychiatry, 58,* 592–603.

Levine, A. (1982). *Love Canal: Science, politics and people.* Lexington, MA: Heath.

Levine, A., & Levine, M. (1977). The social context of evaluative research: A case study. *Evaluation Quarterly, 1,* 515–542.

Levine, A. G. (1977). Women at work in America: History, status and prospects. In H. Kaplan (Ed.), *American minorities and economic opportunity.* Itasca, IL: Peacock.

Levine, D. (2000). The Chinese American challenge to court-mandated quotas in San Francisco's public schools: Notes from a (partisan) participant-observer. *Harvard Black Letter Law Journal, 26,* 39–145.

Levine, D. I. (1984). The authority for the appointment of remedial special masters in federal institutional reform litigation: The history reconsidered. *U.C. Davis Law Review, 17,* 753–805.

Levine, D. I. (1993). The latter stages of enforcement of equitable decrees: The course of institutional reform cases after Dowell, Rufo and Freeman. *Hastings Constitutional Law Quarterly, 20,* 579–648.

Levine, M. (1969). Some postulates of community psychology practice. In F. Kaplan & S. B. Sarason (Eds.), *The Psycho-Educational Clinic papers and research studies.* Springfield, MA: Department of Mental Health.

Levine, M. (1973). Problems of entry in light of some postulates of practice in community psychology. In I. I. Goldenberg (Ed.), *Clinical psychologists in the world of work.* New York: Heath.

Levine, M. (1974). Scientific method and the adversary model: Some preliminary thoughts. *American Psychologist, 29,* 661–677.

Levine, M. (1980a). Investigative reporting as a research method. An analysis of Bernstein and Woodward's All the President's Men. *American Psychologist, 35,* 626–638.

Levine, M. (1980b). *From state hospital to psychiatric center: The implementation of planned organizational change.* Lexington, MA: Lexington Books.

Levine, M. (1981). *The history and politics of community mental health.* New York: Oxford University Press.

Levine, M. (1982). Method or madness: On the alienation of the professional. *Journal of Community Psychology, 10,* 3–14.

Levine, M. (1986). The role of special master in institutional reform litigation: A case study. *Law & Policy, 8,* 275–321.

Levine, M. (1989). Community psychology in Asia. *American Journal of Community Psychology, 17,* 67–71.

Levine, M. (1998). Prevention and community. *American Journal of Community Psychology, 26,* 189–206.

Levine, M. (2000). The family group conference in the New Zealand Children, Young Persons and Their Families Act (CYP&F) of 1989. *Behavioral Sciences & the Law, 18*(4), 517–556.

Levine, M. & Bunker, B. B. (Eds.). (1975). *Mutual criticism.* Syracuse, NY: Syracuse University Press.

Levine, M., Compaan, C., & Freeman, J. (1994). Maltreatment-related fatalities: Issues of policy and prevention. *Law & Policy, 16,* 449–471.

Levine, M., Doueck, H. J., Anderson, E. M., Chavez, F. T., Dietz, R. L., George, N. A., Sharma, A., Skinberg, K. L., & Wallach, L. (1995). *The impact of mandated reporting on the therapeutic process. Picking up the pieces.* Thousand Oaks, CA: Sage.

Levine, M., & Graziano, A. M. (1972). Intervention programs in elementary schools. In S. E. Golann & C. Eisdorfer (Eds.), *Handbook of community mental health* (pp. 541–573). New York: Appleton-Century-Crofts.

Levine, M., & Howe, B. (1985). The penetration of social science into legal culture. *Law & Policy, 7,* 173–198.

Levine, M., & Levine, A. (1992). *Helping children: A social history.* New York: Oxford University Press.

Levine, M., & Perkins, D. V. (1980a). Tailor-making a life events scale. In D. Perkins (Chair), New developments in research on life stress and social support. Symposium presented at the American Psychological Association Convention, Montreal.

Levine, M., & Perkins, D. V. (1980b). Social setting interventions and primary prevention: Comments on the Report of the Task Panel on Prevention to the President's Commission on Mental Health. *American Journal of Community Psychology, 8,* 147–158.

Levine, M., & Perkins, D. V. (1987). *Principles of community psychology.* New York: Oxford University Press.

Levine, M., Reppucci, N. D., & Weinstein, R. S. (1990). Learning from Seymour Sarason. *American Journal of Community Psychology, 18,* 343–351.

Levine, M., Toro, P. A., & Perkins, D. V. (1993). Social and community interventions. *Annual Review of Psychology, 44,* 525–588.

Levine, M., & Wallach, L. (2002). *Psychological problems, social issues and law.* Boston: Allyn and Bacon.

Levy, C. J. (2002). State to survey mentally ill in residences. *New York Times,* December 13, pp. B1, B6.

Levy, L. H. (1976). Self–help groups: Types and psychological processes. *Journal of Applied Behavioral Science, 12,* 310–322.

Levy, L. H. (2000). Self-help groups. In J. Rappaport & E. Seidman (Eds.), *Handbook of community psychology* (pp. 591–613). New York: Kluwer Academic/Plenum.

Levy, R. M., Rubenstein, L. S., Ennis, B. J., & Friedman, P. R. (1996). *The rights of people with mental disabilities: The authoritative ACLU guide to the rights of people with mental illness and mental retardation.* Carbondale: Southern Illinois University Press.

Lewin, K. (1935). *Principles of topological psychology.* New York: McGraw-Hill.

Lewin, K. (1946). Action research and minority problems. *Journal of Social Issues, 2,* 34–46.

Li, C. (1998). The contribution of common land to sense of community. In J. Sanford & B. R. Connell (eds.), *People, places and public policy* (pp. 57–70). Edmond, OK: Environmental Design Research Association.

Li, D. (1989). The effect of role change on intellectual ability and on the ability self-concept in Chinese children. *American Journal of Community Psychology, 17,* 73–81.

Lichtenstein, B. (1996). Needle exchange programs: New Zealand's experience. *American Journal of Public Health, 86,* 1319.

Lidz, C. W., Mulvey, E. P., Arnold, R. P., Bennett, N. S., & Kirsch, B. L. (1993). Coercive interactions in a psychiatric emergency room. *Behavioral Sciences & the Law, 11,* 269–280.

Lieberman, M. A. (1989). Group properties and outcomes: A study of group norms in self-help groups for widows and widowers. *International Journal of Group Psychotherapy, 39*(2), 191–208.

Light, D. W. (1982). Learning to label: The social construction of psychiatrists. In W.R. Gove (Ed.), *Deviance and mental illness.* Beverly Hills, CA: Sage.

Lindemann, E. (1944). Symptomatology and management of acute grief. *American Journal of Psychiatry, 101,* 141–148.

Lindsay, W. R. (1982). The effects of labelling: Blind and nonblind ratings of social skills on schizophrenic and nonschizophrenic control subjects. *American Journal of Psychiatry, 139,* 216–219.

Linehan, P. (2001). Guarding the dumping ground: Equal protection, Title VII, and Justifying the use of race in the hiring of special educators. *Brigham Young University Education and Law Journal, 2001,* 179–212.

Long, N.E. (1958). The local community as an ecology of games. *American Journal of Sociology, 64,* 251–261.

Lorion, R. P., & Ross, J. G. (Eds.). (1992). Programs for Change: Office of Substance Abuse Prevention demonstration models. *Journal of Community Psychology,* OSAP Special Issue.

Low, A. A. (1997). *Mental health through will-training: A system of self-help in psychotherapy as practiced by Recovery, Incorporated* (3rd ed.). Glencoe, IL: Willett.

Lubeck, S., DeVries, M., Nicholson, J., & Post, J. (1997). Head Start in transition. *Early Education and Development, 8*(3), 219–244.

Luce, A., Firth Cozens, J., Midgley, S., & Burges, C. (2002). After the Omagh bomb: Posttraumatic stress disorder in health service staff. *Journal of Traumatic Stress, 15*(1), 27–30. http://www.wkap.nl/journalhome.htm/0894-9867

Luepnitz, D. A. (1991). A comparison of maternal, paternal, and joint custody: Understanding the varieties of post-divorce family life. In J. Folberg (Ed.), *Joint custody and shared parenting* (2nd ed., pp. 105–113). New York: Guilford Press.

Luke, D. A., Rappaport, J., & Seidman, E. (1991). Setting phenotypes in a mutual help organization: Expanding behavior setting theory. *American Journal of Community Psychology, 19,* 147–167.

Luthar, S. S., & Zigler, E. (1991). Vulnerability and competence: A review of research on resilience in childhood. *American Journal of Orthopsychiatry, 61*, 6–22.

Lynn, L. E. Jr. (1990). Managing the social safety net: The job of social welfare executive. In E. C. Hargrove & J. C. Glidewell (Eds.), *Impossible jobs in public management*. Lawrence KS: University Press of Kansas.

MacLean, M. G., Embry, L. E., & Cauce, A. M. (1999). Homeless adolescents' paths to separation from family: Comparison of family characteristics, psychological adjustment, and victimization. *Journal of Community Psychology, 27*, 179–187.

Madara, E. J., & Meese, A. (1988). *The self-help sourcebook. Finding and forming mutual aid self-help groups*. Denville, NJ: St. Clares-Riverside Medical Center.

Malloy, M. (1995). *Mental illness and managed care: A primer for families and consumers*. Arlington, VA: National Alliance for the Mentally Ill.

Mann, P. A. (1978). *Community psychology: Concepts and applications*. New York: Free Press.

Manne, S., & Sandler, I. N. (1984). Coping and adjustment to genital herpes. *Journal of Behavioral Medicine, 7*, 391–410.

Manne, S., Sandler, I. N., & Zautra, A. (1986). Coping and adjustment to genital herpes: The effects of time and social support. *Journal of Behavioral Medicine, 9*, 163–177.

Marchetti, A. G. (1987). Wyatt v. Stickney: A consent decree. *Research in Developmental Disabilities, 8*(2), 249–259.

Markman, H. J., Renick, M. J., Floyd, F. J., Stanley, S. M., & Clements, M. (1993). Preventing marital distress through communication and conflict management training: A 4- and 5-year follow-up. *Journal of Consulting and Clinical Psychology, 61*, 70–77.

Marrow, A. J. (1969). *The practical theorist: The life and work of Kurt Lewin*. NY: Basic Books.

Marsick, V. J., Bitterman, J., & van der Veen, R. (2000). From the learning organization to learning communities toward a learning society. Ohio State U. Info. Series No. 382. ERIC. http://www.ericacve.org/mp_marsick_01.asp

Maslow, A. H. (1998). *Toward a psychology of being* (3rd ed.). New York: Wiley.

Masterpasqua, F. (1989). A competence paradigm for psychological practice. *American Psychologist, 44*, 1366–1371.

Maton, K. (Spring, 1999). SCRA moving onwards: Social policy, multidisciplinary linkages, diversity, and updates. *The Community Psychologist, 32*(2), 4–7.

Maton, K. I. (1988). Social support, organizational characteristics, psychological well-being, and group appraisal in three self-help groups. *American Journal of Community Psychology, 16*, 53–77.

Maton, K. I., & Salem, D. A. (1995). Organizational characteristics of empowering community settings: A multiple case study approach. *American Journal of Community Psychology, 23*, 631–656.

Maton, K. I, Schellenbach, C. J., Leadbeater, B. J., & Solarz A. L. (Eds.). (2004). *Investing in children, youth, families and communities: Strengths-based research and policy*. Washington, DC: American Psychological Association.

McAdams, D. R. (2000). *Fighting to save our urban schools . . . and winning! Lessons from Houston*. New York: Columbia University Press.

McCarroll, J. E., Ursano, R. J., Wright, K. M., & Fullerton, C. S. (1993). Handling bodies after violent death: Strategies for coping. *American Journal of Orthopsychiatry, 63*, 209–214.

McCord, J. (1978). A thirty-year follow-up of treatment effects. *American Psychologist, 33*, 284–289.

McCord, J. (1992). The Cambridge-Somerville Study: A pioneering longitudinal experimental study of delinquency prevention. In J. McCord & R. E. Tremblay (Eds.), *Preventing antisocial behavior: Interventions from birth through adolescence* (pp. 196–206). New York: Guilford Press.

McCurdy, K., & Daro, D. (1993). Current trends in child abuse reporting and fatalities: The results of the 1992 annual fifty state survey. Working Paper No. 808, National Committee for the Prevention of Child Abuse, Chicago, IL.

McGaughey, W. H., & Whalon, M. E. (1992). Managing insect resistance to Bacillus thuringiensis toxins. *Science, 258*, 1451–1455.

McIntosh, J. L. (1999). *1999 Official final statistics*. Washington, DC: American Association of Suicidology.

McLaurin v. Oklahoma State Regents for Higher Education 337 U. S. 637 (1950).

McMillan, B., Florin, P., Stevenson, J., Kerman, B., & Mitchell, R.E. (1995). Empowerment praxis in community coalitions. *American Journal of Community Psychology, 23,* 699–727.

McMillan, D. W., & Chavis, D. M. (1986). Sense of community: A definition and theory. *Journal of Community Psychology, 14,* 6–23.

McNeil, L. M., & Valenzuela, A. (2000). The harmful impact of the TAAS system of testing in Texas: Beneath the accountability rhetoric. The Civil Rights Project, Harvard University. http://www.law.harvard.edu./groups/civilrights/conferences/testing98/drafts/mcneil_valenzuela.html

McNeil, L. M. (2000). *Contradictions of school reform. Educational costs of standardized tests.* New York: Routledge.

Medvene, L. J., & Krauss, D. H. (1989). Causal attributions and parent-child relationships in a self-help group for families of the mentally ill. *Journal of Applied Social Psychology, 19,* 1413–1430.

Meehl, P. E. (1954). *Clinical versus statistical prediction.* Minneapolis: University of Minnesota Press.

Meissen, G. J., Gleason, D. F., & Embree, M. G. (1991). An assessment of the needs of mutual help groups. *American Journal of Community Psychology, 19,* 427–442.

Melvin, D., & Appleby, S. (1995). A sharing experience: Development of a group of families affected by HIV infection. *British Journal of Guidance and Counselling, 23*(1), 7–17.

Merry, S.E. (1987). Crowding, conflict, and neighborhood regulation. In I. Altman & A. Wandersman (Eds.), *Neighborhood and community environments.* New York: Plenum.

Mertig, A. G., Dunlap, R. E., & Morrison, D. E. (2001). In R. E. Dunlap and W. Michelson (Eds.), *Handbook of Environmental Sociology* (pp. 448–481). Westport, CT: Greenwood Press.

Metcalf, G. R. (1983). *From Little Rock to Boston. The history of school desegregation.* Westport, CT: Greenwood Press.

Mezey, S. G. (1998). Systemic reform litigation and child welfare policy: The case of Illinois. *Law & Policy, 20*(2), 203–231.

Milazzo-Sayre, L. J., Henderson, M .J., Manderscheid, R. W., Bokossa, M. C., Evans, C., & Male, A. A. (2001). Persons treated in specialty mental health care programs, United States, 1997. http://www.mentalhealth.org/publications/allpubs/SMA01-3537?chapter15.asp

Milburn, N., & D'Ercole, A. (1991). Homeless women: Moving toward a comprehensive model. *American Psychologist, 46,* 1161–1169.

Miller, G. E., & Iscoe, I. (1990). A state mental health commissioner and the politics of mental illness. In E. C. Hargrove & J. C. Glidewell (Eds.), *Impossible jobs in public management.* Lawrence, KS: University Press of Kansas.

Miller, H. L., Coombs, D. W., Leeper, J. D., & Barton, S. N. (1984). An analysis of the effects of suicide prevention facilities on suicide rates in the United States. *American Journal of Public Health, 74,* 340–343.

Miller, R. L., Klotz, D., Eckholdt, H. M. (1998). HIV prevention with male prostitutes and patrons of hustler bars: Replication of an HIV preventive intervention. *American Journal of Community Psychology, 26,* 97–131.

Milliken v. Bradley, 418 U.S. 717 (1974).

Milner, N. (1987). The right to refuse treatment: Four case studies of legal mobilization. *Law and Society Review, 21*(3), 447–485.

Minnesota Public Radio. (2000). Jailing the mentally ill. http://www.American radioworks.org/features/mentally_ill/poll/stats.html

Mirowsky, J., & Ross, C. E. (1989). *Social causes of psychological distress.* Hawthorne, NY: Aldine de Gruyter.

Mirowsky, J., & Ross, C. E. (1995). Sex differences in distress: Real or artifact? *American Sociological Review, 60*(3), 449–468.

Mischel, W. (1973). Toward a cognitive social learning reconceptualization of personality. *Psychological Review, 80,* 252–283.

Mishara, B. L., & Daigle, M. (2001). Helplines and crisis intervention services: Challenges for the future. In D. Lester (Ed.), *Suicide prevention: Resources for the millennium* (pp. 153–171). Philadelphia: Taylor & Francis.

Monahan, J. (1976). The prevention of violence. In J. Monahan (Ed.), *Community mental health and the criminal justice system.* New York: Pergamon Press.

Monahan, J., & Walker, L. (1986). Social authority: Obtaining, evaluating and establishing social science in law. *University of Pennsylvania Law Review, 134,* 477–517.

Monroe, S. M., & Steiner, S. C. (1986). Social support and psychopathology: Interrelations with preexisting disorder, stress and personality. *Journal of Abnormal Psychology, 95,* 29–39.

Moore, T. (1982). Blacks: Rethinking service. In L. R. Snowden (Ed.), *Reaching the underserved. Mental health needs of neglected populations.* Beverly Hills: Sage.

Moos, R. H. (1973). Conceptualizations of human environments. *American Psychologist, 28,* 652–665.

Moos, R. H. (1976). *The human context: Environmental determinants of behavior.* New York: Wiley.

Moos, R. H. (1979). Social climate measurement and feedback. In R. Munoz, L. Snowden, & J. Kelly (Eds.), *Social and psychological research in community settings.* San Francisco: Jossey-Bass.

Moos, R. H. (1987). Person-environment congruence in work, school, and health care settings. *Journal of Vocational Behavior, 31,* 231–247.

Moos, R. H. (2002). The mystery of human context and coping: An unraveling of clues. *American Journal of Community Psychology, 30*(1), 67–88.

Moos, R. H., & Van Dort, B. (1979). Student physical symptoms and the social climate of college living groups. *American Journal of Community Psychology, 7,* 31–43.

Morell, M. A., Levine, M., & Perkins, D. V. (1982). Study of behavioral factors associated with psychiatric rehospitalization. *Community Mental Health Journal, 18,* 190–199.

Morrow, K. B., & Sorell, G. T. (1989). Factors affecting self-esteem, depression, and negative behaviors in sexually abused female adolescents. *Journal of Marriage and the Family, 51*(3), 677–686.

Morse, S. J. (1978). Crazy behavior, morals and science: An analysis of mental health law. *Southern California Law Review, 51,* 527–564.

Morse, S. J., Roth, L. H., & Wettstein, R. M. (1991). The concept of normality in the law. In D. Offer & M. Sabshin (Eds.), *The diversity of normal behavior: Further contributions to normatology* (pp. 275–301). New York: Basic Books.

Mothers in the Labor Force, 1955–2001. U.S. Department of Labor, Bureau of Labor Statistics. Web: data.bis.gov

Mowbray, C. T., Greenfield, A., & Freddolino, P. P. (1992). An analysis of treatment services provided in group homes for adults labeled mentally ill. *Journal of Nervous and Mental Disease, 180,* 551–559.

Moxley, D. P., Mowbray, C. T., & Brown, K. S. (1993). Supported education. In R. Flexer & P. Solomon (Eds.), *Psychiatric rehabilitation in practice* (pp. 137–153). New York: Butterworth.

Moyers, B. (2001). Trade secrets. A Moyers Report. Produced by Public Affairs Television in association with Washington Media Associates.

Moynihan, D. P. (1965). *The Negro family: The case for national action.* Washington, DC: Office of Planning and Research, U.S. Department of Labor.

Moynihan, D. P. (1969). *Maximum feasible misunderstanding. Community action in the War on Poverty.* New York: Free Press.

Mrazek, P. J., & Haggerty, R. J. (Eds.). (1994). *Reducing risks for mental disorders: Frontiers for preventive intervention research.* Washington, DC: National Academy Press.

Mulvey, E. P., & Cauffman, E. (2001). The inherent limits of predicting school violence. *American Psychologist, 56,* 797–802.

Mulvey, E. P., Geller, J. L., & Roth, L. H. (1987). The promise and peril of involuntary outpatient commitment. *American Psychologist, 42,* 571–584.

Mumford, E., Schlesinger, H. J., Glass, G. V., Patrick, C., & Cuerdon, T. (1998). A new look at evidence about reduced cost of medical utilization following mental health treatment. *Journal of Psychotherapy Practice and Research, 7*(1), 68–86.

Murphy, J. M. (1964). Psychotherapeutic aspects of shamanism on St. Lawrence Island, Alaska. In A. Kiev (Ed.), *Magic, faith and healing.* New York: The Free Press of Glencoe.

Murphy, J. M. (1982). Cultural shaping and mental disorders. In W. R. Gove (Ed.), *Deviance and mental illness.* Beverly Hills, CA: Sage.

Murray, B. (2000). A mirror on the self. *Monitor on Psychology, 31*(4), 16–19.

Murray, H. A. (1938). *Explorations in personality.* New York: Oxford University Press.

Murray J. P. (Ed.). (1983). *Status offenders. A sourcebook.* Boys Town, NE: The Boys Town Center.

Myers, J. K., Weissman, M. M., Tischler, G. L., Holze, C. E., III, Leaf, P. J., Orvaschel, H., Anthony, J. C., Boyd, J. H., Burke, J. D., Jr., Kramer, M. (1984). Six-month prevalence of psychiatric disorders in three communities: 1980–1982. *Archives of General Psychiatry, 41*(10), 959–967.

Myrdal, G. (1944). *An American dilemma* (2 vols). New York: Harper & Row.

Namir, S., & Weinstein, R. S. (1982). Children: Facilitating new directions. In L. R. Snowden (Ed.), *Reaching the underserved: Mental health needs of neglected populations.* Beverly Hills, CA: Sage.

Naroll, R. (1983). *The moral order. An introduction to the human situation.* Beverly Hills, CA: Sage.

Narrow, W. E., Regier, D. A., Rae, D. S., Manderscheid, R. W., & Locke, B. Z. (1993). Use of services by persons with mental and addictive disorders: Findings from the National Institute of Mental Health Epidemiological Catchment Area program. *Archives of General Psychiatry, 50,* 95–107.

Nasar, J. L., & Julian, D.A. (1995). The psychological sense of community in the neighborhood. *Journal of the American Planning Association, 61,* 178–184.

Nathan, V. M. (1979). The use of masters in institutional reform litigation. *Toledo Law Review, 10,* 419–464.

National Academy of Sciences. (1984). *Bereavement: Reactions, consequences, and care.* Washington, DC: National Academy Press.

National Adoption Information Clearinghouse. (2000). http://www.calib.com/naic/pubs/s_number.htm

National Advisory Mental Health Council. (1990). National plan for research on child and adolescent mental disorders. DHHS Publication No. ADM 90-1683. Washington, DC: Alcohol, Drug Abuse, and Mental Health Administration.

National Alliance for the Mentally Ill. (1993). 'Critical need' cited for employment data. *NAMI Advocate, 14,* 1.

National Alliance for the Mentally Ill Staff, & Public Citizen Health Research Group Staff. (1992). *Criminalizing the seriously mentally ill: The abuse of jails as mental hospitals.* Washington, DC: Public Citizen, Inc.

National Association of Psychiatric Health Care Systems. (2001). http://mentalhealthy.about.com/library/sci/0201/bishop0102.htm

National Center for Education Statistics. (2001). http://nces.ed.gov/pubs2002(digest2001)tables/pdf/table_052.pdf

National Center for Health Statistics. (1997). Americans less likely to use nursing home care today. http://www.cdc.gov/nchs/releases97/news/nurshome.htm

National Center for Health Statistics. (2001). http://www.cdc.gov/nchs/fastats/

National Center for HIV, STD and TB Prevention. (2000). STD Surveillance. National Profile, Other Sexually Transmitted Diseases. http://www.cdc.gov/std/stats/2000OtherSTDs.htm

National Center for HIV, STD and TB Prevention. (2002). Tracking the hidden epidemics 2000. Trends in STDs in the United States. http://www.cdc.gov/nchstp/od/news/RevBrochure1pdfHerpes.htm

National Clearinghouse on Child Abuse and Neglect Information. (2001). Foster care national statistics, April, 2001. http://www.calib.co/nccanch/pubs/factsheets/foster.cfm

National Institute of Mental Health. (1999). Statement on the NIMH AIDS research program responding to the report released on December 6, 1999, by the National Alliance for the Mentally Ill and the Stanley Foundation Research Program. http://www.nimh.nih.gov/events/aidsnamifinal.cfm

National Research Council. (1993). *Understanding child abuse and neglect.* Washington, DC: National Academy Press.

Nelson, B. J. (1984). *Making an issue of child abuse.* Chicago, IL: University of Chicago Press.

Nelson, G., & Prilleltensky, I. (Eds.). (in press). *Community psychology: In pursuit of well-being and liberation.* New York: Palgrave Macmillan.

Newbrough, J. R. (1967). The Corresponding Committee of Fifty: An experiment in organizational innovation. *The Clinical Psychologist, 20,* 71–73.

Newbrough, J. R. (1995). Toward community: A third position. *American Journal of Community Psychology, 23,* 9–37.

Norris, F. H., & Murrell, S. A. (1988). Prior experience as a moderator of disaster impact on anxiety symptoms of older adults. *American Journal of Community Psychology, 16,* 665–683.

Norris, F. H., Phifer, J. F., & Kaniasty, K. (1994). Individual and community reactions to the Kentucky floods: Findings from a longitudinal study of older adults. In R. J. Ursano, B. G. McCaughey, & C. S. Fullerton (Eds.), *Individual and community responses to trauma and disaster: The structure of human chaos* (pp. 378–400). London: Cambridge University.

Norris, F. H., & Thompson, M. P. (1995). Applying community psychology to the prevention of trauma and traumatic life events. In J. R. Freedy & S. E. Hobfoll (Eds.), *Traumatic stress: From theory to practice* (pp. 49–71). New York: Plenum.

Norris-Baker, C. (1999). Aging on the old frontier and the new: A behavior setting approach to the declining small towns of the Midwest. *Environment and Behavior, 31,* 240–258.

Novaco, R. W., Kliewer, W., & Broquet, A. (1991). Home environment consequences of commuter travel impedence. *American Journal of Community Psychology, 19,* 881–909.

O'Connor v. Donaldson, 422 U.S. 563 (1975).

O'Donnell, C. R. (2001). School violence, trends, risk factors, prevention, and recommendations. *Law & Policy, 23*(3), 409–415.

Odum, E. P. (1971). *Fundamentals of ecology* (3d ed.). Philadelphia: Saunders.

Ogburn, W. F. (1966). *Social change with respect to cultural and original nature.* New York: Dell Publishing (originally published 1922).

Olasky, M. N. (1995). *Tragedy of American compassion.* Wheaton, IL: Crossway Books.

Olfson, M. (1990). Assertive community treatment: An evaluation of the experimental evidence. *Hospital and Community Psychiatry, 41,* 634–641.

O'Neill, P. O. (1989). Responsible to whom? Responsible for what? Some ethical issues in community intervention. *American Journal of Community Psychology, 17,* 323–341.

Ong, E. K., & Glantz, S. A. (2001). Constructing sound science" and good epidemiology": Tobacco, lawyers, and public relations firms. *American Journal of Public Health, 91,* 1749–1757.

Orfield, G. (1993). *The growth of segregation in American schools: Changing patterns of separation and poverty since 1968.* Cambridge, MA: Harvard Project on School Desegregation.

Orfield, G. (2001). *Schools more separate: Consequences of a decade of resegregation.* Cambridge, MA: The Civil Rights Project, Harvard University.

Orford, J. (1992). *Community psychology: Theory and practice.* Chichester, England: Wiley.

Osipow, S. H., & Fitzgerald, L. F. (1993). Unemployment and mental health: A neglected relationship. *Applied and Preventive Psychology, 2,* 59–64.

O'Sullivan, M. J., Peterson, P. D., Cox, G. B., & Kirkeby, J. (1989). Ethnic populations: Community mental health centers ten years later. *American Journal of Community Psychology, 17,* 17–30.

Pagani, L., Tremblay, R. E., Vitaro, F., Boulerice, B., & McDuff, P. (2001). Effects of grade retention on academic performance and behavioral development. *Development and Psychopathology, 13*(2), 297–315. http://uk.cambridge.org/journals/dpp/

Page, R. (1992). *Data reference book.* San Francisco: California Commission on the Future of the Courts.

Page, S. (1977). Effects of the mental illness label in attempts to obtain accommodations, *Canadian Journal of Behavioural Science, 9,* 85–90.

Page, S. (1983). Psychiatric stigma: Two studies of behaviour when the chips are down. *Canadian Journal of Community Mental Health, 2,* 13–19.

Pakenham, K. I., Dadds, M. R., & Terry, J. (1994). Relationships between adjustment to HIV and both social support and coping. *Journal of Consulting and Clinical Psychology, 62,* 1194–1203.

Parad, H. J., & Parad, L. G. (Eds.). (1999). *Crisis intervention, the practitioner's sourcebook for brief therapy.* Canada: Manticore Publishers.

Pargament, K. I., & Maton, K. I. (2000). Religion in American life: A community psychology perspective. In J. Rappaport & E. Seidman (Eds.), *Handbook of community psychology* (pp. 495–522). New York: Kluwer Academic/Plenum.

Parham v. J.R. and J.L. 442 U.S. 584 (1979).

Pasadena Board of Education v. Spangler, 427 U. S. 424 (1976).

Pattillo McCoy, M. (1998). Church culture as a strategy of action in the Black community. *American Sociological Review, 63*(6), 767–784.

Pauly, P. J. (1994). Is liquor intoxicating? Scientists, Prohibition, and the normalization of drinking. *American Journal of Public Health, 84,* 305–313.

Pearlin, L. I., & Schooler, C. (1978). The structure of coping. *Journal of Health and Social Behavior, 19,* 2–21.

Pedro-Carroll, J. (1997). The children of divorce intervention program: Fostering resilient outcomes for school-aged children (Ch. 10, 213–238). In. G. W. Albee and T. P. Gullotta (Eds), *Primary prevention works.* Thousand Oaks, CA,: Sage.

Peek, L. A., & Mileti, D. S. (2002). The history and future of disaster research. In R. B. Bechtel & A. Churchman (Eds.), *Handbook of environmental psychology.* (pp. 511–524). New York: John Wiley & Sons.

Peirce, N. R., & Steinbach, C. F. (1987). *Corrective capitalism. The Rise of America's Community Development Corporations.* New York: Ford Foundation.

Pellow, D. N. (2002). *Garbage wars: The struggle for environmental justice in Chicago.* Cambridge, MA: MIT Press.

Perkins, C. A., Stephan, J. J., & Beck, A. J. (1995). Jails and jail inmates, 1993–1994. *Bureau of Justice Statistics Bulletin,* April, 1995.

Perkins, D. D. (1988). The use of social science in public interest litigation: A role for community psychologists. *American Journal of Community Psychology, 16,* 465–485.

Perkins, D. D. (1995). Speaking truth to power: Empowerment ideology as social intervention and policy. *American Journal of Community Psychology 23,* 765–794.

Perkins, D. D., Brown, B. B., & Taylor, R. B. (1996). The ecology of empowerment: Predicting participation in community organizations. *Journal of Social Issues, 52,* 85–110.

Perkins, D. D., Crim, B., Silberman, P., & Brown, B. B. (2004). Community development as a response to community-level adversity: Ecological theory and research and strengths-based policy. In K. I. Maton, C. J. Schellenbach, B. J. Leadbeater, & A. L. Solarz (Eds.), *Investing in children, youth, families and communities: Strengths-based research and policy* (pp. 321–340). Washington, DC: American Psychological Association.

Perkins, D. D., Florin, P., Rich, R. C., Wandersman, A., & Chavis, D. M. (1990). Participation and the social and physical environment of residential blocks: Crime and community context. *American Journal of Community Psychology, 18,* 83–115.

Perkins, D. D., Hughey, J., & Speer, P. W. (2002). Community psychology perspectives on social capital theory and community development practice. *Journal of the Community Development Society, 33,* 33–52.

Perkins, D. D., & Long, D. A. (2002). Neighborhood sense of community and social capital: A multi-level analysis. In A. T. Fisher, C. C. Sonn, & B. J. Bishop (Eds.), *Psychological sense of community: Research, applications, and implications* (pp. 291–318). New York: Kluwer Academic/Plenum Publishers.

Perkins, D. D., Meeks, J. W., & Taylor, R. B. (1992). The physical environment of street blocks and resident perceptions of crime and disorder: Implications for theory and measurement. *Journal of Environmental Psychology, 12,* 21–34.

Perkins, D. D., & Taylor, R. B. (1996). Ecological assessments of community disorder: Their relationship to fear of crime and theoretical implications. *American Journal of Community Psychology, 24,* 63–107.

Perkins, D. D., & Zimmerman, M. A. (1995). Empowerment theory, research, and application. *American Journal of Community Psychology, 23,* 569–579.

Perkins, D. V. (1982). The assessment of stress using life events scales. In L. Goldberger & S. Breznitz (Eds.), *Handbook of stress.* New York: Free Press.

Perkins, D. V., & Baker, F. (1991). A behavior setting assessment for community programs and residences. *Community Mental Health Journal, 27,* 313–325.

Perkins, D. V., Burns, T. F., Perry, J. C., & Nielsen, K. P. (1988). Behavior setting theory and community psychology: An analysis and critique. *Journal of Community Psychology, 16,* 355–372.

Perkins, D. V., & Perry, J. C. (1985). Dimensional analysis of behavior setting demands in a community residence for chronically mentally ill women. *Journal of Community Psychology, 13,* 350–359.

Perrotta, P. (1982). The experience of caring for an elderly family member. Unpublished doctoral dissertation, Department of Psychology, SUNY at Buffalo.

Perrow, C. (1984). *Normal accidents: Living with high-risk technologies.* New York: Basic Books.

Peterson, L., & Mori, L. (1985). Prevention of child injury: an overview of targets, methods, and tactics for psychologists. *Journal of Consulting and Clinical Psychology, 53,* 586–594.

Peterson, R. L., Larson, J., & Skiba, R. (2001). School violence prevention: Current status and policy recommendations. *Law & Policy, 23*(3), 345–371.

Petrakis, P. L. (1988). *The Surgeon General's workshop on self-help and public health.* Washington, DC: U.S. Government Printing Office.

Phelps, R. P. (2000). Test bashing part 14. The "new" Rand report. EducationNews.org. http://www.educationnews.org/test_bashing_part_14.htm

Physicians Committee for Responsible Medicine. http://www.pcrm.org/issues/ETHICS_IN_HUMAN_RESEARCH/ethics_human_birthdefects.html

Pilisuk, M. (2001). A job and a home: Social networks and the integration of the mentally disabled in the community. *American Journal of Orthopsychiatry, 71*(1), 49–60.

Pilisuk, M., McAllister, J., & Rothman, J. (1996). Coming together for action: The challenge of contemporary grassroots community organizing. *Journal of Social Issues, 52*(1), 15–37.

Pillow, D. R., Sandler, I. N., Braver, S. L., Wolchik, S. A., & Gersten, J. C. (1991). Theory-based screening for prevention: Focusing on mediating processes in children of divorce. *American Journal of Community Psychology, 19,* 809–836.

Pincus, H. A., Tanielian, T. L., Marcus, S. C., Offson, M., Zarin, D. A., Thompson, J., & Zito, J. M. (1998). Prescribing trends in psychotropic medications. Primary care, psychiatry and other medical specialties. *Journal of the American Medical Association, 279*(7), 526–531.

Pitegoff, P. (1993). Child care enterprise, community development, and work. *The Georgetown Law Journal, 81,* 1897–1943.

Pit-Ten Cate, I. M., & Loots, G. M. P. (2000). Experiences of siblings of children with physical disabilities: An empirical investigation. *Disability and Rehabilitation: An International Multidisciplinary Journal, 22*(9), 399–408.

Planin, E. (2001). Toxic chemical review process faulted. Scientists on EPA advisory panels often have conflicts of interest, GAO says. *Washington Post,* Monday, July 16, p. A-2.

Plas, J. M., & Lewis, S. E. (1996). Environmental factors and sense of community in a planned town. *American Journal of Community Psychology, 24*(1), 109–143.

Plessy v. Ferguson, 163 U.S. 537 (1896).

Poythress, N. G. (1978). Psychiatric expertise in civil commitment: Training attorneys to cope with expert testimony. *Law and Human Behavior, 2,* 1–24.

President's Commission on Mental Health. (1978). *Report to the President from the President's Commission on Mental Health.* Washington, DC: U. S. Government Printing Office.

Pressman, J. L., & Wildavsky, A. B. (1984). *Implementation* (3rd ed.). Berkeley: University of California Press.

Pretty, G. M. H. (1990). Relating psychological sense of community to social climate characteristics. *Journal of Community Psychology, 18,* 16–65.

Pretty, G. M. H. (2002). Young people's development of the community-minded self: considering community identity, community attachment and sense of community. In A. Fisher, C. C. Sonn, & B. Bishop (eds.), *Psychological sense of community: Research, applications, and implications* (pp. 183–203). New York: Plenum.

Prezza, M., Amici, M., Roberti, T., & Tedeschi, G. (2001). Sense of community referred to the whole town: Its relations with neighboring, loneliness, life satisfaction, and area of residence. *Journal of Community Psychology, 29,* 29–52.

Price, R. H., & Moos, R. H. (1975). Toward a taxonomy of inpatient treatment environments. *Journal of Abnormal Psychology, 84,* 181–188.

Prilleltensky, I. (in press). The role of power in wellness, oppression, and liberation: The promise of psychopolitical validity. *Journal of Community Psychology.*

Psychosocial Rehabilitation Journal. (1992). Special issue on clubhouses. *Psychosocial Rehabilitation Journal, 16,* No. 2, October.

Puddifoot, J.E. (1995). Dimensions of community identity. *Journal of Community and Applied Social Psychology, 5,* 357–370.

Putnam, R.D. (2000). *Bowling alone: The collapse and revival of American community.* New York: Simon & Schuster.

Quick, J. C., Barab, J., Hurrell, J. J., Jr., Ivancevich, J. M., Mangelsdorff, A. D., Pelletier, K. R., Raymond, J., Smith, D. C. Vaccaro, V., et al. (1992). Health promotion, education, and treatment. In G. P. Keita, & S. L. Sauter (Eds.), *Work and well being: An agenda for the 1990s* (pp. 47–61). Washington, DC: American Psychological Association.

Rabasca, L. (2000). Self-help sites: A blessing or a bane? *Monitor on Psychology, 31*(4), 28–30.

Rabkin, J. G., & Streuning, E. L. (1976). Life events, stress and illness. *Science, 194,* 1013–1020.

Rabow, J., Hernandez, A. C., & Newcomb, M. D. (1990). Nuclear fears and concerns among college students: A cross-national study of attitudes. *Political Psychology, 11*(4), 681–698.

Rainwater, L., & Yancey, W. L. (1967). *The Moynihan Report & the politics of controversy.* Cambridge, MA: M.I.T. Press.

Rao, P. K. (2000). *Sustainable development: Economics and policy.* Malden, MA: Blackwell.

Rapp, C. A., & Moore, T. D. (1995). The first 18 months of mental health reform in Kansas. *Psychiatric Services, 46,* 580–585.

Rappaport, J. (1977). *Community psychology: Values, research, and action.* New York: Holt, Rinehart & Winston.

Rappaport, J. (1981). In praise of paradox: A social policy of empowerment over prevention. *American Journal of Community Psychology, 9,* 1–26.

Rappaport, J. (1987). Terms of empowerment/exemplars of prevention: Toward a theory for community psychology. *American Journal of Community Psychology 15,* 121–148.

Rappaport, J. (1992). The dilemma of primary prevention in mental health services: Rationalize the status quo or bite the hand that feeds you. *Journal of Community and Applied Social Psychology, 2,* 95–99.

Ravitch, D. (1983). *The troubled crusade: American education, 1945–1980.* New York: Basic Books.

Ravitch, D. (2000). Frank J. Battitsti Memorial Lecture: School reform, past, present, and future. *Case Western Reserve Law Review, 51,* 187–200.

Rawls, P. (2003). 33-year-old Alabama mental health suit ends. Associated Press State and Local Wires.

Redding, R. E. (2001). Sociopolitical diversity in psychology: The case for pluralism. *American Psychologist, 56,* 205–215.

Redding, R. E., & Shalf, S. M. (2001). The legal context of school violence: The effectiveness of federal, state and local law enforcement efforts to reduce gun violence in schools. *Law & Policy, 23*(3), 297–343.

Regehr, C., Cadell, S., & Jansen, K. (1999). Perceptions of control and long-term recovery from rape. *American Journal of Orthopsychiatry, 69*(1), 110–115.

Regier, D. A., Narrow, W. E., Rae, D. S., Manderscheid, R. W., Locke, B. Z., & Goodwin, F. K. (1993). The de facto U.S. mental and addictive disorders service system: Epidemiological Catchment Area prospective 1-year prevalence rates of disorders and services. *Archives of General Psychiatry, 50,* 85–94.

Reinecke, M. A., & DuBois, D. L. (2001). Socioenvironmental and cognitive risk and resources: Relations to mood and suicidality among inpatient adolescents. *Journal of Cognitive Psychotherapy, 15*(3), 195–222.

Reinhardt, J. P. (2001). Effects of positive and negative support received and provided on adaptation to chronic visual impairment. *Applied Developmental Science, 5*(2), 76–85.

Reiss, B. F., & Brandt, L. W. (1965). What happens to applicants for psychotherapy? *Community Mental Health Journal, 1,* 175–180.

Reissman, F. (1965). The 'helper-therapy' principle. *Social Work, 10,* 27–32.

Rennison, C. (2002). Criminal victimization 2001. Changes 2000-01 with trends 1993–2001. Bureau of Justice statistics. National Crime Victimization Survey. NCJ 194610.

Reppucci, N. D., Woolard, J. L., & Fried, C. S. (1999). Social, community, and preventive interventions. *Annual Review of Psychology, 50,* 387–418.

Revkin, A. C., & Seelye, K. Q. (6/19/2003). Report by the E.P.A. leaves out data on climate change. *New York Times.*

Rhodes, J. E. (1998). Family, friends, and community: The role of social support in promoting health. In P. M. Camic & S. J. Knight (Eds.), *Clinical handbook of health psychology: A practical guide to effective interventions* (pp. 481–493). Seattle: Hogrefe & Huber.

Ribisl, K. M., & Humphreys, K. (1998). Collaboration between professionals and mediating structures in the community: Toward a "third way" in health promotion. In S. A. Shumaker, E. B. Schron, J. K. Ockene, & W. L. McBee (Eds.), *The handbook of health behavior change* (2nd ed.). (pp. 535–554). New York: Springer.

Rich, R. C., Edelstein, M., Hallman, W. K., & Wandersman, A. H. (1995). Citizen participation and empowerment: The case of local environmental hazards. *American Journal of Community Psychology, 23,* 657–676.

Richardson, L. A., Keller, A. M., Selby-Harrington, M. L., & Parrish, R. (1996). Identification and treatment of children's mental health problems by primary care providers: A critical review of research. *Archives of Psychiatric Nursing, 10*(5), 293–303.

Riggio, R. E. (1990). *Introduction to industrial/organizational psychology.* Glenview, IL: Scott, Foresman/Little, Brown.

Rind, B., Tromovitch, P., & Bauserman, R. (1998). A meta-analytic examination of assumed properties of child sexual abuse using college samples. *Psychological Bulletin, 124,* 22–53.

Roberts, A. R. (Ed.). (2000). *Crisis intervention handbook: Assessment, treatment and research* (2nd ed.). New York: Oxford University Press.

Roberts, J. T., Toffolon-Weiss, M. M. (2001). *Chronicles from the Environmental justice frontline.* New York: Cambridge University Press.

Roberts, L. J., Salem, D., Rappaport, J., Toro, P. A., Luke, D. A., & Seidman, E. (1999). Giving and receiving help: Interpersonal transactions in mutual-help meetings and psychosocial adjustment of members. *American Journal of Community Psychology, 27*(6), 841–868.

Robins, L. N. (1974). *Deviant children grown up.* Huntington, NY: Krieger.

Robins, L. N., & Rutter, M. (1991). *Straight and devious pathways from childhood to adulthood.* New York: Cambridge University Press.

Roe v. Wade 410 U.S. 113 (1973).

Roen, S. R., & Burnes, A. J. (1968). *The community adaptation schedule: Preliminary manual.* New York: Behavioral Publications.

Roessler, W., Salize, H. J., & Voges, B. (1995). Does community-based care have an effect on public attitudes toward the mentally ill? *European Psychiatry, 10*(6), 282–289.

Rogers, A. (1993). Coercion and "voluntary" admission: An examination of psychiatric patient views. *Behavioral Sciences & the Law, 11,* 259–267.

Rogler, L. (1994). International migrations: A framework for directing research. *American Psychologist, 49,* 701–708.

Rook, K. S. (2001). Emotional health and positive versus negative social exchanges: A daily diary analysis. *Applied Developmental Science, 5*(2), 86–97.

Roosens, E. (1979). *Mental patients in town life. Geel—Europe's first therapeutic community.* Beverly Hills, CA: Sage.

Rosenberg, M. S., & Reppucci, N. D. (1985). Primary prevention of child abuse. *Journal of Consulting and Clinical Psychology, 53,* 576–585.

Rosenhan, D. L. (1973). On being sane in insane places. *Science, 179,* 250–258.

Ross, C. E. (1993). Fear of victimization and health. *Journal of Quantitative Criminology, 9*(2), 159–175.

Rossi, A. M. (1969). Some pre–World War II antecedents of community mental health theory and practice. In A. J. Bindman & A. D. Spiegel (Eds.), *Perspectives in community mental health* (pp. 9–28). Chicago: Aldine.

Rossman, M. (1976). Self-help marketplace. *Social Policy, 7,* 86–91.

Rotheram-Borus, M. J., Koopman, C., Haignere, C., & Davies, M. (1991). Reducing HIV sexual risk behaviors among runaway adolescents. *Journal of the American Medical Association, 266,* 1237–1241.

Rothman, D. J. (1982). The courts and social reform: A postprogressive outlook. *Law and Human Behavior, 6,* 113–19.

Ryan, W. (1969). *Distress in the city.* Cleveland, OH: Press of Case Western Reserve University.

Ryan, W. (1976). *Blaming the victim* (Rev., updated ed.). New York: Vintage Books.

Sabin, J. E., & Daniels, N. (2001). Managed care: Strengthening the consumer voice in managed care: I. Can the private sector meet the public-sector standard? *Psychiatric Services, 52*(4), 461–464.

Saegert, S., & Winkel, G. (1996). Paths to community empowerment: Organizing at home. *American Journal of Community Psychology, 24,* 517–550.

Saegert, S., & Winkel, G. (1998). Social capital and the revitalization of New York City's distressed inner city housing. *Housing Policy Debate, 9,* 17–60.

Sagan, L. A. (1987). *The health of nations.* New York: Basic Books.

Sagarin, E. (1969). *Odd man in: Societies of deviants in America.* Chicago: Quadrangle Books.

St. Lawrence, J. S., Brasfield, T. L., Jefferson, K. W., Alleyne, E., O'Bannon, III, R. E., & Shirley, A. (1995). Cognitive-behavioral intervention to reduce African American adolescents' risk for HIV infection. *Journal of Consulting and Clinical Psychology, 63,* 221–237.

Sakaguchi, Y. (2001). Secondary stressors and mental health after bereavement: Comparison between spouses and children. *Japanese Journal of Family Psychology, 15*(1), 13–24.

Salem, D. A., Seidman, E., & Rappaport, J. (1988). Community treatment of the mentally ill: The promise of self-help organizations. *Social Work, 33,* 403–410.

Salzer, M. S., Blank, M., Rothbard, A., & Hadley, T. (2001). Adult mental health services in the 21st Century. In R. W. Manderscheid, and M. J. Henderson (Eds.), Mental Health, United States, 2000 (Chapter 11). DHHS Pub. No. (SMA) 01-3537. Washington, DC: Supt. of Docs., U.S. Government Printing Office.

Sampson, R. J. (1991). Linking the micro- and macro-level dimensions of community social organization. *Social Forces, 70,* 43–64.

San Antonio Independent School District v. Rodriguez 411 U.S. 1 (1973).

Sarason, I. G., & Sarason, B. R. (1981). Teaching cognitive and social skills to high school students. *Journal of Consulting and Clinical Psychology, 49,* 908–918.

Sarason, S. B. (1972). *The creation of settings and the future societies.* San Francisco: Jossey-Bass.

Sarason, S. B. (1974). *The psychological sense of community: Prospects for a community psychology.* San Francisco: Jossey-Bass.

Sarason, S. B. (1976). Community psychology, networks, and Mr. Everyman. *American Psychologist, 31,* 317–328.

Sarason, S. B. (1978). The nature of problem solving in social action. *American Psychologist, 33,* 370–380.

Sarason, S. B. (1981a). *Psychology misdirected.* New York: Free Press.

Sarason, S. B. (1981b). An asocial psychology and a misdirected clinical psychology. *American Psychologist, 36,* 827–836.

Sarason, S. B. (1982a). *Psychology and social action: Selected papers.* New York: Praeger.

Sarason, S. B. (1982b). *The culture of the school and the problem of change.* 2nd ed. Boston, MA: Allyn & Bacon.

Sarason, S. B. (1990). *The predictible failure of educational reform.* San Francisco: Jossey-Bass.

Sarason, S. B. (1996). *Barometers of change: Individual, educational, and social transformation.* San Francisco: Jossey-Bass.

Sarason, S. B., Carroll, C. F., Maton, K., Cohen, S., & Lorentz, E. (1977). *Human services and resource networks.* San Francisco: Jossey-Bass.

Sarason, S. B., & Doris. J. (1969). *Psychological problems in mental deficiency* (4th ed.). New York: Harper & Row.

Sarason, S. B., & Klaber, M. (1985). The school as a social situation. *Annual Review of Psychology, 36,* 115–140.

Sarason, S. B., Levine, M., Goldenberg, I. I., Cherlin, D. L., & Bennett, E. M. (1966). *Psychology in community settings.* New York: Wiley.

Sarbin, T. R. (1970). A role theory perspective for community psychology: The structure of social identity. In D. Adelson & B. Kalis (Eds.), *Community psychology and mental health: Perspectives and challenges.* Scranton, PA: Chandler.

Sareyan, A. (1994). *The turning point: How men of conscience brought about major change in the care of America's mentally ill.* Washington, DC: American Psychiatric Press.

Scales-Trent, J. (1995). *Notes of a white black woman*. University Park, PA: The Pennsylvania State University Press.

Schacter, J. (2001). Geographical mobility. Current Population Reports P20-538, U.S. Census Bureau, May 2001.

Scheff, T. J. (1966). *Being mentally ill: A sociological perspective*. Chicago: Aldine.

Scheff, T. J. (1984). *Being mentally ill. A sociological theory*. (2nd ed.). New York: Aldine.

Scheff, T. J. (1999). *Being mentally ill: A sociological theory* (3rd ed.). New York: Aldine de Gruyter.

Scherschel, P. M. (1997). Reality bites: How much do students owe? In Student Loan Debt: Problems and Prospects. Proceedings from a National Symposium, December 10, 1997. Washington, DC, pp. 15–38.

Schmuckler, M. A. (2001). What is ecological validity? A dimensional analysis. *Infancy, 2*(4), 419–436.

Schoggen, P., Barker, R. G., & Fox, K. A. (1989). *Behavior settings: A revision and extension of Roger G. Barker's ecological psychology*. Stanford, CA: Stanford University Press.

Schulz, R., & Hanusa, B. H. (1978). Long-term effects of control and predictability-enhancing interventions: Findings and ethical issues. *Journal of Personality and Social Psychology, 36*, 1194–1201.

Schuster, T. I., Kessler, R. C., & Aseltine, R. H., Jr. (1990). Supportive interactions, negative interactions, and depressed mood. *American Journal of Community Psychology, 18*, 423–438.

Schwartz, C. E., & Rogers, M. (1994). Designing a psychosocial intervention to teach coping flexibility. *Rehabilitation Psychology, 39*, 57–72.

Schwebel, M., & Schwebel, B. (1981). Children's reactions to the threat of nuclear plant accidents. *American Journal of Orthopsychiatry, 51*, 260–270.

Scott v. Sanford 60 U.S. 393 (1856).

Scull, A. T. (1977). *Decarceration: Community treatment and the deviant—A radical view*. Englewood Cliffs, NJ: Prentice-Hall.

Seedat, M., & Duncan, N. (Eds.). (2001). *Community psychology: Theory, method and practice: South African and other perspectives*. Cape Town: Oxford University Press Southern Africa.

Segal, S. P., Silverman, C., & Temkin, T. (1993). Empowerment and self-help agency practice for people with mental disabilities. *Social Work, 38*, 705–712.

Seidman, E. (1990). Pursuing the meaning and utility of social regularities for community psychology (pp. 91–100). In P. Tolan et al. (Eds.), *Researching community psychology: Issues of theory and methods*. Washington DC: American Psychological Association.

Select Committee on Children, Youth and Families, U. S. House of Representatives. (1990). *No place to call home: Discarded children in America*. Washington, DC: U. S. Government Printing Office.

Seligman, M. E. P. (2002). *Authentic happiness*. New York: Free Press.

Seller, M. S. (1979). Ethnic communities and education in Buffalo, New York: Politics, power and group identity 1838–1979 (Occasional paper #1). Buffalo Community Studies Graduate Group. Buffalo: SUNY at Buffalo.

Serrano-García, I. (1994). The ethics of the powerful and the power of ethics. *American Journal of Community Psychology, 22*(1), 1–20.

Shinn, M. (1992). Homelessness: What is a psychologist to do? *American Journal of Community Psychology, 20*, 1–24.

Shinn, M., & Felton, B. J. (Eds.). (1981). Institutions and alternatives. *Journal of Social Issues, 37*, 1–176.

Shinn, M., & Perkins, D.N.T. (2000). Contributions from Organizational Psychology. In J. Rappaport, & E. Seidman (Eds.), *Handbook of Community Psychology* (pp. 615–641). New York: Kluwer Academic/Plenum Publishers.

Shinn, M., Rosario, M., Mørch, H., & Chestnut, D.E. (1984). Coping with job stress and burnout in the human services. *Journal of Personality and Social Psychology, 46*, 864–876.

Shinn, M., & Toohey, S. M. (2003). Community contexts of human welfare. *Annual Review of Psychology, 54*, 427–459.

Shinn, M., & Tsemberis, S. (1998). Is housing the cure for homelessness? In X. Arriaga & S. Oskamp (Eds.), *Addressing community problems: Psychological research and interventions* (pp. 52–77). Thousand Oaks, CA: Sage.

Shinn, M., Wong, N.W., Simko, R.A. & Ortiz-Torres, B. (1989). Promoting the well-being of working parents: Coping, social support, and flexible job schedules. *American Journal of Community Psychology, 17,* 31–55.

Shure, M. B. (1997). Interpersonal cognitive problem solving: Primary prevention of early high-risk behaviors in the preschool and primary years (Ch. 8, 167–188). In. G. W. Albee and T. P. Gullotta (Eds.), *Primary prevention works.* Thousand Oaks, CA: Sage.

SIECUS. (2003). Policy update—April 2003. http://www.siecus.org/policy/PUpdates/pdate0056.html#REL.

Sikkema, K. J., Kelly, J. A., Winett, R. A., Solomon, L. J., Cargill, V. A., Roffman, R. A., McAuliffe, T. L., Heckman, T. G., Anderson, E. A., Wagstaff, D. A., Norman, A. D., Perry, M. J., Crumble, D. A., Mercer, M. B. (2000). Outcomes of a randomized community-level HIV prevention intervention for women living in 18 low-income housing developments. *American Journal of Public Health, 90*(1), 57–63.

Silverman, D. C. (1992). Male co-survivors: The shared trauma of rape. In G. C. Mezey & M. B. King (Eds.), *Male victims of sexual assault* (pp. 87–103). New York: Oxford University Press.

Simon, P. (1999). Report on special education troubles administrators. *Buffalo News,* February 5, A-1, 9.

Singer, S. I. (1996). *Recriminalizing delinquency. Violent juvenile crimes and juvenile justice reform.* Cambridge, UK: Cambridge University Press.

Sipuel v. Oklahoma State Board of Regents 332 U. S. 631 (1948).

Skaff, M. M., Finney, J. W., & Moos, R. H. (1999). Gender differences in problem drinking and depressions: Different vulnerabilities? *American Journal of Community Psychology, 27*(1), 25–54.

Slack, P. (1995). *The English poor law, 1531–1782* (1st Cambridge University Press ed.). New York: Cambridge University Press.

Slaikeu, K. A. (1984). *Crisis intervention: A handbook for practice and research.* Boston: Allyn and Bacon.

Smith, K. E., & Bachu, A. (1999). Women's labor force attachment patterns and maternity leave: A review of the literature. Washington, DC: Population Division, U.S. Bureau of the Census.

Smith, R. R. (1978). Two centuries and twenty-four months: A chronicle of the struggle to desegregate the Boston public schools. In H. Kalodner & J. J. Fishman (Eds.), *Limits of justice: The courts' role in school desegregation.* Cambridge: Ballinger.

Smock, P. J., Manning, W. D., & Gupta, S. (1999). The effect of marriage and divorce on women's economic well-being. *American Sociological Review, 64*(6), 794–812. http://www.jstor.org/journals/00031224.html

Snell, T. L., & Morton, D. C. (1994). Women in prison. Bureau of Justice Statistics Special Report. Washington, DC: U.S. Department of Justice.

Snowden, L. R. (Ed.). (1982). *Reaching the underserved: Mental health needs of neglected populations.* Beverly Hills: Sage.

Snowden, L. R. (1993). Emerging trends in organizing and financing human services: Unexamined consequences for ethnic minority populations. *American Journal of Community Psychology, 21,* 1–13.

Snyder, H. (2000). Juvenile arrests 1999. Washington, DC: Office of Juvenile Justice and Delinquency Prevention.

Socall, D. W., & Holtgraves, T. (1992). Attitudes toward the mentally ill: The effects of labels and beliefs. *The Sociological Quarterly, 33,* 3, 435–445.

Social Security Online. (2003). Supplemental Security Income. http://www.socialsecurity.gov

Sommer, R., & Wicker, A. W. (1991). Gas station psychology: The case for specialization in ecological psychology. *Environment and Behavior, 23,* 131–149.

Sorotzkin, B. (2003). The denial or child abuse: The Rind et al. controversy. NARTH, http://www.narth.com/docs/denial.html

Spaulding, J., & Balch, P. (1983). A brief history of primary prevention in the Twentieth Century: 1908 to 1980. *American Journal of Community Psychology, 11,* 59–80.

Speer, P. W., & Hughey, J. (1995). Community organizing: An ecological route to empowerment and power. *American Journal of Community Psychology, 23,* 729–748.

Speer, P. W., Hughey, J., Gensheimer, L. K., & Adams-Leavitt, W. (1995). Organizing for power: A comparative case study. *Journal of Community Psychology, 23,* 57–73.

Speer, P. W., Jackson, C. B., & Peterson, N. A. (2001). The relationship between social cohesion and empowerment: Support and new implications for theory. *Health Education and Behavior, 28*, 716–732.

Spence, S. H., Sheffield, J. K., & Donovan, C. L. (2003). Preventing adolescent depression: An evaluation of the Problem Solving for Life program. *Journal of Consulting and Clinical Psychology, 71*, 3–13.

Spitzer, R. L., & Williams, J. B. W. (1982). The definition and diagnosis of mental disorder. In W. R. Gove (Ed.), *Deviance and mental illness*. Beverly Hills, CA: Sage.

Spivack, G., & Shure, M. B. (1974). *Social adjustment of young children*. San Francisco: Jossey-Bass.

Spivack G., & Shure, M. B. (1985). ICPS and beyond: Centripetal and centrifugal forces. *American Journal of Community Psychology, 13*, 226–243.

Spivack, G., & Shure, M. B. (1989). Interpersonal Cognitive Problem Solving (ICPS): A competence-building primary prevention program. *Prevention in Human Services, 6*, 151–178.

Spivack, G., & Shure, M. B. (1993). *Social adjustment of young children: A cognitive approach to solving real-life problems* (3rd ed.). San Francisco: Jossey-Bass.

Spreitzer, G. M. (1995). An empirical test of intrapersonal empowerment in the workplace. *American Journal of Community Psychology, 23*(5), 601–629.

Srebnik, D. S., & Elias, M. J. (1993). An ecological, interpersonal skills approach to dropout prevention. *American Journal of Orthopsychiatry, 63*, 526–535.

Srole, L., Langner, T. S., Michael, S. T., Opler, M. K., & Rennie, T. A. C. (1962). *Mental health in the metropolis: The midtown Manhattan study*. New York: McGraw-Hill.

Stack, L. C., Lannon, P. B., & Miley, A. D. (1983). Accuracy of clinicians' expectancies for psychiatric rehospitalization. *American Journal of Community Psychology, 11*, 99–113.

Stahl, A. L. (2001). Delinquency cases in juvenile courts, 1998. OJJDP Fact Sheet #31.

Stangor, C., & Crandall, C. S. (2000). Threat and the social construction of stigma. In T. F. Heatherton & R. E. Kleck (Eds.), *The social psychology of stigma* (pp. 62–87). New York: Guilford Press.

Stashenko, J. (1999). Regents ask why so many nonwhite students are in special ed. *Buffalo News*, February 3, A–5.

Steele, C. M. (1992, April). Race and the schooling of Black Americans. *The Atlantic Monthly*, 68–78.

Stefan, S. (2001). *Unequal rights: Discrimination against people with mental disabilities and the Americans with Disabilities Act*. Washington, DC: American Psychological Association.

Stein, L. I., & Test, M. A. (1985). *The Training in Community Living model: A decade of experience*. (New Directions for Mental Health Services, No. 26). San Francisco: Jossey-Bass.

Steinberg, J. (2002). For Head Start children, their turn at testing. *New York Times*, December 4, A-27.

Stepfamily Association of America. (2000). http://www.saafamilies.org/faqs/index.htm

Stephan, W. G. (1978). School desegregation: An evaluation of predictions made in Brown v. Board of Education. *Psychological Bulletin, 85*, 217–238.

Stokols, D. (1992). Establishing and maintaining healthy environments: Toward a social ecology of health promotion. *American Psychologist, 47*, 6–22.

Stokols D. (1996). Translating social ecological theory into guidelines for community health promotion. *American Journal of Health Promotion, 10*, 282–298.

Stone, R. (1995). Panel slams EPA's dioxin analysis. *Science, 268*, 1124.

Stone, R. A., & Levine, A. G. (1985). Reactions to collective stress: Correlates of active citizen participation at Love Canal. *Prevention in Human Services, 4*, 153–177.

Stott, M. W. R., Gaier, E. L., & Thomas, K. B. (1984). Supervised access: A judicial alternative to noncompliance with visitation arrangements following divorce. *Children and Youth Services Review, 6*, 207–217.

Stover, J., Walker, N., Garnett, G. P., Salomon, J. A., Stanecki, K. A., Ghys, P. D., Grassly, N. C., Anderson, R. M., Schwartlander, B. (2002). Can we reverse the HIV/AIDS pandemic with an expanded response? *Lancet, 360*, 73–77.

Stroul, B. A. (1986). *Models of community support services: Approaches to helping persons with long-term mental illness*. Boston: Center for Psychiatric Rehabilitation.

Substance Abuse and Mental Health Services Administration. (2001). www.samhsa.gov/oas/NHSDA/2kNHSDA/chapter3.htm

Suttles, G. D. (1968). *The social order of the slum: Ethnicity and territory in the inner city.* Chicago: University of Chicago Press.

Swann v. Charlotte-Mecklenburg Board of Education 402 U. S. 1 (1971).

Swanson, J. M., & Chenitz, W. C. (1990). Psychosocial aspects of genital herpes: A review of the literature. *Public Health Nursing, 7*(2), 96–104.

Sweatt v. Painter, 339 U. S. 629 (1950).

Swenson, K. (2000). School finance reform litigation: Why are some state supreme courts activist and others restrained? *Albany Law Review, 63,* 1147–1182.

Swindle, R. W., Heller, K., Alexander, D. B., Allen, S. J., & Wyman, M. F. (2001). Sources of stressor-specific negative transactions and depressive symptoms among White and African-American older women. *Applied Developmental Science. 5,* 98–111.

Szasz, T. S. (1963). *Law, liberty and psychiatry.* New York: Macmillan.

Szasz, T. S. (1974). *The myth of mental illness: Foundations of a theory of personal conduct* (Rev. ed.). New York: Harper & Row.

Task Panel on Prevention. (1978b). Report of the Task Panel on Prevention. Task Panel Reports Submitted to the President's Commission on Mental Health, vol. 4. Washington, DC: U. S. Government Printing Office.

Taussig, H. N, Clyman, R. B., & Landswerk, J. (2001). Children who return home from foster care: A 6-year prospective study of behavioral health outcomes in adolescence. *Pediatrics, 108*(1)(July) p. e10 Electronic Article.

Taylor, H. L., Jr. (1990). *African Americans and the rise of Buffalo's post-industrial city, 1940 to present. Volume 1: An introduction to a research report.* Buffalo, NY: Buffalo Urban League, Inc.

Taylor, R.B. (2002). Crime prevention through environmental design (CPTED): Yes, no, maybe, unknowable, and all of the above. In R. B. Bechtel & A. Churchman (Eds.), *Handbook of environmental psychology* (pp. 413–426). New York: John Wiley & Sons.

Taylor, S. E., Kemeny, M. E., Reed, G. M., Bower, J. E., & Gruenewald, T. L. (2000). Psychological resources, positive illusions, and health. *American Psychologist, 55*(1) 99–109.

Tebes, J. A. (1983). Stigma and mental disorder: A review and analysis. Unpublished doctoral qualifying paper, Department of Psychology, SUNY at Buffalo.

Tebes, J. A., & Perkins, D. V. (1984). Converting stress to positive mental health: Evidence from students coping with parental death. Paper presented at the Eastern Psychological Association Convention, Baltimore.

Tebes, J. K., & Kraemer, D. T. (1991). Quantitative and qualitative knowing in mutual support research: Some lessons from the recent history of psychology. *American Journal of Community Psychology, 19,* 739–756.

Telch, C. F., & Telch, M. J. (1986). Group coping skills instruction and supportive group therapy for cancer patients: A comparison of strategies. *Journal of Consulting and Clinical Psychology, 54,* 802–808.

tenBroek, J. (1965). *Equal under law.* London: Collier.

Teplin, L. A. (1983). The criminalization of the mentally ill: Speculation in search of data. *Psychological Bulletin, 94,* 54–67.

Teplin, L. A. (1984). Criminalizing mental disorder: The comparative arrest rate of the mentally disordered. *American Psychologist, 39,* 794–803.

Teplin, L. A. (2001). Police discretion and mentally ill persons. In G. Landsberg & A. Smiley (Eds.), *Forensic mental health: Working with offenders with mental illness* (pp. 28.21–28.11). Kingston, NJ: Civic Research Institute.

Teplin, L. A., Abram, K. M., & McClelland, G. M. (1994). Does psychiatric disorder predict violent crime among released jail detainees? A six-year longitudinal study. *American Psychologist, 49*(4), 335–342.

Teplin, L. A., Abram, K. M., & McClelland, G. M. (1996). Prevalence of psychiatric disorders among incarcerated women: Pretrial jail detainees. *Archives of General Psychiatry, 53*(6), 505–512.

Teplin, L. A., Abram, K. M., & McClelland, G. M. (1997). Mentally disordered women in jail: Who receives services? *American Journal of Public Health, 87*(4), 604–609.

Test, M. A. (1991). The Training in Community Living Model: Delivering treatment and rehabilitation services through a continuous treatment team. In R. Liberman (Ed.), *Handbook of psychiatric rehabilitation.* New York: Pergamon.

The Key. (1999). Successful national summit leads to action plans. *The Key, 5*(3), 1–7.

The Liberator, Defender of Men, 1994, 21.

Thoits, P. A. (1986). Social support as coping assistance. *Journal of Consulting and Clinical Psychology, 54,* 416–423.

Thomas, D., & Veno, A. (1992). *Psychology and social change.* Palmerston, NZ: Dunmore.

Thomas, S. B., & Quinn, S. C. (1991). The Tuskegee syphilis study, 1932 to 1972: Implications for HIV education and AIDS risk education programs in the Black community. *American Journal of Public Health, 81,* 1498–1505.

Timko, C., & Moos, R. H. (1991). A typology of social climates in group residential facilities for older people. *Journal of Gerontology, 46,* S160–169.

Toch, H., & Grant, J. D. (1982). *Reforming human services: Change through participation.* Beverly Hills: Sage.

Tomkins, A. J., Steinman, M., Kenning, M. K., Mohamed, S. & Afrank, J. (1992). Children who witness woman battering. *Law & Policy, 14,* 169–184.

Tönnies, F. (1887/2001). *Community and civil society: Gemeinschaft und gesellschaft* (J. Harris, Ed., J. Harris & M. Hollis, Transl.). New York: Cambridge University Press.

Toro, P. A. (1990). Evaluating professionally operated and self-help programs for the seriously mentally ill. *American Journal of Community Psychology, 18,* 903–908.

Toro, P. A., Rappaport, J., & Seidman, E. (1987). Social climate comparison of mutual help and psychotherapy groups. *Journal of Consulting and Clinical Psychology, 55,* 430–431.

Toro, P. A., Reischl, T. M., Zimmerman, M. A., Rappaport, J., Seidman, E., Luke, D. A., & Roberts, L. J. (1988). Professionals in mutual help groups: Impact on social climate and members' behavior. *Journal of Counseling and Clinical Psychology, 56,* 631–632.

Toro, P. A. & Wall, D. D. (1991). Research on homeless persons: Diagnostic comparisons and practice implications. *Professional Psychology: Research and Practice, 22,* 479–488.

Torrey, E. F. (1990). Economic barriers to widespread implementation of model programs for the seriously mentally ill. *Hospital and Community Psychiatry, 41,* 526–531.

Torrey, E. F., Bowler, A., Taylor, E., & Gottesman, I. I. (1994). *Schizophrenia and manic-depressive disorder.* New York: Basic Books.

Torrey, E. F., Wolfe, S. M., & Flynn, L. M. (1988). *Care of the seriously mentally ill: A rating of state programs* (2nd ed.). Arlington, VA: National Alliance for the Mentally Ill, and Public Citizen Health Research Group.

Toulmin, S. (1958). *The uses of argument.* London: Cambridge University Press.

Travers, J., White, R. E., Boscoe, A. N., & McDonnell, D. D. (2001). Mental well being among caregivers of people with schizophrenia. http://www.nimh.nih.gov/ncdeu/abstracts2001/ncdeu1015.cfm

Trickett, E. J. (1978). Toward a social-ecological conception of adolescent socialization: Normative data on contrasting types of public school classrooms. *Child Development, 49,* 408–414.

Trickett, E. J., Kelly, J. G., & Vincent, T. A. (1985). The spirit of ecological inquiry in community research (pp. 283–333). In E. C. Susskind & D. C. Klein (Eds.), *Community research: Methods, paradigms, and applications.* New York: Praeger.

Trickett, E. J., & Moos, R. H. (1974). Personal correlates of contrasting environments: Student satisfactions in high school classrooms. *American Journal of Community Psychology, 2,* 1–12.

Trussel, J., Koenig, J., Ellerston, C., & Stewart, F. (1997). Preventing unintended pregnancy: The cost-effectiveness of three methods of emergency contraception. *American Journal of Public Health, 87,* 932–937.

Tuckman, J., & Lavell, M. (1959). Attrition in psychiatric clinics for children. *Public Health Reports, Public Health Service, 74,* 309–315.

Tuckman, J., & Lavell, M. (1962). Patients discharged with or against medical advice. *Journal of Clinical Psychology, 13,* 177–180.

Turner, J. C. (1999). Some current issues in research on social identity and self-categorization theories. In N. Ellemers & R. Spears & B. Doosje (Eds.), *Social identity: Context, commitment, content* (pp. 6–34). Malden, MA: Blackwell Publishers, Inc.

Twigger-Ross, C. L., & Uzzell, D. L. (1996). Place and identity processes. *Journal of Environmental Psychology, 16*(3), 205–220.

Uhl, G., & Levine, M. (1990). Group homes and crime. *Hospital and Community Psychiatry, 41,* 1028.

Unger, D. G., & Wandersman, A. (1983). Neighboring and its role in block organizations. *American Journal of Community Psychology, 11,* 291–300.

Unger, D. G., & Wandersman, A. (1985). The importance of neighbors: The social, cognitive, and affective components of neighboring. *American Journal of Community Psychology, 13,* 139–169.

U.S. Advisory Board on Child Abuse and Neglect. (1990). Child abuse and neglect: Critical first steps to a national emergency. Washington, DC: Office of Human Development Services.

U.S. Advisory Board on Child Abuse and Neglect. (1993). Neighbors helping neighbors: A new national strategy for the protection of children. Washington, DC: Administration for Children and Families.

U.S. Advisory Board on Child Abuse and Neglect. (1995). A nation's shame: Fatal child abuse and neglect in the United States. Washington, DC: Administration for Children and Families.

U.S. Bureau of Justice Statistics. (1990). Jail inmates. Washington, DC: U.S. Department of Justice.

U.S. Bureau of the Census. (1997). Statistical abstract of the United States, 1997 (117th ed.). Washington, DC: U.S. Department of Commerce.

U.S. Bureau of the Census. (1998). Statistical abstract of the United States, 1998 (118th ed.). Washington, DC: U.S. Department of Commerce.

U. S. Bureau of the Census. (2002). Statistical Abstract of the United States, 2002 (122 ed.). Washington, DC: U.S. Department of Commerce.

U. S. Bureau of the Census, Census 2000 Summary File, accessed on the internet through the U. S. Census Bureau site.

U. S. Department of Education. (1990). 12th annual report to Congress on the implementation of the Education of the Handicapped Act. Washington, DC: U.S. Department of Education.

U. S. Department of Education. (n.d.). Stronger accountability. Testing for results. Helping families, schools and communities understand and improve student achievement. http:/www.ed.gov/ncbl/accountability/ayp/testingforresults.html

U.S. Department of Health and Human Services. (2000). Healthy People 2000: National health promotion and disease prevention objectives. Washington, DC: U.S. Government Printing Office.

U.S. Department of Health and Human Services. (2001). Child Maltreatment 1999. Washington, DC: U.S. Government Printing Office.

U. S. Department of Justice. (1999). Juvenile offenders in residential placement for 1997. Washington, DC: U.S. Department of Justice.

U.S. Department of Labor, Bureau of Labor Statistics. (2004). Current Population Survey. www.bls.gov

U.S. General Accounting Office. (1993). Foster care. Services to prevent out-of-home placements are limited by funding barriers. Washington, DC: Author.

U.S. House of Representatives Select Committee on Children, Youth and Families. (1990). No place to call home: Discarded children in America. Washington, DC: U.S. Government Printing Office.

U. S. Office of Special Education and Rehabilitative Services. (1990). "To assure the free appropriate education of all handicapped children." 12th Annual Report to Congress on the Implementation of the Education of the Handicapped Act. Washington, DC: U. S. Department of Education.

U.S. Surgeon General. (2001a). Mental Health: A Report of the Surgeon General. http://mentalhealth.about.com/library/sg/

U.S. Surgeon General. (2001b). Report of the Surgeon General's Conference on Children's Mental Health: A National Action Agenda. http://www.surgeongeneral.gov/childreport. htm#fore

U.S. v. Cruickshank 92 U. S. 542 (1875).

Urban Institute. (2000). Millions still face homelessness in a booming economy. http://www.urban.org/news/pressrel/pr000201.html

Vaillant, G. E. (1995). *The natural history of alcoholism revisited.* Cambridge, MA: Harvard University Press.

Vaillant, G. E., & Davis J. T. (2000). Social/emotional intelligence and midlife resilience in schoolboys with low tested intelligence. *American Journal of Orthopsychiatry, 70*(2), 215–222.

van Ryn, M., & Vinokur, A. D. (1992). How did it work? An examination of the mechanisms through which an intervention for the unemployed promoted job-search behavior. *American Journal of Community Psychology, 20,* 577–597.

van Uchelen, C. (2000). Individualism, collectivism, and community psychology. In J. Rappaport & E. Seidman (Eds.), *The handbook of community psychology* (pp. 65–78). New York: Plenum.

Varady, D. (1986). Neighborhood confidence: A critical factor in neighborhood revitalization? *Environment and Behavior, 18,* 480–501.

Varmus, H. E. (1998). *NIMH parity in financing mental health services: Managed Care effects on cost, access and quality.* Washington, DC: National Institutes of Health. http://www.nimh.nih.gov/research/prtyrpt/qualityofcare.html

Veneman, A. M. (2001). Testimony of Secretary of Agriculture Ann M. Veneman before the Senate Committee on Agriculture, Nutrition and Forestry, September 26, 2001.

Videka-Sherman, L. & Lieberman, M. (1985). The effects of self-help and psychotherapy on child loss: The limits of recovery. *American Journal of Orthopsychiatry, 55,* 70–82.

Vincent, T. A., & Trickett, E. J. (1983). Preventive interventions and the human context: Ecological approaches to environmental assessment and change. In R. Felner, L. Jason, J. Moritsugu, & S. Farber (Eds.), *Preventive psychology.* New York: Pergamon.

Vinokur, A. D., Price, R. H., Caplan, R. D., van Ryn, M., & Curran, J. (1995). The Jobs I preventive intervention for unemployed individuals: Short- and long-term effects on reemployment and mental health. In L. R. Murphy & J. J. Hurrell (Eds.), *Job stress interventions* (pp. 125–138). Washington, DC: American Psychological Association.

Vinokur, A. D., van Ryn, M., Gramlich, E. M., & Price, R. H. (1991). Longer-term follow-up and benefit-cost analysis of the Jobs Program: A preventive intervention for the unemployed. *Journal of Applied Psychology, 76,* 213–219.

Vivian, D., & O'Leary, K. D. (1990). Physical aggression in marriage. In F. D. Fincham & T. N. Bradbury (Eds.), *The psychology of marriage: Basic issues and applications* (pp. 323–348). New York: Guilford Press.

Vogel, W. (1991). A personal memoir of the state hospitals of the 1950s. *Hospital and Community Psychiatry, 42,* 593–597.

Vriens, L. (1999). Children, war, and peace: A review of fifty years of research from the perspective of a balanced concept of peace education. In A. Raviv & L. Oppenheimer (Eds.), *How children understand war and peace: A call for international peace education* (pp. 27–58). San Francisco, CA: Jossey-Bass.

Vyner, H. M. (1988). *Invisible trauma: The psychosocial effects of the invisible environmental contaminants.* Lexington, MA: Lexington Books.

Wald, A., Langenberg, A. G. M., Link, K., Izu, A. E., Ashley, R., Warren, T., Tyring, S., Douglas, J. M. Jr., & Corey, L. (2001). Effect of condoms on reducing the transmission of herpes simplex virus type 2 from men to women. *Journal of the American Medical Association. 285,* 3100–3106.

Walter, H. J., & Vaughn, R. D. (1993). AIDS risk reduction among a multiethnic sample of urban high school students. *Journal of the American Medical Association, 270,* 725–730.

Walton, R. E. (1977). The diffusion of new work structures: Explaining why success didn't take. In P. H. Mirvis & D. N. Berg (Eds.), *Failures in organization development and change: Cases and essays for learning.* New York: Wiley.

Wandersman, A., & Florin, P. (Eds.). (1990). Citizen participation, voluntary organizations and community development: Insights for empowerment through research (Special Section). *American Journal of Community Psychology, 18,* 41–177.

Wandersman, A., & Florin, P. (2000). Citizen participation and community organizations. In J. Rappaport & E. Seidman (Eds.), *Handbook of community psychology* (pp. 247–272). New York: Plenum Press.

Wandersman, A., Florin, P., Friedmann, R., & Meier, R. (1987). Who participates, who does not, and why? An analysis of voluntary neighborhood associations in the United States and Israel. *Sociological Forum, 2*, 534–555.

Wandersman, A., Goodman, R. M., & Butterfoss, F. D. (1997). Understanding coalitions and how they operate an open systems" organizational framework. In M. Minkler (Ed.), *Community organizing and community building for health* (pp. 261–277). New Brunswick, NJ: Rutgers University Press.

Wandersman, A. H., & Hallman, W. K. (1993). Are people acting irrationally? Understanding public concerns about environmental threats. *American Psychologist, 48*, 681–686.

Watzlawick, P., Weakland, J. H., & Fisch, R. (1974). *Change: Principles of problem formation and problem resolution.* New York: Norton.

Weick, K. E. (1984). Small wins: Redefining the scale of social problems. *American Psychologist, 39*, 40–49.

Weikart, D. P., & Schweinhart, L. J. (1997). High/Scope Perry Preschool program. In G. W. Albee & T. P. Gullotta (Eds.), *Primary prevention works: Issues in children's and families' lives* (pp. 146–166). Thousand Oaks, CA: Sage.

Weisman, J. (2000). The Texas education myth. Only a test. The New Republic Online. http://www.thenewrepublic.com/041000.html

Weiss, R. S. (1987). Principles underlying a manual for parents whose children were killed by a drunk driver. *American Journal of Orthopsychiatry, 57*, 431–440.

Weissberg, R. P., Barton, H. A., & Shriver, T. P. (1997). The social competence promting program for young adolescents. In G. W. Albee and T. P., Gullotta (Eds.), *Primary prevention works* (pp. 268–290). Thousand Oaks, CA: Sage.

Weissberg, R. P., & Elias, M. J. (1993). Enhancing young people's social competence and health behavior: An important challenge for educators, scientists, policymakers, and funders. *Applied & Preventive Psychology, 2*, 179–190.

Weissberg, R. P., Gullotta, T. P., Hampton, R. L, Ryan, B. A., & Adams, G. R. (Eds.). (1997a). *Enhancing children's wellness.* Thousand Oaks, CA: Sage.

Weissberg, R. P., Gullotta, T. P., Hampton, R. L, Ryan, B. A., & Adams, G. R. (Eds.). (1997b). *Establishing preventive services.* Thousand Oaks, CA: Sage.

Weithorn, L. A. (1988). Mental hospitalization of troublesome youth: An analysis of skyrocketing admission rates. *Stanford Law Review, 40*, 773–838.

Wenocur, S., & Belcher, J. R. (1990). Strategies for overcoming barriers to community-based housing for the chronically mentally ill. *Community Mental Health Journal, 26*(4), 319–333.

Werner, C. M. (2003). Changing homeowners' use of toxic household products: A transactional approach. *Journal of Environmental Psychology, 23*, 33–45.

Werner, C. M., Voce, R., Openshaw, K.-G., & Simons, M. (2002). Designing service-learning to empower students and community: Jackson Elementary builds a nature study center. *Journal of Social Issues, 58*, 557–579.

White, B. J., & Madara, E. J. (2002). The self-help group sourcebook: Your guide to community and online support groups (7th ed) Cedar Knolls, NJ: American Self-Help Group Clearinghouse.

White, R. E., Travers, J., Boscoe, A. N., & McDonnell , D. D. (2001). Healthcare resource use among caregivers ot people with schizophrenia. http://www.nimh.nih.gov/ncdeu/abstracts2001/ncdeu1014.cfm

Whitehead, B. D. (1994). The failure of sex education. *The Atlantic Monthly,* October, 1994. Reprinted in *American Educator, 18*, 22–29, 46–52.

Whyte, W. W. (2001). *The social life of small urban spaces.* New York: Project for Urban Spaces.

Wicker, A. W. (1972). Processes which mediate behavior-environment congruence. *Behavioral Science, 17*, 365–277.

Wicker, A. W. (1984). *An introduction to ecological psychology* (2nd ed.). Cambridge, MA: Cambridge University Press.

Wicker, A. W. (2002). Ecological psychology: Historical contexts, current conception, prospective directions. In R. B. Bechtel & A. Churchman (Eds.), *Handbook of environmental psychology* (pp. 114–126). New York: Wiley.

Wiener, D., Anderson, R. J., & Nietupski, J. (1982). Impact of community-based residential facilities for mentally retarded adults on surrounding property values using realtor analysis methods. *Education and Training of the Mentally Retarded, 17*(4), 278–282.

Wiesenfeld, E. (1998). Paradigms of community social psychology in six Latin American nations. *Journal of Community Psychology, 26*, 229–242.

Wiesenfeld, E., & Sanchez, E. (2002). Sustained participation: A community based approach to addressing environmental problems. In R. B. Bechtel & A. Churchman (Eds.), *Handbook of environmental psychology* (pp. 629–643). New York: Wiley.

Willie, C. V. (1984). *School desegregation plans that work*. Westport, CT: Greenwood Press.

Wills, T. A., & Shinar, O. (2000). Measuring perceived and received social support. In S. Cohen, L. G. Underwood, and B. H,. Gottlieb (Eds.), *Social support measurement and intervention* (pp. 86–135). New York: Oxford University Press.

Wilson, B. D. M., Hayes, E., Greene, G. J., Kelly J. G., & Iscoe, I. (2003). Community psychology. In D. K. Freedheim and I. B. Wiener (Eds.), *Handbook of psychology, Vol. 1: History of psychology* (Chapter 21, pp. 431–449). New York: Wiley.

Wilson, W. J. (1987). *The truly disadvantaged: The inner city, the underclass, and public policy*. Chicago: University of Chicago Press.

Winerip, M. (1985, May 13). School integration in Buffalo is hailed as a model for U.S. *New York Times*, pp. A1, B4.

Wingenfeld, S., & Newbrough, J. R. (2000). Community psychology in international perspective. In J. Rappaport & E. Seidman (Eds.), *Handbook of community psychology*. (pp. 779–810). Dordrecht, Netherlands: Kluwer Academic Publishers.

Witheridge, T. F. (1990). Assertive community treatment: A strategy for helping persons with severe mental illness to avoid rehospitalization. In N. L. Cohen (Ed.), *Psychiatry takes to the streets: Outreach and crisis intervention for the mentally ill* (pp. 80–106). New York: Guilford Press.

Woff, I., Toumbourou, J., Herlihy, E., Hamilton, M., & Wales, S. (1996). Service providers' perceptions of substance use self-help groups. *Substance Use & Misuse, 31*(10), 1241–58.

Wolchik, S. A., Ruehlman, L. S., Braver, S. L., & Sandler, I. N. (1989). Social support of children of divorce: Direct and stress buffering effects. *American Journal of Community Psychology, 17*, 485–501.

Wong, A., Escobar, M., Lesage, A., Loyer, M., Vanier, C., & Sakinofsky, I. (2001). Are UN peacekeepers at risk for suicide? *Suicide and Life Threatening Behavior, 31*(1), 103–112.

Woodward, B. & Bernstein, C. (1976). *The final days*. New York: Simon & Schuster.

Woodworth, T. (2000). DEA Congressional Testimony, U.S. Congress Committee on Education and the Workforce: Subcommittee on Early Childhood, *Youth and Families*, May 16, 2000.

Wright, B., Bryant, P, & Bullard, R. D. (1994). Coping with poisons in Cancer Alley. In R. D. Bullard (Ed.), *Unequal protection: Environmental justice and communities of color*. San Francisco: Sierra Club.

Wyatt v. Stickney 344. F. Supp. 387 (M.D. Ala. 1972); Wyatt v Aderholt 503 F.2d 1305 (5th Cir 1974).

York, P., & York, D. (1987). *Toughlove* (Rev. ed.). Doylestown, PA: Toughlove.

Young, J. (1992). An evaluation of the mutual help organisation, GROW. In D. Thomas and A. Veno (Eds.), *Psychology and Social Change*. Palmerston North, New Zealand: Dunmore.

Young, J., & Williams, C. L. (1988). Whom do mutual-help groups help? A typology of members. *Hospital and Community Psychiatry, 39*, 1178–1182.

Zaff, J., & Devlin, A. S. (1998). Sense of community in housing for the elderly. *Journal of Community Psychology, 26*(4), 381–397.

Zahner, G. E. P., Kasl, S. V., White, M., & Will, J. C. (1985). Psychological consequences of infestation of the dwelling unit. *American Journal of Public Health, 75*, 1303–1307.

Zane, N., Sue, S., Castro, F. G., & George, W. (1982). Service system models for ethnic minorities. In L. R. Snowden (Ed.), *Reaching the underserved: Mental health needs of neglected populations*. Beverly Hills: Sage.

Zapata, B. C., Rebolledo, A., Atalah, E., Newman, B., & King, M. C. (1992). The influence of social and political violence on the risk of pregnancy complications. *American Journal of Public Health, 82*, 685–690.

Zigler, E., & Muenchow, S. (1992). *Head Start: The inside story of America's most successful educational experiment.* New York: Basic Books.

Zigler, E., & Styfco, S. J. (Eds.). (1993). *Head Start and beyond.* New Haven, CT: Yale University Press.

Zigler, E., & Styfco, S. J. (2000). Pioneering steps (and fumbles) in developing a federal preschool intervention. *Topics in Early Childhood Special Education, 20*(2), 67–70, 78.

Zigler, E. F. & Finn-Stevenson, M. (1997). Policy efforts to enhance child and family life: Goals for 2010. In Weisberg, R. P., Gullotta, T. P., Hampton, R. L, Ryan, B. A., & Adams, G. R. (Eds.), *Establishing preventive services* (pp. 27–60). Thousand Oaks, CA: Sage.

Zimmerman, M.A. (2000). Empowerment theory: Psychological, organizational and community levels of analysis. In J. Rappaport & E. Seidman (Eds.), *Handbook of community psychology* (pp. 43–63). New York: Kluwer Academic/Plenum.

Zimmerman, M. A., Israel, B.A., Schulz, A., & Checkoway, B. (1992). Further explorations in empowerment theory: An empirical analysis of psychological empowerment. *American Journal of Community Psychology, 20,* 707–727.

Zimmerman, M. A., Ramirez-Valles, J., Suarez, E., de la Rosa, G., & Castro, M. A. (1997). An HIV/AIDS prevention project for Mexican homosexual men: An empowerment approach. *Health Education and Behavior, 24*(2), 177–190.

Zimmerman, M. A., Reischl, T. M., Seidman, E., Rappaport, J., Toro, P. A., & Salem, D. A. (1991). Expansion strategies of a mutual help organization. *American Journal of Community Psychology, 19,* 251–278.

Zippay, A. (1997). Trends in siting strategies. *Community Mental Health Journal, 33*(4), 301–310.

Zremski, J. (2002). Starting over? President's plan to revamp the federal Head Start program for poor children is drawing mixed reviews. *Buffalo News,* May 24, pp. A-1, 7.

Zusman, J., & Simon, J. (1983). Differences in repeated psychiatric examinations of litigants to a law suit. *American Journal of Psychiatry, 140,* 1300–1304.

Name Index

521

Subject Index

Abortion, 33, 34, 76, 247, 302, 303, 317, 325, 334, 337, 401, 444
Acquired Immune Deficiency Syndrome (AIDS)/HIV Disease, 26–28, 30, 81, 129, 186, 234, 235, 257, 288, 322, 351
prevention of, 28, 186, 262, 273, 284, 313–22, 324, 375
Adaptation between persons and the environment or situations, 8, 34, 39, 41, 43–45, 52, 59, 83, 96, 98–100, 103, 107, 108, 111, 117, 119, 126–28, 131–35, 138–40, 145–51, 153, 156, 161, 162, 175, 186–88, 192–97, 212, 219, 222–25, 232, 239–40, 246, 257–58, 265–66, 277, 300–01, 309, 324, 327, 331, 333–34, 338, 348–50, 352, 428–29, 437, 442, 456
to health problems, 28–30, 34, 48–49, 235–36, 244
to legal change, 142–49, 338, 375
to stressful life events or crises, 92, 103, 107, 108, 220, 224–25, 227–31, 240–43, 249, 259, 263, 266, 302–03, 359
Adolescents. *See* Children and adolescents
Advocacy groups, 73, 76, 129, 144, 168–69, 171, 273, 297, 329, 361–64, 369, 374, 390, 392, 434, 475
Affirmative action, 100, 127–29, 410, 413, 421, 423, 464
Africa, 322
African American. *See also* School desegregation
children in foster care and single-headed households, 35, 62, 95, 98–100, 230
community in Buffalo, New York, 97, 100, 438
community organizations, 97, 319, 336–37, 378, 407, 438–42, 450
coping and support, 62, 96–97, 99–100, 108, 230, 250, 252, 334, 336, 439
HIV/AIDS rates, prevention, and health promotion, 30, 314–316, 319, 322
labeling and discrimination, 62, 96, 98, 128, 133, 213, 229, 252, 314, 336, 404–10, 413, 415, 424, 463
leaders, 412, 439, 440–42
mental health and prevention services, 79, 308, 310, 312
migration, segregation, and mobility, 45, 97, 99, 133, 136, 183, 337, 404, 410–11, 422, 441

schools and students, 8, 96, 394, 408–10, 412–22, 424, 441–42, 463
socio-economic or poverty status, 8, 37, 79, 95–100, 128, 136, 183, 230, 252, 310, 404, 406, 408, 422, 463
victimization, 97–98, 314, 325, 406, 408, 450, 454
Al-Anon, 327–28, 336, 345, 348, 350, 357–60
Alateen, 328
Albany, New York, 446–47
Albuquerque, New Mexico, 412
Alcohol abuse, 15–16, 20–22, 29, 33, 38, 44–45, 71, 80, 94, 103, 107, 111, 121, 123, 168, 202, 207, 215–16, 231, 261, 282–83, 285, 288, 304, 327–28, 332–333, 336, 344–45, 349–50, 352, 355–60. *See also* Substance abuse
Alcoholics Anonymous (AA), 137, 168, 215–16, 327–28, 332–333, 343–45, 348–50, 352, 354, 359–61, 430
ideology in, 342–44
and recovery from alcohol abuse, 355–58
Alliance for the Mentally Ill. *See* National Alliance for the Mentally Ill
Aloneness, loneliness, and social isolation, 14, 28, 44–46, 51–52, 168, 170–71, 201, 207, 234, 246–47, 257, 260, 278, 281, 284–85, 304, 331, 335–36, 338–39, 342, 350–51, 356–57, 359, 364, 422, 437
American Evaluation Association, 470
American Journal of Community Psychology, 124, 171, 179, 403
American Orthopsychiatric Association, 470
American Psychiatric Association, 213, 334
American Psychological Association, 64, 90, 409, 464, 466, 469–70
American Public Health Association, 470
Annals of the American Academy of Political and Social Science, 99
Anthropology, 68, 179, 201, 470–71, 473
Antisocial Personality Disorder or antisocial behavior, 20 (table), 218, 273, 282, 285
Arthur v. Nyquist, 426n.11
Asia, 476. *See also* Hong Kong
Asian Americans and Pacific Islanders, 30, 45, 79, 127, 315, 412–13, 421
Assertive Community Treatment (ACT)/Assertive community supports, 74–75, 106, 151, 192, 263, 390

and hassles, 92, 228–30
and individual vulnerabilities, 107–08, 231
and prevention, 112–115, 243, 289–90, 296,
300, 437, 454–55
research on, 35–36, 45, 51–52, 101, 222,
227–30, 244, 258, 283, 306
and social-situational vulnerabilities, 95, 97,
99–100, 109–12, 300
Stringfellow Acid Pits, California, 109
Substance abuse, 21–23, 38, 50, 70–71, 75–76,
78, 80, 143, 248, 261, 376, 428–29, 432.
See also Alcohol abuse
prevention of, 171, 273–74, 295, 303, 314, 316,
321–22, 324
self-help for, 346, 349, 360
Succession, 136–39, 153, 410, 437
Suicide, 19, 24, 45, 80, 111, 131, 143–44, 147,
247, 249, 335
prevention of, 76, 101–02, 238, 278, 282, 286,
294, 363
Supplemental Security Income, 38, 61, 77, 93,
135
Support groups, 102, 162, 237, 254, 275. *See also*
Self-help groups; Mutual aid
organizations
Support interventions. See Psychosocial
Rehabilitation
Sustainability (in community development),
434 (figure), 436, 454
Swampscott, Massachusetts, conference, 64,
468
Swann v. *Charlotte-Mecklenburg Board of
Education*, 426n.9
Sweatt v. *Painter*, 425n.5
Systems theory, 374–75, 380

Ten Points Coalition, 439
Territoriality, 177–79, 192
Testing, 6, 68, 119–20, 299, 311, 394–400, 415.
See also IQ scores
Texas Assessment of Academic Skills (TAAS),
394–98
Texas Education Agency (TEA), 394, 396
Texas "educational miracle," 393–400. *See also*
Rand study on Texas education
and the Select Committee on Public
Education (SCOPE), 393
"teaching to the test," 397–400
Three Mile Island, Pennsylvania, 31, 109–110
Times Beach, Missouri, 109
Tough Love, 328
Toxic waste. *See* Dioxin; Environmental threats
Transactional Ecological Psychology, Peabody
College graduate program in, 65
Transcendental ecology, 164–65, 223
Transsexuals, 167, 216–17
Trauma-stren conversion, 243–44, 300
Turbulence, of ecosystem, 147, 374–75
Tuscaloosa, Alabama, 109
Tuskegee syphilis study, 314, 318

Unemployment. *See* Employment
United States
Administration for Children, Youth and
Families, 310, 325n.5–6
Advisory Board on Child Abuse and
Neglect, 26, 51, 83, 130–31, 281
Child and Adolescent Service System
Program, 80

Constitution, 140–41, 405–07, 423, 426n.2
Eighteenth Amendment, 459
Fifteenth Amendment, 406
Fourteenth Amendment, 140–42, 406–11,
415–22
Thirteenth Amendment, 406
Constitutional Convention of 1787, 368
Department of Education, 108, 393, 398–99
Department of Justice, 82
Environmental Protection Agency (EPA), 31,
445, 447–48, 451–53, 455, 461
Federal programs assisting needy children,
80–82
Joint Commission on the Mental Health of
Children, 80
Joint Commission on Mental Illness and
Health, 46, 61, 80, 272
No Child Left Behind Act of 2001, 311, 393
Office of Human Development, 113
Personal Responsibility and Work
Opportunity Reconciliation Act, 37,
312. *See also* Welfare, reform
President's Commission on Mental Health,
78, 80, 272
Public Health Service, 81
Select Committee on Children, Youth and
Families, 80
Select Committee on Public Education
(SCOPE), 393
Social Security Administration, 37
Substance Abuse and Mental Health Services
Administration (SAMHSA), 22
Supreme Court
desegregation and, 64, 405–11, 416, 419–20,
422–424, 425n.4, 426n.9
group homes for the retarded and, 215,
387
involuntary hospitalization and, 142, 207
Surgeon General, 20, 25, 46, 80–84, 115, 329
Veterans Administration, 61
Universe of alternatives, 51, 68, 148, 368–69, 428
University of Kansas, 64–65
University of Michigan, 65
University of Rochester, 277
University of Texas, 65
Unwed Parents and Grandparents, 328
Urban Affairs Association, 470
Urban Family Institutes, 441
Urban League, 440
U. S. v. *Cruickshank*, 425n.3

Values
affecting research, 458, 463–67, 477
and community psychology, 4, 6, 9
cultural, 242, 383–84
ecological, 117, 124–25, 149–50, 152–53, 162,
164, 168, 170, 173, 223–24
family, and social support, 254–55
implications for prevention, 282, 284, 299,
315, 324
and leisure, 43–44
as psychological mediators, 94, 103–04,
223–24
of segregated vs. integrated education, 412–13
and setting creation and change, 368–71, 384,
416
shared, and self-help groups, 343
value-free perspective of behaviorism, 67–68
work-related, 42–43